Essentials of
Children's Literature

Essentials of
Children's Literature
Second Edition

Carl M. Tomlinson
Northern Illinois University

Carol Lynch-Brown
Florida State University

Allyn and Bacon
Boston • London • Toronto • Sydney • Tokyo • Singapore

To my parents (C.M.T.)

To my grandson, Logan (C.L.-B.)

Senior Editor: Virginia C. Lanigan
Editorial Assistant: Nihad Farooq
Marketing Manager: Kathy Hunter
Manufacturing Buyer: Aloka Rathnam
Editorial-Production Services: Electronic Publishing Services Inc.
Cover Administrator: Linda Knowles
Cover Designer: Susan Paradise

Copyright © 1996, 1993 by Allyn & Bacon
A Simon & Schuster Company
Needham Heights, Massachusetts 02194

Library of Congress Cataloging-in-Publication Data

Tomlinson, Carl M.
    Essentials of children's literature / Carl M. Tomlinson, Carol Lynch-Brown.
      p. cm.
    Rev. ed. of: Essentials of children's literature / Carol Lynch-Brown. 1993.
    Includes bibliographical references and index.
    ISBN 0-205-16751-9
    1. Children's literature—Study and teaching (Higher)
  2. Children's literature—History and criticism.   3. Children and literature.
  4. Children's literature—Bibliography.   I. Lynch-Brown, Carol.
  II. Lynch-Brown, Carol. Essentials of children's literature.   III. Title.
PN1009.A1L96 1995
809'.89282'0711—dc20   95-18195
                                                          CIP

0-205-16751-9

Printed in the United States of America
10 9 8 7 6 5 4 3   00 99 98 97 96

Acknowledgments are listed on page 386, which constitutes a continuation of the copyright page.

Contents

Preface

Essentials of Children's Literature is a straightforward presentation on literature and sharing literature with children. This textbook is tailored to the undergraduate or beginning survey course in children's literature. The full collaboration between the two authors has continued: we have shared in all decisions and revisions. The reader will note that we alternate use of *he* or *she* by chapter to avoid the sexist overtones of the traditional generic *he* or *she* for teachers and librarians.

Overview

Part One: Children and Literature

The two chapters in Part One cover the introductory material students need in order to begin selecting, reading, and evaluating children's trade books. Chapter 1 defines children's literature, discusses its values, explains its vulnerability to censorship, and provides research evidence supporting its use with children. Concepts about literature, elements of fiction, visual elements, and aspects of book format are treated extensively in Chapter 2. We mention well-known books as examples, when needed, but avoid lengthy reviews. We believe that instructors and their students can conduct in-depth booktalks within the context of their college courses. A facts-only approach is taken in all chapters.

Part Two: Categories of Literature

Each of the eight chapters in Part Two defines and describes a specific category and discusses the types of books that fall within that category. Following the narrative is a list of notable authors (poets, illustrators, compilers, etc.) in the category. Within each chapter are two lists: recommended read-aloud books within the category, and recommended books for students' use in selecting books to read within the category. These eight chapters include more than 2,000 recommended titles in end-of-chapter lists.

Chapter 4 focuses on picture books of all types and genres, and Chapter 10 treats the important topics of multicultural and international literature. It should be noted that multicultural and international books are included throughout this textbook. Some might argue that a separate chapter for multicultural literature reinforces the segregation that persists between cultures today. Our aim in providing a focus chapter for multicultural literature is to make this literature more visible (and easier to find and use) in a society where, until recently, it was all but nonexistent. Chapter 10 features the history and current status of multicultural and international literature in the children's book field and highlights notable writers and artists of this body of literature.

Part Three: Literature in the School

The last two chapters focus on curriculum and teaching strategies. Step-by-step instructions are given for building and setting up a classroom library and library corner, producing a creative drama based on a book, conducting booktalks, and selecting and directing choral poetry. Also discussed are the "basalization" of literature, the literary canon, and the efficacy of written book reports.

Appendices

Award lists and professional resources can be found in the appendices. We indicate genre, type, or topic of the books in the Newbery and Caldecott Award lists to assist students who may be seeking books of a particular type, topic, or genre for their free-choice readings or for their projects and term papers. Professional sources for the study of literature and pedagogy are included in Appendix B, which was compiled and fully annotated by Marie Sorensen. Histories of children's literature that served as references for the development of the historical overview sections are also included in that appendix.

Pedagogy

We believe that the primary focus of an undergraduate course should be reading children's trade books, not reading an exhaustive textbook about children's books. Students need direct experience with these trade books—reading them, reading them aloud to others, writing about them, comparing them, criticizing them, evaluating them, applying them to their own lives, and thinking about using them with their future students. One of our goals is to awaken students to the joy of reading. At the same time, the body of knowledge about literature and about teaching literature to children can be conveyed most efficiently through a textbook, freeing class time for involvement with literature. *Essentials of Children's Literature* presents this body of knowledge in a concise, direct narrative using brief lists, examples, figures, and tables in combination with prose.

Notable Features of the Second Edition

- Author-title index of children's books
- Suggested read-aloud list for each genre
- Up-dated and reorganized end-of-chapter book lists. Includes more than 2,000 recommended book titles for students. Includes a list of books for and about the disabled child in Chapter Seven, Realistic fiction.

- Updated appendices
- A thorough integration of multicultural and international children's literature as well as a separate chapter on these topics
- Expanded discussion of poetry activities
- Introductory poems for each chapter to highlight the importance of introducing and sharing poetry throughout the school year
- Emphasis on the importance of cooperation between teachers and school and public librarians in fostering children's love of books

Acknowledgments

For their generous help, good advice, and valued opinions concerning this revision of *Essentials of Children's Literature*, we wish to express our appreciation to the following people:

Marie Sorensen for again producing an excellent bibliography of resource materials found in Appendix B;

Ginny Moore Kruse and Kathleen Horning at the Cooperative Children's Book Center, Madison, Wisconsin, and Editors of the Australian journal, *Magpies*, for sharing their knowledge and wonderful resources;

Colleagues Barbara Elleman (American Library Association), Charles Larry and Donald Richgels (Northern Illinois University), Pamela Barron and Barbara Tobin (Florida State University) for their wise counsel;

Our graduate students: Edna Brabham, Jenny Jacobs, Michael Lahey, Aimee Nichols, and Karen Wilson for their help in organizing and maintaining our children's literature collections;

Richard Casey for his help in creating the graphics for Chapters 2 and 11; Matthew Brown and Ilga Janouskovec for their computer assistance;

The librarians and children's literature consultants who helped us locate information and books and were always willing to discuss books with us: Carol Fiori (State of Florida Library), Sally Walker (author and children's literature consultant, DeKalb, Illinois), and the children's librarians at the DeKalb Public Library, DeKalb, Illinois.

The reviewers of our manuscript, Marilyn A. Greer, Mt. Vernon Nazarene College; and Margot C. Papworth, Cazenovia College–NY.

The reviewers of the First Edition: Joanne E. Bernstein, Brooklyn College; Carol J. Fox, Illinois State Library; M. Jean Greenlaw, University of North Texas; Judith Hakes, Angelo State University; John Hemphill, Greensboro College; Julie M. Jensen, University of Texas at Austin; Barbara Kiefer, Columbia University; Sam Perez, Western Washington University; Masha Rudman, University of Massachusetts at Amherst; Rosemary Salesi, University of Maine; Donna Wiseman, Texas A & M University.

We are indebted to Patricia Polacco for the splendid cover artwork created especially for this edition of *Essentials of Children's Literature*. In her picture story-books, Polacco imbues her characters with all of the best traits we want to associate with children the world over—curiosity, joy, and the capacity to love and learn. The cover captures these traits and projects the overall message that reading and sharing good books is a joyous, rewarding enterprise.

Chapter 1

Learning about Children and Their Literature

Give Me Books, Give Me Wings

*Give me books,
give me wings,
let me fly
from the page
to a once-upon time
in a long-ago age;
taking off
for an extraterrestrial
place
with brave words
for my flight
through the darkness
of space;
gliding
down
to an ocean's
mysterious
deep
with watery shadows
and pictures to keep;
soaring back
to the earth
and a world
that I know;
give me books,*

give me wings
to climb higher
and grow.

—Myra Cohn Livingston

A child leans forward, head cupped in hands, eyes wide with anticipation, raptly concentrating on hearing a story: this is an image for all time. Whether that child was seated beside an open fire in the Stone Ages, on a rough bench in a medieval fairground, or in a modern-day classroom, the message of the image is the same: Children love a good story.

Definition of Children's Literature

This book is written about literature for children from infancy to adolescence, for you who will be meeting and working with these children as teachers, librarians, and parents. In these roles, your opportunities to lead children to literature will be unparalleled, if you have the prerequisite knowledge.

A definition of children's literature is a logical way to begin an investigation into the world of children's books. *Children's literature* is good quality trade books for children from birth to adolescence, covering topics of relevance and interest to children of those ages, through prose and poetry, fiction and nonfiction. This definition contains several key concepts that will be explained in the following sections. Understanding these concepts will help you find your way around the over 50,000 children's titles currently in print, the more than 4,000 new children's titles being published annually in the United States (Barr, 1994), as well as the additional thousands of children's books published worldwide each year in English.

Content

Children's books are about the experiences of childhood, both good and bad. Although these experiences may be set in the past, present, or future, they should still be relevant to the child of today. Enjoying birthday parties, losing a tooth for the first time, anticipating adulthood, camping out and telling ghost stories, getting a new pet, enduring siblings, and dealing with family problems are experiences common to children today. The content of children's books also includes the amazingly diverse topics that are not a part of childhood but are of interest to children, such as dinosaurs, Egyptian mummies, world records, and fighter planes.

The manner in which content is treated also helps to define children's books. Childhood stories told in a forthright, humorous, or suspenseful manner are appropriate for young readers, whereas stories *about* childhood told in nostalgic or overly sentimental terms are inappropriate. Likewise, when stories show children as victims of natural and human-made disasters, the stories should emphasize the hope for a better future rather than the hopelessness and utter despair of the moment.

The subject matter of children's literature can be expressed in prose or poetry. If the literary work is prose, it must be presented as fiction (a product of the imagination, an invented story), nonfiction (factual), or a combination of the two.

Teachers and librarians distinguish between the terms *textbook* and *trade book.* A *textbook*, by design and content, is for the purpose of instruction. School systems buy textbooks in volume, and each child in a classroom or instructional group typically reads the same textbook for a subject. The textbook for elementary-grade reading instruction, the basal reader, is typically marketed as part of a series through which each student progresses from year to year. In contrast, a *trade book*, by design and content, is primarily for the purposes of entertainment and information. Currently, many teachers use trade books in place of basal readers for reading instruction, and in this situation, it is not uncommon for each child in a classroom to use a different book. Trade books are often referred to as *library books* and *storybooks.* The term *trade books* comes from the fact that they are published for the general public, or trade, rather than for a specific consumer group. The books that we will be discussing in this text will be trade books, not textbooks.

Quality

Not all trade books aimed at young readers are worth attention. Books ranging in quality from excellent to poor are now readily available to parents, teachers, and children in the United States and Canada. Look around and you will see racks of children's books in department stores, drugstores, and even grocery stores. But the question is: Are they *good* children's books?

Quality in writing is never easy to define, but it has to do with originality and importance of ideas, imaginative use of language, and beauty of literary and artistic style that enable a work to remain fresh, interesting, and meaningful for years and years. These books have permanent value.

This is not to say that books of good-but-not-great quality have no value. Children have enjoyed fast-moving, adventure-filled, easily predictable stories from the so-called penny-dreadfuls of the seventeenth and eighteenth centuries to the serial adventures of the Hardy Boys, Nancy Drew, and the Babysitters Club of the twentieth century. These works have won no literary prizes but many young readers enjoy them; and because books such as these encourage newly independent readers to read more, they have worth. However, you will probably not want to select books of this calibre to read aloud to your students. Why deprive them of the pleasure of reading such easy and enjoyable books independently? If a child's entire literary experience were limited to serial adventures and other books of trendy but passing interest, he would miss much of the wonder of the natural world and the human experience. The best children's books offer readers enjoyment as well as memorable characters and situations and valuable insights into the human condition.

Many of the so-called children's books today are actually nothing more than advertisements for television cartoon characters and their associated products, such as candy, clothing, and toys. These books represent the low end of the quality spectrum.

The Personal Value of Literature to Children

Literature for children leads to personal fulfillment and academic gains. Separating the values into personal and academic is an intellectual distinction, since both types benefit the child and are all proper parts of a child's schooling. The distinction is useful, however, since teachers and librarians must often justify the benefits of literature in the classroom and find the academic benefits the most convincing ones for administrators and parents.

Enjoyment

The most important personal gain that good books offer to children is the most obvious one—enjoyment. Those of you who read widely as children will never forget the stories that were so funny that you laughed out loud, or mysteries so scary that your heart thumped with apprehension. Such positive early experiences often lead to a lifetime of reading enjoyment.

Vicarious Experience

When a story is so convincingly written that the reader feels as though he has lived through an experience or has actually been in the place and time where the story is set, the book has given him a vicarious experience. Experiences such as these are broadening for children because they, as readers, are taken to places and times that they could never actually visit—and might not want to! A vicarious experience can also be a good mental exercise for children, since they are asked to view situations from perspectives other than their own. Good books open the doors of our imaginations, and that in itself is valuable.

Empathy

Walking in someone else's shoes often helps children develop a greater capacity to empathize with others. Children around the world can benefit from stories that explain what life is like for people who are restricted by handicaps, politics, or circumstance, or whose lives are different from theirs because of culture or geography.

Moral Reasoning

Often, story characters are placed in situations that require them to make moral decisions. Young readers naturally consider what they would do in such a situation. As the story unfolds and the character's decision and the consequences of that choice are disclosed, readers discover whether their own decisions would have had positive outcomes. Regular experience with these types of stories can help young people formulate their own concepts of right and wrong.

Discovering Literary and Artistic Preferences

Another valuable result of children interacting with literature is that they quickly come to recognize the literary and artistic styles of many authors and illustrators.

This is an important first step to literary awareness—that is, to recognize that the style of one writer or illustrator differs from another and that a piece of writing or an illustration has personal appeal. Children who read regularly from a wide variety of children's books soon develop their own personal preferences for types of books and select favorite authors and illustrators. Good teachers and librarians have long recognized the motivation potential of personal preference and interest as expressed through self-selection of reading materials. They also know that the more children read and the greater the variety of literature they read, the more discerning readers they become.

The more children know about their world, the more they discover about themselves—who they are, what they value, and what they stand for. These personal insights alone are sufficient to warrant making good books an essential part of any child's home and school experiences. But literature is also valuable for its academic benefits, as will be discussed in the following section.

The Academic Value of Literature to Children

In addition to the personal benefits of literature for young readers, there are several important academic benefits.

Reading

Many of you already may have reached the common-sense deduction that reading ability, like any other skill, improves with practice. As educators, you should also know some of the landmark research studies that have confirmed this belief and that have revealed other important findings about the worth of literature for children. Table 1-1 summarizes these studies and their findings.

A glance at Table 1-1 clearly shows that literature can be invaluable in teaching children to read. Two procedures seem especially important: reading aloud to children and silent independent reading by children, both on a daily basis, if possible. To discover another truth, you must read between the lines of the table. Who makes the books available? Who decides to read aloud to the children? Who makes the first decisions about what to read aloud? Who makes a child's first experiences with literature enjoyable? Who makes the experiences interactive by asking thought-provoking questions? The truth is that there must first be someone, more than likely an adult, who has the knowledge, willingness, and patience to guide children to books. Who will this be? For some children, it will be their parents; for many others, it will be you—their teacher or librarian.

Several recent publications have important information for parents and teachers about the role of literature (among other things) in learning to read and in teaching reading. *Becoming a Nation of Readers: The Report of the Commission on Reading* (Anderson, Hiebert, Scott, & Wilkinson, 1985) and *Counterpoint and Beyond: A Response to Becoming a Nation of Readers* (Davidson, 1988) present excellent overviews of reading and what works in reading instruction as based on research findings. The U.S. Department of Education's 65-page monograph, *What Works: Research about Teaching*

TABLE 1–1   Important Studies on Literature and Literacy

Researcher(s)	Subjects	Findings
Reading		
Butler (1975)	Cushla, from ages 4 months to 3 years	Reading aloud from children's picture books to a severely disabled child from age 4 months enabled the child to learn to read.
Durkin (1966)	Children who learned to read before attending school	Children who learned to read before attending school were read to regularly from the age of 3. Early reading and early writing are often linked.
Cohen (1968)	7-year-olds	Reading to children who have not been previously exposed to literature can help them learn to read.
Eldredge and Butterfield (1986)	1,149 beginning readers in 50 classrooms	Use of children's literature to teach reading has a much greater positive effect on students' achievement and attitudes toward reading than does use of basals with traditional homogeneous grouping.
Leinhardt, Zigmond, and Cooley (1981)	Elementary-grade children	The amount of time children spend reading silently in school is associated with their year–to–year gains in reading achievement. Children improve their reading ability by reading a lot.
Fielding, Wilson, and Anderson (1968)	Middle-graders	Students who read a lot at home show larger gains on reading achievement tests.
Applebee (1978)	Children ages 2 to 17	Children's sense of story grows as they mature. Literature has a positive effect on children's language development.
Carlsen and Sherrill (1988)	College students who were committed readers	Conditions that promote a love of reading include: Freedom of choice in reading material Availability of books and magazines Family members who read aloud Adults and peers who model reading Role models who value reading Sharing and discussing books Owning books Availability of libraries and librarians
Writing		
McGonaghy (1990)	First-graders in a literature-based reading and writing program	Children use in their own writing the literary conventions and forms they encounter in literature.

TABLE 1–1   *continued*

Researcher(s)	Subjects	Findings
DeFord (1981)	First-graders in phonics-, skills-, and literature-based reading classes	Children in literature-based reading classrooms tend to produce a wider variety of written forms and better written stories than children in phonics or skills-based reading classes.
Eckhoff (1983)	Second-graders who used basal readers	Children adopt writing styles from their reading texts. Some inappropriate writing structures may be learned from oversimplified reading texts.

Responding to Literature

Lehr (1991)	Children in grades K–4	Degree of sophistication of children's commentary on literature increases with exposure to literature.
Hickman (1992)	Children in grades K–5	Children respond to literature at their level of understanding. Forced responses can destroy the enjoyment of literature.

Other Content Areas

Levstik (1986)	Sixth-grade class that used narrative literature to learn history	Children use "human behavior" schemata to make sense of historical information. Personal narrative descriptions of historical fiction have a greater impact on young students than textbooks' depersonalized explanations.
Kiefer (1994)	Children in grades 1–5	Exposure to picture books can increase children's awareness of art and aesthetics. Children's awareness of stylistic factors in picture books grows developmentally.

and Learning (1986) is a distillation of years of research findings organized into terse (sometimes single-sentence) statements of effective teaching and learning practices in the home, classroom, and school. Since reading instruction in U.S. classrooms is currently dominated by basal reading series, you should also be aware of the *Report Card on Basal Readers* (Goodman, Shannon, Freeman, & Murphy, 1988) in which the shortcomings of basal readers and alternatives to them are discussed. Two summary statements of the *Report Card on Basal Readers* are available from the National Council of Teachers of English. They are entitled *Report on Basal Readers* (Weaver & Watson, 1988) and *Basal Readers and the State of American Reading Instruction: A Call for Action.* These documents are well worth the short time it takes to read them.

Writing

Since people tend to assimilate or adopt what they like of what they read and hear, children may, by listening to and reading literature, begin to develop their own writing "voice," or unique, personal writing style. By listening to and reading excellent literature, children are exposed to rich vocabulary and excellent writing styles, which serve as good models for their own speaking and writing voices. The acquisition of a larger vocabulary through reading offers young writers a better choice for their own stories. Devices found in books such as the use of dialect, dialogue, and precise description are often assimilated into students' own writing.

Content Area Subjects

In reading about and discussing children's literature, you will often hear the phrase *literature across the curriculum.* This means using works of literature as teaching materials in the content areas of reading, social studies and history, science, health, and, possibly, math. Good teachers have always used literature across the curriculum. The logic for this practice is sound. Many trade books contain information relevant to the topics studied in school. Moreover, this information is presented through captivating, sometimes beautifully illustrated, narratives. Information thus presented is interesting to students and, therefore, is more comprehensible and memorable. When using literature across the curriculum, teachers and students are not confined to the textbook as the sole resource. Using resource books such as those that are listed in Appendix B, you can find several trade books on almost any topic. Using several sources of information has always been considered prudent both in and out of school, since doing so usually provides fuller factual coverage of topics and leads to wiser, more informed decisions on issues. Few resources are available to the teacher that will help as much to make learning interesting and memorable to children as good trade fiction and nonfiction. Using literature across the curriculum is particularly appropriate today, given the abundance of masterfully written, information-relevant children's trade books available to teachers and librarians.

Art Appreciation

Illustration in children's picture books can be appreciated both for its ability to help tell the story (cognitive value) and for its value as art (aesthetic value). The cognitive value of illustration in picture books will be dealt with in more detail in Chapter 4, but the point to be emphasized here is that if you appreciate art for its own sake, there is much that you can do in your classroom to instill in your students a similar appreciation. It takes only a moment to call to your students' attention particularly striking and unusual illustrations. By doing so, you show them that you value art. You can also discuss the artist's style, the medium used (watercolor, oils, pastels, etc.), the palette (range of colors), and how the artist's style compares to the style of others. In addition, picture book art serves well as a model for applied art lessons. By suggesting to your students that they use media, techniques, and topics suggested by picture book illustrations in their own artwork, you make good use of a handy, valuable resource and in yet another way show that you value this art.

From the foregoing discussion, it should be clear that students are not the only ones in schools who can benefit from children's literature. As a teacher or librarian, you will find that excellent literature is rich in social, historical, and scientific information about the world and its people and that it has great potential for developing the entire elementary school curriculum.

Approaches to Studying and Interpreting Literature

The scholarly study of literature generally focuses on the meaning to be found in a work. Some people seek insights into the work by studying the author's life. Some interpret the work by associating it with the social and political milieu within which it was written, while others analyze works from the past in light of today's prevailing attitudes. Deep analysis of a work through exact and careful reading is referred to as *structural criticism* or *New Criticism*. In this approach the analysis of the words and structure of a work is the focus; the goal is to find the "correct" interpretation.

Until the 1960s, structural criticism held sway in most literature classrooms. Most teachers who used literature in their classes took the view that there is only one correct interpretation of any work of literature. According to this view, reading is a process of taking from the text only what was put there by the author. Young readers' success with any work of literature was determined by how closely their interpretations matched the "authorized" interpretation. Students' responses to literature were thus limited to naming (or guessing) the "right" answers to teachers' questions.

In 1938, Louise Rosenblatt introduced the *transactional view of reading.* She asserted that what the reader brings to the reading act—his world of experience, personality, and current frame of mind—is just as important in making meaning of the text as is what the author writes. According to this view, reading is a fusion of text and reader. Consequently, any text's meaning will vary from reader to reader and, indeed, from reading to reading of the same text by the same reader. Almost everyone has experienced reading a book only to discover that a friend has reacted to or interpreted the same book quite differently. Although Rosenblatt (1978) points out that the text of any book guides and constrains the interpretation that is made, an important corollary to her view of reading is that personal interpretations, within reason, are valid, permissible, and, in fact, desirable.

Another interesting aspect of Rosenblatt's theory is that reading is done for two distinct purposes: to take knowledge from the text (efferent reading) and to live through a literary experience, in the sense of assuming the identity of a book character (aesthetic reading). Whether we read efferently or aesthetically depends on what we are reading (e.g., a want-ad versus a mystery novel) and why we are reading it (e.g., for information versus for escape). Rosenblatt's view of reading is in tune with teaching practices today and has important implications for the way you will encourage your students to respond to the literature you share with them.

Choosing Books for Children

If given a choice in housing, child care, education, food, or clothing, parents usually choose what they consider to be the best for their children. Why should it be any different with the literature adults choose to share with children? The points made about quality and content of literature at the beginning of this chapter definitely play a part in any book selection for children. In addition, you will also want to consider the following suggestions.

Know the Child

The best teachers tend to know their students well. For instance, you will find it helpful to know your students' long-term and short-term interests, their home environment (family makeup, siblings, pets), their friends and social activities, their hobbies, their skills (athletic, academic, artistic), and their hopes or plans for the future. Children's interests have been shown to be one of the most powerful motivating forces available to teachers. Since there are now books on almost every topic conceivable and written at varying degrees of difficulty, you should be able to assemble a collection of books from which your students will be able to make satisfying selections. In addition, you will want to have a general grasp of your students' reading and listening levels. Often children's abilities to read and listen are on different levels. Young children, in particular, are able to listen to and comprehend more difficult material than they are able to read and comprehend. This difference is one that teachers accommodate by reading aloud more challenging books and providing a choice of easier reading material for students' independent reading.

Know the Books

Teachers and librarians who read children's books regularly, who are familiar with a wide variety of genres, and who are informed about recently published books are likely to be able to interest children in books. Of course, it is advantageous to have read widely and to be able to share and compare your reactions to a book with the children. However, it is not necessary to read every book that your students read in order to be well versed in children's literature or to be an effective promoter of good books. Aside from reading the books, there are a number of other ways to become familiar with them. You can ask librarians for information about the most current titles, share information about books with your colleagues, and read book reviews (see the *Reliable Sources* section below for specific review journals). Your own reading program can be made more effective if you focus on award-winning and notable books, as well as on those selected for their appeal to individual children under your care. Knowledge of children's *classics* (works whose excellent quality and enduring appeal to children through several generations are generally recognized) is also an advantage. After you have read a number of books from a genre, particularly classic examples, you will develop a framework for thinking about books of that kind, whether or not you have read an individual title. You will, of course, want to have read any book you plan to read aloud to a class.

Two other features for teachers and librarians to consider are the readability and conceptual difficulty of books. *Readability* is an estimate of a text's difficulty based upon its vocabulary (common versus uncommon words) and sentence structure (short, simple sentences versus long, complex sentences). *Conceptual difficulty* pertains to the complexity of ideas treated in the work and to how these ideas are presented. Symbolism, abstraction, and lengthy description contribute to the complexity of ideas, just as the use of flashbacks or shifting points of view contributes to the complexity of plot presentation.

Consider the Mode of Delivery

Whether the book is intended for independent reading by children or for reading aloud by an adult is another important consideration in choosing a book for children. Children can listen with good comprehension to a book that is too difficult for them to read independently. In fact, good teachers often select books that challenge their students intellectually so that students can be guided in their appreciation of deeper works of literature.

Censorship

Closely associated with book selection, albeit quite different from it, is censorship. *Censorship* is the removal, suppression, or restricted circulation of literary, artistic, or educational materials on the grounds that they are morally or otherwise objectionable (Reichman, 1988). *Selection* of books for children, on the other hand, is the right to choose certain books and reject others for use with children on the bases of literary quality and knowledge of child development and child psychology; selection does not *insist upon removing the rejected books from the shelves for everyone else* (Jalongo & Creany, 1991). Censorship is a complex issue in that those who attempt to censor come from both conservative and liberal sectors of society and act out of seemingly legitimate concerns, such as protection of children from harm. The essential problem with censorship is that individuals or small groups of people want to decide on the basis of their beliefs the books that the general public may read. In other words, censors want to make moral decisions for all others. In so doing, censors of children's books deny intellectual freedom not only to children, but also to those who often select books for children, such as teachers, librarians, and parents. Because the censor's goal is to ban books or limit access to them, censorship is essentially a negative act. Because the selector's goal is to provide high-quality, honest works of literature for children, selection is essentially a positive act.

Censorship attempts are growing in the United States. According to Judith Krug, editor of the American Library Association (ALA) journal, *Intellectual Freedom*, 697 challenges to children's books were received by the ALA in 1993, and nationwide the number was about four times that many (personal communication, March 1994). The following list of children's books that have been involved in censorship attempts may surprise you, not only because of the high quality of some of the books, but also because of the nature of some of the objections.

Book	Objection
Forever, by Judy Blume (1975)	Deals with sex
The Witches, by Roald Dahl (1983)	Promotes witchcraft
Little Red Riding Hood, retold and illustrated by Trina Hyman (1983)	Promotes alcoholism
Swimmy, by Leo Lionni (1963)	Promotes Communism
Halloween ABC, by Eve Merriam (1987)	Promotes devil worship
The Bridge to Terabithia, by Katherine Paterson (1977)	Deals with death
The Catcher in the Rye, by J.D. Salinger (1951)	Contains profanity
Scary Stories to Tell in the Dark, by Alvin Schwartz (3 vol.; 1981–1991)	Terrorizes children
In the Night Kitchen, by Maurice Sendak (1970)	Contains nudity
Sylvester and the Magic Pebble, by William Steig (1969)	Portrays police as pigs
The Adventures of Huckleberry Finn, by Mark Twain (1884)	Promotes slavery
Daddy's Roommate, by Michael Willhoite (1990)	Promotes homosexuality

Although only a fraction of attempts at censorship ever makes it to court, the effect of these attempts is nonetheless powerful. Teachers and librarians, afraid that some parent might object to an excellent book because of one curse word or the mention of a witch or the devil, may choose not to have the book in their library, or may feel compelled to leave out sections or change words when they read the book aloud. This is particularly true when there are reports of trouble with the book in another community.

In response to the trend toward more censorship attempts, school systems have established literature curriculum committees that present guidelines for school personnel to use in selecting books and for dealing with would-be censors of curriculum or library materials. Being able to prove that any book found in a school or classroom library has met stated selection criteria protects teachers against claims that the material has been negligently or capriciously allowed into a school library. The following criteria are often included in school selection policies:

- The book must be favorably reviewed in national professional review journals.
- The book must be included on one or more national recommended lists. (Lists such as the ALA's annual Notable Books list, for example, should be stated.)

It makes sense for a school to have and use written criteria for evaluating and selecting books that students are going to be asked or invited to read. You would be wise to find out if your school has a book selection policy and, if not, help develop one.

In dealing with censorship attempts, teachers should let their actions be guided by two precepts: (1) a parent has the right to object to his or her child's reading or listening to a specific book, and that right should be respected; and (2) a parent does not have the right to deny everyone else the right to read or hear a book. Teachers often find that censorship problems can be solved by being flexible. For example, if a parent objects to a book that is being read aloud to his or her child, the teacher can allow that child to visit another classroom or the media center when the book is being read.

Teachers and library media specialists also have found that a written procedure is helpful for bringing order and reason into discussions with parents who want to censor school materials. Most procedures call for teachers to give would-be censors a complaint form and ask them to specify their concerns in writing. There are advantages to such a system: Both teachers and parents are given time to reflect on the issue and to control their emotions; and the would-be censor is given time to read the book in its entirety, if he has not done so already. Developing written procedures and complaint forms for dealing with a would-be censor are important tasks for the literature curriculum committee.

The American Library Association's Office for Intellectual Freedom has several publications about censorship such as *Censorship and Selection: Issues and Answers for Schools* (co-published by the American Association of School Administrators, 1988) that provide important and helpful information to schools on this topic. (For a catalog of all ALA publications, write to ALA Publishing, 50 East Huron Street, Chicago, IL 60611.) *People for the American Way*, an organization that provides advice and assistance in combatting school censorship, can be contacted at 2000 M St. NW, Suite 400, Washington, D.C. 20036.

One form of school censorship is so subtle that most teachers, librarians, and students are unaware that it is happening. This form of censorship—just as harmful as publicized cases—occurs when teachers or librarians, for whatever reason, select such a narrow assortment of books for classroom use as to omit perfectly acceptable genres, topics, character types, and authors. Your best defense against this kind of censorship is an awareness of the harm that it can do.

Reliable Sources for Book Titles

Several awards have been established in this century for the purposes of elevating and maintaining the literary standards of children's books and for honoring the authors and illustrators whose work is judged by experts in the field to be the best. These awards lists provide the teacher with one means for selecting excellent works to share with children.

Table 1-2 itemizes what are considered to be the major awards for children's books in the United States, Canada, and Great Britain. Complete lists of the books that won these awards can be found in Appendix A.

Many states have their own awards for children's books, often generated from school children who nominate and vote on books based on appeal or popularity. You will want to check the listings of these state awards in Appendix A, and familiarize yourself with your own state's children's choice award. Teachers and librarians across the country report that children enjoy participating in the selection process and give these award programs high marks for reading motivation.

Because journals are published several times yearly, they are helpful for keeping current with children's book publishing. *The Horn Book Magazine, School Library*

TABLE 1–2   Major U.S., Canadian, and British Children's Book Awards

Award/Country	Period	For/Year Established
Newbery Award/U.S.A.	Annual	The most distinguished contribution to children's literature published in the previous year. Given to a U.S. author. Established 1922.
Caldecott Award/U.S.A.	Annual	The most distinguished picture book for children published in the previous year. Given to a U.S. illustrator. Established 1938.
Laura Ingalls Wilder Award/U.S.A.	Every 3 years	Lifetime work that has made a substantial and lasting contribution to children's literature. Given to a U.S. author or illustrator. Established 1954.
Mildred Batchelder Award/U.S.A.	Annual	The most distinguished translated work for children published in the previous year. Given to a U.S. publisher. Established 1968.
Canadian Library Awards/Canada	Annual	The most distinguished contribution to children's literature by a Canadian published in the previous year. Established 1947. Also the most distinguished children's book published in French. Established 1954.
Amelia Frances Howard-Gibbon Award/Canada	Annual	The most distinguished picture book for children published in the previous year. Given to a Canadian illustrator. Established 1971.
Carnegie Medal/Great Britain	Annual	The most distinguished contribution to children's literature first published in the United Kingdom in the previous year. Given to an author. Established 1936.
Kate Greenaway Award/Great Britain	Annual	The most distinguished picture book for children first published in the United Kingdom in the previous year. Given to an illustrator. Established 1956.
Hans Christian Andersen/International	Every 2 years	Recognition of an entire body of work. Given to an author and an illustrator. Established 1956.

Journal, Booklist, and *Bulletin of the Center for Children's Books* are review journals that evaluate, annotate, and discuss the most recently published trade books on a monthly or semimonthly basis. Two language-related teacher journals often subscribed to by elementary teachers, *Language Arts* and *The Reading Teacher,* have columns devoted to reviewing new children's books in each monthly issue. *The New Advocate* and *The Journal of Children's Literature*, journals dedicated entirely to children's literature and those involved in it, also have extensive reviews of newly published children's books. *Book Links,* an American Library Association bimonthly publication, helps teachers and librarians to integrate the best children's books into their curriculum by presenting annotated lists of books selected around themes and topics. *The WEB*, published three times a year by Ohio State University, presents curriculum webs of books and related teaching suggestions. These journals are readily available in school libraries and the children's section of most public libraries.

In cooperation with various national teaching associations, The Children's Book Council (CBC) publishes annual, annotated lists of the best trade books to supplement content area subjects in grades K–8. Two excellent lists of this kind are Outstanding Science Trade Books for Children (published in cooperation with the National Science Teachers Association) and Notable Children's Trade Books in the Field of Social Studies (published in cooperation with the National Council for the Social Studies).

Extensive lists or bibliographies, often annotated, of both older and newer books are valuable aids in book selection. These are usually organized around subject headings and can be remarkably helpful and efficient when you are developing units of study and topical reading lists for students or when you are seeking read-aloud literature about a specific subject. Some of the most helpful bibliographic sources are the following:

A to Zoo: Subject Access to Children's Picture Books, 4th ed. (Lima, 1993)
The Best in Children's Books: The University of Chicago Guide to Children's Literature, vol. 1, 1966–1972; vol. 2, 1973–1978; vol. 3, 1979–1984; vol. 4, 1985–1990. (Sutherland)
The Bookfinder: A Guide to Children's Literature about the Needs and Problems of Youth Aged 2 and Up, vol. 4. (Dreyer, 1989) See also *The Best of Bookfinder.* (Dreyer, 1992)
The Elementary School Library Collection: A Guide to Books and Other Media, 19th ed. (Lee & Hoyle, 1994)

Literature for the Developing Child

In this section we will discuss types of books and general topics most likely to be appreciated by children of different age levels. Children's physical, cognitive, language, and moral development are important considerations in book selection, as is their developing concept of story. By overlaying this general information with the specific interests of any child, you can recognize and make available literature that the children in your care will select and read with interest and enjoyment.

Ages 0 to 2

Even infants can enjoy and benefit from good literature. In choosing books for them, we must consider such practical aspects of physical development as how well they can see the illustrations and how long they will sit still for a book experience.

For instance, books chosen for babies to hold and look at by themselves should feature clearly defined, brightly colored pictures, usually placed on a plain background. Most often, these books will be brief, plotless, idea books called *concept books,* and they will concern the everyday routines and familiar objects that fill the infants' lives. These books are often constructed of heavy, nontoxic cardboard and are called *board books.* Examples are *Dressing* by Helen Oxenbury and *What Is It?* by Tana Hoban.

Since babies have a strong, positive reaction to any exaggerated patterns in sound or movement, the natural music created by strong rhymes and rhythms in *nursery rhymes,* as well as the brevity and humor of these verses, make them appropriate read-aloud material for children at this age level. For example, see *The Orchard Book of Nursery Rhymes* selected by Zena Sutherland and illustrated by Faith Jaques.

To take advantage of the primacy of the senses and muscular coordination in early learning, you will want to use *interactive books* with children from birth to age 2. In these books, participation (clapping, moving) or manipulation of the book (touching, opening little doors) is encouraged. Examples include *Pat the Bunny* by Dorothy Kunhardt and *Where's Spot?* by Eric Hill.

All of the best baby books, whether wordless or with brief text, invite the reader or readers to "talk the book through." In this way, the books promote oral language development, which is the child's first step toward literacy.

Ages 2 to 4

Many aspects of the recommended books for babies apply as well to books for toddlers. Daily routines and objects familiar to the child remain good topics. For this audience, such topics can be incorporated into *picture storybooks* that feature simple plots, beautiful illustrations that tell part of the story, and interesting, humorous characters and situations. Story characters often exhibit the physical skills, such as running, buttoning and unbuttoning clothes, and locking and unlocking doors, that 2- to 4-year-olds take pride in having accomplished. These books are meant to be read aloud to the child. Shirley Hughes' *Alfie Gets in First* is a good example.

Concept books are excellent for children who are beginning to make sense of their world, and these concepts can now include numbers (*counting books*), letters (*ABC books*), and more complex concepts like opposites. The *illustrated dictionary* or *word book* is another variety of concept book that promotes the naming and labeling of objects, actions, and people, which are so important to children who are rapidly developing their language skills. Examples are *Push-Pull, Empty-Full: A Book of Opposites* by Tana Hoban and *Richard Scarry's Biggest Word Book Ever!* by Richard Scarry.

Children aged 2 to 4 will enjoy nursery rhymes even more than they did as infants and will easily commit these verses to memory. Folktales, an important part of our literary heritage, work well with children at this age level, particularly the repetitive stories such as *Henny Penny* and *The Gingerbread Boy,* both illustrated by Paul Galdone. These stories and verses are also appropriate because their "good" and "bad" characters fit the 2- to 4-year-old's simplistic "right or wrong" sense of morality.

Ages 4 to 7

Picture storybooks will still be the heart of the literature experience for children during these years. Most of these books are meant to be read aloud to children by a fluent reader, but it is common for children at this stage to choose a favorite picture storybook, memorize the text over repeated hearings, and enjoy the book on their own through "play-reading." Folktales are still a favorite for storytelling and read-aloud experiences, as are humorous poems with strong rhyme and rhythm.

During these years many children will acquire the fundamentals of reading: the notion that stories and the words within them carry meaning, the letter–sound relationship, left-to-right and top-to-bottom progression of print on the page, and a sight vocabulary (certain words that children can recognize and say on sight). *Easy-to-read books* support children's enthusiasm for learning to read; these books make use of familiar words, word patterns, informative illustrations, and, in some cases, rhyme to make the text predictable. Examples are *Rosie's Walk* by Pat Hutchins and *Noisy Nora* by Rosemary Wells. Physical growth and increasing independence are signposted by stories in which children interact with other children more than with adults, spend time away from home, and begin school. Examples are *Ira Sleeps Over* by Bernard Waber and *Chrysanthemum* by Kevin Henkes.

Children at this age level exhibit great enthusiasm for finding out about the world and how it works. This interest can be fed and stimulated through *informational books* for the beginning reader. Examples include *Milk Makers* by Gail Gibbons, and *Messages in the Mailbox: How to Write a Letter* by Loreen Leedy.

Ages 7 to 9

During these years most children who have had the benefit of a rich literature experience will become fluent and willing readers. This skill, combined with their increased flexibility in thinking, makes many new story types appropriate for these children. Now that they can understand and accept others' perspectives, they can enjoy reading about the lives of other children of the past, present, or future in *transitional readers* and later in *novels*.

Transitional readers are chapter books with simple, straightforward plots and writing styles for children who are ready to read slightly longer picture books and short chapter books in addition to short picture books. A helpful guide to books of this type is *Beyond Picture Books: A Guide to First Readers* (Barstow & Riggle, 1995). Examples include the "Ramona" and "Henry Huggins" books by Beverly Cleary and the "Julian" books by Ann Cameron. At 8 or 9, children begin to assert their growing abilities to meet their own needs by doing such things as camping out in the backyard or biking to school alone. Fittingly, books for these children often center on the adventures of young characters within their neighborhoods and communities.

Chapter books with more sophisticated writing styles or more complicated plots can be greatly enjoyed as read-alouds in the classroom and as independent reading by the better readers. Also, many picture storybooks are appropriate for independent reading by children at this age level. For example, see William Steig's *Sylvester and the Magic Pebble* and *The Amazing Bone*. Story characters having both good and bad qualities and realistic problems mirror the 7- to 9-year-olds' maturing sense of morality as they begin to recognize that life and people do not fit into neat "good" and "bad" categories and that opinions different from their own may have validity. *A Dog on Barkham Street* and *The Bully of Barkham Street* by Mary Stolz are good examples, especially when they are read back-to-back.

A common phenomenon among children who are learning to read is the penchant for rereading the same book many times. Often misconstrued by adults as somehow wrong, the act of rereading the same text many times is, in fact, good reading practice made palatable to the child by the security of a familiar, or "friendly," text.

Although folktales continue to be popular with many 7-year-olds, studies have shown that interest in this genre generally peaks and falls off by age 8. Children then begin to show more interest in the here and now and begin to shift toward a preference for realism in their stories and poems.

Ages 9 to 12

With their rapidly developing physical and mental skills and abilities, 9- to 12-year-olds are ready for the great variety of literature that awaits them. Plots in novels can now be more complicated, including such devices as flashback and symbolism. Language devices such as speech patterns and dialects of earlier or different cultures can be managed. Both historical fiction and science fiction, which are set in the distant past and distant future, respectively, can be understood and enjoyed. Examples are *Julie of the Wolves* by Jean George, *Tuck Everlasting* by Natalie Babbitt, and *Across Five Aprils* by Irene Hunt.

These children are particularly interested in reading about young people who, like themselves, are growing up, asserting and using their new-found skills, moving toward independence, and experiencing growth through meeting challenges. Survival stories, peer stories, and realistic animal stories intrigue these children. Moreover, stories that present alternative points of view, non-traditional characters, and moral dilemmas are well-suited to young people whose moral development allows them to recognize the legitimacy of opinions, mores, and lifestyles different from their own. Examples include *Shiloh* by Phyllis Reynolds Naylor, *The Great Gilly Hopkins* by Katherine Paterson, *Hatchet* by Gary Paulsen, and *Nothing But the Truth* by Avi.

An interesting parallel to the 7- to 9-year-olds' tendency to reread books occurs at this age level. Many 9- to 12-year-olds discover series books such as the Sweet Valley Twins, the Hardy Boys, or the Three Investigators adventures, and read every book in the series one after the other. This is rereading of a sort, since all books within such a series are written to a formula and vary only slightly one from the other. Reading these books is beneficial to many children, simply due to the hours of reading practice they willingly gain.

Although most 9- to 12-year-olds will be competent readers, there is no valid reason for librarians or teachers to discontinue their read-aloud programs for these children. More challenging novels as well as sophisticated picture books for older children sometimes can be more fully appreciated by children when read aloud by an excellent reader. Examples include *My Brother Sam Is Dead* by James and Christopher Collier, *The Garden of Abdul Gasazi* by Chris Van Allsburg, and *Rabbit Island* by Jörg Steiner with illustrations by Jörg Müller.

Teachers and librarians who are consistently successful in helping children find books they like rapidly narrow the field of choices by first considering general factors such as age level and types of books appropriate for children of that general age level. Then they consider more personal factors such as the child's current reading interests and reading ability in order to select specific titles. Knowing children's general reading preferences provides some guidance in book selection, but there is no substitute for knowing the child.

Children's Reading Preferences

A *reading preference* is a stated or implied choice between several reading options. For example, in response to the question, Which would you rather read: a romance, a mystery, or a science fiction adventure? if you chose the mystery option, you would have stated a reading preference for mystery.

Many studies of children's reading preferences have been conducted during this century. Differences in the choices offered to children and in the ways data were gathered from study to study make extensive generalization difficult, but a few patterns have emerged from these studies (Haynes, 1988):

- There are no significant differences between the preferences of boys and girls before age 9.
- The greatest differences in reading preferences of boys and girls occur between ages 10 and 13.
- Boys and girls in the middle grades (ages 10 to 13) share a pronounced preference for mystery and, to a lesser degree, humor, adventure, and animals.
- Preferences of boys in the middle grades include action and adventure stories and sports stories.
- Preferences of girls in the middle grades include fantasy stories, animal stories, and stories about people.

A teacher or librarian might use the foregoing information to make general predictions about what types of books boys or girls of a certain age might enjoy.

Reading preferences should not be depended on as the sole guide in making specific book recommendations to individuals. The reason for this should be clear when you consider the hypothetical question involving romance, mystery, and science fiction books posed earlier. Even though you had to choose one or the other of the options offered to you, it is quite possible that you rarely, if ever, read any of these types of books; mystery may have been just the least uninteresting to you of the three. Knowing this so-called preference would not benefit, and could possibly hinder, a teacher or librarian who was seeking to help you find a book that you would enjoy.

Children's Reading Interests

Reading interests and reading preferences are not the same. A *preference*, as noted above, implies a forced choice between options selected by someone other than oneself. An *interest*, on the other hand, comes from within oneself, can encompass whatever can be imagined, and implies freedom of choice. Knowledge of children's reading preferences provides information about children in general, but knowledge of children's reading interests is personal and individual. Since most teachers and school librarians work with particular groups of children over an extended time, they can learn the interests of each child within the group. In so doing, they gain powerful, effective knowledge to use in successfully matching children and books.

Common sense tells us that children will apply themselves more vigorously to read or learn something that they are interested in than they will to read or learn something that they find uninteresting or boring. Interest generates motivation, and good teachers and librarians put that motivation to work by guiding students to good books on topics that satisfy individual interests.

Learning your students' interests can be accomplished in several ways. The best way is to get to know your students by talking to them in whole-class sharing and in one-to-one conferences. All people like to talk about themselves and their interests; children are no different. One or more of the following questions might start a productive dialogue between you and a student:

1. What are your favorite things to do?
2. Are you very good at doing something? Tell me about it.
3. What would you like to learn more about?
4. What do you like to spend most of your free time doing?
5. Do you like fiction or nonfiction better?
6. What kinds of stories do you like to hear?
7. What kinds of books do you like to read?
8. Who is in your family? Tell me a little about each family member.

You can also learn about children's interests through their free-choice writing. Journal writing is particularly helpful in this regard. A perfectly valid and more direct approach is to ask children to list their interests. Many teachers keep such lists in their students' writing folders to use during individual conferences. Because children's interests change often, data of this sort must be updated regularly.

Yet another way for teachers and librarians to keep current on students' interests is to conduct their own interest inventories several times a year to assure that the reading selections available in their classroom or school libraries reflect the general interests of their students. The following steps show one way to conduct a classroom interest inventory:

1. Collect 30 to 40 appropriate books that are new to your students and that represent a wide variety of genres and topics.
2. Number the books by inserting paper markers with numbers at the top.
3. Note on a master list the number and genre of each book.
4. Design a response form for students, such as the one shown in Figure 1-1.
5. Hold each book up and tell your students the title, the type, and a one-sentence summary of the book. You might use the Library of Congress summary that is printed with the cataloguing information on the copyright page of each book.

6. Place the books in order on tables and shelves around the classroom or media center.
7. Give the students 20 to 30 minutes to make the circuit, peruse the books, and mark their response forms.
8. Collect and tally the students' responses and compare with your master list to arrive at the types of books in which your students are currently most interested.

Would You Like to Read This Book?

1.	YES	NO	16.	YES	NO
2.	YES	NO	17.	YES	NO
3.	YES	NO	18.	YES	NO
4.	YES	NO	19.	YES	NO
5.	YES	NO	20.	YES	NO

etc.

FIGURE 1-1 Sample Student Response Form for Interest Inventory

As you look at each book, answer this question by circling either YES or NO next to the appropriate book number. Be sure to match the book number and the item number before circling your answer.

Classroom interest inventories not only provide teachers and librarians with helpful information about their students' current interests but also introduce children to new genres, topics, and titles. In this way, teachers and librarians can help accomplish their fundamental task of expanding students' fields of interest and knowledge bases.

Teachers and librarians are often surprised at how extensive and varied their students' interests are. Rockets and space travel? Lizards? Semitrailer trucks? When your students come to you with interests as diverse as these, expecting you to help them find books on these topics, you can, of course, send them to the card catalog or its computerized equivalent. In addition, however, you need to know about such general subject guide indexes as *Children's Catalog* (Isaacson, Hillegas, & Yaakov, 1991) and the annually updated *Subject Guide to Children's Books in Print,* which is a cross-referenced subject guide to all children's books listed in *Children's Books in Print.* (For more information on these resource books, see Appendix B.) There are few reference tools as helpful as a subject guide index for finding books on specific topics.

Research in Children's Literature

As in any field of study, the field of children's literature naturally gives rise to many and varied questions: Does reading literature aloud to young children help them learn to read? How do children's reading preferences differ by age and sex? What are the common features in recent children's books about World War II? What factors help to ensure success in public library summer reading programs? At some point you will read and review books or articles in which some aspect of children's literature has been investigated in an effort to answer such questions. Sometimes the findings of a single research study are enlightening. More important, over time, research can provide a body of evidence that either proves or disproves a claim, theory, generalization, or assumption.

The field of children's literature has attracted the interest of three major groups—educators, children's librarians, and specialists in literature, including literary critics. Generally speaking, researchers in the fields of education and library and information science are primarily interested in children and how literature affects their lives and learning. Literature specialists, on the other hand, are primarily interested in the literature itself, especially in the literary characteristics of children's literature in terms of how they affect a work's quality or how the work compares to other works.

Both approaches to research in children's literature have resulted in valuable knowledge that helps us serve children better in our various roles. One of the most rewarding practices that you can develop as an educator or librarian is to read professional journals and notable new children's trade books regularly. In this way you will benefit from a constant renewal of information and ideas.

References

Anderson, R. C., Hiebert, E. H., Scott, J. A., & Wilkinson, I. A. G. (1985). *Becoming a nation of readers: The report of the commission on reading.* Washington, DC: National Institute of Education.

Applebee, A. N. (1978). *The child's concept of story.* Chicago: University of Chicago.

Babbitt, N. (1975). *Tuck everlasting.* New York: Farrar.

Barr, C. (Ed.). (1994). *The Bowker annual library and book trade almanac* (39th ed.). New Providence, NJ: R.R. Bowker.

Barstow, B., & Riggle, J. (1995). *Beyond picture books: A guide to first readers.* (2nd ed.). New York: R.R. Bowker.

Blume, J. (1975). *Forever.* New York: Bradbury.

Butler, D. (1975). *Cushla and her books.* Boston: Horn Book.

Carlsen, G. R., & Sherrill, A. (1988). *Voices of readers: How we come to love books.* Urbana, IL: National Council of Teachers of English.

Cohen, D. (1968). The effect of literature on vocabulary and reading achievement. *Elementary English, 45,* 209–213, 217.

Collier, J. L. & Collier, C. (1974). *My brother Sam is dead.* New York: Four Winds.

Dahl, R. (1983). *The witches.* Illus. by Q. Blake. New York: Farrar, Straus, & Giroux.

Davidson, J. L. (Ed.). (1988). *Counterpoint and beyond: A response to becoming a nation of readers.* Urbana, IL: National Council of Teachers of English.

DeFord, D. (1981). Literacy, reading, writing, and other essentials. *Language Arts, 58* (5), 652–658.

Dreyer, S. S. (Ed.). (1977–1989). *The bookfinder: A guide to children's literature about the needs and problems of youth aged 2–15* (Vols. 1–4). Circle Pines, MN: American Guidance Service.

————. (1992). *The best of bookfinder: A guide to children's literature about interests and concerns of youth aged 2–18.* Circle Pines, MN: American Guidance Service.

Durkin, D. (1966). *Children who read early.* New York: Columbia Teachers College Press.

Eckhoff, B. (1983). How reading affects children's writing. *Language Arts, 60* (5), 607–616.

Fielding, L. G., Wilson, P. T., & Anderson, R. C.

(1986). A new focus on free reading: The role of trade books in reading instruction. In T. Raphael (Ed.), *The contexts of school-based literacy* (pp. 149–160). New York: Random House.

Galdone, P. (1975). *The gingerbread boy.* New York: Clarion.

———. (1968). *Henny Penny.* New York: Seabury.

George, J. (1972). *Julie of the wolves.* New York: Harper.

Gibbons, G. (1985). *The milk makers.* New York: Macmillan.

Goodman, K. S., Shannon, P., Freeman, Y., & Murphy, S. (1988). *Report card on basal readers.* New York: Richard C. Owen.

Haynes, C. (1988). Explanatory power of content for identifying children's literature preferences. *Dissertation Abstracts International, 49-12A,* p. 3617. (University Microfilms No. DEW8900468).

Henkes, K. (1991). *Chrysanthemum.* New York: Greenwillow.

Hickman, J. (1992). What comes naturally: Growth and change in children's free response to literature. In Temple, C., & Collins, P. (Eds.). *Stories and readers: New perspectives on literature in the elementary classroom.* Norwood, MA: Christopher Gordon.

Hill, E. (1980). *Where's Spot?* New York: Putnam.

Hoban, T. (1972). *Push pull, empty full: A book of opposites.* New York: Macmillan.

———. (1985). *What Is It?* New York: Greenwillow.

Hughes, S. (1982). *Alfie gets in first.* New York: Lothrop.

Hyman, T. S. (reteller and illustrator) (1983). *Little Red Riding Hood.* New York: Holiday.

Isaacson, R., Hillegas, F., & Yaakov, J. (1991). *Children's catalog* (16th ed.). New York: H. W. Wilson.

Jalongo, M. R., & Creany, A. D. (1991). Censorship in children's literature: What every educator should know. *Childhood Education, 67* (3), 143–148.

Kiefer, B. Z. (1995). *The potential of picturebooks: From visual literacy to aesthetic understanding.* Englewood Cliffs, NJ: Prentice Hall.

Kunhardt, D. (1962). *Pat the bunny.* New York: Golden. (1940)

Lee, L. K., & Hoyle, G. D. (Eds.). (1994). *The elementary school library collection: A guide to books and other media* (19th ed.). Williamsport, PA: Brodart.

Leedy, L. (1991). *Messages in the mailbox: How to write a letter.* New York: Holiday.

Lehr, S. (1991). *The child's developing sense of theme: Responses to literature.* New York: Teachers College Press.

Leinhardt, G., Zigmond, N., & Cooley, W. W. (1981). Reading instruction and its effects. *American Educational Research Journal, 18,* 343–361.

Levstik, L. (1986). The relationship between historical response and narrative in a sixth-grade classroom. *Theory and Research in Social Education, 14,* 1–15.

Lima, C. W., & Lima, J. A. (1993). *A to zoo: Subject access to children's picture books* (4th ed.). New York: R.R. Bowker.

Lionni, L. (1963). *Swimmy.* New York: Pantheon.

Livingston, Myra Cohn. (1992). Give me books, give me wings in *I never told and other poems.* New York: McElderry.

McConaghy, J. (1990). *Children learning through literature: A teacher researcher study.* Portsmouth, NH: Heinemann.

Merriam, E. (1987). *Halloween abc.* Illus. by L. Smith. New York: Macmillan.

National Council of Teachers of English. (1988). *Basal readers and the state of American reading instruction: A call for action.* Urbana, IL: Commission on Reading.

Naylor, P. R. (1991). *Shiloh.* New York: Atheneum.

Oxenbury, H. (1981). *Dressing.* New York: Simon & Schuster.

Paterson, K. (1977). *The Bridge to Terabithia.* New York: Crowell.

———. (1978). *The great Gilly Hopkins.* New York: Crowell.

Paulsen, G. (1987). *Hatchet.* New York: Bradbury.

Riechman, H. F. (1988). *Censorship and selection: Issues and answers for schools.* Chicago: American Library Association and American Association of School Administrators.

Rosenblatt, L. (1978). *The reader, the text, the poem.* Carbondale, IL: Southern Illinois University.

Salinger, J. D. (1951). *The catcher in the rye.* Boston: Little, Brown.

Scarry, R. (1985). *Richard Scarry's biggest word book ever!* New York: Random.

Schwartz, A. (1981). *Scary stories to tell in the dark.* Illus. by S. Gammell. New York: Harper.

Sendak, M. (1970). *In the night kitchen.* New York: Harper.

Steig, W. (1969). *Sylvester and the magic pebble.* New York: Windmill.

———. (1976). *The amazing bone.* New York: Farrar.

Steiner, J. (1978). *Rabbit island.* Illus. by J. Müller. New York: Harcourt.

Subject guide to children's books in print. (1994). New York: R.R. Bowker.

Sutherland, Z. (1973–1990). *The best in children's books: The University of Chicago guide to children's literature* (Vols. 1–4). Chicago: University of Chicago Press.

———. (1990). *The orchard book of nursery rhymes.* Illus. by F. Jaques. New York: Orchard.

Twain, M. (1982; 1884). *The adventures of Huckleberry Finn.* New York: Scholastic.

Tway, E. (Ed.). (1981). *Reading ladders for human relations* (6th ed.). Washington, DC: American Council on Education.

Van Allsburg, C. (1979). *The garden of Abdul Gasazi.* New York: Houghton Mifflin.

Waber, B. (1972). *Ira sleeps over.* New York: Houghton Mifflin.

Weaver, C., & Watson, D. (1988). *Report on basal readers.* Urbana, IL: National Council of Teachers of English.

What works: Research about teaching and learning. (1986). Washington, DC: U.S. Department of Education.

Willhoite, M. (1990). *Daddy's roommate.* Boston: Alyson Publications.

Chapter 2

Learning about Books

A Book

I'm a strange contradiction; I'm new and I'm old,
I'm often in tatters, and oft deck'd in gold;
Though I never could read, yet letter'd I'm found;
Though blind, I enlighten; though loose, I am bound—
I am always in black, and I'm always in white;
I am grave and I'm gay, I am heavy and light.
In form too I differ—I'm thick and I'm thin,
I've no flesh, and no bones, yet I'm covered with skin;
I've more points than the compass, more stops than the flute—
I sing without voice, without speaking confute;
I'm English, I'm German, I'm French and I'm Dutch;
Some love me too fondly; some slight me too much;
I often die soon, though I sometimes live ages,
And no monarch alive has so many pages.

—Hannah More

In Chapter 1 it was stated that reading is a fusion of text and reader and that each reading of a particular literary work results in a different transaction. Even rereadings by the same reader will result in a different experience. But if each time a book is read the transaction is different, how, then, can general assessments of literary merit be made? Rosenblatt answers that although the notion of a single, correct reading of a literary work is rejected, *"given agreed-upon criteria,* it is possible to decide that some readings are more defensible than others" (1985, p. 36). Although each reading of a given literary work will be different, there are certain generally agreed-upon interpretations of that work by a community of educated readers. In this chapter, traditional literary elements are reviewed in order to heighten your awareness of literary criticism and to provide a more precise vocabulary for you to express your responses to children's books.

Elements of Fiction

Learning to evaluate children's books can best be accomplished by reading as many excellent books as possible. Gradually your judgment on the merits of individual books will improve. Discussing your responses to these books with children, teachers, and other students and listening to their responses will also assist you in becoming a more appreciative critic. Understanding the different parts, or elements, of a piece of fiction and how they work together can help you to become more analytical about literary works; and this, too, can improve your judgment of literature. The elements of fiction are discussed separately in the following sections, but it is the unity of all these elements that produces the story.

Plot

The events of the story and the sequence in which they are told constitute the plot of the story. In other words, the plot is what happens in the story. Plot is the most important element of fiction to the child reader. Often adults believe that a story for children needs only to present familiar, everyday activities—the daily routines of life. Perhaps 2- and 3-year-olds will enjoy hearing narratives such as this, but by age 4, children want to find more excitement in books. A good plot produces conflict in order to build the excitement and suspense that are needed to keep the reader involved.

The nature of the *conflict* within the plot can arise from different sources. The basic conflict may be one that occurs within the main character, called *person-against-self*. In this type of story, the main character struggles against inner drives and personal tendencies in order to achieve some goal. Stories about adolescence will frequently have this conflict as the basis of the story problem. For example, in *Language of Goldfish* by Zibby O'Neal, 13-year-old Carrie struggles to find herself and to accept herself and others. A conflict usually found in survival stories is the struggle the character has with the forces of nature. This conflict is called *person-against-nature*. Worthy examples are *Island of the Blue Dolphins* by Scott O'Dell and *Hatchet* by Gary Paulsen. In other children's stories, the source of the conflict is found between two characters. Conflicts with peers, problems with sibling rivalries, and stories of children rebelling against an adult are *person-against-person* conflicts. For example, the young badger, Frances, in *A Bargain for Frances* by Russell Hoban, struggles to get a fair deal from her friend, Thelma, who sells Frances a tea set. Occasionally a story for children presents the main character in conflict with society. This conflict in children's stories is most often either about the environment being destroyed by new technology or changing times, or about children caught up in a political upheaval such as war. The conflict is then called *person-against-society. My*

Brother Sam Is Dead by James Lincoln Collier and Christopher Collier and *Across Five Aprils* by Irene Hunt, both war stories, pose this type of conflict.

Plots are constructed in many different ways. The most usual plot structures found in children's stories are *chronological plots,* which cover a particular period of time and relate the events in order within the time period. For example, if a book relates the events of one week, then Monday's events will precede Tuesday's, and so on. An example of a story with a chronological plot is *Charlotte's Web,* by E. B. White. There are two distinct types of chronological plots, progressive and episodic. In books with *progressive plots,* the first few chapters are the exposition, in which the characters, setting, and basic conflict are established. Following the expository chapters, the story builds through rising action to a climax. The climax occurs, a satisfactory conclusion (or denouement) is reached, and the story ends. Figure 2-1 suggests how a progressive, chronological, plot might be visualized.

An *episodic plot* ties together separate short stories or episodes, each an entity in itself with its own conflict and resolution. These episodes are typically unified by the same cast of characters and the same setting. Often, each episode comprises a chapter. Although the episodes are usually chronological, time relationships among the episodes may be nonexistent or loosely connected by "during that same year" or "later that month." An example of a short chapter book with an episodic plot structure is *Beezus and Ramona* by Beverly Cleary. Because episodic plots are less complex, they tend to be easier to read. Thus, the reader who is just making the transition from picture books to chapter books may find these plots particularly appealing. Many easy-to-read books for the beginning reader are also structured in this way. *Frog and Toad Are Friends* by Arnold Lobel is a good example of an episodic plot in an easy-to-read book. Figure 2-2 suggests how a chronological, episodic plot might be visualized. A *flashback* is used by authors to convey information about events that occurred earlier in the story—for example, prior to the beginning of the story. In this case, the chronology of events is disrupted and the reader is taken back to an earlier time. Flashbacks can occur more than once and in different parts of a

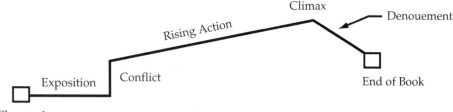

Chapter 1

FIGURE 2-1 Diagram of a Progressive Plot

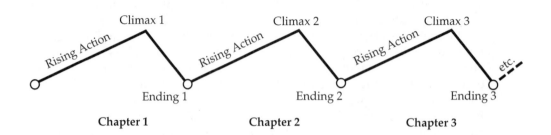

FIGURE 2-2 Diagram of an Episodic Plot

story. The use of a flashback permits authors to begin the story in the midst of the action but later fill in the background for full understanding of the present events. Flashbacks in children's books are mostly found in chapter books for older readers, since such plots can confuse children younger than age 8 or 9. Teachers can help students understand this plot structure by reading aloud good examples of this type of story, such as Jean Craighead George's *My Side of the Mountain.* Class discussion can then focus on the sequence of events and why the author may have chosen to relate the events in this manner. Figure 2-3 illustrates the structure of a flashback in a book.

A stylistic plot device that prepares readers for coming events in a story is *fore-shadowing.* This device gives clues to a later event, possibly even the climax of the story. For example, in *Tuck Everlasting* by Natalie Babbitt the detailed description of the long yellow road in the first chapter foreshadows the long journey the Tuck family members must travel in their lives. You can alert young readers to one of the subtle ways authors prepare them for the outcomes of stories by discussing foreshadowing.

Plot is an important element to all readers, but especially to young readers who enjoy fast-moving, exciting stories. A well-constructed plot contributes substantially to children's acceptance and enjoyment of stories.

Characters

Memorable characters populate the world of children's literature. Ferdinand, the bull; Charlotte, the spider; Frances, the badger; Little Toot, the young tugboat; Karana, the Native-American girl; and Peter, the African-American child with his dog Willie, are all remembered fondly by generations of readers.

Characters, the "actors" in a story, are another element of fiction vital to the enjoyment of a story. A well-portrayed character can become a friend, a role model, or a temporary parent to a child reader. Although exciting events are enjoyed by young readers, the characters involved in those events must matter to the reader or the events no longer seem important. How characters are depicted and how they develop in the course of the story are important to the reader. Two aspects to consider in studying a character are characterization and character development.

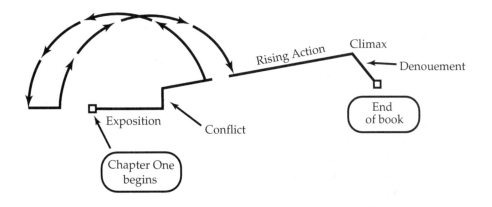

FIGURE 2-3 Diagram of a Flashback

Characterization refers to the way an author helps the reader know a character. The most obvious way an author can do this is to describe the character's physical appearance and personality. Portraying the character's emotional and moral traits or revealing her relationships with other characters are more subtle and effective techniques. In the most convincing characterizations, we see the character through a combination of her own actions and dialogue, the responses of other characters to her, and the narrator's descriptions.

Character development refers to the changes, good or bad, the character undergoes during the course of events in the story. If a character experiences significant, life-altering events, we, as readers, expect that the character will somehow be different as a result of those events. For example, Matt, a boy of age 11 who was left alone for months in the Maine territory to take care of his family's new cabin, becomes a stronger, more independent young man by the end of *The Sign of the Beaver* by Elizabeth George Speare.

In a work of fiction for children there are usually one or two main characters and some minor characters. Ideally each main character, sometimes called the *protagonist,* will be a fully described, complex individual who possesses both good and bad traits, like a real person. Such a character is called a *round character.*

Minor, or secondary, characters may be described in a less complete or partial manner. The extent of description depends on what the reader needs to know about the character for a full understanding of the story. Some of the minor character's traits are described fully, whereas other facets of the character's personality may remain obscure. Because the purpose is to build the story and make it comprehensible, fragmentary knowledge of a minor character may suffice. Occasionally, an author will insert a *flat character*—that is, a character described in a one-sided or underdeveloped manner. Although such persons do not exist in real life, they may be justified within the story to propel the plot. Sometimes the character is shown as an all-evil or all-frivolous person; for instance, folktales present flat characters as symbols of good and evil. In some stories, a flat character plays the role of *character foil,* a person who is in direct juxtaposition to another character (usually the protagonist) and who serves to highlight the characteristics of the other individual. A character foil may occur as a flat or as a round character. The character or force in direct opposition to the main character is called the *antagonist.*

The main characters in an excellent work of fiction for children are rounded, fully developed characters who undergo change in response to life-altering events. Because children generally prefer personified animals or children of their own age, or slightly older, as the main characters of their stories, authors of children's books often face a dilemma. Although in real life children usually have restricted freedom of action and decision making within the confines of a family, the author can develop a more vivid and exciting story if the main characters are "on their own." Thus, in many children's stories parents are absent, no longer living, or no longer functioning. Furthermore, by making up situations, authors are able to focus on just one aspect of life, thereby enabling young readers to see and understand this one facet of life more clearly.

Setting

The time when the story occurs and the place(s) where it occurs constitute the setting of a story. The setting has a more or less important function depending on the story. For example, in historical fiction the authentic re-creation of the period is essential to the comprehension of the story's events. In this situation, the setting, fully described both in time and place, is called an *integral setting.* The story could not be the same if placed in another setting.

On the other hand, the setting in folktales is often vague and general. For example, "long ago in a cottage in the deep woods" is meant to convey a universal, timeless tale, one that could have happened anywhere and almost anytime except the present or very recent past. This type of setting is called a *backdrop setting.* It simply sets the stage and the mood.

Theme

The theme of a story is its underlying meaning or significance. Although we sometimes think of the theme as the message or moral of the story, it can just as likely be an aesthetic understanding, such as an appreciation for nature, or a viewpoint on a current societal issue. To identify the theme, you may ask yourself what the author's purpose was in writing the story, or what the author is saying through this story.

A theme is better expressed by means of a complete sentence than by a single word. For example, students often suggest that a theme found in *Charlotte's Web* by E. B. White is friendship. A better statement of the theme is "Friendship is one of the most satisfying things in the world," as Wilbur the pig tells us in the story. The single word *friendship* may be a topic found in the story, but it is not an expression of the theme.

Themes in children's books should be worthy of children's attention and should convey truth to them. Furthermore, the themes should be based on high moral and ethical standards. A theme, however, must not overpower the plot and characters of the story; children read fiction for enjoyment, not for enlightenment. If the theme is expressed in a heavy-handed, obvious fashion, then the pleasure of the reading experience is diminished. Likewise, overly "teachy" or didactic themes detract from a reader's enjoyment of a story. Certainly a well-written book may convey a moral message, but it should also tell a good story from which the message evolves. In this way the theme is subtly conveyed to the reader.

Often adults write stories not for children's pleasure but to teach morality lessons. Although we think of stories of this sort as the thinly disguised religious tracts found in the early history of children's literature, we must be alert to a tendency for some current authors to use children's literature as a platform to preach about drug abuse, animal rights, and other issues of contemporary interest. If the literary quality of these so-called problem novels is weakened, then the story and characters become secondary to the issue or problem. However, when moral values are embedded within the fabric of a powerful story, children can be led to develop a sense of right and wrong without feeling as if they are being indoctrinated.

Style

Style is the way an author tells the story; it can be viewed as the writing itself, as opposed to the content of the book. However, the style must suit the content of the particular book; the two are intertwined.

Different aspects of style are considered in evaluating a work of fiction. Most obviously, you can look at the *words* chosen to tell the story. Are they long or short, common or uncommon, rhyming or melodic, boring and hackneyed or rich and challenging, unemotional or emotional, standard dialect or regional/minority dialect? The words should be appropriate to the story being told. As an evaluator of books for children, you will want to ask the following questions as you read: Why did the author choose these words? What effect was the author trying to achieve?

The *sentences* may also be considered. Do they read easily? Do they flow without the reader needing to reread to gain the meaning of the text? Sometimes an author chooses to limit the word choices in order to write a book that can be read by a beginning reader. Yet in the hands of a gifted writer, the sentences will remain no less melodic, varied in length and structure, and enjoyable to read and hear than sentences in the best books for the more advanced reader. A good example of a well-written book for beginning readers is Arnold Lobel's *Frog and Toad Are Friends*.

The *organization* of the book may be considered by noting the paragraphs and transitions, length of chapters, headings and chapter titles, preface, endnotes, prologue, epilogue, and length of the book. For the beginning reader it is important whether a story is divided into chapters. After years of looking at, listening to, and reading books without chapters, it is quite an accomplishment for a 6-year-old to move up to so-called chapter books, even if each chapter is only three pages long.

Chapter titles can provoke interest in what will follow, as well as provide the reader with clues to predict story events. Some books provide the readers with a prologue, an introductory statement telling events that precede the start of the story. Some authors include an epilogue, a concluding statement telling events that occur after the story has ended. Gary Paulsen, in speaking to readers about what they bring to the reading act in his prologue to *The Winter Room*, heightens sensitivity to the story that is to follow. In the epilogue of *Tuck Everlasting*, Natalie Babbitt allows the readers to revisit the scene of the story some years later and resolve at least one of the questions they inevitably have at the story's end. Occasionally an author presents information on the sources or historical facts used in the story. In *Friedrich,* for example, Hans Peter Richter adds a chronology of historical events in the endnotes.

Point of view is another aspect of an author's style. If the story is told through the eyes and voice of a *third-person narrator* (the use of *he, she, it*), then the reader can know whatever the narrator knows about the events of the story. In many stories, the narrator is *omniscient* and can see into the minds of all characters and be at many places at the same time. Other stories are narrated from the perspective of only one character in the story. In this case, the story is still told in the third person, but the reader knows only what that particular character can see and understand. This latter technique is called *limited omniscient* point of view.

Other times authors choose to tell the story through a *first-person narrator* (the use of *I*), generally the main character of the story. In such cases the reader gains a sense of closeness to the main character but is not privy to any information unavailable to this character. As you read, you will note that some authors have accomplished a first-person point of view by writing as though their main character were writing a diary or letters, as in *A Gathering of Days: A New England Girl's Journal, 1830-1832* by Joan Blos. Occasionally, a story is told in first person through the eyes of a minor character. For example, *Ben and Me,* by Robert Lawson, is the story of Benjamin Franklin told through the eyes of a mouse in his house. *A shifting point of view* permits the reader to see events from different characters' points of view. This technique is demanding on young readers' skill. When the point of view shifts, the author must carefully cue readers to the changing point of view, as Avi does in *Nothing But the Truth* by identifying sender, receiver, or discussants at the beginning of each letter, memorandum, telephone call, or face-to-face conversation.

Symbolism is an artistic invention used by authors to suggest invisible or intangible meanings by analogy to something else through association, resemblance, or convention. Often a symbol—a person, object, or situation—represents an abstract or figurative meaning in the story in addition to its literal meaning. Some symbols are universal and can be found repeatedly in literary works; others may be particular to the story. For example, a farm often stands for love and security in works of literature. Children often read only on a literal level, but they can be helped by teachers to note more obvious symbols existing in the books they are reading. If the symbolic feature recurs in the story, it is referred to as a *motif.* The number three is a common motif in folktales, for example.

A story for children must be more than a plot and a character study; a story integrates all the elements of fiction into a pleasing whole. In drawing together these elements, authors create new worlds for young readers.

Visual Elements

In many children's books the story is told through both text and pictures. This is particularly true of picture books, but is also true of other books for children in which pictures serve an important function. Many different purposes can be accomplished through book illustrations. They convey meaning and feeling by helping the reader visualize the physical settings and the characters' appearance and actions. They also provide an aesthetic dimension to books by offering the readers additional pleasure and insights beyond the message within the text. Thus, the role of pictures in children's books is both to reflect the text and to extend and enrich it without contradicting its message.

When you read many illustrated books and carefully observe the illustrations and their relationships to the texts, you begin to increase your appreciation of this aspect of children's literature. You may consider the different parts of illustrations as one aspect of your evaluation of illustrations. These parts, or *visual elements*, are line, color, shape, texture, and composition. They can help you become more observant of illustrations so that you will learn to select well-illustrated books.

Line

The stroke marks that form part of a picture and often define its outline are the lines. The line of a picture generally defines the objects within the picture. Artists may choose to use lines that are dark or pale, heavy or light, solid or broken, wide or thin, straight or curved, or have combinations of these elements. The lines may be mostly vertical, horizontal, or on a diagonal. In pictures of the ocean and open prairies, the lines are predominantly horizontal; the impression is one of calm and tranquility. If the ocean is stormy, then the lines are more likely diagonal and upward moving, suggesting action or emotion or both. Each of these choices results in a different visual effect and can help set a different mood. In evaluating the element of line within a picture, you may ask yourself whether the lines of the picture help to create and convey both the meaning and the feeling of the story.

Color

Color, another visual element of a book, may be observed for its hue, lightness, and saturation. Colors may be considered for the actual part of the color spectrum they represent or for their hue. The predominant colors may be from the cool end of the spectrum (the blues, greens, and gray-violets) or from the warm end of the color chart (the reds, oranges, and yellows). The colors may be intense or pale (that is, more or less saturated). The lightness of the colors may range from diaphanous to opaque. The colors used must first complement the text. For example, if the mood of the story is that of calm and contentment, the illustrator may choose soft, warm tones that strengthen the emotional warmth of the story. If the events and mood of the text change during the course of the story, then the colors will change to reflect and signal the shift occurring in the story. In Margaret Wise Brown's *Goodnight Moon* (1947), the colors gradually darken from page to page, as the sun sets and night falls. Sometimes an illustrated book will be noteworthy for its lack of color, which can be very appropriate and effective, as in *Hildilid's Night* by Cheli Durán Ryan, illustrated by Arnold Lobel.

Shape

Shape, or the spatial forms of a picture, is produced by areas of color and by lines joining and intersecting to suggest outlines of forms. Shapes can be evaluated for their simplicity or complexity, their definition or lack of definition, their rigidity (as in geometric shapes) or suppleness (as in organic shapes), and their size. It is easy to see how this visual element can help to create a mood or carry a message. In looking at shapes in a picture, the proportion of one object to another and the spaces surrounding the shapes are noteworthy for the nonverbal messages they carry (the bigger, the more important). The use of negative space or blank space may also be observed for its ability to highlight an object or to show isolation or loneliness.

Texture

The tactile surface characteristics of pictured objects comprise the texture of a picture. More simply, the impression of how a pictured object feels is its texture. Textures may be rough or slick, firm or spongy, hard or soft, jagged or smooth. Textural effects generally offer a greater sense of reality to a picture, as happens in Leo Lionni's *Frederick,* where the torn edges of paper collage lend a convincing furriness to the little mice's bodies. Texture also permits the artist to provide contrasts within the picture.

Composition

Composition includes the arrangement of the visual elements within a picture and the way in which these visual elements relate one to the other and combine to make the picture. Many artists arrange each illustration around a single focal point, which is often a key to understanding composition. The artist decides on proportion, balance, harmony, and disharmony within the various elements to produce the desired visual impact. The total effect should not overpower the story but rather extend and enrich the meaning and mood of the text.

Obviously the details in the illustrations must not conflict with those in the text. Surprisingly, many examples can be cited where the illustrator was not true to the text in all details. Children are keenly observant of these contradictions and find them distracting. Although children accept illustrations that are varied in all visual elements and artistic styles, they have little tolerance for inaccuracies.

Artistic Styles

Children come to note the distinctive features that identify the work of their favorite illustrators. Although the style of a picture is individual to each artist, artwork in general can be grouped by style similarities. Five broad categories of artistic styles are realistic, impressionistic, expressionistic, abstract, and surrealistic. Although an artist's works seldom fit neatly into one single art style, facets of these styles may be merged into the artist's personal expression of the world.

Realistic art represents natural forms and provides accurate representations without idealization. Susan Jeffer's illustrations in *Black Beauty* by Anna Sewell are examples of realistic art, as is Christopher G. Knight's photographic rendering of the story *Sugaring Time* by Kathryn Lasky.

Impressionistic art depicts natural appearances of objects by rendering fleeting visual impressions with an emphasis on light. The illustrations in *Anno's Journey* by Mitsumasa Anno emphasize the play of light in nature.

Expressionistic art communicates an inner feeling or vision by distorting external reality. An example can be found in *A Chair for My Mother* by Vera B. Williams. Graphic art, used heavily in advertising and billboards, can be considered a form of expressionistic art. The intent of the artist is to draw attention to the central message by eliminating competing details. Donald Crews has successfully developed this art style into concept books for the very young child in *Truck* and *Freight Train.*

Abstract art emphasizes intrinsic form and surface qualities with little or no direct representation of objects but rather an emphasis on mood and feeling. The illustrations by Leo and Diane Dillon in *Why Mosquitoes Buzz in People's Ears* by Verna Aardema distort reality and thus convey the feelings evoked by the African tale.

In emphasizing the unconscious, *surrealistic art* often presents incongruous dream and fantasy images, sometimes juxtaposing unlikely objects. Molly Bang's illustrations in *The Grey Lady and the Strawberry Snatcher* present a semirealistic creature, the Grey Lady, in a nightmarish adventure. The unusual use of color and unlikely happenings reassure the reader that this wordless book is an imaginary story.

In addition, *primitive art* and *folk art* styles are seen in books about a particular era or culture. The style of art is reminiscent of the style prevalent at the time the story events occured. In illustrating *Ox-Cart Man* by Donald Hall, Barbara Cooney uses features of Early American art in order to express the culture of early nineteenth-century New England. Folktales from tribal societies also present occasions for artists to choose a folk art style reminiscent of the art from earlier cultures.

Because *cartoons* are popular with children, some artists select this style for their children's books. In this type of art, exaggerated, rounded figures with little or no background are the focal point of the illustrations. Dr. Seuss's many books, such as *Horton Hatches the Egg* and *The Cat in the Hat,* as well as many of William Steig's popular stories, including *The Amazing Bone* and *Caleb and Kate,* have illustrations representative of the cartoon style.

Artistic Media

The artistic media refer to the materials and technical means used by artists to create pictures. Although the variety of techniques and materials used by book illustrators is virtually unlimited, some of the more common media found in children's books are listed here.

Drawing:	Pen and ink, colored pencils, pastels (colored chalk), charcoal pencils
Collage:	Real objects of assorted textures and designs such as lace, birchbark, buttons, torn paper, and cotton used to construct an illustration

Print making: Woodcuts, linoleum prints, block prints, lithography
Photography: Black and white, color
Painting: Oils, acrylics, watercolors, gouache, tempera

Of course, the tools with which the artist applies the paint will affect its look. Tools as varied as brushes, air brushes, and sponges are used for applying paint.

Artists will generally design a picture in one predominant medium, drawing from other media for special effects. Occasionally an artist will choose to combine media more liberally to achieve the desired effect. Brief explanations of the artist's techniques and materials have recently begun to be included on the publishing history page of children's picture books; at other times they appear at the end of illustrated books.

Book Format

Children's books are more than text, or text and pictures combined. Other parts of a book contribute to the final product we call a book. The *dust jacket* is a removable paper cover wrapped around the book; it serves as protection against soiling. It also attracts purchasers and readers as well as informs them about the book, its author, and its illustrator. The *covers* of a book are usually made of two boards, which make the book more durable and allow it to stand on a shelf. When no dust jacket is on a book, the front cover provides the reader with a first impression of the story. The *title,* an important part of the text—usually first seen by the reader on the dust jacket or front cover—combines with the illustrations of the dust jacket or cover to communicate the nature of the story to young readers who choose books primarily by title and cover. Many titles suggest the topic of the story and can assist readers in deciding whether to read the book. Other titles and covers may not offer as much information about the story. In such cases, some explanation by a teacher or librarian in the form of a booktalk may prove invaluable to young readers seeking just such a book.

The *endpapers* are the pages glued to the inside front and back boards of the cover, and the *flyleaf* is the page facing each endpaper. In many fine, well-illustrated books, the endpaper and flyleaf are utilized to provoke curiosity in the reader for what follows, to set a mood, or to evoke an affective response in preparation for the story. Often those first colors and first decorative touches are the visual introduction to the story. When readers turn the flyleaf, they are further prepared by the artist for the story by viewing the title page. The *title page* tells the book's full title and subtitle, if there is one; the names of the author(s) and illustrator(s); and the name and location of the publisher. Occasionally a book will include a *frontispiece,* an illustration facing the title page, which is intended to establish the tone and to entice the reader to begin the story.

On the reverse side of the title page, often referred to as the *verso* of the title page, is the *publishing history* of the book. On this page is the copyright notice, a legal right giving only the holder permission to produce and sell the work. Others who wish to reproduce the work in any way must request permission of the copyright holder. The copyright is indicated by the international symbol ©. This symbol is followed by the name of the person(s) holding the copyright and the date it takes effect, which is the year the book is first published. Later publications are also listed. The country in which the book was printed, the number assigned to the book by the Library of Congress, the International Standard Book Number (ISBN), and the edition of the book are also included on this page. Many publishers now include on this page cataloguing information for libraries, a very brief annotation of the story, and a statement on the media and techniques used in the illustrations.

The title page typically presents the *typeface*, the style of print to be used throughout the book. The size and legibility of the typeface must be suited to the book's intended audience. In children's books this can be extremely important. Books for the young child just learning to read should have large, well-spaced print for easy eye scanning. The print style for an easy-to-read book should be a somewhat larger-than-average standard block print with easily distinguishable and recognizable upper- and lowercase letters. Many children's trade books are now being produced in "big book" size for beginning reading activities with a whole class or group of children. In this case, the print needs to be large enough to be readily seen from a distance of 10 to 12 feet minimum. Legibility is diminished when background colors are used behind the text, leaving insufficient contrast for easy reading.

The size, shape, and darkness of the print type may vary from book to book. The lines may be heavy and strong, or light and willowy. The choice of print type should enhance the overall visual message of the illustrations and fit with the illustrations in style and mood. Note also that the placement of the print on the pages in relation to the illustrations can subtly guide the reader and become a functional part of the story.

Unusual print styles are sometimes selected for a children's book. In a book with a diary format, the use of script print gives the impression of handwriting. In this case, the amount of script print is usually brief, and standard block print is used throughout most of the book for greater ease of reading. In place of print some illustrators choose to hand-letter the text. Classic examples of lettering as part of the illustrative component of a book are found in *Millions of Cats* by Wanda Gág and *The Story of Babar* by Jean De Brunhoff.

The *page layout* is also worth observing. You will notice that illustrations are variously placed one on a page, on facing pages, on alternating pages, or on parts of pages. When the picture extends across the two facing pages, it is called a *doublespread*. A doublespread gives the effect of motion, since the eye is drawn to the next page. It can also give a feeling of grandeur, openness, and expansiveness. Sometimes a picture will begin on a right-hand page and spill over to the following page, the reverse side. This offers a strong sense of continuity from one part of the story to the next. Some pictures have a *frame*. Framing of a picture can work to distance the reader from the action, lend a sense of order to the story, or make the mood more formal. The frame itself may be anything from a simple line to a broad, ornately decorated ribbon of information. Decorations on a frame may repeat certain images or symbols to reinforce the meaning of the story.

Pages are another part of the book makeup. In evaluating the pages, you should ask yourself, What is the quality of the paper? Is it thick, high quality? Is it glossy or textured, white or colored? Are the pages square, rectangular, or shaped in the form of a concrete object? Are they in keeping with the rest of the book? Are unique or unusual page formats, such as half-pages, see-through pages, engineered pages, or partial pages, appropriate and logical?

The *size* of the book is also worth noting. Large picture books are well-suited for reading aloud to a class. Smaller picture books are usually not satisfactory choices for read-alouds, unless, of course, you are reading to only one child or to a small group of children.

Next, consider the *book binding*. Books may be bound in hard cover, paperback, or in some special-purpose material. For example, books for babies are frequently bound in sturdy cardboard or vinyl to withstand the dual role of toy and book. When buying a hardcover book, determine whether the binding is glued or sewn. Look for the stitching. Sewn bindings last much longer than glued ones. Durability relative to cost is the usual trade-off you must weigh in selecting paper or hardcover bindings for classroom or school libraries. Generally speaking, the cost of hardcover books is justified when you expect fairly heavy use.

Balance and Variety in Book Selections

In addition to evaluating the various textual and visual elements that are central to the issue of quality, the child's age and development and the balance and variety among books are also important considerations. In Chapter 1, the age and development of children relative to their reading materials were discussed. Because children in any elementary-grade class have a wide range of reading abilities and reading interests, you need to provide many different types of books, including picture books, easy-to-read books, short chapter books, longer books, and books of prose, poetry, fiction, and nonfiction. Selecting outstanding biographies for an entire year of reading aloud to a class would hardly offer students a range of literary experiences. Thus, balance among the *genres of literature* as well as *variety in topic* are essential. Classroom libraries are usually limited in scope; therefore, school libraries are necessary to provide adequate balance and variety of books for students' research needs and independent reading. Frequent visits to the library by the class and by individual students need to be arranged by the teacher and librarian.

A balance between *male and female main characters* over the course of a year is necessary if you are to meet the needs of children of both sexes and to help members of each sex understand more fully the perspectives, problems, and feelings of members of the opposite sex. Classroom and school library collections need to have a wide range of topics with a balance of male and female main characters.

In addition, understanding and empathy for persons with disabilities can be gained through portrayals in books of children and adults with impairments. A positive image of persons with disabilities needs to be conveyed in these books. Furthermore, children with disabilities need to see characters like themselves in books.

TABLE 2-1 Genres of Children's Literature

Prose				Poetry (3)
Fiction			Nonfiction (9)	
Realistic (7)	Fantasy			
	Traditional Literature (5)	Modern Fantasy (6)		
Family Situations Peer Relationships Growth and Maturity Cultural Differences Sports Mysteries Humorous Stories	Myths Epics Ballads Legends/Tall Tales Folktales Fables Religious Stories	Modern Folktales Animal Fantasy Personified Toys and Objects Unusual Characters/Situations Little People Supernatural Events/Mystery Historical Fantasy Quest Stories Science Fiction/Fantasy	Biological Science Physical Science Social Science Applied Science Humanities Biography	Nursery Rhymes Lyric Poems Narrative Poems
Historical (8)				

The representation of minorities as main characters is also essential if you are to present a realistic view of society and the world. Through well-written *multicultural literature,* children can see that someone from a different race, ethnic group, or religion has many of the same basic needs and feelings that they themselves have. Literature by and about people different from oneself can help to develop an understanding and appreciation for all peoples. Minority children will enjoy reading books in which children from backgrounds similar to their own play the leading, and sometimes, heroic roles. Characters with whom one can identify permit a deeper involvement in literature and at the same time help children to understand situations in their own lives.

International literature—that is, literature from other nations and regions of the world—needs to be included in read-aloud choices and in classroom and library collections in order to guide students toward global understanding. Through reading or listening to the favorite books of children from other nations, your children will experience cultural literacy on a worldwide basis.

Categories of Literature

In Chapters 3 to 10 of this book, the various categories of children's books will be defined and explained, followed by book titles recommended for reading in each of the categories. Most of the chapters focus on the literary genres, as presented in Table 2-1.

However, Chapter 4, Picture Books, diverges from this pattern in that it discusses a book format, and Chapter 10, Multicultural and International Literature, presents books organized by topic. Although multicultural and international books have been placed in a separate chapter for special focus, many multicultural and international titles are also recommended in the genre chapters.

An overview of the genres and their relationships to one another is displayed in Table 2-1. These genres can be used in making balanced choices for library and classroom reading collections and for choosing books to read aloud. The number of the chapter in which each genre of literature is discussed is noted next to the genre.

References

More, H. (1961). A book. In W. Cole (Ed.), *Poems for seasons and celebrations.* Cleveland: World Publishing.

Rosenblatt, L. M. (1985). The transactional theory of the literary work: Implications for research. In C. R. Cooper (Ed.), *Researching response to literature and the teaching of literature: Points of departure* (pp. 33–53). Norwood, NJ: Ablex.

Chapter 3

Poetry

A Word

A word is dead
When it is said,
Some say.
I say it just
Begins to live
That day.

—Emily Dickinson

Poetry is a natural beginning to literature for young children and an enjoyable literary form for all ages. In their earliest years, children acquire language and knowledge of the world around them through listening and observing. Poetry, primarily an oral form of literature that draws heavily on the auditory perceptions of the listeners, is ideally suited to children at this stage. Throughout the elementary and middle school years, poetry that relates to any and every subject can be found and shared orally throughout the school day, providing a flash of humor or a new perspective on the subject. Too often in the classroom poetry is neglected or ignored. For this reason, we have chosen to discuss poetry before other types of literature. We hope you will read and reread favorite poems to your students each day.

Definition and Description

Poetry is the expression of ideas and feelings through a rhythmical composition of imaginative and beautiful words selected for their sonorous effects. In its origin, poetry was oral, and as various minstrels traversed the countryside, they recited poetry and sang songs to groups of listeners of all ages. The musicality of poetry makes it an especially suitable literary form for teachers to read aloud and, at times, to put to music.

Children often believe that rhyme is an essential ingredient of poetry; yet some types of poetry do not rhyme. What, then, distinguishes poetry from prose? The concentration of thought and feeling expressed in succinct, exact, and beautiful language, as well as an underlying pulse or rhythm are the traits that most strongly set poetry apart from prose.

Not all rhyming, rhythmical language merits the label of poetry. *Verse* is a language form in which simple thoughts or stories are told in rhyme with a distinct beat or meter. Nursery rhymes are a good example of well-known, simple verses for children. And, of course, we are all too aware of the *jingle,* a catchy repetition of sounds heard so often in commercials. The most important feature of verses and jingles is their strong rhyme and rhythm. Content is light or even silly. Although verses and jingles can be enjoyable and have a place in the classroom, poetry can enrich children's lives by giving them new insights and fresh views on life's experiences and by bringing forth strong emotional responses.

The term *poetry* is used in this chapter both to refer to a higher quality of language—a form of language that can evoke great depth of feeling and provoke new insights through imaginative and beautiful language—and to refer to favorite verses of childhood.

A wide variety of poetry books is available for use in classrooms by teachers and students. A large, comprehensive *anthology* of poetry for children is a must in every classroom. Anthologies should be organized by subjects for easy retrieval of poems appropriate for almost any occasion. In addition, indices of poets and titles, or first lines, are usually provided in these texts. Works by contemporary and traditional poets can be found in most of these anthologies; they appeal to a wide age range, providing nursery rhymes for toddlers as well as longer, narrative poems for the middle-grade student. An example is *A New Treasury of Children's Poetry: Old Favorites and New Discoveries,* selected by Joanna Cole.

Specialized poetry books are also readily available in which the poems are all by one poet, on one topic, for one age group, or of one poetic form. These specialized collections become necessary adjuncts for a teacher and class who come to love certain kinds of poetry or specific poets. Beautifully illustrated collections are also available and seem to be especially enjoyed by children for independent reading of poetry. Examples include *Words with Wrinkled Knees: Animal Poems* by Barbara Juster Esbensen and *Doodle Soup* by John Ciardi.

Single narrative poems of medium length are presented more frequently in picture book formats. These editions make poetry more appealing and accessible to many children, but in some cases, the illustrations may remove the opportunity for children to form their own mental images from the language created by poets. The poetry section of your school library is worth perusing for interesting poetry books to use in the classroom.

Picture storybooks in verse are treated in Chapter 4, Picture Books. The emphasis of picture books in verse is on the story and rhyme, not on the beauty of the language. By contrast, narrative poems in illustrated versions are first and foremost poetry and often are illustrated only at a later date.

Values of Poetry for Children

Poetry touches our minds and our hearts through drawing on our five senses. Children, too, are reached by poetry, even though the subjects that move them may differ from those that move us. The values of poetry for children are as far reaching and wide ranging as are the topics that one can find in children's poems.

- The most important value of poetry and verse comes from the fun and enjoyment they provide for children. Poetry lends itself to word play; tongue twisters as well as zany rhymes and puns are frequently found in collections of poetry.
- Poetry can help children to see and hear unusual things or to view usual things in a new way. The images and music of poetry have the power to give children wonderment and understanding.
- Poems are excellent to use as bridges between classroom activities, for introducing and concluding new lessons and units, for livening and lightening up the day, or for accenting the events in the class.
- Some poetry and verse are part of a child's literary heritage. Starting with Mother Goose and other nursery rhymes, children can become acquainted with the characters who are in these favorite childhood rhymes and who have become a part of our cultural heritage. Later children can become acquainted with some of the notable poets of the past and present.
- The rhythm and sound elements of poetry make it an especially useful vehicle for the teaching strategy of shared reading that is used with beginning readers. A good resource for the classroom is John Ciardi's *You Read to Me, I'll Read to You* (1962), a book of poems designed for shared reading. (This instructional strategy is described in Chapter 12, Developing Teaching Strategies.)

Elements of Poetry

Just as with a work of fiction, the elements of a poem should be considered if the reader is to understand and evaluate the poem. Each of these parts—meaning, rhythm, sound patterns, figurative language, and sense imagery—is discussed below.

- *Meaning.* Meaning is the underlying idea, feeling, or mood expressed through the poem. As with other literary forms, poetry is a form of communication; it is the way a poet chooses to express emotions and thoughts. Thus, the meaning of the poem is the expressed or implied message the poet conveys.
- *Rhythm.* Rhythm is the beat or regular cadence of the poem. Poetry, usually an oral form of literature, relies on rhythm to help communicate meaning. A fast rhythm is effected through short lines, clipped syllables, sharp, high

vowel sounds such as the sounds represented by the letters *a, e,* and *i,* and abrupt consonant sounds, such as the sounds represented by the letters *k, t, w,* and *p.* A fast rhythm can provide the listener with a feeling of happiness, excitement, drama, and even tension and suspense. A slow rhythm is effected by longer lines, multisyllabic words, full or low vowel sounds such as the sounds represented by the letters *o* and *u,* and resonating consonant sounds such as the sounds represented by the letters *m, n,* and *r.* A slow rhythm can evoke languor, tranquility, inevitability, and harmony, among other feelings. A change in rhythm during a poem signals the listener to a change in meaning.

In the poems that follow, "Song of the Train" exhibits a fast rhythm that evokes the rapid speed of a train; "Slowly" proceeds more slowly in communicating the calm and quiet of summer.

Song of the Train

Clickety-clack,
Wheels on the track,
This is the way
They begin the attack:
Click-ety-clack,
Clickety-clack,
Click-ety-clack-ety,
Click-ety
Clack.

Clickety-clack,
Over the crack,
Faster and faster
The song of the track:
Clickety-clack,
Clickety-clack,
Clickety, clackety,
Clackety
Clack.
Riding in front,
Riding in back,
Everyone hears
The song of the track:
Clickety-clack,
Clickety, clack,
Clickety, clickety,
Clackety
Clack.

—David McCord

Slowly

Slowly the tide creeps up the sand,
Slowly the shadows cross the land.
Slowly the cart-horse pulls his mile,
Slowly the old man mounts the stile.

Slowly the hands move round the clock,
Slowly the dew dries on the dock.
Slow is the snail—but slowest of all
The green moss spreads on the old brick wall.

—James Reeves

- *Sound Patterns.* Sound patterns are made by repeated sounds and combinations of sounds in the words. Words, phrases, or lines are sometimes repeated in their entirety. Also, parts of words may be repeated, as with rhyme, the sound device that children most recognize and enjoy. *Rhyme* occurs when the ends of words (the last vowel sound and any consonant sound that may follow it) have the same sounds. Examples of rhyming words are: *vat, rat, that, brat,* and *flat,* as well as *hay, they, flay, stray,* and *obey. Assonance* is another pattern poets use for effects. In this case, the same vowel sound is heard repeatedly within a line or a few lines of poetry. Assonance is exemplified in these words: *hoop, gloom, moon, moot,* and *boots. Alliteration* is a pattern in which initial consonant sounds are heard frequently within a few lines of poetry. Examples are *ship, shy,* and *shape. Consonance* is similar to alliteration but usually refers to a close juxtaposition of similar final consonant sounds, as in fla*ke*, chu*ck*, and stro*ke. Onomatopoeia* is the device in which the sound of the word imitates the real-world sound. Examples are *buzz* for the sound of a bee and *hiss* for the sound a snake makes.
- *Figurative Language.* Figurative language takes many different forms, but it involves comparing or contrasting one object, idea, or feeling with another one. A *simile* is a direct comparison, typically using *like* or *as* to point out the similarities. A *metaphor* is an implied comparison without a signal word to evoke the similarities. *Personification* is the attribution of human qualities to animate, nonhuman beings or to inanimate objects for the purpose of drawing a comparison between the animal or object and human beings. *Hyperbole* is an exaggeration to highlight reality or to point out ridiculousness. Children often delight in hyperbole because it appeals to their strong sense of the absurd.
- *Sense Imagery.* A poet will play on one or more of the five senses in descriptive and narrative language. *Sight* may be awakened through the depiction of beauty; *hearing* may be evoked by the sounds of a city street; *smell* and *taste* may be recalled through the description of a fish left too long in the sun; and finally, *touch* can be sensitized through describing the gritty discomfort of a wet swimsuit caked with sand from the beach. After listening

to a poem, children can be asked to think about which of the senses the poet is eliciting.

These elements of poetry may be considered in order to select varied types of poems and to group them for presentation. However, little is gained by teaching each of these elements as a separate item to be memorized and/or analyzed. Poetic analysis has caused many students to dislike poetry. On the other hand, students who have teachers who love poetry, who select it wisely, who read it aloud well, and who provide students with many opportunities to enjoy it will come to appreciate poetry.

Evaluation and Selection of Poetry

The criteria to keep in mind in evaluating a poem for use with children are as follows:

- The ideas and feelings expressed are worthy, fresh, and imaginative.
- The expression of the ideas and feelings is unique, often causing the reader to perceive ordinary things in new ways.
- The poem is appropriate to the experiences of children and does not preach to them.
- The poem presents the world through a child's perspective and focuses on children's lives and activities as well as on activities to which people of all ages can relate.
- A poem that panders to children's base instincts is probably best avoided and replaced by other enjoyable, worthy choices.
- Poetry collections should be judged on the quality of the poetry choices. If you decide the poetry is well selected, consider the illustrations and the appearance of the book. Beautiful illustrations do not ensure a good collection of poems within the covers.
- Children report a preference for narrative poems. You will want to include some narrative poems along with other types of poetry.
- Although certain poets may be favored by your students, they will also enjoy the poetry of many other writers. Thus, be sure to share with your students poems by a variety of authors.

In selecting poems to read to students, the list of notable poets at the end of this chapter, the Golden Age poets mentioned later in Table 3-1, and the list of poets who have won the National Council of Teachers of English (NCTE) Award are good starting points. The NCTE Award was established in 1977 in the United States to honor living U.S. poets whose poetry has contributed substantially to the lives of children. This award is given to a poet for the entire body of writing for children ages three through thirteen and is now given every three years.

NCTE Excellence in Poetry for Children Award Winners

1977 David McCord

1978 Aileen Fisher

1979 Karla Kuskin

1980 Myra Cohn Livingston

1981 Eve Merriam

1982 John Ciardi

1985 Lilian Moore

1988 Arnold Adoff

1991 Valerie Worth

1994 Barbara Juster Esbensen

Although more poetry for children is being written and published and many teachers and their students are enjoying this genre of literature, some teachers report that they do not share poetry because of their uncertainty about selecting poems for their students. By learning about students' preferences in poetry and some of the best-loved poems and most respected poets, a teacher can become more skillful at selecting good and enjoyable poems for students. The next section will review research on children's preferences in poetry.

Children's Poetry Preferences

The findings from two surveys of children's poetry preferences can be helpful to teachers in selecting poems for a new group of students. Fisher and Natarella (1982) surveyed primary-grade children and their teachers, and Terry (1974) studied intermediate-grade children. The two age groups were similar, although not identical, in their preferences.

- Both age groups preferred narrative poems over lyric poems.
- Limericks were the favored poetic form of both age groups.
- Free verse and haiku were not well liked by either age group.
- Children of both age groups preferred poems that had pronounced sound patterns of all kinds, but especially enjoyed poems that rhymed.
- Rhythm was also an important element to students of both age groups; they preferred poems with regular, distinctive beats.
- Imagery and figurative language were not as well received by students of both age groups; students reported that they did not always understand poems with considerable figurative language.
- Children of both age groups liked humorous poems, poems about animals, and poems about enjoyable familiar experiences.
- The subjects most preferred by primary-grade children were strange and

fantastic events, animals, and other children; the older children preferred the realistic contents of humor, enjoyable familiar experiences, and animals.

A more recent study by Kutiper and Wilson (1993) was conducted to determine if an examination of school library circulation records would confirm the findings of the earlier poetry preference studies. The findings of this library circulation study indicated that the humorous contemporary poetry of Shel Silverstein and Jack Prelutsky dominated the students' choices. The collections of poetry written by the NCTE award winners did not circulate widely; nor were they widely available in the school libraries studied, even though these poets reflect a higher quality of language and usage than is found in the light verse so popular with students. Kutiper and Wilson stated that real interest in poetry must go beyond Prelutsky and Silverstein. This interest needs to be developed by teachers who provide an array of poetry that builds on students' natural interests.

Children's appreciation of poetry can be broadened and deepened by a good teacher, but you may be wise to proceed with caution on less-liked aspects of poetry until your students become fans of poetry. Thus, a good selection of rhyming, narrative poems with distinct rhythms about humorous events, well-liked familiar experiences, and animals is a good starting point for students who have little experience with poetry.

Historical Overview of Poetry

Poetry for children began centuries ago in the form of nursery rhymes that were recited to babies and toddlers by caregivers. These verses were passed along via the oral tradition. The earliest published collection of nursery rhymes that survives today is *Tommy Thumb's Pretty Song Book* (1744), which is housed in the British Museum (Gillespie, 1970). This songbook contains familiar rhymes such as "Hickory Dickory Dock" and "Mary Mary Quite Contrary." These rhymes and others like them came to be called *Mother Goose rhymes*, but the term *Mother Goose* was first used in France by Charles Perrault in his *Stories and Tales of Past Times with Morals; or, Tales of Mother Goose* (1697) to refer to his collection of fairy tales. Later editions contained nursery rhymes, which became so popular that Mother Goose became a general name for nursery rhymes. The rhymes are light, rhythmical, and often nonsensical verses shared with young children. The rhymes are recited by parents, and children soon become familiar with them and join in the fun. For many, nursery rhymes and other poems were the first forms of literature experienced; these poems symbolize the reassuring sounds of childhood.

Another early type of poetry was quite different from nursery rhymes in nature and was intended for a somewhat older audience of children. Poems of a moral and religious bent were shared with obvious didactic intent, reflecting the strict attitude toward the rearing of children that held sway in the Western world from the Middle Ages to the late nineteenth century. Fear of death and punishment was instilled as

TABLE 3–1   Milestones in Poetry During the Golden Age

Date	Poet	Landmark Work	Country	Characteristic
1846	Edward Lear	A Book of Nonsense	England	Father of nonsense poetry, limericks
1864	Lewis Carroll	"Jabberwocky"	England	Nonsense verses, mostly in Alice's Adventures in Wonderland
1872	Christina Rossetti	Sing Song	England	Poems on children and the small things around them
1885	Robert Louis Stevenson	A Child's Garden of Verses	England	Descriptive poems of childhood memories
1888	Ernest Thayer	"Casey at the Bat"	U.S.A.	Famous ballad on baseball
1890	Laura E. Richards	In My Nursery	U.S.A.	Poems with hilarious situations, wordplay, and strong rhythm
1896	Eugene Field	Poems of Childhood	U.S.A.	Poems reflecting on children and child life
1902	Walter de la Mare	Songs of Childhood	England	Musical and imaginative poetry
1920	Rose Fyleman	Fairies and Chimneys	England	Imaginative poems about fairies
1922	A.A. Milne	When We Were Very Young	England	Poems of fun in which the child's world is observed
1926	Rachel Field	Taxis and Toadstools	U.S.A.	Poems about city and country through the child's eyes

a means of gaining obedience to authority. Ann and Jane Taylor's *Original Poems, for Infant Minds, by Several Young Persons* (1804) provided verse of this kind. Some titles of poems from this early collection are "The Idle Boy," "Greedy Richard," "Meddlesome Matty," and "The Church-Yard." A few purely descriptive, nondidactic poems from this same collection are still remembered today, especially "Twinkle, Twinkle Little Star." Clement Moore's "Visit from St. Nicholas" (1823), another nondidactic, narrative poem, is still enjoyed and known today as "'Twas the Night Before Christmas."

Poetry for children flourished from the middle of the nineteenth century through the 1920s, a period that can be considered the Golden Age of Poetry for Children. Table 3-1 lists the poets, countries, landmark works and dates, and characteristics. The Golden Age of Poetry moved away from moralistic poetry, and instead provided children with poems describing the beauty of life and nature, with poems of humor, nonsense, and word fun, and with imaginative poems that interpreted life from the child's perspective. Much of the Golden Age poetry retains its appeal for today's children; for example, *A Child's Garden of Verses* (1885) by Robert Louis Stevenson remains a favorite collection of poems among parents and children. This positive shift in poetry for children set the standard for poetry for the remainder of the twentieth century.

In the 1960s and 1970s, the general trend toward realism in children's literature was also reflected in poetry. More topics considered suitable for the child audience resulted in protest poetry, poems about girls in nontraditional roles, and irreverent poems. For example, parents, teachers, and other adults became fair game for ridicule and mockery. Minority poets were more frequently published, and their poetry gained in popularity. Most of the early poetry for children prior to the 1950s was by English poets, but during the last half of the century many U.S., Canadian, and Australian poets have gained favor with children. Poems by John Ciardi, Myra Cohn Livingston, Jack Prelutsky, Shel Silverstein, Dennis Lee, and Max Fatchen have engendered popular interest in this genre. As mentioned in the previous section, the National Council of Teachers of English Award for Excellence in Poetry for Children was established in 1977 and has conferred a new importance on poetry for children.

Popularity of poetry in the classroom began in the 1980s and continues into this decade. Developments in the publishing industry attest to this popularity. For example, Boyds Mills Press has a new division devoted to children's poetry, called Windsong. Publishers continue to present both single poems and collections of poems in beautifully illustrated book formats. In the 1980s, Nancy Willard's *A Visit to William Blake's Inn: Poems for Innocent and Experienced Travelers* and Paul Fleischman's *Joyful Noise: Poems for Two Voices* received Newbery Medals, indicating greater recognition of poetry for young people in the United States. In 1994, the Japanese poet Michio Mado was awarded the international Hans Christian Andersen Medal, an honor seldom bestowed on a poet. An increase in the publication of anthologies of poems by and about minorities, such as *Pass It On*, edited by Wade Hudson, has also been noted in the 1990s. This increased publication has also resulted in greater attention to earlier African-American poets, such as Paul Laurence Dunbar, Countee Cullen, and Langston Hughes.

Poetry Types and Forms

Poetry can be classified in many ways; one way is to consider two main types that generally differ in purpose: lyric and narrative poetry. *Lyric poetry* captures a moment, a feeling, or a scene, and is descriptive in nature, whereas *narrative poetry* tells a story or includes a sequence of events. From this definition, you will recognize the following selection to be a lyric poem.

Giraffes

Stilted creatures,
Features fashioned as a joke,
Boned and buckled,
Finger painted,

They stand in the field
On long-pronged legs
As if thrust there.
They airily feed,
Slightly swaying,
Like hammer-headed flowers.

Bizarre they are,
Built silent and high,
Ornaments against the sky.
Ears like leaves
To hear the silken
Brushing of the clouds.

—Sy Kahn

The next selection is an example of a narrative poem:

The Broken-Legg'd Man

I saw the other day when I went shopping in the store
A man I hadn't ever ever seen in there before,
A man whose leg was broken and who leaned upon a crutch—
I asked him very kindly if it hurt him very much.
"Not at all!" said the broken-legg'd man.

I ran around behind him for I thought that I would see
The broken leg all bandaged up and bent back at the knee;
But I didn't see the leg at all, there wasn't any there,
So I asked him very kindly if he had it hid somewhere.
"Not at all!" said the broken-legg'd man.
"Then where," I asked him, "is it? Did a tiger bite it off?
Or did you get your foot wet when you had a nasty cough?
Did someone jump down on your leg when it was very new?
Or did you simply cut it off because you wanted to?"
"Not at all!" said the broken-legg'd man.

"What was it then?" I asked the man, and this is what he said:
"I crossed a busy crossing when the traffic light was red;
A big black car came whizzing by and knocked me off my feet."
"Of course you looked both ways," I said, "before you crossed the street."
"Not at all!" said the broken-legg'd man.

"They rushed me to a hospital right quickly," he went on,
"And when I woke in nice white sheets I saw my leg was gone;
That's why you see me walking now on nothing but a crutch."

"I'm glad," said I, "you told me, and I thank you very much!"
"Not at all!" said the broken-legg'd man.

—John Mackey Shaw

Poetry can also be categorized by its *poetic form,* which refers to the way the poem is structured or put together. *Couplets, tercets, quatrains,* and *cinquains* refer to the number (two, three, four, and five) of lines of poetry in a stanza—a set of lines of poetry grouped together. Couplets, tercets, quatrains, and cinquains usually rhyme, though the rhyme scheme may vary; these poetic forms may constitute an entire poem, or a poem may be comprised of a few stanzas of couplets, tercets, and so on.

Other specific poetic forms frequently found in children's poetry are limericks, ballads, haiku, free verse, and concrete poetry.

A limerick is a humorous, one-stanza, five-line verse form (usually a narrative), in which lines 1, 2, and 5 rhyme and are of the same length and lines 3 and 4 rhyme and are of the same length but shorter than the other lines. The following is an example of a limerick by Edward Lear, the poet who popularized this poetic form in the nineteenth century.

There was a young lady of Firle,
Whose hair was addicted to curl;
It curled up a tree,
And all over the sea,
That expansive young lady of Firle.

—Edward Lear

A *ballad* is a fairly long narrative poem of popular origin, usually adapted to singing. These traditional story poems are often romantic or heroic. "The Outlandish Knight," a 13-stanza ballad, tells the tale of the clever young woman who tricks the man who deceived her.

The Outlandish Knight

An outlandish knight came out of the North,
  To woo a maiden fair,
He promised to take her to the North lands,
  Her father's only heir.

"Come, fetch me some of your father's gold,
  And some of her mother's fee;
And two of the best nags out of the stable,
  Where they stand thirty and three."

She fetched him some of her father's gold
  And some of her mother's fee;

And two of the best nags out of the stable,
  Where they stood thirty and three.

He mounted her on her milk-white steed,
  He on the dapple grey;
They rode till they came unto the sea-side,
  Three hours before it was day.

"Light off, light off thy milk-white steed,
  And deliver it unto me;
Six pretty maids have I drowned here,
  And thou the seventh shall be."

"Pull off, pull off thy silken gown,
  And deliver it unto me;
Methinks it looks too rich and too gay
  To rot in the salt sea."

"Pull off, pull off thy silken stays,
  And deliver them unto me;
Methinks they are too fine and gay
  To rot in the salt sea."

"Pull off, pull off the Holland smock
  And deliver it unto me;
Methinks it looks too rich and gay
  To rot in the salt sea."

"If I must pull off my Holland smock,
  Pray turn thy back unto me,
For it is not fitting that such a ruffian
  A woman unclad should see."

He turned his back towards her,
  And viewed the leaves so green;
She catch'd him round the middle so small,
  And tumbled him into the stream.

He dropped high, and he dropped low,
  Until he came to the tide—
"Catch hold of my hand, my pretty maiden,
  And I will make you my bride."

"Lie there, lie there, you false-hearted man,
  Lie there instead of me;
Six pretty maidens have you drowned here,
  And the seventh has drowned thee."

She mounted on her milk-white steed,
  And led the dapple grey.
She rode til she came to her father's hall,
  Three hours before it was day.

—Traditional

Haiku is a lyric, unrhymed poem of Japanese origin with 17 syllables, arranged on three lines with a syllable count of 5, 7, and 5. Haiku is highly evocative poetry that frequently espouses harmony with and appreciation of nature. Here is an example.

  Small bird, forgive me.
I'll hear the end of your song
   in some other world.

—Anonymous (translated by Harry Behn)

Free verse is unrhymed poetry with little or light rhythm. Sometimes words within a line will rhyme. The subjects of free verse are often abstract and philosophical; they are always reflective.

Last Day of School

Look out!
If you aren't careful
it will happen like this: Someone
will say the word
and that
word
will catapult you   down
the halls   out
the doors   and into
a serious collision
with
SUMMER!

—Barbara Juster Esbensen

Concrete poetry is written and printed in a shape that signifies the subject of the poem. Concrete poems are a form of poetry that must be seen as well as heard in order to be fully appreciated. These poems do not usually have rhyme or definite rhythm; they rely mostly on the words, their meanings and shapes, and the way the words are arranged on the page to evoke images. In "Concrete Cat" you will note through the position of the word that the mouse appears to have met with an accident.

Concrete Cat

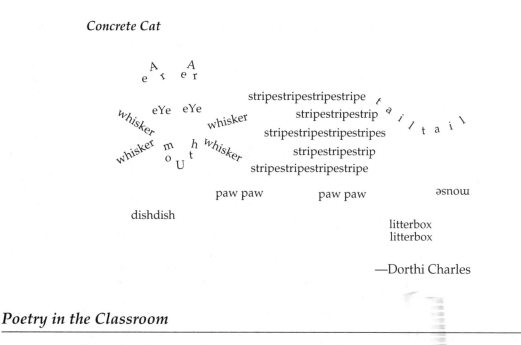

—Dorthi Charles

Poetry in the Classroom

Poetry is enjoyable for students of all ages. It enhances students' development of literacy. Teachers and librarians can entice students into a lifelong love for poetry through making available a well-balanced collection of poetry books and through providing many experiences with poetry.

Students' Listening to and Saying Poems

Teachers and librarians can begin by providing even very young students with many opportunities to hear and say poems. Later, when students have developed a love of poetry and an affinity for the language play in poems, students can read poetry by fine poets and poems by their classmates and can begin to write poems themselves. In other words, poetry needs to be shared in both oral and written forms.

Poetry should be introduced first and often to children in an oral form. As discussed earlier, poetry was in its origins an oral form of literature; it still relies heavily on the auditory perceptions of listeners. Moreover, children's oral language is the basis for their later acquisition of literacy. These two facts combine nicely to make listening to poems and saying poems a natural early introduction to literature for children. Some teachers report that they do not share poetry with their students because of their uncertainty of how to read it aloud. By practicing the poems ahead of time and by reading poetry frequently, a teacher can overcome this reluctance. The rewards to both students and teachers are worth the effort. The next section offers suggestions to help you become an effective reader of poetry.

Reading Aloud Poetry to Children   Poetry should be read aloud to students on a regular, daily basis. Brief, positive encounters with one to three poems at a time are best. Too many poems in one sitting may overwhelm students or make the reading tedious. Introduce the poem to the class before reading it aloud, either by tying the poem in with something else or briefly telling why you chose to read this poem aloud. Then state the title of the poem and begin to read. After reading the poem, be sure to announce the name of the poet so that students discover the writers they especially enjoy. In addition, the following points will help you to read poetry well:

- The most important rule to keep in mind is that poetry should be read for its meaning. Stress the meaning elements of the poem just as you do when reading prose. Often, the words in poetry are phrased in such a way that you must continue past the end of the line to the next line before pausing. In other words, the breaks must be determined by the meaning units of the poem, not by the lines.
- A corollary of the first rule is that a reader should not overemphasize the beat of the poem. Doing so results in an annoying singsong effect. The natural rhythm of the poem will be felt in a more interesting way if you avoid an unnatural, meaningless reading and let the poetic language provide the rhythm.
- Poetry should be enunciated clearly. Each sound and each syllable of a poem are important and must be heard to be appreciated. This often means that you will need to slow down your normal reading pace in order to give full value to each sound.
- Poetry needs to be performed and dramatized. Take some chances and try out different effects (using different voices, elongating words, singing, shouting, whispering, pausing dramatically, and so on) as you read poems aloud. Your voice is a powerful tool: you may change it from louder to softer to only a whisper; you may start at a deep, low pitch and rise to a medium and eventually high pitch; you may speak very quickly in a clipped fashion, and then slow down and drawl out the words.
- Poems may need to be read aloud a number of times because their many meanings may be perceived only after the literal sense is known. Also, favorite poems can be enjoyed again and again, as teachers and students savor one more reading. Another way to provide students with opportunities to listen to poems is by recording audiotapes of poems for the listening center and making them available along with the poem in print, on a chart or in a book, for the student to listen to and read. Commercially made tapes with popular poets reading their works, accompanied by music, are available and are quite popular with children. Some teachers have asked parents to peruse a poetry anthology, select a favorite poem, and then read the poem on tape for use in the listening center.
- After reading a poem aloud, some form of response is usually enjoyed. Sometimes the response students have to a poem is simply the desire to hear it again. Other times students need just a few moments to reflect silently on the poem. Some poems warrant discussion, and students can take the opportunity to tell how the poem made them feel or what it made them think about.

Choral Poetry   A time-honored technique for providing opportunities to say and hear poems over and over again is given by choral poetry. *Choral poetry* consists of interpreting and saying a poem together as a group activity. These poems may either be practiced and recited aloud or rehearsed and read aloud. Students enjoy this way of experiencing poetry because they have a participatory role in the activity. Most poetry, intended to be listened to, is suitable for choral presentation. The following sections explain how to select choral poems and teach them to students.

1. **Selection.**   At first, select a short poem (from one to four stanzas) until your students develop some skill in memorizing, reciting, and performing poems. Humorous narrative poems are good first choices. Later, you will want to experiment with longer poems.
2. **Memorization.**   For most choral presentations, the first step is for the teacher to select and read aloud a poem that is well liked by the students. Then each line or pair of lines is said by the teacher and repeated by the students until they know them. It is preferable for the students to repeat the lines after the teacher and for the teacher to avoid reciting with the class, so that the students will commit the poem to memory instead of waiting for the teacher's voice. Once the entire poem is learned in this way, variations can be added for performing the poem. Although students need to rehearse a poem in order to intone it similarly, some longer poems with older students who read well will not be memorized but will be practiced and read together as a group.
3. **Arrangements.**   Options for reading a poem chorally include unison, two- or three-part, solo voices, cumulative buildup, and simultaneous voices, as is now explained.

   • In unison choral speaking, the students learn the poem and recite it together as a group. Two-part or three-part choral poetry is usually based on arranging students into voice types (for example, high, medium, and low) to achieve different effects, and by selecting lines of the poem for each group to recite or read.
   • Solo voices can be added to either of these presentations and are sometimes used for asking a question or making an exclamation.
   • Some poems lend themselves to cumulative buildup presentations. A cumulative buildup is effected by having, for example, only two voices say the first line, then two more join in on the second, and then two more, gradually building to a crescendo until the entire class says the last line or stanza.
   • Poems can be presented by simultaneous recitation, which forms a presentation similar to a musical round. In this case, group one begins the poem and recites it all the way through. When group one begins the third line, for example, then group two starts the first line, and the two groups recite simultaneously until the end. Other groups can, of course, be added.
   • Poetry selected and arranged for dramatic choral readings on a particular theme infuses an interesting variation into choral poetry. Paul

Fleischman's *Joyful Noise: Poems for Two Voices* (1988) and *I Am Phoenix: Poems for Two Voices* (1985) are collections of poetry on a single theme for older children. These poems are written in a manner already suitable for choral reading. The poems in *Joyful Noise* describe different insects; *I Am Phoenix* contains poems about birds. The poems in each of these collections were written to be read aloud by two readers at once, one reading the left half of the page and one reading the right half. At times, the readers read certain lines simultaneously. Pairs of students may each take a different poem from the collection for presentation.

Many other variations can be developed for use in choral presentations. Let imagination be your guide. Words and lines can be spun into ghostly moans, or barked, or sung, or repeated. Choreography adds visual impact, as do simple props. As soon as children learn that poems do not have to be read sedately through exactly as written, they will begin to find excitement and deeper meaning in poetry.

4. **Performance.**   Incorporating action, gestures, body movements, and finger plays can produce more interesting and enjoyable presentations. Occasionally performing a well-honed choral poem for an audience can bring pride to young performers. Remember, the best audiences are close by—the class next door, the principal, the librarian, the custodian, or a visiting parent. Students truly enjoy this nonthreatening way of sharing poetry. Stimulate creativity by reading different poems and allowing various interpretations to reveal the imagination and insight of your students.

In addition to the group activity of performing choral poetry, teachers can encourage an individual student to learn a poem by heart, voluntarily, and then to recite the poem in a small group or as part of a group performance, perhaps around a theme. For example, a small group of interested students might each select a poem about weather as part of their study about weather in science. Jane Yolen's collection of weather poems, *Weather Report*, could be a resource for this activity.

Students' Reading and Writing Poems

Learning to Read Poetry   Children enjoy reading poetry silently and aloud to others. The classroom library corner should have one or two comprehensive poetry anthologies for students to browse through for general purposes. In addition, two or three specialized collections by a single poet, such as *Garbage Delight* (1978) by Dennis Lee, and another two or three books of poems on a single topic, such as *Cats Are Cats* (1988) by Nancy Larrick, compiler, are needed as well. Students can be encouraged to make copies of their favorite poems from these various collections to develop personal, individual anthologies. Many students choose to illustrate these and arrange the poems in new and inventive ways. Rotating the poetry books occasionally over the course of the school year will spark renewed interest in reading poetry.

Other activities to encourage the reading of poetry by students follow:

- Place students in pairs to take turns reading favorite poems to one another. Make videotapes or audiotapes of these readings and permit students to listen to or watch their own and other students' readings of poetry. Teachers have found that when students listen to their own reading of poetry they begin to note singsong readings and learn to avoid them.
- Ask each student to select three poems by one poet (for example, a Golden Age poet, or an NCTE poet) and find something out about the poet; then place students in small groups of five or six to tell briefly about the poet and read the three poems aloud. Paul B. Janeczko's *The Place My Words Are Looking For: What Poets Say About and Through Their Work* (1990) is an excellent resource for this purpose. Comments on the work of more than forty poets and examples of their poetry can assist students in this activity.
- Have students find three poems on the same topic, such as trees, mice, or friendship; then read them aloud in small groups.
- Students may also find poems that are of the same poetic form—cinquains, limericks and so forth; or that exhibit similar poetic elements—rhyme, alliteration, or onomatopoeia; or that have fast or slow rhythms. These poems can then comprise the poems for reading aloud that day or week.

Learning to Write Poetry   A rich poetry environment stimulates children's interest in writing their own poems. Children need to be very familiar with poetry of many kinds and by many poets before they should be expected to compose poems. The collection of poems, *Inner Chimes: Poems on Poetry* (1992), may be a natural starting place for helping students to think about poetry amd what it is. Poems by various renowned children's poets writing about creating poetry have been selected by Bobbye S. Goldstein for this volume. Another book that provides suggestions on how to include poetry in the classroom is *Sunrises and Songs: Reading and Writing Poetry in an Elementary Classroom* (1990) by Amy McClure, Peggy Harrison, and Sheryl Reed.

Teachers often start the writing of poetry as a collaborative effort. The class brainstorms for ideas, then composes the poem orally as the teacher writes it on the board or on chart paper. As students become comfortable with writing group poetry, they can branch off and begin composing poems in pairs or their own individual poems.

Children should be reminded that poetry is a form of communication and that they should think of an idea, feeling, or event to write about in their poems. They should be reminded that poetry does not have to rhyme, and that they may write about something of interest to them. Children's poetry follows no absolute rules; perfection of form should not be a goal. Other suggestions to foster poetry writing include the following:

- Have students compile personal and class anthologies of their own poems or their favorite poems.

- Design bulletin boards with poetry displays of students' own poems as well as copies of poems by favorite poets.
- Let students rework a narrative poem into a different genre, such as a newspaper article or a letter. In turn, students may attempt the reverse—taking a newspaper article and putting it to verse.
- Suggest to students that they design posters, individually or in groups, to illustrate a favorite poem. Posters are then displayed around the school for a few weeks.
- Encourage students to model the works of professional poets by attempting imitation of a whole poem or of specific techniques.
- Read aloud many poems of one poetic form; then analyze the form with the students to reveal the characteristics of its structure. Quatrains, cinquains, haiku, concrete poems, and limericks can all be used as models with students once they have an appreciation for poetry and for the specific poetic form.

Some poets have suggested other models and patterns for students to follow in writing poetry. Kenneth Koch's *Rose, Where Did You Get That Red?* (1973) and *Wishes, Lies, and Dreams* (1970); Barbara Juster Esbensen's *A Celebration of Bees: Helping Children Write Poetry* (1975); Lee Bennett Hopkins's *Pass the Poetry, Please!* (1987); David McCord's *One at a Time* (1977); Myra Cohn Livingston's *Poem Making: Ways to Begin Writing Poetry* (1991); and Paul Janeczko's *Poetry from A to Z: A Guide for Young Writers* (1994) are useful resources for teachers who want to encourage students to compose poems. (See Appendix B for further information and annotations of these books.) Finally, there is a list of Dos and Don'ts for teaching poetry:

Poetry Do's and Don'ts

Do	*Don't*
Read poetry aloud every day	Limit poetry choices to one or two poets or types of poems
Practice reading a poem before reading it aloud for the first time to students	Choose all poems from one anthology
Choose poetry the students will like	Have poetry "marathon" days or weeks to make up for not sharing poetry regularly
Intersperse classic poems/poets and new poems/poets with more popular poems/poets	Read poems in a "sing-song" style
Make a variety of excellent poetry anthologies and specialized poetry books available in the classroom	Make the analysis of poetry the focus of poetry study
Inspire students to enjoy poetry by reciting poems from memory and by sharing poems you have written	Force students to memorize and recote poems
Encourage students to recite and write poems	Forget to display students' original poems

Direct choral poetry presentations

Feature a notable poet each month

Begin and end each day with a poem

Have students copy poems for handwriting practice

Make the main emphasis of poetry be the writing of formula poems

Forget poetry

References

Charles, D. (1982). Concrete cat. In Kennedy, X. J., & D. M. Kennedy (Eds.), *Knock at a star.* Illus. by K. A. Weinhaus. Boston: Little, Brown.

Dickinson, E. (1951). A word. In Johnson, T. H. (Ed.), *Poems of Emily Dickinson.* Cambridge, MA: Harvard University Press.

Esbensen, B. J. (1975). *A celebration of bees: Helping children write poetry.* Minneapolis: Winston Press.

———. (1984). Last day of school. In B. J. Esbensen, *Cold stars and fireflies: Poems of the four seasons.* Illus. by S. Bonners. New York: Crowell.

Fisher, C. J., & Natarella, M. A. (1982). Young children's preferences in poetry: A national survey of first, second and third graders. *Research in the Teaching of English, 16* (4), 339–354.

Gillespie, M. C. (1970). *Literature for children: History and trends.* Dubuque, IA: Wm. C. Brown.

Hopkins, L. B. (1987). *Pass the poetry please!* New York: Harper & Row.

Janeczko, P. B., Selector. (1990) *The place my words are looking for: What poets say about and through their work.* New York: Bradbury.

Kahn, S. (1967). Giraffes. In Dunning, S., E. Luedens, H. Smith, *Reflections on a gift of watermelon pickle.* New York: Lothrop, Lee and Shepard.

Koch, K. (1973). *Rose, where did you get that red?* New York: Random.

———. (1971). *Wishes, lies and dreams: Teaching children to write poetry.* New York: Random.

Kutiper, K., and P. Wilson. (1993). Updating poetry preferences: A look at the poetry children really like. *The Reading Teacher, 47* (1), 28–35.

McClure, A., P. Harrison, and S. Reed. (1990). *Sunrises and songs: Reading and writing poetry in an elementary classroom.* Portsmouth, NH: Heinemann.

McCord, D. (1952). Song of the train. In D. McCord, *One at a time.* Boston: Little, Brown.

Reeves, J. (1963). Slowly. In E. Blishen (Ed.), *Oxford book of poetry for children.* Illus. by B. Wildsmith. Oxford: Oxford University Press.

Shaw, J. M. (1967). The broken-legg'd man. In J. M. Shaw, *The things I want: Poems for two children.* Tallahassee, FL: Florida State University Library.

Small bird. (1971). In H. Behn (Ed. and Trans.), *More cricket songs.* San Diego: Harcourt.

Terry, A. C. (1974). *Children's poetry preferences: A national survey of upper elementary grades.* Urbana, IL: National Council of Teachers of English.

Notable Poets

Arnold Adoff, recipient of the National Council of Teachers of English (NCTE) Award for Excellence in Poetry for Children. Many poems about relating to people across racial groups. *All the Colors of the Race.*

Dorothy Aldis, a poet known for her narrative poems about everyday activities and emotions. *All Together: A Child's Treasury of Verse.*

Byrd Baylor, a free verse poet whose themes are the desert and harmony with nature. *Hawk, I'm Your Brother.*

Gwendolyn Brooks, an African-American poet known for poems about the lives of urban children. *Bronzeville Boys and Girls.*

John Ciardi, an NCTE award-winning poet known for his humor and, at times, satire in poems for children. *The Man Who Sang the Sillies.*

Walter de la Mare, British poet who gave new importance to early childhood experiences. *Songs of Childhood.*

Barbara Juster Esbensen, contemporary poet and winner of 1994 NCTE Excellence in Poetry Award, noted for her free verse for children. *Cold Stars and Fireflies.*

Eleanor Farjeon, first recipient of the Hans Christian Andersen Medal in 1956. British poet known for well-written poems. *Poems for Children.*

Max Fatchen, Australian poet noted for his poems about children's thoughts and activities. *The Country Mail Is Coming: Poems from Down Under.*

Aileen Fisher, an NCTE award-winning poet whose poems express a closeness to nature and all its inhabitants. *Going Barefoot.*

Paul Fleischman, winner of the Newbery Award for his *Joyful Noise: Poems for Two Voices* in which the poems are composed and printed for two readers to read lines in unison and solo.

Nikki Giovanni, an African-American poet known for her free verse (using mostly lower-case letters) about growing up African-American. *Spin a Soft Black Song: Poems for Children.*

Eloise Greenfield, an African-American poet noted for poems of courage and love. *Under the Sunday Tree.*

Langston Hughes, African-American poet whose protest poems speak of racial pride. *Selected Poems of Langston Hughes.*

X. J. Kennedy, a favorite creator of nonsense and humorous verse about contemporary themes. *One Wonderful Night in August and Other Nonsense Jingles.*

Karla Kuskin, an NCTE award-winning poet known for sometimes serious, sometimes funny poems, including many narrative poems. *Dogs & Dragons, Trees & Dreams: A Collection of Poems.*

Edward Lear, classic Golden Age poet whose nonsense verse and limericks remain favorites today. *The Book of Nonsense.*

Dennis Lee, popular Canadian poet known for humorous poetry. *Alligator Pie.*

Myra Cohn Livingston, an NCTE award-winning poet and an anthologist whose poetry exhibits a balance of perspective and form. *Whispers and Other Poems.*

David McCord, the first winner of the NCTE Award for Excellence in Poetry for Children, known for regular rhythms, agile language, and the use of shape in his poems. *One at a Time.*

Eve Merriam, an NCTE award-winning poet whose poems, often humorous, and sometimes controversial, display an inventive use of language. *A Poem for a Pickle: Funnybone Verses.*

A. A. Milne, English poet whose two collections of poems from the 1920s, *When We Were Very Young* and *Now We Are Six,* remain enjoyable today.

Jack Prelutsky, a popular contemporary poet known for his nonsense poems and poems with humorous characters. *Nightmares: Poems to Trouble Your Sleep.*

Robert Service, classic Canadian poet of well-loved narrative poems. *The Cremation of Sam McGee.*

Shel Silverstein, popular contemporary children's poet who creates nonsense and humorous poetry. *Where the Sidewalk Ends.*

Kaye Starbird, a poet whose poems often feature a dialogue between a child and the reader. *A Snail's a Failure Socially.*

Robert Louis Stevenson, Golden Age poet whose *A Child's Garden of Verses* remains a classic.

Judith Viorst, humorist whose poems are popular with students. *If I Were in Charge of the World and Other Worries: Poems for Children and Their Parents.*

Valerie Worth, an NCTE award-winning poet known for free verse poetry. *Small Poems.*

Recommended Poetry Books

Because poetry is usually of interest to a broad age group, entries of poetry books indicate age only for books mainly suitable for young adults. These books are marked YA.

General Anthologies

Avery, Gillian. *Everyman Anthology of Poetry for Children.* Everyman's, 1994.

Bedrick, Peter, editor. *The Book of a Thousand Poems.* Harper, 1986.

Blishen, Edward, compiler. *Oxford Book of Poetry for Children.* Illustrated by Brian Wildsmith. Watts, 1963.

Booth, David, editor. *'Til All the Stars Have Fallen.* Illustrated by Kady Denton. Viking, 1989.

Cole, Joanna, compiler. *A New Treasury of Children's Poetry; Old Favorites and New Discoveries.* Illustrated by Judith Gwyn Brown. Doubleday, 1984.

Corrin, Sara and Stephen, editors. *Once Upon a*

Rhyme. Illustrated by Jill Bennett. Faber, 1982.

de Regniers, Beatrice Schenk, Eva Moore, Mary Michaels White, and Jean Carr. *Sing a Song of Popcorn: Every Child's Book of Poems.* Scholastic, 1988.

Downie, Mary, and Barbara Robertson, compilers. *The New Wind Has Wings.* Oxford/Merrimack, 1985.

———, compilers. *The Wind Has Wings: Poems from Canada.* Illustrated by Elizabeth Cleaver. Walck, 1968.

Dunning, Stephen, Edward Lueders, and Hugh Smith, compilers. *Reflections on a Gift of Watermelon Pickle.* Scott, Foresman, 1967.

Elledge, Scott, editor. *Wider than the Sky: Poems to Grow Up with.* HarperCollins, 1990.

Ferris, Helen, compiler. *Favorite Poems Old and New.* Illustrated by Leonard Weisgard. Doubleday, 1957.

Hall, Donald, compiler. *The Oxford Book of Children's Verse in America.* Oxford, 1985.

Harrison, Michael, and Christopher Stuart-Clark, editors. *The Oxford Treasury of Children's Poems.* Oxford, 1988.

Janeczko, Paul, editor. *Preposterous: Poems of Youth.* Watts, 1991.

Kennedy, X. J., and Dorothy Kennedy, compilers. *Knock at a Star: A Child's Introduction to Poetry.* Little, Brown, 1982.

Larrick, Nancy. *Piping Down the Valleys Wild.* Illustrated by Ellen Raskin. Delacorte, 1985 (1968).

Moore, Lilian, compiler. *Go with the Poem.* McGraw, 1979.

Opie, Iona, and Peter Opie. *I Saw Esau: The Schoolchild's Pocket Book.* Illustrated by Maurice Sendak. Candlewick, 1992.

Philip, Neil, editor. *A New Treasury of Poetry.* Illustrated by John Lawrence. Stewart, Tabori & Chang, 1990.

Prelutsky, Jack, editor. *The Random House Book of Poetry for Children.* Illustrated by Arnold Lobel. Random House, 1983.

———, editor. *Read-Aloud Rhymes for the Very Young.* Illustrated by Marc Brown. Knopf, 1986.

Rosen, Michael, editor. *Poems for the Very Young.* Illustrated by Bob Graham. Kingfisher, 1993.

Wilner, Isabel. *The Poetry Troupe; An Anthology of Poems to Read Aloud.* Scribner's, 1977.

Untermeyer, Louis, editor. *Rainbow in the Sky.* Illustrated by Reginald Birch. Harcourt, 1985.

Specialized Books
By Poet or Topic

Adoff, Arnold. *All the Colors of the Race.* Illustrated by John Steptoe. Lothrop, 1982.

———. *Chocolate Dreams.* Illustrated by Turi MacCombie. Lothrop, 1989.

———. *Eats.* Illustrated by Susan Russo. Lothrop, 1979.

———. *I Am the Darker Brother.* Illustrated by Benny Andrews. Macmillan, 1968.

———. *I Am the Running Girl.* Illustrated by Ronald Himler. Harper, 1979.

———. *In for Winter, Out for Spring.* Illustrated by Jerry Pinkney. Harcourt, 1991.

———, editor. *My Black Me: A Beginning Book on Black Poetry.* Dutton, 1974.

———. *Sports Pages.* Illustrated by Steve Kuzma. Lippincott, 1986.

Aiken, Conrad. *Cats and Bats and Things with Wings.* Atheneum, 1965.

Baylor, Byrd. *Desert Voices.* Scribner's, 1981.

Bierhorst, John, editor. *The Sacred Path: Spells, Prayers & Power Songs of the American Indians.* Morrow, 1983.

Blake, William. *Songs of Innocence.* Illustrated by Harold Jones. Barnes, 1961.

Blegvad, Lenore. *This Little Pig-a-Wig and Other Rhymes about Pigs.* Illustrated by Erik Blegvad. Atheneum, 1978. Ages 5–7.

Bodecker, N. M. *Hurry, Hurry, Mary Dear! And Other Nonsense Poems.* Illustrated by author. Atheneum, 1976.

———. *Let's Marry Said the Cherry and Other Nonsense Poems.* Illustrated by author. Atheneum, 1974.

Booth, David, editor. *Voices on the Wind: Poems for All Seasons.* Illustrated by Michèle Lemieux. Morrow, 1990.

Brooks, Gwendolyn. *Bronzeville Boys and Girls.* Illustrated by Ronni Solbert. Harper, 1956.

Brown, Margaret Wise. *Under the Sun and the Moon and Other Poems.* Illustrated by Tom Leonard. Hyperion, 1993.

Carlson, Lori M., editor. *Cool Salsa: Bilingual Poems on Growing Up Latino in the United States.* Holt, 1994. Ages: YA.

Carter, Anne, compiler. *Birds, Beasts, and Fishes: A Selection of Animal Poems.* Illustrated by Reg Cartwright. Macmillan, 1991.

Cassedy, Sylvia. *Roomrimes: Poems.* Illustrated by Michele Chessare. Crowell, 1987.

———. *Zoomrimes: Poems about Things that Go.* Illustrated by Michele Chessare. Harper-Collins, 1993.

Cassedy, Sylvia, and Kunihiro Suetake, editors. *Red Dragonfly on My Shoulder.* Illustrated by Molly Bang. Translated from Japanese by editors. HarperCollins, 1992.

Ciardi, John. *Doodle Soup.* Illustrated by Merle Nacht. Houghton, 1985.

———. *Fast and Slow: Poems for Advanced Children of Beginning Parents.* Illustrated by Becky Garver. Houghton Mifflin, 1975.

———. *The Hopeful Trout and Other Limericks.* Illustrated by Susan Meddaugh. Houghton, 1989.

———. *I Met a Man.* Illustrated by Robert Osborn. Houghton, 1961.

———. *The Man Who Sang the Sillies.* Illustrated by Edward Gorey. Lippincott, 1961.

———. *You Read to Me, I'll Read to You.* Illustrated by Edward Gorey. Lippincott, 1962.

Cole, Joanna. *Anna Banana: 101 Jump-rope Rhymes.* Illustrated by Alan Tiegreen. Morrow, 1989.

Cole, William, editor. *Oh, What Nonsense!* Illustrated by Tomi Ungerer. Viking, 1966.

———. *A Zooful of Animals.* Illustrated by Lynn Munsinger. Houghton, 1992.

Cullen, Countee. *The Lost Zoo.* Illustrated by Brian Pinkney. Silver Burdett, 1991 (1969).

Demi, editor-illustrator. *In the Eyes of the Cat: Japanese Poetry for All Seasons.* Translated by Tze-si Hvang. Holt, 1992.

dePaola, Tomie. *Tomie dePaola's Book of Poems.* Putnam, 1988.

Esbensen, Barbara Juster. *Cold Stars and Fireflies: Poems of the Four Seasons.* Illustrated by Susan Bonners. Crowell, 1984.

———. *Who Shrank My Grandmother's House: Poems of Discovery.* Illustrated by Eric Beddows. HarperCollins, 1992.

———. *Words with Wrinkled Knees: Animal Poems.* Illustrated by John Stadler. Crowell, 1986.

Fatchen, Max. *The Country Mail Is Coming: Poems from Down Under.* Little, Brown, 1990.

Feelings, Tom, editor-illustrator. *Soul Looks Back in Wonder.* Dial, 1993.

Fields, Julia. *The Green Lion of Zion Street.* Illustrated by Jerry Pinkney. Macmillan, 1988.

Fisher, Aileen. *Feathered Ones and Furry.* Illustrated by Eric Carle. Crowell, 1971.

———. *Out in the Dark and the Daylight.* Harper, 1980.

Fleischman, Paul. *I Am Phoenix: Poems for Two Voices.* Illustrated by Eric Beddows. Harper, 1985.

———. *Joyful Noise: Poems for Two Voices.* Illustrated by Eric Beddows. Harper, 1988.

Florian, Douglas. *Bing Bang Boing.* Harcourt, 1994.

Frank, Josette, selector. *Snow Toward Evening: A Year in a River Valley/Nature Poems.* Illustrated by Thomas Locker. Dial, 1990.

Froman, Robert. *Seeing Things: A Book of Poems.* Illustrated by Ray Barber. Crowell, 1974.

Gackenbach, Dick, adaptor. *Timid Timothy's Tongue Twisters.* Holiday, 1986.

Giovanni, Nikki. *Spin a Soft Black Song: Poems for Children.* Illustrated by George Martins. Hill & Wang, 1985 (1971).

———, editor. *Grand Mothers: Poems, Reminiscences, and Short Stories about the Keepers of Our Traditions.* Holt, 1994. Ages: YA.

Goldstein, Bobbye S., editor. *Inner Chimes: Poems on Poetry.* Illustrated by Jane Breskin Zalben. Wordsong/Boyds Mills, 1992.

Gordon, Ruth, editor. *Peeling the Onion.* Harper-Collins, 1993. Ages: YA.

———, compiler. *Time Is the Longest Distance: An Anthology of Poems.* HarperCollins, 1991.

Graham, Joan Bransfield. *Splish Splash.* Ticknor & Fields, 1994.

Greenfield, Eloise. *Honey, I Love, and Other Love Poems.* Illustrated by Diane and Leo Dillon. Crowell, 1978.

———. *Under the Sunday Tree.* Illustrated by Amos Ferguson. Harper, 1988.

Grimes, Nikki. *Meet Danitra Brown.* Illustrated by Floyd Cooper. Morrow, 1994.

Harrison, David L. *Somebody Catch My Homework.* Illustrated by Betsy Lewin. Boyds Mills, 1993.

Hoberman, Mary Ann. *Fathers, Mothers, Sisters, Brothers: A Collection of Family Poems.* Illustrated by Marylin Hafner. Little, 1991.

———, editor. *My Song Is Beautiful: Poems and Pictures in Many Voices.* Little, 1994.

Holman, Felice, compiler. *Side by Side: Poems to Read Together.* Illustrated by Hilary Knight. Simon & Schuster, 1988.

———. *The Song in My Head.* Illustrated by Jim Spanfeller. Scribner's, 1985.

———. *Surprises.* Illustrated by Megan Lloyd.

Harper, 1984.

Hopkins, Lee Bennett, editor. *April Bubbles Chocolate: An ABC of Poetry.* Illustrated by Barry Root. Simon & Schuster, 1994.

———, editor. *Dinosaurs.* Illustrated by Murray Tinkelman. Harcourt, 1987.

———, editor. *Ragged Shadows: Poems of Halloween Night.* Illustrated by Giles Laroche. Little, 1993.

Huck, Charlotte, editor. *Secret Places.* Illustrated by Lindsay Barrett George. Greenwillow, 1993.

Hudson, Wade, editor. *Pass It On: African American Poetry for Children.* Illustrated by Floyd Cooper. Scholastic, 1993.

Hughes, Langston. *The Dream Keeper and Other Poems.* Illustrated by Brian Pinkney. Knopf, 1994 (1932).

Hughes, Shirley. *Out and About.* Lothrop, 1988.

Janeczko, Paul B., editor. *Looking for Your Name: A Collection of Contemporary Poems.* Orchard, 1993. Ages: YA.

———, editor. *The Music of What Happens: Poems that Tell Stories.* Watts, 1988.

———. *Poetry from A to Z: A Guide for Young Writers.* Bradbury, 1994.

Kennedy, X. J. *Brats.* Illustrated by James Watts. Atheneum, 1986.

———. *The Forgetful Wishing Well: Poems for Young People.* Illustrated by Monica Incisa. Atheneum, 1985.

———. *Fresh Brats.* Illustrated by James Watts. Macmillan, 1990.

Knudson, R. R., and May Swenson, editors. *American Sports Poems.* Watts, 1988.

Kuskin, Karla. *Dogs & Dragons, Trees & Dreams: A Collection of Poems.* Harper, 1980.

Larrick, Nancy, compiler. *Cats Are Cats.* Illustrated by Ed Young. Philomel, 1988.

———, compiler. *Mice Are Nice.* Illustrated by Ed Young. Philomel, 1990.

———. *To the Moon and Back: A Collection of Poems.* Illustrated by Catharine O'Neill. Delacorte, 1991.

———, compiler. *When the Dark Comes Dancing: A Bedtime Poetry Book.* Illustrated by John Wallner. Philomel, 1983.

Lear, Edward. *The Complete Nonsense Book.* Dodd, 1946.

Lee, Dennis. *Garbage Delight.* Illustrated by Frank Newfeld. Houghton, 1978.

Lenski, Lois. *Sing a Song of People.* Illustrated by Giles Laroche. Little, Brown, 1987.

Levy, Constance. *A Tree Place and Other Poems.* Illustrated by Robert Subuda. Macmillan, 1994.

Lewis, Richard, editor. *In a Spring Garden.* Illustrated by Ezra Jack Keats. Dial, 1965.

Livingston, Myra Cohn. *A Circle of Seasons.* Illustrated by Leonard Everett Fisher. Holiday, 1982.

———. *Roll Along: Poems on Wheels.* Macmillan, 1993.

———. *Sky Songs.* Illustrated by Leonard Everett Fisher. Holiday, 1983.

———. *O Sliver of Liver and Other Poems.* Illustrated by Iris Van Rynbach. Atheneum, 1979.

———, editor. *Thanksgiving Poems.* Illustrated by Stephen Gammell. Holiday, 1985.

———, editor. *Why Am I Grown So Cold? Poems of the Unknowable.* Atheneum, 1982.

McCord, David. *Far and Few: Rhymes of the Never Was and Always Is.* Illustrated by Henry B. Kane. Little, 1952.

———. *One at a Time: Collected Poems for the Young.* Illustrated by Henry B. Kane. Little, 1977.

McNaughton, Colin. *Making Friends with Frankenstein: A Book of Monstrous Poems and Pictures.* Candlewick, 1994.

Merriam, Eve. *Blackberry Ink.* Illustrated by Hans Wilhelm. Morrow, 1985.

———. *Finding a Poem.* Illustrated by Seymour Chwast. Atheneum, 1970.

———. *Halloween ABC.* Illustrated by Lane Smith. Macmillan, 1987.

———. *Out Loud.* Atheneum, 1973.

———. *You Be Good & I'll Be Night: Jump-on-the-Bed Poems.* Illustrated by Karen Lee Schmidt. Morrow, 1988.

Milne, A. A. *The World of Christopher Robin.* Illustrated by Ernest Shepard. Dutton, 1958.

Moore, Lilian. *Something New Begins: New and Selected Poems.* Illustrated by Mary Jane Dunton. Atheneum, 1982.

Morrison, Lillian, compiler. *At the Crack of the Bat: Baseball Poems.* Illustrated by Steve Cieslawsky. Hyperion, 1992.

———, compiler. *Rhythm Road: Poems to Move to.* Lothrop, 1988.

———, compiler. *The Sidewalk Racer and Other Poems of Sports and Motion.* Lothrop, 1977.

Myers, Walter Dean. *Brown Angels: An Album of*

Pictures and Verse. HarperCollins, 1993.

Nash, Ogden. *Custard and Company: Poems by Ogden Nash.* Illustrated by Quentin Blake. Little, 1980.

———, compiler. *The Moon Is Shining Bright as Day.* Illustrated by Rose Shirvanian. Lippincott, 1953.

Nye, Naomi Shihab, editor. *This Same Sky: A Collection of Poems from Around the World.* Four Winds, 1992. Ages: YA.

O'Neill, Mary. *Hailstones and Halibut Bones: Adventures in Color.* Illustrated by Leonard Weisgard. Doubleday, 1989 (1961).

Panzer, Nora, editor. *Celebrate America: In Poetry and Art.* Hyperion, 1994. Ages: YA.

Petersham, Maud, and Miska Petersham. *The Rooster Crows: A Book of American Rhymes and Jingles.* Macmillan, 1945.

Pomerantz, Charlotte. *If I Had a Paka: Poems in Eleven Languages.* Illustrated by Nancy Tafuri. Greenwillow, 1982.

Pooley, Sarah, selector. *A Day of Rhymes.* Knopf, 1988.

Prelutsky, Jack. *The Baby Uggs Are Hatching.* Illustrated by James Stevenson. Greenwillow, 1982.

———. *The Dragons Are Singing Tonight.* Illustrated by Peter Sis. Greenwillow, 1993.

———, editor. *For Laughing out Loud: Poems to Tickle Your Funnybone.* Illustrated by Marjorie Priceman. Knopf, 1991.

———. *The New Kid on the Block.* Illustrated by James Stevenson. Greenwillow, 1984.

———. *Nightmares: Poems to Trouble Your Sleep.* Illustrated by Arnold Lobel. Greenwillow, 1976.

———, selector. *Poems of A. Nonny Mouse.* Illustrated by Henrik Drescher. Knopf, 1989.

———. *Rolling Harvey down the Hill.* Illustrated by Victoria Chess. Greenwillow, 1980.

———. *Something Big Has Been Here.* Illustrated by James Stevenson. Greenwillow, 1990.

———. *Tyrannosaurus Was a Beast: Dinosaur Poems.* Illustrated by Arnold Lobel. Greenwillow, 1988.

Richardson, Polly, editor. *Animal Poems.* Illustrated by Meg Rutherford. Barrons, 1992.

Schmidt, Annie M. G. *Pink Lemonade.* Illustrated by Timothy Foley. Translated by Henrietta Ten Harmsel. Eerdmans, 1992 (1981).

Schwartz, Alvin. *And the Green Grass Grew All Around.* Illustrated by Sue Truesdell. Harper-Collins, 1992.

Seabrooke, Brenda. *Judy Scuppernong.* Dutton, 1990. Ages 9–12.

Silverstein, Shel. *A Light in the Attic.* Illustrated by author. Harper, 1981.

———. *Where the Sidewalk Ends: The Poems and Drawings of Shel Silverstein.* Harper, 1974.

Singer, Marilyn. *Turtle in July.* Illustrated by Jerry Pinkney. Macmillan, 1989.

Smith, William Jay. *Laughing Time.* Illustrated by Juliet Kepes. Little, 1955.

Sneve, Virginia Driving Hawk, selector. *Dancing Teepees: Poems of American Indian Youth.* Illustrated by Stephen Gammell. Holiday, 1989.

Soto, Gary. *A Fire in My Hands.* Scholastic, 1990. Ages 12–YA.

———. *Neighborhood Odes.* Illustrated by David Diaz. Harcourt, 1992.

Starbird, Kaye. *The Covered Bridge House.* Illustrated by Jim Arnosky. Four Winds, 1979.

Stevenson, Robert Louis. *A Child's Garden of Verses.* Chronicle, 1989 (1885).

Strauss, Gwen. *Trail of Stones.* Illustrated by Anthony Browne. Knopf, 1990. Ages 11–YA.

Strickland, Dorothy S., and Michael R., editors. *Families: Poems Celebrating the African American Experience.* Illustrated by John Ward. Wordsong/Boyds Mills, 1994.

Swann, Brian. *A Basket Full of White Eggs: Riddle Poems.* Illustrated by Ponder Goembel. Orchard, 1988.

Thomas, Joyce Carol. *Brown Honey in Broomwheat Tea.* Illustrated by Floyd Cooper. Harper-Collins, 1993.

Viorst, Judith. *If I Were in Charge of the World and Other Worries: Poems for Children and Their Parents.* Illustrated by Lynne Cherry. Atheneum, 1982.

Wallace, Daisy, editor. *Fairy Poems.* Illustrated by Trina Schart Hyman. Holiday, 1980.

———. *Witch Poems.* Illustrated by Trina Schart Hyman. Holiday, 1976.

Westcott, Nadine Bernard, editor. *Never Take a Pig to Lunch: And Other Poems about the Fun of Eating.* Illustrated by Nadine Bernard Wescott. Orchard, 1994.

Whipple, Laura, editor. *Celebrating America: A Collection of Poems and Images of the American Spirit.* Putnam/Philomel, 1994. Ages: YA.

———, compiler. *Eric Carle's Animals Animals.* Illustrated by Eric Carle. Philomel, 1989.

———, compiler. *Eric Carle's Dragons Dragons and Other Creatures that Never Were.* Illustrated by Eric Carle. Philomel, 1991.

Willard, Nancy. *A Visit to William Blake's Inn: Poems for Innocent and Experienced Travelers.* Illustrated by Alice and Martin Provensen. Harcourt, 1981.

———. *The Voyage of the Ludgate Hill: Travels with Robert Louis Stevenson.* Illustrated by Alice and Martin Provensen. Harcourt, 1987.

Woolger, David, editor. *Who Do You Think You Are? Poems about People.* Oxford, 1990.

Worth, Valerie. *More Small Poems.* Illustrated by Natalie Babbitt. Farrar, 1976.

———. *Small Poems.* Illustrated by Natalie Babbitt. Farrar, 1972.

———. *Still More Small Poems.* Illustrated by Natalie Babbitt. Farrar, 1978.

Yolen, Jane. *Best Witches: Poems for Halloween.* Illustrated by Elise Primavera. Putnam, 1988.

———. *Bird Watch: A Book of Poetry.* Illustrated by Ted Lewin. Philomel, 1990.

———, editor. *Sleep Rhymes around the World.* Illustrated by 17 international artists. Wordsong/Boyds Mills, 1994.

———, editor. *Weather Report.* Illustrated by Anne Gusman. Wordsong/Boyds Mills, 1993.

Single Illustrated Poems

Note the distinction between *poems* and *stories told in verse.* Heavily illustrated poems are listed here. Illustrated stories told in verse are included under the heading of Picture Storybooks in Chapter 4.

Adoff, Arnold. *Flamboyan.* Illustrated by Karen Barbour. Harcourt, 1988.

Browning, Robert. *The Pied Piper of Hamelin.* Illustrated by Kate Greenaway. Warne, 1888.

Bryan, Ashley. *Turtle Knows Your Name.* Atheneum, 1989.

cummings, e.e. *hist whist.* Illustrated by Deborah Kogan Ray. Crown, 1989.

———. *little tree.* Illustrated by Deborah Kogan Ray. Crown, 1987.

Fisher, Aileen. *Listen Rabbit.* Illustrated by Symeon Shimin. Crowell, 1964.

Frost, Robert. *Stopping by Woods on a Snowy Evening.* Illustrated by Susan Jeffers. Dutton, 1978.

Johnson, James Weldon. *The Creation.* Illustrated by James Ransome. Holiday, 1994.

Lear, Edward. *The Jumblies.* Illustrated by Ted Rand. Putnam, 1989.

———. *The Owl and the Pussycat.* Illustrated by Jan Brett. Putnam, 1991.

———. *The Scroobious Pip.* Completed by Ogden Nash. Illustrated by Nancy Ekholm Burkert. Harper, 1968.

Lewis, J. Patrick. *A Hippopotamusn't and Other Animal Verses.* Illustrated by Victoria Chess. Dial, 1990.

Lewis, Richard. *In the Night, Still Dark.* Illustrated by Ed Young. Atheneum, 1988.

Little, Lessie Jones. *Children of Long Ago.* Illustrated by Jan Spivey Gilchrist. Putnam, 1988.

Longfellow, Henry Wadsworth. *Paul Revere's Ride.* Illustrated by Ted Rand. Dutton, 1990.

Moore, Clement Clarke. *The Night before Christmas.* Illustrated by Tomie dePaola. Holiday House, 1980.

Rylant, Cynthia. *Waiting to Waltz: A Childhood.* Illustrated by Stephen Gammell. Bradbury, 1984.

Service, Robert W. *The Cremation of Sam McGee.* Illustrated by Ted Harrison. Greenwillow, 1987.

———. *The Shooting of Dan McGrew.* Illustrated by Ted Harrison. Godine, 1988.

Siebert, Diane. *Heartland.* Illustrated by Wendell Minor. HarperCollins, 1989.

———. *Plane Song.* Illustrated by Vincent Nasta. HarperCollins, 1993.

———. *Sierra.* Illustrated by Wendell Minor. HarperCollins, 1991.

———. *Train Song.* Illustrated by Mike Wimmer. HarperCollins, 1990.

Steig, Jeanne. *Consider the Lemming.* Illustrated by William Steig. Farrar, 1988.

Taylor, Jane. *Twinkle, Twinkle, Little Star.* Illustrated by Michael Hague. Morrow, 1992.

Thayer, Ernest Lawrence. *Casey at the Bat.* Illustrated by Patricia Polacco. Putnam, 1992 (1888).

Treece, Henry. *The Magic Wood.* Illustrated by Barry Moser. HarperCollins, 1992 (1945).

Young, Ruth. *Golden Bear.* Illustrated by Rachel Isadora. Viking, 1992.

Chapter 4

Picture Books

My Book!

I did it!
I did it!
Come and look
At what I've done!
I read a book!
When someone wrote it
Long ago
For me to read,
How did he know
That this was the book
I'd take from the shelf
And lie on the floor
And read by myself?
I really read it!
Just like that!
Word by word,
From first to last!
I'm sleeping with
This book in bed,
This is the FIRST book
I've ever read!

—David L. Harrison

In an era when picture books abound and provide many children with a delightful introduction to the world of books, it is difficult to imagine a time when books had no illustrations. Nonetheless, the picture book as we know it is a product of the twentieth century. The development of different types of picture books over the last half century can be seen as a response to our developing awareness of the importance of early learning.

Definition and Description

Picture books are profusely illustrated books in which the illustrations are, to varying degrees, essential to the enjoyment and understanding of the story. For this reason, illustrations in picture books are said to be integral to the story. The illustrations in picture books provide actual plot or concept information as well as clues to character traits, settings, and moods. Without the illustrations, therefore, these books would be diminished, and in some cases the story would make no sense or would be nonexistent.

Many children's books have illustrations but are not picture books. For example, novels and anthologies often have a few, scattered illustrations that depict what has already been described in the text or that serve to decorate the text. These illustrations are said to be *incidental* to the story. When well done, illustrations of this kind are appreciated and enjoyed by readers, but they are not necessary for a complete understanding of the story.

Values of Picture Books

Picture books enable children to enjoy literature from their earliest years, since they can "read" the illustrations to follow the story or to name the objects or characters depicted. Excellent picture books are also created for independent reading by older, fluent readers, but in most cases picture books are first read aloud to children. It is in the read-aloud context that the following important values of the picture book become apparent.

- Hearing good picture books read aloud regularly can help children learn to read and value reading. Reading and discussing picture books bring young children and adults together for an enjoyable shared activity. Of particular value is the practice of *rereading* picture books aloud. Young children often ask for the same book time after time, because they love the story and the words. Quite naturally, they memorize the text and, in this way, learn many of the fundamentals of reading.
- Sharing picture books with children fosters language development. The combination of intriguing text, art, and topics found in the best picture books feeds children ideas, stimulates their imagination and curiosity, and provides them with a rich vocabulary to use in book-related questions and discussions.
- Picture books can foster children's appreciation of art. Many parents, teachers, and librarians take the opportunity to comment on the artwork as they share picture books with children. Their comments range from what they like

about an illustration to calling attention to how artistic styles in different picture books vary and which of the varying styles the children prefer and why.

- Visual clues enable nonreaders and beginning readers to enjoy picture books by themselves. After a picture book has been read to a child, she can return to the book and use picture clues to reproduce enough of the language of the text from memory for a satisfying independent reading.

Evaluation and Selection of Picture Books

Children's first experiences with books must be enjoyable or they will soon not want to be involved with books. Negative experiences could mean that they may never learn to read or to enjoy reading. Over a period of time, evaluation and selection of picture books become a matter of achieving a good balance between what children naturally enjoy and what you want to lead them to enjoy.

The following criteria will help you to identify the best of the picture books.

- The ideas in picture books should be original or presented in an original way. Picture books on topics that children enjoy and find interesting are preferable to books about childhood, in the sense of nostalgia for or reminiscence of childhood. Books of the latter sort are for adults, not children.
- Picture books should avoid racial, ethnic, or sexual stereotyping in text and illustrations. Forms of stereotyping include implying that all members of a group possess the same characteristics, and failing to portray members of a certain group as participating in selected roles.
- Language and writing style should be rich and varied but not so complicated as to be incomprehensible to the child. It is desirable to feature new or unusual vocabulary within the context of interesting situations and complementary illustrations. Avoid overly sentimental and trite language, as well as writing characterized by short, choppy sentences and lifeless vocabulary.
- Illustrations should be appropriate in complexity to the age of the intended audience. In picture books for infants, look for relatively uncomplicated pages showing outlined figures against a plain background. Elements of perspective or unusual page design in which only parts of a figure are shown may not be readily understood or appreciated by very young children.
- Color in illustrations is preferred by children, but color is not essential if illustrations are to work well in picture books. The more important point to consider is whether color or black and white is right for the story.
- Text and illustrations must be well integrated. This means more than that the illustrations on a certain page "go along with" the accompanying text. It means that the illustrations complement or add to the text either by presenting added information about plot, characters, or setting, or by projecting the mood of the story through color and line. Good integration of text and illustrations demands a balance; one must not overwhelm the other.

- When a book is to be shared with a large group, the illustrations must be large enough to be seen from a distance.
- Books selected for infants and toddlers must be durable. Durability is determined by type of cover, type of binding, and paper quality, as discussed in Chapter 2.
- The amount of text on the pages of a picture book determines how long it will take to read the book aloud or for a child to read the book to herself. Generally, the longer the text, the older the intended audience. Note that children's willingness to listen to stories grows with experience, which may result in a younger child who has been read to regularly having a much longer attention span than an older child with no story experience.

Adults sometimes have difficulty perceiving the contributions that illustrations make to picture books. The following general guidelines may improve your ability to "read" illustrations.

- Note characters and actions *not* mentioned in the text. Illustrations can contribute to plot.
- Note how characters' physical characteristics are conveyed through the illustrations. Illustrations can contribute to characterization.
- Note how details such as clothing, architecture, and modes of transportation establish and depict place and era of the story. Illustrations can contribute to setting.
- Note whether and how the story's message is conveyed by or underscored in the illustrations. Illustrations can contribute to theme.

Teachers and librarians often rely on the professional judgment of committees that choose what they consider to be the most outstanding picture books published each year in this country and abroad. The most prestigious picture book award in the United States is the Caldecott Award. The equivalent award in Great Britain is the Kate Greenaway Award, and in Canada, the Amelia Frances Howard-Gibbon Award. (See Appendix A for lists of award winners.) Another reliable source of information about good quality picture books is "The New York Times Best Illustrated Children's Books of the Year," published in early November as a part of *The New York Times Book Review Supplement.*

Historical Overview of Picture Books

Orbis Pictus (Visible World), an ABC book written and illustrated by John Amos Comenius in Moravia and published in 1657, is considered to be the first children's picture book. Comenius's emphasis on using pictures to explain and expand the meaning of the text in books for young people was an important first. But since early books were rare and prohibitively expensive, they were seen by very few children. Moreover, until well into the nineteenth century, Europeans and Americans believed that books were for the serious business of educating and soul saving, not

Excellent Picture Books to Read Aloud

(Books for each level vary in difficulty and should be selected with the students' literary backgrounds in mind.)

Primary Level   Ages 5–8

Alborough, Jez. *Where's My Teddy?* Candlewick, 1992.
Heide, Florence P., and Gilliland, Judith H. *The Day of Ahmed's Secret.* Illustrated by Ted Lewin. Lothrop, 1990.
Henkes, Kevin. *Chrysanthemum.* Greenwillow, 1991.
Hoban, Russell. *A Bargain for Frances.* Illustrated by Lillian Hoban. Harper, 1970.
Hoffman, Mary. *Amazing Grace.* Illustrated by Caroline Binch. Dial, 1991.
Lionni, Leo. *Swimmy.* Pantheon, 1963.
Martin, Bill, Jr. *Chicka Chicka Boom Boom.* Illustrated by Lois Ehlert. Simon and Schuster, 1989.
Ness, Evaline. *Sam, Bangs, and Moonshine.* Holt, 1966.
Waddell, Martin. *Farmer Duck.* Illustrated by Helen Oxenbury. Candlewick, 1992.

Intermediate Level   Ages 8–11

Agee, Jon. *The Incredible Painting of Felix Clousseau.* Farrar, 1988.
Baker, Olaf. *Where the Buffaloes Begin.* Illustrated by Stephen Gammell. Warne, 1981.
Dorros, Arthur. *Abuela.* Illustrated by Elisa Kleven. Dutton, 1991.
Gerstein, Mordicai. *The Mountains of Tibet.* Harper, 1987.
Jukes, Mavis. *Like Jake and Me.* Illustrated by Lloyd Bloom. Knopf, 1984.
Offen, Hilda. *Nice Work, Little Wolf.* Dutton, 1992.
Steig, William. *The Amazing Bone.* Farrar, 1976.
Van Allsburg, Chris. *The Wretched Stone.* Houghton, 1991.
Yorinks, Arthur. *Hey, Al.* Illustrated by Richard Egielski. Farrar, 1986.

Advanced Level   Ages 11–14

Browne, Anthony. *Zoo.* Knopf, 1993.
Gallaz, Christophe, and Innocenti, Roberto. *Rose Blanche.* Illustrated by Roberto Innocenti. Creative, 1985.
Hooks, William H. *The Ballad of Belle Dorcas.* Illustrated by Brian Pinkney. Knopf, 1990.
Kesey, Ken. *Little Tricker the Squirrel Meets Big Double the Bear.* Illustrated by Barry Moser. Viking, 1990.
Polacco, Patricia. *Pink and Say.* Philomel, 1994.
Steiner, Jörg. *The Bear Who Wanted to Be a Bear.* Illustrated by Jörg Müller. Atheneum, 1977.
Van Allsburg, Chris. *The Sweetest Fig.* Houghton, 1993.

for enjoyment! Today's full-color, extravagantly illustrated, highly amusing picture book is the product of the following important developments.

- Technological advances in color printing. Improved four-color printing presses and printing techniques made high-quality illustrations in books more affordable. These advances were a direct result of the Industrial Revolution.

- A more understanding attitude toward childhood. As late as the eighteenth century, the Western world thought of children as miniature adults and expected them to behave and work accordingly. During the nineteenth century, society began to accept the notion of childhood as a time for playing and learning. At the same time, the general economy began to be able to afford the average child the leisure time these activities require.
- Higher standards of excellence in picture book illustrations. The first great children's book illustrators lived in the 1800s. The beauty, charm, and humor of the illustrations of Randolph Caldecott, Kate Greenaway, and Walter Crane brought children's book art to the attention of the general public. The establishment of national awards for excellence in children's book illustration in the twentieth century had the same effect and encouraged more artists to enter the children's book field.
- A greater demand for books. Growth of public school systems and public and school library systems accounted for much of this increase in the number of books for children. In addition, reading came to be recognized as one of the child's best tools for learning and for gaining a worthy source of entertainment.

As a result of these developments, an economic, social, and political infrastructure that would support the widespread publishing of children's books was in place in most of the Western world by the early twentieth century. With its superb children's book illustrators and color printers of the time, England led the world in publishing picture books from the 1860s until the 1930s. Milestones in the development of picture books are highlighted in Table 4-1.

Today, the picture book genre is well established. Current trends in the field are toward an ever-widening audience, more multicultural themes, and realistic themes, as is demonstrated by the controversial picture book, *Daddy's Roommate* (Willhoite, 1990), about a two-father family. Other current trends include greater diversity in formats and more illustrated retellings of folktales. An interesting trend of the 1990s is to publish picture books with high levels of conceptual difficulty and artistic sophistication, intended for middle grade and junior high school students. Another trend (which will be discussed in Chapter 9) is toward greater and more effective use of illustration in informational books. Quite recently, microchip technology has made it possible to produce books that emit sounds or talk when certain pages are opened. A few books are available on CD-ROM and are reader-interactive.

Types of Picture Books

The first picture books were meant to be read aloud to children. The latter half of this century, in response to new educational theories and new markets, has seen the development of new types of picture books to be read and enjoyed independently by a wider range of children than just kindergartners and first-graders. Thus, today's picture books differ in intended audience, purpose, format, and relative

TABLE 4–1   Milestones in the Development of the Picture Book

Date	Event	Significance
1484	Publication of *Aesop's Fables*, illustrated by William Caxton.	One of the first known illustrated books enjoyed by children.
1657	Publication of *Orbis Pictus*, written and illustrated by John Amos Comenius.	Considered to be the first picture book for children.
1860–1900	Golden Age of children's book illustration in Great Britain, led by Randolph Caldecott, Walter Crane, and Kate Greenaway.	Increased awareness, stature, popularity, and appreciation of children's picture books.
1902	Publication of *The Tale of Peter Rabbit* by Beatrix Potter.	Early important modern picture storybook in English.
1928	Publication of *Millions of Cats* by Wanda Gág.	Early important modern American picture storybook.
1938	Establishment of the Caldecott Award for illustration in children's book in the United States.	Promoted excellence in illustrating for children and encouraged talented artists to illustrate children's books.
1940	Publication of *Pat the Bunny* by Dorothy Kunhardt.	One of the first books for babies. Began the move to supply different types of picture books for different child audiences.
1955	Establishment of the Kate Greenaway Award for illustration in children's books in Great Britain.	Promoted excellence in illustrating for children.
1957	Publication of *The Cat in the Hat*, written and illustrated by Dr. Seuss, and *Little Bear*, written by Else Minarik and illustrated by Maurice Sendak.	Introduced the easy-to-read genre of picture books.
1962	Publication of *A Snowy Day*, written and illustrated by Ezra Jack Keats.	One of the first picture books with a minority character as the protagonist to win Caldecott Award.
1967	Publication of *A Boy, a Dog, and a Frog*, illustrated by Mercer Mayer.	Popularized the wordless book genre.
1971	Establishment of Amelia Frances Howard-Gibbon Award for illustration in children's books in Canada.	Promoted excellence in illustrating for children.
1972	Publication of *Push Pull, Empty Full* by Tana Hoban.	Signaled the growing popularity of the concept picture book.
1974	Publication of *Arrow to the Sun: A Pueblo Indian* Tale by Gerald McDermott.	Signaled the emergence of picture books for older readers as a distinct type of picture book.
1981	Publication of "The Baby Board Books" by Helen Oxenbury.	Baby books were established as a distinct and important type of picture book.

TABLE 4–1 *Continued*

Date	Event	Significance
1990	*Color Zoo* by Lois Ehlert wins a Caldecott Honor Award.	Recognition of the engineered book genre.
1991	*Black and White* by David Macaulay wins Caldecott Award.	Denoted acceptance of nontraditional picture book formats.

amount of text and illustration. These differences are not absolute, however; quite often one will find a picture book having characteristics of several specific types. With the understanding that overlap between types is inevitable, you will want to learn to recognize the following kinds of picture books (organized by the intended age of the primary audience from youngest to oldest). Informational picture books are covered in Chapter 9.

Baby Books

Baby books are simply designed, brightly illustrated, durable picture books intended for use with children aged 0 to 2. An example is *Dressing* by Helen Oxenbury. Baby books gained popularity in the 1980s in response to the growing evidence of the remarkable learning capacity of very young children. The types of baby books actually denote the material used in their construction. *Board books* are constructed of heavy, laminated cardboard, and are either bound as a book with pages or are made to fold out in an accordion fashion. *Vinyl books* and *cloth books* are also types of baby books. These books have little or no text. Their content, which deals with the objects and routines familiar to the infant and toddler, is presented mainly by the illustrations. The best baby books, such as those produced by Helen Oxenbury and Jan Ormerod, are intelligently designed to emphasize patterns and associations as well as to promote dialogue between the caregiver and the young child who will often look at these books together.

Interactive Books

Interactive books are picture books that stimulate a child's verbal or physical participation as the book is read. These books ask the child direct questions, invite unison recitation of chants or repeated lines, encourage clapping or moving to the rhythm of the words, or require the child to touch or manipulate the book or find objects in the illustrations. *Each Peach Pear Plum,* Janet and Allan Ahlberg's "I Spy" book featuring well-known nursery rhyme characters, is a good example. The intended audience is usually children aged 2 to 6, and the books are seen as an extension of their world of play. One early example of this type of book that is still greatly enjoyed by toddlers today is Dorothy Kunhardt's *Pat the Bunny* (1940).

Toy Books

Sometimes called *engineered* or *mechanical books,* toy books use paper that has been engineered (i.e., cut, folded, constructed) to provide pop-up, see-through, movable, changeable, or three-dimensional illustrations. Toy books can be found for all ages, but only those that have the simpler types of engineering, such as split pages (as in John Goodall's *Paddy Pork* and *Naughty Nancy* books) or drilled holes for see-through effects (as in Eric Carle's *The Very Hungry Caterpillar*), would be appropriate for most young children. Toy books with fragile or elaborate pop-up features would not last in the hands of a very young child.

Mother Goose and Nursery Rhyme Books

Mother Goose and nursery rhyme picture books are heavily illustrated collections of traditional verse. *Tomie dePaola's Mother Goose,* collected and illustrated by Tomie dePaola, is a good example. Often, a familiar illustration is all a child needs to get her to recite one of these well-loved verses. Collected nursery rhymes first appeared in editions of Charles Perrault's *Tales of Mother Goose* in France in the early eighteenth century. These verses are now part of our children's literary heritage. Also, they have proven to be a wonderful introduction to the world of literature for young children. In societies where countless allusions are made every day to the characters and situations found in nursery rhymes, knowledge of this literature is a mark of being culturally literate.

Because so many of these verses exist, the better collections include large numbers of them thoughtfully organized around themes or topics; they are indexed by titles or first lines. A favorite book of this kind is *The Book of Nursery and Mother Goose Rhymes,* collected and illustrated by Marguerite de Angeli. Some lesser-known traditional verses were collected and illustrated by Arnold Lobel in *The Random House Book of Mother Goose.*

Nursery and Folk Songbooks

Nursery and folk song picture books are heavily illustrated collections of both traditional and modern verses and their musical notation. *Songs from Mother Goose,* compiled by Nancy Larrick and illustrated by Robin Spowart, is a good example. Melody further emphasizes the innate musicality of these verses and turns some verses into games ("Ring Around the Roses") and others into lullabies ("Rock-a-bye Baby"). In choosing a songbook, teachers, librarians, and parents should ascertain that there is a good selection of songs and that the music is well arranged for young voices and playable. Those who plan to work with preschoolers and first- and second-graders will be wise to make these songs part of their repertoire.

Alphabet Books

The alphabet, or ABC, book presents the alphabet letter-by-letter in order to acquaint young children with the shapes, names, and, in some cases, the sounds of the twenty-six letters. For example, see *Eating the Alphabet: Fruits and Vegetables from*

A to Z by Lois Ehlert. Almost all ABC book authors and illustrators choose a theme (animals, elves, fruit, etc.) or device (finding the many objects in the accompanying illustration beginning with the featured letter) to give their books cohesion. Literally hundreds of ABC picture books have been published during the last twenty years, and naturally some are better than others. When choosing an ABC book, consider the appropriateness of the theme or device for students, whether both upper- and lowercase letters are displayed, and the style of print used (Old Gothic print, for example, would be unnecessarily complicated).

Most ABC books are intended for the nonreader or beginning reader. Some authors and illustrators use the alphabet itself as a device for presenting information. In these cases, the intended audience already knows the alphabet. *Ashanti to Zulu,* by Margaret Musgrove and illustrated by Leo and Diane Dillon, presents facts and illustrations about twenty-six African tribes, each beginning with a different letter of the alphabet.

Counting Books

The counting book presents numbers, usually 1 through 10, to acquaint young children with the numerals and their shapes (1, 2, 3 . . .), the number names (one, two, three . . .), the concept of how many each numeral represents, and the counting sequence. *1, 2, 3* by Tana Hoban is a good example of this type of book. As with alphabet books, authors and illustrators of counting books employ themes or devices to make them more cohesive and interesting. Specific considerations in evaluating a counting book include the appeal to children of the theme and objects chosen to illustrate the number concepts, and the clarity with which the illustrator presents the concept of number.

Illustrators often fill their alphabet and counting books with unusual and intriguing objects for children to name and count, such as aardvarks, barracudas, and chameleons. Children pick up a great deal of interesting information and vocabulary in this way. You will be in the best position to decide whether the novelty of these objects will be motivating or confusing to your students.

Concept Books

A concept book is a picture book that explores or explains an idea or concept (e.g., opposites), an object (e.g., a train), or an activity (e.g., working) rather than telling a story. Many concept books have no plot but use repeated elements in the illustrations and text to tie the book together. A good example is *I Touch,* by Rachel Isadora. Limited text and clearly understood illustrations in the best concept books stimulate children's exploratory talk about the concepts, objects, and activities presented.

Alphabet and counting books are considered types of concept books. Another variety of the concept book popular with 2- to 4-year-olds is the naming book, which presents simple, labeled pictures of people, animals, and objects for young children to identify. *Macmillan Picture Wordbook* edited by Judith S. Levey is an example of a naming book.

Wordless Books

The wordless book depends entirely on carefully sequenced illustrations to present the story. There is no text, or the text is limited to one or two pages in the book. *The Gift* by John Prater is a good example of this category. Wordless books are generally intended for prereaders, usually children aged 4 to 6. When children "read" these illustrations in their own words, they benefit from the book's visual story structure in several ways:

- They develop a concept of story as a cohesive narrative with a beginning and an end.
- They use language inventively, which promotes language development.
- They learn the front-to-back, left-to-right page progression in reading.
- They begin to understand that stories can be found not only in books but in themselves.

Publishers began to produce wordless picture books in noticeable quantities in the 1960s. Mercer Mayer, with his wordless book series about a boy, a dog, and a frog, helped to popularize this type of picture book. More sophisticated wordless books for older readers, such as David Weisner's *Tuesday*, are also available.

Picture Storybooks

The picture storybook is a picture book in which both illustrations and text are equally responsible for telling the story. Text and illustration occur with equal frequency in these books, and on most double spreads, both are in view. A good example is *Babushka's Doll* by Patricia Polacco. *The Tale of Peter Rabbit*, written and illustrated by Beatrix Potter and published in England in 1902, has been called the first modern picture book. The first modern American picture storybook, *Millions of Cats*, written and illustrated by Wanda Gág, was published in 1928. The picture storybook is the most common type of picture book.

The text of most picture storybooks is meant to be read aloud to the intended audience of 4- to 7-year-olds, at least for the first time or two, and often includes challenging vocabulary. Many of the best picture storybooks are also read and enjoyed independently by children 8 years old and up.

Easy-to-Read and Pattern Books

Easy-to-read books are created to help the beginning reader read more successfully. They use larger print, more space between lines, limited vocabulary, as well as such devices as word patterns, repeated text, rhyming text, and illustration clues. For example, see The *Josefina Story Quilt* by Eleanor Coerr, illustrated by Bruce Degen. Easy-to-read books that strongly emphasize word patterns are sometimes called *pattern books*. For example, see *Is This a House for Hermit Crab?* by Megan McDonald, illustrated by S. D. Schindler. Easy-to-read picture books were first developed in the 1950s by such authors as Dr. Seuss (*The Cat in the Hat, Fox in Sox*) and Else Holmelund Minarik, who, along with illustrator Maurice Sendak, created the *Little*

Bear series. Easy-to-read books can be used with children whenever they want to learn to read, but the audience for this type of book is usually the 5- to 7-year-old.

The easy-to-read book differs in appearance from the picture storybook in several obvious ways. Because they are intended for independent reading, they do not have to be seen from a distance and are smaller; the text takes up a greater proportion of each page; and the text is often divided into short chapters. Especially in these "chapter" books, the illustrations are proportionately smaller and less profuse than in picture storybooks, occurring on approximately every other page.

Picture Books for Older Readers

Anyone, regardless of age, can enjoy beautiful and interesting illustrations, but, more often than not, picture books are not found in classrooms above grade three. This curious lack of picture books in the intermediate, middle, and junior high school grades may be due, in part, to resistance among adults who influence children in their book choices to include picture books after the primary grades, as Gontarski (1994) found. A wiser approach would be to promote both textual and visual literacy by making appropriate picture books an option in any reading situation. Picture books for older readers are generally more sophisticated, abstract, or complex in themes, stories, and illustrations and are suitable for children aged 10 and older. A good example is *Black and White* by David Macaulay. This type of picture book began to appear in the 1970s, and now artists such as Macaulay, Jörg Steiner, and David Weisner are known for their picture books for older readers. The types of picture books most commonly found for older readers are picture storybooks, wordless books, toy books, and informational picture books.

Transitional Books

Transitional books are a special type of book for the child who can read but who has not yet become a fluent reader. These books, less profusely illustrated and having lengthier text than the other types of books discussed in this chapter, are not considered picture books by some teachers and librarians; in truth, they lie somewhere between picture books and full-length novels. For this reason, we have not included transitional books in the annotated list of titles at the end of this chapter. These titles can be found in the end-of-chapter lists of the appropriate genre chapters.

Characteristic of transitional books are an uncomplicated writing style and vocabulary, an illustration on about every third page, division of text into chapters, and slightly enlarged print. Children who read these books are typically between the ages of 8 and 11. Often, books for the transitional reader occur in series, as in Donald Sobol's *Encyclopedia Brown* books, Ann Cameron's *Julian* books, and Robert Newton Peck's *Soup* books.

With easy-to-read and transitional books in mind, it is wise to remember that children by the age of 5 or 6 have become accustomed to hearing wonderful, richly descriptive stories read and told to them. They are fluent and often sophisticated users of oral language. For children to find themselves suddenly limited to simplistic, boring stories while learning to read would be disheartening, to say the least. To write well for the beginning reader is a real challenge, since these stories must treat interesting topics in vivid language while remaining relatively easy to read. Finding the best of these books for the beginning and transitional readers in your charge will be time well spent.

Within this century the picture book was begun and developed as a genre, diversified to meet the demands of an ever-expanding audience and market, and improved as a result of new and refined printing technology. As researchers came to realize the connections between positive early experiences with good literature, early learning, and future school success, new types of picture books were developed to serve both younger and older audiences. Today, high-quality picture books on nearly every imaginable topic can enrich the lives and imaginations of young children and the classrooms and libraries where they learn.

References

Gontarski, M. (1994). Visual literacy as it relates to picture book use by selected fifth grade students. Unpublished doctoral dissertation, The Florida State University, Tallahassee, FL.

Harrison, David L. (1993). My book! in D. L. Harrison, *Somebody catch my homework*. Illus. by Betsy Lewin. Honesdale, PA: Boyds Mills.

Notable Authors and Illustrators of Picture Books

Janet and Allan Ahlberg, author/illustrator. British. Interactive books. *Each Peach Pear Plum; The Jolly Postman.*

Mitsumasa Anno, author/illustrator. Japanese. Sophisticated wordless and concept books. *Anno's Journey; Anno's Counting Book.*

Molly Bang, author/illustrator. Wordless and concept books illustrated in a variety of styles and media. *The Grey Lady and the Strawberry Snatcher; Ten, Nine, Eight.*

Ludwig Bemelmans, author/illustrator. Creator of "Madeline" series of picture storybooks. *Madeline; Madeline's Rescue.*

Marcia Brown, author/illustrator. Reteller and illustrator of folktales from foreign lands. Three Caldecott Awards, six Caldecott Honor Book Awards. *Once a Mouse . . .; Stone Soup.*

Anthony Browne, author/illustrator. British. Surreal illustrations in picture books for older readers. *Gorilla; The Tunnel.*

Nancy Ekholm Burkert, author/illustrator. Extensive research into the period gives her illustrations authenticity. *Valentine and Orson.*

John Burningham, author/illustrator. British. Picture storybooks often juxtapose adult and child perceptions. *Grandpa; Time to Get Out of the Bath, Shirley.*

Eric Carle, author/illustrator. Unusually formatted picture storybooks and concept books about insects and animals. *The Grouchy Ladybug; The Very Busy Spider.*

Lucille Clifton, author. Creator of "Everett Anderson" series of rhyming picture storybooks about African-American family life. *Amifica; Everett Anderson's Goodbye.*

Barbara Cooney, author/illustrator. Picture storybooks reflect values of New England. *Miss Rumphius.*

Floyd Cooper, illustrator. Uses watercolor and erasers to create characters from many cultures. *The Girl Who Loved Caterpillars.*

Donald Crews, author/illustrator. Concept books about aspects of transportation. *Freight Train; Truck.*

Pat Cummings, illustrator. Realistic illustrations show loving relationships in African-American families. *My Mama Needs Me* (by Mildred Pitts Walter).

Tomie dePaola, author/illustrator. Droll characters like Strega Nona and Big Anthony; uses formal, balanced artistic style. *The Legend of the Bluebonnet; Strega Nona: An Old Tale.*

Jean de Brunhoff, author/illustrator. Creator of "Babar, the Elephant" series of picture storybooks. *The Story of Babar, the Little Elephant; Babar the King.*

Leo and Diane Dillon, illustrators. Illustrators of stories from Black Africa and picture books for older readers. *Ashanti to Zulu; Pish, Posh, Said Hieronymus Bosh.*

Lois Ehlert, author/illustrator. Bold color, geometric shapes, and engineered pages characterize her informational books. *Color Zoo.*

Tom Feelings, illustrator. Inventive artistic techniques used in books about Africans and African Americans. *Moja Means One; Soul Looks Back in Wonder.*

Denise Fleming, author/illustrator. Creates pattern books of handmade paper. *In the Small, Small Pond.*

Stephen Gammell, illustrator. Uses colored pencil in an informal, airy style. *The Relatives Came* (by Cynthia Rylant).

Eric Hill, author/illustrator. Features "Spot," the dog, in toy and board books. *Where's Spot?*

Russell Hoban, author. Creator of "Frances," the badger, in easy-to-read books. *Bedtime for Frances.*

Tana Hoban, author/illustrator. Using photographs, created some of the first and best concept books. *Push Pull, Empty Full; Is It Rough? Is It Smooth? Is It Shiny?*

Shirley Hughes, author/illustrator. British. Picture storybooks about family life. *Alfie Gets in First.*

Pat Hutchins, author/illustrator. British. Pattern books for beginning readers. *Rosie's Walk; Tidy Titch.*

Trina Schart Hyman, illustrator. Illustrator of retold folktales. *Little Red Riding Hood; Hershel and the Hanukkah Goblins.*

Ezra Jack Keats, author/illustrator. One of the first to portray ethnic minorities in the United States as major characters in picture books. *A Snowy Day; Peter's Chair.*

Steven Kellogg, author/illustrator. Uses animals as characters in picture storybooks. *Island of the Skog.*

Leo Lionni, author/illustrator. Uses collage technique to illustrate modern fables. *Swimmy; Frederick.*

Arnold Lobel, author/illustrator. Creator of "Frog and Toad" easy-to-read series. *Days with Frog and Toad; Fables.*

David Macaulay, author/illustrator. Creator of informational picture books and picture books with unusual formats for older readers. *Black and White; Cathedral.*

Robert McCloskey, author/illustrator. Realistic style used in several modern classic picture storybooks. *Make Way for Ducklings; Time of Wonder.*

Patricia McKissack, author. Picture storybooks with African-American characters and themes. *Nettie Jo's Friends* (illustrated by Scott Cook).

James Marshall, author/illustrator. Humorously retold and illustrated folktales. *Goldilocks and the Three Bears.*

Bill Martin, Jr., author. Pattern and rhyming stories for the beginning reader. *Brown Bear, Brown Bear, What Do You See?* (illustrated by Eric Carle).

Mercer Mayer, author/illustrator. One of the first to develop the wordless picture book. *A Boy, A Dog and a Frog.*

Else Holmelund Minarik, author. Her "Little Bear" books were some of the first easy-to-read books. *Little Bear's Visit* (illustrated by Maurice Sendak).

Jörg Müller, illustrator. Swiss. Picture books for older readers. *The Changing City; Rabbit Island* (by Jörg Steiner).

Helen Oxenbury, author/illustrator. British. Board books for babies. *Dressing; Say Goodnight.*

Bill Peet, author/illustrator. Former Disney animator known for humorous picture storybooks about animals and his picture book autobiography. *Merle the High Flying Squirrel; Bill Peet: An Autobiography.*

Jerry Pinkney, illustrator. Represents the African-American experience in realistic, watercolor illustrations. *Mirandy and Brother Wind* (by Patricia McKissack).

Patricia Polacco, author/illustrator. Stories feature homespun characters from varied ethnic backgrounds, particularly Russia. *Baboushka's Doll; Chicken Sunday.*

Leo Politi, author/illustrator. Picture storybooks about ethnic groups in the United States, particularly Mexican Americans. *Song of the Swallows.*

Beatrix Potter, author/illustrator. British. Wrote the first modern, English picture storybook.

The Tale of Peter Rabbit.

Alice and Martin Provensen, authors/illustrator. Use gouache to create charming settings of the past. *The Glorious Flight: Across the Channel with Louis Blériot.*

James Ransome, illustrator. Uses oils in deep, rich colors to portray African-American characters. *Aunt Flossie's Hats (and Crab Cakes Later)* (by Elizabeth Fitzgerald Howard).

H. A. Rey, author/illustrator. Created "Curious George" character in a series of humorous picture storybooks. *Curious George Gets a Medal.*

Cynthia Rylant, author. Picture storybooks set in Appalachia; "Henry and Mudge" easy-to-read series. *The Relatives Came* (illustrated by Stephen Gammell).

Allen Say, author/illustrator. Realistic watercolors depict stories of the Japanese-American experience. *Grandfather's Journey.*

Richard Scarry, author/illustrator. Concept, or naming, books in large format. *Richard Scarry's Biggest Word Book Ever!*

John Schoenherr, illustrator. Crisp, representational style well suited to realistic stories. *Owl Moon* (by Jane Yolen).

Maurice Sendak, author/illustrator. Explores the dreams and imagination of children in complex picture storybooks. *Where the Wild Things Are; Outside Over There.*

Dr. Seuss, (pseudonym for Theodor Geisel), author/illustrator. One of the first to develop the easy-to-read genre. *The Cat in the Hat.*

William Steig, author/illustrator. Animal fantasy picture storybooks. *Dr. De Soto.*

Jörg Steiner, author. Swiss. Picture books for older children (with Jörg Müller). *Rabbit Island; The Bear Who Wanted to Be a Bear.*

John Steptoe, author/illustrator. One of the first successful African-American picture book illustrators. *Stevie; Mufaro's Beautiful Daughters.*

Chris Van Allsburg, author/illustrator. Uses shadow and unusual perspectives to create mysterious moods in picture storybooks for intermediate-grade readers. *Jumanji; The Garden of Abdul Gasazi.*

Julie Vivas, illustrator. Australian. Down-to-earth humor is evident in illustrations. *The Nativity.*

David Wiesner, author/illustrator. Creator of wordless fantasy stories. *Tuesday; Free Fall.*

Rosemary Wells, author/illustrator. Creator of

excellent board books and pattern books. *Hooray for Max; Noisy Nora.*

Brian Wildsmith, author/illustrator. British. Innovative, modernistic illustrations. *Brian Wildsmith's ABC.*

Vera B. Williams, author/illustrator. Expressive artistic style used to depict nontraditional families in picture storybooks. *A Chair for My Mother; Three Days on a River in a Red Canoe.*

Audrey and Don Wood, author/illustrator. Action-filled, humorous illustrations and excellent language characterize rich pattern books. *King Bidgood's in the Bathtub; Heckedy Peg.*

Ed Young, author/illustrator. Chinese-American illustrator of folktales who uses varied media to create mood and textures. *Lon Po Po: A Red-Riding Hood Story from China; Seven Blind Mice.*

Paul O. Zelinsky, illustrator. Illustrates folktales with richly colored oil paintings. *Rumpelstiltskin* (adapted by illustrator).

Charlotte Zolotow, author. Wrote many picture books about family life and emotions. *The Quarreling Book; William's Doll.*

Recommended Picture Books

Ages refer to approximate interest levels. YA = young adult.

Baby Books

These books are generally suitable for ages 0 to 3.

Duke, Kate. *What Bounces?* Dutton, 1986. (Others in the Guinea Pig Board Book series: *Clean-up Day; Bedtime; The Playground.*)

Hoban, Tana. *What Is It?* Greenwillow, 1985.

Kunhardt, Dorothy. *Pat the Bunny.* Golden, 1940.

Ormerod, Jan. *Bend and Stretch.* Lothrop, 1987. (Others in this series: *Making Friends; Mom's Home; This Little Nose*)

Oxenbury, Helen. "Out and About Books." *The Birthday Party.* Dutton, 1983. (Others in this series: *The Car Trip; The Checkup; The Dancing Class; Eating Out; First Day of School; Grandma and Grandpa; Our Dog.*)

———. *I Can.* (Baby Board Book) Random, 1986. (Others in this series: *I Hear; I See; I Touch.*)

———. "The Baby Board Books." *Dressing.* Simon and Schuster, 1981. (Others in this series: *Family; Friends; Playing; Working.*)

———. "Very First Books." *Mother's Helper.* Dial, 1982. (Others in this series: *Shopping Trip; Beach Day; Good Night, Good Morning; Monkey See, Monkey Do.*)

Ricklen, Neil. *Baby's Clothes.* Simon & Schuster, 1994. (Others in this series of 24: *Baby's Friends; Baby's Home; Baby's Toys*)

———. *My Clothes/Mi Ropa.* Macmillan, 1994. (Others in this bilingual English/Spanish series: *My Numbers/Mis Números*)

Tafuri, Nancy. *My Friends.* Greenwillow, 1987.

———. *Where We Sleep.* Greenwillow, 1987.

Wells, Rosemary. "Very First Books." *Max's Bath.* Dial, 1985. (Others in this series: *Max's Bedtime; Max's Birthday; Max's Breakfast; Max's First Word; Max's New Suit; Max's Ride; Max's Toys*)

Interactive Books

Ahlberg, Janet, and Allen Ahlberg. *The Baby's Catalogue.* Little, Brown, 1982. Ages 2–4.

———. *Each Peach Pear Plum: An I–Spy Story.* Viking, 1978. Ages 2–4.

———. *Peek–a Boo!* Viking, 1981. Ages 3–5.

Burton, Marilee Robin. *Tail Toes Eyes Ears Nose.* Harper, 1988. Ages 2–4.

Carlstrom, Nancy White. *Jesse Bear, What Will You Wear?* Illustrated by Bruce Degan. Macmillan, 1986. Ages 2–4. (Others in this series: *Tra–la Tub; Tum–Tum Tickle; Yum–Yum Crumble*)

Christelow, Eileen, reteller. *Five Little Monkeys Jumping on the Bed.* Clarion, 1989. Ages 3–5.

Cook, Trish. *So Much.* Illustrated by Helen Oxenbury. Candlewick, 1994. Ages 3–5.

Dodds, Dayle Ann. *Wheel Away!* Illustrated by Thacher Hurd. Harper, 1989. Ages 5–7.

Hennessy, B. G. *The Missing Tarts.* Illustrated by Tracey Campbell Pearson. Viking, 1989. Ages 3–5.

Hill, Eric. *Where's Spot?* Putnam, 1980. (Others in this series: *Spot's First Walk; Spot's Birthday Party; Spot's First Christmas*) Ages 3–5.

Koch, Michelle. *Hoot, Howl, Hiss.* Greenwillow, 1991. Ages 4–6.

Marzollo, Jean. *I Spy Fantasy: A Book of Picture Riddles.* Illustrated by Walter Wick. Scholastic, 1994.

Ages 5–9. (Others in this series: *I Spy Mystery*)

Noll, Sally. *Jiggle, Wiggle, Prance.* Greenwillow, 1987. Ages 3–5.

———. *Watch Where You Go.* Greenwillow, 1990. Ages 4–6.

Rose, Dorothy. *Follow Me!* Illustrated by Ann Bogart. Simon & Schuster, 1993. Ages 2–5. (Others in this series: *Peek–a–Boo!; What Do Lambs Say?; Where's Your Nose?*)

Shapiro, Arnold. *Who Says That?* Illustrated by Monica Wellington. Dutton, 1991. Ages 3–5.

Spier, Peter. *Crash! Bang! Boom!* Doubleday, 1972. Ages 5–7.

Stolz, Mary. *Say Something.* Illustrated by Alexander Koshkin. HarperCollins, 1993. Ages 4–6.

Tafuri, Nancy. *Have You Seen My Duckling?* Greenwillow, 1984. Ages 3–5.

Watanabe, Shigeo. "I Can Do It All By Myself." *How Do I Put It On?* Illustrated by Yasou Ohtomo. Philomel, 1980. (Also in this series: *What a Good Lunch!; Get Set Go!; I'm King of the Castle; Where's My Daddy?; I Can Ride It!*) Ages 4–6.

Wilkes, Angela. *My First Activity Book.* Knopf, 1990. Ages 3–5.

Williams, Linda. *The Little Old Lady Who Was Not Afraid of Anything.* Illustrated by Megan Lloyd. Crowell, 1986.

Williams, Vera B. *"More More More," Said the Baby.* Greenwillow, 1990. Ages 2–4.

Yoshi. *Who's Hiding Here?* Picture Book Studio, 1987. Ages 5–7.

Toy Books

Baker, Keith. *The Magic Fan.* Harcourt, 1989. Ages 7–9.

Carle, Eric. *The Honeybee and the Robber: A Moving/Picture* Book. Philomel, 1995 (1981). Ages 5–7.

———. *The Very Hungry Caterpillar.* World, 1968. Ages 4–6.

———. *The Very Lonely Firefly.* Putnam, 1995. Ages 2–6.

———. *The Very Quiet Cricket.* Putnam, 1990. Ages 2–6.

Emberley, Ed. *Go Away, Big Green Monster.* Little, Brown, 1992. Ages 3–7.

Goodall, John S. *The Adventures of Paddy Pork.* Harcourt, 1968. Ages 6–8. (Others in this series: *The Ballooning Adventures of Paddy Pork;*

Naughty Nancy; Paddy Pork's Holiday)

———. *The Story of an English Village.* Atheneum, 1979. Ages 7–9.

———. *The Surprise Picnic.* Atheneum, 1977. Ages 6–8.

Hellen, Nancy. *The Bus Stop.* Orchard, 1988. Ages 5–7.

———. *Old MacDonald Had a Farm.* Orchard, 1990. Ages 5–7.

Hill, Eric. *Where's Spot?* Putnam, 1980. Ages 3–5.

Jonas, Ann. *Where Can It Be?* Greenwillow, 1986. Ages 5–7.

Piénkowski, Jan. *The Haunted House.* Heinemann, 1980. Ages 5–7.

Reasoner, Charles. *Whose Mommy Is This?* Price, 1994. Ages 3–6.

Sabuda, Robert. *The Knight's Castle.* Golden, 1994.

———. *The Mummy's Tomb.* Golden, 1994.

Schweninger, Ann. *Birthday Wishes.* Viking, 1986. Ages 6–8.

Mother Goose and Nursery Rhyme Books

These books are generally suitable for ages 2 to 7.

Alderson, Brian. *Cakes and Custard.* Illustrated by Helen Oxenbury. Morrow, 1975.

Arnold, Ted. *Mother Goose's Words of Wisdom: A Book of Months.* Dial, 1990.

Briggs, Raymond. *The Mother Goose Treasury.* Coward–McCann, 1966.

Cauley, Lorinda Bryan. *The Three Little Kittens.* Putnam, 1982.

Cook, Scott. *Mother Goose.* Knopf, 1994.

Cousins, Lucy, illustrator. *The Little Dog Laughed and Other Nursery Rhymes.* Dutton, 1990.

DeAngeli, Marguerite. *Marguerite DeAngeli's Book of Nursery and Mother Goose Rhymes.* Doubleday, 1954.

DeForest, Charlotte B. *The Prancing Pony: Nursery Rhymes from Japan Adapted into English Verse for Children.* Illustrated by Keiko Hida. Walker/Weatherhill, 1968.

dePaola, Tomie, compiler. *Tomie dePaola's Mother Goose.* Putnam, 1985.

Emerson, Sally, selector. *The Nursery Treasury: A Collection of Baby Games, Rhymes and Lullabies.* Illustrated by Moira and Colin MacLean. Doubleday, 1988.

Greenaway, Kate. *Mother Goose, or The Old Nursery Rhymes.* Warne, 1881.

Griego, Margot C., Betsy L. Bucks, Sharon S. Gilbert, and Laurel H. Kimball. *Tortillitas Para Mama.* Illustrated by Barbara Cooney. Holt, 1981.

Hale, Sarah Josepha. *Mary Had a Little Lamb.* Photographs by Bruce McMillan. Scholastic, 1990.

Hoguet, Susan Ramsey. *Solomon Grundy.* Dutton, 1986.

Jeffers, Susan. *Three Jovial Huntsmen.* Bradbury, 1973.

Lines, Kathleen. *Lavender's Blue.* Illustrated by Harold Jones. Watts, 1964.

Lobel, Arnold. *Gregory Griggs and Other Nursery Rhyme People.* Greenwillow, 1978.

———. *Whiskers and Rhymes.* Greenwillow, 1985.

———, selector. *The Random House Book of Mother Goose.* Random, 1986.

Marshall, James. *James Marshall's Mother Goose.* Farrar, 1979.

Opie, Peter and Iona, compilers. *Tail Feathers from Mother Goose: The Opie Rhyme Book.* Little, Brown, 1988.

Provensen, Alice, and Martin Provensen. *The Mother Goose Book.* Random, 1976.

Reed, Philip. *Mother Goose and Nursery Rhymes.* Atheneum, 1963.

Rojankovsky, Feodor. *The Tall Book of Mother Goose.* Harper, 1942.

Spier, Peter. *London Bridge Is Falling Down.* Doubleday, 1967.

———. *To Market, To Market.* Doubleday, 1967.

Sutherland, Zena. *The Orchard Book of Nursery Rhymes.* Illustrated by Faith Jaques. Orchard, 1990.

Tripp, Wallace. *Granfa' Grig Had a Pig and Other Rhymes Without Reason.* Little, Brown, 1976.

Tudor, Tasha. *Mother Goose.* Walck, 1944.

Westcott, Nadine Bernard. *Peanut Butter and Jelly: A Play Rhyme.* Dutton, 1987.

———, adaptor. *The Lady with the Alligator Purse.* Little, Brown, 1988.

Wildsmith, Brian. *Brian Wildsmith's Mother Goose.* Watts, 1963.

Wright, Blanche Fisher. *The Real Mother Goose.* Rand McNally, 1916.

Wyndham, Robert. *Chinese Mother Goose Rhymes.* Illustrated by Ed Young. World, 1968.

Zuromskis, Diane, illustrator. *The Farmer in the Dell.* Little, Brown, 1978.

Nursery and Folk Songbooks

Aliki, pseud. (Aliki Brandenberg). *Go Tell Aunt Rhody*. Macmillan, 1974. Ages 6–10.

Brett, Jan, illustrator. *The Twelve Days of Christmas*. Dodd, 1986. Ages 6–10.

Brown, Marc. *Finger Rhymes*. Dutton, 1980. Ages 5–7.

———. *Hand Rhymes*. Dutton, 1985. Ages 5–7.

dePaola, Tomie. *Tomie dePaola's Book of Christmas Carols*. Putnam, 1987. Ages 6–10.

Durell, Ann, selector. *The Diane Goode Book of American Folk Tales and Songs*. Illustrated by Diane Goode. Dutton, 1989. Ages 6–10.

Fowke, Edith, compiler. *Sally Go Round the Sun: Three Hundred Children's Songs, Rhymes, and Games*. Illustrated by Carlos Marchiori. Doubleday, 1970. Ages 6–10.

Fox, Dan, editor. *Go In and Out the Window: An Illustrated Songbook for Young People*. Holt/ Metropolitan Museum of Art, 1987. Ages 6–10.

Hart, Jane. *Singing Bee: A Collection of Favorite Children's Songs*. Illustrated by Anita Lobel. Lothrop, 1989 (1982). Ages 4–9.

Krull, Kathleen, editor. *Gonna Sing My Head Off! American Folk Songs for Children*. Illustrated by Allen Garns. Knopf, 1992.

Langstaff, John, editor. *What a Morning! The Christmas Story in Black Spirituals*. Illustrated by Ashley Bryan, arrangements for singing and piano by John Andrew Ross. Macmillan, 1987. Ages 6–10.

Larrick, Nancy, compiler. *Songs from Mother Goose: With the Traditional Melody for Each*. Illustrated by Robin Spowart. Harper, 1989. Ages 3–7.

Orozco, José-Luis. *De Colores and Other Latin-American Folk Songs for Children*. Illustrated by Elisa Kleven. Dutton, 1994.

Raffi. *Raffi's Christmas Treasury*. Illustrated by Nadine Bernard Westcott. Crown, 1988. Ages 6–10.

Spier, Peter. *The Fox Went Out on a Chilly Night*. Doubleday, 1961. Ages 6–8.

———. *The Star-Spangled Banner*. Doubleday, 1973. Ages 6–10.

Staines, Bill. *All God's Critters Got a Place in the Choir*. Illustrated by Margot Zemach. Dutton, 1989. Ages 6–10.

Titherington, Jeanne. *Baby's Boat*. Greenwillow, 1992. Ages 3–5.

Yolen, Jane, editor. *The Lullaby Songbook*. Musical arrangements by Adam Stemple. Illustrated by Charles Mikolaycak. Harcourt, 1986. Ages 3–5.

Zemach, Margot. *Hush, Little Baby*. Dutton, 1976. Ages 4–6.

Alphabet Books

These books are generally suitable for ages 3 to 6. Ages will be provided only for those books intended for an older audience.

Anno, Mitsumasa. *Anno's Alphabet*. Crowell, 1975. Ages 7–9.

Aylesworth, Jim. *Old Black Fly*. Illustrated by Stephen Gammell. Holt, 1992.

Azarian, Mary. *A Farmer's Alphabet*. Godine, 1981.

Base, Graeme. *Animalia*. Abrams, 1987. Ages 8–YA.

Baskin, Hosea, Tobias, and Lisa. *Hosie's Alphabet*. Illustrated by Leonard Baskin. Viking, 1972. Ages 7–9.

Berger, Terry, and Alice S. Kandell. *Ben's ABC Day*. Lothrop, 1982.

Brown, Marcia. *All Butterflies: An ABC*. Scribner's, 1974.

Bunting, J. *My First ABC Book*. Dorling Kindersley, 1993.

Duke, Kate. *The Guinea Pig ABC*. Dutton, 1983.

Duvoisin, Roger. *A for the Ark*. Lothrop, 1952.

Ehlert, Lois. *Eating the Alphabet: Fruits and Vegetables from A to Z*. Harcourt, 1989.

Ellis, Veronica Freeman. *Afro-Bets First Book about Africa*. Illustrated by George Ford. Just Us Books, 1990.

Elting, Mary, and Folsom, Michael. *Q Is For Duck: An Alphabet Guessing Game*. Illustrated by Jack Kent. Clarion, 1980. Ages 6–7.

Feelings, Muriel. *Jambo Means Hello: Swahili Alphabet Book*. Illustrated by Tom Feelings. Dial, 1974. Ages 6–8.

Gardner, Beau. *Have You Ever Seen. . .? An ABC Book*. Dodd, 1986.

Geisert, Arthur. *Pigs from A to Z*. Houghton, 1986. Ages 6–10.

Greenaway, Kate. *A– Apple Pie*. Warne, 1886.

Hepworth, Cathi. *ANTics! An Alphabetical Anthology*. Putnam, 1992. Ages 7–9.

Hoban, Tana. *A, B, See!* Greenwillow, 1982.

———. *26 Letters and 99 Cents*. Greenwillow, 1987.

Jonas, Ann. *Aardvarks, Disembark!* Greenwillow, 1990.

Kellogg, Steven. *Aster Aardvark's Alphabet Adventures.* Morrow, 1987.

Kitchen, Bert. *Animal Alphabet.* Dial, 1984.

Lobel, Anita. *Alison's Zinnia.* Greenwillow, 1990.

Lobel, Arnold. *On Market Street.* Illustrated by Anita Lobel. Greenwillow, 1981.

MacDonald, Suse. *Alphabatics.* Bradbury, 1986.

Martin, Bill, Jr., and John Archambault. *Chicka Chicka Boom Boom.* Illustrated by Lois Ehlert. Simon and Schuster, 1989.

Mullins, Patricia. *V for Vanishing: An Alphabet of Endangered Animals.* HarperCollins, 1993. Ages 6–8.

Munari, Bruno. *Bruno Munari's ABC.* World Publishing, 1960.

Musgrove, Margaret. *Ashanti to Zulu: African Traditions.* Illustrated by Leo and Diane Dillon. Dial, 1976. Ages 8–12.

Neumeier, Marty, and Byron Glaser. *Action Alphabet.* Greenwillow, 1985.

Piatti, Celestino. *Celestino Piatti's Animal ABC.* Translated by Jon Reid. Atheneum, 1966.

Provensen, Alice, and Martin Provensen. *A Peaceable Kingdom: The Shaker ABCEDARIUS.* Viking, 1978. Ages 6–8.

Rankin, Laura. *The Handmade Alphabet.* Dial, 1991. Ages 6–11.

Sendak, Maurice. "The Nutshell Library." *Alligators All Around.* Harper, 1962.

Tudor, Tasha. *A Is for Annabelle.* Walck, 1954.

Van Allsburg, Chris. *The Z Was Zapped.* Houghton Mifflin, 1987. Ages 6–10.

Wildsmith, Brian. *Brian Wildsmith's ABC.* Watts, 1962. Ages 6–10.

Wilner, Isabel. *B Is for Bethlehem: A Christmas Alphabet.* Illustrated by Elisa Kleven. Dutton, 1990.

Yolen, Jane. *All in the Woodland Early: An ABC Book.* Illustrated by Jane Breskin Zalben. Collins, 1979.

Counting Books

These books are generally suitable for ages 4 to 7. Ages will be provided only for those books intended for an older audience.

Aker, Susan. *What Comes in 2's, 3's & 4's?* Illustrated by Bernie Karlin. Simon & Schuster, 1990.

Anno, Mitsumasa. *Anno's Counting Book.* Crowell, 1977. Ages 7–9.

Aylesworth, Jim. *One Crow: A Counting Rhyme.* Illustrated by Ruth Young. Lippincott, 1988.

Bang, Molly. *Ten, Nine, Eight.* Greenwillow, 1983.

Carle, Eric. *My Very First Book of Numbers.* Crowell, 1974.

———. *1,2,3 to the Zoo.* Philomel, 1968.

Dunrea, Olivier. *Deep Down Underground.* Macmillan, 1989.

Ehlert, Lois. *Fish Eyes: A Book You Can Count On.* Harcourt, 1990.

Ernst, Lisa Campbell. *Up to Ten and Down Again.* Lothrop, 1986.

Feelings, Muriel. *Moja Means One: Swahili Counting Book.* Illustrated by Tom Feelings. Dial, 1971.

Fleming, Denise. *Count!* Holt, 1992.

Giganti, Paul. *Each Orange Had Eight Slices.* Illustrated by Donald Crews. Greenwillow, 1992.

Hoban, Tana. *1, 2, 3.* Greenwillow, 1985.

———. *26 Letters and 99 Cents.* Greenwillow, 1987.

Hutchins, Pat. *1 Hunter.* Greenwillow, 1982.

Jonas, Ann. *Splash!* Morrow, 1995.

Kitchen, Bert. *Animal Numbers.* Dial, 1987.

Langstaff, John. *Over in the Meadow.* Illustrated by Feodor Rojankovsky. Harcourt, 1957.

Lifesize Animal Counting Book, The. Dorling Kindersley, 1994.

Lindbergh, Reeve. *Midnight Farm.* Illustrated by Susan Jeffers. Dial, 1987.

Lynn, Sara. *123.* Little, Brown, 1986.

McMillan, Bruce. *Counting Wildflowers.* Lothrop, 1986.

Oxenbury, Helen. *Numbers of Things.* Watts, 1968.

Reiss, John. *Numbers.* Bradbury, 1971.

Rowan, Dick. *Everybody In! A Counting Book.* Bradbury, 1968.

Sis, Peter. *Waving: A Counting Book.* Greenwillow, 1988.

Tafuri, Nancy. *Who's Counting?* Greenwillow, 1986.

Testa, Fulvio. *If You Take a Pencil.* Dial, 1982.

Walsh, Ellen S. *Mouse Count.* Harcourt, 1991.

Wildsmith, Brian. *Brian Wildsmith's 1, 2, 3's.* Watts, 1965.

Wise, William. *Ten Sly Piranhas: A Counting Story in Reverse.* Illustrated by Victoria Chess. Dial, 1992.

Concept Books

These books are generally suitable for ages 3 to 5. Ages will be provided only for those books intended for an older audience.

Baer, Gene. *Thump, Thump, Rat-a-Tat-Tat.* Illustrated by Lois Ehlert. Harper, 1989.

Barton, Byron. *Building a House.* Greenwillow, 1981.

———. *Dinosaurs, Dinosaurs.* Crowell, 1989.

———. *Machines at Work.* Crowell, 1987.

Carle, Eric. *My Very First Book of Colors.* Crowell, 1974.

———. *My Very First Book of Shapes.* Crowell, 1974.

Collier, John. *The Backyard.* Viking, 1993. Ages 5–7.

Crews, Donald. *Flying.* Greenwillow, 1986.

———. *Freight Train.* Greenwillow, 1978.

———. *Truck.* Greenwillow, 1980.

Ehlert, Lois. *Growing Vegetable Soup.* Harcourt, 1987.

———. *Red Leaf, Yellow Leaf.* Harcourt, 1991. Ages 5–7.

Emberley, Rebecca. *Jungle Sounds.* Little, Brown, 1989.

Florian, Douglas. *A Summer Day.* Greenwillow, 1988.

———. *A Winter Day.* Greenwillow, 1987.

Fowler, Susi Gregg. *When Summer Ends.* Illustrated by Marisabina Russo. Greenwillow, 1989.

Gerstein, Mordicai. *The Sun's Day.* Harper, 1989.

Henkes, Kevin. *The Biggest Boy.* Illustrated by Nancy Tafuri. Morrow, 1995.

Hoban, Tana. *Color Everywhere.* Morrow, 1995.

———. *Is It Red? Is It Yellow? Is It Blue?* Greenwillow, 1978.

———. *Look Again!* Macmillan, 1971.

———. *Over, Under, and Through and Other Spatial Concepts.* Macmillan, 1973.

———. *Push Pull, Empty Full: A Book of Opposites.* Macmillan, 1972.

Hughes, Shirley. *Alfie Gets in First.* Lothrop, 1982.

———. *Alfie Gives a Hand.* Lothrop, 1984.

———. *Angel Mae.* Lothrop, 1989.

———. *The Big Concrete Lorry.* Lothrop, 1990.

———. *Out and About.* Lothrop, 1988.

———. "Nursery Collection." *Bathwater's Hot.* Lothrop, 1985. (Others in this series: *Noisy*; *When We Went to the Park.*)

Isadora, Rachel. *I Hear.* Greenwillow, 1985. (Also in this series: *I Touch, I See*)

Kalan, Robert. *Blue Sea.* Illustrated by Donald Crews. Greenwillow, 1979.

Kightley, Rosalinda. *Opposites.* Little, Brown, 1986.

———. *Shapes.* Little, Brown, 1986.

Krauss, Ruth. *A Hole Is To Dig.* Illustrated by Maurice Sendak. Harper, 1952.

Lember, Barbara H. *A Book of Fruit.* Ticknor & Fields, 1994.

Levey, Judith S., editor. *Macmillan Picture Wordbook.* Macmillan, 1990.

Lipkind, William. *Finders Keepers.* Illustrated by Nicolas Mordvinoff. Harcourt, 1951.

Lynn, Sara. *Colors.* Little, Brown, 1986.

Lyon, George Ella. *Who Came Down That Road?* Illustrated by Peter Catalanotto. Orchard, 1992. Ages 4–7.

Martin, Bill, Jr., and John Archambault. *Listen to the Rain.* Illustrated by James Endicott. Holt, 1988.

McCloskey, Robert. *Time of Wonder.* Viking, 1957.

McDonald, Golden. pseud. (Margaret Wise Brown). *The Little Island.* Illustrated by Leonard Weisgard. Doubleday, 1946.

McMillan, Bruce. *Becca Backward, Becca Frontward: A Book of Concept Pairs.* Lothrop, 1986.

———. *Dry or Wet?* Lothrop, 1988.

———. *Super Super Superwords.* Lothrop, 1989.

———. *Time To. . . .* Lothrop, 1989.

Miller, Margaret. *Whose Shoe?* Greenwillow, 1991.

My Little Color Library (six books, six colors). Dorling Kindersley, 1993.

Narahashi, Keiko. *I Have a Friend.* Macmillan, 1987.

Parnall, Peter. *Winter Barn.* Macmillan, 1986.

Pearson, Susan. *My Favorite Time of the Year.* Illustrated by John Wallner. Harper, 1988.

Reiss, John. *Colors.* Bradbury, 1969.

———. *Shapes.* Bradbury, 1974.

Rice, Eve. *Oh, Lewis!* Macmillan, 1974.

Rockwell, Anne, and Harlow Rockwell. *The Toolbox.* Macmillan, 1971.

Rogers, Fred. *Making Friends.* Photographs by Jim Judkis. Putnam, 1987.

———. *Moving.* Photographs by Jim Judkis. Putnam, 1987.

Scarry, Richard. *My First Word Book.* Random House, 1986.

———. *Richard Scarry's Biggest Word Book Ever!*

Random House, 1985.

Schwartz, David M. *If You Made a Million*. Illustrated by Steven Kellogg. Photographs by George Ancona. Lothrop, 1989.

Serfozo, Mary. *Who Said Red?* Illustrated by Keiko Narahashi. Macmillan, 1988.

Shulevitz, Uri. *Rain Rain Rivers*. Scribner's, 1967.

Spier, Peter. *Fast-Slow High-Low*. Doubleday, 1972.

Tafuri, Nancy. *In a Red House*. Greenwillow, 1987.

Testa, Fulvio. *If You Look Around You*. Dutton, 1983.

verDorn, Bethea. *Moon Glows*. Illustrated by Thomas Graham. Arcade, 1990.

Voake, Charlotte. *Mrs. Goose's Baby*. Little, Brown, 1989.

Walsh, Ellen Stoll. *Mouse Paint*. Harcourt, 1989.

Winthrop, Elizabeth. *Shoes*. Illustrated by William Joyce. Harper, 1986.

Wolde, Gunilla. "Betsy Books." *This Is Betsy*. Random, 1975. (Also in series: *Betsy's Baby Brother*, 1975; *Betsy's First Day at Nursery School*, 1976; and *Betsy and the Doctor*, 1978.)

Wolff, Ashley. *A Year of Beasts*. Dutton, 1986.

———. *A Year of Birds*. Dodd, Mead, 1984.

Wordless Books

These books are generally suitable for ages 3 to 6. Ages will be provided only for those books intended for an older audience.

Alexander, Martha. *Bobo's Dream*. Dial, 1970.

Anno, Mitsumasa. *Anno's Journey*. Collins, 1978. Ages 8–10.

———. *Topsy-Turvies–Pictures to Stretch the Imagination*. Walker/Weatherhill, 1970.

Baker, Jeannie. *Window*. Greenwillow, 1991. Ages 7–12.

Briggs, Raymond. *The Snowman*. Random, 1978.

Carle, Eric. *Do You Want to Be My Friend?* Harper, 1971.

Collington, Peter. *The Angel and the Soldier Boy*. Knopf, 1987.

———. *On Christmas Eve*. Knopf, 1990.

Day, Alexandra. *Carl Goes Shopping*. Farrar, 1989.

Demarest, Chris L. *Orville's Odyssey*. Prentice Hall, 1986.

Dupasquier, Philippe. *The Great Escape*. Houghton, 1988.

Hutchins, Pat. *Changes, Changes*. Macmillan, 1971.

Krahn, Fernando. *Who's Seen the Scissors?* Dutton, 1975.

Martin, Rafe. *Will's Mammoth*. Illustrated by Stephen Gammell. Putnam, 1989.

Mayer, Mercer. *A Boy, a Dog, and a Frog*. Dial, 1967. (Others in this series: *Frog, Where Are You?*; *A Boy, a Dog, and a Friend*; *Frog on His Own*; *Frog Goes to Dinner*; *One Frog Too Many*, with Marianna Mayer)

McCully, Emily Arnold. *The Christmas Gift*. Harper, 1988.

———. *New Baby*. Harper, 1988.

———. *School*. Harper, 1987.

Prater, John. *The Gift*. Viking, 1986. Ages 6–8.

Spier, Peter. *Noah's Ark*. Doubleday, 1977. Ages 6–8.

———. *Oh, Were They Ever Happy!* Doubleday, 1978. Ages 6–8.

———. *Peter Spier's Rain*. Doubleday, 1982.

Tafuri, Nancy. *Follow Me!* Greenwillow, 1990.

Wiesner, David. *Free Fall*. Lothrop, 1988. Ages 6–10.

———. *Tuesday*. Clarion, 1991. Ages 6–10.

Picture Storybooks

Ackerman, Karen. *Song and Dance Man*. Illustrated by Stephen Gammell. Knopf, 1988. Ages 6–8.

Ada, Alma Flor. *Dear Peter Rabbit*. Illustrated by Leslie Tryon. Atheneum, 1994.

Agee, Jon. *The Incredible Painting of Felix Clousseau*. Farrar, 1988. Ages 7–9.

Alexander, Lloyd. *The Fortune-Tellers*. Illustrated by Trina Schart Hyman. Dutton, 1992. Ages 6–8.

Alexander, Martha. *Nobody Asked Me If I Wanted a Baby Sister*. Dial, 1971. Ages 5–7.

Allard, Harry. *Miss Nelson Is Missing*. Illustrated by James Marshall, Houghton, 1977. Ages 6–8.

———. *The Stupids Have a Ball*. Illustrated by James Marshall. Houghton, 1977. Ages 6–8.

Allard, Harry, and James Marshall. *Miss Nelson Has a Field Day*. Illustrated by James Marshall. Houghton, 1985. Ages 6–8.

Andersen, Hans Christian. *The Little Match Girl*. Illustrated by Rachel Isadora. Putnam, 1987. Ages 7–9. (Modern folktale)

———. *The Tinderbox*. Illustrated by Barry Moser. Little, Brown, 1990. Ages 6–8. (Modern folktale)

Anholt, Catherine. *Truffles in Trouble*. Little, Brown, 1987. Ages 6–8.

———. *Truffles Is Sick*. Little, Brown, 1987. Ages 6–8.

Ardizzone, Edward. *Little Tim and the Brave Sea Captain*. Walck, 1955. Ages 6–8.

Arnold, Ted. *No Jumping on the Bed!* Dial, 1987. Ages 5–7.

Aruego, Jose. *Look What I Can Do.* Scribner's, 1971. Ages 5–7.

Babbitt, Natalie. *The Devil's Other Storybook.* Farrar, 1987. Ages 6–8.

———. *Nellie: A Cat on Her Own.* Farrar, 1989. Ages 6–8.

Baker, Jeannie. *Where the Forest Meets the Sea.* Greenwillow, 1988. Ages 8–10.

Baker, Olaf. *Where the Buffaloes Begin.* Illustrated by Stephen Gammell. Warne, 1981. Ages 8–10.

Bang, Molly. *The Paper Crane.* Greenwillow, 1985. Ages 8–10.

Barber, Antonia. *The Mousehole Cat.* Illustrated by Nicola Bayley. Macmillan, 1990. Ages 6–8.

Baylor, Byrd. *The Best Town in the World.* Illustrated by Ronald Himler. Scribner's, 1983. Ages 7–9.

———. *Hawk, I'm Your Brother.* Illustrated by Peter Parnall. Scribner's, 1976. Ages 7–9.

———. *The Other Way to Listen.* Illustrated by Peter Parnall. Scribner's, 1978. Ages 7–9.

———. *The Table Where Rich People Sit.* Illustrated by Peter Parnall. Scribner's, 1994. Ages 7–10.

Bemelmans, Ludwig. *Madeline.* Viking, 1939. Ages 5–7.

———. *Madeline's Rescue.* Viking, 1953. Ages 5–7.

Birdseye, Tom. *Air Mail to the Moon.* Illustrated by Stephen Gammell. Holiday, 1988. Ages 6–8.

Blos, Joan W. *Old Henry.* Illustrated by Stephen Gammell. Morrow, 1987. Ages 7–9.

Bottner, Barbara. *Bootsie Barker Bites.* Illustrated by Peggy Rathman. Putnam, 1992. Ages 4–7

Brett, Jan. *The Wild Christmas Reindeer.* Putnam, 1990. Ages 6–8.

Bröger, Achim. *The Santa Clauses.* Illustrated by Ute Krause. Dial, 1986. Ages 6–8.

Brown, Marc. *Arthur's Baby.* Little, Brown, 1987. Ages 5–7.

———. *D. W. All Wet.* Little, Brown, 1988. Ages 5–7.

Brown, Margaret Wise. *Goodnight Moon.* Illustrated by Clement Hurd. Harper, 1947. Ages 4–6.

Brown, Ruth. *Our Puppy's Vacation.* Dutton, 1987. Ages 5–7.

Browne, Anthony. *Gorilla.* Knopf, 1985. Ages 7–9.

Bunting, Eve. *Ghost's Hour, Spook's Hour.* Illustrated by Donald Carrick. Clarion, 1987. Ages 7–9.

———. *The Wall.* Illustrated by Ronald Himler. Clarion, 1990. Ages 7–9.

———. *The Wednesday Surprise.* Illustrated by Donald Carrick. Clarion, 1989. Ages 6–10.

Burningham, John. *Grandpa.* Crown, 1985. Ages 5–7.

———. *Mr. Gumpy's Motor Car.* Harper, 1976.

———. *Time to Get Out of the Bath, Shirley.* Crowell, 1978.

Burton, Virginia Lee. *The Little House.* Houghton, 1942. Ages 5–7.

———. *Mike Mulligan and His Steam Shovel.* Houghton, 1939. Ages 5–7.

Carle, Eric. *The Grouchy Ladybug.* Crowell, 1971. Ages 5–7.

———. *The Mixed-Up Chameleon.* Crowell, 1975. Ages 6–8.

———. *The Very Busy Spider.* Philomel, 1984. Ages 5–7.

Carlstrom, Nancy White. *Blow Me a Kiss, Miss Lilly.* Illustrated by Amy Schwartz. Harper, 1990. Ages 5–7.

Carrick, Carol. *What Happened to Patrick's Dinosaurs?* Illustrated by Donald Carrick. Clarion, 1986. Ages 6–8.

Carrick, Donald. *Harald and the Great Stag.* Clarion, 1988. Ages 6–8.

Caudill, Rebecca. *A Pocketful of Cricket.* Illustrated by Evaline Ness. Holt, 1964. Ages 6–8.

Cazet, Denys. *Never Spit on Your Shoes.* Orchard, 1990. Ages 6–10.

Cecil, Laura, editor. *Listen to This.* Illustrated by Emma Chichester Clark. Greenwillow, 1988. Ages 6–8.

Cherry, Lynne. *The Great Kapok Tree: A Tale of the Amazon Rainforest.* Harcourt, 1990. Ages 6–10.

Chetwin, Grace. *Box and Cox.* Illustrated by David Small. Bradbury, 1990. Ages 7–9.

Christelow, Eileen. *The Great Pig Escape.* Clarion, 1994.

Clifton, Lucille. *Amifika.* Illustrated by Thomas DiGrazia. Dutton, 1977. Ages 6–8.

———. *My Friend Jacob.* Illustrated by Thomas DiGrazia. Dutton, 1980. Ages 6–8.

Cohen, Caron Lee. *Whiffle Squeek.* Illustrated by Ted Rand. Dodd, 1987. Ages 6–8.

Cole, Brock. *Alpha and the Dirty Baby.* Farrar, 1991. Ages 5–8.

———. *The Giant's Toe.* Farrar, 1986. Ages 6–8.

Cooney, Barbara. *Hattie and the Wild Waves: A Story from Brooklyn.* Viking, 1990. Ages 6–8.

———. *Island Boy.* Viking, 1988. Ages 6–10.

———. *Miss Rumphius.* Viking, 1982. Ages 6–10.

Cooney, Nancy Evans. *The Umbrella Day.* Illustrated by Melissa Bay Mathis. Putnam, 1989. Ages 5–7.

Craven, Carolyn. *What the Mailman Brought.* Illustrated by Tomie dePaola. Putnam, 1987. Ages 5–7.

Crews, Donald. *Bigmama's.* Greenwillow, 1991. Ages 4–7.

———. *Shortcut.* Greenwillow, 1992. Ages 4–7.

Crowe, Robert. *Clyde Monster.* Illustrated by Kay Chorao. Dutton, 1976. Ages 5–7.

Daly, Niki. *Not So Fast Songololo.* Atheneum, 1986. Ages 6–8.

Day, Alexandra. *Frank and Ernest.* Scholastic, 1988. Ages 6–10.

———. *Frank and Ernest Play Ball.* Scholastic, 1990. Ages 6–10.

de Brunhoff, Jean. *The Story of Babar.* Random House, 1933. Ages 6–8.

———, and Laurent de Brunhoff. *Babar's Anniversary Album: 6 Favorite Stories.* Random House, 1981. Ages 6–8.

deFelice, Cynthia. *Mule Eggs.* Illustrated by Mike Shenon. Orchard, 1994. Ages 5–7.

Denslow, Sharon Phillips. *Night Owls.* Illustrated by Jill Kastner. Bradbury, 1990. Ages 5–7.

Denton, Terry. *Felix and Alexander.* Houghton, 1988. Ages 5–7.

dePaola, Tomie. *The Art Lesson.* Putnam, 1989. Ages 6–8.

———. *Nana Upstairs, Nana Downstairs.* Putnam, 1973. Ages 6–8.

———. *Strega Nona.* Prentice Hall, 1975. Ages 5–7.

Dorros, Arthur. *Abuela.* Illustrated by Elisa Kleven. Dutton, 1991. Ages 5–7.

Dugan, Barbara. *Loop the Loop.* Illustrated by James Stevenson. Greenwillow, 1992. Ages 7–9.

Dumbleton, Mike. *Dial-a-Croc.* Illustrated by Ann James. Orchard, 1991. Ages 4–8.

Duncan, Lois. *Songs from Dreamland.* Illustrated by Kay Chorao. Knopf, 1989. Ages 6–8.

Duvoisin, Roger. *Petunia.* Knopf, 1950. Ages 6–8.

Engel, Diana. *Josephina Hates Her Name.* Morrow, 1989. Ages 5–7.

Ernst, Lisa Campbell. *Zinnia and Dot.* Viking, 1992. Ages 4–7.

Ets, Marie Hall. *Gilberto and the Wind.* Viking, 1963. Ages 6–8.

Ets, Marie Hall, and Aurora Labastida. *Nine Days to Christmas.* Illustrated by Marie Hall Ets. Viking, 1959. Ages 7–9.

Feelings, Tom (selector and illustrator). *Soul Looks Back in Wonder.* Dial, 1993. Ages 8–12.

Flack, Marjorie. *The Story About Ping.* Illustrated by Kurt Wiese. Viking, 1933. Ages 7–9.

Fleischman, Paul. *Time Train.* Illustrated by Clair Ewart. HarperCollins, 1991. Ages 5–8.

Fleischman, Sid. *The Scarebird.* Illustrated by Peter Sis. Greenwillow, 1988. Ages 7–9.

Forrester, Victoria. *Poor Gabriella: A Christmas Story.* Illustrated by Susan Seddon. Calligraphy by John Prestianni. Atheneum, 1986. Ages 7–9.

Fox, Mem. *Hattie and the Fox.* Illustrated by Patricia Mullins. Bradbury, 1987. Ages 6–8.

———. *Night Noises.* Illustrated by Terry Denton. Gulliver, 1989. Ages 6–8.

———. *Shoes from Grandpa.* Illustrated by Patricia Mullins. Orchard, 1990. Ages 6–8.

———. *Wilfrid Gordon McDonald Partridge.* Illustrated by Julie Vivas. Kane/Miller, 1985. Ages 6–8.

Freeman, Don. *Corduroy.* Viking, 1968. Ages 3–5.

———. *A Pocket for Corduroy.* Viking, 1978. Ages 3–5.

Friedman, Ina. *How My Parents Learned to Eat.* Illustrated by Allen Say. Houghton, 1984. Ages 7–9.

Gág, Wanda. *Millions of Cats.* Coward-McCann, 1928. Ages 4–6.

Galbraith, Kathryn. *Laura Charlotte.* Illustrated by Floyd Cooper. Philomel, 1990. Ages 6–8.

Gerstein, Mordicai. *The Mountains of Tibet.* Harper, 1987. Ages 7–9. (Modern folktale)

Goode, Diane. *I Hear a Noise.* Dutton, 1988. Ages 5–7.

Gray, Nigel. *A Country Far Away.* Illustrated by Philippe Dupasquier. Orchard, 1989. Ages 7–9.

Greenfield, Eloise. *Nathaniel Talking.* Illustrated by Jan Spivey Gilchrist. Writers and Readers, 1989. Ages 6–8.

———. *She Come Bringing Me That Little Baby Girl.* Illustrated by John Steptoe. Lippincott, 1974. Ages 6–8.

Grifalconi, Ann. *The Village of Round and Square Houses.* Little, Brown, 1986. Ages 6–8.

Griffith, Helen V. *Grandaddy's Place.* Illustrated by James Stevenson. Greenwillow, 1987. Ages 7–9.

Gross, Theodore. *Faro, Everyone Asked about You.* Illustrated by Sheila White Samton. Philomel,

1990. Ages 6–8.

Grossman, Bill. *Tommy at the Grocery Store.* Illustrated by Victoria Chess. Harper, 1989. Ages 6–10.

Hader, Berta, and Elmer Hader. *The Big Snow.* Macmillan, 1948. Ages 6–8.

Hall, Donald. *Ox-Cart Man.* Illustrated by Barbara Cooney. Viking, 1979. Ages 7–9.

Heide, Florence Parry, and Judith Heide Gilliland. *The Day of Ahmed's Secret.* Illustrated by Ted Lewin. Lothrop, 1990. Ages 6–10.

Hendershot, Judith. *In Coal Country.* Illustrated by Thomas B. Allen. Knopf, 1987. Ages 7–9.

Henkes, Kevin. *Chrysanthemum.* Greenwillow, 1991. Ages 5–7.

———. *Julius, the Baby of the World.* Greenwillow, 1990. Ages 5–7.

———. *Owen.* Greenwillow, 1993. Ages 2–4.

———. *Sheila Rae the Brave.* Greenwillow, 1987. Ages 5–7.

Hest, Amy. *The Midnight Eaters.* Illustrated by Karen Gundersheimer. Four Winds, 1989. Ages 6–8.

———. *Nana's Birthday Party.* Illustrated by Amy Schwartz. Morrow, 1993. Ages 5–9.

Hilton, Nette. *Dirty Dave.* Illustrated by Roland Harvey. Orchard, 1990. Ages 6–8.

Hissey, Jane. *Little Bear's Trousers.* Putnam, 1987. Ages 4–6.

———. *Old Bear.* Putnam, 1986. Ages 4–6.

Hoban, Russell. *A Baby Sister for Frances.* Illustrated by Lillian Hoban. Harper, 1964. (Others in this series: *Bedtime for Frances,* illustrated by Garth Williams, 1969; *Best Friends for Frances.* Illustrated by Lillian Hoban, 1969; *A Bargain for Frances,* illustrated by Lillian Hoban. Harper, 1970.) Ages 4–6.

Hoberman, Mary Ann. *Mr. and Mrs. Muddle.* Illustrated by Catharine O'Neill. Little, Brown, 1988. Ages 4–6.

Hodges, Margaret. *The Wave.* Illustrated by Blair Lent. Houghton, 1957. Ages 7–9.

Hoffman, Mary. *Amazing Grace.* Illustrated by Caroline Binch. Dial, 1991. Ages 5–7.

Hood, Thomas. *Before I Go to Sleep.* Illustrated by Maryjane Begin-Callanan. Putnam, 1990. Ages 5–7.

Houselander, Caryll. *Petook: An Easter Story.* Illustrated by Tomie dePaola. Holiday, 1988. Ages 7–9.

Houston, Gloria. *My Great-Aunt Arizona.* Illustrated by Susan C. Lamb. Harper, 1992. Ages 7–9.

———. *The Year of the Perfect Christmas Tree: An Appalachian Story.* Illustrated by Barbara Cooney. Dial, 1988. Ages 7–9.

Howard, Elizabeth Fitzgerald. *Chita's Christmas Tree.* Illustrated by Floyd Cooper. Bradbury, 1989. Ages 6–8.

———. *Aunt Flossie's Hats (and Crab Cakes Later).* Illustrated by Floyd Cooper. Clarion, 1991. Ages 6–9.

Howe, James. *Pinky and Rex Get Married.* Illustrated by Melissa Sweet. Atheneum, 1990. Ages 5–7.

———. *There's a Monster Under My Bed.* Illustrated by David Rose. Atheneum, 1986. Ages 5–7.

Hughes, Shirley. *An Evening at Alfie's.* Lothrop, 1985. Ages 5–7.

Hurd, Edith Thacher. *I Dance in My Red Pajamas.* Illustrated by Emily Arnold McCully. Harper, 1982. Ages 6–8.

———. *The Pea Patch Jig.* Crown, 1986. Ages 6–8.

Ichikawa, Satomi. *Nora's Castle.* Putnam, 1986. Ages 5–7.

Isaacs, Anne. *Swamp Angel.* Illustrated by Paul O. Zelinsky. Dutton, 1994.

Isadora, Rachel. *Ben's Trumpet.* Greenwillow, 1979. Ages 6–10.

———. *The Pirates of Bedford Street.* Greenwillow, 1988. Ages 6–10.

Johnson, Angela. *Julius.* Illustrated by Dav Pilkey. Orchard, 1993. Ages 6–8.

———. *Tell Me a Story, Mama.* Illustrated by David Soman. Orchard, 1989. Ages 6–8.

Johnson, Crockett. *Harold and the Purple Crayon.* Harper, 1955. Ages 5–7.

Johnson, Tony. *The Quilt Story.* Illustrated by Tomie dePaola. Putnam, 1985. Ages 6–8.

———. *Yonder.* Illustrated by Lloyd Bloom. Dial, 1988. Ages 6–8.

Jonas, Ann. *The Quilt.* Greenwillow, 1984. Ages 7–9.

———. *When You Were A Baby.* Greenwillow, 1982. Ages 6–8.

Joyce, William. *Bently and Egg.* HarperCollins, 1992. Ages 4–8.

———. *Santa Calls.* HarperCollins, 1993. Ages 5–8.

Jukes, Mavis. *I'll See You in My Dreams.* Illustrated by Stacey Schuett. Knopf, 1993. Ages 6–9.

———. *Like Jake and Me.* Illustrated by Lloyd Bloom. Knopf, 1984. Ages 6–8.

Kahl, Virginia. *The Duchess Bakes a Cake.* Scribner's,

1955. Ages 6–8.

Kalman, Maira. *Max Makes a Million.* Viking, 1990. Ages 7–9.

Kasza, Keiko. *The Pigs' Picnic.* Putnam, 1988. Ages 6–8.

Keats, Ezra Jack. *Goggles.* Macmillan, 1969. Ages 5–7.

———. *Peter's Chair.* Harper, 1967. Ages 4–6.

———. *The Snowy Day.* Viking, 1962. Ages 4–6.

———. *Whistle for Willie.* Viking, 1964. Ages 5–7.

Kellogg, Steven. *Pinkerton, Behave!* Dial, 1979. Ages 6–8.

———. *Prehistoric Pinkerton.* Dial, 1987. Ages 6–8.

———. *The Mysterious Tadpole.* Dial, 1977. Ages 6–8.

Kennaway, Mwalimu and Adrienne. *Awful Aardvark.* Little, Brown, 1989. Ages 6–8.

Kennedy, William and Brendan. *Charlie Malarkey and the Singing Moose.* Illustrated by S. D. Schindler. Viking, 1994.

Kesey, Ken. *Little Tricker the Squirrel Meets Big Double the Bear.* Illustrated by Barry Moser. Viking, 1990. Ages 8–11.

Khalsa, Dayal Kaur. *Cowboy Dreams.* Clarkson N. Potter, 1990. Ages 7–9.

———. *My Family Vacation.* Clarkson N. Potter, 1988. Ages 7–9.

Kimmel, Eric A. *The Chanukkah Guest.* Illustrated by Giora Carmi. Holiday, 1990. Ages 7–9.

Kinsey-Warnock, Natalie. *The Wild Horses of Sweetbriar.* Illustrated by Ted Rand. Dutton, 1990. Ages 7–9.

Kitamura, Satoshi. *UFO Diary.* Farrar, 1989. Ages 7–9.

Komaiko, Leah. *Annie Bananie.* Illustrated by Laura Cornell. Harper, 1987. Ages 6–8.

Kraus, Robert. *Leo the Late Bloomer.* Illustrated by José Aruego. Crowell, 1971. Ages 7–9.

———. *Owliver.* Illustrated by José Aruego and Ariane Dewey. Windmill, 1974. Ages 6–8.

Krause, Ute. *Pig Surprise.* Dial, 1989. Ages 6–8.

Kuskin, Karla. *The Philharmonic Gets Dressed.* Illustrated by Marc Simont. Harper, 1982. Ages 6–10.

Lasker, Joe. *A Tournament of Knights.* Crowell, 1986. Ages 8–10.

Lattimore, Deborah Nourse. *The Lady With the Ship on Her Head.* Harcourt, 1990. Ages 8–10.

Leaf, Margaret. *Eyes of the Dragon.* Illustrated by Ed Young. Lothrop, 1987. Ages 7–9.

Leaf, Munro. *The Story of Ferdinand.* Illustrated by Robert Lawson. Viking, 1936. Ages 7–9.

Lent, Blair. *John Tabor's Ride.* Little, Brown, 1966. Ages 7–9.

Levine, Abby. *What Did Mommy Do Before You?* Illustrated by DyAnne DiSalvo-Ryan. Whitman, 1988. Ages 5–7.

Levinson, Riki. *Watch the Stars Come Out.* Illustrated by Diane Goode. Dutton, 1985. Ages 7–9.

Lexau, Joan. *Benjie on His Own.* Illustrated by Don Bolognese. Dial, 1970. Ages 6–8.

Lindbergh, Reeve. *The Day the Goose Got Loose.* Illustrated by Steven Kellogg. Dial, 1990. Ages 5–7.

Lionni, Leo. *Alexander and the Wind-up Mouse.* Pantheon 1967. Ages 6–8.

———. *The Biggest House in the World.* Pantheon, 1968. Ages 5–7.

———. *Inch by Inch.* Astor-Honor, 1960. Ages 5–7.

———. *Swimmy.* Pantheon, 1963. Ages 6–8.

Locker, Thomas. *Sailing with the Wind.* Dial, 1986. Ages 6–8.

———. *Where the River Begins.* Dial, 1984. Ages 6–8.

Loriot, reteller. *Peter and the Wolf.* Illustrated by Jörg Müller. (Original story by Sergei Prokofiev.) Knopf, 1986. Ages 6–10.

Luenn, Nancy. *Nessa's Fish.* Illustrated by Neil Waldman. Atheneum, 1990. Ages 7–9.

Lyon, George Ella. *Come a Tide.* Illustrated by Stephen Gammell. Orchard, 1990. Ages 6–8.

———. *Dreamplace.* Illustrated by Peter Catalanotto. Orchard, 1993.

Macaulay, David. *Why the Chicken Crossed the Road.* Houghton, 1987. Ages 8–10.

MacLachlan, Patricia. *Mama One, Mama Two.* Illustrated by Ruth Lercher Bornstein. Harper, 1982. Ages 8–10.

———. *Through Grandpa's Eyes.* Illustrated by Deborah Ray. Harper, 1979. Ages 7–9.

Mahy, Margaret. *The Great White Man-Eating Shark: A Cautionary Tale.* Illustrated by Jonathan Allen. Dial, 1990. Ages 8–10.

———. *The Rattlebang Picnic.* Illustrated by Steven Kellogg. Dial, 1994. Ages 7–10.

———. *17 Kings and 42 Elephants.* Illustrated by Patricia McCarthy. Dial, 1987. Ages 6–10.

Manson, Christopher. *Two Travellers.* Holt, 1990. Ages 6–8.

Markum, Patricia. *The Little Painter of Sabana Grande.* Macmillan, 1993. Ages 7–9.

Marshall, James. *George and Martha.* Houghton, 1972. Ages 6–8.

———. *George and Martha Round and Round.* Houghton, 1988. Ages 6–8.

Martin, Bill, Jr., and John Archambault. *Knots on a Counting Rope.* Illustrated by Ted Rand. Holt, 1987. Ages 6–8.

———. *White Dynamite and Curly Kid.* Illustrated by Ted Rand. Holt, 1986. Ages 6–8.

Martin, Jacqueline Briggs. *Bizzy Bones and the Lost Quilt.* Illustrated by Stella Ormai. Lothrop, 1988. Ages 6–8.

Mayer, Mercer. *There's a Nightmare in My Closet.* Dial, 1968. Ages 5–7.

McAfee, Annalena. *Kirsty Knows Best.* Illustrated by Anthony Browne. Knopf, 1988. Ages 5–7.

McCloskey, Robert. *Blueberries for Sal.* Viking, 1948. Ages 5–7.

———. *Make Way for Ducklings.* Viking, 1941. Ages 5–7.

———. *One Morning in Maine.* Viking, 1952. Ages 7–9.

McCully, Emily Arnold. *The Evil Spell.* Harper, 1990. Ages 6–8.

McKissack, Patricia C. and Fredrick L. *Christmas in the Big House, Christmas in the Quarters.* Illustrated by John Thompson. Scholastic, 1994. Ages 8–12.

———. *Flossie and the Fox.* Illustrated by Rachel Isadora. Dial, 1986. Ages 7–9.

———. *Nettie Jo's Friends.* Illustrated by Scott Cook. Knopf, 1989. Ages 7–9.

Meddaugh, Susan. *Martha Calling.* Houghton, 1994. Ages 4–8.

———. *Martha Speaks.* Houghton, 1992. Ages 4–8.

Melmed, Laura K. *The Rainbabies.* Illustrated by Jim LaMarche. Lothrop, 1992. Ages 7–9.

Merrill, Jean (adapter). *The Girl Who Loved Caterpillars.* Illustrated by Floyd Cooper. Philomel, 1992. Ages 7–12.

Mollel, Tololwa. *The Orphan Boy.* Illustrated by Paul Morin. Clarion, 1991. Ages 7–9.

Mosel, Arlene, adapter. *The Funny Little Woman.* Illustrated by Blair Lent. Dutton, 1972. Ages 6–8.

Naylor, Phyllis Reynolds. *Keeping a Christmas Secret.* Illustrated by Lena Shiffman. Atheneum, 1989. Ages 6–8.

Nesbit, E. *Melisande.* Illustrated by P. J. Lynch. Harcourt, 1989. Ages 8–10. (Modern folktale)

Ness, Evaline. *Sam, Bangs and Moonshine.* Holt, 1966. Ages 6–8.

Noble, Trinka H. *Jimmy's Boa and the Big Splash Birthday Bash.* Illustrated by Steven Kellogg. Dial, 1989. Ages 6–8.

Nolan, Dennis. *Dinosaur Dream.* Macmillan, 1990. Ages 6–8.

Novak, Matt. *Mouse TV.* Orchard, 1994. Ages 6–8.

Oakley, Graham. *The Church Mice Adrift.* Atheneum, 1977. Ages 6–8.

———. *The Church Mouse.* Atheneum, 1972. Ages 6–8.

Olaleye, Isaac. *Bitter Bananas.* Illustrated by Ed Young. Boyds Mills, 1994.

Paxton, Tom. *Englebert the Elephant.* Illustrated by Steven Kellogg. Morrow, 1990. Ages 6–8.

Peet, Bill. *Cyrus the Unsinkable Sea Serpent.* Houghton, 1975. Ages 5–7.

———. *Merle the High Flying Squirrel.* Houghton, 1974. Ages 5–7.

Peters, Lisa Westberg. *Good Morning River!* Illustrated by Deborah Kogan Ray. Arcade, 1990. Ages 6–8.

Pittman, Helena Clare. *Once When I Was Scared.* Illustrated by Ted Rand. Dutton, 1988. Ages 5–7.

Polacco, Patricia. *Babushka's Doll.* Simon and Schuster, 1990. Ages 6–8.

———. *Chicken Sunday.* Putnam, 1992. Ages 4–9.

———. *The Keeping Quilt.* Simon and Schuster, 1988. Ages 6–8.

———. *Pink and Say.* Philomel, 1994. Ages 8–11.

———. *Thunder Cake.* Putnam, 1990. Ages 6–8.

Politi, Leo. *Song of the Swallows.* Scribner's, 1949. Ages 6–8.

Pomerantz, Charlotte. *The Chalk Doll.* Illustrated by Frané Lessac. Harper, 1989. Ages 7–9.

Potter, Beatrix. *The Tale of Peter Rabbit.* Warne, 1902. (See 20 other titles in the series.) Ages 5–7.

Priceman, Marjorie. *How to Make an Apple Pie and See the World.* Knopf, 1994. Ages 6–8.

Provensen, Alice, and Martin Provensen. *The Glorious Flight: Across the Channel with Louis Blériot.* Viking: 1983. Ages 8–10.

———. *Shaker Lane.* Viking, 1987. Ages 7–9.

Ransome, Arthur. *The Fool of the World and the Flying Ship.* Illustrated by Uri Shulevitz. Farrar, 1968. Ages 6–8.

Ray, Deborah Kogan. *Mr. and Mrs. Pig's Evening Out.* Atheneum, 1976. Ages 6–8.

Rayner, Mary. *Mrs. Pig Gets Cross: And Other Stories.* Dutton, 1987. Ages 6–8.

Rey, Hans A. *Curious George.* Houghton, 1941. (See others in the Curious George series.) Ages 5–7.

Rice, Eve. *Peter's Pockets.* Illustrated by Nancy Winslow Parker. Greenwillow, 1989. Ages 6–8.

Ringgold, Faith. *Aunt Harriet's Underground Railroad in the Sky.* Crown, 1992. Ages 6–9.

———. *Tar Beach.* Crown, 1991. Ages 8–10.

Rogers, Jacqueline. *The Christmas Pageant.* Grosset, 1989. Ages 6–8.

Rogers, Jean. *Runaway Mittens.* Illustrated by Rie Muñoz. Greenwillow, 1988. Ages 5–7.

Russo, Marisabina. *Waiting for Hannah.* Greenwillow, 1989. Ages 6–8.

Ryan, Cheli Duran. *Hildilid's Night.* Illustrated by Arnold Lobel. Macmillan, 1971. Ages 6–8.

Rylant, Cynthia. *Mr. Grigg's Work.* Illustrated by Julie Downing. Orchard, 1989. Ages 7–9.

———. *The Relatives Came.* Illustrated by Stephen Gammell. Bradbury, 1985. Ages 6–10.

———. *When I Was Young in the Mountains.* Illustrated by Diane Goode. Dutton, 1982. Ages 7–9.

San Souci, Robert D. *Sukey and the Mermaid.* Illustrated by Brian Pinkney. Four Winds, 1992. Ages 6–9.

Sanders, Scott Russell. *Aurora Means Dawn.* Illustrated by Jill Kastner. Bradbury, 1989. Ages 7–9.

Say, Allen. *Grandfather's Journey.* Houghton, 1993. Ages 8–10.

———. *Tree of Cranes.* Houghton, 1991. Ages 7–9.

Schertle, Alice. *William and Grandpa.* Illustrated by Lydia Dabcovich. Lothrop, 1989. Ages 6–8.

Schotter, Roni. *Captain Snap and the Children of Vinegar Lane.* Illustrated by Marcia Sewall. Watts, 1989. Ages 6–8.

Schroeder, Alan. *Ragtime Tumpie.* Illustrated by Bernie Fuchs. Little, Brown, 1989. Ages 6–8.

Schwartz, Amy. *Annabelle Swift, Kindergartner.* Orchard, 1988. Ages 5–7.

Scieszka, Jon. *The Stinky Cheese Man and Other Fairly Stupid Tales.* Illustrated by Lane Smith. Viking, 1992. Ages 7–10.

Scott, Ann Herbert. *Hi!* Illustrated by Glo Coalson. Philomel, 1994. Ages 4–6.

———. *Sam.* Illustrated by Symeon Shimin. McGraw-Hill, 1967. Ages 7–9.

Seligson, Susan. *The Amazing Amos and the Greatest Couch on Earth.* Illustrated by Howie Schneider. Little, Brown, 1989. Ages 6–8.

Sendak, Maurice. *In the Night Kitchen.* Harper, 1970. Ages 7–9.

———. *We Are All In the Dumps With Jack and Guy.* HarperCollins, 1993.

———. *Where the Wild Things Are.* Harper, 1963. Ages 5–7.

Seuss, Dr. (pseud. for Theodor S. Geisel). *And To Think That I Saw It On Mulberry Street.* Vanguard, 1937. Ages 5–7.

———. *The 500 Hats of Bartholomew Cubbins.* Vanguard, 1938. Ages 5–7.

———. *Horton Hatches the Egg.* Random, 1940. Ages 6–8.

———. *Oh, the Places You'll Go!* Random, 1990. Ages 6–8.

———. *Thidwick the Big–hearted Moose.* Random, 1948. Ages 6–8.

Seymour, Tres. *Hunting the White Cow.* Illustrated by Wendy A. Halperin. Orchard, 1993. Ages 7–10.

Shannon, David. *How Georgie Radbourn Saved Baseball.* Scholastic, 1994.

Shulevitz, Uri. *Dawn.* Farrar, 1974. Ages 6–8.

———. *One Monday Morning.* Scribner's, 1967. Ages 6–8.

Sís, Peter. *Komodo!* Greenwillow, 1993. Ages 4–7.

———. *The Three Golden Keys.* Doubleday, 1994.

Slobodkina, Esphyr, *Caps for Sale.* Addison-Wesley, 1947. Ages 4–6.

Small, David. *George Washington's Cows.* Farrar, 1994. Ages 7–10.

———. *Imogene's Antlers.* Crown, 1985. Ages 6–8.

Soto, Gary. *Chato's Kitchen.* Illustrated by Susan Guevara. Putnam, 1995.

———. *Too Many Tamales.* Illustrated by Ed Martinez. Putnam, 1993.

Spier, Peter. *Bored—Nothing To Do!* Doubleday, 1978. Ages 7–9.

Steig, William. *The Amazing Bone.* Farrar, 1976. Ages 7–9.

———. *Caleb and Kate.* Farrar, 1977. Ages 7–9.

———. *Doctor De Soto.* Farrar, 1982. Ages 7–9.

———. *Sylvester and the Magic Pebble.* Simon and Schuster, 1969. Ages 7–9.

Steptoe, John. *Baby Says.* Lothrop, 1988. Ages 5–7.

———. *Stevie.* Harper, 1969. Ages 5–7.

Stevenson, James. *July.* Greenwillow, 1990. Ages

6–8.

———. *That Dreadful Day.* Greenwillow, 1985. Ages 6–8.

———. *What's Under My Bed?* Greenwillow, 1983. Ages 5–7.

———. *Will You Please Feed Our Cat?* Greenwillow, 1987. Ages 6–8.

Stock, Catherine. *Armien's Fishing Trip.* Morrow, 1990. Ages 6–8.

———. *Where Are You Going, Manyoni?* Morrow, 1993.

Stolz, Mary. *Storm in the Night.* Illustrated by Pat Cummings. Harper, 1988. Ages 6–8.

Swope, Sam. *The Araboolies of Liberty Street.* Illustrated by Barry Root. Clarkson N. Potter, 1989. Ages 6–8.

Tejima. *Fox's Dream.* Translated from Japanese by Susan Matsui. Philomel, 1987. Ages 6–8.

Testa, Fulvio. *Wolf's Favor.* Dial, 1986. Ages 6–8.

Thomas, Jane Resh. *Saying Goodbye to Grandma.* Illustrated by Marcia Sewall. Clarion, 1988. Ages 7–9.

Thurber, James. *The Great Quillow.* Illustrated by Steven Kellogg. Harcourt, 1994.

Tompert, Ann. *Grandfather Tang's Story.* Illustrated by Robert Andrew Parker. Crown, 1990. Ages 7–9.

Tresselt, Alvin. *White Snow, Bright Snow.* Illustrated by Roger Duvoisin. Lothrop, 1947. Ages 4–6.

Trivas, Irene. *Emma's Christmas.* Orchard, 1988. Ages 5–7.

Turkle, Brinton. *Do Not Open.* Dutton, 1981. Ages 5–7.

Turner, Ann. *Heron Street.* Illustrated by Lisa Desimini. Harper, 1989. Ages 6–8.

Udry, Janice May. *The Moon Jumpers.* Illustrated by Maurice Sendak. Harper, 1959. Ages 5–7.

Ungerer, Tomi. *The Beast of Monsieur Racine.* Farrar, 1971. Ages 6–8.

Updike, David. *An Autumn Tale.* Illustrated by Robert Andrew Parker. Pippin Press, 1988. Ages 6–8.

Van Allsburg, Chris. *Jumanji.* Houghton, 1981. Ages 6–10.

———. *The Sweetest Fig.* Houghton, 1993. Ages 8–11.

———. *The Widow's Broom.* Houghton, 1992. Ages 5–7.

———. *The Wretched Stone.* Houghton, 1991. Ages 8–11.

Van Laan, Nancy. *Possum Come a-Knockin'.* Illustrated by George Booth. Knopf, 1990. Ages 7–9.

Vincent, Gabrielle. *Where Are You, Ernest and Celestine?* Greenwillow, 1986. Ages 6–8.

Viorst, Judith. *Alexander and the Terrible, Horrible, No Good, Very Bad Day.* Illustrated by Ray Cruz. Atheneum, 1972. Ages 5–7.

———. *Alexander Who Used to Be Rich Last Sunday.* Illustrated by Ray Cruz. Atheneum, 1978. Ages 6–8.

———. *I'll Fix Anthony.* Illustrated by Arnold Lobel. Harper, 1969. Ages 4–6.

Waber, Bernard. *Ira Says Goodbye.* Houghton, 1988. Ages 6–8.

———. *Ira Sleeps Over.* Houghton, 1972. Ages 6–8.

Waddell, Martin. *Can't You Sleep, Little Bear?* Illustrated by Barbara Firth. Candlewick, 1992. Ages 2–4.

———. *Farmer Duck.* Illustrated by Helen Oxenbury. Candlewick, 1992. Ages 4–6.

Wahl, Jan. *Humphrey's Bear.* Illustrated by William Joyce. Holt, 1987. Ages 5–7.

Wallace, Barbara Brooks. *Argyle.* Illustrated by John Sandford. Abingdon, 1987. Ages 5–7.

Walter, Mildred Pitts. *My Mama Needs Me.* Illustrated by Pat Cummings. Lothrop, 1983. Ages 5–7.

Watson, Wendy. *Tales for a Winter's Eve.* Farrar, 1988. Ages 6–8.

Wayland, April Halprin. *To Rabbittown.* Illustrated by Robin Spowart. Scholastic, 1989. Ages 6–8.

Weller, Frances Ward. *Riptide.* Illustrated by Robert J. Blake. Philomel, 1990. Ages 6–8.

Wells, Rosemary. *Shy Charles.* Dial, 1988. Ages 4–6.

———. *Timothy Goes to School.* Dial, 1981. Ages 5–7.

Wiesner, David. *June 29, 1999.* Clarion, 1992. Ages 6–9.

Wild, Margaret. *Mr. Nick's Knitting.* Illustrated by Dee Huxley. Harcourt, 1989. Ages 6–8.

———. *The Very Best of Friends.* Illustrated by Julie Vivas. Harcourt, 1990. Ages 6–8.

Wilde, Oscar. *The Happy Prince.* Illustrated by Ed Young. Simon and Schuster, 1989. Ages 7–9. (Modern folktale)

Wildsmith, Brian. *Daisy.* Pantheon, 1984. Ages 6–8.

Wilhelm, Hans. *I'll Always Love You.* Crown, 1985. Ages 6–8.

Willard, Nancy. *The Mountains of Quilt.* Illustrated by Tomie dePaola. Harcourt, 1987. Ages 7–9.

———. *Night Story.* Illustrated by Ilse Plume. Harcourt, 1986. Ages 7–9.

Williams, Margery. *The Velveteen Rabbit.* Illustrated by William Nicholson. Doubleday, 1922. Ages 6–8.

Williams, Sherley Anne. *Working Cotton.* Illustrated by Carole Byard. Harcourt, 1992. Ages 5–7.

Williams, Vera B.. *A Chair for My Mother.* Greenwillow, 1982. Ages 6–8.

———. *Scooter.* Greenwillow, 1993. Ages 8–10.

———. *Something Special for Me.* Greenwillow, 1983. Ages 6–8.

———. *Stringbean's Trip to the Shining Sea.* Illustrated by author and Jennifer Williams. Greenwillow, 1988. Ages 7–9.

Willis, Val. *The Secret in the Matchbox.* Illustrated by John Shelley. Farrar, 1988. Ages 6–8.

Winter, Jeanette. *Come Out to Play.* Knopf, 1986. Ages 5–7.

Winthrop, Elizabeth. *Bear and Mrs. Duck.* Illustrated by Patience Brewster. Holiday, 1988. Ages 5–7.

Wolkstein, Diane. *Little Mouse's Painting.* Illustrated by Maryjane Begin. Morrow, 1992. Ages 3–6.

Wood, Audrey. *Heckedy Peg.* Illustrated by Don Wood. Harcourt, 1987. Ages 6–8.

Xiong, Blia, reteller. *Nine-in-One Grr! Grr!,* adapted by Cathy Spagnoli. Illustrated by Nancy Hom. Children's Book Press, 1990. Ages 6–8.

Yashima, Taro. (pseud. Jun Iwamatsu). *Crow Boy.* Viking, 1955. Ages 7–9.

Yolen, Jane. *Letting Swift River Go.* Illustrated by Barbara Cooney. Little, 1992. Ages 5–11.

———. *Owl Moon.* Illustrated by John Schoenherr. Putnam, 1987. Ages 6–8.

———. *Piggins.* Illustrated by Jane Dyer. Harcourt, 1987. Ages 6–8.

Yorinks, Arthur. *Company's Coming.* Illustrated by David Small. Crown, 1988. Ages 7–9.

———. *Hey, Al.* Illustrated by Richard Egielski. Farrar, 1986. Ages 7–9.

Young, Ed. *Seven Blind Mice.* Philomel, 1992. Ages 6–10. (Modern folktale)

Ziefert, Harriet. *A New Coat for Anna.* Illustrated by Anita Lobel. Knopf, 1986. Ages 6–8.

Zimelman, Nathan. *Treed by a Pride of Irate Lions.* Illustrated by Toni Goffe. Little, Brown, 1990. Ages 6–8.

Zolotow, Charlotte. *If It Weren't for You.* Illustrated by Ben Shecter. Harper, 1966. Ages 6–8.

———. *Mr. Rabbit and the Lovely Present.* Illustrated

by Maurice Sendak. Harper, 1962. Ages 5–7.

———. *Say It!* Illustrated by James Stevenson. Greenwillow, 1980. Ages 6–8.

———. *Something Is Going to Happen.* Illustrated by Catherine Stock. Harper, 1988. Ages 6–8.

———. *William's Doll.* Illustrated by William Pène du Bois. Harper, 1972. Ages 6–8.

Easy-to-Read and Pattern Books

These books are generally suitable for ages 4 to 8.

Appelt, Kathi. *Elephants Aloft.* Illustrated by Keith Baker. Harcourt, 1993.

Asch, Frank. *Monkey Face.* Parent's Magazine Press, 1977.

Barrett, Judi. *Animals Should Definitely Not Act Like People.* Atheneum, 1980.

———. *Animals Should Definitely Not Wear Clothing.* Atheneum, 1977.

Bonsall, Crosby. *The Case of the Cat's Meow.* Harper, 1965.

———. *The Case of the Scaredy Cats.* Harper, 1971.

Brown, Margaret Wise. *Goodnight Moon.* Harper, 1947.

———. *The Runaway Bunny.* Illustrated by Clement Hurd. Harper, 1991 (1942). Ages 2–5.

Bulla, Clyde Robert. *The Chalk Box Kid.* Illustrated by Thomas B. Allen. Random, 1987.

———. *The Christmas Coat.* Illustrated by Sylvie Wickstrom. Knopf, 1990.

———. *Daniel's Duck.* Illustrated by Joan Sandin. Harper, 1979.

Byars, Betsy. *Hooray for the Golly Sisters!* Illustrated by Sue Truesdell. Harper, 1990.

Charlip, Remy. *Fortunately.* Parents' Magazine Press, 1964.

Cherry, Lynne. *Who's Sick Today?* Dutton, 1988.

Coerr, Eleanor. *Chang's Paper Pony.* Illustrated by Deborah Kogan Ray. Harper, 1988.

———. *The Josefina Story Quilt.* Illustrated by Bruce Degen. Harper, 1986.

Cohen, Caron Lee. *Three Yellow Dogs.* Illustrated by Peter Sis. Greenwillow, 1986.

Cohen, Miriam. *First Grade Takes a Test.* Illustrated by Lillian Hoban. Greenwillow, 1980.

———. *It's George!* Illustrated by Lillian Hoban. Greenwillow, 1988.

———. *When Will I Read?* Illustrated by Lillian

Hoban. Greenwillow, 1977.

Cole, Joanna, and Stephanie Calmenson, compilers. *Ready . . . Set . . . Read!: The Beginning Reader's Treasury.* Illustrated by Anne Burgess and Chris Demarest. Doubleday, 1990.

Cuyler, Margery. *That's Good, That's Bad.* Illus. by David Catrow. Holt, 1991.

dePaola, Tomie. *The Comic Adventures of Old Mother Hubbard and Her Dog.* Harcourt, 1981.

de Regniers, Beatrice Schenk. *May I Bring a Friend?* Illustrated by Beni Montresor. Atheneum, 1964.

Ehrlich, Amy. *Leo, Zack, and Emmie.* Illustrated by Steven Kellogg. Dial, 1981.

Emberley, Barbara. *Drummer Hoff.* Illustrated by Ed Emberley. Prentice Hall, 1967.

———. *One Wide River to Cross.* Prentice Hall, 1966.

Fleming, Denise. *In the Small, Small Pond.* Holt, 1993. Ages 4–6.

———. *In the Tall, Tall Grass.* Holt, 1991. Ages 4–6.

Fox, Mem. *Shoes from Grandpa.* Orchard, 1990.

Gág Wanda. *Millions of Cats.* Coward-McCann, 1928.

Gage, Wilson. *Squash Pie.* Illustrated by Glen Rounds. Greenwillow, 1976.

George, Lindsay B. *In the Woods.* Morrow, 1995.

George, William. *Fishing at Long Pond.* Illustrated by Lindsay B. George. Greenwillow, 1991.

Griffith, Helen V. *Alex and the Cat.* Illustrated by Joseph Low. Greenwillow, 1982.

Guarino, Deborah. *Is Your Mama a Llama?* Illustrated by Steven Kellogg. Scholastic, 1989.

Hellen, Nancy. *The Bus Stop.* Orchard, 1988.

Hoban, Lillian. *Arthur's Great Big Valentine.* Harper, 1989.

———. *Arthur's Prize Reader.* Harper, 1978.

Hogrogian, Nonny. *One Fine Day.* Macmillan, 1971.

Hopkins, Lee Bennett, selector. *Good Books, Good Times.* Illustrated by Harvey Stevenson. Harper, 1990.

Hutchins, Pat. *The Doorbell Rang.* Greenwillow, 1986.

———. *Rosie's Walk.* Macmillan, 1968.

———. *Tidy Titch.* Greenwillow, 1991.

———. *Titch.* Macmillan, 1971.

———. *What Game Shall We Play?* Greenwillow, 1990.

———. *The Wind Blew.* Macmillan, 1974.

Johnson, Crockett. *A Picture for Harold's Room.* Harper, 1960.

Joslin, Sesyle. *What Do You Say, Dear?* Addison-Wesley, 1958.

Kessler, Leonard. *Kick, Pass, and Run.* Harper, 1966.

Kraus, Robert. *Leo the Late Bloomer.* Illustrated by José Aruego. Dutton, 1971.

———. *Where Are You Going, Little Mouse?* Illustrated by José Aruego and Ariane Dewey. Greenwillow, 1986.

Lobel, Arnold. *Mouse Soup.* Harper, 1977.

———. "Frog and Toad Series." *Frog and Toad Are Friends.* Harper, 1970. (Others in this series: *Frog and Toad Together,* 1972; *Frog and Toad All Year,* 1976; *Days with Frog and Toad,* 1979.)

Lyon, George Ella. *Who Came Down That Road?* Illustrated by Peter Catalanotto. Orchard, 1992.

Martin, Bill, Jr. *Brown Bear, Brown Bear, What Do You See?* Illustrated by Eric Carle. Holt, 1983.

———. *The Maestro Plays.* Illustrated by Vladimir Radunsky. Holt, 1994.

———. *Polar Bear, Polar Bear, What Do You Hear?* Illustrated by Eric Carle. Holt, 1991. Ages 4–9.

———. *The Wizard.* Illustrated by Alex Schafer. Harcourt, 1994.

McDonald, Megan. *Is This a House for Hermit Crab?* Illustrated by S. D. Schindler. Orchard, 1990.

Minarik, Else Holmelund. *Little Bear.* Illustrated by Maurice Sendak. Harper, 1957. (Others in the *Little Bear* series: *Father Bear Comes Home,* 1959; *Little Bear's Friend,* 1960; *Little Bear's Visit,* 1961; *A Kiss for Little Bear,* 1968.)

Moore, Lilian. *I'll Meet You at the Cucumbers.* Illustrated by Sharon Wooding. Atheneum, 1988.

Numeroff, Laura Joffe. *If You Give a Mouse a Cookie.* Harper, 1985.

Porte, Barbara Ann. *Harry in Trouble.* Illustrated by Yossi Abolafia. Greenwillow, 1989.

Rabin, Staton. *Casey Over There.* Illustrated by Greg Shed. Harcourt, 1994.

Rascha, Chris. *Yo! Yes?* Orchard, 1993.

Rosen, Michael, reteller. *We're Going on a Bear Hunt.* Illustrated by Helen Oxenbury. Macmillan, 1989.

Rylant, Cynthia. *Henry and Mudge.* Illustrated by Suçie Stevenson. Bradbury, 1987. (See others in this series)

———. *Mr. Putter and Tabby Bake a Cake.* Illustrated by Arthur Howard. Harcourt, 1994. (See others in this series)

Seuss, Dr. (pseud. for Theodor S. Geisel). *The Cat in the Hat.* Random, 1957.

———. *The Cat in the Hat Comes Back.* Random, 1958.

————. *Fox in Sox*. Random, 1965.

Shapiro, Arnold. *Who Says That?* Illus. by Monica Wellington. Dutton, 1991.

Shaw, Nancy. *Sheep in a Jeep*. Illustrated by Margot Apple. Houghton, 1986.

————. *Sheep on a Ship*. Illustrated by Margot Apple. Houghton, 1989.

Titherington, Jeanne. *A Child's Prayer*. Greenwillow, 1989.

————. *Pumpkin Pumpkin*. Greenwillow, 1986.

Van Leeuwen, Jean. *Oliver and Amanda's Christmas*. Illustrated by Ann Schweninger. Dial, 1989.

Weiss, Nicki. *Where Does the Brown Bear Go?* Greenwillow, 1989.

Wellington, Monica. *All My Little Ducklings*. Dutton, 1989.

Wells, Rosemary. *A Lion for Lewis*. Dial, 1982.

————. *Noisy Nora*. Dial, 1973.

Williams, Sue. *I Went Walking*. Illustrated by Julie Vivas. Harcourt, 1990.

Winter, Jeanette. *Follow the Drinking Gourd*. Knopf, 1988.

————. *Hush Little Baby*. Pantheon, 1984.

Wood, Audrey. *The Napping House*. Illustrated by Don Wood. Harcourt, 1984.

Zolotow, Charlotte. *Do You Know What I'll Do?* Illustrated by Garth Williams. Harper, 1958.

————. *If It Weren't for You*. Harper, 1966.

Picture Books for Older Readers

Anno, Mitsumasa. *Anno's Britain*. Philomel, 1982. Ages 9–YA.

————. *Anno's Magical ABC: An Anamorphic Alphabet*. Illustrated by Masaichiro Anno. Philomel, 1981. Ages 9–YA.

————. *Anno's U.S.A.* Philomel, 1983. Ages 8–10.

Bang, Molly. *The Paper Crane*. Greenwillow, 1985. Ages 8–10.

Browne, Anthony. *Piggybook*. Knopf, 1986. Ages 9–YA.

————. *The Tunnel*. Knopf, 1990. Ages 8–12.

————. *Zoo*. Knopf, 1993. Ages 8–YA.

Burkert, Nancy Ekholm. *Valentine and Orson*. Farrar, 1989. Ages 9–YA.

Capote, Truman. *A Christmas Memory*. Illustrated by Beth Peck. Knopf, 1989. Ages 8–10.

Carrick, Donald. *Morgan and the Artist*. Clarion, 1985. Ages 8–10.

Cendrars, Blaise. *Shadow*. Illustrated by Marcia Brown. Scribner's, 1982. Ages 8–10.

Clément, Claude. *The Voice of the Wood*. Illustrated by Frédéric Clément. Dial, 1989. Ages 8–10.

Cooper, Susan. *The Silver Cow: A Welsh Tale*. Illustrated by Warwick Hutton. Atheneum, 1983. Ages 8–10.

Damjan, Mischa. *December's Travels*. Illustrated by Dušan Kállay. Dial, 1986. Ages 10–14.

Ekoomiak, Normee. *Arctic Memories*. Holt, 1990. Ages 9–12.

Fields, Julia. *The Green Lion of Zion Street*. Illustrated by Jerry Pinkney. Macmillan, 1988. Ages 8–10.

Freedman, Florence B. *Brothers: A Hebrew Legend*. Illustrated by Robert Andrew Parker. Harper, 1985. 9–12.

Gallaz, Christophe, and Roberto Innocenti. *Rose Blanche*. Illustrated by Roberto Innocenti. Creative Education, 1985. Ages 9–YA.

Goble, Paul. *Buffalo Woman*. Bradbury, 1984. Ages 9–12.

————. *Dream Wolf*. Bradbury, 1990. Ages 9–12.

Hamanaka, Sheila. *The Journey: Japanese Americans, Racism, and Renewal*. Orchard, 1990. Ages 9–YA.

Hartford, John. *Steamboat in a Cornfield*. Crown, 1986. Ages 8–10.

Hastings, Selina. *Sir Gawain and the Loathly Lady*. Illustrated by Juan Wijngaard. Lothrop, 1985. Ages 9–12.

Heide, Florence P. *The Shrinking of Treehorn*. Illustrated by Edward Gorey. Holiday, 1971. See also *Treehorn Times Three* (Dell, 1992), a collection which includes *The Shrinking of Treehorn*. Ages 8–11.

Hodges, Margaret. *Saint George and the Dragon*. Illustrated by Trina Schart Hyman. Little, Brown, 1984. Ages 8–10.

Hooks, William H. *The Ballad of Belle Dorcas*. Illustrated by Brian Pinkney. Knopf, 1990. Ages 10–12.

Keeping, Charles. *Sammy Streetsinger*. Oxford, 1984. Ages 8–10.

Lattimore, Deborah Nourse. *The Flame of Peace: A Tale of the Aztecs*. Harper, 1987. Ages 8–10.

————. *The Lady With the Ship on Her Head*. Harcourt, 1990. Ages 9–12.

————. *The Sailor Who Captured the Sea: A Story of the Book of Kells*. Harper, 1991. Ages 9–YA.

Macaulay, David. *Black and White*. Houghton, 1990.

Ages 8–14.

——. *Motel of the Mysteries*. Houghton, 1979. Ages 11–14.

Maruki, Toshi. *Hiroshima No Pika*. Lothrop, 1980. Ages 9–YA.

McDermott, Gerald. *Arrow to the Sun: A Pueblo Indian Tale*. Viking, 1974. Ages 8–10.

Müller, Jörg. *The Changing City*. Atheneum, 1977. Ages 9–YA.

Musgrove, Margaret. *Ashanti to Zulu*. Illustrated by Leo and Diane Dillon. Dial, 1976. Ages 8–10.

Oakley, Graham. *Henry's Quest*. Atheneum, 1986. Ages 8–10.

Paterson, Katherine. *The Tale of the Mandarin Ducks*. Illustrated by Leo and Diane Dillon. Dutton, 1990. Ages 8–10.

Price, Leontyne. *Aïda*. Illustrated by Leo and Diane Dillon. Harcourt, 1990. Ages 8–12.

Rylant, Cynthia. *Miss Maggie*. Illustrated by Thomas DiGrazia. Dutton, 1983. Ages 8–10.

Sales, Francesc. *Ibrahim*. Illustrated by Eulàlia Sariola. Translated by Marc Simont. Lippincott, 1989. Ages 9–12.

Say, Allen. *El Chino*. Houghton, 1990. Ages 8–10.

——. *The Lost Lake*. Houghton, 1989. Ages 8–10.

Scieszka, Jon. *The True Story of the Three Little Pigs! By A. Wolf*. Illustrated by Lane Smith. Viking, 1989. Ages 8–11.

Sendak, Maurice. *Outside Over There*. Harper, 1981. Ages 9–YA.

Service, Robert William. *The Cremation of Sam McGee*. Illustrated by Ted Harrison. Greenwillow, 1986. Ages 8–11.

Siekkinen, Raija. *The Curious Faun*. Illustrated by Hannu Taina. Translated by Tim Steffa. Carolrhoda, 1990. Ages 8–11.

Stanley, Diane, and Peter Vennema. *Good Queen Bess: The Story of Elizabeth I of England*. Four Winds, 1990. Ages 8–11.

Steiner, Jörg. *The Bear Who Wanted to Be a Bear*. Illustrated by Jörg Müller. Atheneum, 1977. Ages 8–12.

——. *Rabbit Island*. Illustrated by Jörg Müller. Harcourt, 1978. Ages 8–12.

Turner, Ann. *Dakota Dugout*. Illustrated by Ronald Himler. Macmillan, 1985. 9–11.

Van Allsburg, Chris. *The Mysteries of Harris Burdick*. Houghton, 1984. Ages 8–10.

——. *The Wreck of the Zephyr*. Houghton, 1983. Ages 8–10.

Ward, Lynd. *The Biggest Bear*. Houghton, 1952. Ages 7–9.

Willard, Nancy. *Pish, Posh, said Hieronymous Bosh*. Illustrated by Leo and Diane and Lee Dillon. Harcourt, 1991. Ages 9–YA.

Wisniewski, David. *Elfwyn's Saga*. Lothrop, 1990. Ages 8–10.

——. *Rain Player*. Houghton, 1991. Ages 8–10.

Illustrated Traditional and Modern Folktales

See Chapter Five Recommended Books List

Illustrated Books of Poetry

See Chapter Three Recommended Books List

Chapter 5

Traditional Literature

Listen!

Quiet your faces; be crossed every thumb;
 Fix on me deep your eyes . . .
And out of my mind a story shall come—
 Old, and lovely, and wise.

—Walter de la Mare

Visual narratives told by ancient cave paintings in Europe, Asia, and Australia show us that prehistoric humans had stories to tell long before they had a written language. For thousands of years before writing was discovered, the best of these stories were preserved through the art of storytelling from one generation to the next. Surely these stories survived because people enjoyed hearing them. Even today, their entertainment value cannot be denied. In folk literature we have our most ancient stories and a priceless literary heritage that links us to our beginnings as thinking beings.

Definition and Description

Traditional literature is the body of ancient stories and poems that grew out of the human quest to understand the natural and spiritual worlds and that was preserved through time by the oral tradition of storytelling before being eventually written down. Having no known or identifiable authors, these stories and poems are attributed to entire groups of people or cultures. Although in ancient times some traditional stories may have been told as truths or may have been thought to contain elements of truth, today we consider them to be mostly or wholly fantasy.

Traditional literature includes several different types of stories, but because they were all shared orally for so long, they have many features in common. For example, plots are generally shorter than in other genres of literature because all but the essential details were omitted during countless retellings. Action, in turn, is concentrated, which kept audiences alert and interested. Characters in traditional literature tend to have only one outstanding quality, which made them easy to identify. In these stories the audience has no doubt about who is good and who is bad. Settings are unimportant and are described and referred to in the vaguest of terms, such as "In the beginning . . ." or "Long ago in a land far away . . . ." The language, though full of rhythm and melody, is yet sparse, since lengthy explanations and descriptions were also pared down or eliminated by countless retellings. Style is characterized by stock beginnings and endings ("Once upon a time" and "They lived happily ever after"), motifs or recurring features (use of the number three, as in three sisters, three wishes), and repetition of refrains or chants ("Mirror, mirror, on the wall . . ."). Themes most common in these stories are good versus evil, the power of perseverance, and explanations for the ways of the world. One feature that makes these stories particular favorites of young children is that they almost always have a happy ending.

Folklore is still being created, particularly in some of the developing countries where the oral tradition remains the chief means of communication. In our country, urban legends, jokes, and jump-rope rhymes are all part of the constantly evolving body of folklore. These stories and rhymes are of unknown origin, but because they are certainly not ancient, they will not be treated in this chapter. We must also note those stories written in the style of folk stories but by known authors. Because this body of modern, or literary, folktales has known authors and is not of ancient origin, it will be discussed in Chapter 6, Modern Fantasy.

Values of Traditional Literature for Children

Traditional literature connects us to our past, to the roots of our specific cultures and our human condition. These stories are also valuable for the following important reasons.

- Traditional stories are highly entertaining. Their brevity, immediate action, easily understandable characters, chants, fantastic elements, and happy endings make them particularly appealing to children between the ages of 3 and 8.
- Hearing traditional tales helps children to develop a strong sense of story, which in turn provides them with a good foundation for understanding other literary genres. The stock phrases, repetition, and uncomplicated characters typical of traditional tales help children without much story experience to make sense of, remember, and keep up with the action and characters in these stories.

- Traditional literature is an excellent source of stories for storytelling.
- Knowing the characters and situations of traditional literature is part of being culturally literate. Children who grow up unfamiliar with this body of literature will be at a disadvantage when allusions to traditional literature are made in conversations and in print.
- Traditional literature provides an interesting way for children to be introduced to the diverse cultural groups of their country and other countries. Every cultural group has its body of folklore that gives insights into what makes the culture unique.
- Folklore has a core of universality that makes it possible for children to see that all humans are, to some degree, alike. By introducing children to folklore from many lands and by comparing variants of the same story from different cultures, teachers and librarians are building a solid foundation for multicultural and international understanding.
- Traditional stories may help children begin to develop a sense of morality. Because characters in traditional stories are easily identifiable as good or bad and because evil in these stories is punished with clear-cut finality, traditional literature helps children to sort out good and evil in the world and to identify with the good.

Some adults raise concerns that the gruesome violence sometimes found in traditional stories harms or traumatizes children. In recent times, many traditional stories have been rewritten to omit the violence, as in the Disney versions of folktales. In a "softened" version of "Snow White," the evil stepmother is either forgiven by the heroine or banished from the kingdom. More authentic versions of the tale end like this:

> Then she [the stepmother] railed and cursed, and was beside herself with disappointment and anger. First she thought she would not go to the wedding; but then she felt she should have no peace until she went and saw the bride. And when she saw her she knew her for Snow-white, and could not stir from the place for anger and terror. For they had ready red-hot iron shoes, in which she had to dance until she fell down dead. (From Jakob Grimm and Wilhelm Grimm, *Household Stories*, translated by Lucy Crane [Macmillan, 1886].)

Critics of the softened versions of traditional tales claim that altering the stories robs them of their power, their appeal, and their psychological benefit to children who, in the original versions, are reassured that the evil force is gone forever and cannot come back to hurt them. As parents, teachers, and librarians, you will be in a position to choose which versions of traditional literature to share. With apologies to all good stepmothers, we believe that the unaltered versions, shared within the security of the family or classroom, have the greater benefit to children.

Evaluation and Selection of Traditional Literature

For thousands of years, people of all ages were the intended audience for traditional stories. In our scientifically enlightened times, these stories have come to be seen as childlike in their use of the supernatural and magic, but nonetheless charming and entertaining. The following list of evaluation criteria was developed with a general child audience in mind.

- A traditional tale, even though written down, should preserve the narrative, or storytelling, style and should sound as though it is being told.
- Retold versions of traditional tales must preserve the essential content that made the stories vital to people for thousands of years and that makes them relevant to children today.
- A traditional tale should preserve the flavor of the culture or country of its origin through the use of colloquialisms, unusual speech patterns, a few easily understood foreign terms, or proper names common to the culture.
- In illustrated versions of traditional literature, text and illustrations must be of high quality, and illustrations must match the tone of the text and help to capture the essence of the culture of origin. There are instances when it would be tempting to base one's evaluation and selection mainly on illustrations. Not all illustrators are skillful as writers, however.
- Though simple in other respects, traditional tales employ a rich literary style. Even very young children are fascinated by the chants, stylistic flourishes, and colorful vocabulary that are characteristic of masterful storytelling.
- In evaluating collections of traditional literature, it is important to consider all of the criteria listed above, as well as the number and variety of tales in the collection and the quality of reference aids, such as tables of contents and indexes.

Historical Overview of Traditional Literature

Perhaps the world's first stories grew out of the dreams, wishes, ritual chants, or retellings of the notable exploits of our primitive ancestors. No one knows. Little can be said about the early history of this genre except that these stories existed only in oral form for thousands of years.

Folklorists are intrigued by the startling similarity of traditional tales around the world. Cinderella-like tales, for example, can be found in every culture. One explanation for this is that the first humans created these stories and took them along as they populated the globe. We call this theory *monogenesis*, or "single origin." Another theory credits the fundamental psychological similarity of humans for the similarity of their stories. *Polygenesis*, or "many origins," holds that early humans had similar urges and motives and asked similar, fundamental questions about themselves and the world around them, and, logically, created similar stories in response. Both theories have merit; and since the answer lies hidden in ancient pre-history, neither theory has prevailed over the other.

The first known English publication of any traditional literature was that of *Aesop's Fables* in 1484 by William Caxton, the printer. Although this work was instantly popular, further collections of traditional stories in print were slow to come, due mainly to the Puritans, who disapproved of any and all popular literature.

Excellent Traditional Literature to Read Aloud

(Books for each level vary in difficulty and should be selected with students' literary backgrounds in mind.)

Primary Level   Ages 5–8

Brown, Marcia. *Stone Soup.* Scribner's, 1975 (1947).
dePaola, Tomie. *Strega Nona.* Prentice Hall, 1989.
Ivimey, John W. *Three Blind Mice.* Illustrated by Victoria Chess. Little, Brown, 1990.
Marshall, James. *The Three Little Pigs.* Dial, 1989.
Martin, Rafe. *Foolish Rabbit's Big Mistake.* Illustrated by Ed Young. Putnam, 1985.
San Souci, Robert D. *Talking Eggs.* Illustrated by Jerry Pinkney. Dial, 1989.
Stamm, Claus. *Three Strong Women: A Tall Tale from Japan.* Illustrated by Jean and Mou-Sien Tseng. Viking, 1991 (1962).
Steptoe, John. *The Story of Jumping Mouse: A Native American Legend.* Morrow, 1984.
Young, Ed. *Lon Po Po: A Red-Riding Hood Story from China.* Philomel, 1989.

Intermediate Level Ages 8–11

dePaola, Tomie. *The Legend of the Bluebonnet.* Putnam, 1983.
Hodges, Margaret. *The Hero of Bremen.* Illustrated by Charles Mikolaycak. Holiday, 1993.
Lester, Julius. *The Tales of Uncle Remus: The Adventures of Brer Rabbit.* Illustrated by Jerry Pinkney. Dial, 1987.
Mayo, Margaret, reteller. *Magic Tales from Many Lands.* Illustrated by Jane Ray. Dutton, 1993.
McKissack, Patricia C. *The Dark-Thirty: Southern Tales of the Supernatural.* Illustrated by Brian Pinkney. Knopf, 1992.
Mollel, Tololwa. *The Orphan Boy.* Illustrated by Paul Morin. Houghton, 1990.
Osborne, Mary Pope. *American Tall Tales.* Illustrated by Michael McCurdy. Knopf, 1991.
Sutcliff, Rosemary. *Dragonslayer: The Story of Beowulf.* Puffin, 1986 (1966).
Taylor, C. J., *How We Saw the World: Nine Native Stories of the Way Things Began.* Tundra, 1993.
Thuswaldner, Werner, reteller. *Aesop's Fables.* Illustrated by Gisela Dürr. Translated by Anthea Bell. North-South, 1994.

Advanced Level   Ages 11–14

Aliki. *The Gods and Goddesses of Olympus.* HarperCollins, 1994.
Grimm, Jakob and Wilhelm. *Hansel and Gretel.* Illustrated by Anthony Browne. Knopf, 1988 (1981).
Hamilton, Virginia. *In the Beginning: Creation Stories from Around the World.* Illustrated by Barry Moser. Harcourt, 1988.
Kimmel, Eric A., adapter. *I-Know-Not What, I-Know-Not-Where: A Russian Tale.* Illustrated by Robert Sauber. Holiday, 1994.
McKinley, Robin. *Beauty: A Retelling of the Story of Beauty and the Beast.* Harper & Row, 1978.
Pyle, Howard. *Some Merry Adventures of Robin Hood.* Scribner's, 1954.
San Souci, Robert D. *Cut from the Same Cloth: American Women of Myth, Legend, and Tall Tale.* Illustrated by Brian Pinkney. Philomel, 1993.

During the Puritan Movement, which lasted roughly from 1500 to 1700, traditional literature retained its popularity with the common people through the *chapbook*, named after the chapmen, or peddlers, who sold them. These inexpensive paper books of between 32 and 64 pages contained stories of adventure and humor that were loosely based on the epics, legends, and folk heroes of traditional literature.

As the Romantic Movement gradually replaced the Puritan Movement in Europe in the eighteenth century, traditional literature was accepted by all levels of society once more. The first evidence of this change in attitude was the publication by Charles Perrault in 1697 in France of eight "courtly" tales under the title *Tales of Mother Goose.* Included in this collection were "Cinderella," "The Sleeping Beauty," "Little Red Riding Hood," and "Puss in Boots." The popularity of this publication is evidenced by its many editions in both France and England, but it was another hundred years before the next collection of traditional literature appeared.

The publication in 1812 of Jakob and Wilhelm Grimm's *Nursery and Household Tales,* which included such tales as "Rumpelstiltskin," "Snow White and the Seven Dwarfs," and "Hansel and Gretel," gave the world some of its best-loved stories. As the nineteenth century progressed, other important collections of traditional literature appeared in Europe and England for the first time. In Norway, Peter Christian Asbjörnsen and Jörgen Moe collected such folktales as "The Three Billy Goats Gruff," "East o' the Sun and West o' the Moon," "Henny Penny," and "Pancake"; these were published in 1851 in book form under the title *The Norwegian Folktales.* In England, Joseph Jacobs compiled from already printed sources his *English Fairy Tales* (1894), which included "The Three Bears," "The Three Little Pigs," and "The Little Red Hen." Jacobs's adaptations of many tales for a child audience is an important part of his contribution. By the time the Scot, Andrew Lang, published his valuable four-volume collection of folktales from around the world (*The Blue, Red, Green,* and *Yellow Fairy Books,* 1889–1894), the value and importance of traditional literature had been generally accepted. Milestones in the development of traditional literature are highlighted in Table 5-1.

The popularity of traditional literature with children has continued to grow in the twentieth century, due, in part, to a renewed interest in storytelling. Other trends contributing to the popularity of this genre are the publication of single, illustrated retellings of works of traditional literature, publication of cultural variants of traditional tales from around the world, and publication of newly discovered ethnic folk literature of many Canadian and U.S. minorities in collections and single, illustrated works. Surely these trends indicate both a healthy respect for the importance of our folk literary heritage and a general recognition of the worth of all traditional literature.

Types of Traditional Literature

For the beginning student of traditional literature, classification of stories can be confusing. For one, not everyone uses the same terms when referring to certain types of traditional stories. For another, we have a large body of modern stories

TABLE 5–1   Milestones in the Development of Traditional Literature

Date	Event	Significance
Prehistory–1500s	Oral storytelling	Kept ancient stories alive and provided literature to common people
1484	*Aesop's Fables* published by William Caxton in England	First known publication of traditional literature
1500–1700	Puritan Movement	Prevented the publication of traditional literature by the legitimate press
	Chapbooks emerge	Helped keep interest in traditional heroes alive during Puritan Movement
1697	*Tales of Mother Goose* published by Charles Perrault in France	First written version of folktales
1700s	Romantic Movement	Traditional fantasy promoted and embraced in Europe
1812	Wilhelm and Jakob Grimm published *Nursery and Household Tales* in Germany	Contributed to a sense of national identity in Germany. Helped to popularize folk literature worldwide
1851	Asbjörnsen and Moe publihsed *The Norwegian Folktales* in Norway	Contributed to a sense of national identity in Norway. Helped to popularize folk literature worldwide
1894	Joseph Jacobs published *English Fairy Tales* in England	Adapted many tales for a child audience
1889–94	Andrew Lang published 4 volumes of folktales from around the world	Growing popularity and knowledge of folktales worldwide

written by known authors in the style of the traditional ones, but that are not of ancient and unknown origin and, therefore, are not "traditional" in the strict sense.

We have chosen the term *traditional literature* to refer to the entire body of stories passed down from ancient times by the oral tradition. The term *folktale* is sometimes used in the same way. The term *retold tale* refers to a version of a tale that is obviously based upon an earlier, well-known tale but in which the language and bits of the plot have been altered to modernize or further dramatize the story. Nowadays, retold tales are often accompanied by completely new and original illustrations that sometimes give remarkable insights into the deeper meaning or relevancy of these tales. *Variant*, a term often used in reference to folktales, refers to a story that shares fundamental elements of plot or character with other stories, and therefore is said to be in the same story family. There are hundreds of variants of "Cinderella," for example, from all over the world. All of the following types of traditional literature occur in variant and retold tale versions.

Myths

Myths are stories that recount and explain the origins of the world and the phenomena of nature. They are sometimes referred to as *creation stories*. Myths may have originated in ancient religious rituals. The characters in these stories are mainly gods and goddesses, with occasional mention of humans, and the setting is high above earth in the home of the gods. Though often violent, myths nonetheless mirror human nature and the essence of our sometimes primitive emotions, instincts, and desires. Some folklorists believe that myths are the foundation of all other ancient stories. The best-known mythologies are of Greek, Roman, and Norse origin.

Many excellent collections of myths are currently available for children (see the list at the end of this chapter). In addition, single myths are often published in picture book format (see the list at the end of Chapter 4). The complexity and symbolism often found in myths make them appropriate for an older audience (9 years and up) than is usual with traditional literature. Some myths have been simplified for a younger audience, but oversimplification robs these stories of their power and appeal.

Epics

Epics are long stories of human adventure and heroism recounted in many episodes. Some epics are told in verse. Epics are grounded in mythology, and their characters can be both human and divine. However, the hero is always human, or, in some cases, superhuman, as was Ulysses in the *Odyssey,* Beowulf in the epic of that name, and Roland in *The Song of Roland.* The setting is earthly but not always realistic. Because of their length and complexity, epics are perhaps more suitable for students in high school or college, but on the strength of their compelling characters and events, some epics have been adapted and shortened for younger audiences. *Dragonslayer,* an adaptation of *Beowulf* by Rosemary Sutcliff, is a good example.

Legends and Tall Tales

Legends are stories based on either real or supposedly real individuals and their marvelous deeds. Legendary characters such as King Arthur, Lancelot, and Merlin, and legendary settings such as Camelot are a tantalizing mix of realism and fantasy. Although the feats of the heroes of legend defy belief today, in ancient times these stories were considered factual.

Tall tales are highly exaggerated accounts of the exploits of persons, both real and imagined, so they may be considered a subcategory of legends, albeit of much more recent origin. In the evolution of the tall tale, however, as each teller embroidered upon the hero's abilities or deeds, the tales became outlandishly exaggerated and were valued more for their humor and braggadocio than for their factual content. Legends, in contrast, are more austere in tone. Well-known North American tall-tale heroes are Pecos Bill, Paul Bunyan, John Henry, and Johnny Appleseed. Legends, because of their length, seriousness, and complexity, are often suitable for middle graders; the shorter and more humorous tall tales can be enjoyed by children aged 7 and up.

Folktales

Folktales are stories that grew out of the lives and imaginations of the people, or folk. Folktales have always been children's favorite type of traditional literature and are enjoyed by children from about age 3 and up. One of the most interesting and important characteristics of these tales is their universality. No theories adequately explain this phenomenon, but the folktales of all cultures, regardless of geography or other surface cultural differences, are remarkably similar.

Folktales vary in content as to their original intended audiences. Long ago, the nobility and their courtiers heard stories of the heroism, valor, and benevolence of people like themselves—the ruling classes. In contrast, the stories heard by the common people portrayed the ruling classes as unjust or hard taskmasters whose riches were fair game for those common folk who were quickwitted or strong enough to acquire them. These class-conscious tales are sometimes referred to as *castle* and *cottage* tales, respectively.

Some people use the terms *folktale* and *fairy tale* interchangeably. In fact, the majority of these stories have no fairies or magic characters in them, so to use one term in place of the other can be confusing and erroneous. We categorize fairy tales under *magic tales,* a kind of folktale having magic characters such as fairies.

The following is a list of the most prevalent kinds of folktales. Note that some folktales have characteristics of two or more folktale categories.

Cumulative   The cumulative tale uses repetition, accumulation, and rhythm to make an entertaining story out of the barest of plots. Because of its simplicity, rhythm, and humor, the cumulative tale has special appeal to the 3- to 5-year-olds. "The Gingerbread Boy," with its run-away cookie and his growing host of pursuers, is a good example of this kind of tale.

Humorous   The humorous tale revolves around a character's incredibly stupid and funny mistakes. These tales are also known as noodleheads, sillies, drolls, and numbskulls. They have endured, no doubt, for their comic appeal and the guaranteed laughter they evoke. Some famous noodleheads are the Norwegian husband who kept house (and nearly demolished it) and Clever Elsie, who was so addlebrained that she got herself confused with someone else and was never heard from again.

Beast   Beast tales feature talking animals and overstated action. Human characters sometimes occur. Young children accept and enjoy these talking animals, and older children can appreciate the fact that the animals symbolize humans. "Goldilocks and the Three Bears," perhaps the best-loved folktale of all, is a good example of a beast tale.

Magic   Magic tales, also known as wonder tales or fairy tales, contain elements of magic or enchantment in characters, plots, or settings. Fairies, elves, pixies, brownies, witches, magicians, genies, and fairy godparents are pivotal characters in these stories, and they use magic objects or words to weave their enchantments. Talking mirrors, hundred-year naps, glass palaces, enchanted forests, thumb-sized heroines, and magic kisses are the stuff of magic tales. "Aladdin and the Wonderful Lamp" is a well-loved magic tale.

Pourquoi   Pourquoi tales explain phenomena of nature. The word "pourquoi" is French for "why," and these tales can be understood as primitive explanations for the many "why" questions early humans asked. The strong connection between these tales and myths is obvious, which is why some folklorists identify pourquoi tales as the simplest myths. Note, however, that deities play no role in pourquoi tales as they do in myths. Moreover, the setting in pourquoi tales is earthly, while the setting in myths is the realm of the gods. An example of a pourquoi tale is "Why the Sun and the Moon Live in the Sky."

Realistic   Realistic tales are those whose characters, plot, and setting could conceivably have occurred. There is no magic in these tales, and any exaggeration is limited to the possible. Only a few realistic tales exist. "The Hero of Bremen" is a good example.

Fables

The fable is a simple story that incorporates characters—typically animals—whose actions teach a moral lesson or universal truth. Often the moral is stated at the end of the story. Throughout history, fables have appealed to adults as well as to children, for the best of these stories are both simple and wise. Moreover, their use of animals as symbols for human behavior have made them safe, yet effective, political tools. Perhaps because of their adult appeal, fables were put into print far earlier than other forms of traditional literature.

Aesop's fables compose the best-known collection of fables in the Western world, but other collections deserve our notice. From Persia, there are the *Panchatantra Tales;* from India, the *Jataka Tales;* and from France, the collected fables of Jean de La Fontaine.

Religious Stories

Stories based on religious writings or taken intact from religious manuscripts are considered to be religious stories. These stories may recount milestones in the development of a religion and its leadership, or they may present a piece of religious doctrine in narrative form. Stories of the latter sort are usually called *parables.*

Scholars of religion, language, and mythology have found a definite thread of continuity from myth and folk narrative to early religious thinking and writing. Many of the stories, figures, and rituals described in the sacred scriptures of Christianity, Hinduism, and Buddhism, among other religions, have their roots in ancient mythology.

Regardless of whether one considers the religious stories to be fact or fiction, the important point is that these wonderful stories should be shared with children. Because religion in the classroom is potentially controversial, however, many teachers and librarians do not feel comfortable sharing stories with any religious connection. This is unfortunate, since many wonderful stories and some superlative literature, as well as characters, sayings, and situations essential to the culturally literate person, are therefore missed.

Modern Folktales

The main difference between this literature and traditional literature is that it is a creation of the recent past or of the present and is written by known authors. For this reason, modern folktales will be discussed in the following chapter.

Traditional literature, the wealth of ancient stories accumulated over the course of human existence, is one of the treasures of our species. We listen to these endlessly fascinating stories, we reflect on them, and they help to tell us who we are. Good companions of our childhood, they easily become part of us and stay with us throughout our lives. Every child deserves access to this wonderful literary heritage.

References

de la Mare, Walter. (1930). Listen! In W. de la Mare, *Poems for children*. New York: Holt.

Notable Retellers, Collectors, and Illustrators of Traditional Literature

Verna Aardema, reteller of African folktales. *When the Rains Came to Kapiti Plain; Why Mosquitoes Buzz in People's Ears.*

Aesop, supposed Greek slave of the sixth century B.C. and author of a collection of classic fables.

Peter Christian Asbjørnsen, nineteenth-century Norwegian collector of folktales.

Marcia Brown, seven of her nine Caldecott Awards or Honor Book Awards are for illustrating folktales. *Cinderella; Once a Mouse.*

Nancy Ekholm Burkert, author and illustrator whose meticulously detailed, authentic illustrations bring depth to folktales. *Snow White and the Seven Dwarfs* (translated by Randall Jarrell).

Tomie dePaola, reteller, illustrator, and collector of Italian folktales and Bible stories. *Strega Nona.*

Walt Disney, animated film producer whose greatly sentimentalized versions of folktales popularized the genre. "Snow White and the Seven Dwarfs."

Leonard Everett Fisher, reteller and illustrator of Greek and Mexican mythology. *Theseus and the Minotaur.*

Paul Galdone, illustrator of numerous classic folktales. *The Gingerbread Boy; Androcles and the Lion.*

Paul Goble, author/illustrator. Reteller and illustrator of folktales and legends of the North American Indian. *Beyond the Ridge.*

Jakob and Wilhelm Grimm, nineteenth-century German folktale collectors.

Margaret Hodges, reteller of folktales for older children. *Saint George and the Dragon* (illustrated by Trina Schart Hyman).

Warwick Hutton, reteller and illustrator of Bible stories. *Adam and Eve: The Bible Story; Jonah and the Great Fish.*

Trina Schart Hyman, reteller and illustrator of classic folktales. *Little Red Riding Hood; The Sleeping Beauty.*

Joseph Jacobs, nineteenth-century English compiler and adaptor of folktales for children.

Susan Jeffers, illustrator. Representational style used to illustrate folktales, classic stories, and poems. *The Three Jovial Huntsmen* (Mother Goose).

Jean de La Fontaine, seventeenth-century French author of fables.

Andrew Lang, nineteenth-century Scottish collector of folktales from around the world.

James Marshall, reteller and illustrator of humorously irreverent versions of classic folktales. *Goldilocks and the Three Bears.*

Gerald McDermott, reteller and illustrator of Native American myths and folktales. *Raven:*

A Trickster Tale from the Pacific Northwest.

Jörgen Moe, nineteenth-century Norwegian collector of folktales.

Charles Perrault, seventeenth-century French collector of folktales and nursery rhymes. Originator of the term, "Mother Goose."

Patricia Polacco, author and illustrator of Russian folk stories. *Thundercake.*

Ed Young, Chinese-American illustrator of Chinese folktale variants. *Lon Po Po: A Red Riding Hood Story from China; Seven Blind Mice.*

Paul O. Zelinsky, illustrator whose realistic oil paintings provide insights into the meaning of folktales. *Hansel and Gretel; Rumpelstiltskin.*

Margot Zemach, author and illustrator of humorous folktales from many countries. *It Could Always Be Worse: A Yiddish Folk Tale.*

Lisbeth Zwerger, Austrian who won the 1990 Hans Christian Andersen Award for her watercolor illustrations of folktales. *Little Red Cap.*

Recommended Traditional Literature

Ages refer to approximate interest levels. YA = young adult.

Myths

Asimov, Isaac. *Words from the Myths.* Illustrated by William Barss. Houghton, 1961. Ages 9–YA.

Baker, Betty. *At the Center of the World.* Illustrated by Murray Tinkelman. Macmillan, 1973. Ages 8–10.

Barth, Edna. *Cupid and Psyche.* Illustrated by Ati Forberg. Seabury, 1976. Ages 9–12.

Bierhorst, John. *The Woman Who Fell from the Sky: The Iroquois Story of Creation.* Illustrated by Robert A. Parker. Ages 7–10.

Colum, Padraic. *The Children of Odin.* Illustrated by Willy Pogany. Macmillan, 1920. Ages 9–12.

Coolidge, Olivia. *Greek Myths.* Illustrated by Edouard Sandoz. Houghton, 1949. Ages 9–12.

d'Aulaire, Ingri, and Edgar Parin d'Aulaire. *Book of Greek Myths.* Doubleday, 1962. Ages 8–10.

———. *Norse Gods and Giants.* Doubleday, 1967. Ages 8–10.

Evslin, Bernard. *Hercules.* Illustrated by Joseph A. Smith. Morrow, 1984. Ages 9–12.

———, Dorothy Evslin, and Ned Hoopes. *Heroes and Monsters of Greek Myth.* Illustrated by William Hunter. Scholastic, 1970. Ages 9–12.

Farmer, Penelope. *Beginnings: Creation Myths of the World.* Illustrated by Antonio Frasconi. Atheneum, 1979. Ages 9–12.

———. *Daedalus and Icarus.* Illustrated by Chris Connor. Harcourt, 1971. Ages 9–12.

Fisher, Leonard Everett. *The Olympians: Great Gods and Goddesses of Ancient Greece.* Holiday, 1984. Ages 9–12.

Gates, Doris. *The Golden God: Apollo.* Illustrated by Constantinos CoConis. Viking, 1973. Ages 9–12.

———. *Lord of the Sky: Zeus.* Illustrated by Robert Handeville. Viking, 1972. Ages 9–12.

———. *Two Queens of Heaven, The Story of Demeter and Aphrodite.* Illustrated by Trina Schart Hyman. Viking, 1973. Ages 9–12.

———. *The Warrior Goddess: Athena.* Illustrated by Don Bolognese. Viking, 1972. Ages 9–12.

Green, Roger Lancelyn. *Tales of the Greek Heroes.* Penguin Books, 1958. Ages 9–12.

Hamilton, Virginia, reteller. *In the Beginning: Creation Stories from Around the World.* Illustrated by Barry Moser. Harcourt, 1988. Ages 9–12.

Hodges, Margaret. *The Gorgon's Head.* Illustrated by Charles Mikolaycak. Little, Brown, 1972. Ages 8–10.

———. *Persephone and the Springtime, A Greek Myth.* Illustrated by Arvis Stewart. Little, Brown, 1973. Ages 9–12.

Leach, Maria. *How the People Sang the Mountains Up: How and Why Stories.* Illustrated by Glen Rounds. Viking, 1967. Ages 8–10.

Low, Alice. *The Macmillan Book of Greek Gods and Heroes.* Illustrated by Arvis Stewart. Macmillan, 1985. Ages 9–12.

McDermott, Gerald. *Daughter of Earth: A Roman Myth.* Delacorte, 1984. Ages 9–12.

Proddow, Penelope, translator. *Demeter and Persephone.* Illustrated by Barbara Cooney. Doubleday, 1972. Ages 9–12.

Serraillier, Ian. *A Fall from the Sky: The Story of Daedalus.* Illustrated by William Stobbs. Walck, 1966. Ages 9–12.

———. *The Gorgon's Head: The Story of Perseus.* Illustrated by William Stobbs. Walck, 1962. Ages 9–12.

———. *Heracles the Strong.* Illustrated by Rocco Negri. Walck, 1970. Ages 9–12.

Epics

Fisher, Leonard Everett. *Cyclops.* Holiday, 1991. Ages 8–10.

———. *Jason and the Golden Fleece.* Holiday, 1990. Ages 9–12.

———. *The Olympians.* Holiday, 1984. Ages 8–10.

———. *Theseus and the Minotaur.* Holiday, 1988. Ages 9–12.

Hutton, Warwick, reteller. *Theseus and the Minotaur.* Macmillan, 1989. Ages 8–10.

Serraillier, Ian. *The Clashing Rocks: The Story of Jason.* Illustrated by William Stobbs. Walck, 1964. Ages 9–12.

———. *The Way of Danger: The Story of Theseus.* Illustrated by William Stobbs. Walck, 1963. Ages 9–12.

Sutcliff, Rosemary. *Black Ships Before Troy: The Story of the Iliad.* Illustrated by Alan Lee. Delacorte, 1993. Ages 11–14.

Legends and Tall Tales

Bird, E. J. *Ten Tall Tales.* Carolrhoda, 1984. Ages 8–10.

Blair, Walter. *Tall Tale America: A Legendary History of Our Humorous Heroes.* Illustrated by Glen Rounds. Coward-McCann, 1944. Ages 7–9.

Coolidge, Olivia. *Legends of the North.* Illustrated by Edouard Sandoz. Houghton, 1951. Ages 9–12.

Crossley-Holland, Kevin, editor. *The Faber Book of Northern Legends.* Illustrated by Alan Howard. Faber, 1983. Ages 9–12.

Day, Edward C. *John Tabor's Ride.* Illustrated by Dirk Zimmer. Knopf, 1989. Ages 8–10.

dePaola, Tomie, reteller. *The Legend of the Indian Paintbrush.* Putnam, 1988. Ages 6–8.

———. *The Legend of the Poinsettia.* Putnam, 1994. Ages 6–8.

Dewey, Ariane. *The Narrow Escapes of Davy Crockett.* Greenwillow, 1990. Ages 8–10.

———. *Pecos Bill.* Greenwillow, 1983. Ages 7–9.

Fleischman, Sid. *McBroom and the Beanstalk.* Illustrated by Walter Lorraine. Little, Brown, 1978. (Others in the McBroom series: *McBroom Tells a Lie; McBroom and the Great Race; McBroom's Ghost; McBroom's Zoo; McBroom's Ear; McBroom and the Big Wind; McBroom's Almanac.*) Ages 6–8.

Gleiter, Jan, and Kathleen Thompson. *Paul Bunyan and Babe the Blue Ox.* Illustrated by Yoshi Miyake. Raintree, 1985. Ages 7–9.

Goble, Paul. *The Girl Who Loved Wild Horses.* Bradbury, 1978. Ages 7–9.

Greene, Ellin. *The Legend of the Christmas Rose.* Illustrated by Charles Mikolaycak. Holiday, 1990. Ages 6–8.

Hastings, Selina. *Sir Gawain and the Green Knight.* Illustrated by Juan Wijngaard. Lothrop, 1981. Ages 9–12.

———. *Sir Gawain and the Loathly Lady.* Illustrated by Juan Wijngaard. Lothrop, 1985. Ages 9–12.

Hodges, Margaret. *Saint George and the Dragon.* Illustrated by Trina Schart Hyman. Little, Brown, 1984. Ages 8–10.

Keats, Ezra Jack. *John Henry, An American Legend.* Pantheon, 1965. Ages 8–10.

Kellogg, Steven, reteller. *Paul Bunyan.* Morrow, 1984. Ages 6–8.

———. reteller. *Pecos Bill.* Morrow, 1986. Ages 6–8.

Lester, Julius. *John Henry.* Illustrated by Jerry Pinkney. Dial, 1994. Ages 8–10.

Lister, Robin. *The Legend of King Arthur.* Illustrated by Alan Baker. Doubleday, 1990.

McKinley, Robin. *The Outlaws of Sherwood.* Greenwillow, 1988. Ages 12–14.

Pyle, Howard. *The Merry Adventures of Robin Hood.* Scribner's, 1946(1883). Ages 9–12.

———. *Some Merry Adventures of Robin Hood.* Scribner's, 1954. Ages 9–12.

———. *The Story of King Arthur and His Knights.* Scribner's, 1984(1883). Ages 9–12.

Quayle, Eric, reteller. *The Shining Princess: and Other Japanese Legends.* Illustrated by Michael Foreman. Arcade, 1989. Ages 7–9.

Rounds, Glen. *Washday on Noah's Ark: A Story of Noah's Ark According to Glen Rounds.* Holiday, 1985. Ages 6–8.

San Souci, Robert D. *Young Merlin.* Illustrated by Daniel Horne. Doubleday, 1990. Ages 9–12.

Stamm, Claus. *Three Strong Women: A Tall Tale from Japan.* Illustrated by Jean and Mou-sien Tseng. Viking, 1990. Ages 6–8.

Sutcliff, Rosemary. *The Light Beyond the Forest: The Quest for the Holy Grail.* Dutton, 1980. Ages 9–12.

———. *The Road to Camlann.* Dutton, 1982. Ages 9–12.

———. *The Sword and the Circle.* Dutton, 1981. Ages 9–12.

Folktales

(Note country, continent, or culture of origin after each entry.)

Aardema, Verna, reteller. *Borreguita and the Coyote.* Illustrated by Petra Mathers. Knopf, 1991. Ages 5–8. (Mexico)

———, reteller. *Rabbit Makes a Monkey of Lion: A Swahili Tale.* Illustrated by Jerry Pinkney. Dial, 1989. Ages 5–7. (Swahili Africa)

———, reteller. *The Riddle of the Drum.* Illustrated by Tony Chen. Four Winds, 1979. Ages 6–8. (Africa)

———, reteller. *Traveling to Tondo: A Tale of the Nkundo of Zaire.* Illustrated by Will Hillenbrand. Knopf, 1990. Ages 7–9. (Zaire)

———, reteller. *Who's in Rabbit's House?* Illustrated by Leo and Diane Dillon. Dial, 1977. Ages 5–7. (West Africa)

———, reteller. *Why Mosquitoes Buzz in People's Ears.* Illustrated by Leo and Diane Dillon. Dial, 1975. Ages 5–7. (Kenya)

Arkhurst, Joyce Cooper. *The Adventures of Spider: West African Folk Tales.* Illustrated by Jerry Pinkney. Little, Brown, 1964. Ages 6–8. (West Africa)

Asbjörnsen, Peter Christian, and Jörgen E. Moe. *The Three Billy Goats Gruff.* Illustrated by Marcia Brown. Harcourt, 1957. Ages 6–8. (Norway)

Baker, Keith. *The Magic Fan.* Harcourt, 1989. Ages 7–9. (Japan)

Bang, Molly. *Dawn.* Morrow, 1983. Ages 6–8. (United States)

Barth, Edna. *Cupid and Psyche: A Love Story.* Illustrated by Ati Forberg. Houghton Mifflin, 1976. Ages 7–9. (Greece)

Berenzy, Alix. *A Frog Prince.* Holt, 1989. Ages 5–7. (Germany)

Bishop, Gavin. *Chicken Licken.* Oxford, 1984. Ages 6–8. (England)

Brett, Jan. *Beauty and the Beast.* Clarion, 1989. Ages 6–8. (France)

———. *The Mitten.* Putnam, 1989. Ages 5–7. (Ukraine)

Briggs, Raymond. *Jim and the Beanstalk.* Coward, 1970. Ages 5–7. (England; modernized)

Brown, Marcia. *The Bun: A Tale from Russia.* Harcourt, 1972. Ages 6–8. (Russia)

———. *Dick Whittington and His Cat.* Scribner's, 1950. Ages 6–8. (England)

———. *Once a Mouse.* Scribner's, 1961. Ages 7–9. (India)

———. *Stone Soup.* Scribner's, 1947. Ages 6–8. (France)

Bruchac, Joseph. *The First Strawberries: A Cherokee Story.* Illustrated by Anna Vojtech. Dial, 1993. Ages 7–9. (Native-American: Cherokee)

Bryan, Ashley. *Beat the Story-Drum, Pum-Pum.* Atheneum, 1980. Ages 6–8. (Africa)

———. *The Dancing Granny.* Atheneum, 1977. Ages 6–8. (Antilles)

Carew, Jan. *The Third Gift.* Illustrated by Leo and Diane Dillon. Little, Brown, 1974. Ages 7–9. (Africa)

Cauley, Lorinda Bryan. *Goldilocks and the Three Bears.* Putnam, 1982. Ages 4–6. (England)

Chase, Richard. *The Jack Tales.* Illustrated by Berkeley Williams, Jr. Houghton Mifflin, 1943. Ages 6–8. (United States)

Chaucer, Geoffrey. *Canterbury Tales.* Adapted by Barbara Cohen. Illustrated by Trina Schart Hyman. Lothrop, 1988. Ages 8–10. (England)

Climo, Shirley. *The Egyptian Cinderella.* Illustrated by Ruth Heller. Crowell, 1989. Ages 7–9. (Egypt)

———. *The Korean Cinderella.* Illustrated by Ruth Heller. HarperCollins, 1993. Ages 7–9. (Korea)

Cohn, Amy L., editor. *From Sea to Shining Sea: A Treasury of American Folklore and Folk Songs.* Scholastic, 1993. Ages 4–10. (United States)

Cole, Joanna. *Bony-Legs.* Illustrated by Dirk Zimmer. Four Winds, 1983. Ages 4–6. (Russia)

Conover, Chris, reteller. *Mother Goose and the Sly Fox.* Farrar, 1989. Ages 6–8. (France)

Cook, Scott, illustrator. *The Gingerbread Boy.* Knopf, 1987. Ages 5–7. (England)

Cooney, Barbara. *Chanticleer and the Fox.* Crowell, 1958. Ages 6–8. (England)

Cooper, Susan. reteller. *The Selkie Girl.* Illustrated by Warwick Hutton. McElderry, 1986. Ages 7–9. (Scotland)

———, reteller. *The Silver Cow.* Illustrated by Warwick Hutton. Atheneum, 1983. Ages 8–10. (Wales)

———. *Tam Lin.* Illustrated by Warwick Hutton. McElderry, 1991. Ages 8–10. (Scotland)

Corrin, Sara and Stephen, retellers. *The Pied Piper of Hamelin.* Illustrated by Errol Le Cain. Harcourt, 1989. Ages 7–9. (Germany)

d'Aulaire, Ingri, and Edgar Parin d'Aulaire, editors and illustrators. *East of the Sun and West of the Moon.* Viking, 1969 (1938). Ages 7–9. (Norway)

De Beaumont, Madame. *Beauty and the Beast.* Translated and illustrated by Diane Goode. Bradbury, 1978. Ages 7–9. (France)

de la Mare, Walter. *Molly Whuppie.* Illustrated by Errol Le Cain. Farrar, 1983. Ages 6–8. (England)

dePaola, Tomie. *Strega Nona.* Prentice Hall, 1975. Ages 6–8. (Italy)

———. *Tomie dePaola's Favorite Nursery Tales.* Putnam, 1986. Ages 4–6.

Dewey, Ariane. *Febold Feboldson.* Greenwillow, 1984. Ages 6–8. (United States)

Ehlert, Lois. *Moon Rope: A Peruvian Folktale.* Harcourt, 1992. Ages 4–8. (Peru)

Eisen, Armand, reteller. *Goldilocks and the Three Bears.* Illustrated by Lynn Bywaters Ferris. Knopf, 1987. Ages 5–7. (England)

Esbensen, Barbara Juster, reteller. *The Star Maiden: An Ojibway Tale.* Illustrated by Helen K. Davie. Little, Brown, 1988. Ages 7–9. (Native-American)

Frasconi, Antonio. *The House That Jack Built.* Harcourt, 1958. Ages 6–8. (England)

French, Fiona. *Snow White in New York.* Oxford, 1986. Ages 7–10. (Germany; modernized)

Galdone, Paul. *Cinderella.* McGraw-Hill, 1978. Ages 5–7. (France)

———. *The Gingerbread Boy.* Clarion, 1975. Ages 4–6. (England)

———. *Henny Penny.* Seabury, 1968. Ages 5–7. (England)

———. *The House That Jack Built.* McGraw-Hill, 1961. Ages 6–8. (England)

———. *The Little Red Hen.* Seabury, 1973. Ages 5–7. (England)

———. *Old Mother Hubbard and Her Dog.* McGraw-Hill, 1960. Ages 5–7. (England)

———. *The Three Billy Goats Gruff.* Seabury, 1973. Ages 5–7. (Norway)

———. *What's in Fox's Sac? An Old English Tale.* Clarion, 1982. Ages 6–8. (England)

Garner, Alan. *Alan Garner's Book of British Fairy Tales.* Illustrated by Derek Collard. Delacorte, 1985. Ages 6–8. (England)

Geras, Adèle. *My Grandmother's Stories: A Collection of Jewish Folk Tales.* Illustrated by Jael Jordan.

Knopf, 1990. Ages 8–10. (Jewish)

Geringer, Laura, adapter. *The Seven Ravens.* Illustrated by E. S. Gazsi. HarperCollins, 1994. Ages 7–10. (Germany)

Gerstein, Mordicai, reteller. *The Seal Mother.* Dial, 1986. Ages 7–9. (Scotland)

———. *Tales of Pan.* Harper, 1986. Ages 7–9. (Greece)

Goble, Paul. *Buffalo Woman.* Bradbury, 1984. Ages 7–9. (Native-American)

———. *Beyond the Ridge.* Bradbury, 1989. Ages 8–10. (Native-American)

———. *The Girl Who Loved Wild Horses.* Bradbury, 1978. Ages 7–9. (Native-American)

———, reteller. *Iktomi and the Berries: A Plains Indian Story.* Orchard, 1989. Ages 7–9. (Native-American)

———, reteller. *Iktomi and the Boulder: A Plains Indian Story.* Orchard, 1988. Ages 7–9. (Native-American)

Grimm, Jakob, and Wilhelm Grimm. *The Bremen-Town Musicians.* Retold and illustrated by Ilse Plume. Doubleday, 1980. Ages 6–8. (Germany)

———. *The Bremen Town Musicians.* Translated by Elizabeth Shub. Illustrated by Janina Domanska. Greenwillow, 1980. Ages 6–8. (Germany)

———. *The Bremen Town Musicians.* Illustrated by Joseph Palecek. Translated by Anthea Bell. Picture Book Studio, 1988. Ages 6–8. (Germany)

———. *Favorite Tales from Grimm.* Retold by Nancy Garden. Illustrated by Mercer Mayer. Four Winds, 1982. Ages 6–8. (Germany)

———. *Hans in Luck.* Illustrated by Felix Hoffman. Atheneum, 1975. Ages 6–8. (Germany)

———. *Hansel and Gretel.* Illustrated by Anthony Browne. Watts, 1981. Ages 8–14. (Germany)

———. *Hansel and Gretel.* Translated by Elizabeth D. Crawford. Illustrated by Lisbeth Zwerger. Morrow, 1979. Ages 6–8. (Germany)

———. *Hansel and Gretel.* Illustrated by Paul Galdone. McGraw-Hill, 1982. Ages 6–8. (Germany)

———. *Hansel and Gretel.* Retold by Rika Lesser. Illustrated by Paul O. Zelinsky. Dodd Mead, 1984. Ages 7–9. (Germany)

———. *The Juniper Tree and Other Tales from Grimm.* Edited by Lore Segal and Maurice Sendak. Translated by Randall Jarrell. Illustrated by Maurice Sendak. Farrar, 1976. Ages 6–8. (Germany)

———. *Little Red Cap.* Translated by Elizabeth D. Crawford. Illustrated by Lisbeth Zwerger. Morrow, 1983. Ages 6–8. (Germany)

———. *Little Red Riding Hood.* Illustrated by Trina Schart Hyman. Holiday, 1982. Ages 6–8. (Germany)

———. *Rumpelstiltskin.* Retold and illustrated by Paul O. Zelinsky. Dutton, 1986. Ages 7–9. (Germany)

———. *The Seven Ravens.* Translated by Elizabeth D. Crawford. Illustrated by Lisbeth Zwerger. Morrow, 1981. Ages 7–9. (Germany)

———. *The Seven Ravens.* Illustrated by Felix Hoffman. Harcourt, 1963. Ages 7–9. (Germany)

———. *The Sleeping Beauty.* Retold and illustrated by Warwick Hutton. Atheneum, 1979. Ages 7–9. (Germany)

———. *The Sleeping Beauty.* Retold and illustrated by Trina Schart Hyman. Little, Brown, 1974. Ages 7–9. (Germany)

———. *Snow-White and the Seven Dwarfs.* Translated by Randall Jarrell. Illustrated by Nancy Ekholm Burkert. Farrar, 1972. Ages 8–10. (Germany)

———. *Tales from Grimm.* Translated and illustrated by Wanda Gág. Coward-McCann, 1936. Ages 7–9. (Germany)

———. *Thorn Rose or The Sleeping Beauty.* Illustrated by Errol Le Cain. Bradbury, 1975. Ages 6–8. (Germany)

———. *Tom Thumb.* Illustrated by Felix Hoffman. Atheneum, 1973. Ages 6–8. (Germany)

———. *The Twelve Dancing Princesses.* Illustrated by Errol Le Cain. Viking, 1978. Ages 7–9. (Germany)

Hadithi, Mwenye. *Crafty Chameleon.* Illustrated by Adrienne Kennaway. Little, Brown, 1987. Ages 6–8. (Africa)

———. *Hot Hippo.* Illustrated by Adrienne Kennaway. Little, Brown, 1986. Ages 6–8. (Africa)

———. *Lazy Lion.* Illustrated by Adrienne Kennaway. Little, Brown, 1990. Ages 6–8. (Africa)

Hague, Kathleen, and Michael Hague. *East of the Sun and West of the Moon.* Illustrated by Michael Hague. Harcourt, 1980. Ages 7–9. (Norway)

Hale, Lucretia. *The Lady Who Put Salt in Her Coffee.* Adapted and illustrated by Amy Schwartz. Harcourt, 1989. Ages 7–9. (United States; modern folktale)

Haley, Gail E. *Jack and the Bean Tree.* Crown, 1986. Ages 6–8. (United States-Appalachia)

———. *Jack and the Fire Dragon.* Crown, 1988. Ages 6–8. (United States)

———. *A Story, A Story.* Atheneum, 1970. Ages 6–8. (Africa)

Hamilton, Virginia. *The People Could Fly: American Black Folktales.* Illustrated by Leo and Diane Dillon. Knopf, 1985. Ages 8–10. (African-American)

Haviland, Virginia. *Favorite Fairy Tales Told in India.* Illustrated by Blair Lent. Little, Brown, 1973. Ages 7–9. (India)

———. *Favorite Fairy Tales Told in Italy.* Illustrated by Evaline Ness. Little, Brown, 1965. Ages 7–9. (Italy)

———. *Favorite Fairy Tales Told in Norway.* Illustrated by Leonard Weisgard. Little, Brown, 1961. Ages 7–9. (Norway)

———, editor. *North American Legends.* Illustrated by Ann Strugnell. Collins, 1979. Ages 7–9. (North America)

Heyer, Marilee, reteller. *The Weaving of a Dream: A Chinese Folktale.* Viking, 1986. Ages 7–9. (China)

Highwater, Jamake. *Anpao: An American Indian Odyssey.* Illustrated by Fritz Scholder. Lippincott, 1977. Ages 9–12. (Native-American)

Hodges, Margaret. *The Fire Bringer: A Paiute Indian Legend.* Illustrated by Peter Parnall. Little, Brown, 1972. Ages 8–10. (Native-American)

Hogrogian, Nonny. *One Fine Day.* Macmillan, 1971. Ages 4–6. (Armenia)

Hong, Lily Toy, reteller. *Two of Everything: A Chinese Folktale.* Albert Whitman, 1993. Ages 5–8. (China)

Hooks, William H. *The Ballad of Belle Dorcas.* Illustrated by Brian Pinkney. Knopf, 1990. Ages 8–10. (United States)

———, reteller. *Moss Gown.* Illustrated by Donald Carrick. Clarion, 1987. Ages 7–9. (United States; a Cinderella variant)

Huck, Charlotte. *Princess Furball.* Illustrated by Anita Lobel. Greenwillow, 1989. Ages 6–8. (Germany; a Cinderella variant)

Hutton, Warwick. *Beauty and the Beast.* Atheneum, 1975. Ages 7–9. (France)

———, reteller. *The Trojan Horse.* Macmillan/McElderry, 1992. Ages 6–10. (Greece)

Ishii, Momoko, reteller. *The Tongue-Cut Sparrow.* Translated from Japanese by Katherine Paterson. Illustrated by Suekichi Akaba. Lodestar, 1987. Ages 7–9. (Japan)

Ivimey, John W. *The Complete Story of the Three Blind Mice.* Illustrated by Paul Galdone. Clarion, 1987. Ages 6–8. (England; expanded)

——. *Three Blind Mice.* Illustrated by Victoria Chess. Little, Brown, 1990. Ages 7–9. (England)

Jagendorf, Moritz A. *Noodlehead Stories from Around the World.* Illustrated by Shane Miller. Vanguard, 1957. Ages 6–8.

Jaquith, Priscilla. *Bo Rabbit Smart for True: Folktales from the Gullah.* Illustrated by Ed Young. Philomel, 1981. Ages 8–10. (African-American)

Johnston, Tony. *The Badger and the Magic Fan: A Japanese Folktale.* Illustrated by Tomie dePaola. Putnam, 1990. Ages 6–8. (Japan)

Joseph, Lynn. *A Wave in Her Pocket: Stories from Trinidad.* Illustrated by Brian Pinkney. Clarion, 1991. Ages 7–9. (Trinidad)

Karlin, Barbara, reteller. *Cinderella.* Illustrated by James Marshall. Little, Brown, 1989. Ages 6–8. (France)

Kellogg, Steven. *Chicken Little.* Morrow, 1985. Ages 4–6. (United States; modern folktale)

——, reteller. *Johnny Appleseed.* Morrow, 1988. Ages 6–8. (United States)

——. *Paul Bunyan.* Morrow, 1984. Ages 6–8. (United States)

——. *Pecos Bill.* Morrow, 1986. Ages 6–8. (United States)

Kimmel, Eric. *Baba Yaga: A Russian Folktale.* Illustrated by Megan Lloyd. Holiday, 1991. Ages 7–9. (Russia)

——. *The Gingerbread Man.* Illustrated by Megan Lloyd. Holiday, 1993. Ages 5–7. (England)

——. *Iron John.* Illustrated by Trina Schart Hyman. Holiday, 1994. Ages 8–10. (Germany)

Kurtz, Jane. *Fire on the Mountain.* Illustrated by E. B. Lewis. Simon & Schuster, 1994. Ages 7–9. (Ethiopia)

Lang, Andrew, reteller. *Aladdin.* Illustrated by Errol Le Cain. Viking, 1981. Ages 6–8. (Middle East)

Langstaff, John, and Feodor Rojankovsky. *Frog Went A- Courtin'.* Illustrated by Feodor Rojankovsky. Harcourt, 1955. Ages 6–8. (England)

Larry, Charles. *Peboan and Seegwun.* Farrar, 1993. Ages 7–10. (Native-American: Ojibwa)

Lester, Julius. *How Many Spots Does a Leopard Have? and Other Tales.* Illustrated by David Shannon. Scholastic, 1989. Ages 7–9. (African-American)

——. *The Knee-high Man and Other Tales.* Illustrated by Ralph Pinto. Dial, 1972. Ages 7–9. (African-American)

——, reteller. *The Tales of Uncle Remus: The Adventures of Brer Rabbit.* Dial, 1987. (See also: *More Tales of Uncle Remus: Further Adventures of Brer Rabbit, His Friends, Enemies, and Others.* Dial, 1988.) Ages 7–9. (African-American)

Lindbergh, Reeve. *Johnny Appleseed.* Illustrated by Kathy Jakobsen. Little, Brown, 1990. Ages 6–8. (United States)

Lottridge, Celia Barker. *The Name of the Tree: A Bantu Folktale.* Illustrated by Ian Wallace. Macmillan, 1990. Ages 6–8. (Africa)

Louie, Ai-Ling. *Yeh-Shen: A Cinderella Story from China.* Illustrated by Ed Young. Philomel, 1982. Ages 7–9. (China)

MacGill-Callahan, Sheila. *The Children of Lir.* Illustrated by Gennady Spirin. Dial, 1993. Ages 5–8. (Wales)

Mahy, Margaret. *The Seven Chinese Brothers.* Illustrated by Jean and Mou-sien Tseng. Scholastic, 1990. Ages 6–8. (China)

Marshak, Samuel. *The Month-Brothers: A Slavic Tale.* Translated by Thomas P. Whitney. Illustrated by Diane Stanley. Morrow, 1983. Ages 6–8. (Russia)

Marshall, James, reteller. *Fox Be Nimble.* Dial, 1990. Ages 5–7. (England)

——. *Goldilocks and the Three Bears.* Dial, 1988. Ages 5–7. (England)

——. *Red Riding Hood.* Dial, 1987. Ages 6–8. (Germany)

——. *The Three Little Pigs.* Dial, 1989. Ages 5–7. (England)

Martin, Eva, reteller. *Canadian Fairy Tales.* Illustrated by László Gál. Little, Brown, 1984. Ages 7–9. (Canada)

Martin, Rafe, reteller. *Foolish Rabbit's Big Mistake.* Illustrated by Ed Young. Putnam, 1985. Ages 6–8. (India)

——. *The Rough-Face Girl.* Illustrated by David Shannon. Putnam, 1992. Ages 8–10. (Native-American)

Mayer, Marianna. *The Twelve Dancing Princesses.* Illustrated by K. Y. Craft. Morrow, 1989. Ages 6–8. (France)

Mayer, Mercer. *East of the Sun and West of the Moon.* Four Winds, 1980. Ages 7–9. (Norway)

McDermott, Gerald. *Anansi the Spider.* Holt, 1972. Ages 6–8. (Africa)

———. *Arrow to the Sun.* Viking, 1974. Ages 8–10. (Native-American)

———. *Raven: A Trickster Tale from the Pacific Northwest.* Harcourt, 1993. Ages 5–9. (Native-American)

———. *Tim O'Toole and the Wee Folk.* Viking, 1990. Ages 6–8. (Ireland)

———. *Zomo the Rabbit: A Trickster Tale from West Africa.* Harcourt, 1992. Ages 4–8. (Africa)

McVitty, Walter, reteller. *Ali Baba and the Forty Thieves.* Illustrated by Margaret Early. Abrams, 1989. Ages 6–8. (Middle East)

Merrill, Jean. *The Girl Who Loved Caterpillars: A Twelfth-Century Tale from Japan.* Illustrated by Floyd Cooper. Putnam, 1992. Ages 5–8. (Japan)

Mollel, Tololwa M. *The Orphan Boy.* Illustrated by Paul Morin. Clarion, 1990. Ages 7–9. (Tanzania)

Montresor, Beni, adapter. *Little Red Riding Hood.* Doubleday, 1991. Ages 8–10. (Germany)

Mosel, Arlene. *The Funny Little Woman.* Illustrated by Blair Lent. Dutton, 1972. Ages 6–8. (Japan)

———. *Tikki Tikki Tembo.* Illustrated by Blair Lent. Holt, 1968. Ages 6–8. (China)

Ness, Evaline. *Old Mother Hubbard and Her Dog.* Holt, 1972. Ages 5–7. (England)

———. *Tom Tit Tot.* Scribner's, 1965. Ages 4–6. (England)

Newton, Pam. *The Stonecutter: An Indian Folktale.* Putnam, 1990. Ages 7–9. (India)

O'Shea, Pat, reteller. *Finn Mac Cool and the Small Men of Deeds.* Illustrated by Steven Lavis. Holiday, 1987. Ages 7–9. (Ireland)

Parks, Van Dyke, and Malcolm Jones, adaptors and retellers. (Original story by Joel Chandler Harris.) *Jump!: The Adventures of Brer Rabbit.* Illustrated by Barry Moser. Harcourt, 1986. (See also: *Jump Again!: More Adventures of Brer Rabbit,* 1987; *Jump on Over!: The Adventures of Brer Rabbit and His Family,* 1989.) Ages 7–9. (African-American)

Paterson, Katherine. *The Tale of the Mandarin Ducks.* Illustrated by Leo and Diane Dillon. Lodestar, 1990. Ages 7–9. (Japan)

Perrault, Charles. *Cinderella.* Illustrated by Marcia Brown. Scribner's, 1954. Ages 6–8. (France)

———. *Cinderella, or The Little Glass Slipper.* Illustrated by Errol Le Cain. Bradbury, 1973. Ages 6–8. (France)

———. *The Glass Slipper: Charles Perrault's Tales of Times Past.* Translated by John Bierhorst. Illustrated by Mitchell Miller. Four Winds, 1981. Ages 6–8. (France)

———. *Puss in Boots.* Illustrated by Fred Marcellino. Farrar, 1990. Ages 6–8. (France)

———. *Puss in Boots.* Illustrated by Marcia Brown. Scribner's, 1952. Ages 6–8. (France)

———. *The Sleeping Beauty.* Translated and illustrated by David Walker. Crowell, 1976. Ages 6–8. (France)

Polacco, Patricia. *Babushka Baba Yaga.* Philomel, 1993. Ages 7–9. (Russia)

Ransome, Arthur. *The Fool of the World and the Flying Ship.* Illustrated by Uri Schulevitz. Farrar, 1968. Ages 6–8. (Russia)

Robinson, Gail. *Raven the Trickster.* Illustrated by Joanna Troughton. Atheneum, 1982. Ages 6–8. (Native-American)

Rounds, Glen, reteller. *Old MacDonald Had A Farm.* Holiday, 1989. Ages 4–6. (England)

San Souci, Robert D. *Sootface: An Ojibwa Cinderella Story.* Illustrated by Daniel San Souci. Doubleday, 1994. Ages 5–8. (Native-American: Ojibwa)

———. *The Talking Eggs: A Folktale from the American South.* Illustrated by Jerry Pinkney. Dial, 1989. Ages 7–9. (African-American)

Sawyer, Ruth. *Journey Cake, Ho!* Illustrated by Robert McCloskey. Viking, 1953. Ages 4–6. (United States)

Schwartz, Alvin. *Flapdoodle: Pure Nonsense from American Folklore.* Illustrated by John O'Brien. Lippincott, 1980. Ages 6–12. (United States)

———. *Witcracks: Jokes and Jests from American Folklore.* Illustrated by Glen Rounds. Lippincott, 1973. Ages 6–12. (United States)

Shannon, George. *More Stories to Solve: Fifteen Folktales from Around the World.* Illustrated by Peter Sís. Greenwillow, 1990. Ages 7–10.

Singer, Isaac Bashevis. *The Golem.* Illustrated by Uri Shulevitz. Farrar, 1982. Ages 8–10. (Jewish)

———. *Mazel and the Shlimazel, or the Milk of the Lioness.* Illustrated by Margot Zemach. Farrar, 1967. Ages 8–10. (Jewish)

———. *When Shlemiel Went to Warsaw and Other Stories.* Translated by the author and Elizabeth Shub. Illustrated by Margot Zemach. Farrar,

1968. Ages 8–10. (Jewish)

Sleator, William. *The Angry Moon.* Illustrated by Blair Lent. Little, Brown, 1970. Ages 7–9. (Native-American)

Snyder, Diane. *The Boy of the Three-Year Nap.* Illustrated by Allen Say. Houghton, 1988. Ages 7–9. (Japan)

Steel, Flora Annie. *Tattercoats.* Illustrated by Diane Goode. Bradbury, 1976. Ages 6–8. (England)

Steptoe, John, reteller. *Mufaro's Beautiful Daughters: An African Tale.* Lothrop, 1987. Ages 6–8. (Africa)

———. *The Story of Jumping Mouse.* Lothrop, 1984. Ages 7–9. (Native-American)

Stevens, Janet, adaptor. *How the Manx Cat Lost Its Tail.* Harcourt, 1990. Ages 6–8. (England; Isle of Man)

Stolz, Mary. *Zekmet, the Stone Carver: A Tale of Ancient Egypt.* Illustrated by Deborah Nourse Lattimore. Harcourt, 1988. Ages 8–10. (Egypt)

Tashjian, Virginia. *Once There Was and Was Not, Armenian Tales Retold.* Illustrated by Nonny Hogrogian. Little, Brown, 1966. Ages 7–9. (Armenia)

Taylor, C. J. *How We Saw the World: Nine Native Stories of the Way Things Began.* Tundra, 1993. Ages 8–10. (Native-American)

Tejima. *Ho-Limlim: A Rabbit Tale from Japan.* Philomel, 1990. Ages 6–8. (Japan)

Tompert, Ann. *Bamboo Hats and a Rice Cake.* Illustrated by Demi. Crown, 1993. Ages 7–9. (Japan)

Toye, William. *The Loon's Necklace.* Illustrated by Elizabeth Cleaver. Oxford, 1977. Ages 7–9. (Native-American)

Trivizas, Eugene. *The Three Little Wolves and the Big Bad Pig.* Illustrated by Helen Oxenbury. Macmillan/McElderry, 1993. Ages 5–9. (England; a Three Little Pigs variant)

Watson, Richard Jesse, reteller. *Tom Thumb.* Harcourt, 1989. Ages 6–8. (England)

Whitney, Thomas P. *Vasilisa the Beautiful.* Illustrated by Nonny Hogrogian. Macmillan, 1970. Ages 6–8. (Russia)

Williams, Linda. *The Little Old Lady Who Was Not Afraid of Anything.* Illustrated by Megan Lloyd. Crowell, 1986. Ages 6–8. (United States)

Williams-Ellis, Amabel, selector. *Tales from the Enchanted World.* Illustrated by Moira Kemp. Little, Brown, 1988. Ages 7–9.

Winthrop, Elizabeth. *Vasilissa the Beautiful.* Illustrated by Alexander Koshkin. HarperCollins, 1991. Ages 7–9. (Russia)

Wisniewski, David. *Elfwyn's Saga.* Lothrop, 1990. Ages 8–10. (Iceland)

Yagawa, Sumiko. *The Crane Wife.* Translated by Katherine Paterson. Illustrated by Suekichi Akaba. Morrow, 1981. Ages 6–8. (Japan)

Yolen, Jane. *Tam Lin.* Illustrated by Charles Mikolaycak. Harcourt, 1990. Ages 7–9. (Scotland)

Young, Ed. *Lon Po Po: A Red Riding-Hood Story from China.* Philomel, 1989. Ages 7–9. (China)

Zelinsky, Paul O., reteller. *Rumpelstiltskin.* Dutton, 1986. Ages 6–8. (Germany)

Zemach, Harve. *Duffy and the Devil.* Illustrated by Margot Zemach, Farrar, 1973. Ages 6–8. (England)

Zemach, Margot. *It Could Always Be Worse.* Farrar, 1977. Ages 6–8. (Jewish)

———. *The Three Little Pigs: An Old Story.* Farrar, 1988. Ages 6–8. (England)

Fables

Aesop. *Aesop's Fables.* Selected and illustrated by Michael Hague. Holt, 1985. Ages 7–9.

———. *Aesop's Fables.* Illustrated by Heidi Holder. Viking, 1981. Ages 7–9.

———. *The Lion and the Mouse.* Illustrated by Ed Young. Doubleday, 1980. Ages 6–8.

Anno, Mitsumasa, reteller. *Anno's Aesop: A Book of Fables by Aesop and Mr. Fox.* Orchard, 1989. Ages 7–9.

Brett, Jan. *Town Mouse, Country Mouse.* Putnam, 1994. Ages 6–8.

Brown, Marcia. *Once a Mouse.* Scribner's, 1961. Ages 6–8.

Cauley, Lorinda Bryan, reteller. *The Town Mouse and the Country Mouse.* Putnam, 1984. Ages 6–8.

Clark, Margaret, reteller. *The Best of Aesop's Fables.* Illustrated by Charlotte Voake. Little, Brown, 1990. Ages 7–9.

De Roin, Nancy. *Jataka Tales: Fables from the Buddha.* Illustrated by Ellen Lanyon. Houghton, 1975. Ages 7–9.

Galdone, Paul. *Three Aesop Fox Fables.* Seabury, 1971. Ages 6–8.

Gatti, Anne. *Aesop's Fables.* Illustrated by Safaya Salter. Harcourt, 1992. Ages 7–10.

Lobel, Arnold. *Fables.* Harper, 1980. Ages 6–8.

Paxton, Tom, reteller. *Belling the Cat and Other Aesop's Fables.* Illustrated by Robert Rayevsky. Morrow, 1990. Ages 7–9.

Stevens, Janet. *The Town Mouse and the Country Mouse: An Aesop Fable.* Holiday, 1987. Ages 6–8.

Testa, Fulvio, illustrator. *Aesop's Fables.* Barron, 1989. Ages 8–10.

Religious Stories

Bach, Alice, and J. Cheryl Exum. *Moses' Ark: Stories from the Bible.* Illustrated by Leo and Diane Dillon. Delacorte, 1989. Ages 6–8.

Bible, New Testament. *Christmas: The King James Version.* Illustrated by Jan Pieńkowski. Knopf, 1984. Ages 6–10.

———. *Easter: The King James Version.* Illustrated by Jan Pieńkowski. Knopf, 1989. Ages 6–8

Bierhorst, John, translator. *Spirit Child: A Story of the Nativity.* Illustrated by Barbara Cooney. Morrow, 1984. Ages 7–9.

Bolliger, Max, reteller. *Noah and the Rainbow.* Translated by Clyde Robert Bulla. Illustrated by Helga Aichinger. Crowell, 1972. Ages 6–8.

Chaikin, Miriam. *Joshua in the Promised Land.* Illustrated by David Frampton. Clarion, 1982. Ages 7–9.

———, adaptor. *Exodus.* Illustrated by Charles Mikolaycak. Holiday, 1987. Ages 6–8.

Cohen, Barbara. *I Am Joseph.* Illustrated by Charles Mikolaycak. Lothrop, 1980. Ages 7–9.

dePaola, Tomie. *The Legend of Old Befana.* Harcourt, 1980. Ages 6–8.

———. *The Story of Three Wise Kings.* Putnam, 1983. Ages 6–8.

———. *Tomie dePaola's Book of Bible Stories.* Putnam, 1990. Ages 6–10.

Evslin, Bernard. *Signs and Wonders: Tales from the Old Testament.* Illustrated by Charles Mikolaycak. Four Winds, 1981. Ages 6–10.

Fisher, Leonard Everett. *The Seven Days of Creation.* Holiday, 1981. Ages 7–9.

Geisert, Arthur. *The Ark.* Houghton, 1988. Ages 6–8.

Graham, Lorenz. *David He No Fear.* Illustrated by Ann Grifalconi. Crowell, 1971. Ages 7–9.

———. *Every Man Heart Lay Down.* Illustrated by Colleen Browning. Crowell, 1970. Ages 7–9.

———. *Hongry Catch Foolish Boy.* Illustrated by James Brown, Jr. Crowell, 1973. Ages 7–9.

———. *A Road Down in the Sea.* Illustrated by Gregorio Prestopino. Crowell, 1970. Ages 7–9.

Hutton, Warwick. *Jonah and the Great Fish.* Atheneum, 1983. Ages 6–8.

———, adaptor. *Adam and Eve: The Bible Story.* Macmillan, 1987. Ages 6–8.

———, reteller. *Moses in the Bulrushes.* Atheneum, 1986. Ages 6–8.

Johnson, James Weldon. *The Creation.* Illustrated by James E. Ransome. Holiday, 1994.

Kimmel, Eric A., reteller. *The Spotted Pony: A Collection of Hanukkah Stories.* Illustrated by Leonard Everett Fisher. Holiday, 1992.

Menotti, Gian Carlo. *Amahl and the Night Visitors.* Illustrated by Michele Lemieux. Morrow, 1986. Ages 8–10.

Mikolaycak, Charles. *Babushka: An Old Russian Folktale.* Holiday, 1984. Ages 6–8.

Robbins, Ruth. *Baboushka and Three Kings.* Illustrated by Nicolas Sidjakov. Parnassus, 1960. Ages 6–8.

Spier, Peter. *The Book of Jonah.* Doubleday, 1985. Ages 6–8.

———. *Noah's Ark.* Doubleday, 1977. Ages 6–8.

Turner, Philip. *Brian Wildsmith's Illustrated Bible Stories.* Illustrated by Brian Wildsmith. Watts, 1969. Ages 6–10.

Vivas, Julie. *The Nativity.* Harcourt, 1988. Ages 6–10.

Weil, Lisl. *Esther.* Atheneum, 1980. Ages 7–9.

Winthrop, Elizabeth. *A Child Is Born.* Illustrated by Charles Mikolaycak. Holiday, 1983. Ages 6–8.

———. *He Is Risen.* Illustrated by Charles Mikolaycak. Holiday, 1985. Ages 6–8.

Chapter 6

Modern Fantasy

Silverly
Silverly,
> *Silverly,*
Over the
> *Trees*
The moon drifts
> *By on a*
Runaway
> *Breeze.*

Dozily,
> *Dozily,*
Deep in her
> *Bed,*
A little girl
> *Dreams with the*
Moon in her
> *Head.*

—Dennis Lee

Modern fantasy has its roots in traditional fantasy from which motifs, characters, stylistic elements, and, at times, themes have been drawn. Many of the most revered works of children's literature fall under the genre of modern fantasy. *The Adventures of Pinocchio, Alice's Adventures in Wonderland, The Wizard of Oz, The Wind in the Willows, Winnie-the-Pooh, Pippi Longstocking,* and *Charlotte's Web* immediately come to mind. The creation of stories that are highly imaginative—yet believable— is the hallmark of this genre.

Definition and Description

Modern fantasy refers to the body of literature in which the events, the settings, or the characters are outside the realm of possibility. A fantasy is a story that cannot happen in the real world, and for this reason this genre has been called the literature of the fanciful impossible. In these stories, animals talk, inanimate objects come to life, people are giants or thumb-sized, imaginary worlds are inhabited, and future worlds are explored, just to name a few of the possibilities. Modern fantasies are written by known authors, and this distinguishes the genre from traditional literature in which the tales are handed down through the oral tradition and have no known author. Although the events could not happen in real life, modern fantasies often contain truths that help the reader to understand today's world.

The *cycle format* in which one book is linked to another through characters, settings, or both is especially prevalent in modern fantasy. Elleman (1987) states, "Events in [fantasy] cycle books are often strung out over three or four volumes. Authors attempt to make each novel self-contained with varying degrees of success, but usually readers need the entire series for full impact" (p. 418). The cycle format appeals to readers who become attached to certain characters and then delight in reading the next book in the series. An example of the cycle format can be found in the chronicles of the creatures of Redwall Abbey, a series of animal fantasies by Brian Jacques.

Values of Modern Fantasy for Children

When reading a work of fantasy, children can delight in imagining other worlds and the limitless possibilities that can be opened up in the human mind. Fantasy enables the reader to see the realities that extend beyond the normal range of human vision.

- Children can develop their imaginations through the vicarious experience of entering a different world from the present one. Trying to imagine something that does not exist in reality and putting shape, color, form, and sound to it can be challenging as well as enjoyable.
- Children can increase their ability to think divergently through modern fantasy. In fantasies, the normal "rules" of the physical world are suspended, permitting the reader to gain a new perspective on the world of reality. Children can consider other ways of living, other ways the world might have been, or perhaps other ways the world might become.
- Modern fantasy provides a temporary escape from reality for all children. Moreover, not all children's lives are easy and lighthearted. Children whose grim experiences make realistic stories seem artificial may relish the opportunity to visit the world of fantasy where good overcomes evil and justice prevails. Getting lost in a story and leaving behind the everyday world and its baggage of reality let the young reader, temporarily at least, become thin, graceful, athletic, loved, curly haired or straight haired, and, of course, a little older—a whole new person, a participant in another world.

- Modern fantasy can entertain through its humor. The suspension of reality, a trait of fantasy, gives authors the leeway to produce humorous situations. Two universal sources of humor are exaggeration and the ridiculous or far-fetched; both of these characteristics are often found in modern fantasies. In Carlo Collodi's *The Adventures of Pinocchio,* the reader is delighted by the ever-longer nose as Pinocchio tells more lies, and in E. B. White's *Charlotte's Web,* the reader is amused and touched by the phrase *"SOME PIG"* found in Charlotte's spider web to describe Wilbur.
- Children can be inspired by an author's treatment of serious themes in modern fantasies. Within the context of fantastic situations or characters, strong messages in modern fantasy seem less somber or didactic than if presented within the framework of serious realistic fiction. The theme of love conquering evil can sometimes be accepted more readily in a fantasy than in realistic fiction, where such a message can appear overly sentimental or preachy.

Evaluation and Selection of Modern Fantasy

The usual standards for fine fiction must also be met by authors of modern fantasy. Believable and well-rounded characters who develop and change, well-constructed plots, well-described settings with internal consistency, a style appropriate to the story, and worthy themes are elements to be expected in all fiction. In addition, the following criteria apply specifically to modern fantasy.

- Authors of modern fantasy have the challenge of persuading readers to open themselves up to believing that which is contrary to reality, strange, whimsical, or magical, yet that has an internal logic and consistency. Sometimes authors will accomplish this through beginning the story in a familiar and ordinary setting with typical, contemporary, human beings as characters. A transition is then made from this realistic world to the fantasy world. An example of this literary device is found in C. S. Lewis's *The Lion, the Witch, and the Wardrobe,* in which the children in the story enter a wardrobe in an old house only to discover that the back of the wardrobe leads into the land of Narnia, a fantasy world with unusual characters. Other fantasies begin in the imagined world, but manage, through well-described settings and consistent well-rounded characters, to make this new reality believable. Either way, the plot, characters, and setting must be so well developed that the child reader is able to suspend disbelief and to accept the impossible as real.
- For a modern fantasy to be truly imaginative, the author must provide a unique setting. In some stories, the setting may move beyond the realistic in both time (moving to the past, future, or holding time still) and place (imagined worlds); in other stories only one of these elements (place or time) will go beyond reality. Moreover, a modern fantasy author's creation must be original, a fresh vision from a mind with special insight.

Excellent Modern Fantasy to Read Aloud

(Books for each level vary in difficulty and should be selected with the students' literary backgrounds in mind.)

Primary Level   Ages 5–8

Andersen, Hans Christian. *The Ugly Duckling*. Illustrated by Alan Marks. Translated by Anthea Bell. Picture Book Studio, 1989.

Grahame, Kenneth. *The Wind in the Willows*. Illustrated by E. H. Shepard. Scribner's, 1908.

Heide, Florence Parry. *The Shrinking of Treehorn*. Illustrated by Edward Gorey. Holiday, 1971.

Jansson, Tove. *Finn Family Moomintroll*. Waulk, 1965.

Lawson, Robert. *Rabbit Hill*. Viking, 1944.

Le Guin, Ursula K. *Catwings*. Illustrated by S. D. Schindler. Orchard, 1988.

Milne, A. A. *Winnie-the-Pooh*. Illustrated by Ernest Shepard. Dutton, 1926.

Nöstlinger, Christine. *Konrad*. Watts, 1977.

Williams, Jay. *The Practical Princess and Other Liberating Fairy Tales*. Parents' Magazine, 1978.

Yolen, Jane. *Sleeping Ugly*. Illustrated by Diane Stanley. Coward, 1981.

Intermediate Level   Ages 8–11

Andersen, Hans Christian. *The Nightingale*. Illustrated by Nancy E. Burkert. Translated by Eva Le Gallienne. Harper, 1965.

Babbitt, Natalie. *Tuck Everlasting*. Farrar, 1975.

Brittain, Bill. *The Wish Giver*. Illustrated by Andrew Glass. Harper, 1983.

Dahl, Roald. *James and the Giant Peach*. Illustrated by Nancy E. Burkert. Knopf, 1961.

Jacques, Brian. *Redwall*. Illustrated by Gary Chalk. Philomel, 1987.

Kendall, Carol. *The Gammage Cup*. Illustrated by Erik Blegvad. Harcourt, 1959.

King-Smith, Dick. *Babe: The Gallant Pig*. Illustrated by Mary Rayner. Crown, 1985.

Lewis, Clive Staples. *The Lion, the Witch, and the Wardrobe*. Illustrated by Pauline Baynes. Macmillan, 1950.

O'Brien, Robert C. *Mrs. Frisby and the Rats of NIMH*. Illustrated by Zena Bernstein. Atheneum, 1971.

Peck, Richard. *The Ghost Belonged to Me*. Viking, 1975.

Waugh, Sylvia. *The Mennyms*. Morrow, 1994.

White, E. B. *Charlotte's Web*. Illustrated by Garth Williams. Harper, 1952.

Advanced Level   Ages 11–14

Alexander, Lloyd. *The Book of Three*. Holt, 1964.

Arkin, Alan. *The Lemming Condition*. Illustrated by Joan Sandin. Harper, 1976.

Conrad, Pam. *Stonewords: A Ghost Story*. Harper, 1990.

Cooper, Susan. *Over Sea, Under Stone*. Illustrated by Margery Gill. Harcourt, 1965.

Engdahl, Sylvia. *Enchantress from the Stars*. Atheneum, 1970.

Hamilton, Virginia. *The Magical Adventures of Pretty Pearl*. Harper, 1983.

Le Guin, Ursula K. *A Wizard of Earthsea*. Parnassus, 1968.

Lowry, Lois. *The Giver*. Houghton, 1993.

McCaffrey, Anne. *Dragonsong*. Atheneum, 1976.

Park, Ruth. *Playing Beatie Bow*. Atheneum, 1982.

Historical Overview of Modern Fantasy

Imaginative literature did not appear until the eighteenth century. These stories were not intended primarily for children but were political satires that came to be enjoyed by children as well as adults. *Gulliver's Travels* (1726) by the Irish clergyman, Jonathan Swift, is the most noteworthy of such books. In this adult satire ridiculing the antics of the English court and its politics, the hero Gulliver travels to strange, imaginary places, one inhabited by six-inch Lilliputians, another inhabited by giants. These imaginary worlds were described in fascinating detail and with sufficient humor to appeal to a child audience.

Charles Kingsley's *The Water Babies* (1863) took a contemporary child and set him in another world. Kingsley's unique tale was marred by heavy didactic passages; however, it paved the way for the classic masterpiece of fantasy. In England in 1865, Charles Lutwidge Dodgson, an Oxford don who used the pen name Lewis Carroll, wrote *Alice's Adventures in Wonderland* that tells of a fantastic journey Alice takes to an imaginary world. The total absence of didacticism—replaced by humor and fantasy—resulted in the book's lasting appeal and world fame. Other fantasies that originated in England shortly after the appearance of *Alice* include *The Light Princess* (1867) and *At the Back of the North Wind* (1871) by George MacDonald, *The Magic Fishbone* (1868) by Charles Dickens, and *Just-So Stories* (1902) by Rudyard Kipling. This early development of modern fantasy for children in England was unrivaled by any other country and established the standard for the genre worldwide.

Modern fantasy has continued to thrive in England during the twentieth century. Noteworthy contributions from England include Beatrix Potter's *The Tale of Peter Rabbit* (1902), *The Wind in the Willows* (1908) by Kenneth Grahame, *The Velveteen Rabbit* (1922) by Margery Bianco, *Winnie-the-Pooh* (1926) by A. A. Milne, *Mary Poppins* (1934) by Pamela Travers, *The Hobbit* (1937) by J. R. R. Tolkien, *The Lion, the Witch, and the Wardrobe* (1950) by C. S. Lewis, *The Borrowers* (1953) by Mary Norton, and *The Children of Green Knowe* (1955) by Lucy M. Boston.

Early books of modern fantasy from other countries include *The Adventures of Pinocchio* (1881) by Carlo Collodi (Carlo Lorenzini) from Italy and *Journey to the Center of the Earth* (1864), *Twenty Thousand Leagues Under the Sea* (1869), and *Around the World in Eighty Days* (1872) by the Frenchman, Jules Verne. Verne's works are considered the first science fiction novels and remain popular today with adults and children. Later in France, Jean de Brunhoff wrote an internationally popular series of animal fantasies about a family of elephants. The first of these was *The Story of Babar* (1937).

Some works of fantasy from Scandinavia also deserve recognition. Hans Christian Andersen, a Dane, published many modern folktales, stories very similar in literary elements to the traditional tales. However, Hans Christian Andersen was the originator of most of his tales, for which his own life experiences were the inspiration. "The Ugly Duckling," "The Emperor's New Clothes," and "Thumbelina" are three of the most loved of Andersen's stories. His tales were published in 1835 and are considered the first modern fairy tales. In 1907, Selma Lagerlöf produced *The Wonderful Adventures of Nils*, a geographic sortie around Sweden by a small boy-turned-elf who flies on the back of a goose. Almost half a century later, another Swedish author, Astrid Lindgren, produced *Pippi Longstocking* (1945). Pippi, a lively, rambunctious, and very strong heroine who throws caution to the wind, lives an independent life of escapades envied by children the world over. From Finland in 1964 came *The Tales of Moominvalley* by Tove Jansson, the first of a series of books focusing on small imaginary creatures called Moomins, who hibernate in the winter and frolic and adventure in the summer.

The United States also produced some outstanding early modern fantasies, beginning with *The Wonderful Wizard of Oz* (1900) by L. Frank Baum, which is considered to be the first classic U.S. modern fantasy for children. Other landmark U.S. works of modern fantasy are the memorable animal fantasy *Rabbit Hill* (1944) by Robert Lawson; *Charlotte's Web* (1952) by E. B. White, the best-known and best-loved U.S. work of fantasy; *The Book of Three* (1964), the first of the Prydain Chronicles by Lloyd Alexander; and *A Wrinkle in Time* (1962) by Madeleine L'Engle, considered a modern classic in science fiction for children.

Science fiction, the most recent development in modern fantasy, is said to owe its birth to the nineteenth-century novels of Jules Verne (*Journey to the Center of the Earth*, 1864, and *20,000 Leagues Under the Sea*, 1869) and H. G. Wells (*Time Machine*, 1895). Adults, not children, were the primary audience for these novels, however. It was not until the twentieth century that science fiction began to be aimed specifically at children. The *Tom Swift* series by Victor Appleton (collective pseudonym for the Stratemeyer Syndicate), although stilted in style and devoid of female characters, can be considered the first science fiction for children, appearing in 1910 (*Tom Swift and His Airship*) with additional titles of the series appearing in rapid succession.

Then, in 1963, Madeleine L'Engle's novel, *A Wrinkle in Time*, was awarded the Newbery Medal. From this point forward, many science fiction novels for children began to appear. In the late 1960s and 1970s, the theme of mind control was popular. John Christopher's Tripods trilogy and William Sleator's *House of Stairs* are good examples. Space travel and future worlds were frequent science fiction topics in the 1980s. Examples are H. M. Hoover's *The Shepherd Moon* (1984) and Pamela Sargent's *Earthseed* (1987). Milestones in the development of modern fantasy are highlighted in Table 6-1.

Modern fantasy is a genre for children that remains strong, especially in Great Britain and other English-speaking countries. Although personified toys and animals remain popular and prevalent in children's books, growth in this genre appears to be in stories in which fantasy is interwoven into other genres—science fiction, science fantasy, and historical fantasy. This blurring of traditional genres can also be seen in the interesting mixture of the logic of realistic mystery stories with supernatural elements, as in the popular mysteries of John Bellairs and Mary Downing Hahn. Modern fantasy is likely to continue to be a popular genre with children and authors, both in the more traditional modes as well as in the current direction of hybrid stories. The rich literary works of modern fantasy will continue to challenge children's imaginations and enhance their lives.

TABLE 6–1   Milestones in the Development of Modern Fantasy

Date	Event	Significance
1726	*Gulliver's Travels* by Jonathan Swift (England)	An adult novel prototype for children's fantasy adventures
1835	*Fairy Tales* by Hans Christian Andersen (Denmark)	First modern folktales
1864	*Journey to the Center of the Earth* by Jules Verne (France)	First science fiction novel (for adults)
1865	*Alice's Adventures in Wonderland* by Lewis Carroll (England)	First children's masterpiece of modern fantasy
1881	*The Adventures of Pinocchio* by Carlo Collodi (Italy)	Early classic personified toy story
1900	*The Wonderful Wizard of Oz* by L. Frank Baum (U.S.A.)	First classic U.S. modern fantasy for children
1908	*Wind in the Willows* by Kenneth Grahame (England)	Early classic animal fantasy
1910	*Tom Swift and His Airship* by Victor Appleton (U.S.A.)	First science fiction novel for children
1926	*Winnie-the-Pooh* by A. A. Milne (England)	Early classic personified toy story
1926	*Amazing Stories*, science fiction magazine, begun	Formal recognition of science fiction as a literary genre
1937	*The Hobbit* by J. R. R. Tolkien (England)	Early quest adventure with a cult following
1945	*Pippi Longstocking*, by Astrid Lindgren (Sweden)	Classic unusual-character fantasy
1947	*Rocket Ship Galileo* by Robert Heinlein (U.S.A.)	Science fiction novel for children about a journey to the moon
1950	*The Lion, the Witch, and the Wardrobe* by C. S. Lewis (England)	Early classic quest adventure for children; first of the Narnia series
1952	*Charlotte's Web* by E.B. White (U.S.A.)	Classic U.S. animal fantasy
1953	*The Borrowers* by Mary Norton (England)	Classic little people fantasy
1962	*A Wrinkle in Time* by Madeleine L'Engle (U.S.A.)	Classic U.S. science fiction novel for children
1964	*The Book of Three* by Lloyd Alexander (U.S.A.)	First book in classic quest series, the Prydain Chronicles
1967	*The White Mountains* by John Christopher (England)	First book in classic science fiction series, the Tripod series
1985	*The Hero and the Crown* by Robin McKinley (U.S.A.)	A quest fantasy with a female protagonist; won the Newbery Medal
1987	*Redwall* by Brian Jacques (England)	First book of exciting animal fantasy series
1993	*The Giver* by Lois Lowry (U.S.A.)	Popular futuristic fiction novel; Newbery Medal winner

Types of Modern Fantasy

In modern fantasy, as in other genres, the distinctions between types are not totally discrete. The types of modern fantasy listed below are a starting point for thinking about the variety of fantastic stories, motifs, themes, and characters that gifted authors have created. Additional categories could be listed, and you will find that some stories may fit appropriately in more than one category. For example, *The Root Cellar* by Janet Lunn has been discussed as an historical fantasy due to its authentic historical setting, but its inclusion of spirits from the past also categorizes this story under the label of Supernatural Events and Mystery Fantasy.

Modern Folktales

Modern folktales, or *literary folktales* as they are also called, are tales told in a form similar to that of a traditional tale with the accompanying typical elements: little character description, strong conflict, fast-moving plot with a sudden resolution, vague setting, and, in some cases, magical elements. But these modern tales have a known, identifiable author who has written the tale in this form. In other words, the tales do not spring from the cultural heritage of a group of people through the oral tradition but rather from the mind of one creator. However, this distinction does not matter at all to children, and they delight in these tales as much as they do in the old folktales.

The tales of Hans Christian Andersen are the earliest and best known of these modern tales. More recently, others, including Jane Yolen (*The Girl Who Loved the Wind* and *The Emperor and the Kite*) and Robin McKinley (*Beauty*) have become known for their modern folktales.

Modern folktales are an important counterbalance to traditional tales. As was noted in Chapter 5, many of the traditional tales present an old-fashioned, stereotypic view of male and female characters. Many of the modern tales present more assertive female characters who are clearly in charge of their own destinies. Examples include *The Practical Princess* and *Petronella* by Jay Williams.

Animal Fantasy

Animal fantasies are stories in which animals behave as human beings in that they experience emotions, talk, and have the ability to reason. Usually the animals in fantasies will (and should) retain many of their animal characteristics. In the best of these animal fantasies, the author will interpret the animal for the reader in human terms without destroying the animal's integrity or removing it from membership in the animal world. For example, a rabbit character in an animal fantasy will retain her natural abilities of speed and camouflage to outsmart her adversaries. At the same time, however, the author will permit the reader to see human qualities such as caring and love by having the rabbit carry on conversations with family members.

Animal fantasies can be read to very young children who enjoy the exciting but reassuring adventures in books. Examples are *The Tale of Peter Rabbit* by Beatrix Potter and *Runaway Bunny* by Margaret Wise Brown. Books for children in primary grades include somewhat longer stories, often in a humorous vein, such as Beverly Cleary's mouse stories, *Runaway Ralph* and *The Mouse and the Motorcycle*; Deborah and James Howe's humor-filled books, *Bunnicula,* and *Howliday Inn;* and Michael Bond's *Paddington Bear.* Enjoyable animal fantasies for the young reader often have easy-to-follow, episodic plots.

Fully developed novels of modern fantasy with subtle and complex characterizations and a progressive plot are especially suitable for reading aloud to children in their elementary school years. *Charlotte's Web* by E. B. White remains a favorite read-aloud book; *The Cricket in Times Square* by George Selden is also popular. A beautifully written book with richly drawn characterizations is *The Wind in the Willows* by Kenneth Grahame, who describes in artistic detail the life of animal friends along a riverbank. This book features an episodic plot structure but has a challenging style appropriate to intermediate-grade students. *The Lemming Condition* by Alan Arkin, a short novel with a progressive plot, is also appreciated by intermediate-grade students who enjoy discussing the risks of being a follower. Although the interest in animal fantasy peaks at age 8 or 9, many children and adults continue to enjoy well-written animal fantasies. In animal fantasies for older readers, an entire animal world is usually created with all of the relationships among its members that might be found in a novel portraying human behavior. *Mrs. Frisby and the Rats of NIMH* by Robert C. O'Brien, *Watership Down* by Richard Adams, and *Redwall* by Brian Jacques are examples of complex, fully developed animal fantasy novels for readers in fifth grade through adulthood.

Personified Toys and Objects

Stories in which admired objects or beloved toys are brought to life and believed in by a child or adult character in the story are the focus of this type of fantasy. An early classic example of these stories is *The Adventures of Pinocchio* by Carlo Collodi (Carlo Lorenzini), in which a mischievous puppet comes to life, runs away from his master, and has many exciting and dangerous escapades. In these stories, the object, toy, or doll becomes real to the human protagonist and, in turn, becomes real to the child reader (who has perhaps also imagined a toy coming to life). An example of a personified machine story can be found in Virginia Lee Burton's *Mike Mulligan and His Steam Shovel,* in which a close relationship exists between a steam shovel and his human operator. The responsibilities of parenthood are often assumed by the child protagonist who must nourish, protect, assist, and extricate the toy-come-to-life from various predicaments. This motif of responsibility is found in the recent story, *The Castle in the Attic,* by Elizabeth Winthrop. Personified toy and object stories appeal to children from preschool through upper-elementary grades.

Unusual Characters and Strange Situations

Some authors approach fantasy through reality, but take it beyond reality to the ridiculous or exaggerated. Generally those stories can be best described as having unusual characters or strange situations. Without doubt, *Alice's Adventures in Wonderland* by Lewis Carroll is the best known of this type of modern fantasy. More recent writers of modern fantasy have described such strange situations as a boy sailing across the Atlantic Ocean in a giant peach (*James and the Giant Peach* by Roald Dahl) and such unusual characters as a perfect, factory-made boy (*Konrad* by Christine Nöstlinger).

Modern fantasy appeals to readers of all ages. Florence Parry Heide's *The Shrinking of Treehorn* portrays a young boy who, one day, starts to shrink, but no one notices. The story is fascinating for middle-school students. Jean Merrill's *The Pushcart War* also is enjoyed by somewhat older students. This preposterous and amusing satire tells of a struggle between pushcart peddlers and truck drivers in New York City. In *Tuck Everlasting*, Natalie Babbitt explores the theme of immortality and its consequences, a provocative theme for children and adults.

Worlds of Little People

Some authors have written about worlds inhabited by miniature people who have developed a culture of their own in this world or who live in another world. In Mary Norton's *The Borrowers*, small people live in our world but take our discards to create their own world. It is, of course, eventually human beings who threaten their existence and cause them to seek safety elsewhere. Carol Kendall has described the Land Between the Mountains where the Minnipins live in *The Gammage Cup*, a story about little people struggling against the pressure to conform. A recent version of *Gulliver's Travels* can be found in *The Minpins* (1991) by Roald Dahl. Stories of little people delight children because they can identify with the indignities foisted upon little and powerless people and because the "big people" in these stories are invariably outdone by the more ingenious little people.

Supernatural Events and Mystery Fantasy

Many recent fantasies evoke the supernatural. One common form of supernatural literature found in children's books is the ghost story. Some ghost stories intrigue younger children, especially when the topic is treated humorously and reassuringly, as in *The Ghosts of Hungryhouse Lane* by Sam McBratney. In this story, children find out about three ghosts in their new home but unearth ways to satisfy the needs of the ghosts. Ghosts in children's books can be fearful threats or helpful protectors. The ghost of the priest in John Bellairs's *The Curse of the Blue Figurine* is the very soul of evil, whereas *Whispers from the Dead* by Joan Lowery Nixon features a ghost who prevents a murder.

Many authors write mysteries for children in which the solution is partially supernatural or arrived at with supernatural assistance. One author who is well known for many such fantasy mysteries is John Bellairs.

Witchcraft and other aspects of the occult sometimes play a role in children's fantasy books. Witches are often portrayed as the broom-wielding villains of both traditional and modern tales, such as the Russian stories of Baba Yaga. Halloween and its traditions are also frequently presented in children's stories. Witchcraft has recently been the focus of criticism because of an upsurge of sects whose members refer to themselves as witches. Also, some parents' groups have attempted to censor children's books featuring witches, Halloween, and other elements of the occult. Chapter 1 has a full discussion on censorship and schools' responsibilities in these situations. An interesting realistic novel, *Save Halloween!* by Stephanie S. Tolan (1993), presents the issue of banning Halloween in a school as seen through the eyes of a teenage girl from a preacher's family.

Historical Fantasy

Historical fantasy, sometimes called *time-warp fantasy,* is a story in which a present-day protagonist goes back in time to a different era. A contrast between the two time periods is shown to readers through the modern-day protagonist's discoveries of and astonishment with earlier customs. Historical fantasies must fully and authentically develop the historical setting, both time and place, just as in a book of historical fiction. Canadian Janet Lunn in *The Root Cellar* succeeds in producing this type of mixed-genre story. Kevin Major's *Blood Red Ochre,* an historical fantasy, alternates chapters between the present and past time. Belinda Hurmence in *A Girl Called Boy* and David Wiseman in *Jeremy Visick* also present interesting historical fantasies that will appeal to intermediate-grade students and older.

Quest Stories

Quest stories are adventure stories with a search motif. The quest may be pursuit for a lofty purpose, such as justice or love, or for a rich reward, such as a magical power or a hidden treasure. Quest stories that are serious in tone are sometimes called *high fantasy.* Many of these novels are set in medieval times and are reminiscent of the search for the holy grail. In these high fantasies, an imaginary otherworld fully portrays the society, its history, family trees, geographic location, population, religion, customs, and traditions. The conflict in these tales usually centers on the struggle between good and evil. Often characters are drawn from myth and legend. The protagonist is engaged in a struggle against external forces of evil and internal temptations of weakness. Thus, the quest usually represents a journey of self-discovery and personal growth for the protagonist, in addition to the search for the reward. *The Hobbit,* written by J. R. R. Tolkien in 1937, is one of the first of these high fantasies; it retains a cult of followers even today. Because of the greater complexity of these novels, their allure is for children in fifth grade and higher, including adults, of course. Good examples are C. S. Lewis's series starting with *The Lion, the Witch, and the Wardrobe,* Lloyd Alexander's series starting with *The Book of Three,* and Susan Cooper's series starting with *Over Sea, Under Stone.*

Science Fiction and Science Fantasy

Science fiction is a form of imaginative literature that provides a picture of something that could happen based on real scientific facts and principles. Therefore, story elements in science fiction must have the appearance of scientific plausibility or technical possibility. Hypotheses about the future of humankind and the universe presented in science fiction appear plausible and possible to the reader because settings and events are built on extensions of known technologies and scientific concepts.

In novels of science fiction such topics as mind control, genetic engineering, space technologies and travel, visitors from outer space, and future political and social systems all seem possible to the readers. These novels especially fascinate many young people because they feature characters who must learn to adjust to change and to become new persons, two aspects of living that adolescents also experience. In addition, science fiction stories may portray the world, or one very much like it, that young people will one day inhabit; for this reason, science fiction has sometimes been called *futuristic fiction*.

Science fiction is a type of fiction that you will want to know about because of its growing popularity among children and adolescents. If you are reluctant to read science fiction, or have never read it, you may want to start with some books by William Sleator (*Interstellar Pig; The Duplicate*), H. M. Hoover (*Children of Morrow; This Time of Darkness*), or John Christopher (*The White Mountains*).

The distinction between science fiction and science fantasy is not clearly defined or universally accepted. *Science fantasy* is a popularized type of science fiction in which a scientific explanation, though not necessarily plausible, is offered for imaginative leaps into the unknown. Science fantasy presents a world that often mixes elements of mythology and traditional fantasy with scientific or technological concepts, resulting in a setting that has some scientific basis but never has existed or never could exist. A worthy example is *Collidescope* by Grace Chetwin. These novels, which usually appear in series, appeal to adolescents and young adults and, like many series, are sometimes formulaic and of mixed quality.

The *science fantasy gamebook* is a trend in science fantasy that appeals to a wide age range of young people, particularly boys, from age 8 to upper teen years. Gamebooks involve fantasies developed in numbered segments so that the reader may choose from alternatives in determining the outcome of the story. These science fantasies, book adaptations of the computer games programmed for participation and decision making, usually contain violent scenes and characters. Marshall (1988) points out that because of the violent nature of these gamebooks some adults tend to be concerned, whereas others "see the popularity of the books as a change from the well-documented findings that interest in reading declines fast, in teenage boys" (p. 44). For example, see *Talisman of Death* by Steve Jackson and Ian Livingstone.

Modern fantasy has appeal for persons with nonliteral minds, for people who go beyond the letter of a story to its spirit. Children, with their lively imaginations, are especially open to reading fantasies. The many types and topics within this genre—animal fantasies, little people stories, tales of personified toys, mystery fantasies, stories of unusual people and situations, quest tales, science fiction, and so on—offer children a breadth of inspiring and delightful entertainment. Since the level of conceptual difficulty varies considerably in this genre, modern fantasy offers many excellent stories for children, from the youngest to the oldest.

References

Elleman, B. (1987). Current trends in literature for children. *Library Trends, 35* (3): 413–426.

Lee, D. (1989). Silverly. In D. Booth (Ed.), *'Til all the stars have fallen.* Illus. by K. M. Denton. New York: Viking.

Marshall, M. R. (1988). *An introduction to the world of children's books* (2nd ed.). Brookfield, VT: Gower.

Notable Authors of Modern Fantasy

Lloyd Alexander, author of high fantasy based on Welsh mythology, noted for the Prydain series with *The Book of Three* and four other titles.

Hans Christian Andersen, nineteenth-century Dane, father of modern folktales. Author of such literary folktales as *The Ugly Duckling* and *The Little Mermaid.*

Natalie Babbitt, author of *Tuck Everlasting,* a book about immortality.

John Bellairs, author of mysteries containing supernatural elements. The *House with a Clock in Its Walls* is the first book of a trilogy.

John Christopher, British science fiction author who created the Tripods series set in the twenty-first century. *The White Mountains; City of Gold and Lead.*

Carlo Collodi, (pseud. for Carlo Lorenzini), Italian author who created the classic puppet tale, *The Adventures of Pinocchio,* in 1880.

Susan Cooper, author of high fantasies based on Arthurian legends. *Over Sea, Under Stone* is the first in a five-book series.

Roald Dahl, British author of many popular fantasies known for humor and exaggerated characters. *James and the Giant Peach; Charlie and the Chocolate Factory.*

Peter Dickinson, British author of modern fantasies including science fiction novels. *Eva; Heartsease.*

Sylvia Engdahl, science fiction author who created a future society in *Enchantress from the Stars.*

Kenneth Grahame, author of *The Wind in The Willows,* the British classic about animal life on a riverbank.

Mary Downing Hahn, author of popular mystery novels. *Wait Till Helen Comes: a Ghost Story; The Doll in the Garden: A Ghost Story.*

Virginia Hamilton, African-American author of stories with supernatural elements. *Sweet Whispers, Brother Rush; Justice and Her Brothers.*

H. M. Hoover, young adult science fiction writer who presents future worlds. *Children of Morrow.*

Monica Hughes, Canadian science fiction author whose themes often center on the role of free will. *The Keeper of the Isis Light.*

Mollie Hunter, Scottish author of modern fantasies. *The Mermaid Summer; A Stranger Came Ashore.*

Brian Jacques, author of the Redwall Abbey animal fantasy series. *The Bellmaker; Mossflower.*

Dick King-Smith, British author of animal fantasies. *Pigs Might Fly; Babe: The Gallant Pig.*

Robert Lawson, author of animal fantasies and biographical fiction. *Rabbit Hill; Ben and Me.*

Ursula Le Guin, creator of the Earthsea trilogy, a quest adventure series set in a world of magic. *The Wizard of Earthsea; The Tombs of Atuan.*

Madeleine L'Engle, noted for a popular science fiction milestone book, *A Wrinkle in Time,* and its sequels.

C. S. Lewis, British creator of the Chronicles of Narnia, a series of adventure quest stories. *The Lion, the Witch, and the Wardrobe.*

Astrid Lindgren, Swedish creator of the irrepressible Pippi of *Pippi Longstocking.*

Lois Lowry, winner of the 1994 Newbery Medal for *The Giver,* a popular work of science fiction.

Margaret Mahy, New Zealand author of fantasies with supernatural elements. *The Visitors; The Changeover.*

Anne McCaffrey, science fiction author who writes of Menolly, a young woman with special musical talents in *Dragonsong.*

Robin McKinley, author of quest tales with a female protagonist and a mythical setting. *The Blue Sword; The Hero and the Crown.*

A. A. Milne, British author of the whimsical classic, *Winnie-the-Pooh.*

Mary Norton, British author of *The Borrowers,* a series of little people stories.

George Selden, author of humorous animal fantasies. *The Cricket in Times Square; The Genie of Sutton Place.*

William Sleator, author of science fiction novels. *Interstellar Pig; The Duplicate.*

J. R. R. Tolkien, British author of *The Hobbit,* well-known fantasy set in Middle-earth, an imaginary world.

E. B. White, author of the classic animal fantasy, *Charlotte's Web.*

Betty Ren Wright, author of popular mystery novels. *The Dollhouse Murders; The Ghost Witch.*

Patricia Wrightson, Australian author of modern fantasies drawing on Aboriginal myths. *The Nargun and the Stars.*

Recommended Modern Fantasy Books

Ages refer to approximate interest levels. YA = young adult readers.

Modern Folktales

Andersen, Hans Christian. *The Fir Tree.* Illustrated by Nancy E. Burkert. Harper, 1970. Ages 8–11. (Andersen's *Fairy Tales* were first published in 1835.)

———. *The Nightingale.* Illustrated by Nancy E. Burkert. Translated by Eva Le Gallienne. Harper, 1965. Ages 7–10.

———. *The Snow Queen.* Illustrated by Susan Jeffers. Dial, 1982. Ages 8–10.

———. *The Steadfast Tin Soldier.* Illustrated by Marcia Brown. Translated by M. R. James. Scribner's, 1953. Ages 7–10.

———. *Thumbelina.* Illustrated by Lisbeth Zwerger. Translated by Anthea Bell. Picture Book Studio, 1985. Ages 6–9.

———. *The Ugly Duckling.* Illustrated by Alan Marks. Translated by Anthea Bell. Picture Book Studio, 1989. Ages 6–9.

Brooke, William J. *Teller of Tales.* Illustrated by Eric Beddows. HarperCollins, 1994. Ages 10–YA.

———. *A Telling of the Tales: Five Stories.* Illustrated by Richard Egielski. Harper, 1991. Ages 10–YA.

Isaacs, Anne. *Swamp Angel.* Illustrated by Paul Zelinsky. Dutton, 1994. Ages 7–10.

MacDonald, George. *At the Back of the North Wind.* Illustrated by George and Doris Hauman. Macmillan, 1871.

McKinley, Robin. *Beauty: A Retelling of the Beauty and the Beast.* Harper, 1978. Ages 10–YA.

Nolen, Jerdine. *Harvey Potter's Balloon Farm.* Illustrated by Mark Buehner. Lothrop, 1994. Ages 5–9.

Thurber, James. *The Great Quillow.* Harcourt, 1994. Ages 8–10.

Willard, Nancy. *Beauty and the Beast.* Illustrated by Barry Moser. Harcourt, 1992. Ages 8–11.

Williams, Jay. *Petronella.* Parents' Magazine, 1973. Ages 6–9.

———. *The Practical Princess and Other Liberating Fairy Tales.* Parents' Magazine, 1978. Ages 6–9.

Yolen, Jane. *The Emperor and the Kite.* Illustrated by Ed Young. World, 1967. Ages 7–10.

———. *The Girl Who Loved the Wind.* Illustrated by Ed Young. Crowell, 1972. Ages 7–10.

———. *Sleeping Ugly.* Illustrated by Diane Stanley. Coward, 1981. Ages 7–10.

Animal Fantasies

Adams, Richard. *Watership Down.* Macmillan, 1974. Ages 12–YA.

Alexander, Lloyd. *The Cat Who Wished to Be a Man.* Dutton, 1978. Ages 9–12.

Arkin, Alan. *The Lemming Condition.* Illustrated by Joan Sandin. Harper, 1976. Ages 10–YA.

Atwater, Richard and Florence. *Mr. Popper's Penguins.* Illustrated by Robert Lawson. Little, 1938. Ages 8–11.

Cleary, Beverly. *The Mouse and the Motorcycle.* Illustrated by Louis Darling. Morrow, 1965. Ages 7–11.

———. *Ralph S. Mouse.* Illustrated by Paul O. Zelinsky. Morrow, 1982. Ages 7–11.

———. *Runaway Ralph.* Illustrated by Louis Darling. Morrow, 1970. Ages 7–11.

Grahame, Kenneth. *The Wind in the Willows.* Illustrated by E. H. Shepard. Scribner's, 1908. Ages 8–12.

Howe, Deborah, and James Howe. *Bunnicula; A Rabbit-Tale of Mystery.* Illustrated by Alan Daniel. Atheneum, 1979. Ages 8–11.

Howe, James. *Howliday Inn.* Atheneum, 1982. Ages 8–11.

Jacques, Brian. *Redwall.* Illustrated by Gary Chalk. Philomel, 1987 Ages 11–YA. Others in the Redwall series are *Mossflower, Mattimeo, Mariel of Redwall, Salamandastron, The Bellmaker.*

Jarrell, Randall. *The Bat-Poet.* Illustrated by Maurice Sendak. Macmillan, 1967. Ages 8–12.

King-Smith, Dick. *Ace: The Very Important Pig.* Illustrated by Lynette Hemmant. Crown, 1990. Ages 7–11.

———. *Babe: The Gallant Pig.* Illustrated by Mary Rayner. Crown, 1985. Ages 7–11.

———. *Harry's Mad.* Illustrated by Jill Bennett. Crown, 1987. Ages 7–9.

———. *Pigs Might Fly.* Illustrated by Mary Rayner. Viking, 1982. Ages 8–11.

———. *Three Terrible Trins.* Illustrated by Mark Teague. Crown, 1994. Ages 8–11.

Kipling, Rudyard. *Just So Stories.* Doubleday, 1902. Ages 6–10.

Lawson, Robert. *Rabbit Hill.* Viking, 1944. Ages 8–11.

Le Guin, Ursula K. *Catwings.* Illustrated by S. D. Schindler. Orchard, 1988. Ages 7–10.

———. *Catwings Return.* Illustrated by S. D. Schindler. Orchard, 1989. Ages 7–10.

Lisle, Janet Taylor. *Forest.* Watts, 1993. Ages 9–12.

Marshall, James. *Rats on the Range and Other Stories.* Dial, 1993. Ages 5–8.

———. *Rats on the Roof and Other Stories.* Dial, 1991. Ages 6–9.

Michels, Tilde. *Rabbit Spring.* Harcourt, 1988. Ages 7–10.

Selden, George. *Chester Cricket's New House.* Illustrated by Garth Williams. Farrar, 1960. Ages 8–11.

———. *The Cricket in Times Square.* Illustrated by Garth Williams. Farrar, 1960. Ages 8–11.

———. *Harry Cat's Pet Puppy.* Illustrated by Garth Williams. Farrar, 1974. Ages 8–11.

———. *Tucker's Countryside.* Illustrated by Garth Williams. Farrar, 1969. Ages 8–11.

Sharp, Margery. *The Rescuers.* Illustrated by Garth Williams. Little, Brown, 1959. Ages 7–10.

Steig, William. *Abel's Island.* Farrar, 1976. Ages 8–11.

———. *Dominic.* Farrar, 1972. Ages 811.

Stevenson, James. *The Mud Flat Olympics.* Greenwillow, 1994. Ages 7–9.

White, E. B. *Charlotte's Web.* Illustrated by Garth Williams. Harper, 1952. Ages 8–11.

———. *Stuart Little.* Illustrated by Garth Williams. Harper, 1945. Ages 8–11.

Personified Toys and Objects

Bailey, Carolyn. *Miss Hickory.* Illustrated by Ruth Gannett. Viking, 1968. Ages 8–11.

Bond, Michael. *A Bear Called Paddington.* Illustrated by Peggy Fortnum. Houghton, 1960. Ages 7–10.

Cassedy, Sylvia. *Behind the Attic Wall.* Crowell, 1983. Ages 10–13.

Clarke, Pauline. *The Return of the Twelves.* Illustrated by Bernarda Bryson. Coward, 1964. Ages 9–12.

Collodi, Carlo. (pseud. for Carlo Lorenzini). *The Adventures of Pinocchio.* Illustrated by Attilio Mussino. Translated by Carol Della Chiesa. Macmillan, 1881.

Fleming, Ian. *Chitty-Chitty-Bang-Bang: The Magical Car.* Illustrated by John Burningham. Random, 1964. Ages 8–11.

Godden, Rumer. *The Dolls' House.* Illustrated by Tasha Tudor. Viking, 1960. Ages 7–10.

———. *Impunity Jane.* Illustrated by Adrienne Adams. Viking, 1954. Ages 7–10.

Milne, A. A. *The House at Pooh Corner.* Illustrated by Ernest Shepard. Dutton, 1928. Ages 6–9.

———. *Winnie-the-Pooh.* Illustrated by Ernest Shepard. Dutton, 1926. Ages 6–9.

O'Connell, Jean. *The Dollhouse Caper.* Illustrated by Erik Blegvad. Crowell, 1976. Ages 8–11.

Waugh, Sylvia. *The Mennyms.* Morrow, 1994. Ages 8–12.

Winthrop, Elizabeth. *The Battle for the Castle.* Holiday, 1993. Ages 8–12.

———. *The Castle in the Attic.* Holiday, 1985. Ages 8–12.

Unusual Characters and Strange Situations

Aiken, Joan. *Is Underground.* Delacorte, 1993. Ages 10–13.

Babbitt, Natalie. *The Search for Delicious.* Farrar, 1969. Ages 9–12.

———. *Tuck Everlasting.* Farrar, 1975. Ages 10–YA.

Barrie, Sir James. *Peter Pan.* Illustrated by Nora Unwin. Scribner's, 1911. Ages 8–11.

Baum, L. Frank. *The Wonderful Wizard of Oz.* Illustrated by W. W. Denslow. Morrow, 1900. Ages 8–11.

Boston, Lucy M. *The Children of Green Knowe.* Illustrated by Peter Boston. Harcourt, 1955. Ages 8–11. The first of a series of fantasies set in an English mansion. Others include *Enemy at Green Knowe, River at Green Knowe, Stranger at Green Knowe,* and *Treasure of Green Knowe.*

Butterworth, Oliver. *The Enormous Egg.* Illustrated by Louis Darling. Little, Brown, 1956. Ages 8–11.

Carroll, Lewis. (pseud. for Charles Lutwidge Dodgson). *Alice's Adventures in Wonderland* and *Through the Looking Glass*. First published in 1865. A recent edition is illustrated by Anthony Browne. Knopf, 1988. Ages 9–13.

Dahl, Roald. *Charlie and the Chocolate Factory*. Illustrated by Joseph Schindelman. Knopf, 1964. Ages 8–11.

———. *James and the Giant Peach*. Illustrated by Nancy E. Burkert. Knopf, 1961. Ages 8–11.

———. *Matilda*. Illustrated by Quentin Blake. Viking, 1988. Ages 8–11.

Farmer, Nancy. *The Ear, the Eye and the Arm*. Orchard, 1994. Ages 11–14. Humorous.

Garner, Alan. *Elidor*. Walck, 1967. Ages 9–12.

———. *The Owl Service*. Walck, 1968. Ages 9–12.

Heide, Florence Parry. *The Shrinking of Treehorn*. Illustrated by Edward Gorey. Holiday, 1971. Ages 7–10. See also *Treehorn Times Three* (Dell, 1992).

Hunter, Mollie. *The Kelpie's Pearls*. Illustrated by Joseph Cellini. Funk & Wagnalls, 1966. Ages 9–12.

———. *The Mermaid Summer*. Harper, 1988. Ages 9–YA.

———. *A Stranger Came Ashore*. Harper, 1975. Ages 11–YA.

Jones, Diana Wynne. *Castle in the Air*. Greenwillow, 1991. Ages 11–YA.

———. *Howl's Moving Castle*. Greenwillow, 1986. Ages 11–YA.

———. *The Lives of Christopher Chant*. Greenwillow, 1988. Ages 10–13.

Juster, Norton. *The Phantom Tollbooth*. Illustrated by Jules Feiffer. Random, 1961. Ages 10–13.

Langton, Jane. *The Astonishing Stereoscope*. Illustrated by Erik Blegvad. Harper, 1971. Ages 9–12.

———. *The Fledgling*. Harper, 1980. Ages 10–YA.

Lindgren, Astrid. *Pippi Longstocking*. Translated by Florence Lamborn. Viking, 1950. Ages 8–11.

Mahy, Margaret. *Blood-and-Thunder Adventure on Hurricane Peak*. McElderry, 1989. Ages 9–12.

———. *The Pirates' Mixed-up Voyage: Dark Doings in the Thousand Islands*. Dial, 1993. Ages 8–12.

———. *Tick Tock Tales: Twelve Stories to Read Aloud Around the Clock*. Illustrated by Wendy Smith. McElderry, 1994. Ages 5–8.

Mayne, William. *Earthfasts*. Dutton, 1967. Ages 12–YA.

Merrill, Jean. *The Pushcart War*. Illustrated by Ronni Solbert. Harper, 1964. Ages 10–YA.

Nöstlinger, Christine. *Konrad*. Watts, 1977. Ages 8–11.

Sandburg, Carl. *Rootabaga Stories*. Illustrated by Maud and Miska Petersham. Harcourt, 1922. Ages 8–12.

Travers, P. L. *Mary Poppins*. Illustrated by Mary Shepard. Harcourt, 1934. Ages 9–12.

Worlds of Little People

Dahl, Roald. *The Minpins*. Illustrated by Patrick Benson. Viking, 1991. Ages 5–8.

Jansson, Tove. *Finn Family Moomintroll*. Walck, 1965. Ages 7–10.

Kendall, Carol. *The Firelings*. Atheneum, 1982. Ages 9–12.

———. *The Gammage Cup*. Illustrated by Erik Blegvad. Harcourt, 1959. Ages 8–12.

———. *The Whisper of Glocken*. Harcourt, 1965. Ages 8–12.

Norton, Mary. *The Borrowers*. Illustrated by Beth and Joe Krush. Harcourt, 1953. Ages 8–11. This is the first of a series of little people fantasies, including *The Borrowers Afield, The Borrowers Afloat, The Borrowers Aloft,* and *The Borrowers Avenged.*

Supernatural Events and Mystery Fantasy

Alcock, Vivien. *The Stonewalkers*. Delacorte, 1983. Ages 10–13.

———. *Singer to the Sea God*. Delacorte, 1993. Ages 12–YA.

Alexander, Lloyd. *The Wizard in the Tree*. Illustrated by Laszlo Kubinyi. Dutton, 1975. Ages 10–YA.

Babbitt, Natalie. *The Devil's Other Storybook*. Farrar, 1987. Ages 8–11.

———. *Knee-Knock Rise*. Farrar, 1970. Ages 9–12.

Bauer, Marion Dane. *A Taste of Smoke*. Houghton, 1993. Ages 8–12.

Bellairs, John. *The Curse of the Blue Figurine*. Dial, 1983. Ages 10–YA.

———. *A Figure in the Shadows*. Illustrated by Mercer Mayer. Dial, 1975. Ages 10–13.

Bond, Nancy. *Another Shore*. McElderry, 1988. Ages 11–YA.

———. *A String in the Harp*. Atheneum, 1976. Ages 11–14.

Brittain, Bill. *Dr. Dredd's Wagon of Wonders*. Illustrated by Andrew Glass. Harper, 1987. Ages 8–12.

———. *The Wish Giver*. Illustrated by Andrew

Glass. Harper, 1983. Ages 9–12.

Charbonneau, Eileen. *The Ghosts of Stony Clove.* Orchard, 1988. Ages 10–YA.

Cohen, Daniel. *Young Ghosts.* Dutton, 1994. Ages 9–12.

Conrad, Pam. *Stonewords: A Ghost Story.* Harper, 1990. Ages 8–12.

Cooper, Susan. *The Boggart.* McElderry, 1993. Ages 9–12.

Duncan, Lois. *Locked in Time.* Little, Brown, 1985. Ages 9–12.

———. *Third Eye.* Little, Brown, 1984. Ages 9–12.

Fleischman, Sid. *The Midnight Horse.* Illustrated by Peter Sís. Greenwillow, 1990. Ages 8–11.

Garfield, Leon. *The Empty Sleeve.* Delacorte, 1988. Ages 10–YA.

Hahn, Mary Downing. *The Doll in the Garden: A Ghost Story.* Clarion, 1989. Ages 9–12.

———. *Wait Till Helen Comes: A Ghost Story.* Clarion, 1986. Ages 9–13.

Hamilton, Virginia. *Justice and Her Brothers.* Greenwillow, 1978. Ages 12–YA.

———. *The Magical Adventures of Pretty Pearl.* Harper, 1983. Ages 11–YA.

———. *Sweet Whispers, Brother Rush.* Philomel, 1982. Ages 11–YA.

Hilgartner, Beth. *The Feast of the Trickster.* Houghton, 1991. Ages 12–YA.

Key, Alexander. *Escape to Witch Mountain.* Illustrated by Leon B. Wisdom, Jr. Westminster, 1968. Ages 10–12.

Klause, Annette Curtis. *The Silver Kiss.* Delacorte, 1990. Ages 12–YA.

Lively, Penelope. *The Ghost of Thomas Kempe.* Illustrated by Anthony Maitland. Dutton, 1973. Ages 9–12.

Mayne, William. *Hob and the Goblins.* Illustrated by Norman Messenger. Dorling Kindersley, 1994. Ages 7–10.

Mahy, Margaret. *Dangerous Spaces.* Viking, 1991. Ages 8–12.

———. *The Haunting.* Atheneum, 1983. Ages 10–YA.

———. *Memory.* McElderry, 1988. Ages 11–YA.

———. *The Tricksters.* McElderry, 1987. Ages 11–YA.

McBratney, Sam. *The Ghosts of Hungryhouse Lane.* Holt, 1989. Ages 7–10.

McKissack, Patricia C. *The Dark-Thirty: Southern Tales of the Supernatural.* Illustrated by Brian Pinkney. Knopf, 1992. Ages 9–12.

Nixon, Joan Lowery. *Whispers from the Dead.* Delacorte, 1989. Ages 10–YA.

Norton, Andre. *Lavender-green Magic.* Illustrated by Judith Gwyn Brown. Crowell, 1974. Ages 11–YA.

Pearce, Philippa. *Tom's Midnight Garden.* Lippincott, 1959. Ages 9–12.

Peck, Richard. *The Ghost Belonged to Me.* Viking, 1975. Ages 11–YA.

Pierce, Meredith Ann. *The Darkangel.* Little, Brown, 1982. Ages 11–14.

———. *A Gathering of Gargoyles.* Little, 1984. Ages 11–14.

———. *The Pearl of the Soul of the World.* Little, 1990. Ages 11–14.

Price, Susan. *The Ghost Drum: A Cat's Tale.* Farrar, 1987. Ages 8–12.

———. *Ghost Song.* Farrar, 1992. Ages 9–12.

Sherman, Josepha. *Child of Faerie, Child of Earth.* Walker, 1992. Ages 11–YA.

Smith, Sherwood. *Wren's Quest.* Harcourt, 1993. Ages 10–YA.

Westall, Robert. *Ghost Abbey.* Scholastic, 1989. Ages 10–YA.

Wright, Betty Ren. *The Dollhouse Murders.* Holiday, 1983. Ages 9–12.

———. *The Ghost Witch.* Illustrated by Ellen Eagle. Holiday, 1993. Ages 8–11.

Wrightson, Patricia. *Balyet.* McElderry, 1989. Ages 10–13.

———. *A Little Fear.* Atheneum, 1983. Ages 10–13.

———. *The Nargun and the Stars.* Atheneum, 1974. Ages 10–13.

Historical Fantasy

Alphin, Elaine M. *The Ghost Cadet.* Holt, 1991. Ages 9–12.

Bellairs, John. *The Ghost in the Mirrors.* Dial, 1993. Ages 10–14.

Chetwin, Grace. *Friends in Time.* Bradbury, 1992. Ages 9–12.

Cresswell, Helen. *Moondial.* Macmillan, 1987. Ages 10–YA.

Dickinson, Peter. *A Bone from a Dry Sea.* Delacorte, 1993. Ages 12–YA.

Griffin, Peni R. *Switching Well.* McElderry, 1993. Ages 10–14.

Hurmence, Belinda. *A Girl Called Boy.* Clarion, 1982. Ages 10–13.

Lawson, Robert. *Ben and Me*. Little, 1939. Ages 9–12.

Lunn, Janet. *The Root Cellar*. Scribner's, 1983. Ages 10–13.

Major, Kevin. *Blood Red Ochre*. Doubleday, 1989. Ages 12–YA.

Park, Ruth. *Playing Beatie Bow*. Atheneum, 1982. Ages 10–YA.

Slepian, Jan. *Back to Before*. Philomel, 1993. Ages 10–13.

Voigt, Cynthia. *Building Blocks*. Atheneum, 1984. Ages 9–11.

Wiseman, David. *Jeremy Visick*. Houghton, 1981. Ages 10–13.

Yolen, Jane. *The Devil's Arithmetic*. Viking 1988. Ages 10–13.

Quest Stories

Alexander, Lloyd. *The Beggar Queen*. Dutton, 1984. Ages 10–13.

———. *The Book of Three*. Holt, 1964. Ages 10–YA. The first of the Prydain Chronicles, a series of five quest fantasies, including *The Black Cauldron, The Castle of Llyr, The High King,* and *Taran Wanderer*.

———. *The First Two Lives of Lukas-Kasha*. Dutton, 1978. Ages 9–12.

———. *The Kestrel*. Dutton, 1982. Ages 10–YA.

———. *The Marvelous Misadventures of Sebastian*. Dutton, 1970. Ages 9–12.

———. *The Remarkable Journey of Prince Jen*. Dutton, 1991. Ages 10–YA.

———. *Westmark*. Dutton, 1981. Ages 10–YA.

Cooper, Susan. *Over Sea, Under Stone*. Illustrated by Margery Gill. Harcourt, 1965. Ages 10–YA. This is the first of a five-book Arthurian quest series, including *The Dark Is Rising, Greenwitch, The Grey King,* and *Silver on the Tree*.

Dickinson, Peter. *Merlin Dreams*. Illustrated by Alan Lee. Delacorte, 1988. Ages 10–YA.

Kelleher, Victor. *The Red King*. Dial, 1990. Ages 12–YA.

Le Guin, Ursula K. *A Wizard of Earthsea*. Parnassus, 1968. Ages 11–YA. Other books in this series are *The Farthest Shore, The Tombs of Atuan,* and *Tehanu: The Last Book of Earthsea*.

Lewis, Clive Staples. *The Lion, the Witch, and the Wardrobe*. Illustrated by Pauline Baynes. Macmillan, 1950. Ages 9–12. The first in a series of quest fantasies, including *The Horse and His Boy, The Last Battle, The Magician's Nephew, Prince Caspian, The Silver Chair,* and *The Voyage of the Dawn Treader*.

McGowen, Tom. *The Magical Fellowship*. Dutton, 1991. Ages 9–13.

———. *The Magician's Apprentice*. Dutton, 1987. Ages 9–13.

———. *A Trial of Magic*. Dutton, 1992. Ages 9–13.

McKillip, Patricia A. *The Riddle-Master of Hed*. Atheneum, 1976. Ages 10–13.

McKinley, Robin. *The Blue Sword*. Greenwillow, 1982. Ages 11–YA.

———. *The Hero and the Crown*. Greenwillow, 1984. Ages 11–YA.

———. *A Knot in the Grain and Other Stories*. Morrow, 1994. Ages 12–YA.

Snyder, Zilpha Keatley. *Below the Root*. Illustrated by Alton Raible. Atheneum, 1975. Ages 10–YA.

Sutcliff, Rosemary. *The Light Beyond the Forest*. Dutton, 1980. Ages 12–YA.

———. *The Road to Camlaan: The Death of King Arthur*. Dutton, 1982. Ages 12–YA.

Tolkien, J. R. R. *The Hobbit*. Houghton, 1938. Ages 10–YA.

Wrede, Patricia C. *Calling on Dragons*. Harcourt, 1993. Ages 9–12.

———. *Dealing with Dragons*. Harcourt, 1990. Ages 9–12.

———. *Searching for Dragons*. Harcourt, 1991. Ages 9–12.

Yolen, Jane. *Dragon's Blood*. Delacorte, 1982. Ages 10–13.

Science Fiction and Science Fantasy

Alcock, Vivien. *The Monster Garden*. Delacorte, 1988. Ages 10–14.

Brittain, Bill. *Shape-Changer*. HarperCollins, 1994. Ages 8–12.

Cameron, Eleanor. *The Wonderful Flight to the Mushroom Planet*. Illustrated by Robert Henneberger. Little, 1954. Ages 7–9.

Chetwin, Grace. *Collidescope*. Bradbury, 1990. Ages 11–YA.

Christopher, John. *Beyond the Burning Lands*. Macmillan, 1971. Ages 11–YA.

———. *The City of Gold and Lead*. Macmillan, 1967. Ages 11–YA.

————. *The Guardians.* Macmillan, 1970. Ages 11–YA.

————. *The Pool of Fire.* Macmillan, 1968. Ages 11–YA.

————. *The White Mountains.* Macmillan, 1967. Ages 11–YA.

Conly, Jane Leslie. *Racso and Rats of NIMH.* Illustrated by Leonard Lubin. Harper, 1986. Ages 9–12.

————. *R.T., Margaret, and the Rats of NIMH.* HarperCollins, 1990. Ages 9–12.

Dickinson, Peter. *Eva.* Delacorte, 1989. Ages 12–YA.

————. *Heartsease.* Little, 1969. Ages 10–YA.

————. *The Weathermonger.* Little, 1969. Ages 10–YA.

du Bois, William Pène. *The Twenty-One Balloons.* Viking, 1947. Ages 8–12.

Engdahl, Sylvia. *Enchantress from the Stars.* Atheneum, 1970. Ages 11–YA.

————. *The Far Side of Evil.* Atheneum, 1971. Ages 11–YA.

————. *This Star Shall Abide.* Atheneum, 1972. Ages 11–YA.

Hoover, H. M. *Away Is a Strange Place to Be.* Dutton, 1989. Ages 9–12.

————. *Children of Morrow.* Four Winds, 1973. Ages 11–YA.

————. *Orvis.* Viking, 1987. Ages 10–YA.

————. *The Shepherd Moon.* Viking, 1984. Ages 11–YA.

————. *This Time of Darkness.* Viking, 1980. Ages 11–YA.

Hughes, Monica. *The Crystal Drop.* Simon and Schuster, 1993. Ages 10–YA.

————. *Devil on My Back.* Atheneum, 1985. Ages 9–YA.

————. *The Dream Catcher.* Atheneum, 1987. Ages 9–YA.

————. *The Keeper of the Isis Light.* Atheneum, 1984. Ages 9–YA.

Key, Alexander. *The Forgotten Door.* Westminster, 1965. Ages 10–12.

Klause, Annette Curtis. *Alien Secrets.* Delacorte, 1993. Ages 10–13.

Lawrence, Louis. *The Patchwork People.* Clarion, 1994. Ages 11–YA.

L'Engle, Madeleine. *Many Waters.* Farrar, 1986. Ages 11–YA.

————. *A Swiftly Tilting Planet.* Farrar, 1978. Ages 11–YA.

————. *A Wind in the Door.* Farrar, 1973. Ages 11–YA.

————. *A Wrinkle in Time.* Farrar, 1962. Ages 11–YA.

Lowry, Lois. *The Giver.* Houghton, 1993. Ages 11–YA.

McCaffrey, Anne. *Dragonsinger.* Atheneum, 1977. Ages 11–YA.

————. *Dragonsong.* Atheneum, 1976. Ages 11–YA.

O'Brien, Robert C. *Mrs. Frisby and the Rats of NIMH.* Illustrated by Zena Bernstein. Atheneum, 1971. Ages 9–12. (See sequels by Conly.)

————. *Z for Zachariah.* Atheneum, 1975. Ages 11–YA.

Paton Walsh, Jill. *The Green Book.* Illustrated by Lloyd Bloom. Farrar, 1982. Ages 8–11.

Pinkwater, Daniel Manus. *Alan Mendelson, the Boy from Mars.* Dutton, 1979. Ages 10–YA.

————. *Fat Men from Space.* Dodd, 1977. Ages 8–11.

Rubinstein, Gillian. *Beyond the Labyrinth.* Watts, 1990. Ages 12–YA.

Sargent, Pamela. *Earthseed.* Harper, 1983. Ages 12–YA.

Service, Pamela F. *Stinker from Space.* Scribner's, 1988. Ages 9–12.

Sleator, William. *The Boy Who Reversed Himself.* Dutton, 1986. Ages 10–YA.

————. *The Duplicate.* Dutton, 1988. Ages 11–YA.

————. *House of Stairs.* Dutton, 1974. Ages 11–YA.

————. *Interstellar Pig.* Dutton, 1984. Ages 11–YA.

Stevermer, Caroline. *River Rats.* Harcourt, 1992. Ages 12–YA.

Chapter 7

Realistic Fiction

Stories that could happen - real people, animals
Factual

Listening to grownups quarreling,
standing in the hall against the
wall with my little brother, blown
like leaves against the wall by their
voices, my head like a pingpong ball
between the paddles of their anger:
I knew what it meant
to tremble like a leaf.

Cold with their wrath, I heard
the claws of the rain
pounce. Floods
poured through the city,
skies clapped over me,
and I was shaken, shaken
like a mouse
between their jaws.

—Ruth Whitman

Children's lives are sometimes sad and harsh. Realistic stories of today openly address these situations as well as the happy and humorous situations of life. Children of all ages appreciate stories about people who seem like themselves or who are involved in familiar activities. These realistic fiction stories have appealed to children for many years and continue to do so today.

Definition and Description

Realism in literature is a complex, multifaceted concept. Marshall (1988) considers various components of realism in literature, including factual, situational, emotional, and social. *Factual realism* is provided by the description of actual persons, places, and events in a book. When this occurs, the facts need to be recorded accurately. For example, usually in historical fiction and occasionally in realistic fiction, the names and locations of actual places are included in the story, with accurate and complete descriptions. *Situational realism* is provided by a situation that is not only possible but also quite likely, often in an identifiable location with characters of an identifiable age and social class, making the whole treatment believable. The survival story, which often hinges on a life-threatening situation, is an example of a story built on situational realism. *Emotional realism* is provided by the appearance of believable feelings and relationships among characters. Rite-of-passage or growing-up stories often employ emotional realism. *Social realism* is provided by an honest portrayal of society and its conditions of the moment, including both healthy and adverse conditions. In almost all good realistic stories several of these components of realism occur, with varying degrees of emphasis.

Realistic fiction refers to stories that could indeed happen to people and animals; that is, it is within the realm of possibility that such events could occur or could have occurred. The protagonists of these stories are fictitious characters created by the author, but their actions and reactions are quite like those of real people or real animals. Sometimes events in these stories are exaggerated or outlandish—hardly probable but definitely possible. These stories, too, fit under the definition of realistic fiction.

Contemporary realism is a term used to describe stories that take place in the present time and portray attitudes and mores of the present culture. Unlike realistic books of several decades ago that depicted only happy families and were never controversial, today's contemporary realism often focuses on current societal issues, such as alcoholism, racism, poverty, and homelessness. These contemporary books still tell of the happy, funny times in children's lives, but they also include the harsh, unpleasant times that are, sadly, also a part of many children's lives. Child abuse and neglect, peer problems, the effects of divorce on children, drug abuse, physical and mental disabilities, disillusionment, and alienation from the mainstream of society are all topics included in the contemporary realistic novel.

Authors of contemporary realistic fiction set their stories in the present or recent past. But, in time, features of these stories, such as dialogue and allusions to popular culture, customs, and dress become dated and the stories are therefore no longer contemporary, though they may still be realistic. Older stories that obviously no longer describe today's world, though they may have once been contemporary realistic fiction, are now simply realistic fiction.

The *problem novel* is a contemporary realistic story in which the conflict overwhelms the plot and characterization. The problem novel is written to provide the author with a soapbox from which to lecture or as a vehicle for capitalizing on whichever societal problem is currently at the forefront. Generally, these stories lack depth, have weak character development and consist of little, if any, plot. Problem novels remind us that it is always necessary to read literature carefully in order to find books worthy of children's attention.

Topics for realistic fiction are drawn from all aspects of life—stories of humorous, everyday escapades of well-adjusted children in happy families and stories about animals portrayed realistically. Other topics common to realistic fiction are mysteries, adventures, romances, sports stories, and stories about children from other countries.

Values of Realistic Fiction for Children

Although a work of realistic fiction may be several times older than the child who reads it, it can still have great value for the child. Some books never lose their appeal and their ability to speak to the reader. The following values can be found in both older and contemporary realistic fiction:

- Realistic fiction stories are easy for children to relate to and enjoy. Children can often see their own lives, or lives much like their own, in these stories. Intermediate-grade children report on reading interest surveys that realistic fiction is their favorite genre. Of course, some children may prefer other categories, but realistic fiction does hold high appeal for many children at all grade levels.
- Realistic fiction permits children to see how other people live their lives and solve their problems. By understanding human relationships through stories, children can come to a better understanding of themselves and their own relationships with others.
- Some works of realistic fiction depict the lives of children from other cultures. In reading these stories, children can discover different ways people live their daily lives as well as explore the many commonalities in basic human values across cultures.
- Children can become aware that not all children's lives are as warm and secure as theirs may be and, as a result, they may become more sensitive to problems being experienced by other children.

Evaluation and Selection of Realistic Fiction

The criteria for evaluating realistic fiction are the same as for any work of fiction. Well-developed characters who manifest change as a result of significant life events, a well-structured plot with sufficient conflict and suspense to hold the reader's interest, a time and place suitable to the storyline, and a worthy theme are basic literary elements expected of any work of fiction, including works of realistic fiction.

- Some realistic novels portray adverse and discouraging social situations, such as homelessness and poverty; yet it remains important that the stories permit some cause for optimism. Children need to trust that this world can be a good place in which to live and that it can be made a better place through the efforts of individuals. Children also need to understand that problems can be overcome or ameliorated.

- Themes in realistic stories often convey moral values, such as the rewards of kindness and generosity to others. However, these moral values must spring naturally from the story, as a by-product of the story itself, not as the main reason for the story. At times, adults write books for children with the sole intent of teaching or preaching, and the story itself is nothing more than a thin disguise for a heavy-handed moral lesson. This may have been acceptable in the past, but today a good story must be the *raison d'être* of a children's book. The moral must not overwhelm the story, but may be its logical outcome.

- A novel of realistic fiction must be believable, even though all aspects may not be probable. Some adults and children have a tendency to criticize a story when the events are not probable. An example is *Homecoming* by Cynthia Voigt in which four children manage to travel hundreds of miles alone with almost no money to reach their grandmother's house. Admittedly this storyline may be improbable, yet it is certainly possible. Other aspects of *Homecoming* are more ordinarily realistic; for example, the characters are well developed and the relationships among the characters seem quite ordinary. Sometimes an author goes closer to the edge of the believable range in order to produce a more exciting, suspense-filled story. In fiction, the story is of paramount importance and the sacrifice of some probability for a good story does not usually interfere with the pleasure children gain from a book. It may instead help to create interest in the story.

- Much of the controversy involving children's books centers on topics often found in realistic fiction novels, such as premarital sex, pregnancy, homosexuality, and the use of profanity. Many of these controversial books fall within the type of realism labeled "Adolescent Issues" in the recommended list at the end of this chapter. Chapter 1 provides a full discussion of issues surrounding controversial books and censorship.

- An aspect of writing style greatly appreciated by students is humor. Although humor may be found in stories of any genre, it is more often found in realistic fiction. Humorous stories feature characters caught up in silly situations or involved in funny escapades. Children often are amused by the incongruities presented in these predicament stories. Other humorous stories draw on word play for their humor. *Bagthorpes Unlimited* by Helen Cresswell is a good example of a humorous story. In the list of recommended books at the end of this chapter, humorous books are indicated.

Selection of realistic fiction for classroom and library collections and for read-alouds should be balanced among the different types of realistic stories. A steady diet of humorous read-alouds does not offer the richness of experience to children that they deserve, nor does it provide for the varied reading interests of a group of children. It is extremely important to read aloud some books with females as main

Excellent Realistic Fiction to Read Aloud

(Books for each level vary in difficulty and should be selected with the students' literary backgrounds in mind.)

Primary Level   Ages 5–8

Cameron, Ann. *More Stories Julian Tells.* Illustrated by Ann Strugnell. Knopf, 1986.
Cleary, Beverly. *Ramona and Her Father.* Illustrated by Alan Tiegreen. Morrow, 1977. Humorous.
Estes, Eleanor. *The Moffats.* Illustrated by Louis Slobodkin. Harcourt, 1941.
Gardiner, John Reynolds. *Stone Fox.* Illustrated by Marcia Sewall. Crowell, 1980.
Henry, Marguerite. *Misty of Chincoteague.* Illustrated by Wesley Dennis. Rand, 1947.
Leverich, Kathleen. *Best Enemies.* Illustrated by Susan Lamb. Greenwillow, 1989.
Lindgren, Astrid. *The Six Bullerby Children.* Methuen, 1961.
Lord, Bette Bao. *In the Year of the Boar and Jackie Robinson.* Illustrated by Marc Simont. Harper, 1984.
Mathis, Sharon Bell. *The Hundred Penny Box.* Illustrated by Leo and Diane Dillon. Viking, 1975.

Intermediate Level   Ages 8–11

Cleary, Beverly. *Dear Mr. Henshaw.* Illustrated by Paul Zelinsky. Morrow, 1983.
Cresswell, Helen. *Ordinary Jack.* Macmillan, 1977. Humorous.
George, Jean Craighead. *My Side of the Mountain.* Dutton, 1959.
Lowry, Lois. *Anastasia at Your Service.* Illustrated by Diane de Groat. Houghton, 1982. Humorous.
Paterson, Katherine. *The Great Gilly Hopkins.* Crowell, 1978.
Myers, Walter Dean. *Scorpions.* Harper, 1988.
Naidoo, Beverley. *Journey to Jo'burg: A South African Story.* Illustrated by Eric Velasquez. Lippincott, 1986.
Naylor, Phyllis Reynolds. *Shiloh.* Atheneum, 1991.
Park, Barbara. *Skinnybones.* Knopf, 1982. Humorous.
Raskin, Ellen. *The Westing Game.* Dutton, 1978.
Slote, Alfred. *The Trading Game.* Lippincott, 1990.
Wallace, Barbara Brooks. *Peppermints in the Parlor.* Atheneum, 1980.

Advanced Level   Ages 11–14

Avi. *Nothing But the Truth.* Orchard, 1991.
Bauer, Joan. *Squashed.* Delacorte, 1992. Humorous.
Bridgers, Sue Ellen. *Notes for Another Life.* Knopf, 1981. Mental illness.
Byars, Betsy. *The Summer of the Swans.* Illustrated by Ted CoConis. Viking, 1970.
Cole, Brock. *The Goats.* Farrar, 1987.
Doherty, Berlie. *Dear Nobody.* Orchard, 1992. Teen pregnancy and its consequences.
George, Jean Craighead. *Julie.* HarperCollins, 1994.
Oneal, Zibby. *The Language of Goldfish.* Viking, 1980. Mental illness.
Paulsen, Gary. *Hatchet.* Bradbury, 1987.
Rawls, Wilson. *Summer of the Monkeys.* Doubleday, 1976. Humorous.
Staples, Suzanne Fisher. *Shabanu: Daughter of the Wind.* Knopf, 1989.

characters, and some with males as main characters, and some with minorities as main characters. The Edgar Allan Poe Award for Juvenile Mystery Novels can be helpful to you in selecting good mysteries—the most popular story type of all for intermediate-grade students. This award was established in 1961 by the Mystery Writers of America and is awarded annually in order to honor U.S. authors of mysteries for children. The list of winners is included in Appendix A.

Historical Overview of Realistic Fiction

The earliest realistic stories were didactic ones intending to teach morality and manners to young readers. The characters of the children's stories of the 1700s were usually wooden, lifeless boys and girls whose lives were spent in good works; however, in England during this period two significant events affecting the future of children's literature occurred. *Robinson Crusoe* by Daniel Defoe was published in 1719 for adults, but became a popular book among children. This forerunner of the adventure-survival story for children recounts the tale of a shipwrecked sailor who struggles against the forces of nature for survival on an island. Then in 1744, John Newbery began to publish, expressly for a child audience, books of realistic fiction intended to entertain as well as to educate. These two events laid the groundwork for establishing children's literature as a separate branch of literature. Milestones in the development of realistic fiction are highlighted in Table 7-1.

The first type of realistic fiction for children that avoided the heavy didactic persuasion was the adventure story. Imitators of *Robinson Crusoe* were many, including the very popular *Swiss Family Robinson* by Johann Wyss of Switzerland in 1812. Later adventure stories of renown from England were *Treasure Island* (1883) and *Kidnapped* (1886) by Robert Louis Stevenson; and from the United States, *The Adventures of Tom Sawyer* (1876) and *The Adventures of Huckleberry Finn* (1884) by Samuel Clemens (pseud. Mark Twain). Clemens, through the addition of sharp humor and characters who were in many ways less than admirable but nonetheless appealing, took an important step toward increased realism in stories.

Realistic family stories also came on the scene during the 1800s with *Little Women* (1868) by Louisa May Alcott and *Five Little Peppers and How They Grew* (1880), the first of a series of family stories by Harriet M. Lothrop (pseud. Margaret Sydney). The family story remains a favorite in the twentieth century, with early memorable books such as *Rebecca of Sunnybrook Farm* (1903) by Kate Douglas Wiggins, the series *Anne of Green Gables* (1908) by Canadian Lucy Maud Montgomery, and *The Secret Garden* (1909) by Frances Hodgson Burnett. Since Anne of *Anne of Green Gables* and Mary of *The Secret Garden* were orphans, the books by Burnett and Montgomery can be considered precursors of adjustment stories that addressed the special needs of children with problems. Stories of happy and often large families continued to thrive and peaked in the 1940s and 1950s in family story series about the Moffat family by Eleanor Estes and about the Melendy family by Elizabeth Enright. Beverly Cleary's *Henry Huggins* stories and Sydney Taylor's *All-of-a-Kind*

TABLE 7–1   Milestones in the Development of Realistic Fiction

Date	Event	Significance
1719	*Robinson Crusoe* by Daniel Defoe (England)	Early survival/adventure on a desert island; many imitators
1812	*Swiss Family Robinson* by Johann Wyss (Switzerland)	Most successful imitation of *Robinson Crusoe*
1865	*Hans Brinker, or The Silver Skates* by Mary Mapes Dodge (U.S.A.)	An early story set in another land (Holland)
1867	*Little Women* by Louisa May Alcott (U.S.A.)	An early family story of great popularity
1876	*The Adventures of Tom Sawyer* by Mark Twain (U.S.A.)	Classic adventure story set along the Mississippi
1877	*Black Beauty* by Anna Sewell (England)	Early horse story deploring inhumane treatment of animals
1880	*Heidi* by Johanna Spyri (Switzerland)	An early international story popular in the United States
1883	*Treasure Island* by Robert Louis Stevenson (England)	Classic adventure story with pirates
1894	*Beautiful Joe* by Margaret M. Saunders (Canada)	Early dog story, popular and sentimental
1908	*Anne of Green Gables* by Lucy Maud Montgomery (Canada)	Early family story about an orphan and her new family
1911	*The Secret Garden* by Frances Hodgson Burnett (U.S.A.)	A classic sentimental novel of two children adjusting to life
1934	*The Good Master* by Kate Seredy (U.S.A.)	Newbery winner set in Hungary
1938	*The Yearling* by Marjorie Kinnan Rawlings (U.S.A.)	Classic animal story and coming–of–age story
1941	*In My Mother's House* by Ann Nolan Clark (U.S.A.)	Early story featuring Native Americans
1945	*Strawberry Girl* by Lois Lenski (U.S.A.)	Regional story set in Florida
1960	*The Incredible Journey* by Sheila Burnford (Canada)	Classic animal survival story with two dogs and a cat
1964	*Harriet the Spy* by Louise Fitzhugh (U.S.A.)	The beginning of the new realism movement
1970	*Are You There, God? It's Me, Margaret* by Judy Blume (U.S.A.)	Early book with frank treatment of sex
1972	*The Planet of Junior Brown* by Virginia Hamilton (U.S.A.)	Realistic novel featuring minority main characters by an African–American author
1986	*A Fine White Dust* by Cynthia Rylant (U.S.A.) and *On My Honor* by Marion Dane Bauer (U.S.A.)	Newbery Honor Books that feature clear moral dilemmas
1990	*Maniac Magee* by Jerry Spinelli (U.S.A.)	Newbery Medal winner presenting the importance of family
1991	*Nothing but the Truth* by Avi (U.S.A.)	Newbery Honor Book, documentary novel

Family series continued this tradition into the 1950s and 1960s. These stories are often referred to as the *happy family* stories, and, compared with much of today's contemporary realism for children, these stories do seem almost lighthearted.

Children from other lands is another theme that can be found in many realistic stories for children. *Hans Brinker, or The Silver Skates* (1865) by Mary Mapes Dodge and *Heidi* (1880) by Johanna Spyri of Switzerland are set in Holland and Switzerland respectively and were two of the earliest *other lands* books. In the United States, Kate Seredy was awarded a Newbery Medal for *The Good Master* (1934), which was set in Hungary. One of the purposes of these early stories was to provide children with an understanding and appreciation of foreign cultures. This theme continues to be seen in recent books published both by U.S. authors and by authors from other countries whose works are later published in the United States.

Realistic animal stories for children began to appear in the latter half of the nineteenth century. *Black Beauty* (1877) by Anna Sewell was a plea for humane treatment of animals and, though quite sentimental in places and completely personified (i.e., the animal is given human qualities), is still appreciated by some readers. *Beautiful Joe* (1894) by Margaret Marshall Saunders of Canada was a sentimental but well-loved dog story from this era. In 1894, Rudyard Kipling's *The Jungle Books*—exciting animal stories set in India—appeared, and these stories continue to hold the attention of readers today. Animal stories showing the maturing of the young human protagonist who assists the animal in the story have remained popular throughout the twentieth century. Canadian authors, such as Sheila Burnford, have been especially recognized for their contributions to this type of story.

Regional stories and stories about children of minority groups began to appear with more frequency in the 1940s. *Strawberry Girl* (1945), by Lois Lenski, featured rural Florida, and was one of the first regional stories. *In My Mother's House* (1941), by Ann Nolan Clark, featured Pueblo Indians; *Bright April* (1946) by Marguerite De Angeli discussed prejudice toward African Americans. However, it was only in the 1960s and 1970s that books written by minorities began to achieve national recognition. *Zeely* (1967) by Virginia Hamilton and *Stevie* (1969) by John Steptoe portray African-American childhood experiences and are two of the earliest and most noteworthy books representing this trend toward increased minority authorship—a trend that continues today.

A new era in realistic fiction for children was ushered in with the publication of *Harriet the Spy* by Louise Fitzhugh in 1964. This story of an unhappy and, at times, unpleasant girl depicted Harriet, her parents, and her classmates as anything but ideal or sympathetic human beings. This trend toward a more graphic and explicitly truthful portrayal of life and the inclusion of many topics previously considered taboo continued to grow in children's books in the 1970s and 1980s and still prevails today. For example, Judy Blume's books are especially frank about sexual development and the emotional reactions to that development. Other controversial topics such as death, divorce, drugs, pacifism, alcoholism, and handicaps, which have always been a part of childhood, became permissible topics in children's books. Parents and other adults began to be shown, at times, as less than perfect, and families began to be portrayed as they truly are, not as one might believe they should be. This newer, franker brand of realism, sometimes referred to as the *new realism*, changed the world of children's books. The rosy cheer and avoidance of unpleasantness of earlier times were replaced by head-on discussion of all topics reflective of contemporary experience. The new realism books may be less light-hearted than their predecessors, but they are also more truthful and more real. At the present time censorship of materials for children, including children's trade books, is rampant, due, in part, to a trend toward more conservative family values.

Types of Realistic Fiction

The subject matter of realistic fiction includes the child's whole world of relationships with self and others: the joys, sorrows, challenges, adjustments, anxieties, and satisfactions of human life. A single realistic book will often treat more than one aspect of human life within its pages; however, each book emphasizes one or the other of these aspects by which it is defined.

Families

Stories about the *nuclear family*—children and their relationships with parents and siblings—are a natural subject of books for children. Childhood for most children is spent in close contact with family members. Family stories for younger children often portray a happy child with loving parents. In these stories the everyday activities are shown—from brushing teeth to cooking dinner. Easy chapter books appealing to newly independent readers can be found within this type. These stories often show the child at play and sometimes explore sibling relationships as well. *Anastasia Krupnik* by Lois Lowry and *Ramona Quimby, Age 8* by Beverly Cleary are good examples of this type of book.

Extended families can also be found in children's books. Aunts, uncles, grandparents, and cousins are important in the real lives of many children and may also be enjoyed in stories written for children. Sometimes a book will tell of a child being raised by a member of the extended family; other times a relative is portrayed as a supportive family member. See *Arthur for the Very First Time* by Patricia MacLachlan and *The Unmaking of Rabbit* by Constance C. Greene.

The *alternative family* of today's world is also depicted in family stories. Not all family stories present the safe and secure world of healthy, intact families. Separation, divorce, single-parent families, and reconstructed families of stepparents and stepchildren are often the backdrop of stories today. For example, see *The Night Daddy* by Maria Gripe, *Mom, the Wolfman and Me* by Norma Klein, and *Something to Count On* by Emily Moore. The difficulty children and adults encounter in adjusting to these new family situations becomes the primary conflict in some stories. Temporary family situations, such as foster care for children, are also described in books about family life. It is important for children to see families other than the typical mother, father, and two children portrayed positively in books.

Peers

In addition to adapting to one's family situation, children must also learn to cope with their peers. Many realistic stories show children struggling for *acceptance by peers* in a group situation. School settings are common in these stories. Examples include *Blubber* by Judy Blume and *Skinnybones* by Barbara Park. Neighborhoods, clubhouses, and summer camps are other common settings. For instance, see *The Goats* by Brock Cole and *Jennifer, Hecate, MacBeth, William McKinley, and Me, Elizabeth* by E. L. Konigsburg.

Developing *close friendships* is another focus of stories about peer relationships. Friends may be of the same sex or the opposite sex, of the same age or a very different age, or of the same culture or a different culture. A concern for friendship and how to be a good friend to someone are shared traits of these stories. *Bridge to Terabithia* by Katherine Paterson and *Onion John* by Joseph Krumgold are good examples of this type of book.

Adolescent Issues

From birth to age 10, most children's lives revolve around family, friends, and classmates, but during the preteen and teen years a shift toward *self-discovery and independence* occurs. During these years, rapid growth and change are seen in the physical, emotional, moral, and intellectual domains of life. These changes are reflected in books for adolescent children aged 10 and older. Sometimes books that deal with the trials and tribulations encountered during growth from childhood to adulthood are called *rite-of-passage* books, such as *A Fine White Dust* by Cynthia Rylant and *The 18th Emergency* by Betsy Byars.

Children become aware of their *growing sexuality* during preteen and teen years as they begin to mature. Some stories for older teens show attraction between members of the opposite sex as well as members of the same sex, with the beginning of sexual activity sometimes depicted in relationships. See *Deliver Us from Evie* by M. E. Kerr and *Then Again, Maybe I Won't* by Judy Blume.

Maturity is achieved through *facing and overcoming fears*. These fears may be of internal forces as well as external dangers. Stories of dealing with fears of emotional and psychological dangers feature protagonists who fear being different, making commitments, and being rejected. Sometimes the characters are excessively fearful of life itself. For example, see *Different Dragons* by Jean Little.

Survival and Adventure

Facing physical danger, an external force, also contributes to the maturing process. Stories of *survival and adventure* are ones in which the young protagonist must rely on will and ingenuity to survive a life-threatening situation. Although most survival stories are set in isolated places, a growing number are being set in cities where gangs, drug wars, and abandonment are indeed life threatening. Adventure stories may be set in any environment where the protagonist has freedom of action. *Hatchet* by Gary Paulsen and *Scorpions* by Walter Dean Myers are examples of this type of book.

Persons with Disabilities

Many children live with disabilities—their own, or those of a family member or friend. These disabilities may be physical, such as scoliosis, emotional, such as depression, mental, such as mental retardation, or multiple disabilities. Yet children do not like to appear different or strange to others. Authors of children's books are becoming increasingly sensitive to the need for positive portrayals of individuals with disabilities. Well-written, honest stories of such individuals in children's books can help other children to gain an understanding of disabilities and to empathize with those who have disabilities. As inclusion of special education students into regular classrooms becomes a more common practice, this trend in children's literature can be an important educational resource. As an example, Jane Leslie Conly's Newbery Medal winner, *Crazy Lady!*, deals with mental retardation.

Cultural Diversity

Part of growing up involves the discovery that not all people are the same; part of becoming a healthy and humane adult is accepting the differences in oneself and in others. Today's children are growing up in a multicultural society in which an understanding and appreciation of cultural and linguistic differences among peoples are essential for societal harmony and cooperation. *Multicultural books* are those in which the main characters are from a racial, language, religious, or ethnic minority such as African Americans, Asian Americans, Hispanic Americans, Jewish Americans, or Native Americans. These books can be instrumental in developing in all children new understanding and appreciation for others as well as providing characters with whom minority children themselves may more readily identify. *Yellow Bird and Me* by Joyce Hansen is a good example. Each year more authors and illustrators from minority groups are recognized for their contributions to children's literature.

As our earth hastens toward becoming an international community, children will be members of an international community. Books set in *foreign countries* may be written by U.S. authors about life in another culture or by a foreign author about his own country. These books can help children develop an awareness of people from other countries and an appreciation for children whose lives differ from their own. Examples include *Buster's World* by Bjarne Reuter and *Shabanu: Daughter of the Wind* by Suzanne Fisher Staples. For further discussion of multicultural and international children's literature of a variety of genres, see Chapter 10.

Popular Topics in Realistic Fiction

Certain types of realistic fiction are consistently sought out by children for their independent reading. Although the quality of some of these books may be mediocre, others are well written and deserve children's attention. What these books provide is "light reading" for the developing reader. By reading many of these stories, children improve their vocabularies, comprehension, and fluency at this stage of their reading development. You can help students by making them aware of the best books available in these categories.

Sports stories often present a story in which a child protagonist struggles to become accepted as a member of a team and does eventually succeed through determination and hard work. *Undercover Tailback* by Matt Christopher is a good example of a sports story. Although traditionally written with boys as the main characters, some sports stories are now available that feature girls as protagonists.

Mysteries, popular with boys and girls, range from simple "whodunits" to complex character stories. The element of suspense is a strong part of the appeal of these stories. Mysteries have won more state children's choice awards than any other type of story, a fact that suggests that mysteries are truly favorites of many children. See *Encyclopedia Brown* by Donald J. Sobol and *The Dollhouse Murders* by Betty Ren Wright.

Animal stories remain an ever-popular genre with children, with dog and horse stories being the most popular. In realistic animal stories, the animal protagonist behaves like an animal and is not personified. Usually a child is also a protagonist in these stories. Examples are *The Black Stallion* by Walter Farley and *The Incredible Journey* by Sheila Burnford.

Series stories have appealed to children for generations. The Nancy Drew series and Hardy Boys series, with their quick-moving, linear plots, ordinary vocabulary, and easy syntax, offer children the satisfaction of reading a chapter book on their own. The young reader knows that a series book, once completed, can be quickly followed by another similar book from the same shelf. The ease of reading and the ease of availability make the series books popular with the newly independent reader. These series books are called *formula fiction* and appear as mysteries, fantasy and science fantasy adventures, and romances. The authors who are hired by a syndicate follow a set structure in developing each book. Three or four plots and a set number of characters are established and implemented in the writing of each book of the series.

Many recent series released in quantity are *romances,* such as *Babysitters Club, Sweet Valley Twins, Wild Fire,* and *Sweet Dreams.* Although no one claims that these books are literature, their success in the market cannot be ignored. Elleman (1987) points out that an especially unfortunate aspect of these series romances is their dependence on stereotyped characters and reflection of white, middle-class, suburban life. The stereotyping of girls in traditional roles in which success is too often defined in terms of popularity among boys is a debilitating message to convey to today's girls.

Stories in the realistic fiction genre present familiar situations with which children can readily identify, often reflect contemporary life, and portray settings not so different from the homes, schools, towns, and cities known to today's children. The protagonists of these stories are frequently testing themselves as they grow toward adulthood; young readers can therefore empathize and gain insight into their own predicaments. Your challenge will be to stay abreast of good realistic stories in order to provide a wide range of books that will both entertain, encourage, and inspire your students.

References

Elleman, B. (1987). Current trends in literature for children. *Library Trends, 35* (3), 413–426.

Marshall, M. R. (1988). *An introduction to the world of children's books* (2nd ed.) Brookfield, VT: Gower.

Whitman, R. (1968). Listening to grownups quarreling. In R. Whitman. *The marriage wig and other stories.* Orlando, FL: Harcourt.

Notable Authors of Realistic Fiction

Judy Blume, author of popular, sometimes controversial, novels focusing on problems of preteens and teens. *Are You There God? It's Me, Margaret; Tales of a Fourth Grade Nothing.*

Sue Ellen Bridgers, author of adolescent novels on family relationships. *All Together Now.*

Bruce Brooks, author who presents problems of adolescence in Newbery Honor books. *What Hearts.*

Sheila Burnford, Canadian author of a popular animal survival story, *The Incredible Journey.*

Betsy Byars, author of stories about children who face and overcome family and personal problems. *The Pinballs; Summer of the Swans.*

Eleanor Cameron, Canadian author whose realistic novels have strong character portrayals. *That Julia Redfern.*

Matt Christopher, author of many sports stories. *Dirt Bike Racer.*

Beverly Cleary, author of humorous family stories about everyday happenings. *Ramona Quimby, Age 8; Dear Mr. Henshaw.*

Vera and Bill Cleaver, authors of Appalachian-based realistic fiction. *Where the Lilies Bloom.*

Paula Fox, recipient of Hans Christian Andersen Medal who writes stories about family relationships. *Blowfish Live in the Sea; One-Eyed Cat.*

Jean Craighead George, author of ecological fiction and survival in nature stories. *Julie of the Wolves; My Side of the Mountain.*

Virginia Hamilton, author of stories about the African-American experience. *Zeely; The Planet of Junior Brown.*

Marguerite Henry, author of many horse stories. *King of the Wind; Misty of Chincoteague.*

S. E. Hinton, author of young adult novels about peers and contemporary problems. *The Outsiders.*

James Houston, Canadian author of survival stories. *Frozen Fire; White Fang.*

Elaine L. Konigsburg, author of sensitive and humorous stories of preteens and teens. *From the Mixed-Up Files of Mrs. Basil E. Frankweiler; (George).*

Jean Little, Canadian author who writes family-adjustment stories. *Mine for Keeps; Mama's Going to Buy You a Mockingbird.*

Sharon Bell Mathis, author of African-American family experiences. *The Hundred Penny Box.*

Nicholasa Mohr, author of adolescent novels set in Puerto Rican neighborhoods of New York City. *Nilda.*

Farley Mowat, author of popular animal stories set in Canada. *Owls In the Family.*

Walter Dean Myers, author of novels about African-American adolescents in city settings. *Scorpions; Fast Sam, Cool Clyde, and Stuff.*

Joan Lowery Nixon, popular author of suspenseful mysteries. *The Other Side of Dark.*

Peggy Parish, author of *Amelia Bedelia* series of humorous books on literalmindedness.

Katherine Paterson, author of stories featuring relationships with peers and family. *The Great Gilly Hopkins; Bridge to Terabithia.*

Gary Paulsen, author of nature survival adventures often set in northern United States or Canada. *Hatchet; Dogsong.*

Ellen Raskin, author of intriguing, complex mysteries. *The Westing Game; Figgs & Phantoms.*

Wilson Rawls, author of poignant animal stories set in the Ozarks. *Where the Red Fern Grows; Summer of the Monkeys.*

Cynthia Rylant, author of introspective realistic stories often set in Appalachia. *Every Living Thing; Missing May.*

Jan Slepian, author of books on overcoming handicaps and adjusting to change. *The Broccoli Tapes; The Alfred Summer.*

Alfred Slote, author of sports stories. *The Trading Game; Hang Tough, Paul Mather.*

Zilpha Keatley Snyder, author of mystery stories. *The Famous Stanley Kidnapping Case; The Egypt Game.*

Donald Sobol, author of a mystery series for transitional readers. *Encyclopedia Brown* series.

Ivan Southall, Australian author of high-risk adventure stories. *Ash Road; To the Wild Sky.*

Colin Thiele, Australian author of adventure stories that often include Aboriginal characters. *Fire in the Stone; Storm Boy.*

Cynthia Voigt, author of stories about the Tillerman family of four children and their friends. *Dicey's Song; A Solitary Blue.*

Laurence Yep, author of novels about the Asian-American experience. *Child of the Owl; Dragonwings.*

Recommended Realistic Fiction Books

Ages refer to approximate interest levels. YA = young adult readers.

Families

Alcock, Vivien. *A Kind of Thief.* Delacorte, 1992. Ages 10–14.

Bauer, Marion Dane. *A Question of Trust.* Scholastic, 1994. Ages 10–13.

Bawden, Nina. *Humbug.* Clarion, 1992. Ages 9–12.

———. *Kept in the Dark.* Lothrop, 1982. Ages 10–YA.

———. *The Outside Child.* Lothrop, 1989. Ages 10–YA.

Brooks, Bruce. *Everywhere.* HarperCollins, 1990. Ages 11–YA.

Burch, Robert. *Queenie Peavy.* Illustrated by Jerry Lazare. Viking, 1966. Ages 10–YA.

Byars, Betsy C. *After the Goat Man.* Illustrated by Ronald Himler. Viking, 1974. Ages 9–12.

———. *Cracker Jackson.* Viking, 1985. Ages 10–14.

———. *The House of Wings.* Illustrated by Daniel Schwartz. Viking, 1972. Ages 8–12.

———. *The Night Swimmers.* Illustrated by Troy Howell. Delacorte, 1980. Ages 8–11.

Cameron, Ann. *More Stories Julian Tells.* Illustrated by Ann Strugnell. Knopf, 1986. Ages 7–11.

Cameron, Eleanor. *Julia's Magic.* Illustrated by Gail Owens. Dutton, 1984. Ages 9–12.

———. *That Julia Redfern.* Dutton, 1982. Ages 9–12.

Cassedy, Sylvia. *Lucie Babbidge's House.* Crowell, 1989. Ages 9–12.

———. *M. E. and Morton.* Crowell, 1987. Ages 11–YA.

Cleary, Beverly. *Dear Mr. Henshaw.* Illustrated by Paul Zelinsky. Morrow, 1983. Ages 9–12.

———. *Ramona and Her Father.* Illustrated by Alan Tiegreen. Morrow, 1977. Ages 7–10. Humorous.

———. *Ramona and Her Mother.* Illustrated by Alan Tiegreen. Morrow, 1977. Ages 7–10. Humorous.

———. *Ramona Quimby, Age 8.* Illustrated by Alan Tiegreen. Morrow, 1981. Ages 7–10. Humorous.

———. *Ramona the Brave.* Illustrated Alan Tiegreen. Morrow, 1975. Ages 5–8. Humorous.

———. *Ramona the Pest.* Illustrated by Louis Darling. Morrow, 1968. Ages 5–8. Humorous.

Cleaver, Vera and Bill. *I Would Rather Be a Turnip.* Lippincott, 1971. Ages 11–13.

———. *Lady Ellen Grae.* Illustrated by Ellen Raskin. Lippincott, 1968. Ages 9–12.

———. *Trial Valley.* Lippincott, 1977. Ages 11–YA.

———. *Where the Lilies Bloom.* Illustrated by Jim Spanfeller. Lippincott, 1969. Ages 11–YA.

Corcoran, Barbara. *Annie's Monster.* Atheneum, 1990. Ages 10–YA.

Cresswell, Helen. *Bagthorpes Liberated: Being the Seventh Part of the Bagthorpe Saga.* Macmillan, 1989. Ages 8–12. Humorous.

———. *Bagthorpes Unlimited.* Penguin, 1978. Ages 10–12. Humorous.

———. *Ordinary Jack.* Macmillan, 1977. Ages 8–12. Humorous.

Cutler, Jane. *No Dogs Allowed.* Illustrated by Tracey Campbell Pearson. Farrar, 1992. Ages 8–11.

Ellis, Sarah. *A Family Project.* Macmillan, 1988. Ages 10–14.

———. *Next-Door Neighbors.* Macmillan, 1990. Ages 9–13.

Estes, Eleanor. *The Moffats.* Illustrated by Louis Slobodkin. Harcourt, 1941. Ages 7–10.

Feiffer, Jules. *The Man in the Ceiling.* HarperCollins, 1993. Ages 9–12.

Fox, Paula. *Blowfish Live in the Sea.* Bradbury, 1970. Ages 12–YA.

———. *How Many Miles to Babylon?* Illustrated by Paul Giovanipoulos. White, 1967. Ages 11–YA.

———. *Monkey Island.* Watts, 1991. Ages 9–12.

———. *The Moonlight Man.* Bradbury, 1986. Ages 11–YA.

———. *One-Eyed Cat.* Bradbury, 1984. Ages 9–12.

———. *The Village by the Sea.* Watts, 1988. Ages 10–13.

———. *Western Wind.* Orchard, 1993. Ages 9–12.

Greene, Constance C. *Al(exandra) the Great.* Viking, 1982. Ages 8–12.

———. *Beat the Turtle Drum.* Illustrated by Donna Diamond. Viking, 1976. Ages 10–YA.

———. *The Unmaking of Rabbit.* Viking, 1972. Ages 9–11.

Gripe, Maria. *The Night Daddy.* Illustrated by Harald Gripe. Translated from the Swedish by Gerry Bothmer. Delacorte, 1971. Ages 9–11.

Hamilton, Virginia. *Cousins.* Putnam, 1990. Ages 9–13.

Henkes, Kevin. *Words of Stone.* Greenwillow, 1992. Ages 9–12.

Hughes, Dean. *Family Pose.* Atheneum, 1989. Ages 10–13.

Hunt, Irene. *Lottery Rose.* Scribner's, 1976. Ages 9–12.

———. *Up a Road Slowly.* Follett, 1966. Ages 11–YA.

Johnson, Angela. *Toning the Sweep.* Orchard, 1993. Ages 11–YA.

Johnston, Julie. *Adam and Eve and Pinch-Me.* Little, 1994. Ages 11–YA.

Keller, Beverly. *No Beasts! No Children!* Lothrop, 1983. Ages 8–12.

Kinsey-Warnock, Natalie. *The Canada Geese Quilt.* Illustrated by Leslie W. Bowman. Dutton, 1989. Ages 8–12.

Klein, Norma. *Mom, the Wolf Man, and Me.* Pantheon, 1972. Ages 11–YA.

Konigsburg, E. L. *From the Mixed-Up Files of Mrs. Basil E. Frankweiler.* Atheneum, 1967. Ages 9–12.

———. *Journey to an 800 Number.* Atheneum, 1982. Ages 10–13.

L'Engle, Madeleine. *Meet the Austins.* Vanguard, 1960. Ages 9–12.

Levin, Betty. *The Trouble with Gramary.* Greenwillow, 1988. Ages 10–13.

Lindgren, Astrid. *The Six Bullerby Children.* Methuen, 1961. Ages 5–8.

Little, Jean. *Mama's Going to Buy You a Mockingbird.* Viking, 1985. Ages 10–13.

Lowry, Lois. *All About Sam.* Illustrated by Diane de Groat. Houghton, 1988. Ages 8–12. Humorous.

———. *Anastasia at Your Service.* Illustrated by Diane de Groat. Houghton, 1982. Ages 8–12. Humorous.

———. *Anastasia Krupnik.* Houghton, 1985. Ages 8–12. Humorous.

———. *Attaboy, Sam!* Illustrated by Diane de Groat. Houghton, 1992. Ages 7–11. Humorous.

———. *The One Hundredth Thing about Caroline.* Houghton, 1983. Ages 8–12.

———. *Rabble Starkey.* Houghton, 1987. Ages 10–13.

———. *A Summer to Die.* Houghton, 1977. Ages 10–13.

MacLachlan, Patricia. *Arthur for the Very First Time.* Illustrated by Lloyd Bloom. HarperCollins, 1980. Ages 8–11.

———. *Baby.* Delacorte, 1993. Ages 10–YA.

———. *Journey.* Illustrated by Barry Moser. Delacorte, 1991. Ages 10–14.

Mahy, Margaret. *The Good Fortunes Gang.* Illustrated by Marion Young. Delacorte, 1993. Ages 8–11.

———. *Tangled Fortunes.* Illustrated by Marion Young. Delacorte, 1994. Ages 9–12.

Major, Kevin. *Hold Fast.* Delacorte, 1980. Ages 13–YA.

Marino, Jan. *The Day That Elvis Came to Town.* Little, Brown, 1991. Ages 12–YA.

Mathis, Sharon Bell. *The Hundred Penny Box.* Illustrated by Leo and Diane Dillon. Viking, 1975. Ages 7–10.

McEwan, Ian. *The Daydreamer.* HarperCollins, 1994. Ages 10–YA.

McKay, Hilary. *The Exiles.* Macmillan,1992. Ages 9–12. Humorous.

Moore, Emily. *Something to Count On.* Unicorn Books, 1980. Ages 11–YA.

Naylor, Phyllis Reynolds. *Reluctantly Alice.* Atheneum, 1991. Ages 8–11.

Paterson, Katherine. *The Great Gilly Hopkins.* Crowell, 1978. Ages 9–12.

Procházková, Iva. *The Season of Secret Wishes.* Translated by Elizabeth D. Crawford. Lothrop, 1989. Ages 9–12.

Rodowsky, Colby. *The Gathering Room.* Farrar, 1981. Ages 10–YA.

———. *H, My Name Is Henley.* Farrar, 1982. Ages 10–13.

Rylant, Cynthia. *A Blue-Eyed Daisy.* Bradbury, 1985. Ages 9–12.

———. *A Fine White Dust.* Bradbury, 1986. Ages 9–12.

———. *Missing May.* Orchard, 1992. Ages 10–YA.

Sachs, Marilyn. *The Bears' House.* Illustrated by Louis Glanzman. Doubleday, 1971. Ages 9–12.

Slepian, Jan. *The Broccoli Tapes.* Philomel, 1989. Ages 10–13.

Smith, Doris Buchanan. *The Pennywhistle Tree.* Putnam, 1991. Ages 9–12.

———. *Return to Bitter Creek.* Viking, 1986. Ages 10–13.

Stolz, Mary. *The Bully of Barkham Street.* Illustrated by Leonard Shortall. Harper, 1963.

———. *A Dog on Barkham Street.* Harper, 1960. Ages 8–11.

———. *Stealing Home.* HarperCollins, 1992. Ages 8–12.

Talbert, Marc. *Pillow of Clouds.* Dial, 1991. Ages 11–YA.

Taylor, Sydney. *All-of-a-Kind Family.* Illustrated by Helen John. Follett, 1951. Ages 7–10.

Voigt, Cynthia. *Homecoming.* Atheneum, 1981. Ages 9–12.

———. *A Solitary Blue*. Atheneum, 1983. Ages 10–YA.

———. *Sons from Afar*. Atheneum, 1987. Ages 10–YA.

Walter, Mildred Pitts. *Justin and the Best Biscuits in the World*. Illustrated by Catherine Stock. Lothrop, 1986. Ages 8–11.

Williams, Vera B. *Scooter*. Morrow, 1993. Ages 8–12.

Peers

Bauer, Marion Dane. *On My Honor*. Clarion, 1986. Ages 8–12.

Blume, Judy. *Tales of a Fourth Grade Nothing*. Illustrated by Roy Doty. Dutton, 1972. Ages 8–12. Humorous.

Byars, Betsy C. *Bingo Brown, Gypsy Lover*. Viking, 1990. Ages 11–YA.

———. *The Burning Questions of Bingo Brown*. Viking, 1988. Ages 9–12.

Cole, Brock. *The Goats*. Farrar, 1987. Ages 11–YA.

Estes, Eleanor. *The Hundred Dresses*. Illustrated by Louis Slobodkin. Harcourt, 1944. Ages 8–11.

Fine, Anne. *Alias Madame Doubtfire*. Little, Brown, 1988. Ages 9–12.

———. *The Book of the Banshees*. Little, Brown, 1992. Ages 11–YA.

Fitzhugh, Louise. *Harriet the Spy*. Harper, 1964. Ages 9–12.

———. *The Long Secret*. Harper, 1965. Ages 9–12.

Gantos, Jack. *Heads or Tails: Stories from the Sixth Grade*. Farrar, 1994. Ages 10–14.

Geller, Mark. *What I Heard*. Harper, 1987. Ages 10–13.

Gilson, Jamie. *Sticks and Stones and Skeleton Bones*. Illustrated by Dee deRosa. Lothrop, 1991. Ages 8–11.

Greene, Bette. *Philip Hall Likes Me, I Reckon Maybe*. Illustrated by Charles Lilly. Dial, 1974. Ages 9–12.

Greene, Constance C. *A Girl Called Al*. Illustrated by Byron Barton. Viking, 1969. Ages 8–12.

Haas, Jessie. *Skipping School*. Greenwillow, 1992. Ages 12–YA.

Hamilton, Virginia. *The Planet of Junior Brown*. MacMillan, 1971. Ages 12–YA.

Henkes, Kevin. *Words of Stone*. Greenwillow, 1992. Ages 8–12.

Hurwitz, Johanna. *Class Clown*. Illustrated by Sheila Hamanaka. Morrow, 1987. Ages 6–9.

———. *Russell and Elisa*. Morrow, 1989. Ages 6–9.

Klein, Robin. *Enemies*. Illustrated by Noela Young. Dutton, 1989. Ages 9–12.

Kline, Suzy. *Herbie Jones and the Class Gift*. Illustrated Richard Williams. Putnam, 1987. Ages 8–11.

———. *What's the Matter with Herbie Jones?* Illustrated by Richard Williams. Putnam, 1986. Ages 8–11.

Konigsburg, E. L. *Jennifer, Hecate, MacBeth, William McKinley, and Me, Elizabeth*. Atheneum, 1967. Ages 8–12.

Krumgold, Joseph. *Onion John*. Illustrated by Symeon Shimin. HarperCollins, 1959. Ages 9–12.

Lisle, Janet Taylor. *Afternoon of the Elves*. Watts, 1989. Ages 9–12.

MacLachlan, Patricia. *The Facts and Fictions of Minna Pratt*. Harper, 1988. Ages 7–11.

Mark, Jan. *Handles*. Atheneum, 1985. Ages 11–YA.

———. *Thunder and Lightnings*. Crowell, 1979. Ages 11–YA.

Park, Barbara. *Almost Starring Skinnybones*. Knopf, 1988. Ages 9–12. Humorous.

———. *Skinnybones*. Knopf, 1982. Ages 9–12. Humorous.

Paterson, Katherine. *Bridge to Terabithia*. Illustrated by Donna Diamond. Crowell, 1977. Ages 9–13.

———. *Flip-Flop Girl*. Dutton, 1994. Ages 8–12.

Peck, Richard. *Remembering the Good Times*. Delacorte, 1985. Ages 11–YA.

Pfeffer, Susan Beth. *The Year Without Michael*. Bantam, 1987. Ages 12–YA.

Phipson, Joan. *Hit and Run*. Atheneum, 1985. Ages 10–YA.

Porte, Barbara Ann. *I Only Made Up the Roses*. Greenwillow, 1987. Ages 12–YA.

Rodowsky, Colby. *Sydney. Herself*. Farrar, 1989. Ages 11–YA.

Sachar, Louis. *Wayside School is Falling Down*. Lothrop, 1989. Ages 7–10. Humorous.

Shreve, Susan. *The Gift of the Girl Who Couldn't Hear*. Morrow, 1991. Ages 10–13.

Smith, Doris Buchanan. *A Taste of Blackberries*. Illustrated by Charles Robinson. Crowell, 1973. Ages 9–12.

Snyder, Zilpha Keatley. *The Changeling*. Atheneum, 1970. Ages 9–12.

———. The *Egypt Game*. Illustrated by Alton Raible. Atheneum, 1967. Ages 10–13.

Spinelli, Jerry. *Maniac Magee*. Little, Brown, 1990. Ages 9–12.

Thesman, Jean. *The Rain Catchers.* Houghton, 1991. Ages 12–YA.

Tolan, Stephanie S. *Save Halloween!* Morrow, 1993. Ages 9–12.

Williams, Vera B. *Scooter.* Greenwillow, 1993. Ages 9–12.

Yarbrough, Camille. *The Shimmershine Queens.* Putnam, 1988. Ages 9–12.

Adolescent Issues

Avi. *Nothing But the Truth.* Orchard, 1991. Ages 12–YA.

Bauer, Joan. *Squashed.* Delacorte, 1992. Ages 11–14. Humorous.

Bauer, Marion Dane, editor. *Am I Blue? Coming Out from the Silence.* HarperCollins, 1994. Ages 14–YA.

Block, Francesca Lia. *Witch Baby.* Harper Collins, 1991. Ages 14–YA.

Blume, Judy. *Are You There God? It's Me, Margaret.* Bradbury, 1970. Ages 10–YA.

———. *Blubber.* Bradbury, 1974. Ages 9–12.

———. *It's Not the End of the World.* Bradbury, 1972. Ages 12–YA.

———. *Then Again, Maybe I Won't.* Bradbury, 1971. Ages 10–YA.

Brooks, Bruce. *What Hearts.* HarperCollins/Laura Geringer, 1992. Ages 14–YA.

Brooks, Martha. *Traveling on into the Light: And Other Stories.* Orchard, 1994. Ages 12–YA.

———. *Two Moons in August.* Little, Brown, 1992. Ages 12–YA.

Byars, Betsy. *The 18th Emergency.* Illustrated by Robert Grossman. Viking, 1973. Ages 9–12.

Cleary, Beverly. *Strider.* Illustrated by Paul O. Zelinsky. Morrow, 1991. Ages 9–13.

Clements, Bruce. *Tom Loves Anna Loves Tom.* Farrar, 1990. Ages 12–YA.

Cole, Brock. *Celine.* Farrar, 1989. Ages 12–YA.

Coman, Caroline. *Tell Me Everything.* Farrar, 1993. Ages 11–YA.

Cormier, Robert. *The Bumblebee Flies Anyway.* Pantheon, 1983. Ages 13–YA.

———. *The Chocolate War.* Pantheon, 1974. Ages 12–YA.

Davis, Jenny. *Goodbye and Keep Cold.* Watts, 1987. Ages 13–YA.

Doherty, Berlie. *Dear Nobody.* Orchard, 1992. Ages 12–YA.

———. *Granny Was a Buffer Girl.* Watts, 1988. Ages 13–YA.

———. *White Peak Farm.* Watts, 1990. Ages 11–YA.

Ehrlich, Amy. *Where It Stops, Nobody Knows.* Dial, 1988. Ages 12–YA.

Fine, Anne. *Flour Babies.* Little, Brown, 1994. Ages 10–YA.

———. *My War with Goggle-Eyes.* Little, Brown, 1989. Ages 11–14.

Grant, Cynthia D. *Keep Laughing.* Atheneum, 1991. Ages 12–YA.

Hall, Barbara. *Dixie Storms.* Harcourt, 1990. Ages 12–YA.

Hamilton, Virginia. *Plain City.* Scholastic, 1993. Ages 10–YA.

Harris, Rosemary. *Zed.* Farber, 1982. Ages 11–YA.

Hermes, Patricia. *Mama, Let's Dance.* Little, 1991. Ages 10–YA.

Hesse, Karen. *Phoenix Rising.* Holt, 1994. Ages 12–YA.

Hinton, S. E. *The Outsiders.* Viking, 1967. Ages 13–YA.

———. *That Was Then, This Is Now.* Viking, 1967. Ages 13–YA.

Kerr, M. E. *Deliver Us from Evie.* HarperCollins, 1994. Ages 13–YA.

———. *Fell.* Harper, 1987. Ages 13–YA.

———. *Fell Down.* HarperCollins, 1991. Ages 12–YA.

Koertge, Ron. *The Harmony Arms.* Little, 1992. Ages 12–YA. Humorous.

Little, Jean. *Different Dragons.* Illustrated by Laura Fernandez. Viking Kestrel, 1987. Ages 8–12.

Mahy, Margaret. *The Catalogue of the Universe.* McElderry, 1986. Ages 14–YA.

———. *Underrunners.* Viking, 1992. Ages 12–YA.

Marsden, John. *Letters from the Inside.* Houghton, 1994. Ages 12–YA.

———. *So Much to Tell You.* Joy Street, 1989. Ages 12–YA.

Myers, Walter Dean. *The Mouse Rap.* Harper, 1990. Ages 11–YA.

———. *Scorpions.* Harper, 1988. Ages 10–YA.

———. *Somewhere in the Darkness.* Scholastic, 1992. Ages 12–YA.

Naylor, Phyllis Reynolds. *Alice in April.* Atheneum, 1993. Ages 10–13.

Nelson, Theresa. *Earthshine.* Watts, 1994. Ages 12–YA.

Paterson, Katherine. *Jacob Have I Loved.* Crowell, 1980. Ages 12–YA.

———. *Park's Quest.* Lodestar/Dutton, 1988. Ages

13–YA.

Peck, Robert Newton. *A Day No Pigs Would Die.* Knopf, 1973. Ages 11–YA.

Plummer, Louise. *My Name Is Sus5an Smith. The 5 Is Silent.* Delacorte, 1991. Ages 13–YA.

Salisbury, Graham. *Blue Skin of the Sea.* Delacorte, 1992. Ages 12–YA.

Walker, Kate. *Peter.* Houghton, 1993. Ages 14–YA.

Wolff, Virginia Euwer. *Make Lemonade.* Holt, 1993. Ages 12–YA.

Survival and Adventure

Aiken, Joan. *The Wolves of Willoughby Chase.* Illustrated by Pat Marriott. Doubleday, 1963. Ages 10–13.

Buss, Fran Leeper, and Daisy Cubias. *Journey of the Sparrows.* Dutton, 1991. Ages 12–YA.

Cross, Gillian. *The Great American Elephant Chase.* Holiday, 1993. Ages 9–12.

George, Jean Craighead. *Julie.* HarperCollins, 1994. Ages 11–YA.

———. *Julie of the Wolves.* Illustrated by John Schoenherr. Harper, 1972. Ages 11–YA.

———. *The Missing Gator of Gumbo Limbo: An Ecological Mystery.* HarperCollins, 1992. Ages 10–12.

———. *My Side of the Mountain.* Dutton, 1959. Ages 9–12.

Holman, Felice. *Slake's Limbo.* Scribner's, 1974. Ages 10–13.

Houston, James A. *Frozen Fire.* Atheneum, 1977. Ages 11–YA.

Paulsen, Gary. *Hatchet.* Bradbury, 1987. Ages 9–12.

———. *The Haymeadow.* Illustrated by Ruth Wright Paulsen. Delacorte, 1992. Ages 12–YA.

———. *The River.* Delacorte, 1991. Ages 11–YA.

———. *The Voyage of the Frog.* Bradbury, 1989. Ages 12–YA.

Pullman, Philip. *The Ruby in the Smoke.* Knopf, 1987. Ages 14–YA. London, 1800s.

Ross, Ramon Royal. *Harper & Moon.* Atheneum, 1993. Ages 10–YA.

Naylor, Phyllis Reynolds. *The Fear Place.* Atheneum, 1994. Ages 11–YA.

Sperry, Armstrong. *Call It Courage.* Macmillan, 1940. Ages 8–12.

Thiele, Colin. *Shadow Shark.* Harper, 1988. Ages 10–13.

Persons with Disabilities

Anderson, Rachel. *The Bus People.* Holt, 1992. Ages 10–14. Character portrayals, different disabilities.

Bawden, Nina. *The Witch's Daughter.* Clarion, 1991 (1966). Ages 9–12. Visual impairment.

Blume, Judy. *Deenie.* Bradbury, 1973. Ages 12–YA. Scoliosis.

Booth, Barbara D. *Mandy.* Illustrated by Jim LaMarche. Lothrop, 1991. Ages 7–9. Hearing impairment. Picture book.

Brooks, Bruce. *The Moves Make the Man.* Harper, 1984. Ages 12–YA. Emotional disability.

Bridgers, Sue Ellen. *All Together Now.* Knopf, 1979. Ages 11–YA. Mental retardation.

———. *Notes for Another Life.* Knopf, 1981. Ages 12–YA. Emotional disability.

Byars, Betsy. *The Summer of the Swans.* Illustrated by Ted CoConis. Viking, 1970. Ages 10–14. Mental retardation.

Carrick, Carol. *Stay Away from Simon.* Illustrated by Donald Carrick. Clarion, 1985. Ages 7–9. Mental retardation. Picture book.

Cleaver, Vera and Bill. *Me Too.* Lippincott, 1973. Ages 12–YA. Mental retardation.

Clifton, Lucille. *My Friend Jacob.* Illustrated by Thomas DiGrazia. Dutton, 1980. Ages 5–8. Mental retardation. Picture book.

Conly, Jane Leslie. *Crazy Lady!* HarperCollins, 1993. Ages 10–YA. Mental retardation.

Cowen-Fletcher, Jane. *Mama Zooms.* Scholastic, 1993. Ages 5–8. Physical disability. Picture book.

Fassler, Joan. *Howie Helps Himself.* Illustrated by Joe Lasker. Whitman, 1974. Ages 7–10. Paraplegic.

Fleming, Virginia. *Be Good to Eddie Lee.* Illustrated by Floyd Cooper. Philomel, 1993. Ages 6–8. Down's syndrome. Picture book.

Friis-Baastad, Babbis. *Don't Take Teddy.* Translated from the Norwegian by Lise Sömme McKinnon. Scribner's, 1967. Ages 9–12. Mental retardation.

Garrigue, Sheila. *Between Friends.* Scholastic, 1986. Ages 10–13. Down's syndrome.

Hines, Anna Grossnickle. *Gramma's Walk.* Greenwillow, 1993. Ages 5–8. Physical disability. Picture book.

Howard, Ellen. *Edith Herself.* Illustrated by Ronald Hinter. Atheneum, 1987. Ages 7–11. Epilepsy.

Johnston, Julie. *Hero of Lesser Causes.* Little, 1993. Ages 11–YA. Poliomyelitis.

Killilea, Marie. *Karen.* Illustrated by Bob Riger. Dodd, Mead, 1954. Ages 10–YA. Cerebral palsy.

Klein, Robin. *Boss of the Pool.* Penguin, 1986. Ages 8–11. Down's syndrome.

Konigsburg, E. L. *(George).* Atheneum, 1970. Ages 12–YA. Emotional disability.

Laird, Elizabeth. *Loving Ben.* Delacorte, 1988. Ages 10–YA. Hydrocephalic infant.

Lasker, Joe. *He's My Brother.* Illustrated by the author. Whitman, 1974. Ages 7–10. Learning disability.

Little, Jean. *From Anna.* Illustrated by Joan Sandin. Harper & Row, 1972. Ages 9–12. Visual impairment.

———. *Listen for the Singing.* HarperCollins, 1991. Ages 10–13. Visual impairment.

———. *Mine for Keeps.* Illustrated by Lewis Parker. Little, 1962. Ages 9–12. Cerebral palsy.

———. *Take Wing.* Little, Brown, 1968. Ages 9–12. Mental retardation.

Madsen, Jane M., and Bockoras, Diane. *Please Don't Tease Me . . .* Illustrated by Kathleen T. Brinko. Judson, 1983. Ages 11–14. Physical disability.

Oneal, Zibby. *The Language of Goldfish.* Viking, 1980. Ages 12–YA. Emotional disability.

Osofsley, Audrey. *My Buddy.* Illustrated by Ted Rand. Holt, 1994. Ages 6–8. Muscular dystrophy.

Paulsen, Gary. *The Monument.* Delacorte, 1991. Ages 11–YA. Physical disability.

Philbrick, Rodman. *Freak the Mighty.* Blue Sky, 1993. Ages 12–YA. Learning disability.

Pollock, Penny. *Keeping it Secret.* Illustrated by Donna Diamond. Putnam, 1982. Ages 11–14. Hearing impairment.

Riskind, Mary. *Apple is My Sign.* Houghton Mifflin, 1981. Ages 10–13. Hearing impairment.

Rodowsky, Colby. *What About Me?* Watts, 1976. Ages 8–12. Mental retardation.

Rubin, Susan Goldman. *Emily Good as Gold.* Harcourt, 1993. Ages 12–YA. Mental retardation.

Shyer, Marlene. *Welcome Home Jellybean.* Scribner's, 1978. Ages 8–12. Mental retardation.

Slepian, Jan. *The Alfred Summer.* Macmillan, 1980. Ages 11–14. Cerebral palsy.

———. *Lester's Turn.* Macmillan, 1981. Ages 11–14. Cerebral palsy.

———. *Risk n' Roses.* Putnam, 1990. Ages 11–YA. Mental retardation.

Southall, Ivan. *Let the Balloon Go.* Illustrated by Jon Weiman. Bradbury, 1968. Ages 11–14. Spasms and stuttering.

Spence, Eleanor. *The Devil Hole.* Illustrated by Malcolm Green. Lothrop, 1977. Ages 10–YA. Mental disability. (Published in Great Britain under the title, *The October Child,* Oxford University Press in 1976.)

Taylor, Theodore. *Tuck Triumphant.* Doubleday, 1991. Ages 10–YA. Hearing impairment.

Thesman, Jean. *When the Road Ends.* Houghton, 1992. Ages 10–YA. Physical disability.

Thiele, Colin. *Jodie's Journey.* Harper, 1988. Ages 10–13. Rheumatoid arthritis.

Voigt, Cynthia. *Dicey's Song.* Atheneum, 1983. Ages 10–YA. Mental illness.

Wilson, Nancy Hope. *The Reason for Janey.* Macmillan, 1994. Ages 10–13. Mental retardation.

Wolff, Virginia Euwer. *Probably Still Nick Swanson.* Holt, 1988. Ages 12–YA. Learning disability.

Cultural Diversity

See also Chapter 10, Multicultural and International Literature.

Aamundsen, Nina Ring. *Two Short and One Long.* Translated from the Norwegian by the author. Houghton, 1990. Ages 8–11.

Beake, Lesley. *The Song of Be.* Holt, 1993. Ages 12–YA.

Berry, James. *The Future-Telling Lady and Other Stories.* HarperCollins, 1993. Ages 10–YA.

Bonham, Frank. *Durango Street.* Dutton, 1965. Ages 12–YA.

Casey, Maude. *Over the Water.* Holt, 1994. Ages 12–YA.

Gordon, Sheila. *Waiting for the Rain: A Novel of South Africa.* Watts, 1987. Ages 11–YA.

Hansen, Joyce. *The Gift-Giver.* Clarion, 1980. Ages 9–12.

———. *Yellow Bird and Me.* Clarion, 1986. Ages 9–12.

Ho, Minfong. *The Clay Marble.* Farrar, 1991. Ages 11–14.

Lord, Bette Bao. *In the Year of the Boar and Jackie Robinson.* Illustrated by Marc Simont. Harper, 1984. Ages 7–10.

Maartens, Maretha. *Paper Bird: A Novel of South Africa.* Translated by Madeleine van Biljon. Clarion, 1991. Ages 10–YA.

Mohr, Nicholasa. *Felita.* Illustrated by Ray Cruz. Dial, 1979. Ages 8–11.

Naidoo, Beverley. *Chain of Fire.* Illustrated by Eric Velasquez. Lippincott, 1990. Ages 11–YA.

———. *Journey to Jo'burg: A South African Story.* Illustrated by Eric Velasquez. Lippincott, 1986. Ages 8–12.

Namioka, Lensey. *Yang the Youngest and His Terrible Ear.* Little, 1992. Ages 9–12.

Reuter, Bjarne. *Buster's World.* Translated from the Danish by Anthea Bell. Dutton, 1989. Ages 9–12.

———. *The Sheik of Hope Street.* Translated from the Danish by Anthea Bell. Dutton, 1991. Ages 9–12.

Staples, Suzanne Fisher. *Haveli: A Young Woman's Courageous Struggle for Freedom in Present-day Pakistan.* Knopf, 1993. Ages 12–YA.

———. *Shabanu: Daughter of the Wind.* Knopf, 1989. Ages 12–YA.

Temple, Frances. *Grab Hands and Run.* Orchard, 1993. Ages 12–YA.

———. *Taste of Salt: A Story of Modern Haiti.* Watts, 1992. Ages 12–YA.

Walter, Mildred Pitts. *Have a Happy* ———. Illustrated by Carole Byard. Lothrop, 1989. Ages 9–12.

Wojciechowska, Maia. *Shadow of a Bull.* Illustrated by Alvin Smith. Atheneum, 1964. Ages 9–12.

Sports

Christopher, Matt. *Centerfield Ballhawk.* Illustrated by Ellen Beier. Brown/Springboard, 1992. Ages 7–9.

———. *Return of the Home Run Kid.* Illustrated by Paul Casale. Little, 1992. Ages 9–12.

———. *Tackle Without a Team.* Illustrated by Margaret Sanfilippo. Little, Brown, 1989. Ages 10–14.

———. *Undercover Tailback.* Illustrated by Paul Casale. Little, 1992. Ages 8–11.

Cohen, Barbara. *Thank You, Jackie Robinson.* Illustrated by Richard Cuffari. Lothrop, 1974. Ages 8–11.

Crutcher, Chris. *Athletic Shorts: Six Short Stories.* Greenwillow, 1991. Ages 13–YA.

Lynch, Chris. *Iceman.* HarperCollins, 1994. Ages 14–YA.

———. *Shadow Boxer.* HarperCollins, 1993. Ages 12–YA.

Slote, Alfred. *Hang Tough, Paul Mather.* Lippincott, 1973. Ages 9–12.

———. *The Trading Game.* Lippincott, 1990. Ages 9–12.

Smith, Robert Kimmel. *Bobby Baseball.* Illustrated by Alan Tiegreen. Delacorte, 1989. Ages 8–11.

Mysteries

Aiken, Joan. *Blackhearts in Battersea.* Doubleday, 1964. Ages 10–14.

———. *Midnight Is a Place.* Penguin, 1974. Ages 10–14.

Avi. *The Man Who Was Poe.* Orchard, 1989. Ages 10–YA.

Bunting, Eve. *Coffin on a Case.* HarperCollins, 1992. Ages 9–12.

Corbett, Scott. *Grave Doubts.* Little, Brown, 1982. Ages 9–12.

Cross, Gillian. *A Map to Nowhere.* Holiday, 1989. Ages 10–13.

———. *On the Edge.* Holiday, 1985. Ages 10–13.

———. *Wolf.* Holiday, 1991. Ages 10–13.

Garfield, Leon. *The December Rose.* Viking, 1987. Ages 10–YA.

Newman, Robert. *The Case of the Frightened Friend.* Atheneum, Ages 10–13.

———. *The Case of the Murdered Players.* Atheneum, 1985. Ages 10–13.

———. *The Case of the Vanishing Corpse.* Atheneum, 1980. Ages 10–13.

Nixon, Joan Lowery. *The Name of the Game Was Murder.* Delacorte, 1993. Ages 11–14.

Pearce, Philippa. *The Way to Sattin Shore.* Illustrated by Charlotte Voake. Greenwillow, 1984. Ages 10–13.

Prather, Ray. *Fish & Bones.* HarperCollins, 1992. Ages 11–YA.

Raskin, Ellen. *Figgs & Phantoms.* Dutton, 1989. Ages 9–12.

———. *The Westing Game.* Dutton, 1978. Ages 9–12.

Reaver, Chap. *A Little Bit Dead.* Delacorte, 1992. Ages 12–YA.

———. *Mote.* Delacorte, 1990. Ages 12–YA.

Sobol, Donald J. *Encyclopedia Brown.* Lodestar/Dutton, 1963. Ages 8–10.

Wallace, Barbara Brooks. *Peppermints in the Parlor.* Atheneum, 1980. Ages 9–12.

———. *The Twin in the Tavern.* Atheneum, 1993. Ages 9–12.

Wright, Betty Ren. *The Dollhouse Murders.* Holiday House, 1983. Ages 9–12.

Animals

Burnford, Sheila. *The Incredible Journey.* Illustrated by Carl Burger. Little, 1961. Ages 8–11.

Cutler, Jane. *No Dogs Allowed.* Illustrated by Tracey Campbell Pearson. Farrar, 1992. Ages 8–11.

Doty, Jean. *Dark Horse.* Morrow, 1983. Ages 9–11.

Eckert, Allan W. *Incident at Hawk's Hill.* Illustrated by John Schoenherr. Little, Brown, 1971. Ages 10–YA.

Farley, Walter. *Black Stallion.* Illustrated by Keith Ward. Random House, 1941. Ages 8–11.

Fleischman, Sid. *Jim Ugly.* Illustrated by Jos. A. Smith. Greenwillow, 1992. Ages 9–12.

Gardiner, John Reynolds. *Stone Fox.* Illustrated by Marcia Sewall. Crowell, 1980. Ages 7–11.

George, Jean Craighead. *The Cry of the Crow.* Harper, 1980. Ages 10–13.

Gipson, Fred. *Old Yeller.* Illustrated by Carl Burger. Harper, 1956. Ages 10–YA.

Haas, Jessie. *A Horse like Barney.* Greenwillow, 1993. Ages 8–12.

———. *Keeping Barney.* Greenwillow, 1982. Ages 9–12.

———. *The Sixth Sense: And Other Stories.* Greenwillow, Ages 11–YA.

———. *Working Trot.* Greenwillow, 1983. Ages 8–11.

Hall, Lynn. *Danza.* Scribner's, 1982. Ages 8–11.

———. *The Something Special Horse.* Scribner's, 1985. Ages 8–11.

Henry, Marguerite. *Brighty of the Grand Canyon.* Illustrated by Wesley Dennis. Macmillan, 1953. Ages 8–10.

———. *King of the Wind.* Illustrated by Wesley Dennis. Rand, 1948. Ages 7–11.

———. *Misty of Chincoteague.* Illustrated by Wesley Dennis. Rand, 1947. Ages 7–11.

Hesse, Karen. *Sable.* Holt, 1994. Ages 8–11.

Kjelgaard, Jim. *Big Red.* Illustrated by Bob Kuhn. Holiday, 1945. Ages 9–12.

Mowat, Farley. *Owls In the Family.* Illustrated by Robert Frankenberg. Little, 1962. Ages 9–12.

Naylor, Phyllis Reynolds. *Shiloh.* Atheneum, 1991. Ages 8–11.

North, Sterling. *Rascal: A Memoir of a Better Era.* Illustrated by John Schoenherr. Dutton, 1963. Ages 11–14.

———. *Wolfling.* Puffin, 1992 (1969). Ages 8–11.

Peyton, K. M. *Darkling.* Doubleday, 1990. Ages 8–11.

Rawls, Wilson. *Summer of the Monkeys.* Doubleday, 1976. Ages 9–11. Humorous.

———. *Where the Red Fern Grows.* Doubleday, 1961. Ages 9–11.

Reaver, Chap. *Bill.* Delacorte, 1994. Ages 11–YA.

Rylant, Cynthia. *Every Living Thing.* Illustrated by S. D. Schindler. Bradbury, 1985. Ages 11–YA.

Sewell, Anna. *Black Beauty.* Illustrated by John Speirs. Simon and Schuster, 1982. Ages 9–11.

Springer, Nancy. *A Horse to Love.* HarperCollins, 1987. Ages 8–12.

Taylor, Theodore. *The Trouble with Tuck.* Doubleday, 1981. Ages 7–10. See disabilities list for sequel, *Tuck Triumphant.*

Wallace, Bill. *Beauty.* Holiday, 1988. Ages 8–11.

Chapter 8

Historical Fiction

Ancestors

On the wind-beaten plains
  once lived my ancestors.
In the days of peaceful moods,
  they wandered and hunted.
In days of need or greed,
  they warred and loafed.
Beneath the lazy sun, kind winds above,
  they laughed and feasted.
Through the starlit night, under the moon.
  they dreamed and loved.
Now, from the wind-beaten plains,
  only their dust rises.

—Grey Cohoe

Historical fiction brings history to life by placing appealing child characters in accurately described historical settings. By telling the stories of these characters' everyday lives as well as presenting their triumphs and failures, authors of historical fiction provide young readers with the human side of history, making it more real and more memorable.

Definition and Description

Historical fiction is realistic fiction set in a time remote enough from the present to be considered history. That is, although the story is imaginary, it is within the realm of possibility that such events could have occurred. In these stories historical facts blend with imaginary characters and plot. The facts are actual historical events, authentic period settings, and real historical figures. An imaginary story is constructed around these facts. In the *Reference Guide to Historical Fiction for Children and Young Adults,* Adamson (1987) states as follows:

> Historical fiction recreates a particular historical period with or without historical figures as incidental characters. It is generally written about a time period in which the author has not lived or no more recently than one generation before its composition. For example, fiction written in 1987 must be set, at the latest, in 1967, to be considered historical. Fiction written in 1930 but set in 1925 does not fulfill this criterion for legitimate historical fiction. (p. ix)

In the most common form of historical fiction, the main characters of the story are imaginary, but some secondary characters may be actual historical figures. An example of this type of historical fiction is the 1944 Newbery Award winner, *Johnny Tremain* by Esther Forbes. Set in the U.S. Revolutionary War period, this story tells of Johnny, a fictitious character, who is apprenticed to a silversmith. In the course of the story, Samuel Adams, John Hancock, and Paul Revere are introduced as minor characters.

In another form of historical fiction, the past is described complete with the social traditions, customs, morals, and values of the period but with no mention of an actual historical event nor actual historical figures as characters. The physical location is also accurately reconstructed for the readers. An example of this story type is *The Witch of Blackbird Pond* by Elizabeth George Speare. The Puritan way of life in Connecticut in the 1600s is depicted in this story about young Kit from Barbados who becomes involved in a witchcraft trial. The locales and traditions are accurate reconstructions of Puritan life of that era, whereas the characters, dialogue, day-to-day events, and details are fictitious. Both these forms of historical stories qualify as historical fiction under the definition of this genre.

A third type of historical story is one in which elements of fantasy are found, and therefore the tale is not within the realm of possibility. For example, time warps and other supernatural features may be found in Canadian Janet Lunn's *The Root Cellar* and in Belinda Hurmence's *A Girl Called Boy.* These stories are *historical fantasy* and are included in Chapter 6, Modern Fantasy. Picture books in the historical fiction genre are discussed in Chapter 4, Picture Books.

Values of Historical Fiction for Children

Historical fiction can enliven the dry facts of history by presenting those facts through the everyday lives of children who lived long ago. Reading about and recognizing the feelings and thoughts a child of that era might have experienced enables today's young readers to relate on a more personal level with the events and people of history. Of course, with historical fiction—as with any form of good literature—the primary value is enjoyment and reading pleasure. Other values of historical fiction include the following:

- Readers see that their lives have been affected by those who lived before them. They also realize that their lives will affect the lives of those who will come after them.
- The human, everyday side of history is seen. Children understand that history was made by people like themselves.
- Children understand how people lived and enjoyed their lives in different historical times.
- An appreciation of the universality of human needs across history is developed.
- Children learn about their own ethnic or national heritage.
- Readers acquire a sense of time and, gradually, a sense that history consists of stories about what happened in the past.
- Readers develop greater interest in the study of social studies—history, geography, and anthropology.

Evaluation and Selection of Historical Fiction

Historical fiction must first be evaluated for its story strength. It must tell an engaging story. The author must develop rounded, complex characters with whom children can identify. The author should also develop a universal theme that is worthy and thought provoking, without being didactic. In addition, the author of historical fiction must present historical facts with as much accuracy and objectivity as books of history. This means that a setting must be described in sufficient detail as to provide an authentic sense of that time and that place without overwhelming the story. Details such as hair and clothing styles, home architecture and furnishings, foods and food preparation, and modes of transportation must be subtly woven into the story to provide a convincing, authentic period setting. The characters must act within the traditions and norms of their times.

Expressing the language or dialect of the period presents a particular challenge to the author of historical stories. Dialogue that occurs within the text often becomes problematic for the writer. If the speech of the period is greatly different from that of today, then the author faces a decision: remain true to the language of the time but cause readers difficulties in comprehending, or present the language in today's dialect but lose the flavor and authenticity of the language of the period. In any case, it seems important that the language not jar the reader by its obvious inappropriateness, nor lose the reader by its extreme difficulty. Most children's authors strive to attain the middle ground—some flavor of a language difference but modified in order to be understandable to the child reader. Young listeners adapt easily to dialects when they are modeled well by their teachers, and may even find occasion to use the dialect to lend flavor to their subsequent writing.

Many adults today are unaware that the history they learned as children may have been biased or one-sided. Some authors attempt to include more modern interpretations of historical events in historical fiction by setting the record straight or adding a minority presence to the story. However, as previously mentioned, care must be taken that the characters behave in an historically accurate fashion.

In summary, the criteria for evaluating historical fiction are as follows:

- An engrossing story with well-developed characters
- An interesting plot
- Worthy but subtle themes
- An authentic, well-described setting that informs the reader but does not overwhelm the story
- Historical accuracy in describing places, events and facts, morals, manners, customs, and behaviors of the people

The Scott O'Dell Award, an award established in 1981 by the author Scott O'Dell and administered by Zena Sutherland, University of Chicago, honors what is judged to be the most outstanding work of children's historical fiction published in the previous year. The work must be written by a U.S. citizen and be set in the New World. The list of the Scott O'Dell Award winners found in Appendix A can be a source for selecting outstanding historical fiction for use with students. The National Council of Social Studies publishes a list of the most notable trade books in the field of social studies from the preceding year in the April/May issue of its journal, *Social Education.* This list includes many works of historical fiction, as well as nonfiction works, and is a useful source to locate recent books of this genre.

Early Books and Trends in Historical Fiction

Although historical stories were written for children as early as the 1800s, few titles remain of interest from those early years. The early books placed an emphasis on exciting events and idealized real-life characters—much in the style of heroic legends. Howard Pyle's works were an exception to this pattern. Two of his historical novels, *Otto of the Silver Hand* (1888) and *Men of Iron* (1891), set in the Middle Ages, approach in quality many of the more recent works. However, few other stories written prior to World War I had memorable characters presented as well-rounded, complex individuals. Most of these stories seem unconvincing today.

Between World War I and World War II, historical stories appeared in which well-developed characters involved in realistic events were portrayed in authentic period settings. In 1929, Eric Kelly won the Newbery Medal for *The Trumpeter of Krakow,* set in Poland in the Middle Ages. This exciting adventure features two children who outwit the Tartars who have captured one of their fathers. From the 1930s, a few truly remarkable books remain popular with children today. *Calico Bush* (1931) by Rachel Field tells the story of Marguerite Ledoux, a French servant girl who settles in Maine in 1743. Between 1932 and 1943, the first eight books of the *Little House* series by Laura Ingalls Wilder were published. These stories have continued to grow in popularity, partially as a result of the long-lasting television series based on the books. *Caddie Woodlawn* by Carol Ryrie Brink tells the story of Caddie, a tomboy growing up in Wisconsin during the 1860s; this story was first published

Excellent Historical Fiction to Read Aloud

(Books for each level vary in difficulty and should be selected with the students' literary backgrounds in mind.)

Primary Level   Ages 5–8

Brenner, Barbara. *Wagon Wheels.* Harper, 1978.
Bulla, Clyde Robert. *Viking Adventure.* Crowell, 1963.
Dalgliesh, Alice. *The Courage of Sarah Noble.* Scribner's, 1954.
Fritz, Jean. *The Cabin Faced West.* Coward, 1958.
Gauch, Patricia. *This Time, Tempe Wick?* Coward, 1974.
Hamilton, Virginia. *The Bells of Christmas.* Illustrated by Lambert Davis. Harcourt, 1989.
MacLachlan, Patricia. *Sarah, Plain and Tall.* Harper, 1985.
Monjo, F. N. *The Drinking Gourd.* Harper, 1970.
Wilder, Laura Ingalls. *Little House in the Big Woods.* Harper, 1932.

Intermediate Level Ages 8–11

Avi. *The Barn.* Orchard/Richard Jackson, 1994.
Caudill, Rebecca. *Tree of Freedom.* Illustrated by Dorothy Bayley. Viking, 1949.
Conlon-McKenna, Marita. *Under the Hawthorn Tree.* Illustrated by Donald Teskey. Holiday, 1990.
Dorris, Michael. *Morning Girl.* Hyperion, 1992.
Lowry, Lois. *Number the Stars.* Houghton, 1989.
O'Dell, Scott. *Island of the Blue Dolphins.* Houghton, 1960.
Orlev, Uri. *The Island on Bird Street.* Translated from the Hebrew by Hillel Halkin. Houghton, 1983.
Paulsen, Gary. *Nightjohn.* Delacorte, 1993.
Reeder, Carolyn. *Shades of Gray.* Macmillan, 1989.
Skurzynski, Gloria. *What Happened in Hamelin.* Four Winds, 1979.
Speare, Elizabeth George. *The Sign of the Beaver.* Houghton, 1983.

Advanced Level   Ages 11–14

Berry, James. *Ajeemah and His Son.* HarperCollins, 1992.
Cushman, Karen. *Catherine, Called Birdy.* Clarion, 1994.
Fleischman, Paul. *Bull Run.* HarperCollins, 1993.
———. *Coming-and-Going Men: Four Tales.* Illustrated by Randy Gaul. Harper, 1985.
Hudson, Jan. *Sweetgrass.* Philomel, 1989.
Lasky, Kathryn. *Beyond the Divide.* Macmillan, 1983.
Paterson, Katherine. *Lyddie.* Dutton, 1991.
Richter, Hans Peter. *Friedrich.* Translated from the German by Edite Kroll. Holt, 1970.
Taylor, Mildred. *Roll of Thunder, Hear My Cry.* Dial, 1976.
Temple, Frances. *The Ramsay Scallop.* Orchard, 1994.

in 1936 and is still read with enjoyment by children today. *Johnny Tremain* by Esther Forbes was awarded the Newbery Award in 1944. This Revolutionary era novel is considered a children's classic.

The period after World War II saw a flowering of historical fiction for children in both English and American literature. Many outstanding books were published in the fifteen years following the war. Examples are *The Door in the Wall* by Marguerite deAngeli, published in 1949; *The Buffalo Knife* by William O. Steele, published in 1952; *The Courage of Sarah Noble* by Alice Dalgliesh, published in 1954; *The Sword in the Tree* by Clyde Robert Bulla, published in 1956; *Calico Captive*, by Elizabeth George Speare, published in 1957; the best-selling Newbery Award-winning book, *The Witch of Blackbird Pond*, by Elizabeth George Speare, published in 1958; *The Cabin Faced West* by Jean Fritz, published in 1958; and *The Lantern Bearers* by Rosemary Sutcliff, published in 1959. In 1954, the Laura Ingalls Wilder Award was awarded to (and named for) Laura Ingalls Wilder, an author of historical fiction. This award, the "Hall of Fame" of children's authors and illustrators, honors an author or illustrator whose books, published in the United States, have made a substantial and lasting contribution to children's literature. By 1960, the genre of historical fiction was well established as a fine resource for children's enjoyment and enrichment. Milestones in the development of historical fiction are highlighted in Table 8-1.

Historical fiction continues to flourish today. Some older historical fiction novels have been criticized for portraying some cultural groups in an extremely negative light. For example, two Newbery Medal winners, *Caddie Woodlawn* by Carol Ryrie Brink and *The Matchlock Gun* by Walter D. Edmonds, have been faulted for their negative portrayals of Native Americans. However, minority authors have written a number of excellent works based on the early experiences of their cultural groups in North America; for example, see *Song of the Trees* and its sequels by Mildred Taylor and *Journey to Topaz* and its sequel by Yoshiko Uchida. Of special note are also many outstanding, recently published books set during the years leading up to and including World War II. The establishment in 1981 of the Scott O'Dell Award for Historical Fiction has begun to offer additional recognition for authors of this genre. In 1989, Elizabeth George Speare was selected to receive the Laura Ingalls Wilder Award for the entire body of her work, which comprises four outstanding works of historical fiction for children.

Topics in Historical Fiction

Two ways of considering the topics treated in historical fiction novels are by the universal themes presented in the books and by the historical periods in which the books are set. First, some *common themes* that can be found within historical fiction novels for children are suggested with titles of books in which the theme is developed. Next, six *historical periods* in which historical fiction novels can be found are reviewed in capsule form.

TABLE 8–1   Milestones in the Development of Historical Fiction

Date	Event	Significance
1888	*Otto of the Silver Hand* by Howard Pyle	Early recognized work of historical fiction
1928	The Newbery Award given to *The Trumpeter of Krakow* by Eric Kelly	National recognition for an early work of historical fiction
1932–1943	Publication of the first eight books of *Little House* series by Laura Ingalls Wilder	Classic historical fiction
1944	*Johnny Tremain* by Esther Forbes given the Newbery Award	Classic historical adventure set during the American Revolution era
1949–1960	Many historical novels published, including *The Door in the Wall*, by Marguerite de Angeli, *Witch of Blackbird Pond* by Elizabeth George Speare, *The Lantern Bearers* by Rosemary Sutcliff	Dramatic increase in the quality and quantity of historical novels for children
1954	Establishment of the Laura Ingalls Wilder Award, first awarded to Wilder	Recognition of an historical fiction author for the entire body of her work
1961	Scott O'Dell's *Island of the Blue Dolphins* awarded the Newbery medal	Landmark book of historical fiction with a strong female protagonist from a minority culture
1962	Scott O'Dell awarded the Hans Christian Andersen Prize	International recognition of a U.S. author of historical novels
1971	*Journey to Topaz* by Yoshiko Uchida	Early historical work about and by a minority–Japanese American
1975	*The Song of the Trees* by Mildred Taylor	First in a series of books about an African-American family's struggle starting in the Depression era
1981	Establishment of the Scott O'Dell Award	Award given for outstanding historical novel set in North America brings recognition to the genre
1989	Elizabeth George Speare awarded the Laura Ingalls Wilder Award	Recognition of an author of historical fiction for her substantial contribution to children's literature
1989	*Number the Stars* by Lois Lowry	Newbery Medal book about the Holocaust set in World War II Denmark
1993	*Bull Run* by Paul Fleischman	Novel set during the U.S. Civil War and told through personal episodes
1994	*Catherine, Called Birdy* by Karen Cushman	Novel set in medieval England and told through a girl's journal

Themes in Historical Fiction

Common themes that extend across time and place in historical stories can be an approach for presenting historical fiction to children. For example, a theme, such as seeking new frontiers, is explored through a small group of books set in different times and places. Some possible themes for development in this manner are listed below with suggestions of books that might be selected for the study of the theme. Other themes may be discovered when you read historical fiction novels and consider the commonalities to be found among them.

Seeking New Frontiers

The Cabin Faced West by Jean Fritz.
Little House in the Big Woods by Laura Ingalls Wilder.
Wagon Wheels by Barbara Brenner.
Beyond the Divide by Kathryn Lasky.
The Far-off Land by Rebecca Caudill.
On to Oregon by Honoré Morrow.

Search for Freedom from Persecution

Jump Ship to Freedom by James Lincoln Collier and Christopher Collier.
The Island on Bird Street by Uri Orlev.
The Upstairs Room by Johanna Reiss.
The Wild Children by Felice Holman.
Sing Down the Moon by Scott O'Dell.
The Endless Steppe by Esther Hautzig.
The Witch of Blackbird Pond by Elizabeth George Speare.

Effects of War

My Brother Sam Is Dead by James Lincoln Collier and Christopher Collier.
Zoar Blue by Janet Hickman.
Across Five Aprils by Irene Hunt.
Summer of My German Soldier by Bette Greene.
Shades of Gray by Carolyn Reeder.

Family Closeness in Times of Adversity

Journey Home by Yoshiko Uchida.
Journey to America by Sonia Levitin.
Roll of Thunder, Hear My Cry by Mildred Taylor.
Upon the Head of the Goat by Aranka Siegal.
Sounder by William H. Armstrong.

Periods of History in Fiction

The natural relationship of historical fiction stories to the study of history and geography suggests building whole units of study around periods of both world and

U.S. history in which good stories for children are set. The following capsule statements on seven historical periods will give you an idea of how these units might be organized. At the end of the chapter (under Recommended Books), you will find works of historical fiction organized by these seven historical periods.

Beginnings of Civilization up to 3000 B.C.   This period represents prehistoric cultures and civilizations. Early peoples (Java, Neanderthals, Cro-Magnons) and early civilizations in the Middle East and Asia are included. Egyptians, Syrians, and Phoenicians developed civilizations, and Hebrews produced a religious faith, Judaism, that resulted in the Old Testament. The subcontinent of India was the site of Aryan civilizations. Chinese dynasties were responsible for excellent works of art and agricultural systems of irrigation. An example of an historical novel set in this time period is A. Linevski's *An Old Tale Carved Out of Stone.*

Civilizations of the Ancient World, 3000 B.C. to A.D. 600   The era of the Greek city-states was followed by a period of Roman rule in western Europe. Christianity was founded in Jerusalem and spread throughout Europe. Ancient Asia was the site of enduring civilizations that bred two remarkable men born about 560 B.C.: the Indian religious leader, Buddha, and the Chinese philosopher, Confucius. Both have had a lasting influence on their civilizations. One novel set in this time period retells the story of Moses leading his people from Egypt to the promised land in Sonia Levitin's *Escape from Egypt.*

Civilizations of the Medieval World, 600 to 1500   The eastern part of the Roman Empire maintained its stability and preserved the civilization from the capital of Constantinople. This civilization, the Byzantine Empire, created a distinct culture and branch of the Christian Church—the Orthodox Church—which influenced Russia to adopt both the religion and the culture. Following the fall of the Roman Empire, western Europe dissolved into isolated separate regions without strong governments. Many of the responsibilities of government were carried out by the Christian Church. The Church dominated the economic, political, cultural, and educational life of the Middle Ages in western Europe. These feudal societies eventually gave rise to the separate nations of modern Europe. During this era, early African and American civilizations arose independently. The great civilizations of China and Japan continued to flourish throughout these centuries. As examples, Marguerite De Angeli's *A Door in the Wall* and Karen Cushman's *Catherine, Called Birdy* portray medieval life in England.

Emergence of Modern Nations, 1500 to 1800   The Renaissance, a literary and artistic movement, swept western Europe. Many important developments of this period included the invention of the printing press, a new emphasis on reason, a reformation of the Christian Church, and advances in science. During this same period, central governments throughout Europe increased their power. Spain, and then France, dominated Europe in the 1500s and 1600s. In the 1700s, Russia, Austria, and Prussia rose to power. This was also a time when Europeans explored and settled in Africa, India, and the Americas. The Portuguese and Spanish took the lead in explorations and acquired many foreign colonies. England, the Netherlands, France, and Russia also colonized and influenced East Asia, India, Africa, and the Americas.

Revolutions created new governments and new nations. The American Revolution (1776–1781) created a new nation; the French Revolution in 1789 affected the direction of governments toward democracy in all of Europe. Napoleon built an empire across Europe, resulting in the uniting of European nations to defeat Napoleon. The nations of Latin America also began to gain their independence. China expanded gradually under the Ming and Ch'ing dynasties. Japan prospered under the Tokugawa shogunate. The United States and Canada were the sites of rapid population increases due to immigration; the settlements in North America were predominantly along the eastern coasts. Some westward expansion was beginning in the United States and Canada. For example, a story relating the challenges of settling the Maine frontier in the 1700s is Elizabeth George Speare's *The Sign of the Beaver.*

Development of Industrial Society, 1800 to 1914   The 1800s were marked by a rapid shift from agricultural societies to industrial societies. Great Britain was an early site for this change. The factory system developed and prospered, while working and living conditions deteriorated for the worker. Two stories about life as a millworker in this period are Katherine Paterson's *Lyddie* and James Lincoln Collier and Christopher Collier's *The Clock.* New technology—railroad trains, steamboats, the telegraph and telephone—affected transportation and communications. Advances in science and medicine helped explain the nature of life and improved the quality of life. Education developed into an important institution in western Europe and North America. Europe underwent revolutions that readjusted boundaries and eventually led to the unification of new nations.

The westward movement was fully realized as pioneers settled across the United States and Canada. The building of railroads hastened the establishment of new settlements. Native Americans struggled for survival in the face of these massive population shifts. Black slavery had existed in the American colonies from earliest days, but in the 1800s, slavery became a social and economic issue resulting in the Civil War (1861–1865). Slavery was abolished and the Union was preserved at the cost of 600,000 lives and a major rift between the North and the South. Carolyn Reeder's *Shades of Gray* portrays a family torn apart by this war.

The United States grew in economic and political strength. An age of imperialism resulted in firm control of large areas of the world by other world powers such as England, France, and Belgium. Great Britain dominated India, parts of Africa, and continued its influence over Canada, Australia, and New Zealand, while Japan became a powerful force in east Asia. Alki Zei's *The Sound of Dragon's Feet* describes events occurring in Russia during the end of the 1800s.

World Wars in the Twentieth Century, 1914 to 1945   This era includes World War I (1914–1918) in Europe, in which the United States and Canada joined and fought with the Allies (Great Britain, France, Russia, Greece, and Rumania); the between-wars period that included the Great Depression; Hitler's rise to power in 1933; and World War II (1939–1945) in Europe and Asia, in which Canada and the United States joined forces with England, France, and Russia to battle Germany, Italy, and

Japan. In 1917, the Bolshevik Revolution established a communist government in Russia. In 1931, Great Britain recognized Canada, Australia, New Zealand, and South Africa as completely independent. However, each nation declared its loyalty to the British monarch and continued its cultural ties with Great Britain. The Holocaust during World War II—the persecution and killing of Jewish and other people by the Nazi regime—stands out as one of the most atrocious periods in modern history. Hans Peter Richter's *Friedrich* tells of the horrors of the Holocaust as it affected a Jewish boy's life. World War II ended shortly after nuclear devices were dropped on Hiroshima and Nagasaki by the United States.

Post-World War II Era, 1945 to 1970s   During this era, the United States and Western European nations were involved in a struggle for world influence against the communist nations, particularly the Soviet Union and China. A massive arms buildup, including nuclear weapons, was undertaken by the major nations of both sides. The Korean War (1950-1953) and the Vietnam War (1965–1973) were major conflicts in which the United States fought in order to contain communist expansion. The Korean War, combined with the postwar economic recovery of Japan, drew attention to the growing importance of East Asia in world affairs. A novel for children, *The Purple Heart* by Marc Talbert, describes the Vietnam War era. The Soviet Union launched a series of satellites beginning with Sputnik I on October 4, 1957, inaugurating the space age. An explosion of scientific knowledge occurred as a result of increased spending for weapons development and space exploration. The 1950s and 1960s have been described as the Cold War decades because of the increasing hostility between the Soviet Union and the United States. In the 1970s, public pressure mounted in the United States to reduce the nation's external military commitments.

During the 1960s a strong civil rights movement, led by Martin Luther King, Jr. and other prominent figures of the era, fought for equal treatment of African Americans. The movement led to desegregation of schools, restaurants, transportation, and housing. Equal rights for women were also sought during the feminist movement in the 1970s. An example of a book set in the 1960s is Trudy Krisher's *Spite Fences*, a story of race relations in Georgia.

Many fine works of historical fiction for children can now be found. Children have an opportunity to live vicariously the lives of people from long ago—people from different cultures and from different parts of the world.

References

Adamson, L. G. (1987). *A reference guide to historical fiction for children and young adults*. Westport, CT: Greenwood Press.

Cohoe, G. (1972). Ancestors. In T. Allen (Ed.), *The whispering wind: Poetry by young american Indians*. New York: Doubleday.

Notable Authors of Historical Fiction

Patricia Beatty, author of U.S. and British historical novels. *Hail Columbia; Turn Homeward, Hannalee.*

Patricia Clapp, author of novels set in U.S. colonial and Revolutionary War eras. *I'm Deborah Sampson: A Soldier in the War of the Revolution.*

James Lincoln Collier and Christopher Collier, authors of novels set in U.S. Revolutionary War era. *My Brother Sam Is Dead.*

Esther Forbes, author of 1944 Newbery Award winner, *Johnny Tremain,* set in U.S. Revolutionary War period.

Erik Christian Haugaard, author of historical novels set in many different eras, including the Viking explorations and England in the Middle Ages. *Messenger for Parliament.*

Mollie Hunter, Scottish writer whose novels are set in early Scotland. *The Stronghold.*

Lois Lowry, author of the historical fiction novel *Number the Stars,* Newbery Medal winner in 1990. Also noted for realistic fiction and modern fantasy novels.

Patricia MacLachlan, Newbery Award-winning author noted for a wide range of literature for children, including works of historical fiction. *Sarah, Plain and Tall; Skylark.*

Scott O'Dell, author of many stories based on Native-American and Mexican-American cultures. *Island of the Blue Dolphins.*

Uri Orlev, noted Israeli author of historical fiction novels treating the Holocaust and its aftermath. *The Island on Bird Street; Lydia, Queen of Palestine.*

Hans Peter Richter, author of holocaust novels set in Germany during World War II. *Friedrich.*

Elizabeth George Speare, winner of Scott O'Dell, Newbery, and Laura Ingalls Wilder Awards for her works of historical fiction. *The Sign of the Beaver.*

Rosemary Sutcliff, English author of many memorable books recreating the early history of England. *Song for a Dark Queen.*

Mildred Taylor, author of seven stories of an African-American land-owning family, beginning in the 1930s and set in rural Mississippi. *Roll of Thunder, Hear My Cry.*

Yoshiko Uchida, author of historical novels about the life of Japanese Americans during the Depression and during and immediately following World War II. *Journey to Topaz.*

Laura Ingalls Wilder, author of *Little House* series based on the Ingalls family experiences as pioneers in the Midwest.

Laurence Yep, author of historical fiction about Chinese Americans and their adjustments to life in the United States. *Dragonwings.*

Alki Zei, author of international historical novels, three of which have won the Batchelder Award. *The Sound of Dragon's Feet.*

Recommended Historical Fiction Books

Ages refer to approximate interest levels. YA = young adult readers. Locales and dates of settings are noted. Historical biographies are arranged by these same eras and placed at the end of Chapter 9.

Beginnings of Civilization up to 3000 B.C.

Behn, Harry. *The Faraway Lurs.* World, 1963. Ages 12–15. Northern Europe, 3500 B.C.

Linevski, A. *An Old Tale Carved Out of Stone.* Translated by Maria Polushkin. Crown, 1973. Ages 10–14. Early Siberia.

Osborne, Chester. *The Memory String.* Atheneum, 1984. Ages 8–12. Siberian Peninsula, 25,000 B.C.

Steele, William O. *The Magic Amulet.* Harcourt, 1979. Ages 10–14. North America, 10,000 B.C.

Treece, Henry. *The Dream-Time.* Meredith, 1968. Ages 11–14. British Isles, 11,000 B.C..

Wibberley, Leonard. *Attar of the Ice Valley.* Farrar, 1968. Ages 11–YA. Europe, 50,000 B.C.

Civilizations of the Ancient World, 3000 B.C. to A.D. 600

Hunter, Mollie. *The Stronghold.* Harper, 1974. Ages 9–12. British Isles, 100 B.C.

Levitin, Sonia. *Escape from Egypt.* Little, Brown, 1994. Ages 14–YA. Jews, 1200 B.C.

McGraw, Eloise Jarvis. *Mara, Daughter of the Nile.* Penguin, 1953. Ages 11–YA. Ancient Egypt, 1550 B.C.

Paton Walsh, Jill. *Children of the Fox.* Farrar, 1978. Ages 10–14. Ancient Persia, 400 B.C.

Speare, Elizabeth George. *The Bronze Bow.* Houghton, 1961. Ages 10–14. Jerusalem, A.D. 30.

Sutcliff, Rosemary. *Song for a Dark Queen.* Crowell, 1978. Ages 10–14. British Isles, A.D. 50.

————. *Sun Horse, Moon Horse.* Dutton, 1978. Ages 10–14. British Isles, 100 B.C.

Civilizations of the Medieval World, 600 to 1500

Bulla, Clyde Robert. *Viking Adventure.* Crowell, 1963. Ages 7–10. Norway, 900s.

Cushman, Karen. *Catherine, Called Birdy.* Clarion, 1994. Ages 11–YA. England, manor life, 1290s.

De Angeli, Marguerite. *The Door in the Wall.* Doubleday, 1949. Ages 9–12. England, 1300s.

Dorris, Michael. *Morning Girl.* Hyperion, 1992. Ages 9–12. Taino Indians, 1490s.

Fleischman, Sid. *The Whipping Boy.* Greenwillow, 1986. Ages 9–11. England, Middle Ages.

Haugaard, Erik Christian. *Hakon of Rogen's Saga.* Houghton, 1963. Ages 9–12. Vikings, 900s.

Kelly, Eric. *The Trumpeter of Krakow.* Macmillan, 1928. Ages 11–14. Poland, 1400s.

Skurzynski, Gloria. *Manwolf.* Houghton, 1981. Ages 10–14. Poland, 1380s.

————. *What Happened in Hamelin.* Four Winds, 1979. Ages 10–14. Germany, 1200s.

Stolz, Mary. *Pangur Ban.* Harper, 1988. Ages 11–14. Ireland, 800s, 1100s.

Temple, Frances. *The Ramsay Scallop.* Orchard, 1994. Ages 12–YA. England, 1299.

The Emergence of Modern Nations, 1500 to 1800

Avi. *The Fighting Ground.* Lippincott, 1984. Ages 10–14. U.S. Revolutionary War era, 1770s.

————. *Night Journeys.* Pantheon, 1979. Ages 8–11. U.S. colonial era, 1770s.

Bosse, Malcolm. *The Examination.* Farrar, 1994. Ages 11–YA. China, sixteenth-century Ming Dynasty.

Bowen, Gary. *Stranded at Plimoth Plantation 1626.* Illustrated by Gary Bowen. HarperCollins, 1994. Ages 9–12. Jamestown, settler life, 1620s.

Caudill, Rebecca. *The Far-off Land.* Viking, 1964. Ages 11–14. U.S. frontier, 1780s.

————. *Tree of Freedom.* Illustrated by Dorothy Bayley. Viking, 1949. Kentucky, U.S. Revolutionary War era.

Clapp, Patricia. *Constance: A Story of Early Plymouth.* Lothrop, 1968. Ages 10–14. U.S. colonial era, 1620s.

————. *I'm Deborah Sampson: A Soldier in the War of the Revolution.* Lothrop, 1977. Ages 9–12. U.S., 1770s.

————.*Witches' Children: A Story of Salem.* Lothrop, 1982. Ages 10–YA. U.S. colonial era, 1690s.

Collier, James Lincoln, and Christopher Collier. *Jump Ship to Freedom.* Delacorte, 1981. Ages 9–12. U.S. slavery, 1780s.

————. *My Brother Sam Is Dead.* Four Winds, 1974. Ages 10–14. U.S. Revolutionary War era, 1770s.

————. *War Comes to Willy Freeman.* Delacorte, 1983. Ages 9–12. U.S., U.S. slavery, 1780s.

Colver, Anne. *Bread-and-Butter Journey.* Holt, 1970. Ages 7–10. U.S. pioneers, 1780s.

Dalgliesh, Alice. *The Courage of Sarah Noble.* Scribner's, 1954. Ages 7–9. U.S. pioneers, early 1700s.

Fleischman, Paul. *Saturnalia.* Harper, 1990. Ages 12–YA. Boston, Narraganset Indians, 1680s.

Forbes, Esther. *Johnny Tremain.* Houghton, 1943. Ages 10–13. U.S. Revolutionary War era, 1770s.

Fritz, Jean. *The Cabin Faced West.* Coward, 1958. Ages 7–10. U.S. pioneers, 1700s.

Gauch, Patricia. *This Time, Tempe Wick?* Coward, 1974. Ages 7–10. U.S. Revolutionary War era, 1780s.

Greene, Jacqueline Dembar. *One Foot Ashore.* Walker, 1994. Ages 8–12. Brazil, slaves, Portuguese Inquisition.

Haugaard, Erik Christian. *The Boy and the Samurai.* Houghton Mifflin, 1991. Ages 10–13. Sixteenth-century Japan.

————. *A Messenger for Parliament.* Houghton, 1976. Ages 10–14. England, 1640s.

Hunter, Mollie. *The 13th Member.* Harper, 1971. Ages 12–YA. Scotland, 1500s.

Lasky, Kathryn. *Beyond the Burning Time.* Scholastic, 1994. Ages 11–YA. U. S. Salem witch trials, 1690s.

Llorente, Pilar Molina. *The Apprentice.* Illustrated by Juan Ramón Alonso. Translated from the Spanish by Robin Longshaw. Farrar, 1993. Ages 11–YA. Florence, Renaissance.

Namioka, Lensey. *The Coming of the Bear.* HarperCollins, 1992. Ages 10–YA. Japan, 1600s.

O'Dell, Scott. *The Captive.* Houghton, 1979. Ages 10–14. Mexico, 1500s.

————. *Sarah Bishop.* Houghton, 1980. Ages 10–14.

U.S. Revolutionary War era, 1770s.

Petry, Ann. *Tituba of Salem Village*. Crowell, 1964. Ages 10–14. U.S. colonial era, 1690s.

Rinaldi, Ann. *A Break with Charity: A Story about the Salem Witch Trials*. Harcourt, 1992. Ages 12–YA. Salem witch trials, 1692.

————. *The Fifth of March: A Story of the Boston Massacre*. Harcourt, 1993. Ages 11–YA. Boston, indentured servant, 1770s.

————. *A Stitch in Time*. Scholastic, 1994. Ages 12–YA. Salem, Massachusetts, family saga, 1788–91.

Speare, Elizabeth George. *The Sign of the Beaver*. Houghton, 1983. Ages 8–12. Maine frontier, 1700s.

————. *The Witch of Blackbird Pond*. Houghton, 1958. Ages 10–14. U.S. colonial era, 1680s.

Sutcliff, Rosemary. *Bonnie Dundee*. Dutton, 1984. Ages 10–14. Scotland, 1600s.

Van Leeuwen, Jean. *Going West*. Illustrated by Thomas B. Allen. Doubleday/Dial, 1992. Ages 5–8. Wagon train, picture book.

The Development of Industrial Society, 1800 to 1914

Aiken, Joan. *The Teeth of the Gale*. Harper, 1988. Ages 9–YA. Spain, 1820s.

Angell, Judie. *One-Way to Ansonia*. Bradbury, 1985. Ages 10–YA. U.S. immigrants, 1890s.

Armstrong, William H. *Sounder*. Harper, 1969. Ages 9–12. U.S. South, African Americans, early 1900s.

Avi. *The Barn*. Orchard/Richard Jackson, 1994. Ages 9–12. Oregon Territory, 1850s.

————. *The True Confessions of Charlotte Doyle*. Orchard, 1990. Ages 8–12. England, United States, 1830s.

Beatty, Patricia. *Charley Skedaddle*. Morrow, 1987. Ages 11–14. U.S. Civil War, 1860s.

————. *Jayhawker*. Morrow, 1991. Ages 10–14. Kansas, slavery, underground railroad, 1800s.

————. *Turn Homeward, Hannalee*. Morrow, 1984. Ages 10–14. U.S. Civil War, 1860s.

————. *Who Comes with Cannons?* Morrow, 1992. Ages 9–12. North Carolina, underground railroad, mid-1800s.

Berry, James. *Ajeemah and His Son*. HarperCollins, 1992. Ages 12–YA. Slavery, U.S., 1807.

Bilson, Geoffrey. *Death over Montreal*. Kids Can Press, 1982. Ages 8–11. Scotland, Canada, 1830s.

Blos, Joan. *A Gathering of Days: A New England Girl's Journal, 1830–32*. Scribner's, 1979. Ages 8–11. New England, 1830s.

Brandis, Marianne. *The Tinderbox*. Porcupine's Quill, 1982. Ages 11–14. Canada, 1830s.

Brenner, Barbara. *Wagon Wheels*. Harper, 1978. Ages 7–9. U.S. pioneers, African Americans, 1870s.

Brink, Carol Ryrie. *Caddie Woodlawn*. Macmillan, 1935. Ages 8–11. Wisconsin frontier, 1860s.

Collier, James Lincoln, and Christopher Collier. *The Clock*. Delacorte, 1992. Ages 9–12. Connecticut mill life, early 1800s.

Conlon-McKenna, Marita. *Under the Hawthorn Tree*. Illustrated by Donald Teskey. Holiday, 1990. Ireland, mid-1800s.

————. *Wildflower Girl*. Illustrated by Donald Teskey. Holiday, 1992. Ages 9–12. Ireland and Boston, immigration, 1850s.

Conrad, Pam. *Prairie Songs*. Harper, 1985. Ages 10–14. Nebraska, late 1800s.

De Felice, Cynthia. *Weasel*. Macmillan, 1990. Ages 9–12. Ohio frontier, 1830s.

DeVries, David. *Home at Last*. Dell, 1992. Ages 10–13. Orphan train, New York to Nebraska, 1800s.

Fleischman, Paul. *The Borning Room*. Harper, 1991. Ages 11–YA. Ohio farm life, 1800s.

————. *Bull Run*. HarperCollins, 1993. Ages 10–YA. U.S. Civil War era, 1860s.

————. *Coming-and-Going Men: Four Tales*. Illustrated by Randy Gaul. Harper, 1985. Ages 11–YA. Vermont, 1800.

Forman, James D. *Becca's Story*. Scribner's, 1992. Ages 10–YA. Michigan, U.S. Civil War era.

Fox, Paula. *The Slave Dancer*. Bradbury, 1973. Ages 11–YA. U.S. slave trade, 1840s.

Fritz, Jean. *Brady*. Coward, 1960. Ages 9–12. Pennsylvania, underground railroad, 1830s.

German, Tony. *A Breed Apart*. McClelland and Stewart, 1985. Ages 11–YA. Canadian Northwest, early 1800s.

Hamilton, Virginia. *The Bells of Christmas*. Illustrated by Lambert Davis. Harcourt, 1989. Ages 8–11. Ohio, African Americans, 1890s.

Hansen, Joyce. *The Captive*. Scholastic, 1994. Ages 11–YA. U.S. slave trade, Civil War era.

————. *Which Way Freedom?* Walker, 1986. Ages

11–YA. U.S., slavery, Civil War era.

Harris, Christie. *Cariboo Trail*. Longman, 1957. Ages 12–14. U.S., Minnesota, western Canada, 1860s.

Harvey, Brett. *Cassie's Journey: Going West in the 1860's*. Illustrated by Deborah Kogan Ray. Holiday, 1988. Ages 7–9. U.S. frontier, 1860s.

Hickman, Janet. *Zoar Blue*. Macmillan, 1978. Ages 9–12. U.S. Civil War era, 1860s.

Highwater, Jamake. *Legend Days*. Harper, 1984. Ages 10–YA. U.S., Northern Plains Indians, 1800s.

Holland, Isabelle. *Behind the Lines*. Scholastic, 1994. Ages 11–YA. U.S. Civil War.

Holman, Felice. *The Wild Children*. Scribner's, 1983. Ages 9–12. Russia, early 1900s.

Hudson, Jan. *Sweetgrass*. Philomel, 1989. Ages 11–YA. Canada, Dakota Indians, 1830s.

Hunt, Irene. *Across Five Aprils*. Follett, 1964. Ages 10–YA. U.S. Civil War era, 1860s.

Irwin, Hadley. *Jim-Dandy*. Macmillan, 1994. Ages 11–YA. General Custer, horse story, 1870s.

Kudlinsky, Kathleen V. *Night Bird: A Story of the Seminole Indians*. Viking, 1993. Ages 8–11. Florida, Seminole Indians, 1850s.

Lasky, Kathryn. *Beyond the Divide*. Macmillan, 1983. Ages 12–YA. Westward expansion, 1849.

———. *The Bone Wars*. Morrow, 1988. Ages 11–YA. U.S. frontier, mid-1800s.

———. *The Night Journey*. Warne, 1981. Ages 10–14. Russia, United States, early 1900s.

Lawlor, Laurie. *George on His Own*. Whitman, 1993. Ages 9–12. Frontier life, homesteading in South Dakota, early 1900s.

Lunn, Janet. *Shadow in Hawthorn Bay*. Scribner's, 1986/Dennys, 1986. Ages 12–YA. Canada frontier, early 1800s.

Lyons, Mary E. *Letters from a Slave Girl: The Story of Harriet Jacobs*. Scribner's, 1992. Ages 10–YA. North Carolina, slavery, early 1800s.

MacLachlan, Patricia. *Sarah, Plain and Tall*. Harper, 1985. Ages 7–10. U.S. frontier, 1850s.

———. *Skylark*. HarperCollins, 1994. Ages 8–11. Sequel to *Sarah, Plain and Tall*.

Moeri, Louise. *Save Queen of Sheba*. Dutton, 1981. Ages 9–12. U.S. frontier, 1800s.

Monjo, F. N. *The Drinking Gourd*. Harper, 1970. Ages 6–9. New England, underground railroad, 1850s.

Morrow, Honoré. *On to Oregon!* Morrow, 1954.

Ages 9–12. U.S. frontier, 1840s.

Myers, Walter Dean. *The Glory Field*. Scholastic, 1994. Ages 12–YA. U.S. slavery era to present.

Nixon, Joan Lowery. *A Family Apart*. Bantam, 1987. Ages 10–13. New York City, Orphan Train, 1860s.

O'Dell, Scott. *Island of the Blue Dolphins*. Houghton, 1960. Ages 10–14. Pacific island, Native Americans, mid-1800s.

———. *Sing Down the Moon*. Houghton, 1970. U.S., Navajo Indians, 1860s.

———, and Elizabeth Hall. *Thunder Rolling in the Mountains*. Houghton, 1992. Ages 10–14. Native American removal to reservations, 1870s.

Paterson, Katherine. *Lyddie*. Dutton, 1991. Ages 12–YA. Massachusetts, mill life, mid-1800s.

Paton Walsh, Jill. *Grace*. Farrar, 1992. Ages 11–YA. Northumbrian coast of England, lighthouse keeper's daughter, 1830s.

Paulsen, Gary. *Nightjohn*. Delacorte, 1993. Ages 11–YA. U.S. slavery.

Reeder, Carolyn. *Shades of Gray*. Macmillan, 1989. Ages 9–12. U.S. Civil War era, 1860s.

Rinaldi, Ann. *In My Father's House*. Scholastic, 1993. Ages 12–YA. U.S. Civil War era, 1860s.

Savage, Deborah. *To Race a Dream*. Houghton, 1994. Small Minnesota town, horse story, early 1900s.

Schur, Maxine Rose. *The Candlemaker*. Dial, 1994. Ages 11–YA. Russia, Ukraine, Jewish boy, 1852.

Skurzynski, Gloria. *The Tempering*. Clarion, 1983. Pennsylvania steel mills, turn of twentieth-century.

Smucker, Barbara. *Underground to Canada*. Clarke Irwin, 1977. Ages 12–YA. Canada, Ontario, 1800s.

Stolz, Mary. *Cezanne Pinto: A Memoir*. Knopf, 1994. Ages 11–YA. Georgia plantation, underground railroad to Canada, 1860s.

Turner, Ann. *Grasshopper Summer*. Macmillan, 1989. Ages 9–12. U.S., Kentucky to Dakota Territory, 1870s.

Weitzman, David. *Thrashin' Time: Harvest Days in the Dakotas*. Godine, 1991. Ages 10–13. U.S. western settlements, 1912.

Wilder, Laura Ingalls. *Little House in the Big Woods*. Harper, 1932. Ages 7–10. Wisconsin frontier, 1800s.

Wisler, G. Clifton. *Jericho's Journey*. Dutton, 1993. Ages 9–12. Move from Tennessee to Texas, pioneer life.

Yee, Paul. *Tales from Gold Mountain: Stories of the Chinese in the New World*. Illustrated by Simon Ng. Macmillan, 1990. U.S. and Canada, 1800s.

Yep, Laurence. *Dragon's Gate*. HarperCollins, 1993. Ages 9–12. Sierra Nevada, transcontinental railroad, 1867.

————. *Dragonwings*. Harper, 1979. Ages 9–12. California, early 1900s.

————. *The Serpent's Children*. Harper, 1984. Ages 9–12. China, 1830s.

Zei, Alki. *The Sound of Dragon's Feet*. Dutton, 1979. Ages 10–14. Russia, late 1800s.

World Wars in the Twentieth Century, 1914 to 1945

Anderson, Rachel. *Paper Faces*. Holt, 1993. Ages 12–YA. England, World War II.

Avi. *Who Was That Masked Man, Anyway?* Orchard, 1992. Ages 9–12. U.S., World War II.

Bawden, Nina. *Henry*. Illustrated by Joyce Powzyk. Lothrop, 1988. Ages 9–12. England, World War II era.

Chang, Margaret, and Raymond Chang. *In the Eye of the War*. Macmillan, 1990. Ages 10–12. China, World War II.

Coerr, Eleanor. *Mieko and the Fifth Treasure*. Putnam, 1993. Ages 9–12. World War II, Nagasaki bombardment, Japan, 1945.

DeJong, Meindert. *House of Sixty Fathers*. Harper, 1956. Ages 8–12. China, World War II.

Disher, Garry. *The Bamboo Flute*. Ticknor & Fields, 1993. Ages 10–14. Australia, 1932.

Frank, Rudolf. *No Hero for the Kaiser*. Translated by Patricia Crampton. Illustrated by Klaus Steffens. Lothrop, 1986 (originally published in 1931). Ages 10–YA. Poland, World War I.

Garrigue, Sheila. *The Eternal Spring of Mr. Ito*. Bradbury, 1985. Ages 8–11. Canada, Japanese-Canadian internment, World War II.

Gee, Maurice. *The Fire-Raiser*. Houghton, 1992. Ages 11–YA. New Zealand, World War I era.

Greene, Bette. *Summer of My German Soldier*. Dial, 1973. U.S., World War II.

Hahn, Mary Downing. *Stepping on the Cracks*. Clarion, 1991. Ages 10–13. U.S., Maryland, World War II.

Hautzig, Esther. *The Endless Steppe*. Harper, 1968. Ages 10–14. Russia, Jews, World War II.

Hesse, Karen. *Letters from Rifka*. Holt, 1992. Ages 9–12. Russian immigration to U.S., 1919.

Heuck, Sigrid. *The Hideout*. Translated from the German by Rika Lesser. Dutton, 1988. Ages 9–12. Germany, Jews, World War II.

Hooks, William H. *Circle of Fire*. Atheneum, 1982. Ages 9–12. Rural North Carolina, Ku Klux Klan, 1930s.

Hughes, Monica. *Blaine's Way*. Irwin, 1986. Ages 12–YA. Canada, World War II.

Hunter, Bernice Thurman. *That Scatterbrain Booky*. Scholastic-TAB, 1981. Ages 12–YA. Canada, Depression, 1930s.

Kogawa, Joy. *Naomi's Road*. Oxford, 1986. Ages 9–12. Canada, British Columbia, Japanese Canadian internment, World War II.

Koller, Jackie. *Nothing to Fear*. Harcourt, 1991. Ages 10–13. Irish immigrant family in New York City, 1929.

Levitin, Sonia. *Anne's Promise*. Atheneum, 1993. Ages 10–14. German immigration to U.S., World War II era.

————. *Journey to America*. Atheneum, 1970. Ages 10–14. Germany, Jews, World War II era.

Little, Jean. *From Anna*. Harper, 1972. Ages 9–12. Canada, 1930s. Germany, Canada, 1930s.

Lowry, Lois. *Number the Stars*. Houghton, 1989. Ages 8–12. Denmark, World War II.

Lyon, George Ella. *Borrowed Children*. Watts, 1988. Ages 10–14. Kentucky, Depression era, 1930s.

Magorian, Michelle. *Good Night, Mr. Tom*. Harper, 1982. Ages 11–14. England, World War II.

Matas, Carol. *Lisa's War*. Scribner's, 1989. Ages 10–13. Denmark, Jews, World War II.

Morpurgo, Michael. *Waiting for Anya*. Viking, 1991. Ages 10–14. Southern France, Jews, World War II.

Myers, Anna. *Red-Dirt Jessie*. Walker, 1993. Ages 9–12. Oklahoma, Great Depression, early 1900s.

Orlev, Uri. *The Island on Bird Street*. Translated from the Hebrew by Hillel Halkin. Houghton, 1983. Ages 9–13. Poland, Jews, World War II.

————. *Lydia, Queen of Palestine*. Translated from the Hebrew by Hillel Halkin. Houghton, 1993. Ages 8–12. Escape to Palestine from Romania, World War II era.

————. *The Man from the Other Side*. Translated from the Hebrew by Hillel Halkin. Houghton,

1991. Ages 12–YA. Poland, Jews, World War II.

Pearson, Kit. *Looking at the Moon*. Viking, 1992. Ages 10–YA. Toronto, World War II, 1943.

Pendergraft, Patricia. *As Far as Mill Springs*. Philomel, 1991. Ages 10–13. U.S. east coast, 1929 Depression era.

Paulsen, Gary. *The Cookcamp*. Orchard, 1991. Ages 10–13. U.S., road crew, World War II.

Pelgrom, Els. *The Winter When Time Was Frozen*. Translated from the Dutch by Maryka and Rafael Rudnik. Morrow, 1980. Ages 9–12. Holland, World War II.

Reiss, Johanna. *The Upstairs Room*. Crowell, 1972. Ages 10–14. Holland, Jews, World War II.

Reuter, Bjarne. *The Boys from St. Petri*. Translated from Danish by Anthea Bell. Dutton, 1994. Ages 12–YA. Denmark, World War II.

Richter, Hans Peter. *Friedrich*. Translated from the German by Edite Kroll. Holt, 1970. Ages 10–14. Germany, Jews, World War II.

———. *I Was There*. Translated from the German. Puffin, 1987. Ages 10–YA. Germany, Jews, World War II.

Ross, Ramon Royal. *Harper & Moon*. Atheneum, 1993. Ages 10–YA. World War II.

Salisbury, Graham. *Under the Blood-Red Sun*. Delacorte, 1994. Japanese residents of Hawaii, World War II era.

Siegal, Aranka. *Upon the Head of the Goat: A Childhood in Hungary 1939–44*. Farrar, 1981. Ages 12–YA. Hungary, World War II.

Skurzynski, Gloria. *Good-Bye Billy Radish*. Bradbury, 1992. Ages 10–14. Pennsylvania steel mill town, World War I era.

Snyder, Zilpha Keatley. *Cat Running*. Delacorte, 1994. Ages 9–12. California, U.S. depression, 1933.

Taylor, Mildred. *Let the Circle Be Unbroken*. Dial, 1981. Ages 10–14. U.S. South, African Americans, 1930s.

———. *Road to Memphis*. Dial, 1990. Ages 12–YA. U.S. South, African Americans, 1941.

———. *Roll of Thunder, Hear My Cry*. Dial, 1976. Ages 10–14. U.S. South, African Americans, 1930s.

Taylor, Theodore. *The Cay*. Doubleday, 1969. Ages 8–12. Caribbean, World War II era.

———. *Timothy of the Cay: A Prequel-Sequel*. Harcourt, 1993. Ages 11–13. Carribean, 1884 and World War II era.

Uchida, Yoshiko. *Journey to Topaz*. Illustrated by Donald Carrick. Scribner's, 1971. Ages 10–14. U.S., internment of Japanese Americans, World War II.

Vos, Ida. *Anna Is Still Here*. Translated from the Dutch by Terese Idelstein and Inez Smidt. Houghton, 1993. Ages 9–13. Holland, World War II era.

———. *Hide and Seek*. Translated from the Dutch by Terese Edelstein and Inez Smidt. Houghton, 1991. Ages 9–13. Jews, World War II.

Westall, Robert. *The Kingdom by the Sea*. Farrar, 1991. Ages 10–13. England, World War II.

Zei, Alki. *Petros' War*. Translated from the Greek by Edward Fenton. Dutton, 1972. Ages 12–YA. Greece, World War II.

———. *Wildcat under Glass*. Translated from the Greek by Edward Fenton. Holt, 1968. Ages 11–YA. Greece, 1930s.

Post-World War II Era, 1946 to 1970s

Bauer, Marion Dane. *Rain of Fire*. Clarion, 1983. Ages 10–13. U.S., post-World War II era.

Brooks, Martha. *Two Moons in August*. Little, 1992. Ages 12–YA. Canada, August 1959.

de Jenkins, Lyll Becerra. *The Honorable Prison*. Lodestar, 1988. Ages 12–YA. South America, 1950s.

Doyle, Brian. *Angel Square*. Groundwood Books, 1984. Ages 9–12. Canada, Ottawa, post-World War II.

Härtling, Peter. *Crutches*. Translated from the German by Elizabeth D. Crawford. Lothrop, 1988. Ages 9–14. Austria, post-World War II.

Hendry, Diana. *Double Vision*. Candlewick, 1993. Ages 13–YA. England, seaside community, 1950s.

Hewitt, Marsha, and Claire MacKay. *One Proud Summer*. Women's Press, 1981. Ages 10–YA. Canada, Quebec, 1946.

Ho, Minfong. *Rice without Rain*. Lothrop, 1988. Ages 11–14. Thailand, class struggles, 1970s.

Krisher, Trudy. *Spite Fences*. Delacorte, 1994. Ages 13–YA. Georgia, race relations, 1960s.

Myers, Walter Dean. *Fallen Angels*. Scholastic, 1988. Ages 14–YA. Vietnam War.

Nelson, Vaunda Micheaux. *Mayfield Crossing*. Illustrated by Leonard Jenkins. Putnam, 1993.

Ages 9–12. U.S. school integration, race relations, baseball, 1960s.

Perera, Hilda. *Kiki: A Cuban Boy's Adventures in America*. Translated from Spanish by Warren Hampton and Hilda Gonzales. Pickering, 1992. Miami, Cuba, Florida's Seminole and Miccosukee tribes, 1960s.

Sacks, Margaret. *Beyond Safe Boundaries*. Lodestar, 1989. Ages 12–YA. South Africa, Jews. 1960s.

Slepian, Jan. *Risk n' Roses*. Putnam, 1990. Ages 11–14. Bronx, New York, 1948.

Talbert, Marc. *The Purple Heart*. HarperCollins, 1992. Ages 10–13. U.S., Vietnam War era.

Uchida, Yoshiko. *Journey Home*. Illustrated by Charles Robinson. Atheneum, 1978. Ages 10–13. U.S., Japanese Americans, post-World War II.

Young, Ronder Thomas. *Learning by Heart*. Houghton, 1993. Ages 9–12. Southern U.S., 1960s.

Chapter 9

Nonfiction: Biography and Informational Books

Questions at Night

Why
Is the sky?

What starts the thunder overhead?
Who makes the crashing noise?
Are the angels falling out of bed?
Are they breaking all their toys?

Why does the sun go down so soon?
Why do the night-clouds crawl
Hungrily up to the new-laid moon
And swallow it, shell and all?

If there's a bear among the stars,
As all the people say,
Won't he jump over those pasture-bars
And drink up the Milky Way?

Does every star that happens to fall
Turn into a firefly?
Can't it ever get back to Heaven at all?
And why
Is the sky?

—Louis Untermeyer

Children are naturally curious. Their interest in the world around them is boundless. Teachers, librarians, and parents want to nourish that curiosity with lively, intelligent answers, provocative questions, and stimulating books that provide answers and a thirst for further knowledge. Today's constantly innovative and improving works of nonfiction are an excellent source of information for children and the adults who guide their learning.

Definition and Description

By now it should be understood that in children's literature there are no absolute genre definitions. For example, nonfiction for children is not limited to works containing only facts. Instead, this genre can best be defined in terms of emphasis. The content emphasis of children's nonfiction is documented fact; its primary purpose is to inform. In contrast, the content of fictional literature is largely, if not wholly, a product of the imagination, and the purpose is to entertain.

Some countries now recognize a third type of literature that has elements of both fiction and nonfiction and call it *faction.* Mogens Jansen, president of the Danish National Association of Reading Teachers, describes *faction* as "'nonfiction' the presentation of which is mainly sustained by 'fiction elements': the well-told nonfiction which has fictional overtones, but *is* nonfictional—and absolutely correct" (Jansen, 1987, p. 16). Although North America has not designated faction as an independent genre, but considers it a part of nonfiction, adults who deal with books and children are well aware of this type of literature and its appeal to 8- to 12-year-old boys, in particular. Today a great number of books present factual information on a ribbon of narrative. Examples are *Cathedral* by David Macaulay and *My Place in Space* by Robin and Sally Hirst, illustrated by Roland Harvey with Joe Levine.

Informational books can be written on any aspect of the physical, biological, and social world, including what is known of outer space. Thus, it should come as no surprise that in most children's collections in school and public libraries well over half of the titles are nonfiction, with some estimates as high as 70 percent. In school libraries, at least, more nonfiction circulates than fiction, and informed sources say that more than half of children's books being published currently are nonfiction. Although fictional literature is better known to the general public (due to book awards and a tendency for adults to equate children's literature with stories), nonfiction is enormously popular with children as recreational reading material.

Biography deals with the life of an actual person of the past or present with the intent of commemorating the subject and inspiring the reader by example. Biographers report the experiences, influences, accomplishments, and legacies of their subjects. An *autobiography* is about the author's own life. *Bill Peet: An Autobiography* by Bill Peet is an example of an autobiography.

Some comment on the formats of nonfiction books is in order. Book format has to do with how information is presented on the book page, rather than with the information itself. Any topic could conceivably be presented in a number of different ways. The most common distinct formats in which informational books for children are currently being produced are as follows:

- *Nonfiction chapter book.*   This format, widely used in nonfiction, features a large amount of text that is organized into chapters. Graphics and illustrations are common in the more recent nonfiction chapter books but are still less important than the text. Almost all biographies, with the exception of picture book biographies, appear in this format. Examples include *Rescue: The Story of How Gentiles Saved Jews in the Holocaust* by Milton Meltzer and *Amos Fortune, Free Man* by Elizabeth Yates.
- *Nonfiction picture book.*   This format features large, uncomplicated illustrations and brief text in large typeface on oversized pages. The illustrations help to convey the information. The main types of informational picture books are concept books, including ABC and counting books (discussed in Chapter 5), and picture book biographies. Examples include *A Picture Book of Eleanor Roosevelt* by David A. Adler, illustrated by Robert Casilla, and *The King's Day* by Aliki.
- *Science and social science concept picture book.*   Originally conceived for 4- to 8-year-olds, this book presents one or two scientific or social concepts via brief, uncomplicated text accompanied by numerous, large illustrations. It also encourages participation by including an experiment or hands-on activity. These books are now available for older children as well. *Evolution* by Joanna Cole, illustrated by Aliki, and the *Science Book* series by Neil Ardley are good examples of this type of book.
- *Photo essay.*   Presentation of information in the photo essay is equally balanced between text and illustration. Excellent, information-bearing photographs, and crisp, condensed writing style are hallmarks of this nonfictional format. Photo essays are generally written for children in the intermediate grades and up. Examples include *Lincoln: A Photobiography* by Russell Freedman and *The American Family Farm* by George Ancona, with text by Joan Anderson.
- *Fact books.*   Presentation of information in these books is mainly through lists, charts, and tables. Examples include almanacs, books of world records, and sports trivia and statistics books. For example, see *The Guinness Book of World Records* published annually by Sterling Publishing Company.

Values of Nonfiction for Children

When the best nonfictional literature is shared regularly with children, the ultimate benefit to them is that they acquire a love of learning. In addition, the following important values of children's nonfiction are worth considering.

- High-quality nonfiction provides accurate information in understandable and interesting language and illustrations, proving to children that learning can be enjoyable.

- Nonfiction provides children with a ready source of factual information about their personal questions, interests, hobbies, and problems.
- Nonfiction can be an excellent resource for content area classes, providing varied sources of information about topics and different points of view about issues.
- The best nonfiction offers students excellent models of the scientific method of observation, hypothesis formulation, data gathering, experimentation, and evaluation.
- Well-written biographies can inspire children to overcome obstacles and formulate goals and can help them to understand and accept themselves and others.

Teachers stand to benefit from good nonfiction as much as children, if they use it as a resource for their content area teaching. It stands to reason that the examples, anecdotes, and interesting facts chosen by world-class researchers and writers might add considerably to most teachers' presentations. Besides, good teaching demands that classroom resources not be confined to the single point of view and selective coverage offered by the average school textbook. It is much more interesting and instructive for children to be presented with a variety of resources to be read, heard, or seen, and then discussed and compared.

Evaluation and Selection of Nonfiction

Criteria for evaluating children's nonfiction bear some similarity to those for evaluating fiction, since authors of both kinds of literature have stories to tell. In nonfiction, however, the story must be true. The criteria listed below will help you to distinguish the worthier books of nonfiction from the not so worthy. However, it is important to remember that every work of nonfiction need not meet every criterion to be worthy and that no one book can cover a topic completely. By offering children a variety of satisfactory books to be read and compared, you more than compensate for the shortcomings of a good-but-not-great book.

- Children's nonfiction must be written in a clear, direct, easily understandable style. In recent years, a tight, compressed, but conversational, writing style has come to be favored in nonfictional text. Such stylistic devices as questions and the second-person pronoun *you*, as in "Have you ever wondered how chameleons change colors?" stimulate readers' interest and involvement.
- Captions and labels must be clearly written and informative. Though brief, these pieces of text serve the vital function of explaining the significance of illustrations or of drawing the reader's attention to important or interesting details pictured.
- Facts must be accurate and current. Since today's children's book editors avoid heavy documentation, evaluators must be careful to check the resources or resource persons used by the author and listed in the introduction,

reference lists, or appendix as indicators of the book's accuracy. Another reliable check is to compare the information with that found in other recently published sources on the topic.

- Nonfiction must distinguish between fact, theory, and opinion. When not clearly stated as such, theories or opinions are flagged in good nonfiction by carefully placed phrases such as "may be," "is believed to be," or "perhaps."
- Attributing human qualities to animals, material objects, or natural forces is called *personification* and is part of the charm of works of traditional and modern fantasy. In nonfiction, however, this same device is to be avoided, because the implication is factually inaccurate. Saying in a work of nonfiction that a horse "feels proud to carry his master" is an example of this device. A similar rhetorical device to be avoided in nonfiction is *teleology,* or giving humanlike purpose to natural phenomena. People sometimes say that nature has "donned its finery" when they are admiring springtime blossoms, and this is perfectly acceptable in our daily conversation. But to explain the forces of nature in such human terms in a work of nonfiction is unscientific.
- Works of nonfiction must be attractive to the child. An intriguing cover, impressive illustrations, and balance of text and illustrations make books look interesting to a child. Dense text that fills up each page and dull, infrequent illustrations can make a book unattractive to young readers.
- Presentation of information should be from known to unknown, general to specific, or simple to more complex to aid conceptual understanding and encourage analytical thinking. Judicious use of subheadings can make text much easier to read and comprehend. Reference aids such as tables of contents, indexes, pronunciation guides, glossaries, maps, charts, and tables also serve to make information in books easier to find and retrieve, more comprehensible, and more complete. Information presented in these ways is not only easier to understand but it also provides models for students' own expository writing.
- Stereotyping must be avoided. The best nonfiction goes beyond mere avoidance of sexist or racist language and stereotyped images in text and illustrations. It also shows positive images of cultural diversity.
- Format and artistic medium should be appropriate to the content. The exactness, clarity, and precision of photography, for example, make this medium useful to authors whose purpose is to present the world as it is. Sometimes, however, a drawing is preferable to a photograph when an illustrator wishes to highlight a specific feature by omitting irrelevant details. Engineered paper or pop-up illustrations are appropriate when three dimensions are required to give an accurate sense of placement of the parts of a whole, as in human anatomy.
- Depth and complexity of subject treatment must be appropriate for the intended audience. If an explanation must be simplified to the extent that facts must be altered before a child can begin to understand, perhaps the concept or topic should be taken up when the child is older.

Selecting the best of nonfiction for children can be a challenge. With an annual North American production of over 2,000 new nonfiction titles on such divergent and complicated topics as black holes and the internal combustion engine, few individuals have time to read more than a fraction of the new titles, let alone know enough about the topics to be able to judge the technical accuracy of these books. Many teachers and librarians find the following professional review sources helpful in identifying the outstanding informational books on topics of interest to them and their students.

> *Eyeopeners* by Beverly Kobrin: A good, general introduction to children's nonfiction and an annotated list of 500 recommended informational books
>
> *The Kobrin Letter:* A monthly newsletter that reviews informational books, both new and old, on selected topics
>
> *Appraisal: Children's Science Books:* A quarterly periodical featuring reviews by content specialists of books with more advanced scientific content
>
> "Outstanding Science Trade Books for Children": An annual, annotated list of notable books in the field of science
>
> "Notable Children's Trade Books in the Field of Social Studies": An annual, annotated list of notable books in the field of social studies
>
> *Historical Figures in Fiction* by Donald K. Hartman and Gregg Sapp: A bibliography of biographies for children and young adults

For further information on these sources, see the Reference List in Appendix B.

In addition to these review sources, the Orbis Pictus Award for Outstanding Nonfiction for Children offers yet another source of good nonfiction titles. The National Council of Teachers of English (NCTE) announces at its November convention the award winner, up to five Honor Books, and other outstanding nonfiction choices published during the previous year. For a complete listing of the Orbis Pictus award winners and honor books, see Appendix A.

Historical Overview of Nonfiction

The history of children's nonfiction begins in 1657 with the publication of John Amos Comenius's *Orbis Pictus, The World in Pictures.* Not only was this the first children's picture book but it was also a work of nonfiction. This auspicious beginning for nonfiction was cut short, however, by the Puritan Movement. For nearly two hundred years the vast majority of books published for and read by children were intended more for moralistic instruction than for information.

Although books of nonfiction continued to be written in the eighteenth and nineteenth centuries, much of the growth and development of this genre occurred

Excellent Nonfiction for Reading Aloud

(Books for each level vary in difficulty and should be selected with students' literary backgrounds in mind.)

Primary Level   Ages 5–8

Coerr, Eleanor. *Sadako*. Illustrated by Ed Young. Putnam, 1993.
Gray, Nigel. *A Country Far Away*. Illustrated by Philippe Dupasquier. Orchard, 1989.
Heller, Ruth. *Chickens Aren't the Only Ones*. Grosset & Dunlap, 1981.
Kuskin, Karla. *The Philharmonic Gets Dressed*. Illustrated by Marc Simont. Harper, 1982.
Provensen, Alice and Martin. *The Glorious Flight: Across the Channel with Louis Blériot*. Viking, 1983.
Robbins, Ken. *Make Me a Peanut Butter Sandwich and a Glass of Milk*. Scholastic, 1991.
Pfeffer, Wendy. *From Tadpole to Frog*. Illustrated by Holly Keller. HarperCollins, 1994.
Simon, Seymour. *Autumn Across America*. Hyperion, 1993.

Intermediate Level   Ages 8–11

Alexander, Sally H. *Mom Can't See Me*. Photographs by George Ancona. Macmillan, 1990.
Brooks, Bruce. *Making Sense: Animal Perception and Communication*. Farrar, 1993.
Cummings, Pat. *Talking With Artists*. Bradbury, 1992.
Fenner, Carol. *Gorilla, Gorilla*. Illustrated by Symeon Shimin. Random, 1973.
Fritz, Jean. *And Then What Happened, Paul Revere?* Illustrated by Tomie dePaola. Coward, McCann, 1973.
Krull, Kathleen. *Lives of the Musicians*. Illustrated by Kathryn Hewitt. Harcourt, 1993.
Peet, Bill. *Bill Peet: An Autobiography*. Houghton, 1989.
Perl, Lila. *The Great Ancestor Hunt: The Fun of Finding Out Who You Are*. Clarion, 1989.
Tsuchiya, Yukio. *Faithful Elephants*. Illustrated by Ted Lewin. Translated by Tomoko Tsuchiya Dykes.

Advanced Level   Ages 11–14

Brandenburg, Jim. Edited by Joann Bren Guernsey. *To the Top of the World: Adventures with Arctic Wolves*. Walker, 1993.
Freedman, Russell. *Lincoln: A Photobiography*. Clarion, 1987.
Hamilton, Virginia. *Many Thousand Gone: African Americans from Slavery to Freedom*. Illustrated by Leo and Diane Dillon. Knopf, 1993.
Latham, Jean Lee. *Carry On, Mr. Bowditch*. Houghton, 1955.
Lyons, Mary E. *Letters from a Slave Girl: The Story of Harriet Jacobs*. Scribner's, 1992.
Meltzer, Milton. *Columbus and the World Around Him*. Franklin Watts, 1990.
Rogasky, Barbara. *Smoke and Ashes: The Story of the Holocaust*. Holiday, 1988.
Stanley, Jerry. *Children of the Dust Bowl: The True Story of the School at Weedpatch*. Crown, 1992.

in the twentieth century. Writing in 1953 about history and biography for children, Elizabeth Nesbitt commented, "In comparison with the present, the early 1900s seem poverty-stricken in these two fields, in regard to both number of books and to significance of presentation" (Meigs, Eaton, Nesbitt, & Viguers, 1953, p. 392). The growth of public school and library systems in the United States and Canada called for more nonfiction trade books to meet the curricular demands of schools. With few exceptions, however, much of the children's nonfiction written during the first half of the twentieth century was decidedly unremarkable in quality.

Then, in 1957, the former Soviet Union launched *Sputnik*, the first artificial space satellite, and the United States was galvanized into action in an effort to catch up and win the race for space and technology. The National Defense Education Act funneled federal money into science education, and children's book publishers responded with a wave of improved science trade books on every conceivable topic. The gush of federal funding and the emphasis on science in schools lasted through most of the 1960s, during which time nonfiction continued a gradual evolution in style and format and a growing trend toward publication in series. Generous use of illustrations in nonfiction, introduced in the "picture histories" and "picture geographies" of the 1940s and 1950s, was taken to a new level in the science concept picture book, which appeared in the early 1960s (Giblin, 1988). These books, exemplified by the *Let's Read and Find Out* series (Crowell), successfully delivered science concepts to preschool and primary-grade audiences for the first time by using numerous, large, high-quality illustrations. Popular with children accustomed to watching television, this trend toward more illustrations and less text in nonfiction has continued to the present time and has resulted in the adoption (from *Life* magazine), development, and refinement of yet another format for children's nonfiction—the photo essay.

As the stature of nonfiction rose and more top-flight authors and illustrators were engaged in its production, the quality of research, writing, and art in these books improved. The inaccuracies of fictionalizing, the dullness of lengthy and stiff or overly sentimental prose, and the incidental nature of infrequent and colorless illustrations common in nonfiction through the 1950s were no longer tolerated. A lighter, yet factual, tone balanced with high-quality, informative illustrations and graphics emerged as the preferred nonfiction style of the 1980s (Elleman, 1987).

Meanwhile, children's biographies were greatly affected by the more liberal attitudes and relaxed topic restrictions that revolutionized children's fiction in the 1960s. Prior to this time, certain subjects (ethnic minorities, women, infamous people) and topics (the subjects' personal weaknesses, mistakes, and tragedies) were not often found in children's biographies. It was thought that subjects worthy of being commemorated should be placed on a pedestal. By the mid-1960s, this had changed, as Russell Freedman (1988) pointed out in his Newbery Award acceptance speech: "The hero worship of the past has given way to a more realistic approach, which recognizes the warts and weaknesses that humanize the great" (p. 447).

Long in the literary shadow of fiction (less than 10 percent of the Newbery winners were nonfiction as of 1980), nonfiction finally achieved equal stature in the 1980s. Nancy Willard won a Newbery Award for her biographical poem, *A Visit to William Blake's Inn: Poems for Innocent and Experienced Travelers* (Harcourt Brace

Jovanovich, 1981), and Russell Freedman won a Newbery Award for his photo essay, *Lincoln: A Photobiography* (Clarion, 1987) in 1988. Moreover, six works of nonfiction were among the Newbery Honor Books between 1980 and 1990.

As the decade of the nineties began, it was widely recognized in the children's book industry that nonfiction was *the* hot topic in book selection for the young. But this surge of interest in nonfiction was not the result of massive government funding, as in the 1950s and 1960s. Rather, it was the result of parents and librarians who were willing to supply their children with the best learning materials possible.

The trend toward respect and recognition of children's nonfiction culminated in 1990 with the establishment of the Orbis Pictus Award for Outstanding Nonfiction for Children. This award program, sponsored by the National Council of Teachers of English, is for the purpose of promoting and recognizing excellence in the writing of nonfiction for children. The award itself is made annually to the author of what has been judged to be the most outstanding work of nonfiction (excluding textbooks, historical fiction, folklore, and poetry) published during the previous year. Named in honor of Comenius's book written some 300 years earlier, this award calls to mind how far children's nonfiction has come. Recent multimedia publication (book and CD-ROM versions) of nonfictional books such as David Macaulay's *The Way Things Work* suggests an exciting future for this genre. Milestones in the development of nonfiction for children are highlighted in Table 9-1.

Types of Biographies

In adult nonfiction, biographies must be completely documented to be acceptable. In biographies for children, more latitude is allowed, and biographers use varying degrees of invention. This invention ranges from choosing what aspect of the subject the biographer wants to emphasize as the theme of the book (e.g., great energy or love of freedom) to actually inventing fictional characters and conversation.

Biographies, then, can be classified by degree of documentation, as follows:

Authentic biography   In this type of biography, all factual information is documented through eyewitness accounts, written documents, letters, diaries, and, more recently, audio and videotape recordings. Details in the lives of people who lived long ago, such as conversations, are often difficult to document, however. So, for the sake of art, biographers must use such devices as interior monologue (telling what someone probably thought or said to himself or herself based on known actions), indirect discourse (reporting the gist of what someone said without using quotation marks), attribution (interpretation of known actions to determine probable motives), and inference to make their stories lively and appealing and worth the children's time to read. Skillful biographers such as Jean Fritz are able to employ these devices without altering the truth or fictionalizing. Still, it is advisable to read and compare several biographies of a subject, if possible, in order to counteract any bias an author might have. *The Great Little Madison* by Jean Fritz is an example of an authentic biography.

TABLE 9–1   Milestones in the Development of Nonfiction for Children

Date	Event	Significance
1657	*Orbis Pictus* by John Amos Comenius	First known work of nonfiction for children
1671	*A Token for Children, Being an Exact Account of the Conversions, Holy and Exemplary Lives and Joyful Deaths of Several Young Children* by James Janeway	A didactic biography believed to be the most widely read children's book in the Puritan era
1683	*New England Primer*	First concept book for American children; reflected didacticism of the Puritan era
1921	*The Story of Mankind* by Hendrik Van Loon	Won the first Newbery award; greatly influenced children's books with its lively style and creative approach
1939	*Abraham Lincoln* by Ingri and Edgar Parin d'Aulaire	One of the first picture book biographies for younger children
1940	*Daniel Boone* by James H. Daugherty	First biography to win the Newbery Award
1948	*The Story of the Negro* by Arne Bontemps	The first important history of the Negro
1952	*Diary of a Young Girl* by Anne Frank	Classic autobiography; helped many to understand the tragedy of the Jewish Holocaust
1960	*Let's-Read-and-Find-Out* series by Franklyn Branley and Roma Gans	Introduced the science concept picture book for young children
1969	*To Be a Slave* by Julius Lester	African-American nonfiction chosen as Newbery Honor Book
1987	*Lincoln: A Photobiography* by Russell Freedman	First nonfictional photo essay to win a Newbery Award
1990	First Orbis Pictus Award for Nonfiction (*The Great Little Madison* by Jean Fritz)	Nonfiction as a genre is recognized

Fictionalized biography   This type of biography is also based on careful research, but the author creates dramatic episodes from known facts by using imagined conversation. The conversation is, of course, carefully structured around what pertinent facts are known, but the actual words are invented by the author. An example of this type of biography is *Carry On, Mr. Bowditch* by Jean Lee Latham.

Biographical fiction   This type of biography allows much artistic license, including invented dialogue, fictional secondary characters, and some reconstructed action. The known achievements of the biographical subjects are reported accurately, but in other respects these works are as much fiction as fact. Examples include *Anthony Burns: The Defeat and Triumph of a Fugitive Slave* by Virginia Hamilton and *Ben and Me* by Robert Lawson.

Biographies can also be classified by coverage of the subject's life. Quality in biography for young readers, as determined by accuracy of information, coverage, and writing style, will vary. In evaluating the following types of biographies, you will want to look for a balance between the need for adequate coverage and the tolerance that the target child audience has for detail.

- The *complete biography* covers the entire life of the subject from birth to death. An example is *Columbus and the World Around Him* by Milton Meltzer.
- The *partial biography* covers only part of the life of the subject. Biographies for very young children will often be of this type, as will, of course, the biographies of living persons. An example is *Teammates* by Peter Golenbock, illustrated by Paul Bacon.
- The *collected biography* includes the life stories of several people in one book, organized into chapters. An example is *Indian Chiefs* by Russell Freedman.
- The *biography series* is a multivolume set of books with each book containing one separate biography. Most series of this type feature subjects with some common attribute, accomplishment, or skill, such as leadership or legendary sports ability. For example, the *Women of Our Time* series, published by Viking, includes biographies on such subjects as Grandma Moses, Babe Didrikson, Diana Ross, and Margaret Thatcher; and the *First Biographies* series by David A. Adler, published by Holiday House, written for beginning independent readers in grades 2 through 4, includes biographies on such subjects as Thomas Jefferson, Martin Luther King, and Jackie Robinson.

Topics of Informational Books

Although nonfiction is confined to just one chapter in this book, it is by far the largest single genre in children's literature in that everything known to humankind is a conceivable topic. Organization of such an enormous variety of topics could, of course, be done in a variety of satisfactory ways, one of which is the scientific approach used here. First, the world of information is divided into the biological, the physical, the social, and the applied sciences; then the humanities and biography are dealt with separately.

The Biological Sciences

The biological sciences deal with living organisms and the laws and phenomena that relate to any organism or group of organisms. A topic particularly interesting to children within this field is the human body—its anatomy, senses, nutrition, reproduction, health, handicaps, and heredity. Equally interesting to children are information books about pets and their care, breeding, and training, as well as the habits, habitats, life cycles, and migrations of wild animals. Ecology and the environment will be of interest and concern to more and more children who recognize the fragility of our global ecology and their responsibility to help protect it from destruction. Informational books can help children to understand what harms our ecology and to learn how they can participate in its protection and healing. Examples include *Going Green: A Kid's Handbook to Saving the Planet* by John Elkington, Julia Hailes, Douglas Hill, and Joel Makower, illustrated by Tony Ross; and *The Human Body* by Jonathan Miller, designed by David Pelham.

The Physical Sciences

The physical sciences, sometimes referred to as the natural sciences, deal primarily with nonliving materials. Rocks, landforms, oceans, the stars, and the atmosphere and its weather and seasons are all likely topics that children could learn about within the fields of geology, geography, oceanography, astronomy, and meteorology that comprise the physical sciences. Not only will children be able to satisfy their curiosity about such topics in this category as volcanoes and earthquakes, but teachers will also find the many books about the planets and our solar system helpful in presenting these topics in class. Examples include *Weather Words and What They Mean* by Gail Gibbons and *Volcano: The Eruption and Healing of Mount St. Helens* by Patricia Lauber.

The Social Sciences

The social sciences deal with the institutions and functioning of human society and the interpersonal relationships of individuals as members of society. Through books in this field children can learn about various forms of government, religions, different countries and their cultures, money, and transportation. Most children have a natural interest in books about careers, family relationships, and leisure activities and will appreciate finding answers to their questions without always having to ask an adult. An example is *Celebrating Kwanzaa* by Diane Hoyt-Goldsmith, illustrated by Lawrence Migdale.

The Applied Sciences

The applied sciences deal with the practical applications of pure science that people have devised. All machines, for example—from simple levers to super computers, from bicycles to space rockets—are part of this field, and many children are naturally interested in finding out how they work. Interest in the applied sciences can be developed in children by pointing out how their lives are affected by these applications. For example, children get sick and medicine helps to cure them. How? Children get hungry and food appears. What are the processes by which the food is produced, prepared, packaged, and marketed? Children like toys and buy them in stores. Who designs the toys and how are they manufactured? The answers to questions like these can be found in today's nonfictional literature. For example, see *The Way Things Work* by David Macaulay and *Milk* by Donald Carrick.

A specific type of book within the applied sciences—the experiment or how-to book—capitalizes on children's natural curiosity and fondness for hands-on activities. Its contents range from directions for conducting various scientific experiments to cookbooks, guides to hobbies, and directions for small construction projects, like clubhouses. For example, see *How to Make a Chemical Volcano and Other Mysterious Experiments* by Alan Kramer.

The Humanities

The humanities deal with those branches of learning that primarily have a cultural or artistic character. Of greatest interest to children and their teachers are books about the fine arts of drawing, painting, and sculpture; the performing arts of singing, dancing, making instrumental music, and acting; and handicrafts of all sorts. Since many children are artistically creative and often study dance, music, and drawing, they can be led to read about the arts and artists to learn new techniques or to draw inspiration from the experiences of others. Some might read these books to decide whether they are interested in trying to develop their artistic talent. Some books make the arts more accessible or real to children by explaining what to look for in paintings or an opera, for example, or by revealing the hard work required of an artist to achieve a spectacular performance or an intriguing work of art. Examples include *A Very Young Musician* by Jill Krementz and *Great Painters* by Piero Ventura.

As never before, today's nonfictional literature for children is able to meet the needs and interests of young readers in quality, variety, and reader appeal. With these books, children's appetites for learning can be fed while their curiosity for more information is piqued.

References

Elleman, Barbara. (1987). Current trends in literature for children. *Library Trends, 35* (3), 413–426.

Freedman, Russell. (1988). Newbery medal acceptance. *The Horn Book, 64* (4), 444–451.

Giblin, James Cross. (1988). The rise and fall and rise of juvenile nonfiction, 1961–1988. *School Library Journal, 35* (2), 27–31.

Jansen, Mogens. (1987). *A little about language, words, and concepts—Or what may happen when children learn to read.* Translated by Lotte Rosbak Juhl. Dragör, Denmark: Landsforeningen af Læsepædagoger.

Meigs, C., Eaton, A. T., Nesbitt, E., & Viguers, R. H. (1953). *A critical history of children's literature.* New York: Macmillan.

Untermeyer, Louis. (1969). Questions at Night. In L. Untermeyer (Selector), *The golden treasury of poetry.* London: Collins.

Notable Authors of Nonfiction

Aliki, author/illustrator of informational picture books for older readers. *The King's Day; A Medieval Feast.*

George Ancona, illustrator/author of photoessays. *The American Family Farm.*

Rhoda Blumberg, author of accounts of important explorations in U.S. history. *The Incredible Journey of Lewis and Clark; Commodore Perry in the Land of the Shogun.*

Franklyn Branley, originator of the science concept picture book.

Clyde Robert Bulla, author of biographies for beginning independent readers. *Squanto, Friend of the White Man.*

Joanna Cole, author of a variety of informational books for beginning independent readers. *Magic School Bus* series.

Ingri and Edgar Parin d'Aulaire, authors/illustrators of several oversized picture book biographies for 5- to 7-year-olds. *Christopher Columbus; Abraham Lincoln.*

Russell Freedman, author of biographies of famous Americans and of informational books about U.S. history. *Lincoln: A Photobiography; Children of the Wild West.*

Jean Fritz, biographer of political leaders during the U.S. Revolutionary War era. *Can't You Make Them Behave, King George?; And Then*

What Happened, Paul Revere?

Gail Gibbons, author/illustrator of numerous informational books for the 5- to 7-year-old that explain how everyday things work or get done. *The Post Office Book; Check It Out! The Book About Libraries.*

Virginia Hamilton, biographer of several important African Americans. *Anthony Burns: The Defeat and Triumph of a Fugitive Slave; W.E.B. DuBois.*

Jill Krementz, author of nonfiction series on children's hobbies and coping with difficult situations. *How It Feels To Live with a Physical Disability.*

Kathryn Lasky, author of well-regarded works of photojournalism and works concerning archaeology. *Sugaring Time; Dinosaur Dig.*

Patricia Lauber, author of definitive nonfiction on popular topics such as volcanoes, mummies, and dinosaurs. *Volcano: The Eruption and Healing of Mt. St. Helens; Tales Mummies Tell.*

David Macaulay, author/illustrator of several books of faction about construction of monumental buildings and informational picture books for older readers. *Cathedral; The Way Things Work.*

Milton Meltzer, author who presents the minority perspective in historical informational books. *The Black Americans: A History in Their Own Words.*

Dorothy Hinshaw Patent, zoologist who writes informational books about animals. *Farm Animals; Whales: Giants of the Deep.*

Laurence Pringle, author of many informational books that express concern for the environment. *Nuclear Energy: Troubled Past, Uncertain Future.*

Anne Rockwell, creator of concept books for preschoolers. *Willy Can Count.*

Jack Denton Scott, author of photo essays about well-known American birds and animals. *Alligator; Little Dogs of the Prairie.*

Millicent E. Selsam, author of informational books about plants and "A First Look" nonfiction series for primary-grade children. *The Amazing Dandelion; A First Look at Animals That Eat Other Animals.*

Seymour Simon, author of over 100 science-related books that often contain practical activities. *The Planets* series; *Icebergs and Glaciers.*

Diane Stanley, author of picture book biographies for older readers. *Good Queen Bess: The Story of Elizabeth I of England; Shaka: King of the Zulus.*

Yoshiko Uchida, author of an autobiographical account of the internment of Japanese Americans during World War II. *Journey to Topaz; Journey Home.*

Recommended Nonfiction Books

Ages refer to approximate reading levels. YA = young adult readers. Biography is organized by historical era as in Chapter 8.

Biography

Civilizations of the Ancient World, 3000 B.C. to A.D. 600

Lasker, Joe. *The Great Alexander the Great.* Viking, 1983. Ages 7–9.

Lasky, Kathryn. *The Librarian Who Measured the Earth.* Illustrated by Kevin Hawkes. Little, Brown, 1994. Ages 7–10.

Civilizations of the Medieval World, 600 to 1500

d'Aulaire, Ingri and Edgar Parin. *Columbus.* Doubleday, 1955. Ages 7–9.

Meltzer, Milton. *Columbus and the World Around Him.* Watts. 1990. Ages 12–YA.

The Emergence of Modern Nations, 1500 to 1800

Bulla, Clyde Robert. *Squanto, Friend of the White Man.* Illustrated by Peter Burchard. Crowell, 1954. Ages 7–9.

Fritz, Jean. *And Then What Happened, Paul Revere?* Illustrated by Tomie dePaola. Coward/McCann, 1973. Ages 8–10.

———. *Can't You Make Them Behave, King George?* Illustrated by Tomie dePaola. Coward/McCann, 1976. Ages 8–10.

———. *The Double Life of Pocahontas.* Illustrated by Ed Young. Putnam, 1983. Ages 8–10.

———. *The Great Little Madison.* Putnam, 1989. Ages 9–12.

———. *Traitor: The Case of Benedict Arnold.* Putnam, 1981. Ages 9–12.

———. *What's the Big Idea, Ben Franklin?* Illustrated by Margot Tomes. Coward/McCann,1978. Ages 8–10.

———. *Where Do You Think You're Going, Christopher Columbus?* Illustrated by Margot Tomes. Putnam, 1980. Ages 8–10.

———. *Where Was Patrick Henry on the 29th of May?* Illustrated by Margot Tomes. Coward/McCann, 1975. Ages 8–10.

———. *Why Don't You Get a Horse, Sam Adams?* Illustrated by Trina Schart Hyman. Coward/McCann, 1974. Ages 8–10.

———. *Will You Sign Here, John Hancock?* Illustrated by Trina Schart Hyman. Coward/ McCann, 1976. Ages 8–10.

Gerrard, Roy. *Sir Francis Drake: His Daring Deeds.* Farrar, 1988. Ages 9–12.

Giblin, James C. *Thomas Jefferson: A Picture Book Biography.* Illustrated by Michael Dooling. Scholastic, 1994. Ages 8–10.

Lawson, Robert. *Ben and Me.* Little, Brown, 1951 (1939).

Lyons, Mary E. *Letters from a Slave Girl: The Story of Harriet Jacobs.* Scribner's, 1992. Ages 10–14.

Meltzer, Milton. *George Washington and the Birth of Our Nation.* Watts, 1986. Ages 12–YA.

———. *Thomas Jefferson: The Revolutionary Aristocrat.* Watts, 1991. Ages 12–YA.

Ross, Stewart. *Shakespeare and Macbeth: The Story Behind the Play.* Illustrated by Tony Karpinski. Viking, 1994. Ages 9–12.

Stanley, Diane, and Peter Vennema. *Bard of Avon: The Story of William Shakespeare.* Illustrated by Diane Stanley. Morrow, 1992. Ages 8–13.

———. *Good Queen Bess: The Story of Elizabeth I of England.* Four Winds, 1990. Ages 8–10.

Willard, Nancy. *A Visit to William Blake's Inn: Poems for Innocent and Experienced Travelers.* Illustrated by Alice and Martin Provensen. Harcourt, 1981. Ages 8–10.

Yates, Elizabeth. *Amos Fortune, Free Man.* Illustrated by Nora S. Unwin. Dutton, 1950. Ages 8–12.

The Development of Industrial Society, 1800 to 1914

Blair, Gwenda. *Laura Ingalls Wilder.* Illustrated by Thomas B. Allen. Putnam, 1981. Ages 8–10.

Blumberg, Rhoda. *Commodore Perry in the Land of the Shogun.* Lothrop, 1985. Ages 9–12.

———. *The Incredible Journey of Lewis and Clark.* Lothrop, 1987. Ages 9–12.

d'Aulaire, Ingri and Edgar Parin. *Abraham Lincoln.* Doubleday, 1939, 1957. Ages 7–9.

Freedman, Russell. *Indian Chiefs.* Holiday, 1987. Ages 9–12.

———. *Lincoln: A Photobiography.* Clarion, 1987. Ages 9–12.

———. *The Wright Brothers: How They Invented the Airplane.* Holiday, 1991. Ages 9–12.

Fritz, Jean. *Bully for You, Teddy Roosevelt!* Putnam, 1991. Ages 8–10.

Hamilton, Virginia. *Anthony Burns: The Defeat and Triumph of a Fugitive Slave.* Knopf, 1988. Ages 11–YA.

Klausner, Janet. *Sequoyah's Gift: A Portrait of the Cherokee Leader.* HarperCollins, 1993.

Krull, Kathleen. *Lives of the Musicians: Good Times, Bad Times (and What the Neighbors Thought).* Harcourt, 1993. Ages 8–10.

———. *Lives of the Writers: Comedies, Tragedies (and What Their Neighbors Thought).* Illustrated by Kathryn Hewitt. Harcourt, 1994. Ages 8–10.

Kunhardt, Edith. *Honest Abe.* Illustrated by Malcah Zeldis. Greenwillow, 1993. Ages 7–9.

Latham, Jean Lee. *Carry On, Mr. Bowditch.* Houghton, 1955. Ages 10–12.

Meltzer, Milton. *Lincoln: In His Own Words.* Illustrated by Stephen Alcorn. Harcourt, 1993. Ages 10–14.

Russell, Marion. Adapted by Ginger Wadsworth. *Along the Santa Fe Trail: Marion Russell's Own Story.* Illustrated by James Watling. Whitman, 1993. Ages 7–10.

Sandburg, Carl. *Abe Lincoln Grows Up,* reprinted from *Abraham Lincoln: The Prairie Years.* Illustrated by James Daugherty. Harcourt, 1928. Ages 9–12.

Stanley, Diane, and Peter Vennema. *Charles Dickens: The Man Who Had Great Expectations.* Illustrated by Diane Stanley. Morrow, 1993. Ages 9–12.

———. *The Last Princess: The Story of Princess Ka'iulani of Hawaii.* Four Winds, 1991. Ages 8–10.

———. *Shaka: King of the Zulus.* Illustrated by Diane Stanley. Morrow, 1988. Ages 7–9.

Whiteley, Opal. Selected by Jane Boulton. *Only Opal.* Illustrated by Barbara Cooney. Philomel, 1994. Ages 7–10.

World Wars of the Twentieth Century, 1914 to 1945

Adler, David A. *A Picture Book of Eleanor Roosevelt.* Holiday, 1991. (See others in the *First Biogra-*

phies series.) Ages 6–8.

Cleary, Beverly. *A Girl from Yamhill: A Memoir.* Morrow, 1988. Ages 8–10.

Freedman, Russell. *Franklin Delano Roosevelt.* Clarion, 1990. Ages 9–12.

———. *Eleanor Roosevelt: A Life of Discovery.* Clarion, 1993. Ages 9–12.

Fritz, Jean. *China Homecoming.* Putnam, 1985. Ages 8–10.

———. *Homesick: My Own Story.* Illustrated by Margot Tomes. Putnam, 1982. Ages 8–10.

Lyons, Mary E. *Sorrow's Kitchen: The Life and Folklore of Zora Neale Hurston.* Scribner's, 1990. Ages 12–YA.

Meltzer, Milton. *Dorothea Lange, Life through the Camera.* Illustrated by Donna Diamond. Viking, 1985. Ages 9–12.

Peet, Bill. *Bill Peet: An Autobiography.* Houghton, 1989. Ages 8–10.

Say, Allen. *El Chino.* Houghton, 1990. Ages 8–10.

Toll, Nelly S. *Behind the Secret Window: A Memoir of a Hidden Childhood During World War Two.* Dial, 1993. Ages 10–14.

Uchida, Yoshiko. *The Invisible Thread.* Messner, 1992. Ages 10–13.

———. *Journey to Topaz.* Scribner's, 1971. (Sequel: *Journey Home,* Atheneum, 1978.) Ages 9–12.

van der Rol, Ruud, and Rian Verhoeven. *Anne Frank: Beyond the Diary: A Photographic Remembrance.* Translated by Tony Langham and Plym Peters. Viking, 1993. Ages 10–YA.

Post-World War II Era, 1946 to 1970s

Adoff, Arnold. *Malcolm X.* Crowell, 1970. Ages 8–10.

Bray, Rosemary L. *Martin Luther King.* Illustrated by Malcah Zeldis. Morrow, 1995.

Coerr, Eleanor. *Sadako.* Illustrated by Ed Young. Putnam, 1993. Ages 8–12.

———. *Sadako and the Thousand Paper Cranes.* Illustrated by Ronald Himler. Putnam, 1977.

Filipovic, Zlata. *Zlata's Diary: A Child's Life in Sarajevo.* Viking, 1994. Ages 10–14.

Golenbock, Peter. *Teammates.* Illustrated by Paul Bacon. Harcourt, 1990. Ages 7–9.

Hyman, Trina Schart. *Self-Portrait: Trina Schart Hyman.* Addison-Wesley, 1981. Ages 7–9.

Littlefield, Bill. *Champions: Stories of Ten Remarkable Athletes.* Illustrated by Bernie Fuchs. Little, Brown, 1993. Ages 11–14.

Myers, Walter Dean. *Malcolm X: By Any Means Necessary.* Scholastic, 1993. Ages 12–14.

Turner, Glennette Tilley. *Take a Walk In Their Shoes.* Illustrated by Ellen C. Fox. Dutton/Cobblehill, 1989. Ages 8–10.

Winter, Jonah. *Diego.* Translated by Amy Prince. Illustrated by Jeanette Winter. Knopf, 1991. Ages 6–9.

Women of Our Time Series. Viking. Ages 9–12.

Zemach, Margot. *Self-Portrait, Margot Zemach.* Addison-Wesley, 1978. Ages 8–10.

Zhensun, Zheng, and Alice Low. *A Young Painter: The Life and Paintings of Wang Yani—China's Extraordinary Young Artist.* Scholastic, 1991. Ages 8–14.

Informational Books

The Biological Sciences

Arnold, Caroline. *On the Brink of Extinction: The California Condor.* Photos by Michael Wallace. Harcourt, 1993. Ages 9–11.

———. *Saving the Peregrine Falcon.* Photographs by Richard R. Hewett. Carolrhoda, 1985. Ages 8–10.

Arnosky, Jim. *Deer at the Brook.* Lothrop, 1986. Ages 6–8.

———. *Raccoons and Ripe Corn.* Lothrop, 1987. Ages 6–8.

Banish, Roslyn. *Let Me Tell You about My Baby.* Harper, 1988. Ages 7–9.

Bash, Barbara. *Shadows of the Night: The Hidden World of the Little Brown Bat.* Sierra Club, 1993. Ages 7–12.

———. *Tree of Life: The World of the African Baobab.* Little, Brown, 1989. Ages 7–9.

Brandenburg, Jim. Edited by Joann Bren Guernsey. *To the Top of the World: Adventures with Arctic Wolves.* Walker, 1993. Ages 9–YA.

Brinkloe, Julie. *Fireflies!* Macmillan, 1985. Ages 6–8.

Brooks, Bruce. *Nature by Design.* Farrar, 1991. Ages 11–13.

———. *Predator!* Farrar, 1991. Ages 11–13.

Brown, Laurene Krasny, and Marc Brown. *Dinosaurs Alive and Well!: A Guide to Good Health.* Little, Brown, 1990. Ages 6–8.

Brown, Marc. *Your First Garden Book.* Atlantic-Little, 1981. Ages 4–6.

Cajacob, Thomas, and Teresa Burton. *Close to the Wild: Siberian Tigers in a Zoo.* Photographs by Thomas Cajacob. Carolrhoda, 1986. Ages 7–9.

Cole, Henry. *Jack's Garden.* Morrow, 1995. Ages 5–9.

Cole, Joanna. *Evolution.* Illustrated by Aliki. Crowell, 1990. Ages 6–8.

———. *A Horse's Body.* Photographs by Jerome Wexler. Morrow, 1981. (Others in the series: *A Snake's Body,* 1981; *A Cat's Body,* 1982; *A Big Bird's Body,* 1983.) Ages 6–8.

———. *How You Were Born.* (rev. ed.) Photos by Margaret Miller. Morrow, 1993. Ages 5–8.

———. *The Human Body: How We Evolved.* Illustrated by Walter Gaffney-Kessel and Juan Carlos Barberis. Morrow, 1987. Ages 6–8.

———. *Large As Life: Nighttime Animals Life Size.* Illustrated by Kenneth Lilly. Knopf, 1985. Ages 6–8.

———. *My Puppy Is Born.* (rev. ed.) Photographs by Jerome Wexler. Morrow, 1991. Ages 6–8.

———. *The Magic Schoolbus: Inside the Human Body.* Illustrated by Bruce Degen. Scholastic, 1989. Ages 7–9.

Durell, Ann, and Jean C. George, Katherine Paterson (Editors). *The Big Book for Our Planet.* Dutton, 1993. Ages 7–YA.

Ehlert, Lois. *Eating the Alphabet: Fruits and Vegetables from A–Z.* Harcourt, 1989. Ages 4–6.

———. *Growing Vegetable Soup.* Harcourt, 1987. Ages 4–6.

Esbensen, Barbara Juster. *Great Northern Diver: The Loon.* Illustrated by Mary Barrett Brown. Little, Brown, 1990. Ages 8–10.

Flackham, Margery. *And Then There Was One: The Mysteries of Extinction.* Illustrated by Pamela Johnson. Little, Brown, 1990. Ages 8–12.

———. *Do Not Disturb: The Mysteries of Animal Hibernation and Sleep.* Illustrated by Pamela Johnson. Little, Brown, 1989. Ages 8–12.

Freedman, Russell. *Dinosaurs and Their Young.* Illustrated by Leslie Morrill. Holiday, 1983. Ages 8–10.

———. *Sharks.* Holiday, 1985. Ages 8–10.

George, Jean C. *One Day in the Woods.* Illustrated by Gary Allen. Crowell, 1988. (See also: *One Day in the Tropical Rain Forest,* 1990.) Ages 7–9.

George, William T. *Box Turtle at Long Pond.* Illustrated by Lindsay Barrett George. Greenwillow, 1989. Ages 6–8.

Goodall, Jane. *The Chimpanzee Family Book.* Photographs by Michael Neugebauer. Picture Book Studio, 1989. Ages 8–10.

Goor, Ron and Nancy. *Insect Metamorphosis: From Egg to Adult.* Photographs by Ron Goor. Atheneum, 1990. Ages 7–9.

Harris, Robie H. *It's Perfectly Normal: A Book about Changing Bodies, Growing Up, Sex, and Sexual Health.* Illustrated by Michael Emberley. Candlewick, 1994. Ages 11–14

Hausherr, Rosemarie. *My First Kitten.* Four Winds, 1985. Ages 6–8.

Jasperson, William. *Cranberries.* Houghton, 1991. Ages 8–10.

Johnston, Ginny, and Judy Cutchins. *Scaly Babies: Reptiles Growing Up.* Morrow, 1988. Ages 7–9.

Kitzinger, Sheila. *Being Born.* Photographs by Lennart Nilsson. Grosset, 1986. Ages 6–YA.

Lauber, Patricia. *Fur, Feathers, and Flippers: How Animals Live Where They Do.* Scholastic, 1994. Ages 8–12.

———. *The News about Dinosaurs.* Bradbury, 1989. Ages 8–12.

———. *Seeds Pop! Stick! Glide!* Photographs by Jerome Wexler. Crown, 1981. Ages 8–12.

Lavies, Bianca. *Backyard Hunter: The Praying Mantis.* Dutton, 1990. Ages 7–9.

———. *Lily Pad Pond.* Dutton, 1989. Ages 7–9.

———. *Tree Trunk Traffic.* Dutton, 1989. Ages 7–9.

Lewis, Naomi. *Swan.* Illustrated by Deborah King. Lothrop, May 1986. Ages 7–9.

Mabey, Richard. *Oak and Company.* Illustrated by Clare Roberts. Greenwillow, 1983. Ages 6–8.

Martin, James. *Hiding Out: Camouflage in the Wild.* Illustrated by Art Wolfe. Crown, 1993. Ages 8–10.

Mason, Cherie. *Wild Fox: A True Story.* Illustrated by Jo Ellen A. Stammen. Down East, 1993. Ages 7–9.

Matthews, Downs. *Polar Bear Cubs.* Photographs by Dan Guravich. Simon and Schuster, 1989. Ages 6–8.

McClung, Robert M. *America's Endangered Birds: Programs & People Working to Save Them.* Illustrated by George Founds. Morrow, 1979. Ages 9–12.

McLaughlin, Molly. *Earth Worms, Dirt, and Rotten Leaves: An Exploration in Ecology.* Macmillan, 1988. Ages 9–12.

McNulty, Faith. *Peeping in the Shell: A Whooping Crane is Hatched.* Illustrated by Irene Brady. Harper, 1986. Ages 8–10.

Miller, Jonathan. *The Human Body.* Designed by David Pelham. Viking, 1983. Ages 9–12.

Norsgaard, E. Jaediker. *How to Raise Butterflies.* Photographs by Campbell Norsgaard. Putnam, 1988. Ages 7–9.

Parker, Nancy Winslow, and Joan Richards Wright. *Bugs.* Illustrated by Nancy Winslow Parker. Greenwillow, 1987. Ages 7–9.

Patent, Dorothy Hinshaw. *Farm Animals.* Photographs by William Muñoz. Holiday, 1984. Ages 6–8.

———. *A Picture Book of Cows.* Photographs by William Muñoz. Holiday, 1982. Ages 6–8.

———. *Where the Bald Eagles Gather.* Photographs by William Muñoz. Clarion, 1984. Ages 6–8.

Patterson, Francine. *Koko's Kitten.* Photographs by Ronald H. Cohn. Scholastic, 1985. Ages 6–10.

———. *Koko's Story.* Photographs by Ronald H. Cohn. Scholastic, 1988. Ages 6–10.

Pringle, Laurence. *Death Is Natural.* Four Winds, 1977. Ages 7–9.

———. *Dinosaurs and Their World.* Harcourt, 1968. Ages 7–9.

Ryder, Joanne. *Where Butterflies Grow.* Illustrated by Lynne Cherry. Lodestar, 1989. Ages 7–9.

———. *White Bear, Ice Bear.* Illustrated by Michael Rothman. Morrow, 1989. Ages 7–9.

Sattler, Helen Roney. *Dinosaurs of North America.* Illustrated by Anthony Rao. Lothrop, 1981. Ages 6–8.

———. *The Illustrated Dinosaur Dictionary.* Illustrated by Pamela Carroll, Anthony Rao, and Christopher Santuro. Lothrop, 1983. Ages 6–10.

Scott, Jack Denton. *Alligator.* Photographs by Ozzie Sweet. Putman, 1984. Ages 7–9.

———. *Swans.* Photographs by Ozzie Sweet. Putnam, 1988. Ages 7–9.

Selsam, Millicent E. *Cotton.* Photographs by Jerome Wexler. Morrow, 1982. Ages 7–9.

Simon, Seymour. *The Smallest Dinosaur.* Illustrated by Anthony Rao. Crown, 1982. Ages 7–9.

Wexler, Jerome. *Flowers, Nuts, Seeds.* Prentice-Hall, 1988. Ages 7–9.

Yoshida, Toshi. *Elephant Crossing.* Putnam, 1989. Ages 7–9.

———. *Young Lions.* Putnam, 1989. Ages 7–9.

The Physical Sciences

Arnold, Caroline. *Dinosaurs Down Under: And Other Fossils from Australia.* Photographs by Richard Hewett. Clarion, 1990. Ages 8–10.

Branley, Franklyn. *The Christmas Sky,* revised edition. Illustrated by Stephen Fieser. Crowell, 1990. Ages 6–8.

———. *Eclipse: Darkness in Daytime,* revised edition. Illustrated by Donald Crews. Crowell, 1988. Ages 6–8.

———. *Uranus: The Seventh Planet.* Illustrated by Yvonne Buchanan. Crowell, 1989. Ages 6–8.

Cole, Joanna. *The Magic Schoolbus: Inside the Earth.* Illustrated by Bruce Degen. Scholastic, 1987. Ages 7–9.

———. *The Magic Schoolbus: Lost in the Solar System.* Illustrated by Bruce Degen. Scholastic, 1990. Ages 7–9.

Dunphy, Madeleine. *Here Is the Arctic Winter.* Illustrated by Alan J. Robinson. Hyperion, 1993. Ages 6–8.

Elkington, John, Julia Hailes, Douglas Hill, and Joel Makower. *Going Green: A Kid's Handbook to Saving the Planet.* Illustrated by Tony Ross. Puffin, 1990. Ages 8–12.

Gibbons, Gail. *Weather Words and What They Mean.* Holiday, 1990. Ages 6–8.

Hirst, Robin, and Sally Hirst. *My Place in Space.* Illustrated by Roland Harvey with Joe Levine. Orchard, 1988. Ages 9–13.

Iverson, Diane. *I Celebrate Nature.* Dawn, 1993.

Lasky, Kathryn. *Dinosaur Dig.* Illustrated by Christopher Knight. Morrow, 1990. Ages 8–10.

———. *Surtsey: The Newest Place on Earth.* Photos by Christopher G. Knight. Hyperion, 1992. Ages 10–14.

———. *Traces of Life: The Origins of Humankind.* Illustrated by Whitney Powell. Morrow, 1990. Ages 9–12.

Lauber, Patricia. *Dinosaurs Walked Here and Other Stories Fossils Tell.* Bradbury, 1987. Ages 8–12.

———. *Journey to the Planets.* Crown, 1982. Ages 8–12.

———. *Volcano: The Eruption and Healing of Mount St. Helens.* Bradbury, 1986. Ages 9–12.

Peters, Lisa Westberg. *The Sun, the Wind, and the Rain.* Illustrated by Ted Rand. Holt, 1988. Ages 7–9.

Polacco, Patricia. *Meteor!* Dodd, 1987. Ages 7–9.

Pringle, Laurence. *Dinosaurs and People: Fossils, Facts, and Fantasies.* Harcourt, 1978. Ages 7–9.

———. *Global Warming: Assessing the Greenhouse Threat.* Arcade, 1990. Ages 7–9.

Ride, Sally, and Susan Okie. *To Space and Back.* Lothrop, 1986. Ages 9–12.

Selsam, Millicent E. *How to Be a Nature Detective.* Illustrated by Ezra Jack Keats. Harper, 1963. Ages 7–9.

Selsam, Millicent, and Joyce Hunt. *Keep Looking!* Illustrated by Normand Chartier. Macmillan, 1989. Ages 7–9.

Simon, Seymour. *Jupiter.* Morrow, 1985. (Others in The Planets series: *Mars,* 1987; *Saturn,* 1985; *Uranus,* 1987.) Ages 8–10.

———. *The Long Journey from Space.* Crown, 1982. Ages 8–10.

———. *The Long View into Space.* Crown, 1979. Ages 8–10.

———. *Soap Bubble Magic.* Illustrated by Stella Ormai. Lothrop, 1985. Ages 7–9.

———. *The Stars.* Morrow, 1986. Ages 8–10.

———. *Storms.* Morrow, 1989. Ages 8–10.

———. *The Sun.* Morrow, 1986. Ages 8–10.

———. *Volcanoes.* Morrow, 1988. Ages 8–10.

Temple, Lannis, ed. *Dear World: How Children around the World Feel About Our Environment.* Random, 1993. Ages 7–12.

Wilkes, Angela. *My First Nature Book.* Knopf, 1990. Ages 6–8.

The Social Sciences

Abells, Chana Byers. *The Children We Remember.* Photographs from the Archives of Yad Vashem, the Holocaust Martyrs' and Heroes' Remembrance Authority, Jerusalem, Israel. Greenwillow, 1986. Ages 12–YA.

Alexander, Sally Hobart. *Mom Can't See Me.* Photographs by George Ancona. Macmillan, 1990. Ages 4–6.

Aliki. *Communication.* Greenwillow, 1993. Ages 7–9.

———. *The King's Day: Louis XIV of France.* Crowell, 1989. Ages 7–9.

———. *A Medieval Feast.* Crowell, 1983. Ages 8–10.

Ancona, George. *The American Family Farm.* Text by Joan Anderson. Harcourt, 1989. Ages 8–10.

———. *Powwow.* Harcourt, 1993. Ages 8–10.

Ancona, George and Mary Beth. *Handtalk Zoo.* Photographs by George Ancona. Four Winds, 1989. Ages 6–8.

Anderson, Joan. *Born to the Land: An American Portrait.* Photographs by George Ancona. Harcourt, 1989. Ages 7–9.

———. *The First Thanksgiving Feast.* Photographs by George Ancona. Clarion, 1984. Ages 7–9.

Atkin, S. Beth. *Voices from the Fields: Children of Migrant Farmworkers Tell Their Stories.* Little, Brown, 1993. Ages 8–12.

Baer, Edith. *This Is the Way We Go to School: A Book about Children Around the World.* Illustrated by Steve Bjorkman. Scholastic, 1990. Ages 6–10.

Ballard, Robert D. *Exploring the Titanic.* Illustrated by Ken Marschall. Scholastic, 1988. Ages 7–9.

Barton, Byron. *I Want to Be an Astronaut.* Crowell, 1988. Ages 7–9.

Bial, Raymond. *Frontier Home.* Houghton, 1993. Ages 9–12.

Blumberg, Rhoda. *Commodore Perry in the Land of the Shogun.* Lothrop, 1985. Ages 9–12.

———. *The Great American Gold Rush.* Bradbury, 1989. Ages 9–12.

———. *The Incredible Journey of Lewis and Clark.* Lothrop, 1987. Ages 9–12.

Brown, Laurene Krasny, and Marc Brown. *Dinosaurs' Divorce: A Guide for Changing Families,* Atlantic Monthly Press, 1986. Ages 6–8.

Bunting, Eve. *The Wall.* Illustrated by Ronald Himler. Clarion, 1990. Ages 6–8.

Carrick, Carol. *Whaling Days.* Illustrated by David Frampton. Clarion, 1993. Ages 8–11.

Carter, Jimmy. *Talking Peace: A Vision for the Next Generation.* Dutton, 1993. Ages 10–14.

Chang, Ina. *A Separate Battle: Women and the Civil War.* Lodestar, 1991. Ages 10–13.

Charlip, Remy and Mary Beth. *Handtalk Birthday: A Number and Story Book in Sign Language.* Photographs by George Ancona. Four Winds, 1987. Ages 7–9.

Cohn, Janice. *I Had a Friend Named Peter: Talking to Children about the Death of a Friend.* Illustrated by Gail Owens. Morrow, 1987. Ages 6–10.

Cole, Joanna. *A Gift from Saint Francis: The First Creche.* Illustrated by Michelle Lemieux. Morrow, 1989. Ages 7–9.

Day, Alexandra. *Frank and Ernest.* Scholastic, 1988. Ages 7–9.

———. *Frank and Ernest Play Ball.* Scholastic, 1990. Ages 7–9.

dePaola, Tomie. *My First Chanukah.* Putnam, 1987. Ages 6–8.

Ehrlich, Amy. *The Story of Hanukkah.* Illustrated by Ori Sherman. Dial, 1989. Ages 7–9.

Ellis, Veronica Freeman. *Afro-Bets First Book about Africa.* Illustrated by George Ford. Just Us

Books, 1990. Ages 4–6.

Fisher, Leonard Everett. *The Great Wall of China.* Macmillan, 1986. Ages 9–12.

———.*The Wailing Wall.* Macmillan, 1989. Ages 9–12.

Freedman, Russell. *An Indian Winter.* Illustrated by Karl Bodmer. Holiday, 1992. Ages 11–14.

———. *Kids at Work: Lewis Hine and the Crusade against Child Labor.* Photos by Lewis Hine. Clarion, 1994. Ages 9–12.

Fritz, Jean. *Shh! We're Writing the Constitution.* Illustrated by Tomie dePaola. Putnam, 1987. Ages 8–10.

Gelfand, Marilyn. *My Great-Grandpa Joe.* Photographs by Rosemarie Hausherr. Four Winds, 1986. Ages 7–9.

Giblin, James Cross. *Be Seated: A Book about Chairs.* HarperCollins, 1993. Ages 8–14.

———. *From Hand to Mouth: Or, How We Invented Knives, Forks and Spoons and the Tablemanners To Go with Them.* Harper, 1987. Ages 6–10.

———. *Unicorns.* Illustrated by Michael McDermott. HarperCollins, 1991. Ages 10–12.

Girard, Linda Walvoord. *Adoption Is for Always.* Illustrated by Judith Friedman. Albert Whitman, 1986. Ages 8–10.

Goodall, John. *The Story of an English Village.* Atheneum, 1979. Ages 7–9.

Greenfeld, Howard. *The Hidden Children.* Ticknor & Fields, 1993. Ages 10–14.

Hamilton, Virginia. *Many Thousand Gone: African Americans from Slavery to Freedom.* Illustrated by Leo and Diane Dillon. Random, 1992. Ages 10–14.

Handler, Andrew, and Susan Meschel. *Young People Speak: Surviving the Holocaust in Hungary.* Watts, 1993. Ages 10–14.

Harrison, Ted. *O Canada.* Ticknor & Fields, 1993. Ages 7–9.

Haskins, Jim. *Get On Board: The Story of the Underground Railroad.* Scholastic, 1993. Ages 10–14.

Hausherr, Rosemarie. *Children and the AIDS Virus: A Book for Children, Parents, and Teachers.* Clarion, 1989. Ages 8–12.

Hirschi, Ron. *Who Lives in . . . the Mountains?* Photographs by Galen Burrell. Putnam, 1989. Ages 6–8.

———. *Who Lives in . . . the Prairies?* Photographs by Galen Burrell. Putnam, 1989. Ages 6–8.

Hoyt-Goldsmith, Diane. *Celebrating Kwanzaa.* Illustrated by Lawrence Migdale. Holiday, 1993. Ages 7–9.

———. *Day of the Dead: A Mexican-American Celebration.* Illustrated by Lawrence Migdale. Holiday, 1994. Ages 7–9.

———. *Totem Pole.* Photographs by Lawrence Migdale. Holiday, 1990. Ages 7–9.

Jenness, Aylette. *Families: A Celebration of Diversity, Commitment, and Love.* Houghton, 1990. Ages 8–10.

Keegan, Marcia. *Pueblo Boy: Growing up in Two Worlds.* Cobblehill: Dutton, 1991. Ages 9–11.

Kehoe, Michael. *A Book Takes Root: The Making of a Picture Book.* Carolrhoda, 1993. Ages 7–9.

Knight, Amelia Stewart. Adapted by Lillian Schlissel. *The Way West: Journal of a Pioneer Woman.* Illustrated by Michael McCurdy. Simon & Schuster, 1993. Ages 7–12.

Koralek, Jenny. *Hanukkah: The Festival of Lights.* Illustrated by Juan Wijngaard. Lothrop, 1990. Ages 7–9.

Krementz, Jill. *How It Feels To Live with a Physical Disability.* Simon & Schuster, 1992. Ages 8–14.

Kuklin, Susan. *Speaking Out: Teenagers Take on Sex, Race and Identity.* Putnam, 1993. Ages 12–17.

———. *Thinking Big: The Story of a Young Dwarf.* Lothrop, 1986. Ages 7–9

———. *What Do I Do Now?: Talking about Teenage Pregnancy.* Putnam, 1991. Ages 11–YA.

Kuskin, Karla. *Jerusalem, Shining Still.* Illustrated by David Frampton. Harper, 1987. Ages 8–10.

———. *The Philharmonic Gets Dressed.* Illustrated by Marc Simont. Harper, 1982. Ages 6–8.

Lasker, Joe. *Merry Ever After: The Story of Two Medieval Weddings.* Viking, 1976. Ages 8–10.

Lawrence, Jacob. *The Great Migration: An American Story.* HarperCollins, 1993. Ages 8–12.

Leedy, Loreen. *Messages in the Mailbox: How to Write a Letter.* Holiday, 1991. Ages 7–9.

Lessem, Don. *The Iceman.* Crown, 1994. Ages 9–12.

Lester, Julius. *To Be a Slave.* Dial, 1968. Ages 12–YA.

Levine, Ellen. *Freedom's Children: Young Civil Rights Activists Tell Their Own Stories.* Putnam, 1993. Ages 11–17.

Loverance, Rowena. *Ancient Greece.* Illustrated by Bill LeFever and others. Viking, 1993. Ages 10–14. (Others in the See Through History series: *Ancient Egypt; The Middle Ages; The Renaissance.*)

Machotka, Hana. *What Do You Do at a Petting Zoo?*

Morrow, 1990. Ages 6–8.

Macy, Sue. *A Whole New Ball Game: The Story of the All-American Girls Professional Baseball League.* Holt, 1993. Ages 10–14.

Maestro, Betsy. *The Story of Money.* Illustrated by Giulio Maestro. Clarion, 1993. Ages 7–10.

———. *The Story of the Statue of Liberty.* Illustrated by Giulio Maestro. Lothrop, 1986. Ages 9–12.

McFarlan, Donald, ed. *The Guinness Book of World Records.* Sterling Publishing Company. Published annually. Ages 7–13.

McKissack, Patricia, and Fredrick McKissack. *The Civil Rights Movement in America from 1865 to the Present.* Childrens Press, 1987. Ages 9–YA.

Meltzer, Milton. *The Amazing Potato: a Story in Which the Incas, Conquistadors, Marie Antoinette, Thomas Jefferson, Wars, Famines, Immigrants, and French Fries All Play a Part.* HarperCollins, 1992. Ages 10–13.

———. *The American Revolutionaries: A History in Their Own Words 1750–1800.* Crowell, 1988. Ages 12–YA.

———. *Rescue: The Story of How Gentiles Saved Jews in the Holocaust.* Harper, 1988. Ages 12–YA.

———. *Voices from the Civil War: A Documentary History of the Great American Conflict.* Crowell, 1989. Ages 12–YA.

Monroe, J. *Censorship.* Macmillan, 1990. Ages 10–14.

Müller, Jörg. *The Changing City.* Atheneum, 1977. Ages 8–12.

———. *The Changing Countryside.* Atheneum, 1977. Ages 8–12.

Munro, Roxie. *Christmastime in New York City.* Dodd, 1987. Ages 6–8.

———. *The Inside-Outside Book of Washington, D.C.* Ages 6–8. Dutton, 1987.

Murphy, Jim. *Across America on an Immigrant Train.* Clarion, 1993. Ages 11–14.

———. *The Boy's War: Confederate and Union Soldiers Talk About the Civil War.* Clarion, 1990. Ages 12–YA.

———. *The Long Road to Gettysburg.* Clarion Books, 1992. Ages 11–14.

Myers, Walter Dean. *Now Is Your Time!: The African-American Struggle for Freedom.* HarperCollins, 1991. Ages 10–14.

Onyefulu, Ifeoma. *A Is for Africa.* Cobblehill, 1993. Ages 5–8.

Perl, Lila. *The Great Ancestor Hunt: The Fun of Finding Out Who You Are.* Clarion, 1989. Ages 8–10.

Peterson, Jeanne Whitehouse. *I Have a Sister, My Sister Is Deaf.* Illustrated by Deborah Ray. Harper, 1977. Ages 7–9.

Pinkney, Andrea Davis. *Seven Candles for Kwanzaa.* Illustrated by Brian Pinkney. Dial, 1993. Ages 5–9.

Pringle, Laurence. *Throwing Things Away: From Middens to Resource Recovery.* Crowell, 1988. Ages 8–10.

Rockwell, Harlow. *My Dentist.* Greenwillow, 1975. Ages 3–5.

———. *My Doctor.* Macmillan, 1973. Ages 3–5.

———. *My Nursery School.* Greenwillow, 1976. Ages 3–5.

Rockwell, Anne, and Harlow Rockwell. *The Supermarket.* Macmillan, 1979. Ages 4–6.

Roessel, Monty. *Kinaaldá: A Navajo Girl Grows Up.* Lerner, 1993. Ages 8–10.

Rogasky, Barbara. *Smoke and Ashes: The Story of the Holocaust.* Holiday, 1988. Ages 12–YA.

Rogers, Fred. *Let's Talk about It: Adoption.* Illustrated by Jim Judkis. Putnam, 1995.

———. *Making Friends.* Photographs by Jim Judkis. Putnam, 1988. Ages 4–6.

———. *Moving.* Photographs by Jim Judkis. Putnam, 1988. Ages 4–6.

Rosenberg, Maxine B. *Brothers and Sisters.* Photographs by George Ancona. Clarion, 1991. Ages 6–8.

Sancha, Sheila. *The Luttrell Village: Country Life in the Middle Ages.* Crowell, 1982. Ages 9–12.

Schmitt, Lois. *Smart Spending: A Young Consumer's Guide.* Scribner's, 1989. Ages 7–9.

Sewall, Marcia. *The Pilgrims of Plimoth.* Atheneum, 1986. Ages 8–10.

Spier, Peter. *We the People: The Constitution of the United States of America.* Doubleday, 1987. Ages 8–10.

Stanley, Jerry. *Children of the Dust Bowl: The True Story of the School at Weedpatch.* Crown, 1992. Ages 9–13.

Thomson, Ruth, and Neil Thomson. *A Family in Thailand.* Lerner Publications, 1988. (See others in *A Family in . . .* series.) Ages 7–9.

Tsuchiya, Yukio. *Faithful Elephants.* Illustrated by Ted Lewin. Translated by Tomoko Tsuchiya Dykes. Houghton, 1988. Ages 9–12.

Van Loon, Hendrik Willem. *The Story of Mankind.* Liveright, 1921, 1984. Ages 9–12.

Wilcox, Charlotte. *Trash*. Photographs by Jerry Bushey. Carolrhoda, 1988. Ages 8–10.

The Applied Sciences

Aliki. *How a Book Is Made*. Crowell, 1986. Ages 6–8.

Anno, Mitsumasa. *Anno's Math Games I*. Philomel, 1987. (*Math Games II*, 1989; *Math Games III*, 1991). Ages 6–10.

Carrick, Donald. *Milk*. Greenwillow, 1985. Ages 5–7.

Ceserani, Gian Paolo. *Grand Constructions*. Illustrated by Piero Ventura. Putnam, 1983. Ages 9–YA.

Cole, Joanna. *The Magic Schoolbus: At the Waterworks*. Illustrated by Bruce Degen. Scholastic, 1986. Ages 7–9.

dePaola, Tomie. *Charlie Needs a Cloak*. Prentice Hall, 1973. Ages 6–8.

DeSantis, Kenny. *A Dentist's Tools*. Photographs by Patricia A. Agre. Dodd, 1988. Ages 6–8.

———. *A Doctor's Tools*. Photographs by Patricia A. Agre. Dodd, 1985. Ages 6–8.

Gibbons, Gail. *Trains*. Holiday, 1987. Ages 5–7.

———. *Up Goes the Skyscraper!* Four Winds, 1986. Ages 5–7.

Jasperson, William. *Ice Cream*. Macmillan, 1988. Ages 8–10.

Kramer, Alan. *How to Make a Chemical Volcano and Other Mysterious Experiments*. Franklin Watts, 1989. Ages 8–10.

Kuklin, Susan. *From Head to Toe: How a Doll Is Made*. Hyperion, 1994. Ages 7–9.

Lasky, Kathryn. *Sugaring Time*. Photographs by Christopher Knight. Macmillan, 1983. Ages 8–10.

Macaulay, David. *Castle*. Houghton, 1977. Ages 10–YA.

———. *Cathedral: The Story of Its Own Construction*. Houghton, 1973. Ages 10–YA.

———. *Ship*. Harcourt, 1993. Ages 8–12.

———. *The Way Things Work*. Houghton, 1988. Ages 10–YA. [CD-ROM version: Dorling Kindersley, 1995.]

Morris, Ann. *Bread, Bread, Bread*. Photographs by Ken Heyman. Lothrop, 1989. Ages 8–10.

Robbins, Ken. *Tools*. Four Winds, 1983. Ages 6–8.

Rockwell, Anne. *Things That Go*. Dutton, 1986. Ages 4–6.

Simon, Seymour. *The Paper Airplane Book*. Illustrated by Byron Barton. Viking, 1971. Ages 8–10.

The Humanities

Björk, Christina. *The Other Alice: The Story of Alice Liddell and Alice in Wonderland*. Illustrated by Inga-Karen Eriksson. R&S, 1993. Ages 8–10.

Cummings, Pat, compiler-editor. *Talking with Artists*. Illustrated by various artists. Bradbury, 1992. Ages 8–12.

Davidson, Rosemary. *Take a Look: An Introduction to the Experience of Art*. Viking, 1994. Ages 8–12.

Greenberg, Jan, and Sandra Jordan. *The Painter's Eye: Learning to Look at Contemporary American Art*. Delacorte, 1991. Ages 11–14.

Isaacson, Philip M. *Round Buildings, Square Buildings, and Buildings that Wiggle Like a Fish*. Knopf, 1988. Ages 8–10.

Janeczko, Paul B. *The Place My Words Are Looking For: What Poets Say About and Through Their Work*. Bradbury, 1990. Ages 9–12.

Krementz, Jill. *A Very Young Musician*. Simon & Schuster, 1991. (See others in *A Very Young . . .* series) Ages 8–10.

Monroe, Jean G., and Ray Williamson. *First Houses: Native American Homes and Sacred Structures*. Illustrated by Susan Carlson. Houghton, 1993. Ages 9–12.

Mühlberger, Richard. *What Makes a Van Gogh a Van Gogh?* The Metropolitan Museum of Art/Viking, 1993. (Others in this series: Bruegal, Degas, Monet, Raphael, Rembrandt)

Nichol, Barbara. *Beethoven Lives Upstairs*. Illustrated by Scott Cameron. Orchard, 1994. Ages 8–10.

Pope, Joyce. *Kenneth Lilly's Animals: A Portfolio of Paintings*. Illustrated by Kenneth Lilly. Lothrop, 1988. Ages 8–10.

Ventura, Piero. *Great Painters*. Translated by Geoffrey Culverwell. Putnam, 1984. Ages 9–YA.

Welton, Jude. *Drawing: A Young Artist's Guide*. Dorling Kindersley, 1994. Ages 8–14.

Chapter 10

Multicultural and International Literature

Human Family

I note the obvious differences
in the human family.
Some of us are serious,
some thrive on comedy.

Some declare their lives are lived
as true profundity,
and others claim they really live
the real reality.

The variety of our skin tones
can confuse, bemuse, delight,
brown and pink and beige and purple,
tan and blue and white.

I've sailed upon the seven seas
and stopped in every land,
I've seen the wonders of the world,
not yet one common man.

I know ten thousand women
called Jane and Mary Jane,
but I've not seen any two
who really were the same.

Mirror twins are different
although their features jibe,
and lovers think quite different thoughts
while lying side by side.

We love and lose in China,
we weep on England's moors,
and laugh and moan in Guinea,
and thrive on Spanish shores.

We seek success in Finland,
are born and die in Maine.
In minor ways we differ,
In major we're the same.

I note the obvious differences
between each sort and type,
but we are more alike, my friends,
than we are unalike.

We are more alike, my friends,
than we are unalike.

We are more alike, my friends,
than we are unalike.

—Maya Angelou

This chapter is presented in two parts. The first part focuses on literature written about the major racial, religious, and language cultural groups in the United States other than the Anglo-Saxon group. The second part focuses on literature written originally for children living in other lands but also read and enjoyed by children in the United States.

According to Banks and Banks (1993), each modern nation-state has a shared core culture—a *macroculture*—and a number of *microcultures* that are part of or integrated into the macroculture to greater or lesser degrees. It must be noted that the Anglo-Saxon group, although it has been traditionally the prevailing culture in the United States, is itself a microculture and *not* the macroculture. Because the Banks' schema and nomenclature are inclusive in their emphasis on the contributions of *all* citizens of a country to that country's overarching culture, we have chosen to use their terms in this chapter. We will refer to the Anglo-Saxon group as Euro-American.

You will have noted many references to multicultural and international books and authors throughout the previous genre chapters in discussions of trends and issues, notable author and illustrator lists, and end-of-chapter recommended booklists. In an ideal, culturally integrated world, such inclusion would be sufficient. But the groups represented in multicultural literature have, until recently, been totally absent from or misrepresented in books for children. Furthermore, neither multi-cultural nor international literature is well known or recognized by the educational mainstream. We have chosen to include this special focus chapter to draw attention to these two important bodies of literature.

SECTION ONE: MULTICULTURAL LITERATURE

Definition and Description

Multicultural literature refers to trade books, regardless of genre, that have as the main character a person who is a member of a racial, religious, or language micro-culture other than the Euro-American one. This section of the chapter will focus on the five most populous microcultures in the United States, each of which has an established and growing body of children's literature that describes its experience. These groups are African American; Asian American (including people of Chinese, Japanese, Korean, and Vietnamese descent); Hispanic American (including Cuban Americans, Mexican Americans, Puerto Ricans, Latino Americans, and others of Spanish descent); Jewish American; and Native American (a general term referring to the many tribes of American Indians.)

Values of Multicultural Literature for Children

Multicultural literature has value for all children. All modern nation-states benefit from cooperation and friendship among the people living within their borders. The violence and destruction that often result from racial and religious prejudice hurt everyone. From a non-mainstream perspective, one step toward effective, confident citizenship in a multicultural society is to understand one's particular social and cultural heritage. From a mainstream perspective, the first thing that people must do in order to accept those different from themselves is to learn about them, and reading provides one of the best ways to do this. Knowledge gained through reading then makes understanding possible, and understanding often leads to appreciation.

Multicultural literature, then, is valuable for the following reasons:

- This body of literature includes excellent stories worthy of children's attention.
- Children who see people like themselves positively represented in excellent multicultural literature derive self-esteem and pride in their own heritage. Every child has a right to self-respect. Until recently, however, only Euro-Americans were well represented in children's books in Canada and the United States.
- Reading multicultural literature is a way for Euro-American children (and their parents, teachers, and librarians) to learn about or to become aware of other peoples and their cultures. Euro-American children who find only

people like themselves represented in literature could easily get the impression that they are somehow better or more worthy as a group than others. Multicultural literature shows Euro-American children that other groups are not only worthy but also that they have something to teach others. Also, school-based studies have shown that emotional involvement and vicarious experience with multicultural characters through works of literature reduce students' prejudices toward the microculture. (For a summary of these studies, see *Social Education,* April/May, 1988.)

- Multicultural literature often addresses issues and problems peculiar to children of a specific microculture from the perspective of story characters who themselves are members of the group. Reading about such problems as racial or religious prejudice and how book characters deal with them may help children of that microculture to cope with the same problems themselves.

Evaluation and Selection of Multicultural Literature

With respect to multicultural literature, your first concern as a teacher, librarian, or parent should be that well-written books of this kind are available to the children under your care. This task is often not as simple as it may at first seem. Some cultural groups in the United States are not yet well represented in children's books. Also, a wide variety of the most current and best multicultural books are not readily available everywhere. Someone, perhaps you, has to take the time and the effort to learn about, read, evaluate, and then introduce the best of this literature into a school or community. The following criteria should be considered when evaluating multicultural books:

- Some evaluation criteria remain constant regardless of the type of literature. Multicultural literature should exhibit high literary and artistic quality, worthy themes, and appropriate reading levels for the intended audience.
- Racial and cultural stereotyping should be avoided; instead, multifaceted, well-rounded characters of the featured microculture should be found in these stories. The nature of stereotyping is that it unfairly assigns a fixed image or fixed characteristics to everyone within a group, thereby denying everyone within the group the right to any individuality or choice. No one likes to be the victim of stereotyping.
- Traditional racial, religious, and language group stereotypes that have developed over the years in the United States make clear the damage and unwarranted denigration that can result from the practice. In evaluating children's books, you will want to be alert to any generalized portrayal of African Americans as coarse-featured, musical, and poor; of Asian Americans as sly, overly diligent, and obsequious; of Hispanic Americans as lazy, holiday-minded, and impoverished; of Jewish Americans as greedy, aggressive, and penurious; and of Native Americans as savage, primitive, and warlike. Books perpetuating such stereotypes have no place in the classroom.

- Positive images of characters should be evident. Good multicultural books go beyond avoidance of stereotypes to provide characters and situations that project positive, believable images of these people in family, school, work, and play.
- Cultural details must be accurate. Much of what distinguishes the literature of a particular group from that of other groups is found in the details, such as idioms and dialect used in dialogue, descriptions of clothing, hairstyles, and food, architecture of homes, and customs. Just as important, these details must be accurate when they describe subgroups *within* a microculture. For example, customs of Native Americans vary greatly from tribe to tribe.
- Variety is a concern in selecting multicultural books for a young readership. Not only should there be books about the microcultures represented in a classroom, but there also should be books about the many other microcultures living in this country. Likewise, there should be multicultural books of various genres and multicultural characters in these books from a variety of backgrounds.

Variety also extends to authorship. Multicultural books written by both non-Euro-Americans and Euro-Americans should be readily available to children. In her landmark book, *Shadow and Substance,* Rudine Sims (1982) established a classification system for books about African Americans that can be applied to any multicultural literature and can be helpful in evaluation and selection of these books. Adapting her labels and definitions to include all multicultural literature, there exist the following categories:

Social conscience books.   These books about microcultural groups other than Euro-American are written to help all readers know the condition of their fellow humans. Examples are *The Slave Dancer* by Paula Fox and *Iggie's House* by Judy Blume.

Melting pot books.   These books, which feature multicultural characters, are written for all young readers on the assumption that everyone needs to be informed that children of all microcultures are exactly alike, except for the color of their skins, their language, or their religious preference. Examples include *A Snowy Day* by Ezra Jack Keats and *Jennifer, Hecate, Macbeth, William McKinley, & Me, Elizabeth* by E. L. Konigsburg.

Culturally conscious books.   These books are written primarily (though not exclusively) by microcultural authors other than Euro-American for readers belonging to that microculture. An attempt is made to reveal the true, unique character of that microculture. Examples are *Stevie* by John Steptoe and *Roll of Thunder, Hear My Cry* by Mildred Taylor.

Having examples of all three types of multicultural books in your classroom will assure that your students will be able to read from the perspective of both the Euro-American author and the authors of other microcultures. Students of less integrated microcultures in particular should have the experience of reading stories written about children like themselves from the perspective of someone within their microculture.

Several book selection aids focus on multicultural books. *Multicultural Children's and Young Adult Literature: A Selected Listing of Books by and about People of Color* is a carefully selected, regularly updated, annotated listing of multicultural books of all genres produced by the University of Wisconsin, Madison's Cooperative Children's Book Center. *The Black Experience in Children's Literature* (Pine, 1994), an annotated book list published about every five years by the New York Public Library, offers a comprehensive collection of African-American books in print at the time of publication. The nearly 400 entries in the latest edition are organized by genre. *Literature for Children about Asians and Asian Americans: Analysis and Annotated Bibliography, with Additional Reading for Adults* (Jenkins & Austin, 1987) is arranged by nation and subdivided into genres. *Books without Bias: Through Indian Eyes, Vol. 2* (Slapin & Seale, 1988), contains articles, essays, and poems written by Native Americans. *Resource Reading List 1990: Annotated Bibliography of Resources by and about Native People* (Verrall & McDowell, 1990) focuses on Native Canadians. *Books in Spanish for Children and Young Adults* (Schon, 1989), a guide for choosing Spanish-language books for Hispanic children, is organized by country of origin, including a large section on the United States. These books are of all genres, and some are bilingual. (For further information on these resources, see Appendix B.)

Book awards for special content also can guide teachers and librarians toward high-quality multicultural books. The best known of these is the Coretta Scott King Award, founded in 1969 and, since 1979, sponsored by the American Library Association. This annual award is given to the African-American author and (since 1974) illustrator whose books published in the preceding year are judged to be the most outstanding inspirational and educational literature for children. (For a complete list of award winners, see Appendix A.)

In recent years small presses have given teachers and librarians a source of multicultural books particularly valuable for their distinctly multicultural (versus Euro-American) point of view. The following publishers have focused on multicultural literature, and so their catalogues are a treasure trove for those looking for such literature.

> Arte Publico, University of Houston, Houston, TX 77004. This alternative press publishes children's books with a Latino perspective.

> Black Butterfly/ Writers and Readers, 625 Broadway, Suite 903, New York, NY 10012. This company produces children's books with an Afrocentric perspective and written by African-American writers and artists.

> Children's Book Press, 6400 Hollis Street, Emeryville, CA 94608. This company publishes folktales and contemporary stories, often bilingual, in picture book format for Native American, Asian-American, and Hispanic-American children.

> Cross Cultural Education Center, P.O. Box 92, Welling, OK 74471. This Cherokee-owned company produces a variety of children's literature with a distinctly Cherokee point of view.

> Japanese American Curriculum Project, P.O. Box 367, San Mateo, CA 94401. In addition to its own publications, this company distributes Asian-American books from other small and large presses.

Just Us Books, 301 Main Street, Suite 22-24, Orange, NJ 07050. This company produces the Afrocentric *Afro-Bets* and *Feeling Good Books* to enhance the self-esteem of African-American children.

Lee & Low Books, 228 East 45th Street, New York, NY 10017. This Asian-American-owned company stresses authenticity in its contemporary stories for Asian-American, Hispanic-American, and African-American children. Its Hispanic titles are also offered in Spanish.

Pemmican Publications, Unit #2—1635 Burrows Avenue, Winnipeg, Canada, R2X 0T1. This company publishes excellent realistic stories about contemporary Native American children and educational books for the Métis people about Métis history and culture.

Evaluating, selecting, and then bringing multicultural literature to your classroom, though essential, is not enough to assure that your students will actually read the books. Since children, without adult guidance, tend to choose books about children like themselves (Rudman, 1984), you must also purposefully expose mainstream children to multicultural books through reading aloud, booktalking, and selecting particular titles for small group reading.

Historical Overview of Multicultural Literature

Members of many microcultures living in the United States were long ignored as subjects for children's books. On the few occasions that representatives of these groups did appear, they did so as crudely stereotyped characters, objects of ridicule, or shadowy secondary characters. Helen Bannerman's *The Story of Little Black Sambo* (1900), Claire Bishop's *The Five Chinese Brothers* (1938), Sara Cone Bryant's *Epaminondas and His Auntie* (1907), and Hugh Lofting's *The Voyages of Dr. Dolittle* (1922) come under this category. Today, books such as these have either been rewritten to eliminate the racism or have disappeared from children's library shelves.

Although many of the Newbery Award winners and honor books of the 1920s and 1930s were set in foreign countries, almost none had to do with multicultural groups in the United States. Laura Adams Armer's novel about Native Americans, *Waterless Mountain,* the Newbery winner in 1932, was the only exception.

The 1940s offered little improvement. Although Florence Crannell Means wrote sympathetic and informative novels such as *The Moved-Outers* (1945) about American ethnic microcultures during the 1930s and 1940s, negative stereotypes, such as those of Native Americans as savages projected in Newbery winners *Daniel Boone* by James Daugherty (1939) and *The Matchlock Gun* by Walter D. Edmonds (1941), were more prevalent by far.

The first harbinger of change came in 1949 when an African-American author, Arne Bontemps, won a Newbery Honor Award for his *Story of the Negro* and became the first member of a multicultural group to receive this honor. A more sympathetic attitude toward American microcultures, at least in literature, emerged in the 1950s, as evidenced by the positive treatment of multicultural characters in such

Newbery winners as *Amos Fortune, Free Man* by Elizabeth Yates (1950) and . . .*And Now Miguel* by Joseph Krumgold (1953).

The Civil Rights movement of the 1960s focused attention on the social inequities and racial injustices that prevailed in the United States. The spirit of the times resulted in two landmark publications. The first of these was *The Snowy Day* by Ezra Jack Keats (1962), the first Caldecott Award-winning book to have an African American as the protagonist. The great popularity of this book no doubt encouraged other authors, from the Euro-American and other microcultures, to produce books with multicultural protagonists. The second publication was a powerful article by Nancy Larrick entitled "The All-White World of Children's Books." In this article, which appeared in the September 11, 1965, issue of *Saturday Review,* Larrick reported that in nearly all U.S. children's books the African American was either omitted entirely or was scarcely mentioned (p. 63). American trade book publishers, the education system, and the public library system were called upon to fill this void.

For a time, the spirit of social consciousness born in the 1960s had good results. In 1966, the Council on Interracial Books for Children was founded and helped to promote young, African-American authors. In 1969, the Coretta Scott King Award was established to recognize distinguished writing in children's books by African-American authors. Also, a number of books with multicultural protagonists or themes were chosen as Newbery winners in the early seventies: *Sounder* by William H. Armstrong won in 1970; *Julie of the Wolves* by Jean Craighead George won in 1973; and *The Slave Dancer* by Paula Fox won in 1974. Judging from this record, the establishment had accepted multicultural protagonists in award-winning books; but it was not until 1975 that an author of color, Virginia Hamilton, author of *M. C. Higgins, the Great,* won a Newbery Award.

In quick succession, other African- and Asian-American authors were recognized for their outstanding literary and artistic efforts. In 1976, Leo Dillon (in collaboration with his wife, Diane Dillon) won a Caldecott Award for *Why Mosquitoes Buzz in People's Ears* (Aardema, 1975) and Sharon Bell Mathis and Laurence Yep received Newbery Honor Awards for *The Hundred Penny Box* and *Dragonwings,* respectively. The following year, 1977, Mildred D. Taylor, author of *Roll of Thunder, Hear My Cry,* became the second African American to win the Newbery Award. After 1975, the prevailing opinion among U.S. children's book publishers and professional reviewers seemed to be that members of a microcultural group were the ones most able to write authoritatively about their own particular cultures and experiences. Euro-American authors were no longer as likely to win major awards for writing about minorities as they were in the early 1970s.

The politically conservative 1980s were not conducive to a continued flowering of multicultural literature in the United States. Fewer books with multicultural characters or themes were published and fewer multicultural authors won awards than in the 1970s. In the early 1990s the number of multicultural books published by large, corporate publishers increased only slightly (Horning, 1993). In response to the continuing dearth of good multicultural literature for children, a number of small, alternative presses devoted exclusively to multicultural literature have been founded. Currently there is a renewed interest in multicultural literature, and the number of multicultural authors and illustrators entering the field, though still very small, is increasing. The Asian-American presence, in particular, has come to the fore in the 1990s with the picture books of Ed Young, a Chinese American, and Allen Say, a Japanese American. Bilingual books, particularly those in English and Spanish, are also on the rise, partially in response to the demand for such books in ESOL (English for Speakers of Other Languages) programs.

As microcultural groups intermingle, children of mixed heritage will be born. Already this group is growing fast. Perhaps the experience of growing up with a mixed heritage will be a topic featured in the multicultural literature of the future, as in Lawrence Yep's *Child of the Owl*. Milestones in the development of multicultural literature are highlighted in Table 10-1.

Types of Multicultural Literature

Although the last several decades have seen positive changes in the status of multicultural literature in the United States, there is still a marked shortage of books of this kind. Multicultural authors and illustrators of children's books are also in short supply. In 1991, for instance, only 70 of the 4,000 children's books published in the United States were written or illustrated by African Americans (Kruse & Horning, 1991).

A newfound public interest in family heritage that began in the 1980s in the United States began to be reflected in multicultural literature by the end of the decade. Interest in books about ethnic heritage has helped multicultural authors and illustrators to regain some of the publishing momentum of the 1970s. Awakening to the meaning and importance of one's heritage is a recurring theme in all genres of multicultural literature.

Before discussing the literature of each microculture, a general caution is in order. Each of these groups contains sub-groups that differ remarkably one from the other in country of origin, language, race, traditions, and present location. Teachers must be especially conscious of and sensitive to these differences and guard against presenting these groups as completely uniform or of selecting literature that does so. Gross overgeneralization is not only inaccurate but is a form of stereotyping.

African-American Literature

Of all multicultural groups living in the United States, African Americans have produced the largest and most rapidly growing body of children's literature. Every genre is well represented in African-American literature, but none better than poetry. Because it is so personal, poetry portrays a culture well, as is evident in the sensitive yet powerful work of poets Arnold Adoff, Gwendolyn Brooks, Nikki Giovanni, Eloise Greenfield, and Langston Hughes. For example, see *Honey, I Love and Other Love Poems* by Eloise Greenfield.

Tapping into their rich oral tradition, African Americans have contributed Anansi the Spider, Brer Rabbit, High John the Conqueror, and John Henry the Steel Drivin' Man to the list of favorite U.S. folklore characters. Even today, authors are bringing folktales to the United States from Africa. Examples include *Why*

TABLE 10–1   Milestones in the Development of Multicultural Literature

Date	Event	Significance
1932	*Waterless Mountain* by Laura Armer wins Newbery Medal	One of the few children's books about minorities in the first half of the twentieth century
1945	*The Moved-Outers* by Florence C. Means wins Newbery Honor	A departure from stereotyped depiction of minorities begins
1949	*Story of the Negro* by Anne Bontemps wins Newbery Honor	First minority author to win a Newbery Honor
1950	*Song of the Swallows* by Leo Politi wins Caldecott Award	First picture book with an Hispanic–American protagonist to win the Caldecott Award
1962	*The Snowy Day* by Ezra Jack Keats wins Caldecott Award	First picture book with an African–American protagonist to win the Caldecott Award
1965	"The All-White World of Children's Books" by Nancy Larrick published in *Saturday Review*	Called the nation's attention to the lack of multicultural literature
1969	Coretta Scott King Award founded	African-American literature and authors begin to be promoted and supported
1975	*M. C. Higgins, the Great* by Virginia Hamilton wins Newbery Award	First book by a minority author to win the Newbery Award
1976	*Why Mosquitoes Buzz In People's Ears* illustrated by Leo and Diane Dillon wins Caldecott Award	First picture book illustrated by an African American to win the Caldecott Award
1990	*Lon Po Po: A Red-Riding Hood Story from China* translated and illustrated by Ed Young wins Caldecott Award	First picture book illustrated by a Chinese American to win the Caldecott Award
1994	*Grandfather's Journey* written and illustrated by Allen Say wins Caldecott Award	First picture book illustrated by a Japanese American to win the Caldecott Award

Mosquitoes Buzz in People's Ears by Verna Aardema and *The Village of Round and Square Houses* by Ann Grifalconi.

In some cases, African Americans have reclaimed their tales by retelling (without racist elements) stories first written down in this country by Euro-American authors, as Julius Lester has done in his retelling of Joel Chandler Harris's *The Tales of Uncle Remus: The Adventures of Brer Rabbit.* More recent memories and family stories have begun to be written by African-American authors as modern folktales. For example, see *Mirandy and Brother Wind* by Patricia McKissack.

African Americans have told the stories of their lives in the United States through both historical and realistic fiction. The stories for older readers often include harsh but painfully accurate accounts of racial oppression, as in James Berry's slavery story, *Ajeemah and His Son*, or Mildred Taylor's historical fiction saga of the close-knit Logan family (*The Song of the Trees; Roll of Thunder, Hear My Cry; Let the Circle Be Unbroken;* and *The Road to Memphis*) and in Walter Dean Myers's contemporary realistic novel, *The Scorpions*. The characters, settings, and incidents created by these authors will be recognized by many African Americans who have lived through similar experiences; others will appreciate these stories as windows on understanding today's racial situation. Teachers can see to it that such stories are balanced, however, with more positive, encouraging contemporary stories.

Recently, African-American faces have begun to appear more frequently in picture books. While these books tend to address universal topics rather than those dealing specifically with race, they can still be culturally conscious. The works of illustrators Floyd Cooper, Donald Crews, Leo and Diane Dillon, Tom Feelings, Jerry Pinkney, Brian Pinkney, and John Steptoe deserve special notice. Examples include *Mufaro's Beautiful Daughters* by John Steptoe and *Aïda* retold by Leontyne Price and illustrated by Leo and Diane Dillon.

African-American nonfiction is mainly biography. In the 1960s and 1970s, a large percentage of these biographical subjects were sports heroes, but more recent subjects have come from a broader spectrum of achievement. For example, see *Sojourner Truth: Ain't I a Woman?* by Patricia and Fredrick McKissack.

Asian-American Literature

Asian-American children's literature is mainly represented in the United States by stories about Chinese Americans and Japanese Americans, possibly because these groups have lived as microcultures in this country longer than others such as Vietnamese Americans. A major theme in much of the fiction and nonfiction for older readers is the oppression that drove the people out of their homelands and the prejudice that they faced as newcomers in this country. A more positive theme is that of learning to appreciate one's cultural heritage while adjusting to life in the United States. Examples include *Dragonwings* and *Child of the Owl* by Laurence Yep and *In the Year of the Boar and Jackie Robinson* by Bette Bao Lord.

Traditional stories from Asia retold in English have contributed many interesting folktales and folktale variants to American and Canadian children's libraries. Characters generally thought of as European, such as Little Red Riding Hood and Cinderella, have their Asian counterparts. Examples are *Lon Po Po: A Red-Riding Hood Story from China* translated and illustrated by Ed Young, and *Yeh Shen: A Cinderella Story from China* by Ai-Ling Louie, illustrated by Ed Young.

Asian-American artists have brought the sophisticated style and technical artistry of the Orient to U.S. children's book illustration. Ed Young's use of screenlike panels, Allen Say's precision, and Yoshi's unusual fabric paintings are especially noteworthy. Examples are *The Boy of the Three-Year Nap* by Diane Snyder, illustrated by Allen Say, and *Who's Hiding Here?* by Yoshi.

The body of Asian-American children's literature is small. Nonfiction, poetry, and fantasy are almost unrepresented, with the notable exception of Rhoda Blumberg's

1986 Newbery Honor book, a work of nonfiction, *Commodore Perry in the Land of the Shogun*. The recently established small press, Lee & Low Books, will help to improve this situation with such titles as *Baseball Saved Us*, by Ken Mochizuki and illustrated by Dom Lee. There is no special U.S. award for Asian-American literature.

Hispanic-American Literature

Of the five microcultures focused on in this section, Hispanic Americans currently have the smallest body of children's literature and an insufficient amount of high-quality literature. This is especially regrettable since Hispanic Americans are the fastest growing of the large microcultures in the United States. The available books are mainly about Puerto Ricans and Mexican Americans, with the works of Nicholasa Mohr and, more recently, Gary Soto being outstanding examples. Leo Politi's books about Mexican Americans have been popular for many years, but do not describe the current minority experience. Examples are *Felita* by Nicholasa Mohr and *The Skirt* by Gary Soto.

Some developments hold promise for improvement in the status of Hispanic-American literature. The rise of small press publishers, such as Children's Book Press, which focuses on Hispanic-American literature, has already resulted in more literature being written for and about this group. The trend toward marketing more Spanish-English bilingual texts in the United States also will improve the availability of Hispanic-American books, particularly to younger children who are learning to read. For example, see *Uncle Nacho's Hat/El Sombrero del Tío Nacho* adapted by Harriet Rohmer, Spanish version by Rosalina Zubizarreta.

Jewish-American Literature

Without doubt the terrible experience of the Jewish Holocaust in Europe during the 1930s and 1940s has had a tremendous influence on Jewish-American children's literature. The prejudice and cruelty that led to the holocaust and the nightmare of the death camps themselves are recurring themes in both fiction and nonfiction for older readers. Since many Jewish people immigrated to the United States as the Nazi threat grew in Europe, much holocaust literature has been written by eyewitnesses or by those whose relatives were victims. Examples are *The Upstairs Room* by Johanna Reiss, *Upon the Head of the Goat* by Aranka Siegal, and *Smoke and Ashes: The Story of the Holocaust* by Barbara Rogasky.

Jewish emigration from Europe during the war years brought to the United States many outstanding artists whose work has greatly influenced children's book illustration. Two subjects often presented in Jewish-American picture books are Jewish holidays and folktales. Illustrated Jewish folktale collections, particularly those by Isaac Bashevis Singer, offer excellent, witty stories and high literary quality. Examples include *Hershel and the Hanukkah Goblins* by Eric Kimmel, illustrated by Trina Schart Hyman; *Zlateh the Goat and Other Stories* by Isaac Bashevis Singer, illustrated by Maurice Sendak; and *It Could Always Be Worse* by Margot Zemach.

The Jewish-American community has produced a number of excellent authors and illustrators of children's books. Literary creativity is promoted through two book award programs: the National Jewish Book Awards and the Association of Jewish Libraries Awards.

Native-American Literature

Almost from the moment that European explorers landed on this continent some five hundred years ago, Native Americans have suffered at the hands of Euro-Americans. Consequently, in books written from the Native-American perspective, oppression by the white population is a pervasive theme. Appreciation, celebration, and protection of nature—central tenets of Native-American cultures—are other recurrent themes in this body of literature. Examples are *Sing Down the Moon* by Scott O'Dell and *Morning Girl* by Michael Dorris.

Although much has been written *about* Native Americans, relatively little has been written *by* members of this microculture. Small press publishers specializing in literature by Native Americans may help to change this situation. Northland Press, for example, features the work of Native Americans of the southwestern United States. Native Americans known for their children's books include Virginia Driving Hawk Sneve and Michael Dorris for their novels, Joseph Bruchac for his retold stories, and Michael Lacapa and Shonto Begay for their illustrations. Examples are *When Thunders Spoke* by Virginia Driving Hawk Sneve and *The Mud Pony* by Carol Cohen, illustrated by Shonto Begay.

Numerous other writers and illustrators have told and retold the folktales and history of Native Americans in picture books, historical fiction, and informational books. Paul Goble is particularly well known for his impressively illustrated retellings of the legends of the Plains Indians, as are Scott O'Dell and Canadian Jan Hudson for their award-winning works of historical fiction featuring young Native-American women. The body of nonfictional works about Native Americans is particularly rich, with the works of Ann Nolan Clark, Russell Freedman, Milton Meltzer, John Bierhorst, Brent Ashabranner, and Alex Bealer being outstanding. Examples include *The Girl Who Loved Wild Horses* by Paul Goble, *Island of the Blue Dolphins* by Scott O'Dell, and *Only the Names Remain: The Cherokees and the Trail of Tears* by Alex Bealer.

SECTION TWO: INTERNATIONAL LITERATURE

Definition and Description

International literature in the United States is defined as literary selections originally published for the children in a country other than the United States in a language of that country and later published in the United States. The key elements of this definition are the book's country of origin and the determination of the primary audience for the book. If a book was written and published in France for French children, then translated and published for U.S. children, it is considered an international book in the United States. Books classified as international literature by this definition include the following:

1. English language books, written and published originally in English in another country, such as Canada or Australia, then published or distributed in the United States.

2. Translated books, written and published in a foreign language and then translated into English and published in the United States.
3. Foreign language books, written and published in a foreign language in another country for children of that country and later published or distributed in the United States in the foreign language.

If a book is written and published in the United States about Australian life, then the primary audience is U.S. children and the book is not considered international. Such books written and published in the United States about other countries are included in the lists of recommended books in the genre chapters.

Sometimes it is difficult to ascertain a book's country of origin. The publishing history page is the most reliable source of this information. (Note that in some foreign books, this publishing history is placed at the end of the book.) In any case, a careful reading will inform you of the book's original date and place of publication.

Values of International Literature for Children

The value of international children's literature in developing an understanding and appreciation for other cultures is undeniable. The understanding of people of other countries must be fostered early and allowed to grow throughout life.

- Through this literature, the history, traditions, and people of other countries are brought to life.
- By interpreting events in the everyday lives of their characters and by depicting long-term changes in the characters' lives, authors present a truer and more understandable picture of life in other countries than does the crisis-prone, single-event coverage of television and newspapers.
- Compelling stories build students' interest in the people and places they are reading about and pave the way to a deeper understanding and appreciation of the geography and history content encountered in textbooks.
- Literature written by natives of the country or region under study gives authenticity and an international perspective to classroom materials.
- Today many students in the United States speak a foreign language and have a foreign heritage. International literature reflects the cultural and language diversity often found in classrooms today. By reading international books, students can learn to respect the heritage of others and take pride in their own.
- Through international literature, children are given an opportunity to enjoy the best-loved stories of their peers around the world. This, in turn, can help students develop a bond of shared experience with children of other nations and can enable them to acquire cultural literacy with a global perspective.

In a study by Monson, Howe, and Greenlee (1989), two hundred U.S. children, ages 9 to 11, were asked what they would like to know about their counterparts in other countries. Their responses, categorized into nine questions, then formed the basis for a comparison of eight social studies textbooks and fifteen works of fiction appropriate for the age group about one country, Australia. It was found that both textbooks and trade books gave information about the country. The novels answered more of the children's questions, however, and were richer in detail of daily life and human emotion than the textbooks. The social studies texts gave many facts about the country, while the novels showed the implications of the facts for children's lives and helped the readers "live in" the country for a time.

Evaluation and Selection of International Literature

International books, both chapter books and picture books, should first be judged by the standards for all good literature.

- Translated works should exhibit a good, fluent writing style that is not stilted or awkward. Some flavor of the country of origin should remain. For example, place and character names should usually remain true to the original text in order to foster in children a tolerance and an appreciation of other languages and customs. Some translated books include a glossary of foreign words, meanings, and pronunciations. This permits readers to risk new and different words and sounds with no loss of confidence. Although too many words left untranslated can be annoying to the reader, a few can be enjoyable and can provoke an interest in foreign languages. The translation should not violate the tone of the book by being so idiomatic as to jar the reader. For example, a book from Czechoslovakia rings untrue if the translation of the young people's language sounds like hip American slang or street talk.

- Teachers and librarians may note in some international books differences in writing and illustrating styles. International chapter books for intermediate and upper-grade readers lean toward introspection by the main character. Examples are 1990 Hans Christian Andersen Medalist Tormod Haugen's *Night Birds* and *Zeppelin*. Students could be alerted to the differences and could be asked to reflect on why the author may have chosen that manner of telling the story. In some cases, illustrations in international books are more abstract than is usual for U.S. picture books. Aspects of plot and theme in these books are heavily embedded in the pictorial details. For example, many layers of meaning can be unraveled with repeated readings of the story personifying the months of the year in *December's Travels*, illustrated by Dušan Kállay, 1988 Hans Christian Andersen Medalist.

With the increase of internationalism in all domains of our social and cultural life, more international children's books are becoming available in the United States. A number of selection sources will prove useful and necessary in locating international children's book titles. *Bookbird: World of Children's Books*, the International

Board on Books for Young People (IBBY) journal, announces recent international award-winning books and national award winners from many nations and is, therefore, an important source for current information on international books. It also features articles on international children's literature. The *USBBY Newsletter* from the United States section of IBBY, and the international page of *Reading Today,* the bulletin of the International Reading Association, highlight events of interest in the United States and other countries related to this field.

The lists of past winners of the Hans Christian Andersen Award, the Mildred L. Batchelder Award, and the British, Australian, New Zealand, and Canadian awards for children's books are excellent sources of international titles and authors. (See Appendix A.) The major children's book review sources include reviews of notable international books in their monthly review columns. (See Appendix B for lists of these journals.) *Booklist,* a review journal published by the American Library Association, has occasional summary booklists on translated books and on foreign language books.

Marianne Carus, who grew up in Nazi Germany, made a commitment when founding the children's magazine, *Cricket,* to include "translated stories from as many countries as possible and about as many cultures as possible" because of her belief that "the earlier in life we lay the foundation for international understanding and tolerance, the sounder will be the bridges built later and the more ready for peaceful traffic and exchange back and forth" (Carus, 1980, pp. 174–175). This outstanding magazine, a good source for short read-alouds, features U.S. and international short stories of high quality for children from ages 6 to 12. Although international children's books are published each year by many of the largest U.S. publishers, their numbers are relatively small. Many small press publishers have taken the lead in this field and in publishing multicultural books. A publication that lists small, alternative publishers of children's books with a description of their emphases is *Alternative Press Publishers of Children's Books: A Directory* (4th edition) by Kathleen T. Horning. (For further information see Appendix B.)

A few publishers have specialized in international children's books and deserve special mention here.

> African Imprints Library Services, 410 West Falmouth Highway, Box 350, West Falmouth, MA 02574. This catalogue includes recent children's books available from 20 African nations.
>
> Atheneum/Margaret K. McElderry Books, Macmillan Publishing Company, 866 Third Avenue, New York, NY 10022. This company publishes picture books and chapter books from other English-speaking countries and translated children's chapter books. Margaret K. McElderry, a children's book editor, is recognized for her leadership in bringing more translated children's books to the United States.
>
> Farrar, Straus, and Giroux, 19 Union Square West, New York, NY 10003. As a result of a translation and distribution agreement with the largest Swedish publisher of children's books, Rabén and Sjögren, this company publishes a number of translated Swedish books every year.

Henry Holt and Company, 115 West 18th Street, New York, NY 10114-0378. This publishing firm has recently begun a new imprint, Edge Books, that features international fiction and picture books.

Kane/Miller Book Publishers, P.O. Box 529, Brooklyn, NY 11231-0005. This small press specializes in translated foreign children's picture books from around the world under the Cranky Nell imprint.

Lerner Publications Company/Carolrhoda Books, Inc., 241 First Avenue North, Minneapolis, MN 55401. This company publishes many multicultural and international nonfiction and fiction children's books.

Picture Book Studio, P.O. Box 9139, 10 Central Street, Saxonville, MA 01701. This company publishes many international picture books, some being collaborative works between Europeans and Americans.

Tundra Books of Northern New York, Box 1030, Plattsburgh, NY 12901. This company specializes in Canadian and French/English bilingual books for children.

Turton and Chambers Ltd., Station Road, Woodchester Stroud, Glos GL5 5EQ, England. This firm specializes in translating into English and publishing foreign children's books for distribution in England and Australia. Books can be ordered by catalog from England.

Wellington Publishing Company, P.O. Box 14877, Chicago, IL 60614. This small press specializes in translated children's books.

Historical Overview of International Literature

Much of the children's literature available in the United States during the seventeenth, eighteenth, nineteenth, and early twentieth centuries came from Europe. These early children's books are an important part of our cultural heritage, but we seldom think of the fact that they were originally published in other countries and many in other languages. They are so familiar to us in United States that we consider them our children's classics, and indeed they have become so. Table 10-2 lists a sampling of international children's classics published from the end of the seventeenth century up to World War II.

With the rapid growth in the U.S. children's book field in the twentieth century, the flow of books from other countries became overshadowed by large numbers of U.S. publications. In addition, during World War II, little cultural exchange occurred across international borders. The end of World War II saw a change in the international mood, and two developments occurred that had far-reaching effects on the children's book field: (1) children's books in translation began to be published in unprecedented numbers (Carus, 1980), and (2) the international children's book field was established and fostered by an international organization, awards, and publishers' bookfairs of children's books.

The establishment of an international children's book field was advanced by Jella Lepman, who described these early developments in *A Bridge of Children's Books* (1969). Lepman, a German-born Jew who left Germany during World War II

TABLE 10–2 Early Milestones in International Children's Literature

Date	Event	Significance
1657	*Orbis Pictus* by John Amos Comenius	Earliest nonfiction picture book
1697	*Tales of Mother Goose* by Charles Perrault	Earliest folktales from France
1719	*Robinson Crusoe* by Daniel Defoe	Two early adult adventure books from
1726	*Gulliver's Travels* by Jonathan Swift	England, adopted by children
1812	*Nursery and Household Tales* by Jakob and Wilhelm Grimm	Traditional folktales from Germany
1836	*Fairy Tales* by Hans Christian Andersen	Early modern folktales from Denmark
1846	*Book of Nonsense* by Edward Lear	Early humorous poetry from England
1865	*Alice's Adventures in Wonderland* by Lewis Carroll	Classic English modern fantasy
1880	*Heidi* by Johanna Spyri	Early realistic story from Switzerland
1881	*The Adventures of Pinocchio* by Carlo Collodi	Modern fantasy from Italy
1883	*Treasure Island* by Robert Louis Stevenson	Adventure tale from England by a Scottish author
1885	*A Child's Garden of Verses* by Robert Louis Stevenson	Classic collection of Golden Age poems from England
1894	*The Jungle Book* by Rudyard Kipling	Animal stories set in India by an English author
1901	*The Tale of Peter Rabbit* by Beatrix Potter	Classic English picture book
1906	*The Wonderful Adventures of Nils* by Selma Lagerlöf	A fantasy trip around Sweden
1908	*Wind in the Willows* by Kenneth Grahame	Animal fantasy from England
1908	*Anne of Green Gables* by Lucy M. Montgomery	Realistic family story from Canada
1926	*Winnie-the-Pooh* by A.A. Milne	Personified toy story from England
1928	*Bambi* by Felix Salten	Personified deer story from Germany
1931	*The Story of Babar* by Jean de Brunhoff	Personified elephant story from France
1945	*Pippi Longstocking* by Astrid Lindgren	Classic fantasy from Sweden
1949	*Finn Family Moomintroll* by Tove Jansson	Fantasy about small creatures in Finland

for England, returned to Germany after the war to work in the field of children's books as a way to promote international understanding and world peace. Lepman began a traveling exhibit of children's books for German children, which in 1949 was established as the International Youth Library (IYL) in Munich. The IYL is the largest collection of children's books from around the world and currently holds well over 400,000 books. In reflecting on these accomplishments, Lepman concludes in her book that "in many parts of the world children were holding books in their hands and meeting over a bridge of children's books" (p. 154).

Lepman also worked with others from many countries in establishing the International Board on Books for Young People (IBBY) in 1953. IBBY is organized by sections from member countries. The members of national sections are children's book editors, agents, librarians, publishers, educators, translators, authors, and illustrators—anyone who works in the children's book field. In 1956, IBBY founded the Hans Christian Andersen Medal, an international award program that honors outstanding authors of children's literature. The first recipient of this medal was Eleanor Farjeon of Great Britain. The medal is given every two years, and in 1966 an award to outstanding illustrators was added. Alois Carigiet of Switzerland was the 1966 Medal winner for illustrations. (See Appendix A for other Hans Christian Andersen Award winners.) IBBY holds a biennial world congress in September; the first congress held in North America was in Williamsburg, Virginia, in 1990. Canadian professor Ronald Jobe served as president of IBBY from 1990 to 1994.

In 1963, IBBY founded *Bookbird,* an international quarterly periodical on literature for children and young people. In 1993, the publication of *Bookbird* moved to the United States. North America has thus increased its role in the affairs of IBBY in recent years.

In 1967, the Biennale of Illustrations Bratislava (BIB), an international exposition of children's book illustrations, was established and takes place every other year in Bratislava, Czechoslovakia. An international jury selects prize-winning children's book illustrations for a Grand Prix, the highest award, and recognizes honor books.

In 1968, the first Mildred L. Batchelder Award was announced by the American Library Association in honor of a U.S. publisher of the most distinguished translated children's book published in the preceding year. This award is given annually to encourage the translation and publication of international books in the United States. (See Appendix A for the award list.)

An international children's bookfair is convened in Bologna, Italy, every April for children's book publishers. This forum has proved to be an important one for the international exchange of children's books—a time when publishers display their best in the interests of attracting publishers from other nations to publish the new books in their own countries. Three prizes are awarded at this fair, one selected by a jury of children from ages 6 to 9.

The future of international children's literature depends upon our success in several arenas. First, we must encourage the development of stronger national literatures from developing nations where most literature remains at the stage of the oral tradition. We must also promote more literary exchange with nations whose literature is now growing rapidly in order to bring more of the world's best literature to our children's attention. Finally, we must support those organizations that can assist in these endeavors. Milestones in the development of an international children's book field are highlighted in Table 10-3.

International Books by World Regions

Quite logically, the international books most often available in the United States have been and continue to be books from other English-speaking countries. These *English language* books originate in many different countries, but the largest numbers

TABLE 10–3   Milestones in the Development of an International Children's Book Field

Date	Event	Significance
1949	Founding of the International Youth Library in Munich, Germany	A center for the collection and study of world children's literature
1953	Establishment of the International Board on Books for Young People (IBBY)	An organization for exchange among professional working in the international children's book field
1956	IBBY awards the Hans Christian Andersen Medal to Eleanor Farjeon, England	The first international award for authors of children's books
1966	IBBY awards the Hans Christian Andersen Medal to Alois Carigiet, France	The first international award for illustrators of children's books
1966	Children's book fair begun in Bologna, Italy	An international exchange for publishers of children's books; awards given for the best books
1966	*Bookbird*, quarterly journal from IBBY, begun	A journal for international exchange on children's literature
1967	Establishment of the Biennale of Illustrations, Bratislava	An international exposition of children's book illustrations
1968	The Mildred L. Batchelder Award given to Knopf for Eric Kästner's *The Little Man*	An award established by the American Library Association to recognize U.S. publishers of translated children's books
1969	*A Bridge of Children's Books* by Jella Lepman	Publication of a book intended to promote the international exchange of children's books
1990	IBBY held its biennial congress in Williamsburg, Virginia	First IBBY Congress held in North America
1993	Bookbird publication moved to the United States	More important role for North America in the affairs of IBBY

of them come from Great Britain, Australia, Canada, and New Zealand. Although the books do not require translation, they are often published in the United Sates with other changes: spelling, characters' names, place names, and, sometimes titles and cover illustrations. These changes are made ostensibly in order to increase the marketability of the books in this country, and may indeed accomplish that end in some cases. Due to the shared primary language and some cultural commonalities among these nations, the literary exchange has been relatively easy. Teachers are often surprised to discover that one of their favorite authors is British, Canadian, or Australian. An example is *The Jolly Postman* by Janet and Allan Ahlberg, a book first published in England. However, many English language books do feature cultural attitudes and customs not typically found in the United States that warrant comparison and discussion by students. The major awards and award winners from English-speaking countries are listed in Appendix A.

Translated books come to the United States from around the world, but the largest numbers come from Europe. Today, many books come from Sweden, Norway, Denmark, Switzerland, the Netherlands, Germany, France, and Belgium, and in considerably smaller numbers from eastern European countries, especially Czechoslovakia and the former Soviet Union. A few books come from Italy and Spain. An example from Norway is *Two Short and One Long* by Nina Aamundsen.

Translated children's literature from Asia originates mostly in Japan, but books from Korea, China, and Thailand can occasionally be found. Japan has an extremely sophisticated field of book illustrating, and many beautifully illustrated picture books are now making their way into the U.S. market. An example from Sri Lanka is *The Umbrella Thief*, by Sybil Wettasinghe.

African nations have produced little children's literature that has been exported to the United States. The reasons for this are many, but probably the most influential one is that of economics. Publishing books is expensive, especially in full color; thus, the publishing industry is not firmly established in developing countries. An example from Ghana is *Cat in Search of a Friend* by Meshack Asare. Central and South American countries suffer from similar economic problems. Traditional literature is usually the first genre of children's literature to be published in a developing nation and, therefore, is often the only literature available to our students from those countries. Books of realistic fiction in which contemporary life in another country is portrayed are rare, but worth locating. An example is Lesley Beake's *The Song of Be*, a novel set in Namibia that deals with reconciling present political realities with ancient traditions.

The difficulties of locating and translating good books from non-English-speaking countries contribute to the dearth of available titles. Certain publishing companies have been attempting to overcome this dearth of foreign literature in our country by focusing solely on foreign children's literature, whereas other publishers have made a concerted effort to increase the percentage of foreign books among their titles. These efforts are encouraging. As more librarians, teachers, and parents become interested in purchasing this body of literature, more publishers will become willing to meet the market need.

There is reason to hope that the current unrest between cultures will not always be the case. Ethnic prejudice and bias are not natural behaviors; they are learned. One of the most intriguing challenges to those who work with children is to combat the ignorance that is at the root of racial, cultural, and religious prejudice and intolerance. Children's literature, particularly the rich multicultural and international selections currently available, is a powerful tool in this effort, for it shows that the similarities between all people are much more fundamental than the differences.

References

Angelou, Maya. (1990). Human Family. In *I shall not be moved*. New York: Random.

Banks, J.A., & Banks, C. A. (1993). *Multicultural education: Issues and perspectives*. Boston: Allyn and Bacon.

Carus, M. (1980). Translation and internationalism in children's literature. *Children's Literature in Education, 11* (4), 171–179.

Horning, K. T. (Ed.). (1991). *Alternative press publishers of children's books: A directory (4th ed.).*

Madison, WI: Friends of the CCBC.

———. (1993). The contributions of alternative press publishers to multicultural literature for children. *Library Trends, 41,* 524–540.

Jenkins, E. C., & Austin, M. C. (1987). *Literature for children about asians and asian americans: Analysis and annotated bibliography, with additional readings for adults.* New York: Greenwood Press.

Kruse, G. M. & Horning, K. T. (1991). *Multicultural literature for children and young adults: A selected listing of books, 1980–1990, by and about people of color (3rd ed.).* Madison, WI: Wisconsin Department of Public Instruction.

Larrick, N. (1965). The all-white world of children's books. *Saturday Review* (September 11), 63–65, 84–85.

Lepman, J. (1969). *A bridge of children's books.* Chicago: American Library Association.

Pine, S. (Ed.). (1994). *The black experience in children's books.* New York: New York Public Library.

Rudman, M. (1984). *Children's literature: An issues approach* (2nd ed.). New York: Longman.

Schon, I. (1978–1992). *Books in Spanish for children and young adults: An annotated guide.* (Series I–VI). Metuchen, NJ: Scarecrow.

Sims, R. (1982). *Shadow and substance: Afro-American experience in contemporary children's fiction.* Urbana, IL: NCTE.

Slapin, B. & Seale, D. (1991). *Through Indian eyes: The native experience in books for children* (Vol. 3). Philadelphia: New Society Publishers.

Verrall, C. & McDowell, P. (1990). *Resource reading list 1990: Annotated bibliography of resources by and about Native People.* Toronto: Canadian Alliance in Solidarity with the Native Peoples.

Notable Authors and Illustrators of Multicultural Literature

African American

Verna Aardema, reteller of African folktales. *Bringing the Rain to Kapiti Plain; Why Mosquitoes Buzz in People's Ears.*

Arnold Adoff, author of several books of poetry about the African-American experience. *Black Is Brown Is Tan.*

Ashley Bryan, collector, teller, and illustrator of African songs and folktales. *I'm Going to Sing: Black American Spirituals.*

Lucille Clifton, author of the *Everett Anderson* series of picture story books. *Everett Anderson's Good-bye.*

Leo and Diane Dillon, illustrators of two Caldecott Award-winning books. Leo Dillon is the first African American to win a Caldecott Award. *Why Mosquitoes Buzz in People's Ears; Ashanti to Zulu.*

Tom Feelings, illustrator who uses inventive artistic techniques in books about Africans and African Americans. *Moja Means One; Soul Looks Back in Wonder.*

Eloise Greenfield, author and poet whose work centers on the theme of African-American family life. *Night on Neighborhood Street; She Come Bringing Me That Little Baby Girl.*

Virginia Hamilton, award-winning author whose books about African Americans include realistic fiction, mystery, fantasy, myth, and biography. *M. C. Higgins, the Great; Zeely.*

Langston Hughes, leading African-American poet of the twentieth century; not primarily a children's poet. *The Dream Keeper.*

Lynn Joseph, author of stories from Trinidad. *The Mermaid's Twin Sister.*

Ezra Jack Keats, author/illustrator whose picture book character, Peter, was the first African-American protagonist in a Caldecott Award-winning book. *The Snowy Day; Peter's Chair.*

Julius Lester, author of nonfiction and collector and reteller of African-American folktales. *To Be a Slave.*

Patricia McKissack, author of modern African-American folktales and informational books. *Mirandy and Brother Wind.*

Walter Dean Myers, author of sometimes gritty contemporary realistic fiction about African Americans growing up. *The Scorpions; Fallen Angels.*

Jerry Pinkney, illustrator whose light-filled watercolors capture the beauty of African Americans. *The Talking Eggs.*

Faith Ringgold, author/illustrator of story quilts. *Tar Beach.*

John Steptoe, first African-American author/illustrator to gain fame in the United States. *Stevie; Mufaro's Beautiful Daughters.*

Mildred Taylor, author whose award-winning books of historical fiction chronicle the experience of growing up Black in southern United States in the 1940s and 1950s. *Roll of Thunder, Hear My Cry; The Friendship.*

Asian American

Allen Say, author/illustrator whose realistic watercolors depict stories of the Japanese-American experience. *Grandfather's Journey; Tree of Cranes.*

Yoshiko Uchida, author of autobiographical accounts of U.S. imprisonment of Japanese-American citizens during World War II. *Journey to Topaz; Journey Home.*

Paul Yee, author who writes about the Chinese Canadian experience. *Tales from Gold Mountain: Stories of the Chinese in the New World.*

Laurence Yep, author of historical and contemporary realistic fiction about growing up as an Asian American. *Dragonwings; Child of the Owl.*

Ed Young, first Asian-American illustrator to win the Caldecott Award. *Lon Po Po: A Red-Riding Hood Story from China.*

Hispanic American

Nicholasa Mohr, author of several novels about Puerto Rican life in New York City. *Felita; Going Home.*

Frané Lessac, illustrator of Caribbean island stories and poems. *Caribbean Canvas; The Chalk Doll.*

Leo Politi, author/illustrator of several award-winning picture books having Hispanic-American characters. *Pedro, the Angel of Olvera Street; Juanita.*

Gary Soto, author of contemporary stories about the Mexican-American experience. *Trading Places; The Skirt.*

Jewish American

Eric Kimmel, reteller of tales, many of which are from the Jewish culture. *Hershel and the Hanukkah Goblins; The Chanukkah Guest.*

Milton Meltzer, author of important nonfictional works about several U.S. minorities. *Remember the Days: A Short History of the Jewish American.*

Isaac Bashevis Singer, Nobel prize-winning author of several collections of tales that tell much about Jewish traditions and customs. *When Shlemiel Went to Warsaw and Other Stories.*

Native American

Brent Ashabranner, author of nonfictional books about Native American life, past and present. *To Live in Two Worlds: American Indian Youth Today.*

John Bierhorst, collector of traditional literature of Native Americans and South American and Mexican Indians. *The Fire Plume: Legends of the American Indians.*

Ann Nolan Clark, one of the first authors to write for and about Native Americans. *Secret of the Andes.*

Michael Dorris, author of stories written from a Native American perspective. *Morning Girl.*

Paul Goble, reteller and illustrator of the folktales and legends of the Native Americans of the Great Plains. *The Girl Who Loved Wild Horses.*

Jamake Highwater, author of the Ghost Horse Cycle in which many aspects of the Native American heritage are examined. *Legend Days.*

Scott O'Dell, author of several works of award-winning historical fiction featuring strong female Native-American heroines. *Island of the Blue Dolphins.*

Virginia Driving Hawk Sneve, author of contemporary realistic novels about life on Native-American reservations. *When Thunders Spoke.*

Notable Authors, Illustrators, and Translators of International Literature

Lena Anderson, Swedish illustrator of the Linnea books by Christina Björk, and her own *Baby Bunny* series.

Mitsumasa Anno, Japanese author/illustrator of sophisticated wordless picture books and concept books; 1984 recipient of the Hans Christian Andersen Award. *Topsy Turvies: Pictures to Stretch the Imagination; Anno's Journey.*

Jeannie Baker, Australian artist who uses relief collages in her illustrations. *Where the Forest Meets the Sea; Home in the Sky.*

Graeme Base, Australian illustrator of large, elaborate format picture books. *Animalia; The Eleventh Hour.*

Anthea Bell, British award-winning translator from German, Dutch, and Danish languages. Translated *Buster's World* by Bjarne Reuter and *Konrad* by Christine Nöstlinger.

Quentin Blake, British illustrator popular for his irreverently humorous style. *Quentin Blake's ABC; Nonstop Nonsense* by Margaret Mahy.

Cecil Bödker, Danish author of stories set in Africa; recipient of 1976 Hans Christian Andersen Award. *The Leopard.*

Martha Brooks, Canadian author of adolescent novels and short stories. *Paradise Café and Other Stories; Two Moons in August.*

Anthony Browne, British author/illustrator whose stark surrealism reveals modern social ills. *Wally the Wimp; Gorilla.*

Roald Dahl, British author of extremely popular and wildly humorous modern fantasies. *James and the Giant Peach; Charlie and the Chocolate Factory.*

Peter Dickinson, British author of science fiction. *Heartsease; Tulku.*

Berlie Doherty, British author of adolescent fiction. *Dear Nobody; Granny Was a Buffer Girl.*

Mem Fox, Australian author of picture storybooks often employing Australian animals. *Possum Magic; Koala Lou.*

Bob Graham, Australian author and illustrator of whimsical picture books. *Greetings from Sandy Beach; Rose Meets Mr. Wintergarden.*

Maria Gripe, Swedish author of contemporary realistic fiction novels; recipient of the 1974 Hans Christian Andersen Medal. *The Night Daddy; Hugo and Josephine.*

Ted Harrison, Canadian illustrator particularly noted for his interpretations of the frozen north. *A Northern Alphabet; The Cremation of Sam McGee* by Robert Service.

Peter Härtling, German author of World War II historical fiction novels. *Crutches; Old John.*

Tormod Haugen, Norwegian author of introspective novels for adolescents; recipient of 1990 Hans Christian Andersen Award. *Night Birds; Zeppelin.*

James Houston, Canadian author of survival stories and tales of Inuit Indians. *The Falcon Bow; The White Archer.*

Monica Hughes, Canadian author of contemporary fiction and science fiction. *The Keeper of the Isis Light; The Dream Catcher.*

Tove Jansson, Finnish creator of the *Moomin* fantasy stories; recipient of the 1966 Hans Christian Andersen Award. *Finn Family Moomintroll.*

Dušan Kállay, Czechoslovakian illustrator and winner of the Bratislava Grand Prix and the 1988 Hans Christian Andersen Award. Illustrated *December's Travels* by Mischa Damjan.

Dennis Lee, Canadian poet known for humorous poetry. *Alligator Pie; Garbage Delight.*

Astrid Lindgren, Swedish author of classic fantasy, *Pippi Longstocking,* and realistic novels; second recipient of the Hans Christian Andersen Medal. *The Brothers Lionheart.*

Jean Little, Canadian author of realistic chapter books featuring children with emotional and physical disabilities. *Mine for Keeps; Mama's Going to Buy You a Mockingbird.*

Janet Lunn, Canadian author of historical fantasy novels. *The Root Cellar; Shadow in Hawthorn Bay.*

Margaret Mahy, New Zealand author of modern fantasies with supernatural elements. *The Haunting; The Changeover.*

Kevin Major, Canadian award-winning author of popular adolescent novels. *Hold Fast; Blood Red Ochre.*

Lucy M. Montgomery, Canadian author of *Anne of Green Gables* stories.

Farley Mowat, Canadian author of animal stories. *Owls in the Family; Never Cry Wolf.*

Jörg Müller, Swiss illustrator and 1994 Hans Christian Andersen medalist who unifies social conscience with experimentation in aesthetic form. *Rabbit Island.*

Mary Norton, British author of *The Borrowers* series about personified little people.

Christine Nöstlinger, Austrian author of humorous fantasy; 1984 recipient of the Hans Christian Andersen Award. *Konrad.*

A. Philippa Pearce, British author of modern fantasies and contemporary mysteries. *Tom's Midnight Garden; The Way to Sattin Shore.*

Stéphane Poulin, Canadian artist known for the *Josephine* cat stories and a bilingual ABC. *Ah! Belle Cité / A Beautiful City ABC.*

Annie M. G. Schmidt, poet and author from the

Netherlands and winner of the Hans Christian Andersen Medal. Known for her humorous narrative poems. *Pink Lemonade.*

Ivan Southall, Australian author of realistic adventure stories. *Josh; Ash Road; Let the Balloon Go.*

Rosemary Sutcliff, British author of historical fiction novels. *The Lantern Bearers; Bonnie Dundee.*

Colin Thiele, Australian author of realistic novels whose isolated settings reveal the enormity of the country. *Fire in the Stone; Storm Boy.*

Julie Vivas, Australian illustrator of picture books. *Possum Magic; Wilfrid Gordon McDonald Partridge.*

Brian Wildsmith, British illustrator noted for his innovative and modernistic designs. *Brian Wildsmith's ABC; Brian Wildsmith's Mother Goose.*

Patricia Wrightson, Australian author of contemporary novels with Aboriginal folk spirits; received the Hans Christian Andersen Award in 1986. *The Nargun and the Stars; A Little Fear.*

Alki Zei, Greek author of historical fiction novels; three-time recipient of the Mildred L. Batchelder Award. *Wildcat Under Glass; The Sound of Dragon's Feet.*

Lisbeth Zwerger, Austrian illustrator and recipient of the 1990 Hans Christian Andersen Award; particularly noted for her illustrations of traditional folktales, including tales of the Brothers Grimm. *Hansel and Gretel;* and *Little Red Cap.*

Recommended Multicultural Books

Ages refer to approximate interest levels. YA = young adult readers.

African American

Aardema, Verna. *Bringing the Rain to Kapiti Plain: A Nandi Tale.* Illustrated by Beatriz Vidal. Dial, 1981. Ages 7–9. (picture book)

———. *Why Mosquitoes Buzz in People's Ears.* Illustrated by Leo and Diane Dillon. Dial, 1975. Ages 5–7. (picture book)

Adoff, Arnold. *Black Is Brown Is Tan.* Harper, 1973. Ages 8–10. (poetry)

Armstrong, William H. *Sounder.* Harper, 1969. Ages 9–12. (chapter book)

Berry, James. *Ajeemah and His Son.* HarperCollins, 1992. Ages 9–12. (chapter book)

Binch, Caroline. *Gregory Cool.* Dial, 1994. Ages 6–9. (picture book)

Bontemps, Arne. *The Story of the Negro.* Knopf, 1948. Ages 9–12. (chapter book)

Bryan, Ashley. *Turtle Knows Your Name.* Atheneum, 1989. Ages 6–8. (picture book)

Clifton, Lucille. *Everett Anderson's Good-bye.* Illustrated by Ann Grifalconi. Holt, 1988. Ages 5–7. (picture book)

Collier, James, and Christopher Collier. *Jump Ship to Freedom.* Delacorte, 1981. (Others in the Arabus Family Saga: *War Comes to Willy Freeman,* 1983; *Who Is Carrie?,* 1984.) Ages 9–12. (chapter book)

Davis, Ossie. *Langston: A Play.* Delacorte, 1982. Ages 8–10.

De Treviño, Elizabeth Borton. *I, Juan de Pareja.* Farrar, 1965. Ages 9–12. (chapter book)

Ellis, Veronica Freeman. *Afro-Bets First Book about Africa.* Just Us Books, 1990. Ages 4–6. (picture book)

Feelings, Muriel. *Jambo Means Hello: Swahili Alphabet Book.* Dial, 1974. Ages 6–8. (picture book)

———. *Moja Means One: Swahili Counting Book.* Illustrated by Tom Feelings. Dial, 1971. Ages 6–8. (picture book)

Flournoy, Valerie. *The Patchwork Quilt.* Illustrated by Jerry Pinkney. Dial, 1985. Ages 5–7. (picture book)

Fox, Paula. *The Slave Dancer.* Bradbury, 1973. Ages 9–12. (chapter book)

Greene, Bette. *Philip Hall Likes Me. I Reckon Maybe.* Illustrated by Charles Lilly. Dial, 1974. Ages 8–10. (chapter book)

Greenfield, Eloise. *Honey, I Love and Other Love Poems.* Viking, 1978. Ages 6–10. (poetry)

———. *Nathaniel Talking.* Illustrated by Jan Spivey Gilchrist. Black Butterfly, 1989. Ages 6–10. (picture book)

———. *Under the Sunday Tree.* Illustrated by Amos Ferguson. Harper, 1988. Ages 6–10. (poetry)

Grifalconi, Ann. *The Village of Round and Square Houses.* Little, Brown, 1986. Ages 7–9. (picture book)

Haley, Gail. *A Story, a Story.* Atheneum, 1970. Ages 7–9. (picture book)

Hamilton, Virginia. *The All Jahdu Storybook.* Illustrated by Barry Moser. Harcourt, 1991. Ages 7–9. (story collection)

———. *Cousins.* Philomel, 1990. Ages 9–12. (chapter book)

———. *The House of Dies Drear.* Illustrated by Eros Keith. Macmillan, 1968. (See sequel: *The Mystery of Drear House,* Greenwillow, 1987.) Ages 9–12. (chapter book)

———. *M. C. Higgins, the Great.* Macmillan, 1974. Ages 9–12. (chapter book)

———. *The Magical Adventures of Pretty Pearl.* Harper, 1983. Ages 7–9. (chapter book)

———. *Many Thousand Gone: African Americans from Slavery to Freedom.* Illustrated by Leo and Diane Dillon. Random, 1992. (chapter book)

———. *The Planet of Junior Brown.* Macmillan, 1971. Ages 12–YA. (chapter book)

———. *Zeely.* Illustrated by Symeon Shimin. Macmillan, 1967. Ages 7–9. (chapter book)

Harris, Joel Chandler. *Jump! the Adventures of Brer Rabbit.* Adapted by Van Dyke Parks. Illustrated by Barry Moser. Harcourt, 1986. (See also: *Jump Again! More Adventures of Brer Rabbit,* 1987.) Ages 7–9. (picture book)

Haskins, Francine. *I Remember "121."* Children's Book Press, 1991. Ages 6–8. (picture book)

Howard, Elizabeth Fitzgerald. *Aunt Flossie's Hats (and Crab Cakes Later).* Illustrated by James Ransome. Clarion, 1991. Ages 6–8. (picture book)

Hurmence, Belinda. *A Girl Called Boy.* Clarion, 1982. Ages 9–12. (chapter book)

Johnson, Angela. *Toning the Sweep.* Orchard, 1993. (chapter book)

Joseph, Lynn. *A Wave in Her Pocket: Stories from Trinidad.* Illustrated by Brian Pinkney. Clarion, 1991. Ages 7–9. (collected stories)

———. *The Mermaid's Twin Sister.* Illustrated by Donna Perrone. Clarion, 1994. (collected stories)

Keats, Ezra Jack. *Goggles.* Macmillan, 1969, Ages 5–7. (picture book)

———. *Peter's Chair.* Harper, 1967. Ages 5–7. (picture book)

Lester, Julius. *How Many Spots Does a Leopard Have?* Illustrated by David Shannon. Scholastic, 1989. Ages 7–9. (collected stories)

———. *John Henry.* Illustrated by Jerry Pinkney. Dial, 1994. Ages 7–10. (picture book)

———, reteller. *The Tales of Uncle Remus: The Adventures of Brer Rabbit.* Illustrated by Jerry Pinkney. Dial, 1987. (See also: *More Tales of Uncle Remus: Further Adventures of Brer Rabbit, His Friends, Enemies, and Others,* 1988; *The Last Tales of Uncle Remus,* 1994.) Ages 7–9. (collected stories)

———. *To Be a Slave.* Dial, 1968. Ages 9–12. (chapter book)

Lewin, Hugh. *Jafta.* Illustrated by Lisa Kopper. Carolrhoda, 1983. (See others in the *Jafta* series.) Ages 7–9. (picture book)

Lyons, Mary E. *Raw Head, Bloody Bones: African-American Tales of the Supernatural.* Scribner's, 1991. (collected stories)

———. *Sorrow's Kitchen: The Life of Zora Neale Hurston.* Scribner's, 1990. Ages 12–YA. (chapter book)

Mathis, Sharon Bell. *The Hundred Penny Box.* Illustrated by Leo and Diane Dillon. Viking, 1975. Ages 7–9. (chapter book)

McKissack, Patricia. *Mirandy and Brother Wind.* Illustrated by Jerry Pinkney. Knopf, 1988. Ages 7–9. (picture book)

———, and Fredrick McKissack. *Christmas in the Big House, Christmas in the Quarters.* Illustrated by John Thompson. Scholastic, 1994. Ages 8–11. (chapter book)

———. *A Long Hard Journey: The Story of the Pullman Porter.* Walker, 1989. Ages 8–10. (chapter book)

———. *Sojourner Truth: Ain't I a Woman?* Scholastic, 1992. Ages 12–YA. (chapter book)

Meltzer, Milton. *The Black Americans: A History in Their Own Words, 1619–1983.* Crowell, 1984. Ages 12–YA. (chapter book)

Monjo, F. N. *The Drinking Gourd.* Illustrated by Fred Brenner. Harper, 1970. Ages 6–8. (picture book)

Musgrove, Margaret. *Ashanti to Zulu: African Traditions.* Illustrated by Leo and Diane Dillon. Dial, 1976. Ages 8–10. (picture book)

Myers, Walter Dean. *The Glory Field.* Scholastic, 1994. Ages 11–14. (chapter book)

———. *Now Is Your Time: The African-American Struggle for Freedom.* Harper, 1991. Ages 9–12. (chapter book)

———. *Scorpions.* Harper, 1988. Ages 9–12. (chapter book)

Nicola-Lisa, W. *Bein' with You This Way.* Illustrated by Michael Bryant. Lee and Low, 1994. Ages 4–6. (picture book)

Price, Leontyne. *Aïda.* Illustrated by Leo and

Diane Dillon. Harcourt, 1990. Ages 8–10. (picture book)

Ringgold, Faith. *Aunt Harriet's Underground Railroad in the Sky.* Crown, 1992. (picture book)

———. *Tar Beach.* Crown, 1991. Ages 6–8. (picture book)

Sanfield, Steve. *The Adventures of High John the Conqueror.* Illustrated by John Ward. Watts, 1989. Ages 9–12. (chapter book)

Steptoe, John. *Mufaro's Beautiful Daughters.* Lothrop, 1987. Ages 7–9. (picture book)

Taylor, Mildred. *Roll of Thunder, Hear My Cry.* Dial, 1976. (See others in the Logan family saga: *The Song of the Trees,* 1975; *Let the Circle Be Unbroken,* 1981; *Road to Memphis,* 1990.) Ages 9–12. (chapter book)

Turner, Glennette Tilley. *Take a Walk in Their Shoes.* Cobblehill, 1989. Ages 9–12. (chapter book)

Walter, Mildred Pitts. *Brother to the Wind.* Illustrated by Leo and Diane Dillon. Lothrop, 1985. Ages 6–8. (picture book)

———. *Justin and the Best Biscuits in the World.* Illustrated by Catherine Stock. Lothrop, 1986. Ages 6–8. (picture book)

Williams, Sherley Anne. *Working Cotton.* Illustrated by Carole Byard. Harcourt, 1992. (picture book)

Yarbrough, Camille. *Cornrows.* Illustrated by Carole Byard. Coward-McCann, 1979. Ages 6–8. (picture book)

Yates, Elizabeth. *Amos Fortune, Free Man.* Illustrated by Nora S. Unwin. Dutton, 1950. Ages 8–10. (chapter book)

Asian American

Blumberg, Rhoda. *Commodore Perry in the Land of the Shogun.* Lothrop, 1985. Ages 9–12. (chapter book)

Brown, Tricia. *Lee Ann: The Story of a Vietnamese-American Girl.* Photographs by Ted Thai. Putnam, 1991. Ages 6–8. (picture book)

Choi, Sook Nyul. *Year of Impossible Goodbyes.* Houghton, 1991. Ages 9–12. (chapter book)

Dooley, Norah. *Everybody Cooks Rice.* Illustrated by Peter J. Thornton. Carolrhoda, 1991. Ages 6–8. (picture book)

Friedman, Ina R. *How My Parents Learned to Eat.* Illustrated by Allen Say. Houghton, 1984. Ages 7–9. (picture book)

Ishii, Momoko. *The Tongue-Cut Sparrow.* Illustrated by Suekichi Akaba. Translated by Katherine Paterson. Dutton, 1987. Ages 7–9. (picture book)

Levin, Ellen. *I Hate English!* Illustrated by Steve Bjorkman. Scholastic, 1989. Ages 7–9. (picture book)

Levine, Arthur A. *The Boy Who Drew Cats: A Japanese Folktale.* Illustrated by Frédéric Clément. Dial, 1994. Ages 7–9. (picture book)

Lord, Bette Bao. *In the Year of the Boar and Jackie Robinson.* Illustrated by Marc Simont. Harper, 1984. Ages 7–9. (chapter book)

Mochizuki, Ken. *Baseball Saved Us.* Illustrated by Dom Lee. Lee and Low, 1993. Ages 7–10. (picture book)

Morimoto, Junko. *My Hiroshima.* Viking, 1990. Ages 8–10. (picture book)

Nelson, Theresa. *And One for All.* Orchard, 1989. Ages 12–YA. (chapter book)

Nhuong, Huynh Quang. *The Land I Lost: Adventures of a Boy in Vietnam.* Illustrated by Vo-Dinh Mai. Harper, 1982. Ages 9–12. (chapter book)

Rattigan, Jama Kim. *Dumpling Soup.* Illustrated by Lillian Hsu-Flanders. Little, 1993. Ages 7–9. (picture book)

Sakai, Kimiko. *Sachiko Means Happiness.* Illustrated by Tomie Arai. Children's Book Press, 1990. Ages 7–9. (picture book)

Say, Allen. *Grandfather's Journey.* Houghton, 1993. Ages 7–9. (picture book)

———. *Lost Lake.* Houghton, 1989. Ages 7–9. (picture book)

Shea, Pegi Deitz. *The Whispering Cloth: A Refugee's Story.* Illustrated by Anita Riggio and You Yang. Boyd's Mills, 1995. Ages 8–10. (picture book)

Snyder, Diane. *The Boy of the Three-Year Nap.* Illustrated by Allen Say. Houghton, 1988. Ages 7–9. (picture book)

Tompert, Ann. *Grandfather Tang's Story: A Tale With Tangrams.* Illustrated by Robert Andrew Parker. Crown, 1990. Ages 7–9. (picture book)

Uchida, Yoshiko. *The Bracelet.* Illustrated by Joanna Yardley. Philomel, 1993. Ages 8–11. (picture book)

———. *Journey to Topaz.* Scribner's, 1971. (See sequel: *Journey Home,* Atheneum, 1978.) Ages 9–12. (chapter book)

Wallace, Ian. *Chin Chiang and the Dragon's Dance.* Atheneum, 1984. Ages 7–9. (picture book)

Waters, Kate. *Lion Dancer: Ernie Wan's Chinese New Year.* Illustrated by Martha Cooper. Scholastic, 1990. Ages 7–9. (picture book)

Xiong, Blia. *Nine-in-One, Grr! Grr!* Adapted by Cathy Spagnoli. Illustrated by Nancy Hom. Children's Book Press, 1989. Ages 6–8. (picture book)

Yee, Paul. *Roses Sing on New Snow.* Illustrated by Harvey Chan. Macmillan, 1991. (picture book)

———. *Tales from Gold Mountain: Stories of the Chinese in the New World.* Macmillan, 1990. Ages 8–10. (collected stories)

Yep, Laurence. *Child of the Owl.* Harper, 1977. Ages 12–YA. (chapter book)

———. *Dragon's Gate.* HarperCollins, 1993. Ages 12–YA. (chapter book)

———. *Dragonwings.* Harper, 1975. Ages 9–12. (chapter book)

———. *Tongues of Jade.* Illustrated by David Wiesner. HarperCollins, 1991. Ages 8–12. (collected stories)

Yoshi. *Who's Hiding Here?* Picture Book Studio, 1987. Ages 3–5. (picture book)

Young, Ed. *Seven Blind Mice.* Philomel, 1992. Ages 6–10. (picture book)

Hispanic American

Aardema, Verna. *Borreguita and the Coyote.* Illustrated by Petra Mathers. Knopf, 1991. Ages 6–8. (picture book)

———. *The Riddle of the Drum: A Tale from Tizapan, Mexico.* Illustrated by Tony Chen. Four Winds, 1979. Ages 7–9. (picture book)

Belpré, Pura. *Once in Puerto Rico.* Illustrated by Christine Price. Warne, 1973. Ages 8–10. (picture book)

Buss, Fran Leeper, with assistance of Daisy Cubias. *Journey of the Sparrows.* Lodestar, 1991. Ages 9–12. (chapter book)

Carlson, Lori M. *Cool Salsa: Bilingual Poems on Growing Up Latino in the United States.* Holt, 1994. (poetry)

Carlson, Lori M., and Cynthia L. Ventura, eds. *Where Angels Glide at Dawn: New Stories from Latin America.* Illustrated by José Ortega. Lippincott, 1990. Ages 12–YA. (collected stories)

Castañeda, Omar S. *Among the Volcanoes.* Lodestar, 1991. Ages 12–YA. (chapter book)

Delacre, Lulu. *Arroz con Leche: Popular Songs and Rhymes from Latin America.* Scholastic, 1989. Ages 6–10. (poetry)

———. *Vejigante Masquerader.* Scholastic, 1993. Ages 6–10. (poetry)

De Treviño, Elizabeth Borton. *El Güero: A True Adventure Story.* Illustrated by Leslie W. Bowman. Farrar, 1989. Ages 8–10. (chapter book)

Dorros, Arthur. *Abuela.* Illustrated by Elisa Kleven. Dutton, 1991. Ages 6–8. (picture book)

———. *Radio Man: A Story in English and Spanish.* Translation by Sandra Marulanda Dorros. HarperCollins, 1993. Ages 7–9. (picture book)

Ets, Marie Hall, and Aurora Labastida. *Nine Days to Christmas: A Story of Mexico.* Illustrated by Marie Hall Ets. Viking, 1959. Ages 6–8. (picture book)

Griego y Maestas, José, and Rudolfo A. Anaya. *Cuentos: Tales from the Hispanic Southwest.* Illustrated by Jaime Valdez. Museum of New Mexico, 1980. Ages 7–9. (collected stories)

Gunning, Monica. *Not a Copper Penny in Me House: Poems from the Caribbean.* Illustrated by Frané Lessac. Wordsong, 1993. Ages 7–10. (poetry)

Haseley, Dennis. *Ghost Catcher.* Illustrated by Lloyd Bloom. Harper, 1991. Ages 6–8. (picture book)

Holman, Felice. *Secret City, U.S.A.* Scribner's, 1990. Ages 8–10. (chapter book)

Jagendorf, M. A., and R. S. Boggs. *The King of the Mountains: A Treasury of Latin American Folk Stories.* Vanguard, 1960. Ages 7–9. (collected stories)

Krumgold, Joseph. *. . . And Now Miguel.* Illustrated by Jean Charlot. Crowell, 1953. Ages 8–10. (chapter book)

Kurtycz, Marcos, and Ana Garcia Kobeh. *Tigers and Opossums: Animal Legends.* Little, Brown, 1984. Ages 7–9. (collected stories)

Mangurian, David. *Children of the Incas.* Macmillan, 1979. Ages 8–10. (chapter book)

Markum, Patricia. *The Little Painter of Sabana Grande.* Macmillan, 1993. Ages 7–9. (picture book)

Meyer, Carolyn, and Charles Gallenkamp. *The Mystery of the Ancient Maya.* Atheneum, 1985. Ages 8–10. (chapter book)

Mohr, Nicholasa. *Felita.* Illustrated by Ray Cruz. Dial, 1979. Ages 8–10. (chapter book)

O'Dell, Scott. *Carlota.* Houghton, 1981. Ages 9–12. (chapter book)

Politi, Leo. *Song of the Swallows.* Scribner's, 1949. Ages 6–8. (picture book)

Pomerantz, Charlotte. *The Chalk Doll.* Illustrated by Frané Lessac. HarperCollins, 1989. (picture book)

Presilla, Maricel E. *Feliz Nochebuena, Feliz Navidad: Christmas Feasts of the Hispanic Caribbean.* Illustrated by Espinosa Ferrer. Holt, 1994. (picture book)

Rohmer, Harriet, adapter. *Uncle Nacho's Hat.* Illustrated by Veg Reisberg. Children's Book Press, 1989 (Bilingual, English-Spanish). Ages 6–8. (picture book)

Soto, Gary. *Baseball in April and Other Stories.* Harcourt, 1990. Ages 9–12. (collected stories)

———. *Chato's Kitchen.* Illustrated by Susan Guevara. Putnam, 1995. Ages 6–9. (picture book)

———. *Trading Places.* Harcourt, 1993. Ages 10–13. (chapter book)

Sullivan, Charles, editor. *Here Is My Kingdom: Hispanic-American Literature and Art for Young People.* Abrams, 1994. Ages 13–YA. (collected stories and poems)

Winter, Jonah. *Diego.* Illustrated by Jeanette Winter. Knopf, 1991 (Bilingual, English-Spanish). Ages 7–9. (picture book)

Zubizarreta, Rosalma, Harriet Rohmer, and David Schecter. From a poem by Alejandro Cruz Martinez. *The Woman Who Outshone the Sun.* Illustrated by Fernando Olivera. Children's Book Press, 1991 (Bilingual, English-Spanish). Ages 6–8. (picture book)

Jewish American

Adler, David A. *Hilde and Eli: Children of the Holocaust.* Holiday, 1994. Ages 8–10. (picture book)

———. *The Number on My Grandfather's Arm.* Illustrated by Rose Eichenbaum. UAHC Press, 1987. Ages 7–9. (picture book)

———. *A Picture Book of Hanukkah.* Illustrated by Linda Heller. Holiday, 1982. Ages 6–8. (picture book)

———. *A Picture Book of Jewish Holidays.* Illustrated by Linda Heller. Holiday, 1981. Ages 6–8. (picture book)

Bar-Nissim, Barbara. *The Jews: One People.* Illustrated by Marlene Lobell Ruthen. United Synagogue of America, 1989. Ages 7–11. (chapter book)

Barrie, Barbara. *Lone Star.* Delacorte, 1990. Ages 9–12. (chapter book)

Chaikin, Miriam. *Aviva's Piano.* Illustrated by Yossi Abolafia. Clarion, 1986. (picture book)

Cohen, Barbara. *Carp in the Bathroom.* Illustrated by Joan Halpern. Lothrop, 1972. Ages 7–10. (picture book)

———. *Molly's Pilgrim.* Illustrated by Michael Deraney. Lothrop, 1983. Ages 6–9. (picture book)

Drucker, Malka. *The Family Treasury of Jewish Holidays.* Illustrated by Nancy Patz. Little, 1994. Ages 6–YA. (chapter book)

Ehrlich, Amy. *The Story of Hanukkah.* Illustrated by Ori Sherman. Dial, 1989. Ages 6–8. (picture book)

Feinstein, Steve. *Israel in Pictures.* Lerner, 1988. (picture book)

Geras, Adèle. *My Grandmother's Stories: A Collection of Jewish Folk Tales.* Illustrated by Jael Jordan. Knopf, 1990. Ages 8–10. (collected stories)

Goldin, Barbara Diamond. *Cakes and Miracles: A Purim Tale.* Illustrated by Erika Weihs. Viking, 1991. Ages 7–9. (picture book)

———. *Just Enough Is Plenty.* Illustrated by Seymour Chwast. Viking, 1988. Ages 6–9. (picture book)

Hirsh, Marilyn. *Potato Pancakes All Around.* Jewish Publishing Society, 1982. Ages 6–9. (picture book)

Hutton, Warwick. *Moses in the Bulrushes.* Atheneum, 1986. Ages 6–8. (picture book)

Hautzig, Esther. *The Endless Steppe: A Girl in Exile.* Crowell, 1968. Ages 9–12. (chapter book)

Khalsa, Dayal Kaur. *Tales of a Gambling Grandma.* Potter, 1986. Ages 7–9. (picture book)

Kimmel, Eric, adapter. *Days of Awe: Stories for Rosh Hashanah and Yom Kippur.* Illustrated by Erika Weihs. Viking, 1991. Ages 8–10. (collected stories)

———. *Hershel and the Hanukkah Goblins.* Illustrated by Trina Schart Hyman. Holiday, 1989. Ages 7–9. (picture book)

Kuskin, Karla. *A Great Miracle Happened There: A Chanukkah Story.* Illustrated by Robert Andrew Parker. HarperCollins, 1993. Ages 7–10. (picture book)

Lasky, Kathryn. *The Night Journey.* Warne, 1981. Ages 9–12. (chapter book)

Lawton, Clive. *I Am a Jew.* Illustrated by Chris Fairclough. Franklin Watts, 1985. Ages 5–7. (picture book)

Levinson, Riki. *Watch the Stars Come Out.* Illustrated

by Diane Goode. Dutton, 1985. Ages 7–9. (picture book)

Levitin, Sonia. *Journey to America.* Atheneum, 1970. (See sequel: *Silver Days,* 1989.) Ages 12–YA. (chapter book)

Livingston, Myra Cohn. *Poems for Jewish Holidays.* Illustrated by Lloyd Bloom. Holiday, 1986. Ages 6–10. (poetry)

Lowry, Lois. *Number the Stars.* Houghton, 1989. Ages 7–9. (chapter book)

Manushkin, Fran. *Latkes and Applesauce.* Illustrated by Robin Spowart. Scholastic, 1990. Ages 7–9. (picture book)

Meltzer, Milton. *Never to Forget: The Jews of the Holocaust.* Harper, 1976. Ages 12–YA. (chapter book)

———. *Remember the Days: A Short History of the Jewish American.* Illustrated by Harvey Dinnerstein. Doubleday, 1974. Ages 12–YA. (chapter book)

———. *Rescue: The Story of How Gentiles Saved Jews in the Holocaust.* Harper, 1988. Ages 9–12. (chapter book)

Polacco, Patricia. *The Keeping Quilt.* Simon and Schuster, 1988. Ages 7–9. (picture book)

Reiss, Johanna. *The Upstairs Room.* Crowell, 1972. Ages 9–12. (chapter book)

Rogasky, Barbara. *Smoke and Ashes: The Story of the Holocaust.* Holiday, 1988. Ages 12–YA. (chapter book)

Schwartz, Amy. *Mrs. Moskowitz and the Sabbath Candlesticks.* Jewish Publication Society, 1985. Ages 7–9. (picture book)

Schwartz, Lynn S. *The Four Questions.* Illustrated by Ori Sherman. Dial, 1989. (picture book)

Siegal, Aranka. *Upon the Head of the Goat: A Childhood in Hungary 1939–1944.* Farrar, 1981. (See sequel: *Grace in the Wilderness: After the Liberation, 1945–1948,* 1985.) Ages 9–12. (chapter book)

Singer, Isaac Bashevis. *The Golem.* Illustrated by Uri Shulevitz. Farrar, 1982. Ages 8–10. (picture book)

———. *When Shlemiel Went to Warsaw & Other Stories.* Illustrated by Margot Zemach. Farrar, 1968. Ages 8–10. (collected stories)

Singer, Isaac Bashevis, and Elizabeth Schub, translator. *Zlateh, the Goat, and Other Stories.* Illustrated by Maurice Sendak. Harper, 1966. Ages 7–9. (collected stories)

Slepian, Jan. *Risk n' Roses.* Putnam, 1990. Ages 9–11. (chapter book)

Yolen, Jane. *The Devil's Arithmetic.* Penguin, 1988. Ages 10–13. (chapter book)

Zemach, Margot. *It Could Always Be Worse.* Farrar, 1977. Ages 6–8. (picture book)

Native American

Andrews, Jan. *Very Last First Time.* Illustrated by Ian Wallace. McElderry, 1986. Ages 6–8. (picture book)

Armer, Laura Adams. *Waterless Mountain.* Longmans, 1931. Ages 9–12. (chapter book)

Ashabranner, Brent. *Morning Star, Black Sun: The Northern Cheyenne Indians and America's Energy Crisis.* Photographs by Paul Conklin. Dodd, 1982. Ages 9–12. (chapter book)

———. *To Live in Two Worlds: American Indian Youth Today.* Photographs by Paul Conklin. Dodd, 1984. Ages 9–12. (chapter book)

Ata, Te. *Baby Rattlesnake.* Adapted by Lynn Moroney. Illustrated by Veg Reisberg. Children's Book Press, 1989. Ages 4–6. (picture book)

Baker, Olaf. *Where the Buffaloes Begin.* Illustrated by Stephen Gammell. Warne, 1981. Ages 7–9. (picture book)

Baylor, Byrd. *The Desert Is Theirs.* Illustrated by Peter Parnall. Scribner's, 1975. Ages 7–9. (picture book)

———. *A God on Every Mountain Top: Stories of Southwest Indian Mountains.* Illustrated by Carol Brown. Scribner's, 1981. Ages 8–10. (collected stories)

———. *Hawk, I'm Your Brother.* Illustrated by Peter Parnall. Scribner's, 1976. Ages 8–10. (picture book)

Bealer, Alex. *Only the Names Remain: The Cherokees and the Trail of Tears.* Little, Brown, 1972. Ages 9–12. (chapter book)

Benchley, Nathaniel. *Only Earth and Sky Last Forever.* Harper, 1972. Ages 11–YA. (chapter book)

Bierhorst John, editor. *Black Rainbow: Legends of the Incas and Myths of Ancient Peru.* Farrar, 1976. Ages 9–12. (collected stories)

———. *Doctor Coyote: A Native American Aesop's Fables.* Illustrated by Wendy Watson. Macmillan, 1987. Ages 7–9. (collected stories)

———, editor. *The Hungry Woman: Myths and Legends of the Aztecs.* Morrow, 1984. Ages 8–10. (collected stories)

————, editor. *The Monkey's Haircut and Other Stories Told by the Maya.* Illustrated by Robert Andrew Parker. Morrow, 1986. Ages 8–10. (collected stories)

————, translator. *Spirit Child: A Story of the Nativity.* Illustrated by Barbara Cooney. Morrow, 1984. Ages 6–8. (picture book)

Bruchac, Joseph. *The First Strawberries.* Illustrated by Anna Vojtech. Dial, 1993. (picture book)

Caduto, Michael, and Joseph Bruchac. *Keepers of the Earth: Native American Stories and Environmental Activities for Children.* Fulcrum, 1993. Ages 8–10. (collected stories)

Clark, Ann Nolan. *Secret of the Andes.* Illustrated by Jean Charlot. Viking, 1952. Ages 10–12. (chapter book)

————. *Year Walk.* Viking, 1975. Ages 9–12. (chapter book)

Coatsworth, Emerson, and David Coatsworth, editors. *The Adventures of Nanabush: Ojibway Indian Stories.* Illustrated by Francis Kagige. Atheneum, 1980. Ages 8–10. (collected stories)

Cohen, Carol. *The Mud Pony.* Illustrated by Shonto Begay. Scholastic, 1988. Ages 6–8. (picture book)

DeArmond, Dale, reteller. *The Boy Who Found the Light.* Little, Brown, 1990. Ages 8–10. (picture book)

dePaola, Tomie. *The Legend of the Bluebonnet.* Putnam, 1983. Ages 6–8. (picture book)

Ekoomiak, Normee. *Arctic Memories.* Holt, 1990 (Bilingual, English-Inuktitut). Ages 9–12. (picture book)

Fleischman, Paul. *Saturnalia.* Harper, 1990. Ages 12–YA. (chapter book)

Freedman, Russell. *Buffalo Hunt.* Holiday, 1988. Ages 9–12. (chapter book)

————. *Indian Chiefs.* Holiday, 1987. Ages 9–12. (chapter book)

George, Jean Craighead. *Julie.* HarperCollins, 1994. Ages 10–14. (chapter book)

————. *Julie of the Wolves.* Harper, 1972. Ages 9–12. (chapter book)

————. *The Talking Earth.* Harper, 1983. Ages 9–12. (chapter book)

Goble, Paul. *Beyond the Ridge.* Bradbury, 1989. Ages 8–10. (picture book)

————. *The Gift of the Sacred Dog.* Bradbury, 1980. Ages 8–10. (picture book)

————. *The Girl Who Loved Wild Horses.* Bradbury, 1978. Ages 6–8. (picture book)

————. *Iktomi and the Buffalo Skull.* Orchard, 1991. (See other *Iktomi* trickster tales.) Ages 7–9. (picture book)

Highwater, Jamake. *Anpao: An American Indian Odyssey.* Illustrated by Fritz Scholder. Lippincott, 1977. Ages 9–12. (chapter book)

————. *Legend Days.* Harper, 1984. Ages 9–12. (chapter book)

Hobbs, Will. *Bearstone.* Atheneum, 1989. Ages 11–14. (chapter book)

Hoyt-Goldsmith, Diane. *Totem Pole.* Photographs by Lawrence Migdale. Holiday, 1990. Ages 6–8. (picture book)

Hudson, Jan. *Sweetgrass.* Philomel, 1989. Ages 12–YA. (chapter book)

Keegan, Marcia. *Pueblo Boy: Growing Up in Two Worlds.* Cobblehill, 1991. Ages 7–9. (picture book)

Kesey, Ken. *The Sea Lion.* Illustrated by Neil Waldman. Viking, 1991. Ages 8–10. (picture book)

Larry, Charles. *Peboan and Seegwun.* Farrar, 1993. Ages 7–10. (picture book)

Luenn, Nancy. *Nessa's Fish.* Atheneum, 1990. Ages 7–9. (picture book)

Martin, Bill, and John Archambault. *Knots on a Counting Rope.* Holt, 1987. Ages 6–8. (picture book)

McDermott, Gerald. *Raven: A Trickster Tale from the Pacific Northwest.* Harcourt, 1993. Ages 7–9. (picture book)

Miles, Miska. *Annie and the Old One.* Illustrated by Peter Parnall. Little, Brown, 1971. Ages 7–9. (picture book)

Manitonquat, adapter. *The Children of the Morning Light: Wampanoag Tales.* Illustrated by Mary Arquette. Macmillan, 1994. Ages 8–11. (collected stories)

Mowat, Farley. *Lost in the Barrens.* Illustrated by Charles Geer. McClelland and Stewart, 1984. Ages 9–12. (chapter book)

O'Dell, Scott. *Black Star, Bright Dawn.* Houghton, 1988. Ages 9–12. (chapter book)

————. *Island of the Blue Dolphins.* Houghton, 1960. Ages 9–12. (chapter book)

————. *Sing Down the Moon.* Houghton, 1970. Ages 12–YA. (chapter book)

Paulsen, Gary. *Dogsong.* Bradbury, 1988. Ages 12–YA. (chapter book)

Seattle, Chief. *Brother Eagle, Sister Sky.* Illustrated by Susan Jeffers. Dial, 1991. Ages 6–10.

(picture book)

Sneve, Virginia Driving Hawk, selector. *Dancing Teepees: Poems of American Indian Youth.* Illustrated by Stephen Gammell. Holiday, 1989. Ages 9–12. (poetry)

———. *High Elk's Treasure.* Illustrated by Oren Lyons. Holiday, 1972. Ages 9–12. (chapter book)

———. *Jimmy Yellow Hawk.* Illustrated by Oren Lyons. Holiday, 1972. Ages 9–12. (chapter book)

———. *When Thunder Spoke.* Illustrated by Oren Lyons. Holiday, 1974. Ages 9–12. (chapter book)

Speare, Elizabeth George. *The Sign of the Beaver.* Houghton, 1983. Ages 8–10. (chapter book)

Steptoe, John. *The Story of Jumping Mouse.* Lothrop, 1984. Ages 7–9. (picture book)

Taylor, C. J. *How We Saw the World: Nine Native Stories of the Way Things Began.* Tundra, 1993. Ages 9–12. (collected stories)

Toye, William. *The Loon's Necklace.* Illustrated by Elizabeth Cleaver. Oxford, 1977. Ages 7–9. (picture book)

Wood, Nancy. *Spirit Walker.* Illustrated by Frank Howell. Doubleday, 1993. Ages 12–14. (poetry)

Recommended International Books

Ages refer to approximate interest levels. YA = young adult readers. Country of original publication is noted.

English Language Books

Ahlberg, Janet, and Allan Ahlberg. *Each Peach Pear Plum.* Viking, 1979. Ages 3–6. U.K.

———. *The Jolly Christmas Postman.* Heinemann, 1991. Ages 5–8. U.K.

Aiken, Joan. *Bridle the Wind.* Delacorte, 1983. Ages 11–YA. U.K.

———. *The Wolves of Willoughby Chase.* Doubleday, 1962. Ages 11–YA. U.K.

Alcock, Vivien. *The Cuckoo Sister.* Delacorte, 1986. Ages 12–YA. U.K.

Allen, Pamela. *Who Sank the Boat?* Putnam, 1982.

Ages 4–7. Australia.

Andrews, Jan. *Very Last First Time.* Illustrated by Ian Wallace. Macmillan, 1986. Canadian.

Argent, Kerry, and Rod Trinca. *One Woolly Wombat.* Kane/Miller, 1985. Ages 3–6. Australia.

Asare, Meshack. *Cat in Search of a Friend.* Kane/Miller, 1986. Ages 4–10. Ghana.

Baker, Jeannie. *Window.* Julia McRae, 1991. Ages 8–11. Australia.

———. *Where the Forest Meets the Sea.* Greenwillow, 1987. Ages 7–12. Australia.

Beake, Lesley. *The Song of Be.* Holt/Edge, 1993. Ages 12–YA. South Africa.

Base, Graeme. *Animalia.* Viking, 1986. Ages 6–YA. Australia.

Bell, William. *Forbidden City.* Doubleday, 1990. Ages 12–YA. Canada.

Bishop, Gavin. *Hinepau.* Ashton Scholastic, 1993. Ages 5–8. New Zealand.

Blades, Ann. *Mary of Mile 18.* Tundra, 1971. Ages 7–10. Canada.

Brooks, Martha. *Paradise Café and Other Stories.* Little, Brown, 1988. Ages 12–YA. Canada.

———. *Traveling on into the Light: And Other Stories.* Orchard, 1994. Ages 12–YA. Canada.

———. *Two Moons in August.* Little, 1992. Ages 12–YA. Canada.

Brott, Ardyth. *Jeremy's Decision.* Illustrated by Michael Martchenko. Kane/Miller, 1990. Ages 4–7. Canada.

Browne, Anthony. *Gorilla.* Knopf, 1985. Ages 5–8. U.K.

———. *Willy the Champ.* Knopf, 1986. Ages 4–8. U.K.

———. *Zoo.* Julia McRae, 1992. U.K.

Burnford, Sheila. *The Incredible Journey.* Little, Brown, 1961. Ages 8–12. Canada.

Burningham, John. *Mr. Gumpy's Motor Car.* Crowell, 1976. Ages 4–8. U.K.

Bush, John. *The Fish Who Could Wish.* Illustrated by Korky Paul. Kane/Miller, 1991. Ages 4–8. U.K.

Carmody, Isobelle. *The Gathering.* Penguin, 1993. Ages 8–11. Australia.

Casey, Maude. *Over the Water.* Holt, 1994. Ages 11–14. U.K.

Catterwell, Thelma. *Sebastian Lives in a Hat.* Illustrated by Kerry Argent. Kane/Miller, 1990. Ages 2–5. Australia.

Christopher, John. *Fireball.* Dutton, 1981. Ages 10–YA. U.K.

———. *The White Mountains.* Macmillan, 1967.

Ages 10–YA. U.K.

Clark, Mavis Thorpe. *If the Earth Falls In.* Houghton, 1975. Ages 9–12. Australia.

Cresswell, Helen. *The Secret World of Polly Flint.* Macmillan, 1984. Ages 9–12. U.K.

Crew, Gary. *Angel's Gate.* Heinemann, 1993. Ages 9–YA. Australia.

———. *First Light.* Illustrated by Peter Gouldthorpe. Lothian, 1993. Ages 6–9. Australia.

Dahl, Roald. *Matilda.* Illustrated by Quentin Blake. Viking, 1988. Ages 9–12. U.K.

Dickinson, Peter. *Merlin Dreams.* Delacorte, 1988. Ages 10–13. U.K.

Disher, Garry. *The Bamboo Flute.* Ticknor & Fields, 1993. Ages 10–14. Australia.

Doherty, Berlie. *Dear Nobody.* Hamish Hamilton, 1991. Ages 12–YA. U.K.

Duder, Tessa. *Alessandra: Alex in Rome.* Oxford, 1991. Ages 9–12. New Zealand.

Ellis, Sarah. *Next-Door Neighbors.* Macmillan, 1989. Ages 10–12. Canada.

Fienberg, Anna. *The Magnificient Nose and Other Marvels.* Illustrated by Kim Gamble. Little, 1992. Ages 5–8. Australia.

Fine, Anne. *Flour Babies.* Hamish Hamilton, 1992. Ages 12–YA. U.K.

———. *My War with Goggle Eyes.* Joy Street, 1989. Ages 10–YA. U.K.

Fox, Mem. *Possum Magic.* Illustrated by Julie Vivas. Abingdon, 1987. Ages 4–7. Australia.

———. *Wilfrid Gordon McDonald Partridge.* Illustrated by Julie Vivas. Kane/Miller, 1985. Ages 5–10. Australia.

Freeman, Bill. *Danger on the Tracks.* Lorimer, 1987. Ages 11–YA. Canada.

Garfield, Leon. *The December Rose.* Viking, 1987. Ages 10–YA. U.K.

Gay, Marie-Louise. *Moonbeam on a Cat's Ear.* Stoddart, 1986. Ages 5–8. Canada.

Gee, Maurice. *The Fire Raiser.* Houghton, 1992. Ages 11–YA. New Zealand.

Gordimer, Nadine, and David Goldblatt. *Lifetimes Under Apartheid.* Knopf, 1986. Ages 11–YA. South Africa.

Gordon, Sheila. *Waiting for the Rain: A Novel of South Africa.* Watts, 1987. Ages 11–YA. South Africa.

Graham, Bob. *Crusher Is Coming!* Viking, 1987. Ages 7–10. Australia.

———. *Greetings from Sandy Beach.* Kane/Miller,

1992. Ages 4–8. Australia.

———. *Rose Meets Mr Wintergarden.* Viking/Penguin, 1992. Ages 6–9. Australia.

Harrison, Ted, Illustrator. *O Canada.* Ticknor & Fields, 1993. Ages 7–10. Canada.

Hathorn, Elizabeth. *The Tram to Bondi Beach.* Illustrated by Julie Vivas. Kane/Miller, 1989. Ages 4–8. Australia.

Haugaard, Erik C. *Leif the Unlucky.* Houghton, 1982. Ages 11–YA. U.K.

Houston, James. *The Falcon Bow.* Macmillan, 1986. Ages 10–13. Canada.

———. *The White Archer: An Eskimo Legend.* Harcourt, 1990. Ages 9–13. Canada.

Hughes, Monica. *Blaine's Way.* Irwin, 1986. Ages 12–YA. Canada.

———. *The Crystal Drop.* Simon and Schuster, 1993. Ages 10–YA. Canada.

———. *The Dream Catcher.* Atheneum, 1987. Ages 10–YA. Canada.

———. *Hunter in the Dark.* Atheneum, 1983. Ages 11–YA. Canada.

———. *Keeper of the Isis Light.* Nelson, 1980. Ages 11–YA. Canada.

Ingpen, Robert, adapter and illustrator. *Click Go the Shears.* Collins, 1984. Ages 6–10. Australia.

Jam, Teddy. *Night Cars.* Illustrated by Eric Beddows. Watts, 1988. Ages 5–8. Canada.

Johnston, Julie. *Hero of Lesser Causes.* Little, 1993. Ages 11–YA. Canada.

Kelleher, Victor. *Master of the Grove.* Penguin, 1982. Ages 11–YA. Australia.

———. *Taronga.* Viking, 1986. Ages 11–YA. Australia.

Khalsa, Dayal Kaur. *Tales of a Gambling Grandma.* Tundra, 1986. Ages 6–9. Canada.

Klein, Robin. *Dresses of Red and Gold.* Viking, 1993. Ages 12–YA. Australian.

———. *Hating Alison Ashley.* Viking, 1987. Ages 9–12. Australia.

Kogawa, Joy. *Naomi's Road.* Illustrated by Matt Gould. Oxford, 1986. Ages 9–12. Canada.

Lawson, Julie. *The Dragon's Pearl.* Illustrated by Paul Morin. Oxford, 1992. Ages 5–8. Canada.

Lee, Dennis. *Alligator Pie.* Macmillan, 1974. Ages 5–10. Canada.

———. *Jelly Belly.* Macmillan, 1983. Ages 5–10. Canada.

Lewis, C. S. *The Lion, the Witch, and the Wardrobe.* Macmillan, 1950. Ages 10–YA. U.K.

Lightburn, Ron. *Waiting for the Whales.* Illustrated by Sheryl McFarlane. Orca Books, 1991. Ages 6–8. Canada.

Little, Jean. *Different Dragons.* Illustrated by Laura Fernandez. Viking, 1986. Canada.

———. *Mama's Going to Buy You a Mockingbird.* Viking, 1985. Ages 10–YA. Canada.

Lottridge, Celia Barker. *The Name of the Tree.* Illustrated by Ian Wallace. McElderry, 1989. Ages 5–8. Canada.

———. *Ten Small Tales.* Illustrated by Joanne Fitzgerald. Groundwood, 1993. Ages 5–7. Canada.

———. *Ticket to Curlew.* Groundwood, 1992. Ages 10–13. Canada.

Lunn, Janet. *Amos' Sweater.* Illustrated by Kim LaFave. Groundwood, 1988. Ages 5–9. Canada.

———. *The Root Cellar.* Scribner's, 1983. Ages 11–YA. Canada.

———. *Shadow in Hawthorn Bay.* Scribner's, 1987. Ages 11–YA. Canada.

Mahy, Margaret. *The Blood-and-Thunder Adventure on Hurricane Peak.* McElderry, 1989. Ages 9–12. New Zealand.

———. *The Girl with the Green Ear.* Illustrated by Shirley Hughes. Knopf, 1992. Ages 5–10. New Zealand.

———. *The Good Fortunes Gang.* Illustrated by Marion Young. Delacorte, 1993. Ages 8–11. New Zealand.

———. *The Haunting.* Atheneum, 1983. Ages 10–YA. New Zealand.

———. *The Pirates' Mixed-up Voyage: Dark Doings in the Thousand Islands.* Dial, 1993. Ages 8–12. New Zealand.

———. *Tangled Fortunes.* Illustrated by Marion Young. Delacorte, 1994. Ages 9–12. New Zealand.

———. *The Three-Legged Cat.* Illustrated by Jonathan Allen. Viking, 1993. Ages 5–7. New Zealand.

———. *Tick Tock Tales: Twelve Stories to Read Around the Clock.* Illustrated by Wendy Smith. McElderry, 1994. Ages 5–8. New Zealand.

———. *Underrunners.* Viking, 1992. Ages 10–YA. New Zealand.

Major, Kevin. *Blood Red Ochre.* Delacorte, 1989. Ages 13–YA. Canada.

———. *Eating Between the Lines.* Doubleday, 1991. Ages 10–YA. Canada.

———. *Hold Fast.* Delacorte, 1980. Ages 13–YA. Canada.

Mark, Jan. *Thunder and Lightnings.* Crowell, 1979. Ages 10–YA. U.K.

Marchetta, Melina. *Looking for Alibrandi.* Penguin, 1991. Ages 9–12. Australia.

Marsden, John. *Letters from the Inside.* Houghton, 1994. Ages 12–YA. Australia.

———. *So Much to Tell You.* Joy Street, 1989. Ages 12–YA. Australia.

Matas, Carol. *Lisa's War.* Scribner's, 1989. Ages 10–YA. Canada.

McKay, Hilary. *The Exiles.* Macmillan, 1992. Ages 9–12. U.K.

McKee, David. *Tusk Tusk.* Kane/Miller, 1990. Ages 5–9. U.K.

Melling, O. R. *The Singing Stone.* Viking, 1986. Ages 11–YA. Canada.

Mollel, Tololwa M. *The Orphan Boy.* Illustrated by Paul Morin. Clarion, 1991. Ages 5–8. Canada.

Montgomery, Lucy M. *Anne of Green Gables.* Bantam, 1908. Ages 9–13. Canada.

Moore, Inga. *The Truffle Hunter.* Kane/Miller, 1987. Ages 4–9. U.K.

Morris, Sandra. *One Lonely Kakapo.* Hodder & Stoughton, 1991. Ages 5–8. New Zealand.

Mowat, Farley. *Owls in the Family.* Little, Brown, 1962. Ages 8–11. Canada.

Muller, Robin. *The Magic Paintbrush.* Doubleday, 1989. Ages 5–9. Canada.

Munsch, Robert. *Pigs.* Illustrated by Michael Martchenko. Annick, 1989. Ages 5–8. Canada.

Naidoo, Beverley. *Chain of Fire.* Lippincott, 1990. Ages 11–YA. South Africa.

———. *Journey to Jo'burg.* Lippincott, 1986. Ages 10–YA. South Africa.

Nilsson, Eleanor. *The House Guest.* Viking, 1991. Ages 9–12. Australia.

Noonan, Diana. *A Dolphin in the Bay.* Scholastic, 1993. Ages 11–YA. New Zealand.

Norton, Mary. *The Borrowers.* Harcourt, 1953. Ages 8–12. U.K.

Ottley, Reginald. *No More Tomorrow.* Harcourt, 1971. Ages 9–YA. Australia.

Park, Ruth. *Playing Beatie Bow.* Macmillan, 1980. Ages 10–YA. Australia.

Paterson, A. B. *Waltzing Matilda.* Illustrated by Desmond Digby. HarperCollins, 1991. Ages 4–10. Australia.

Pearson, Kit. *Looking at the Moon*. Viking, 1992. Ages 10–YA. Canada.

Pearce, Philippa. *Tom's Midnight Garden*. Lippincott, 1959. Ages 9–12. U.K.

Phipson, Joan. *Hit and Run*. Macmillan, 1986. Ages 11–YA. Australia.

———. *Six and Silver*. Illustrated by Margaret Horder. Harcourt, 1971. Ages 10–YA. Australia.

Poulin, Stéphane. *Benjamin and the Pillow Saga*. Annick, 1990. Ages 5–9. Canada.

———. *Have You Seen Josephine?* Tundra, 1988. Ages 5–8. Canada.

Richler, Mordecai. *Jacob Two-Two Meets the Hooded Fang*. Bantam, 1987. Ages 5–8. Canada.

Rodda, Emily. *Pigs Might Fly*. Illustrated by Noela Young. Greenwillow, 1986. Ages 8–11. Australia.

Ross, Christine. *Lily and the Present*. Methuen, 1992. Ages 5–8. New Zealand.

Rousseau, May. *Everyone Is Dressing Up*. Kane/Miller, 1991. Ages 2–5. Canada.

Rubinstein, Gillian. *Space Demons*. Dial, 1986. Ages 10–14. Australia.

Service, Robert. *The Cremation of Sam McGee*. Illustrated by Ted Harrison. Greenwillow, 1986. Ages 10–YA. Canada.

———. *The Shooting of Dan McGrew*. Illustrated by Ted Harrison. Godine, 1988. Ages 10–YA. Canada.

Sheldon, Dyan. *The Whale's Song*. Illustrated by Gary Blythe. Dial, 1990. Ages 5–8. U.K.

Smucker, Barbara. *Incredible Jumbo*. Viking, 1990. Ages 10–YA. Canada.

———. *Jacob's Little Giant*. Illustrated by Laura Fernandez. Penguin, 1987. Ages 8–11. Canada.

———. *Underground to Canada*. Puffin, 1978. Ages 11–YA. Canada.

Southall, Ivan. *Ash Road*. Greenwillow, 1978. Ages 10–YA. Australia.

———. *Josh*. Macmillan, 1988. Ages 12–YA. Australia.

———. *Rachel*. Farrar, 1986. Ages 11–YA. Australia.

Speare, Jean. *A Candle for Christmas*. Illustrated by Ann Blades. Macmillan, 1986. Ages 7–10. Canada.

Spence, Eleanor. *The Devil Hole*. Lothrop, 1977. Ages 10–YA. Australia. (Published in Great Britain under the title, *The October Child*, Oxford University Press in 1976.)

Stone, Ted. *The Ghost of Peppermint Flats and Other Stories*. Western Producer Prairie, 1989. Ages 9–12. Canada.

Sutcliff, Rosemary, reteller. *Black Ships Before Troy*. Illustrated by Alan Lee. Frances Lincoln, 1993. Ages 8–12. U.K.

———. *Flame-colored Taffeta*. Farrar, 1986. Ages 10–YA. U.K.

Swindells, Robert. *Stone Cold*. Hamish Hamilton, 1993. Ages 10–YA. U.K.

Thiele, Colin. *Fire in the Stone*. Harper, 1974. Ages 10–YA. Australia.

Thomas, Valerie. *Winnie the Witch*. Illustrated by Korky Paul. Kane/Miller, 1987. Ages 4–8. U.K.

Trezise, Percy. *Turramulli the Giant Quinkin*. Illustrated by Dick Roughsey. Gareth Stevens, 1988. Ages 5–9. Australia.

Trinca, Rod, and Kerry Argent. *One Woolly Wombat*. Illustrated by Kerry Argent. Kane/Miller, 1982. Ages 5–7. Australia.

Vaughn, Marcia K. *Wombat Stew*. Illustrated by Pamela Lofts. Silver Burdett, 1986. Ages 4–7. Australia.

Wagner, Jenny. *The Bunyip of Berkeley's Creek*. Illustrated by Ron Brooks. Bradbury, 1973. Ages 6–9. Australia.

———. *John Brown, Rose and the Midnight Cat*. Illustrated by Ron Brooks. Bradbury, 1977. Australia.

Wallace, Ian. *Chin Chiang & the Dragon's Dance*. Macmillan, 1984. Ages 4–8. Canada.

———. *Morgan the Magnificent*. Macmillan, 1988. Ages 5–9. Canada.

Westall, Robert. *Ghost Abbey*. Scholastic, 1989. Ages 11–YA. U.K.

———. *The Promise*. Scholastic, 1990. Ages 12–YA. U.K.

Wildsmith, Brian. *Fishes*. Oxford, 1985. Ages 4–8. U.K.

Wrightson, Patricia. *The Nargun and the Stars*. Macmillan, 1986. Ages 9–13. Australia.

———. *A Racecourse for Andy*. Harcourt, 1968. Ages 9–12. Australia.

Wynne-Jones, Tim. *Some of the Kinder Planets*. Groundwood, 1993. Ages 10–13. Canada.

Yee, Paul. *The Curses of Third Uncle*. Illustrated by Don Besco. Lorimer, 1986. Ages 10–YA. Canada.

———. *Tales from Gold Mountain: Stories of the Chinese in the New World*. Macmillan, 1990. Ages 7–12. Canada.

Yerxa, Leo. *Last Leaf First Snowflake to Fall*. Groundwood, 1993. Ages 5–8. Canada.

Translated Books

Aamundsen, Nina R. *Two Short and One Long.* Houghton, 1990. Ages 9–13. Norway.

Aleichem, Sholom. *Holiday Tales of Sholom Aleichem.* Translated from the Yiddish by Aliza Shevrin. Macmillan, 1985. Israel.

Anno, Mitsumasa and Others. *All in a Day.* Translated from the Japanese. Putnam, 1987. Ages 3–11. Japan.

Atlan, Liliane. *The Passersby.* Translated by Rochelle Owens. Illustrated by Lisa Desimini. Holt/Edge, 1993. Ages 12–YA. France.

Barbot, Daniel. *A Bicycle for Rosaura.* Illustrated by Morella Fuenmayor. Kane/Miller, 1991. Ages 4–8. Venezuela.

Beck, Martine. *The Wedding of Brown Bear and White Bear.* Illustrated by Marie H. Henry. Translated by Aliyah Morgenstern. Little, Brown, 1990. Ages 4–8. France.

Beckman, Gunnel. *Mia Alone.* Translated from the Swedish by Joan Tate. Dell, 1978. Ages 12–YA. Sweden.

Bergman, Tamar. *Along the Track.* Translated from the Hebrew by Michael Swirsky. Houghton, 1991. Ages 10–YA. Israel.

———. *The Boy from Over There.* Translated from the Hebrew by Hillel Halkin. Houghton, 1988. Ages 12–YA. Israel.

Björk, Christina. *Linnea in Monet's Garden.* Illustrated by Lena Anderson. Translated from the Swedish by Joan Sandin. Farrar (R & S), 1987. Ages 7–11. Sweden.

———. *Linnea's Windowsill Garden.* Illustrated by Lena Anderson. Translated from the Swedish by Joan Sandin. Farrar (R & S), 1988. Ages 7–11. Sweden.

———. *The Other Alice: The Story of Alice Liddell and Alice in Wonderland.* Illustrated by Inga-Karen Eriksson. Translated from the Swedish by Joan Sandin. Farrar (R & S), 1993. Ages 10–YA. Sweden.

Bödker, Cecil. *The Leopard.* Translated from the Danish by Gunnar Poulsen. Atheneum, 1975. Ages 10–14. Denmark.

Bohdal, Susi. *The Magic Honey Jar.* Translated from the German by Anthea Bell. North-South (Holt), 1987. Ages 4–8. Austria.

Bojunga-Nunes, Lygia. *The Companions.* Illustrated by Larry Wilkes. Translated from the Portuguese by Ellen Watson. Farrar (R & S), 1989. Ages 7–10. Brazil.

Bos, Burny. *Prince Valentino.* Illustrated by Hans de Beer. North-South, 1990. Ages 5–8. Netherlands.

Bour, Daniéle. *The House from Morning to Night.* Kane/Miller, 1985. Ages 3–8. France.

Bröger, Achim. *The Day Chubby Became Charles.* Illustrated by Emily Arnold McCully. Translated from the German by Renée Vera Cafiero. Lippincott, 1990. Ages 8–11. Germany.

Brunhoff, Jean de. *The Story of Babar.* Translated from the French by Merle Haas. Random, 1933. France.

Calders, Pere. *Brush.* Illustrated by Carme Solé Vendrell. Translated from the Spanish by Marguerite Feitlowitz. Kane/Miller, 1986. Ages 3–7. Spain.

Carrier, Roch. *The Champion.* Illustrated by Sheldon Cohen. Translated from the French by Sheila Fischman. Tundra, 1991. Ages 7–10. Canada.

———. *The Hockey Sweater.* Translated from the French by Sheila Fischman. Tundra, 1984. Canada.

Clément, Claude. *The Painter and the Wild Swans.* Illustrated by Frédéric Clément. Translated from the French by Robert Levine. Dial, 1986. Ages 7–11. Canada.

———. *The Voice of the Wood.* Illustrated by Frédéric Clément. Translated from the French by Lenny Hort. Dial, 1989. Ages 7–11. France.

Cohen, Peter. *Olson's Meat Pies.* Illustrated by Olaf Landström. Translated from the Swedish by Richard E. Fisher. Farrar (R & S), 1989. Ages 5–9. Sweden.

Collodi, Carlo. *The Adventures of Pinocchio.* Translated from the Italian by Marianna Mayer. Macmillan, 1981 (1881). Ages 6–9. Italy.

Damjan, Mischa. *December's Travels.* Illustrated by Dušan Kállay. Translated from the German by Anthea Bell. Dial, 1986. Ages 5–9. Germany.

Dekkers, Midas. *Arctic Adventures.* Translated from the Dutch. Watts, 1987. Ages 10–14. Netherlands.

Diaz, Jorge. *The Rebellious Alphabet.* Illustrated by Øivind S. Jorfald. Tramslated from the Norwegian by Geoffry Fox. Holt/Edge, 1993. Ages 12–YA. Chile, Spain.

Donnelly, Elfie. *So Long, Grandpa.* Translated from the German by Anthea Bell. Crown, 1981. Ages 8–11. Germany.

Duran, Cheli, editor. *The Yellow Canary Whose Eye Is So Black: Poems from Spanish-speaking Latin America.* Translated from the Spanish by Cheli Duran. Macmillan, 1977. Ages 12–YA.

Eriksson, Eva. *The Tooth Trip.* Translated from the Swedish. Carolrhoda, 1985. Ages 4–7. Sweden.

Escudié, René. *Paul and Sebastian.* Illustrated by Ulises Wensell. Translated from the French by Roderick Townley. Kane/Miller, 1988. Ages 4–8. France.

Fährmann, Willi. *The Long Journey of Lukas B.* Translated from the German by Anthea Bell. Bradbury, 1985. Ages 11–YA. Germany.

Frank, Anne. *Anne Frank: The Diary of a Young Girl.* Translated from the Dutch by B. M. Mooyaart. Doubleday, 1967. Netherlands.

Frank, Rudolf. *No Hero for the Kaiser.* Translated from the German by Patricia Crampton. Lothrop, 1986. Ages 12–YA. Germany.

Friedman, Carl. *Nightfather.* Translated from the Dutch by Arnold and Erica Pomerans. Persea, 1994. Ages 11–14. Netherlands.

Friis-Baastad, Babbis. *Don't Take Teddy.* Translated from the Norwegian by Lise Sömme McKinnon. Scribner's, 1967. Ages 9–12. Norway.

Fukami, Haruo. *An Orange for a Bellybutton.* Translated from the Japanese by Cathy Hirano. Carolrhoda, 1990. Ages 5–8. Japan.

Gajadin, Chitra, reteller. *Amal and the Letter from the King.* Illustrated by Helen Ong. Boyds Mills, 1992. Ages 5–8. Netherlands.

Gallaz, Christophe, and Roberto Innocenti. *Rose Blanche.* Translated from the French by Martha Coventry and Richard Graglia. Creative Education, 1985. Ages 9–YA. France.

Gehrts, Barbara. *Don't Say a Word.* Translated from the German by Elizabeth D. Crawford. Macmillan, 1986. Ages 11–YA. Germany.

Gomi, Taro. *Everyone Poops.* Translated from the Japanese by Amanda Mayer Stinchecum. Kane/Miller, 1993. Ages 2–5. Japan.

Grimm Brothers. *Hansel and Gretel.* Illustrated by Lisbeth Zwerger. Translated from the German by Elizabeth D. Crawford. Picture Book Studio, 1988. Ages 5–8. Germany.

Gripe, Maria. *Agnes Cecilia.* Translated from the Swedish by Rika Lesser. Harper, 1990. Ages 12–YA. Sweden.

———. *Elvis and His Secret.* Translated from the Swedish by Sheila LaFarge. Dell, 1979. Ages 8–11. Sweden.

———. *The Night Daddy.* Translated from the Swedish by Gerry Bothmer. Delacorte, 1971. Ages 9–12. Sweden.

Härtling, Peter. *Crutches.* Translated from the German by Elizabeth D. Crawford. Lothrop, 1988. Ages 11–YA. Germany.

———. *Old John.* Translated from the German by Elizabeth D.Crawford. Lothrop, 1990. Ages 10–12. Germany.

Haugen, Tormod. *Night Birds.* Translated from the Norwegian by Sheila LaFarge. Delacorte, 1982. Norway.

———. *Zeppelin.* Translated from the Norwegian by David Jacobs. Turton & Chambers, Ltd., 1991. Norway.

Heine, Helme. *Prince Bear.* McElderry, 1989. Ages 6–9. Germany.

Hertz, Ole. *Tobias Has a Birthday.* Translated from the Danish by Tobi Tobias. Carolrhoda, 1983. Ages 4–9. Denmark.

Heuck, Sigrid. *The Hideout.* Translated from the German by Rika Lesser. Dutton, 1988. Ages 10–13. Germany.

Heymans, Annemie, and Margriet Heymans. *The Princess in the Kitchen Garden.* Translated from the Dutch by Johanna H. Prins and Johanna W. Prins. Farrar, 1993. Netherlands.

Hidaka, Masako. *Girl from the Snow Country.* Translated from the Japanese by Amanda Mayer Stinchecum. Kane/Miller, 1986. Ages 4–8. Japan.

Holm, Anne. *North to Freedom.* Translated from the Danish by L. W. Kingsland. Harcourt, 1984. Ages 10–13. Denmark.

Isami, Iksuyo. *The Fox's Egg.* Translated from the Japanese by Cathy Hirano. Carolrhoda, 1989. Ages 4–8. Japan.

Jansson, Tove. *Finn Family Moomintroll.* Translated from the Finnish by Elizabeth Portch. Farrar, 1989. Ages 6–9. Finland.

Johansen, Hanna. *7 × 7 Tales of a Sevensleeper.* Illustrated by Käthi Bhend. Translated from the German by Christopher Franschelli. Dutton, 1989. Ages 6–8. Switzerland.

Kaldhol, Marit. *Goodbye Rune.* Illustrated by Wenche Öyen. Translated from the Norwegian. Kane/Miller, 1987. Ages 5–10. Norway.

Kästner, Erich. *The Little Man.* Translated from the

German by James Kirkup. Knopf, 1966. Ages 8–12. Germany.

Korschunow, Irina. *The Foundling Fox.* Illustrated by Reinhard Michl. Translated from the German by James Skofield. Harper, 1985. Ages 4–8. Switzerland.

———. *Small Fur Is Getting Bigger.* Illustrated by Reinhard Michl. Translated from the German by James Skofield. Harper, 1990. Ages 6–9. Switzerland.

Krause, Ute. *Pig Surprise.* Dial, 1989. Ages 5–8. Germany.

Kullman, Harry. *The Battle Horse.* Translated from the Swedish by George Blecher and Lone Thygesen-Blecher. Bradbury, 1981. Ages 12–YA. Sweden.

Lagercrantz, Rose, and Samuel Lagercrantz. *Is It Magic?* Illustrated by Eva Eriksson. Translated from the Swedish by Paul Norlen. Farrar (R & S), 1990. Ages 4–7. Sweden.

Likhanov, Albert. *Shadows Across the Sun.* Translated from the Russian by Richard Lourie. Harper, 1983. Ages 10–YA. Russia.

Lindgren, Astrid. *Lotta's Bike.* Illustrated by Ilon Wiklund. Farrar (R & S), 1989. Ages 3–6. Sweden.

———. *Pippi Longstocking.* Illustrated by Louis S. Glanzman. Translated by Florence Lamborn. Viking, 1950. Ages 8–11. Sweden.

———. *Rasmus and the Vagabond.* Translated from the Swedish by Gerry Bothmer. Puffin, 1960. Ages 9–12. Sweden.

———. *Ronia, the Robber's Daughter.* Translated from the Swedish by Patricia Crampton. Viking, 1983. Ages 10–YA. Sweden.

Lindström, Eva. *The Cat Hat.* Translated from the Swedish by Stephen Croall. Kane/Miller, 1989. Ages 7–9. Sweden.

Llorente, Pilar Molina. *The Apprentice.* Illustrated by Juan Ramón Alonso. Translated from the Spanish by Robin Longshaw. Farrar, 1993. Ages 11–YA. Spain.

Maartens, Maretha. *Paper Bird.* Translated from the Afrikaans by Madeleine van Biljon. Clarion, 1991. Ages 9–12. South Africa.

Mandelbaum, Pili. *You Be Me, I'll Be You.* Translated from the French. Kane/Miller, 1990. Ages 5–8. Belgium.

Marshak, Samuel. *The Month-Brothers; A Slavic Tale.* Translated from the Russian by Thomas Whitney. Morrow, 1983. Ages 5–9. Russia.

———. *The Pup Grew Up.* Illustrated by Vladimir Radunsky. Translated from the Russian by Richard Pevear. Holt, 1989. Ages 7–10. Russia.

Maruki, Toshi. *Hiroshima No Pika.* Translated from the Japanese. Lothrop, 1982. Ages 9–YA. Japan.

Mebs, Gudrun. *Sunday's Child.* Translated from the German by Sarah Gibson. Dial, 1986. Ages 8–11. Switzerland.

Merino, José María. *The Gold of Dreams.* Translated from the Spanish by Helen Lane. Farrar, 1991. Ages 9–12. Spain.

Michels, Tilde. *Rabbit Spring.* Illustrated by Käthi Bhend. Translated from the German by Alison James. Harcourt, 1988. Ages 6–9. Switzerland.

Morgenstern, Susie Hoch. *It's Not Fair!* Illustrated by Kathie Abrams. Translated from the French. Farrar, 1983. Ages 9–12. France.

Newth, Mette. *The Abduction.* Translated from the Norwegian by Tina Nunnally and Steve Murray. Farrar, 1989. Ages 13–YA. Norway.

Nilsson, Ulf. *If You Didn't Have Me.* Illustrated by Eva Eriksson. Translated from the Swedish by George Blecher and Lone Thygesen-Blecher. McElderry, 1987. Ages 7–10. Sweden.

Nomura, Takaaki. *Grandpa's Town.* Translated from the Japanese by Amanda Mayer Stinchecum. Kane/Miller, 1991. Ages 4–8. Japan.

Nöstlinger, Christine. *The Cucumber King.* Translated from the German by Anthea Bell. Bergh, 1984. Ages 6–9. Austria.

———. *Konrad.* Translated from the German by Anthea Bell. Watts, 1977. Ages 9–12. Austria.

Orlev, Uri. *The Island on Bird Street.* Translated from the Hebrew by Hillel Halkin. Houghton, 1984. Ages 9–12. Israel.

———. *Lydia, Queen of Palestine.* Translated from the Hebrew by Hillel Halkin. Houghton, 1993. Ages 8–12.

———. *The Man from the Other Side.* Translated from the Hebrew by Hillel Halkin. Houghton, 1991. Ages 10–13. Israel.

Pelgrom, Els. *The Winter when Time Was Frozen.* Translated from the Dutch by Maryka and Rafael Rudnik. Morrow, 1980. Ages 11–14. Netherlands.

Preussler, Otfried. *The Tale of the Unicorn.* Illustrated by Gennady Spirin. Translated from the German by Lenny Hort. Dial, 1989. Ages 5–8. Germany.

Rettich, Margret. *Suleiman the Elephant.* Translated from the German by Elizabeth D. Crawford. Lothrop, 1986. Ages 6–9. Germany.

Reuter, Bjarne. *The Boys from St. Petri.* Translated from the Danish by Anthea Bell. Dutton, 1994. Ages 12–YA. Denmark.

———. *Buster's World.* Translated from the Danish by Anthea Bell. Dutton, 1989. Ages 9–12. Denmark.

———. *The Sheik of Hope Street.* Translated from the Danish by Anthea Bell. Dutton, 1991. Ages 9–12. Denmark.

Richter, Hans Peter. *Friedrich.* Translated from the German by Edite Kroll. Holt, 1970. Ages 11–YA. Germany.

Sales, Francesc. *Ibrahim.* Illustrated by Eulàlia Sariola. Translated from the Catalon by Marc Simont. Lippincott, 1989. Ages 8–12. Spain.

Sato, Satoru. *I Wish I Had a Big, Big Tree.* Illustrated by Tsutomu Murakami. Translated from the Japanese by Hitomi Jitodai and Carol Eisman. Lothrop, 1989. Ages 5–8. Japan.

Schami, Rafik. *A Hand Full of Stars.* Translated from the German by Rika Lesser. Dutton, 1990. Ages 10–YA. Germany.

Schmidt, Annie M. G. *Pink Lemonade.* Illustrated by Timothy Foley. Translated from the Dutch by Henrietta Ten Harmsel. Eerdmans, 1992 (1981). Ages 6–10. Netherlands.

Schubert, Ingrid, and Dieter Schubert. *The Magic Bubble Trip.* Translated from the Dutch. Kane/Miller, 1985. Ages 3–8. Netherlands.

Siekkinen, Raija. *The Curious Faun.* Illustrated by Hannu Taina. Translated from the Finnish by Tim Steffa. Carolrhoda, 1990. Ages 6–9. Finland.

———. *Mister King.* Illustrated by Hannu Taina. Translated from the Finnish by Tim Steffa. Carolrhoda, 1987. Ages 6–9. Finland.

Singer, Isaac. *When Schlemiel Went to Warsaw & Other Stories.* Translated from the Yiddish by Elizabeth Shub. Farrar, 1968. Ages 7–10. Israel.

———. *Zlateh the Goat & Other Stories.* Translated from the Yiddish by Elizabeth Shub. Harper, 1984. Ages 7–10. Israel.

Solotareff, Grégoire. *Don't Call Me Little Bunny.* Translated from the French. Farrar, 1988. Ages 4–8. France.

———. *The Ogre and the Frog King.* Translated from the French. Greenwillow, 1988. Ages 4–8. France.

Spyri, Johanna. *Heidi.* Crown, 1880. Ages 9–12. Switzerland.

Steiner, Jörg. *The Bear Who Wanted to Be a Bear.* Illustrated by Jörg Müller. Translated from the German. McElderry, 1977. Ages 8–12. Switzerland.

———. *Rabbit Island.* Illustrated by Jörg Muller. Translated from the German by Ann Conrad Lammers. Harcourt, 1978. Ages 8–12. Switzerland.

Sundvall, Viveca. *Mimi and the Biscuit Factory.* Illustrated by Eva Eriksson. Translated from the Swedish by Eric Bibb. Farrar (R & S), 1989. Ages 4–7. Sweden.

Svedberg, Ulf. *Nicky the Nature Detective.* Translated from the Swedish by Ingrid Selberg. Illustrated by Lena Anderson. Farrar (R & S), 1988. Ages 7–11. Sweden.

Takeshita, Fumiko. *The Park Bench.* Illustrated by Mamoru Suzuki. Translated from the Japanese by Ruth A. Kanagy. Kane/Miller, 1988. Ages 3–8. Japan.

Tejima, Keizaburo. *Owl Lake.* Translated from the Japanese. Putnam, 1987. Ages 4–9. Japan.

Tolstoy, Leo. *The Lion and the Puppy and Other Stories for Children.* Illustrated by Claus Sievert. Translated from the Russian by James Riordan. Holt, 1988. Ages 9–YA. Russia.

van der Rol, Ruud, and Rian Verhoeven. *Anne Frank, Beyond the Diary: A Photographic Remembrance.* Translated from the Dutch by Tony Longham and Plym Peters. Viking, 1993. Ages 11–YA. Netherlands.

Van Iterson, S. R. *Pulga.* Translated from the Dutch by Alexander and Alison Gode. Morrow, 1972. Ages 10–14. Netherlands.

Vincent, Gabrielle. *Ernest and Celestine.* Greenwillow, 1982. Ages 3–7. France.

Wettasinghe, Sybil. *The Umbrella Thief.* Kane/Miller, 1987. Ages 4–8. Sri Lanka.

Zei, Alki. *Petros' War.* Translated from the Greek by Edward Fenton. Dutton, 1972. Ages 10–14. Greece.

———. *The Sound of Dragon's Feet.* Translated from the Greek by Edward Fenton. Dutton, 1979. Ages 9–12. Greece.

———. *Wildcat Under Glass.* Translated from the Greek by Edward Fenton. Holt, 1968. Ages 10–YA. Greece.

Chapter 11

Planning the Literature Curriculum

Sixty seconds make a minute
How much good can I do in it?
Sixty minutes make an hour—
All the good that's in my power.

—Traditional

Literature is not a regularly mandated part of the elementary school curriculum as is reading, mathematics, or social studies. Yet knowing how literature works can be valuable. Knowledge of the elements and devices of writing and illustration enriches our appreciation of an interesting story, just as knowing something of music or architecture enhances our appreciation of a beautiful song or a handsome building.

This chapter deals with long-range planning for literature instruction (short-range planning is dealt with in Chapter 12). First, the literature curriculum is defined, and ways to organize such a curriculum are presented. A discussion of literature in reading programs presents another way that literature can be integrated into the elementary school curriculum. The latter part of the chapter introduces some practical guidelines for long-term planning for literature.

The Literature Curriculum

Literature is more than a collection of well-written stories and poems. Literature also has its own body of knowledge. A term sometimes used to label this treatment of literature is *discipline-based literature instruction.* The object of such a course of study is to teach children the mechanics of literature: the terms used to define it, its components or elements, its genres, and the craft of creating it. The terms and elements of literature are presented in Chapter 2; the genres and their characteristics are presented in Chapters 3–10.

Organizing the Literature Curriculum

Some teachers plan for a year-long strand of literature instruction organized variously by genre, by author or illustrator, by literary element or device, by notable books, by topic or theme, or by some combination of these. In each case, there should be goals for the course of study, specific children's trade books to be read or listened to by each child, guidelines for selection of materials, a schedule, and criteria for evaluating the course of study.

Genre

By organizing a literature curriculum around literary genres, teachers provide a context for students to learn about the various types of literature and the characteristics of each. In the beginning, the teacher will have to direct students' attention to similarities in books of like genre—for example, the students will learn that works of historical fiction are always set in the past or that characters in folktales are two-dimensional. Soon, however, students will begin to read with more genre awareness and will enjoy finding common elements within and differences between genres.

One advantage of this plan is that students over the school year can be exposed to a wide variety of literature. Knowledge of different genres gives students useful schemata—frameworks for understanding borne of prior experience—for story types. A genre approach can work in all grade levels, given thoughtful selection of titles and delivery of literary concepts. Planning involves choosing the genres to be studied, selecting the representative children's books for each, and determining the order in which the genres will be studied.

Author or Illustrator

The goal of a curriculum in literature organized by author or illustrator is to make students more familiar with the works and styles of selected children's book authors and illustrators. An additional goal may be knowledge of the authors' or illustrators' lives insofar as these life experiences influenced the subjects' works. The choice of authors and illustrators will naturally be guided both by students' reading interests and the teacher's desire to introduce students to important authors, illustrators, and their works. The number of works chosen to represent an author or illustrator will vary, but even when an author's books are lengthy, more than one work is recommended.

As a class experiences a sampling of the chosen author's or illustrator's work, attention will be focused on trademark stylistic elements such as unusual use of words or color or media, as well as themes, characters, character types, or settings common to these works. Later, information about the person's life can be introduced through reports, audio- and videotaped interviews, and even guest appearances by the author or illustrator. Many resources, including biographies and biographical reference volumes, such as *Something about the Author* (Commire), provide information about children's book authors and illustrators. (For more information about this resource, see Appendix B.)

Success of author and illustrator studies is not necessarily defined by wholesale student approval of the featured artists. Students must be allowed to decide whether they like a person's work or not and should be encouraged to discover why they have these feelings. Wholesale *disapproval* by students of the works of a featured author or illustrator, however, is an important form of *teacher* evaluation that should not be ignored. In such a case, the teacher's choice of author or books to be studied was not appropriate for this purpose and should be reconsidered. Students are evaluated informally through observation of their recognition of featured authors' or illustrators' works and their ability to compare literary and artistic styles of various authors and illustrators.

Literary Element and Device

When teachers say that their teaching of literature is organized by literary element, they are usually referring to the elements of fiction (as presented in Chapter 2): plot, character, setting, theme, and style. Other elements, such as artistic styles, media, and book format, could be addressed as well. A *literary device* is "any literary technique deliberately employed to achieve a special effect" (Baldick, 1990, p. 55). Irony, symbolism, parody, and foreshadowing are examples of devices that add richness to stories.

The goal of a literature curriculum organized by literary elements and devices is to give students a better understanding of the craft of writing so that they can read more perceptively and appreciatively and possibly apply this knowledge to their own writing. Since this approach is analytical and somewhat abstract, it is more appropriate for students in the fourth grade or above.

Careful selection of children's books to accompany the investigation of each literary element or device is crucial to the success of this approach. The featured element must be prominent and must have been used by the author with extraordinary skill. In addition, the story itself must captivate young readers. Note that in this approach, books of various genres can be grouped to demonstrate the same literary element. Note also that picture books are particularly good at presenting literary elements and devices clearly and in relatively simple contexts so that they can be understood more easily. An excellent resource for selecting picture books for this use is Hall's *Using Picture Books to Teach Literary Devices*, Vols. I and II (1990; 1994).

Students' acquaintance with the literary elements and devices can go far beyond mere definition. Close reading of key passages reveals the author's craft at developing character, establishing mood, authenticating setting, or using such devices as inference, symbolism, or foreshadowing. Re-creation of these elements and devices in their own art, drama, and writing not only gives students a personal and more complete understanding of these concepts, but also gives teachers a way to evaluate their students' grasp of these concepts.

Notable Book

Many teachers organize a literature curriculum by notable books, that is, books widely recognized for their literary excellence. Each of these books may exemplify one or more aspects of the literature curriculum that is to be taught, and so the order in which these books are read and studied determines the order in which the content of the literature study will be presented. Since the notable books are read aloud to all the students by the teacher in this approach, it is particularly important that the selections be well-matched to students' general interests and abilities. A problem with this approach can be that the list of notable books does not vary from year to year, regardless of student variation from class to class. Teachers who use this approach successfully must remain flexible in their book selections so that their choices reflect students' current preferences and interests.

In this approach, the teacher reads aloud one or more chapters of the selected book each day and holds class discussions on the book in terms of its meanings and how different students perceive its meaning. Traditionally, these discussions are teacher-led; but some instructors have found that student-led discussions in small groups, if well-managed, are just as effective and have the added advantage of giving students practice in leading and contributing to serious discussions.

Theme or Topic

Teachers who choose to organize a study of literature by theme or topic want their students generally to become aware of the power of literature to explain the human condition. Themes and topics will vary according to ages and circumstances of students. For example, primary-grade children will be interested in themes and topics having to do with school and family life. Those in the middle grades, on the other hand, will be more intrigued by themes and topics dealing with the discovery and use of inner resources to become more independent or even to survive.

Possible themes that a seventh- or eighth-grade class might explore through a year include the following:

Surviving in the Modern World
Alienation
Coping with Parents and Younger Siblings
Teen-Agers Through History: The Same Old Problems?
Dependence and Independence
The Future World
Beneath the Skin: What Is the True Nature of Difference?

Possible themes and topics for a younger group might include these:

Families Come in All Shapes and Sizes
School Now and in the Past
Use Your Wits
The Importance of Having Good Friends
Stories from Other Countries
Old Ones and Young Ones Together
Famous People Were Children Too

Using this approach, each child reads or listens to the book or books chosen by the teacher to accompany each theme. Following the reading, students explore the theme through discussion, writing, drama, art, and further reading on the theme or topic. Those who take a whole language approach to teaching find that this method of organizing a literature curriculum works particularly well.

Themes and topics are chosen by the teacher on the basis of students' needs and interests, current events, and prior successes with previously developed thematic units. The length of time spent on any one theme or topic can vary from a school year to a day, but several weeks' duration is the norm.

Two pitfalls of thematic learning curriculum models must be avoided. The first is choosing a unit theme or topic just because a few related books are at hand. Remember: The unit theme or topic drives literature selection, not vice versa. The second pitfall is choosing literature just because it relates to the theme or topic but with no regard to its quality or appropriateness for the students. Boring books make boring thematic instructional units.

Literature in the Reading Program

Teaching literature and teaching reading are similar in some respects: both use similar materials—stories; both have the purpose of making meaning from texts; and both have the ultimate goal of a greater or deeper understanding of and response to the written text. Because of these similarities, literature and reading can be taught simultaneously.

A critical goal of teachers in grades K through 8 is to help students become literate—that is, to be able to read and write. Inservice and preservice teachers of the 1990s will encounter two different approaches to literacy subscribed to in schools and teacher training institutions: the basal reader approach and the literature-based reading approach. Underlying the differences in these two approaches are the different learning theories upon which each is based. Your approach to literacy development will depend on your own philosophy of teaching and learning, that is, the ideas you believe in strongly enough to act on.

The philosophy you accept will affect many aspects of your teaching: the materials you choose and how you present them to your students, how you arrange your classroom furniture, the activities you engage your students in, how you behave in class, and how you encourage your students to behave. In the following discussion it is important to note the theoretical differences underlying each curriculum model in literature. You should begin to form your own philosophy of learning and literacy development.

Literature-Based Reading

Literature-based reading is an approach to teaching reading through the exclusive use of trade books. The learning theory in which literature-based reading is grounded is that children learn by searching for meaning in the world around them, constantly forming hypotheses, testing them to see if they work, and subsequently accepting or rejecting them. For young children, language has meaning only when it is used in the context of *wholes* (stories, conversations, messages, etc.) and when they have sufficient prior knowledge to support the acquisition of new knowledge. Consequently, from the very beginning of literature-based reading instruction, children are presented with whole (not fragmented) language, mostly in the form of excellent stories. As they hear and see these stories, they naturally begin to form hypotheses about sound-symbol relationships, accepting those that seem to work and rejecting those that do not.

Teachers using the literature-based approach to reading will structure a classroom environment in which children are immersed in good literature. In these classrooms, children hear literature read aloud several times a day, they see good readers reading voluntarily, they discover that good books can entertain them and tell them things they want to know, and they constantly practice reading books that they themselves have chosen because they are interested in the topics.

Key elements of the literature-based reading classroom include:

- Daily reading aloud of good literature by the teacher
- Quantities of good trade books in the classroom (five or more books per child) selected to match specific interests and approximate reading abilities of the students in the class
- Reading experiences that stand on the merits of the literature alone (i.e., stories are not inevitably followed by exercises)
- Daily silent reading by students of books that they choose
- Daily opportunities for students to share their reactions to books orally
- Daily opportunities for students to respond to literature in a variety of ways, including writing, drama, and art
- Reading skills taught when needed, and then within meaningful contexts and never in isolation
- Frequent individual student-teacher reading conferences (See the discussion of individual conferences in Chapter 12.)

Decisions about what to teach, when to teach it, and what materials to use are made by the teacher in the literature-based reading classroom. These decisions and the responsibility for materials selection and acquisition may make literature-based reading more demanding of teachers' professional judgment than other reading instruction methods; however, when it is managed well, this approach has proven to be very effective, not only in teaching students to read but also in creating a positive attitude toward reading. The stimulus of new and exciting materials and students' unique personal responses to them can make teaching less based on rote and more exciting.

The absence of a prescribed, lockstep program is one of the greatest strengths of literature-based reading, but it also makes this approach vulnerable to many abuses. The following practices have no place in the literature-based reading classroom:

- Using quantities of mediocre literature in the reading program solely on the basis of having them at hand and with no regard to their interest to students or their suitability to curricular goals

- Regularly using class sets of single trade books with a predetermined reading schedule and fill-in-the-blank worksheets (This practice is referred to as the "basalization of literature.")
- Reading works of literature by "round-robin" reading
- Selecting and assigning every title read by students
- Assigning book reports regularly under the guise of book "response" to check comprehension
- Excluding multicultural and international titles, poetry, and a balance of genres and character types from the classroom selection

There is no one right way to teach literature-based reading. The method cannot be packaged. Your best protection against bogus claims, materials, and practices is to have a complete understanding of the theory behind the practice. *Transitions* and *Invitations* by Routman (1988; 1992); *Literature-Based Reading Programs at Work* (1987), edited by Hancock and Hill; and *How to Teach Reading with Children's Books* by Veatch (1968) are a few of the excellent, practical resources available to provide this information. (For further information on these resources, see Appendix B.)

Literature-based reading fits within a larger philosophy of teaching and learning called the *whole language approach.* Whole language is an entire philosophy about teaching and learning whose key tenets are materials that have meaning and relevance to students' lives, teachers who are co-learners and resources rather than authoritarians, and a curriculum that is tailored by teachers to students' interests and talents. We believe that the potential for students to learn about literature is greatest in a whole language, literature-based classroom.

Basal Reading Program Supplemented by Children's Literature

Just as children bring a variety of learning styles and needs to the task of learning, so do teachers bring a variety of teaching styles and needs to teaching. A single approach to teaching reading cannot suit all teachers or all students. The most common approach to the teaching of reading is the *basal reading approach supplemented by children's literature.*

The basal reading program has been the traditional approach to teaching reading in U.S. elementary schools for decades. According to Durkin (1987), it is "composed of a series of readers said to be written at successively more difficult levels" (p. 417). The core materials include a student reader, a teacher's manual, student workbooks, ditto masters, and tests. The strength of the basal program is that it provides teachers with an organized instructional framework upon which to build (Lapp, Flood, & Farnan, 1992). In other words, the teacher using this approach does not develop a reading program by selecting materials and planning the related activities. Basal reading programs offer teachers considerable guidance and help with the decisions and challenges involved in teaching children to read.

The learning theory upon which basal reading materials have been based for most of this century is that learning complex skills begins with mastering the simplest components of that skill before attempting the next larger components, and so on until the whole skill is learned. In terms of learning to read, this means that the letters of the alphabet are learned first, followed by letter-sound patterns, words, and then sentences. Finally, when the components of reading are learned, whole works of literature, such as stories, plays, and poems, are read. As late as the beginning of the 1980s, the embodiment of this philosophy was the basal reader—with its emphasis on progressive skill and subskill mastery and its use of short and simple sentences and a controlled vocabulary. The concern with basals of the 1950s, 1960s, and 1970s was with the limitations of the story selections—specifically, the controlled vocabulary, the uninteresting plots, and the poor writing styles.

In the 1980s, U.S. publishers of basal readers made some changes in their products. These changes were made in response to two indicators: (1) criticism by teachers and teacher educators about the low literary quality and the lockstep system in basals and (2) the convincing literacy statistics from New Zealand (100 percent literacy), where a national literature-based reading program was begun nearly thirty years ago. The quality of stories written specifically for the basals was improved. Multicultural characters began to appear in basal stories with more frequency than in the past. Most important, excerpts from high-quality trade books and some whole, albeit brief, literary works were integrated into basal readers. These changes were incorporated while retaining the skill-based instruction (particularly phonics instruction for beginning readers) regarded by researchers as important to well-rounded reading programs (Anderson, Hiebert, Scott, and Wilkinson, 1985).

Even with these changes, basals are not designed to be a complete substitute for trade books. Even though some basal stories are good literature, not excerpted or adapted, the brevity of these selections is a problem for intermediate grades. Most students in these grades are capable of reading novel-length chapter books and should be doing so on a regular basis in their school reading program. Students in classes where anthologies and basal readers are used exclusively are denied the all-important self-selection of reading material from a wide variety of books.

Perhaps basal readers are most effective when used in concert with a wide variety of trade books that reflect students' interests and reading abilities. In this arrangement, the basal provides guidance and structure to both teaching and learning, while the trade books provide the variety, opportunity for self-selection, and interest that motivates children to want to read.

Ideally, each teacher should be allowed to choose the approach to teaching reading that best suits his or her philosophy of learning and teaching style. In many school districts across the United States, however, the use of a basal approach to teach reading is mandated. Even so, many teachers in this situation have begun to move away from a slavish, "read-every-page-or-bust" attitude toward these programs. They have found ways to improve their teaching of reading by using their basal programs in innovative ways that eliminate some of the skills exercises of this approach and allow time for literature as well. Some guidelines drawn from the example of these teachers are as follows:

- Use only the best literary selections the basal offers. Substitute good trade literature for the rest.
- Let students read some of the better written basal selections simply for

enjoyment. It is the joy and wonder of reading marvelous tales or interesting information that motivates children to learn to read, not the tests on their comprehension of these stories. Use the time saved from skill, drill, and comprehension questions for silent reading.

- Eliminate the stigma of ability grouping by forming one, whole-class, heterogeneous reading group. Use the time saved from planning and conducting three or four different reading lessons to hold individual reading conferences.

- Use basal readers' phonics lessons and drills only when, in the teacher's opinion, an individual student or group of students will benefit from them. (This need is exhibited by students in their individual reading conferences and in their writing.) Children do not learn according to an imposed schedule, but only when they are ready to learn. Use the time saved from ineffective exercises to read aloud from good books or for silent reading from self-choice books.

- Avoid comprehension questions at the end of basal reading lessons that trivialize the stories or demean the students. Use the time saved to allow children to share their personal reactions to the story, to offer literary criticisms of the selection, or to respond to the story in writing, drama, or art.

- Make phonics instruction a regular but brief (10–15 minutes) part of primary-grade reading instruction. Avoid letting phonics instruction become the main attraction of reading. That role should be reserved for good stories.

Developing the Literature Curriculum

Planning for a literature curriculum involves many important practical considerations in addition to choosing the approach one takes to teaching literature. The classroom environment must be constructed, the materials collected, and the plans written.

Designing the Classroom Environment

Much can be learned about a teacher's philosophy of learning and teaching simply by taking a look around the classroom. The two classrooms depicted in Figures 11-1 and 11-2 were purposely designed to emphasize the differences possible in classroom arrangement. What sorts of interactions seem to be encouraged in these classrooms as indicated by the arrangement of desks?

The traditional classroom arrangement (Figure 11-1) implies a more teacher-centered environment: The teacher is the center of attention and the main source of information. The preponderant type of discourse in this classroom is most likely a whole-class lecture, and its direction is from teacher to student. The interactive classroom arrangement (Figure 11-2) implies a more student-centered environment. Various types of discourse seem to be encouraged here: student-to-student discussions, small group activities, and teacher-student conferences. The direction of this discourse is as much from student to student and student to teacher as it is teacher to student.

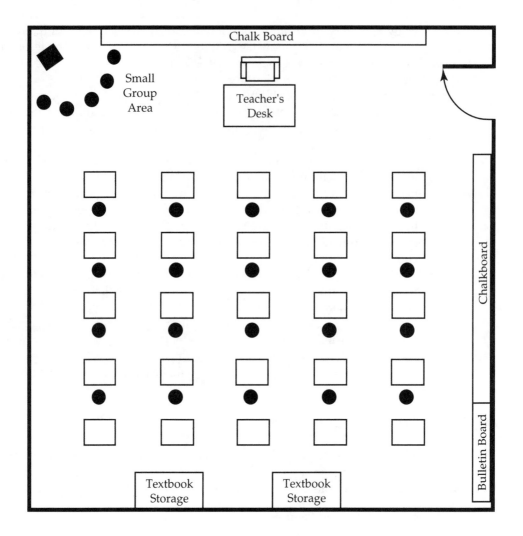

FIGURE 11-1 Traditional Classroom

In addition to room arrangement, other aspects of a classroom reveal the nature of what goes on from day to day. What materials and resources are most apparent? What is the nature of displays and bulletin boards? What level of thinking and inquiry is indicated by the student work on display? Teachers who recognize the importance of good literature will design an attractive and comfortable classroom environment in which books are featured.

Many teachers promote literature and literature-related activities by designating a specific area of the classroom as the *library corner.* The library corner is made conducive to reading by being located as far as possible from noisy activities and by being outfitted with comfortable seating (carpeting, pillows, soft chairs) and lots of conveniently placed and easy-to-find books, as in the interactive classroom in Figure 11-2. The library corner houses the classroom library and can be the setting

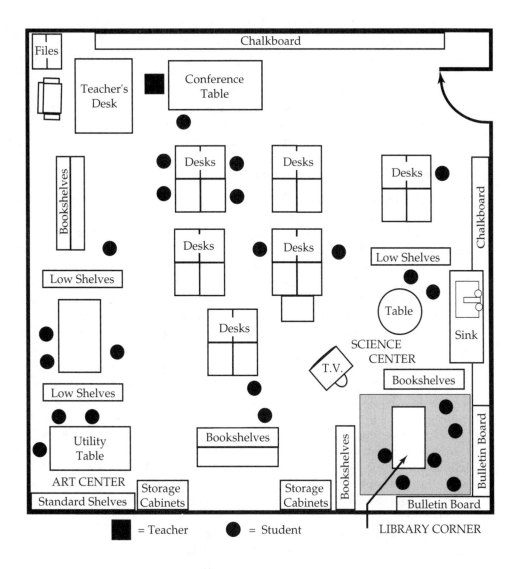

FIGURE 11-2 Interactive Classroom

for independent silent reading, paired and small group reading, and whole-class read-aloud sessions during the day. Low shelving can serve many purposes: it provides boundaries for the corner; sound buffers; and storage for books, book circulation records, book club order forms, and audio- and videotapes relating to books.

The library corner is a logical place to display students' book-related writing and artwork, such as student-produced books, students' book reviews, charts showing the class's favorite books and authors, and letters to and from authors and illustrators. Walls and bulletin boards in this way become an integral part of the library corner.

Teachers with self-contained classrooms might have several centers, each devoted to a specific curricular subject such as science or health, mathematics, and writing. By outfitting each center with appropriate books and displaying student writing and art related to their work in these areas, teachers naturally integrate the subject areas and show students the relationships between them. The interactive classroom shown in Figure 11-2 shows how this might be arranged. Another noticeable feature of the interactive classroom is the proximity and availability of books. Providing students with a rich supply of trade literature is also the result of planning.

Building a Classroom Library Collection

Most, if not all, of the responsibility for acquiring a sufficiently large and varied collection of books in your classroom will be yours. With perseverance, it can be done. Most good classroom libraries have a permanent collection as well as a collection that comes from the school or public library and changes regularly. Beginning teachers who are willing to plan ahead with their school and public librarians can borrow enough books for adequate temporary classroom libraries while they build their own collections. Even after a large permanent collection is established, a rotating selection from the school and public library can be coordinated with specific units of study, providing depth and breadth to the unit content and to the students' learning experience.

Careful selection of titles for the classroom library makes the most of limited resources. Children's librarians can provide invaluable advice in selecting titles for a classroom library and should be consulted. If this is not an option, browsing in a well-stocked children's bookstore and consulting publishers' catalogues are alternative ways of finding out what is available. Publishers of children's books issue one or two catalogues annually in which they describe their new publications and list their previous publications that are currently available (the backlist). If your school or public librarian does not have these catalogues, publishers will supply them on request. Some teachers use catalogues to get an overview of what is available before going to a bookstore.

Your own permanent trade book collection can be built inexpensively by using several proven approaches. These include the following:

- Requesting an allocation from your principal or PTO for purchase of books
- Writing a small grant proposal ($250–$1000) to your school district or professional organization for purchase of trade books
- Taking advantage of bonus books offered by student paperback book clubs
- Informing students' parents that you are building a collection and would like to have first refusal of any children's books that they plan to discard
- Establishing a "give a book to the classroom" policy for parents who want to celebrate their child's birthday or a holiday at school in some way
- Frequenting garage sales and library book sales, where good books can often be purchased for pennies

Most bookstores offer a 20 percent discount to teachers who use their own money to buy books to add to their classroom collections. An alternative to the bookstore is the book "jobber," or wholesale dealer for many publishers. Jobbers offer even greater discounts to teachers, sometimes up to 40 percent, but it is important to remember that most jobbers do not carry small press publications. Your school librarian probably uses a jobber and can assist you in setting up a staff account with the same firm. Some of the larger firms include Baker & Taylor, Brodart, and Ingram Book Company.

With these methods and sources, classroom collections grow quickly. From the beginning, you will need to devise a coding system for your permanent collection to streamline shelving and record keeping. Many teachers find that color coding their books by genre with colored tape on the spines works well. If at all possible, students should be trained and given the responsibility for color coding, checking in and out, repairing, and reshelving books.

Remember that the whole point of building a classroom library is to promote reading, not to provide a handsome display. Inevitably, if children use their classroom library, books will be lost and damaged. Severe reprimands for losing or damaging a book may work against your ultimate goal.

Outlining a Year-Long Literature Curriculum

Planning for the school year permits the teacher to have resources available when they are needed. In outlining for a year-long literature curriculum, several steps must be taken.

Determining the Approach   A teacher must first determine which literature curriculum to teach: genre, author/illustrator, literary element or device, notable book, or topic/theme. Another alternative is to create a hybrid literature curriculum by including aspects of several of these approaches in the plan.

Establishing Goals   Goals in a literature curriculum are those aims one expects to accomplish by the end of the course of study. The term objectives refers to short-range aims to be accomplished day by day or week by week. Central to this part of the planning process is deciding on the literary concepts to be taught. Since goals largely determine the parameters of the course of study, they must be established early in the planning process.

Goals for a literature curriculum are established by individual teachers and sometimes by schools or school districts. Likely goals for a fifth-grade teacher who has determined to use a mixed genre/author organization to teaching literature would be these:

- Students will enjoy reading a variety of genres of literature.
- Students will be familiar with the characteristics of traditional literature, modern fantasy, historical fiction, contemporary realistic fiction, mystery, and science fiction, and will be able to classify a book as belonging to one of the featured genres when reading it.

- Students will become familiar with several leading authors of each of the above genres and will be able to identify characteristics of the writing of each author.

Determining Units of Study   After goals have been identified and set, the next step in outlining a literature curriculum is to determine the units of study through which the literature content will be delivered. In this way, a tentative schedule can be set in order to foresee needs in terms of time and materials.

Selecting Focus Books   Each unit will require certain trade books for reading aloud by the teacher and trade books for class or small group study or independent reading. Early selection of these titles is important for several reasons. Balance in the overall book selection, for instance, is achieved much more easily in the planning stages. *Balance in book selection,* as presented in Chapter 2, means that the books selected present a diversity of characters (type, sex, age, ethnicity, place of origin), settings (urban, rural, familiar, foreign), and themes. Another advantage of early selection is being able to estimate the time necessary for each unit. Some units will take longer than others, depending on such variables as the extent of content to be covered, the length and difficulty of books to be read, and the type and complexity of planned book extension activities. A sample list of units, books, and featured authors for a fifth-grade teacher who is implementing a combined genre/author organization for teaching literature would be as follows:

Unit 1: Traditional Literature

Mythology

The Macmillan Book of Greek Gods and Heroes by Alice Low. Illustrated by Arvis Stewart.
Theseus and the Minotaur adapted by Leonard Everett Fisher.

Legends

The Legend of King Arthur retold by Robin Lister. Illustrated by Alan Baker.
Sir Gawain and the Loathly Lady by Selina Hastings. Illustrated by Juan Wijngaard.
Dragonslayer: The Story of Beowulf by Rosemary Sutcliff.

Folktales

Snow White and the Seven Dwarfs translated by Randall Jarrell. Illustrated by Nancy Ekholm Burkert.
Snow White in New York by Fiona French.

Read-Aloud

Sir Gawain and the Green Knight by Selina Hastings. Illustrated by Juan Wijngaard.

Unit 2: Modern Fantasy

Tuck Everlasting by Natalie Babbitt.
A Stranger Came Ashore by Mollie Hunter.
Konrad by Christine Nöstlinger.

Read-Aloud

The Lion, the Witch, and the Wardrobe by C. S. Lewis.
Featured Author: C. S. Lewis

Unit 3: Historical Fiction (World War II)

The Island on Bird Street by Uri Orlev.
The Upstairs Room by Johanna Reiss.
Summer of My German Soldier by Bette Greene.
Rose Blanche by Christophe Gallaz and Roberto Innocenti.

Read-Aloud

Journey to Topaz by Yoshiko Uchida.
Featured Author: Yoshiko Uchida

Unit 4: Contemporary Realistic Fiction

The Bridge to Terabithia by Katherine Paterson.
Trading Places by Gary Soto.
Monkey Island by Paula Fox.
Two Short and One Long by Nina Ring Aamundsen.

Read-Aloud

Hatchet by Gary Paulsen.
Featured Author: Gary Paulsen

Unit 5: Mystery

Peppermints in the Parlor by Barbara Brooks Wallace.
The Mystery of Dies Drear by Virginia Hamilton.
The Man Who Was Poe by Avi.
The Dollhouse Murders by Betty Ren Wright.

Read-Aloud

Midnight Is a Place by Joan Aiken.
Featured Author: Joan Aiken

Unit 6: Science Fiction

The Green Book by Jill Paton Walsh.
The White Mountains by John Christopher.
Collidescope by Grace Chetwin.
The Giver by Lois Lowry.

Read-Aloud

A Wrinkle in Time by Madeleine L'Engle.
Featured Author: Madeleine L'Engle

An issue often discussed among children's literature instructors is the efficacy of a *literary canon* of children's literature, an official list of children's books judged by experts to be worthy of inclusion in a literature curriculum. Elementary teachers and librarians have largely rejected the idea of a literary canon mainly because its sole criterion for selection is literary excellence, with no consideration for a book's appeal or relevance to children. Moreover, teachers know that they are in the best position to select books that match their students' interests and their own planned curricula. A literary canon is rarely revised and quickly becomes dated. Being so rigid and select, it cannot reflect the varied and changing interests of a particular group of children. Although the term *literary canon* most often refers to a nationally recognized booklist, teachers should be aware that when they stick rigidly to the same set of books year after year, they are, in effect, proclaiming that their own personal literary canon of children's literature is more important than the needs and interests of the children they teach.

Scheduling   With an overview of the plan established, the teacher can begin to set dates and time allotments for each unit and for activities within units. With each year of experience, the teacher's time estimates become more accurate. At this point, it is still easy to adjust the year-long plan if it becomes obvious that too much or too little has been planned.

Planning makes it possible to integrate the literature curriculum with other areas of study. For example, the literature unit presented in Figure 11-3 could be scheduled to coincide with the U.S. history unit on World War II presented in the previous section.

Fleshing Out the Units of Study

Thinking through, organizing, and writing down the details of daily lessons and activities are the final steps in planning for a literature curriculum. Two methods of organizing the details of units of study are to create webs and literature units.

Webs   Webbing is a way of creating a visual overview of a unit of study complete with its focus, related book titles, and activities, as demonstrated in the web in Figure 11-3. Ideas for a web are generated through brainstorming. The main advantage of webbing is that the process clarifies and even suggests ties or associations between concepts, books, and activities. Webs can be organized around a theme or topic, a single book, a book genre, an author or illustrator, or a literary concept. Activities can be drawn from all skill areas—writing, reading, listening, thinking, speaking, art, crafts, drama, and music.

Information about and examples of webs are available in several resources. *The WEB* (Wonderfully Exciting Books), a quarterly book review journal produced by the Reading Center at The Ohio State University, includes a literature web in every issue. *Webbing with Literature: Creating Story Maps with Children's Books* by Bromley (1991) explores webbing as a way for children to respond to literature. Teachers who use webbing as a way to plan literature units will appreciate the many topics, themes, and resources suggested in *Book Links,* a journal published by the American Library Association. (For further information on these resources, see Appendix B.)

A disadvantage of webbing is that it gives no indication of the chronology of events or time allotments. Eventually the web must be transferred to a more linear format, which is similar to the literature unit.

Literature Units   The literature unit resembles an outline organized by day or by week. As with webs, units can be organized around a theme or topic, a single book, a book genre, an author or illustrator, or a literary concept or device. Specificity will vary according to the needs and experience of the teacher, but each day's plan usually includes the following components:

- *Objectives.*   These are short-term aims that can conceivably be met by the end of the day or week. For example, a teacher writing a literature unit around Uchida's *Journey to Topaz* may state as an objective for the second week of his literature unit that he will read aloud Chapters 6–10 of this book. During that same week, a likely objective for his students would be that they note and share descriptions of characters' experiences in the various books of historical fiction that they are reading independently or in small groups, and that they begin to notice the attention to accuracy of details in works of historical fiction.

- *Procedures and methods.*   This part of the unit tells what the teacher does, in what order, and with what materials. The procedures of the teacher conducting the *Journey to Topaz* unit may call for him to let the students choose a way to "put themselves in the shoes" of either the victims or the oppressors in the stories they are reading and to exhibit representative behavior by either group during these times. The teacher suggests some of the ways this might be done (dramatize a book episode, assume the persona of a book character and write a letter to the class, draw a scene as suggested in a book) and asks students to suggest other ways. Likewise, he projects what materials are likely to be needed for these activities so that he might have them on hand.

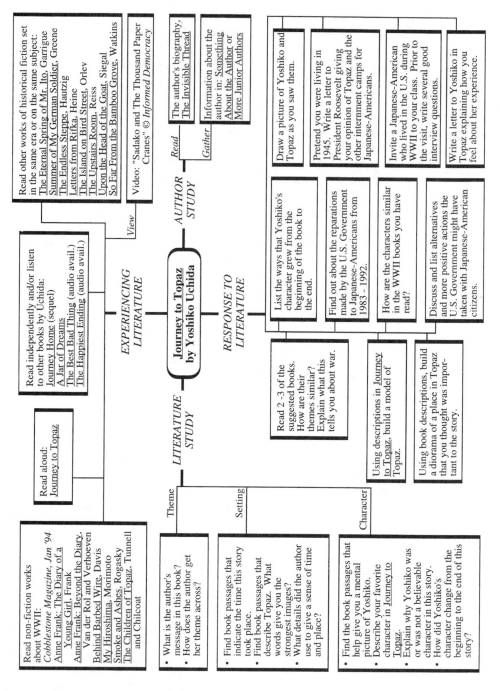

Read non-fiction works about WWII:
Cobblestone Magazine, Jan '94
Anne Frank: The Diary of a Young Girl, Frank
Anne Frank: Beyond the Diary, Van der Rol and Verhoeven
Behind Barbed Wire, Davis
My Hiroshima, Morimoto
Smoke and Ashes, Rogasky
The Children of Topaz, Tunnell and Chilcoat

Read other works of historical fiction set in the same era or on the same subject:
The Eternal Spring of Mr. Ito, Garrigue
Summer of My German Soldier, Greene
The Endless Steppe, Hautzig
Letters from Rifka, Heine
The Island on Bird Street, Orlev
The Upstairs Room, Reiss
Upon the Head of the Goat, Siegal
So Far From the Bamboo Grove, Watkins

Read independently and/or listen to other books by Uchida:
Journey Home (sequel)
A Jar of Dreams
The Best Bad Thing (audio avail.)
The Happiest Ending (audio avail.)

Read aloud:
Journey to Topaz

Video: "Sadako and The Thousand Paper Cranes" © *Informed Democracy*

The author's biography, The Invisible Thread

Information about the author in: Something About the Author or More Junior Authors

Draw a picture of Yoshiko and Topaz as you saw them.

Pretend you were living in 1945. Write a letter to President Roosevelt giving your opinion of Topaz and the other internment camps for Japanese-Americans.

Invite a Japanese-American who lived in the U.S. during WWII to your class. Prior to the visit, write several good interview questions.

Write a letter to Yoshiko in Topaz explaining how you feel about her experience.

List the ways that Yoshiko's character grew from the beginning of the book to the end.

Find out about the reparations made by the U.S. Government to Japanese-Americans from 1983 - 1992.

How are the characters similar in the WWII books you have read?

Discuss and list alternatives and more positive actions the U.S. Government might have taken with Japanese-American citizens.

Read 2 -3 of the suggested books. How are their themes similar? Explain what this tells you about war.

Using descriptions in Journey to Topaz, build a model of Topaz.

Using book descriptions, build a diorama of a place in Topaz that you thought was important to the story.

What is the author's message in this book?
How does the author get her theme across?

Find book passages that indicate the time this story took place.
Find book passages that describe Topaz. What words give you the strongest images?
What details did the author use to give a sense of time and place?

Find the book passages that help give you a mental picture of Yoshiko.
Describe your favorite character in Journey to Topaz.
Explain why Yoshiko was or was not a believable character in this story.
How did Yoshiko's character change from the beginning to the end of this story?

EXPERIENCING LITERATURE

View

AUTHOR STUDY

Read

Gather

Journey to Topaz by Yoshiko Uchida

RESPONSE TO LITERATURE

LITERATURE STUDY

Theme

Setting

Character

FIGURE 11-3 Literature Web

- *Evaluation.* Teachers must consider how they intend to evaluate each day's activities both in terms of how well they worked (a form of self-evaluation) and how well the students met the objectives.

Because units of study are several weeks long, they usually include a culminating activity that gives students an opportunity to reflect on what they have learned, review major points, and sometimes celebrate the focus of the unit in some way. Culminating activities for the *Journey to Topaz* unit might include table and bulletin board displays of books and other resources the students have read, artwork, poems, plays, letters, and stories written in response to these literary experiences, and a debate about the World War II internment issue.

An overall unit evaluation is valuable to a teacher, particularly if he intends to use the unit with another group of students. Revisions can make the unit even more successful in succeeding years. The unit plan should indicate how the unit will be evaluated.

Commercially developed literature units can be found. Beginning teachers may find good ideas in such resources but should avoid considering these units as complete or unalterable. Rather, these prepared units should be tailored by you to reflect your students' prior experiences, interests, and abilities, and your goals and objectives. Many of these commercially published units consist of little more than basal-like worksheets.

Implementing a Schoolwide Curriculum in Literature

Having a schoolwide curriculum in literature has many benefits for teachers and students and is worth pursuing. The main benefit to students is that their teachers' efforts will be coordinated from year to year. Repetition of content and titles will be avoided and continuity will be improved. The main benefits to teachers are that ideas, expertise, and materials will be shared and planning will be facilitated by knowing what experiences with literature incoming students have had or should have.

The impetus for planning a schoolwide curriculum in literature often comes from one person or a small group of people committed to the idea. In your school, that person could be you. The task of developing a schoolwide literature curriculum, however, should be shared by a committee that has a representative from each grade level and the library media specialist. Having individuals on the committee who are knowledgeable about children's books is essential.

A literature curriculum committee's function is to determine what literature content will be presented at each grade level. A set of trade books appropriate for delivering the literature curriculum at each grade level can also be suggested by the committee, although the ultimate choice of books to be used in a classroom will be the individual teacher's decision. Literature curriculum committees often select and update their schoolwide read-aloud list. Such a list helps to prevent duplication of teachers' read-aloud choices at different grade levels and to assure that students hear a well-balanced selection of books over the years. Having such a list may also convince some teachers to begin a read-aloud program.

The Library Media Center   The well-stocked, efficiently run library media center is the heart of a school, and the knowledgeable media center director has his finger on the pulse of each classroom. Gone are the days when the library was synonymous with dry speeches about the Dewey Decimal System and the proper way to do research reports. Lately, as literature-based reading and literature across the curriculum have gained acceptance, library media specialists and teachers have been moving toward a shared responsibility for teaching. They work as a team to provide students with the richest educational experience that their combined resources can provide. Teachers tell librarians their resource needs, and librarians help teachers by identifying and locating appropriate resources, keeping teachers updated with the newest literature and suggesting ways to present books to students. For these reasons, the librarian should be encouraged to play a key role in planning and developing a schoolwide curriculum in literature.

Book Clubs   A marketing phenomenon of our times is the publisher-owned book club. These clubs send monthly catalogues to teachers who then distribute them to students, collect and process student book orders, and receive bonus points for each item ordered. Paperback books representing a full range of quality from award-winning books to joke books, posters, and stickers are offered at prices far below bookstore cost. Children and teachers who lack access to well-stocked libraries are especially dependent on these clubs. Another advantage of book clubs is that the selection, ownership, and reading of these books involves parents.

A recent national study has revealed that book clubs are the major suppliers of reading matter used in literature-based language arts programs in U.S. elementary schools (Strickland & Sandmann, 1993). This study also revealed that the offerings of the major book clubs are heavy on popular, easy-reading fiction, but that they also include books from all the major genres, major authors and illustrators from diverse cultural groups, and some books that could challenge the strongest readers. Being knowledgeable about children's literature enables you to help your students select the best book club titles. You can gently redirect children's choices from the "junk" offerings to the better books by going over the catalogue with students and giving booktalks about the titles you recommend. Care should be given to verify topic and age appropriateness of any selections with which you are unfamiliar.

Teachers who participate in these clubs often use their bonus points to build their classroom book collections. With this in mind, you may want to subscribe to more than one club in order to have a wider choice of titles.

Bookfairs and School Bookstores   Bookfairs and school bookstores are two ways that schools can bring literature to children and their parents. Both entities are important in the overall development of a schoolwide literature curriculum. A bookfair is a book sale that is organized by a book vendor, such as a bookstore owner, and held in the school building for one or more days. Books are attractively displayed so that children and their parents can browse and select items for purchase. Bookfairs always call attention to literature and reading and can even be considered a reading motivator. They are especially appropriate in areas where there are no children's bookstores or well-stocked libraries.

Bookfairs send strong messages to children and their parents about a school's stance on reading and about what sorts of reading materials teachers and librarians in the school endorse. Children and parents who attend bookfairs in which joke collections, scented stickers, stamps, commercialized series books, coloring books, and posters are prominent will assume that this is what reading means to the teachers in these schools. Bookfairs in which a wide variety of good literature is prominent send an entirely different (and more defensible) message about reading to parents and children. Excellent bookfairs are the result of careful planning and active involvement in selection of books by teachers and school librarians. Book selection should not be left solely to the book vendor.

The school bookstore is a permanent part of the school. It is often a Parent-Teacher Organization project and is run by parent volunteers, but students and teachers are often enlisted or volunteer to help run the store. Most books are sold at cost, but arrangements are sometimes made for any profits to support a giveaway program in which students exchange credits for good performance in class for books.

Book selection is just as important to the school bookstore as to the school bookfair and for the same reasons. Teachers and librarians should be actively involved in selecting their bookstore stock and in advising parents on selections. Teachers who are involved in book selection can arrange for titles related to their unit themes and topics to be available in the bookstore.

Parent Involvement   In most communities parents and other adult members of students' families want to be involved in some way in their children's learning. In some instances parents are willing to help in classrooms on a regular basis. These people and their efforts must be integrated into the teacher's plans. In a school with an established curriculum in literature, teachers can develop a list of suggestions for using parent volunteers in the literature program. Such a list would be especially useful for new teachers. Some of the ways that parents can help teachers include the following:

- Listen to children read orally
- Read aloud to small groups or individual students
- Take children to the school library
- Type, assemble, and bind the storybooks that children write
- Read stories and poems on audiotapes for listening
- Help maintain the classroom library (code, repair, shelve, check out books)
- Fill out book club orders
- Make book bags for carrying books back and forth from home
- Type lists of good read-aloud books for children to take home and share with parents

Parental involvement in literature also means getting support for the school reading program at home. Parents are almost always willing to promote their children's academic efforts at home if they are told how to do it. Many teachers give parents lists of activities that support reading, including brief, carefully worded explanations where necessary. Some typical suggestions include the following:

- Read to your child at night (Lists of good read-alouds can be sent home regularly.)
- Listen to your child read aloud

- Participate in shared reading with your child (shared reading techniques for beginning readers are explained in Chapter 12)
- Take your child to the library to select books
- Give books to your child as gifts (lists of good gift book suggestions can be sent home prior to birthdays and holidays)

Guest Authors and Illustrators   Professional children's authors and illustrators often visit schools to speak to children about their careers and their books. Teachers are usually instrumental in selecting, inviting, and organizing these visits. Guest authors and illustrators may be chosen on the basis of availability, but more often they are chosen because of the students' interest in their books or the relevance of their work to a topic that students are studying.

The standard procedure is to contact the marketing director or editor of the author's or artist's publishing house to determine availability and terms. Since most established children's authors and illustrators charge an honorarium and travel expenses, schools within a system often share the author and the costs.

Careful selection, pre-visit promotion and preparation, and scheduling can result in author or illustrator visits that are inspiring to all concerned. At the very least, planners will want to assure that many copies of the guest's books are bought, distributed, and widely read by students for weeks before the guest arrives. As the day of the visit approaches, children can be led to think about and respond to the guest's books in many ways, to develop thought-provoking and worthwhile questions to ask the guest speaker, and to find out as much as possible about the individual. A visit from an author or illustrator can be the culminating event in an instructional unit or of an entire year-long literature curriculum. It deserves careful planning.

Many state reading associations have developed lists of children's authors and illustrators who live in state. These lists can usually be found in public libraries.

Local Public Library   The community has no more valuable resource than its public library. Each time students, teachers, and parents seek the educational resources they need in their public libraries, the natural link between schools and public libraries is reaffirmed. Public libraries provide many services in addition to loaning books. Consider the impact of the following services:

- The interlibrary loan system which gives patrons access to library holdings throughout the state, region, or nation
- Summertime reading programs for children
- Summertime bookmobile programs
- Special observances, such as National Book Week, Banned Book Week, and Hans Christian Andersen Day which help to bring important literacy issues to the public's attention
- Story hour for young children
- Audiovisual versions of many books
- Guest appearances of authors and illustrators

Teachers can help to make the public library more effective by making students and their parents aware of the library and its programs and services.

Evaluating the Literature Program

Ongoing evaluation is part of responsible teaching, since it reveals strengths and weaknesses in instruction and indicates where revision is suggested. In today's schools, reading and mathematics skills are given the lion's share of attention in standardized evaluation programs, and all too often no attention is paid to children's growth in literary understanding. But many teachers believe that student growth in literary understanding and appreciation is important and should be assessed. The question, then, is How?

Observation and Assessment of Student Learning   Evaluation of students in relation to a literature curriculum will focus mainly on the curriculum's effect on student behaviors rather than on the students' grasp of concepts. Consequently, the evaluation will be accomplished primarily by observing students rather than by testing them. An important principle to remember when planning for evaluation of teaching and learning is that evaluation must parallel the goals and objectives of the instructional plan. To look for conceptual understandings or behaviors in students when those concepts or behaviors have not been taught or encouraged is to invite failure and disappointment.

Experienced teachers often develop checklists to use in observation and assessment of various aspects of their literature programs. Also, generic checklists can be developed by teams of teachers and librarians at each grade level in a school and then may be tailored by individual teachers to fit their own specific plans.

Checklist for Student Involvement with Books   Some of the behaviors that teachers look for in their students' interaction with literature will vary by grade level and the students' development. Other behaviors will show up on checklists for all grade levels. For example, preschool or first-grade teachers would be likely to look for evidence that their students know the terms *author* and *illustrator,* use the terms correctly in their discussions of books, and recognize the work of specific authors and illustrators. Middle-grade teachers, on the other hand, would be more likely to look for evidence that students are choosing and reading novel-length stories independently. Teachers at all grade levels will be looking for evidence that their students are enjoying reading and voluntarily choosing to read. The following generic checklist gives an idea of what such an evaluation instrument might look like.

Checklist for Student Involvement with Literature

Behavior	*Yes*	*No*	*Comment*
Reading			
Student reads voluntarily and willingly	___	___	_____
Student enjoys reading	___	___	_____

Checklist for Student Involvement with Literature *Continued*

Behavior	*Yes*	*No*	*Comment*
Reading			
Student reads during silent reading time	____	____	_____
Student reads for entertainment	____	____	_____
Student reads for information	____	____	_____
Student reads a variety of books and poems	____	____	_____
Response to Literature			
Student talks intelligently about books read or heard	____	____	_____
Student shares responses to books with peers	____	____	_____
Student is attentive during read-aloud sessions	____	____	_____
Student is able to discuss a book in terms of			
character	____	____	_____
plot	____	____	_____
setting	____	____	_____
theme	____	____	_____
style	____	____	_____
Student is able to accept that different people may have different responses to the same story	____	____	_____
Student is able to relate stories to personal experience, where applicable	____	____	_____
Selection of Literature			
Student knows how to select appropriate books for independent reading	____	____	_____
Student is developing personal preferences in literature	____	____	_____
Student tries new book genres	____	____	_____

Checklist for Classroom Environment   The environment of a classroom is determined mainly by what the resident teacher values in learning and teaching. These values, in turn, determine how the classroom is arranged, which materials are available, and what sorts of events and activities are regularly scheduled. The following checklist incorporates all of these features.

Checklist for Promoting Literature through Classroom Environment

Behavior	Yes	No	Comment
Physical Plant			
Desks are arranged to promote student-to-student discussion	___	___	_____
Room arrangement provides quiet areas for reading and thinking	___	___	_____
Reading area is well lighted	___	___	_____
Reading area has comfortable seating	___	___	_____
Reading area has adequate and convenient shelving for books	___	___	_____
Reading area is well organized and orderly	___	___	_____
Student response projects are displayed	___	___	_____
Materials			
Classroom has a trade book library	___	___	_____
Classroom library is adequate in			
scope (variety of genres)	___	___	_____
depth (variety of books within a genre)	___	___	_____
quality (light reading for entertainment to excellent quality for study)	___	___	_____
providing for varying reading abilities	___	___	_____
recent books	___	___	_____
multicultural and international books	___	___	_____
poetry collections	___	___	_____
Classroom has a temporary collection	___	___	_____
Temporary collection			
addresses gaps in permanent collection	___	___	_____
is exchanged regularly	___	___	_____
provides for varying student interests	___	___	_____
is coordinated with topics of study	___	___	_____
Classroom library materials are	___	___	_____
easy for students to reach and reshelve	___	___	_____
coded and organized logically	___	___	_____

Checklist for Promoting Literature through Classroom Environment   *Continued*

Behavior	*Yes*	*No*	*Comment*
Scheduling			
Time is provided for self-choice reading every day	____	____	_____
Time is provided for browsing and selection of books regularly	____	____	_____
Time is provided for response to literature	____	____	_____

Checklist for Teaching Activities   Success in making children lovers of books and reading certainly does not depend upon generous supplies of equipment or a certain physical layout, although these can facilitate the job. In the end, it is what the teacher does with literature that makes the biggest impression on children. Activities that make the learning experience positive and nonthreatening are generally the most successful with children. This point of view is evident in the following checklist of teaching activities.

Checklist for Promoting Literature through Teaching Activities

Teaching Activity	*Yes*	*No*	*Comment*
Making Literature Enjoyable			
Read aloud daily (high quality literature)	____	____	_____
Select books for read-aloud that reflect students' interests	____	____	_____
represent a wide variety of genres	____	____	_____
represent outstanding examples of each genre	____	____	_____
Share poetry orally on a regular basis	____	____	_____
Popular poets	____	____	_____
NCTE Award-Winning poets	____	____	_____
Golden Age poets	____	____	_____
Share stories through storytelling	____	____	_____
Motivating Students to Read			
Introduce books regularly through booktalks	____	____	_____
Encourage student response to literature by asking open-ended or divergent questions	____	____	_____
by encouraging varied responses	____	____	_____

Checklist for Promoting Literature through Teaching Activities *Continued*

Teaching Activity	*Yes*	*No*	*Comment*
oral response	____	____	_____
written response	____	____	_____
graphic response	____	____	_____
Allow students to choose books for independent reading	____	____	_____
Take class to school library weekly or more frequently for book browsing or selection	____	____	_____
Take class to public library for a field trip	____	____	_____
Invite a librarian to your class to booktalk and tell stories	____	____	_____
Modeling Reading Behaviors			
Read during silent reading time	____	____	_____
Talk enthusiastically about books read	____	____	_____
Show students how to select books	____	____	_____
Showing the Relevance of Literature			
Integrate literature across the curriculum	____	____	_____
health/science	____	____	_____
social studies/history	____	____	_____
language arts/reading	____	____	_____
mathematics	____	____	_____
Encouraging Literature Appreciation			
Present a year-long literature curriculum	____	____	_____
Reaching Beyond the Classroom			
Send read-aloud suggestions to parents	____	____	_____
Encourage parents to visit library with their children	____	____	_____
Invite parents and community leaders to be guest readers for read-aloud	____	____	_____
Evaluation			
Record student growth			
in understanding literary concepts	____	____	_____
in choices of books to read	____	____	_____
in attitude toward reading	____	____	_____

References

Anderson, R. C., Hiebert, E. H., Scott, J. A., & Wilkinson, I. A. (1985). *Becoming a nation of readers: The report of the commission on reading.* Champaign, IL: Center for the Study of Reading.

Baldick, C. (1990). *The concise Oxford dictionary of literary terms.* New York: Oxford University Press.

Bromley, K. D. (1991). *Webbing with literature: Creating story maps with children's books.* Boston: Allyn and Bacon.

Commire, A. (Ed.). (1990). *Something about the author* (Vol. 59). Detroit: Gale Research.

Durkin, D. (1987). *Teaching young children to read* (4th ed.). Boston: Allyn and Bacon.

Hall, S. (1990). *Using picture storybooks to teach literary devices: Recommended books for children and young adults.* Phoenix: Oryx.

———. (1994). *Using picture storybooks to teach literary devices: Recommended books for children and young adults* (Vol. 2). Phoenix: Oryx.

Hancock, J. & Hill, S. (1987). *Literature-based reading programs at work.* Portsmouth: Heinemann.

Lapp, D., Flood, J., & Farnan, N. (1992). Basal readers and literature: A tight fit or a mismatch? In K. D. Wood & A. Moss (Eds.), *Exploring literature in the classroom: Content and methods* (pp. 33–57). Norwood, MA: Christopher-Gordon.

Routman, R. (1988). *Transitions: From literature to literacy.* Portsmouth: Heinemann.

———. (1991). *Invitations: Changing as teachers and learners K–12.* Portsmouth: Heinemann.

Sixty Seconds in a Minute. In Untermeyer, Louis (Ed.). *Rainbow in the sky.* Harcourt, 1935.

Strickland, D., & Sandmann, A. L. (1993). Study shows teachers rely on book clubs for most K–5 literature. *The Council Chronicle: The National Council of Teachers of English, 2* (4), pp. 1, 6.

Veatch, J. (1968). *How to teach reading with children's books* (2nd ed.). New York: Richard C. Owen.

Chapter 12

Developing Teaching Strategies

Reading

> *. . . We get no good*
> *By being ungenerous even to a book,*
> *   And calculating profits . . . so much help*
> *By so much reading. It is rather when*
> *We gloriously forget ourselves and plunge*
> *Soul-forward, headlong, into a book's profound,*
> *Impassioned for its beauty and salt of truth—*
> *'Tis then we get the right good from a book.*

> — Elizabeth Browning

The teacher is the key to a well-planned, effective literature program. In the previous chapter, we addressed the long-term aspects of planning and preparing for the literature program. This chapter will focus on the strategies teachers need to carry out such a program. Having students experience and respond to literature are two major responsibilities that a teacher must assume in order to ensure a good literature program.

Experiencing Literature

Many teaching strategies can be used to provide students with opportunities to experience enjoyable, exciting, and thought-provoking literature. Students experience prose, poetry, fiction, and nonfiction (1) by having it read aloud to them by a skillful oral reader; (2) by reading it silently to themselves; (3) through shared reading activities with a parent, librarian, teacher, or peer; (4) through stories told to them; and (5) through other media such as audio- and videotapes.

Reading Aloud by Teachers

Reading aloud to students is a powerful way to provide them with literary experiences; it is the centerpiece of a curriculum in literature. Beginning in their infancy and throughout their elementary school years and beyond, children should hear books read aloud. Although some teachers at the intermediate-grade level do not read aloud, this teaching strategy is just as important in the development of readers at this stage as it is in kindergarten.

Some of the more important reasons that teachers read aloud are as follows:

1. To share with students exciting and stimulating reading material that is beyond their reading ability, but well within their listening ability
2. To build background and interest in subject matter that will soon be taught in an upcoming content area unit of instruction
3. To introduce new genres of literature or new literary concepts, such as a particular element of fiction or poetry
4. To contribute to students' knowledge of their literary heritage by reading aloud the works of notable authors and illustrators, as well as the masterpieces of traditional literature
5. To assist students in developing their meaning vocabularies, their ability to comprehend connected discourse, and their ability to think critically
6. To make students aware of the delight to be found in books and poems—a delight that they can later provide to themselves through reading good books
7. To have the opportunity to share emotional, funny, exciting, and stimulating moments with students.

Three distinct aspects of the read-aloud experience need to be examined in order to make it as effective a teaching strategy as possible. Those aspects are (1) selecting the literature to read, (2) preparing the students for read-aloud time, and (3) reading the book aloud. Each aspect needs to be taken into consideration for a successful read-aloud experience.

Book Selection   No matter which book you choose to read aloud, it is essential that you first read the book to yourself. When you preread a book, you can determine whether you find the story enjoyable and worthy of children's time and whether you believe it is of an appropriate level of difficulty for your students. You also can begin to note ways in which the story lends itself to student response.

Over the course of a school year you will want to read aloud a variety of literature: poems, picture books, and chapter books of different genres and types. You will also want to ensure that there is a balance of males and females as main characters in the books, and that the main characters come from different backgrounds and settings, including multicultural and international ones.

The most recognized works in children's literature, though sometimes complex, deserve to be shared with students over the course of their elementary school years. When a book or poem is challenging for students, you need to be prepared to guide the students' understanding. Without this help, many children would never experience and enjoy some of the more difficult, but worthy, pieces of literature. Conversely, you will want to avoid choosing books for reading aloud that students can and will consume eagerly on their own, reserving those books for students' independent reading.

When first reading aloud to a new class, however, you will want to start with shorter and easier works, known to be popular with students, and gradually build up to longer and more challenging works as you become better acquainted with your students, their interests, and their abilities. For more discussion of students' preferences in literature, refer to Chapter 1, Learning about Children and Their Literature, and Chapter 3, Poetry.

Preparation   Once a selection is made, the next step is to prepare the class for read-aloud time. For students to profit from read-aloud experiences, they need to be attentive. You can prepare students for reading aloud by having them remove distractions, such as pencils and other objects, from their immediate vicinity; by having them sit quietly in the designated place for read-aloud time; and by asking them to be ready to listen. If the book has concepts that you believe will baffle your students, you may want to clarify their meaning before beginning to read.

Introduce the book by stating the title, author, and illustrator of the book, even with the smallest children. This will teach children that books are written by real people called authors, and that the illustrations are made by people called illustrators. Sometimes you may want to ask the students to predict what they believe the story will be about from looking at the cover and the title; other times you may want to explain briefly why you chose this book to read to them. For example, you may say that you are going to read this book because "it's another story by one of our favorite authors, William Steig" or that "the book will tell us more about what it was like to live on the prairie in the nineteenth century." Introductions should be kept short. They serve the purpose of preparing students to be attentive to and interested in the story.

In preparing for reading aloud, some teachers set up a tape recorder so they can record the read-aloud sessions. The tapes may be used by students who were absent and by other students who enjoy hearing repetitions of the story while following along in the book. Next, strategies for reading aloud picture books and chapter books need to be considered.

Reading Aloud Picture Books Effectively   Consider the following steps:

- Position yourself close to the class so that all students can see the pictures. Many teachers choose to have students gather on the floor (if it is carpeted) in a semi-circle around the teacher who sits in a low chair just above them. In this way the students can approach more closely than they can on chairs or at desks.
- Show the pictures as you read the book. Most teachers accomplish this by holding the book out to the side where both students and teacher can see it at the same time. If you find this method unmanageable, you can turn the book back and forth for you, and then for the students, to see each page. Some

primary-grade teachers become expert at upside-down reading and can hold the book in front of them while reading it. Whatever system you use will be fine so long as students see the pictures as you read the book. Remember that in a good picture book the text and pictures are carefully integrated to convey the story as a whole. Hearing and seeing picture books should be simultaneous.

- After the introduction, begin reading the book aloud, placing emphasis on the meaning of the story. Think of reading aloud as a type of mini-dramatic performance. Read enthusiastically and provide drama through taking on different voices for different characters, pausing for effect at exciting moments, and varying your voice in pitch (low to high), in volume (soft to loud), and in pace (slow to fast). Good oral readers often start the reading with a soft voice, of medium pace and pitch, so that as the story builds they can alter pitch, volume, and pace for special effects.
- Your body movements and facial expressions can also be used to enhance the drama of the read-aloud experience. Leaning forward during a scary, suspenseful part of a story and smiling or chuckling during a funny part can convey to the students your involvement in the story.
- Maintain eye contact with your students. Be sure you are aware of their nonverbal responses to this reading experience. Good eye contact with the students helps you to maintain class control and permits you to observe when a word of explanation may be needed.
- Read the book from beginning to end without interruptions except on an as-needed basis. Constant interruptions of the story by too many explanations or side comments interfere with the students' enjoyment of the story. On the other hand, if an illustration has a key element that needs to be observed if the listeners are to understand the story, then pointing it out when on that page may be worthwhile. If a child makes a spontaneous comment, you should recognize the response quickly and go on. Interruptions by the teacher should be made only to prevent confusion, misunderstanding, or longer interruptions by students.
- Some books, such as concept books and interactive books, do call for interruptions in the read-aloud process. This is particularly true for informational books.

Reading Aloud Chapter Books Effectively   Many of the same considerations discussed in reading aloud picture books also hold true with chapter book read-alouds. Of course, chapter books have few if any illustrations, so holding the book for students to see the pictures is not necessary. In addition, chapter books are usually read aloud over a relatively long period of time, from a few days to many weeks. In a qualitative study on reading aloud in grades 4 to 6, Lynch-Brown and Tomlinson (1988) found that experienced teachers include four identifiable phases in the process of reading aloud novel-length chapter books:

1. *Orientation.* This brief, pre-book phase of the read-aloud experience includes an introduction of the author and title of the book, predictions about the story based on the title, statements by the teacher on the story

setting, location of the story setting on a map, and elicitation of student knowledge of the time and place of the setting. This orientation phase is completed during the first session of the read-aloud experience; then the teacher begins reading aloud.

2. *Exposition.* This phase typically lasts from four to seven days. It is a period of protracted reading aloud, involving few planned extension activities. At this point, it is as though the teacher allows the book to get its grip on the students' imaginations and does not want to break the spell of the book with any diversions. Teachers note students' nonverbal responses, such as facial expressions or restlessness, which might indicate confusion or lack of understanding, and quickly supply any clarification or information needed. In this phase, as throughout, students are given the opportunity to share their responses to the book.

   The teachers view this phase as a difficult but important period for bringing the students into the story. Some teachers help their students through this period by summarizing the story events at the end of each day's reading during the first several days. Some teachers report negative student reactions to the stories during this phase until the establishment of characters, setting, and problem is supplanted by the rising action of the plot with the conflict and suspense reaching full play.

3. *Extension.* During this phase, the teacher generally reads the middle and end of the story. Students are thoroughly engrossed with the story at this point and want the teacher to read on as quickly as possible. A characteristic of this phase is that enrichment activities are interspersed with the oral reading by the teacher. In contrast to the activities seen in the exposition phase, these activities tend to carry the students beyond the book.

4. *Completion.* Like the orientation phase, this phase is quite brief, generally confined to one session beginning after the oral reading is finished. During this phase, the teacher encourages students to discuss their affective responses to the completed book in order to interpret and savor it. In this phase the teacher conducts brief activities sufficient to bring closure to the read-aloud experience without giving the flavor of a rehash.

Listed below are some practices that teachers have used successfully during the exposition and extension phases of chapter book read-alouds to help "hook" the students on the book and to keep them tuned in and involved.

- Keep a chart of the characters—their names, relationships, and roles in the story—as the characters appear. This strategy is especially helpful if the story has a large number of characters. For example, in *The Westing Game* (1978) by Ellen Raskin, the many characters of this mystery must be remembered for the plot to make sense.
- Design and display a map of the story setting in order to track the events of the story in sequence. In most quest fantasies this visual aid can assist students in following the characters' journey for the quest.
- Develop a time line, somewhat like a horizontal mural, on which the dates are set at intervals above the line and the story events placed below the line

at the appropriate date. For historical fiction and biographies, a time line can serve as a mnemonic device for the storyline as well as for the historic events of the era. For this purpose, the dates and historic events would be noted on a third tier of the time line.

Although each teacher may handle the chapter book read-aloud situation differently, all teachers in the 1988 study took their cues from the students and from the book, letting students' verbal and nonverbal responses and the plot and setting of the book guide them in their choice of strategies.

Silent Reading by Students

Another way for students to experience good literature is to read it to themselves. Indeed, the ultimate goal of a literature program is to turn students into readers who, of their own free will, read self-selected, good literature with enjoyment, understanding, and appreciation. To assist students in becoming independent, life-long readers, teachers in grades K-8 need to set aside time each day for students to read silently in these formative years of reading development. The amount of time for silent reading must be tailored to the reading attention spans of students. Kindergarten and first-grade students may spend only five to ten minutes reading independently, but fourth- and fifth-grade students will often read silently for up to an hour.

Many schools have instituted sustained silent reading (SSR) programs on a schoolwide basis in order to promote the reading habit in students. In these SSR programs, a certain time each day is set aside for all students, teachers, librarians, coaches, principals, custodians, and office and kitchen staff to take a "reading break." The philosophy behind SSR programs is that students need to see adults who read and who place a high priority on reading. In SSR programs, students read materials of their own choosing and are not required to write book reports or give oral reports on these materials.

Whether or not you are in a school that has an SSR program, you will want to provide your students with silent reading time each day. Teachers often indicate that their students have time to read because they can read as soon as their other work is finished. This practice is not adequate in that generally the same students never finish their work and, of course, never have time to read; and these are sometimes the very students who most need encouragement to become avid readers.

Here are some tips for having successful silent reading periods.

- Have a well-stocked classroom collection of books—poetry books, picture books, novels, and information books. See Chapter 11 for more information on this topic.
- Conduct booktalks regularly so students become aware of books they may wish to read. These booktalks can be given by teachers and librarians. Many librarians keep a file of booktalks they have given and will gladly serve as resource persons for teachers.

- Utilize other techniques to introduce books to students. For example, displaying new books attractively in the classroom and showing videos of notable authors talking about their books and craft are effective in "selling" books to children.
- Schedule the same time each day for silent reading and adhere to it. Permit no activities other than silent reading during this time. Allow enough time for students to get well into their books and to achieve some level of satisfaction from the reading.
- Insist on attentiveness to books during this time. With primary-grade students, quiet talking in pairs about books or individual lipreading aloud may be on-task behavior, but children in intermediate grades can probably read silently and should be expected to do so.
- Spend the silent reading period engrossed in books, setting yourself as an example of a reader. Be knowledgeable of and interested in the books the students are reading.
- Provide students with an opportunity to talk *voluntarily* with you or one another about their books after the silent reading period is over.

Booktalks

A booktalk is an oral presentation by a teacher, a librarian, or a student who tells about a book in order to stimulate the students' interest and motivate them to read it. Booktalks are not book reports, analyses of the author's style, or the old-fashioned book report that discusses characters, setting, theme, and plot (Bodart, 1980). Booktalks have been used effectively for years by librarians who have developed this strategy into an art for the purpose of encouraging students to check out books from the library. Teachers can give booktalks on five to ten books each week from their classroom and school library collections; in this way, they can entice students to read and experience good literature.

Booktalks can be given on any book, but they are especially needed to inspire students to read chapter books. Because chapter books take longer to read and have few illustrations, students appreciate booktalks on the books' content to assist them in making wise reading choices. Booktalks can be judged a success when students read the books following the booktalks.

Some teachers who give frequent booktalks also advocate having students give booktalks in order to induce other students to read the suggested books. A regular feature of "Reading Rainbow," the public television program about children's books, is children giving booktalks. One teacher taped two or three of these "Reading Rainbow" booktalks and showed them in class in order to help her students learn how to give good booktalks. The following are recommendations for giving a good booktalk.

- Be sure you have read the book before trying to do a booktalk on it.
- Choose books that you have liked, wholly or in part, or that you think your students will enjoy. Sincere enthusiasm for a book is stimulating and infectious.

- Have the book available to show to the students as you give the booktalk. Format aspects—such as cover illustrations, length, size, and shape of the books—which also influence book choices, can be weighed by students only if they can see the book.
- Keep the booktalk brief, generally no more than two or three minutes. Do not tell too much about the book or the students will see no reason to read it. For most books, four to six sentences will suffice. At first you will want to write out your booktalks until you have a sure feel for how to give them.
- Tell the topic and something about the action in the story, but *do not tell the plot.* Feature a scene or character that the story revolves around, but do not discuss the scene that gives away the ending.
- Some booktalks may feature a short excerpt from the book. You can read aloud an interesting beginning of the book or a suspenseful event, but the outcome is, of course, not told.
- You may want to compare the book with other books known to the students, suggesting that if they liked a certain book they may enjoy this one. Other times you may wish to point out that the book is by a favorite author; you may recall for the students the other titles by the author.
- A booktalk can be about a group of books that share the same theme; in this case you will want to talk briefly about each book and how it fits with the others.

The following is an example of a short booktalk:

The Slave Dancer (1974) by Paula Fox. Back in the 1800s, Jessie Bollier played his fife on the docks of New Orleans for spare change from passersby. But one day he was thrown into a canvas bag and taken aboard a slave ship destined for Africa. The ship's captain wanted a fife player on board so that the black slaves who were going to be transported back from Africa would exercise and remain healthy on the return trip. Thus, Jessie, a white boy, found himself to be the first slave on board. The story of Jessie's journey and the people he met—some of them cruel and some kind—are told in this book, *The Slave Dancer,* which is based on an incident that really happened.

After you have given the booktalk, place the book back on the reading table for students to peruse and to consider for reading. Over time, you should give booktalks on a variety of books at different levels of reading difficulty, on different topics, and with male and female protagonists from many cultures. In this way, you will appeal to the wide range of interests and abilities that exist among students in a classroom.

Storytelling

Storytelling is the oldest medium for sharing literature. Oral literature flourished for thousands of years before writing was invented and books became commonly available. When a teacher tells stories, another delightful means for children to experience literature becomes available to the class. By bringing stories to life through personal expression and interpretation, a storyteller establishes a close communication with the audience. A storyteller begins by selecting a good story. Next, she practices it until she is able to tell it with ease, and then tells it to different audiences again and again.

Selection of a Story   Good stories take time to find. First, you must genuinely like the story. To find possible stories for telling, begin with collections of folktales and short stories. Read some of these until you find a few you especially like. Then consider these two points:

- The first stories you tell should take no longer than ten minutes. As you develop your gifts of storytelling, you may want to tell longer stories.
- Good stories for telling usually have few characters (from two to five), high conflict, action that builds to a climax, and a quick conclusion that ties together all the threads of the story. Humorous elements are also worth seeking.

Preparation for Telling   Once you have selected a story to tell, outline the story content in terms of the plot. Many storytellers note on 3" × 5" cards the title and source of the tale, the characters' names and story events, and any other information that may be helpful. These cards can then be consulted quickly just before one tells a story. A story file can be a nice resource to keep as more stories are prepared for telling. One tapes her stories and then uses them to refresh her memory for later retellings.

Practice   Tell the story aloud to yourself again and again. Do not memorize the story, but keep in mind the characters and sequence of main story events. Each time you tell the story, it will change a bit, becoming more and more your own story as you include personal touches.

The children's imaginations and your voice and facial expressions are the foundations for good storytelling experiences. Some storytellers find props useful, whereas others believe props diminish the closeness between audience and storyteller. If used, props should enhance the story, not overpower or distract from it. Experiment with props to find out what works best for you. They can be simple (a hat, a stick-on mustache, or a stuffed toy) or more elaborate (a mask, a puppet, or a costume).

When puppets are used, a separate puppet is made for each character and is held by the storyteller while the character speaks. Puppets can be purchased or made by the storyteller. Another more elaborate use of props is the feltboard story—a storytelling aid some teachers especially enjoy. Pictures or objects are attached to a feltboard or display board and are moved around during the story. Cumulative stories, especially, lend themselves to feltboard presentations.

The art of storytelling can be developed with practice. Teachers who tell stories in their classrooms report that their students are appreciative listeners and soon begin telling stories themselves.

Shared Reading

Shared reading is a term being used here to describe a number of teaching strategies that attempt to draw on the natural literacy learning that has long occurred in book-loving homes around the world. These various strategies—shared-book experience, assisted reading, and paired reading—provide children with opportunities to experience good literature as they are learning to read. The strategies have in common a semi-structured modification of the parent-child interaction with repeated readings of favorite books as the child gradually acquires an understanding of print and its relationship to our sound system or to the words we speak. A list of predictable books suitable for use in shared reading activities can be found at the end of Chapter 4, Picture Books.

Shared-Book Experience   Don Holdaway is well known for proposing an adaptation of the home-learning experience. He proposed the shared-book experience and developed Big Books, enlarged-text books of approximately 24" × 30", in order to replicate a natural home-learning strategy with groups of beginning readers in school settings. A typical classroom teaching-learning sequence of shared-book experience as proposed by Holdaway (1982) can be summarized in five steps:

- *Opening activity.*   Favorite poems and songs are repeated by the students and teacher while the teacher points to the text of a Big Book. Then a new poem or song is taught.
- *Review of a familiar story.*   The teacher and students review a favorite story in an enlarged format. This story is used to teach skills in context. Students participate by saying the story in unison. Sometimes the story is then informally dramatized.
- *Language play.*   The teacher involves the students in alphabet games, rhymes, and songs that use letter names. The purpose is to have fun with words and sounds and to avoid isolated phonic drills.
- *Presentation of a new story.*   The teacher and students read aloud a new story from a Big Book. The teacher encourages students to use word-solving strategies (contextual clues and prediction) to confirm words that are new to them.
- *Output activities.*   Students read independently from a wide selection of favorites, participate in art activities stemming from the new story, and compose original stories, often using structures from the new story. Sometimes several children enjoy playing school—one acting as teacher—while they read a favorite story together. (p. 299)

This sequence encapsulates the strategy developed by Holdaway and his colleagues in New Zealand to use children's books in classrooms in a manner similar to the one used by many parents whose preschoolers readily and naturally learned to read.

Assisted Reading   The natural reading approach has been adapted for various situations. For example, Hoskisson, Sherman, and Smith (1974) proposed *assisted reading* as a one-to-one strategy for use with impaired readers. In assisted reading, the child and the adult sit side by side with a book. The child reads aloud until she has difficulty, at which point the adult supplies the word.

Paired Reading   *Paired reading* is guided practice with an adult who reads in a soft voice and invites the child to fill in words when the adult pauses and the child knows the word. Paired reading can also be enjoyed by two children of compatible personalities who read back and forth to one another.

In all of these strategies, well-chosen literature is important; the nature of the experience is companionable, not authoritative; and the child reader must see the text and hear the words simultaneously. Sometimes the adult places a finger under each word as it is being read in order to draw the child's attention to the print. Selecting favorite, loved stories is essential because the success of these strategies is contingent on frequent rereadings of the same book. Although the primary purpose of these strategies is to provide a favorable situation in which children can acquire literacy, the effect of the strategies can be the promotion of a love of literature.

Literature Across the Curriculum

Students may also experience good literature in other content area classes, such as social studies, science, and health, when teachers supplement or replace textbooks with trade books for instruction. In this way, trade books can enhance the teaching of other subjects while providing students with rich literary experiences. The use of literature to teach content area subjects is not new, but it is becoming a more frequent practice in schools as teachers discover the wealth of trade books suitable for their content curricula. Many advantages accrue to content-area teachers who incorporate trade books into their teaching.

Trade books make social studies content more memorable because the stories are presented from a child's point of view. Children see the world through a narrative framework. In learning about their world, stories and narrative are more real to children than informational texts. Children are more likely to understand history if it is presented as a story with characters, settings, and events. Later, they move from an interest in the narrative to an interest in the history itself.

Trade books also permit students to read multiple perspectives on topics, which helps them develop critical thinking. Comparing historical information from various sources is a valued practice that helps students encounter differing perspectives on any particular era of history. Students may start with the textbook, then research the facts from other books, or read a work of fiction and then seek to verify to what extent the facts within the story are accurate. In addition, trade books couch political and social events in terms of the moral events related to them. Children can see how these events affected the lives of real people and can better understand the morality underlying their choices. Unlike textbook authors who must write to please all viewpoints, authors of children's literature are more likely to face controversial issues head-on.

Trade books can benefit all subjects. For example, many trade books on health and science present information in interesting ways through graphs, tables, figures, authentic photographs and other visual presentations, coupled with a lively style of writing in the text. Comparison of information from different sources can be readily provided when students are not limited to a single source for their information. Teachers who support the whole language philosophy draw on materials of various types for their instruction. They have discovered that literature has the power to educate the mind, while enlightening the spirit and warming the heart.

Bibliotherapy

Bibliotherapy is the use of selected books to help children deal with their social and emotional problems and, at the same time, to experience good literature. The practice is controversial because of the possibility of its misuse by teachers and librarians untrained in clinical psychology. The technical meaning of the term *bibliotherapy* is the use of books by professionally trained therapists in treating emotionally disturbed individuals. Most teachers and librarians are not trained as psychologists and misguided bibliotherapy may damage students. In addition, using books to guide students' lives could become an extremely didactic practice. If books are always or often selected to correct students or to preach to them about something we want them to change in their lives, students may rebel against reading itself. This would defeat the purpose of the bibliotherapy and could result in a dislike of reading and books.

On the other hand, we know that our students benefit psychologically from reading and talking about powerful stories and the thoughts, feelings, and actions of characters in these stories. Children all face difficult situations at times; discovering that other children have faced similar problems is reassuring. Learning how others have coped successfully with problems gives children confidence that they too will be able to solve problems that may arise later in their lives.

Stories of many different genres and types may offer useful insights to students. Realistic fiction stories can help children realize that everyone faces problems in life—neighborhood bullies, siblings, social rejections. By reading about the problems others face, children can be better prepared to confront the challenges of their own lives. Through fantasy, children's imaginations are set free to explore creative solutions to life and how it may be lived. Biographies of famous persons can provide students with role models and can make students realize that, by setting goals for themselves, they may achieve beyond their present life situations.

A strategy for bibliotherapy sometimes used by teachers is to read aloud a story that may have indirect application to a problem occurring in the classroom. For example, if groups of students are being cliquish and cruel to certain students on the playground, the teacher might read Eleanor Estes's *The Hundred Dresses*, the story of a girl ostracized by other girls in her class, or Brock Cole's *The Goats*, the story of a boy and a girl at camp who are singled out for rejection and mistreatment by other campers. Books like these can help students develop understanding and empathy. Care should be taken that the situation described in the book is not so close to the real one that students will recognize it as such, because this could cause embarrassment for the ostracized students. Discussion in class of how the students think they might feel if they were similarly mistreated may help them to develop awareness and understanding of the effects of their unkind behaviors. With sensitive and caring teachers and librarians, bibliotherapy in its informal sense lends itself to a natural use of literature. Bibliotherapy in its technical sense should, however, be left to professional therapists.

Audiotapes and Videotapes

Many tapes are available today to bring literature to students. Recently, some well-known actors have made excellent audio recordings of favorite children's stories. Animated and iconographic videos are also readily available. *Animated videos* are cartoons or images that move; *iconographic videos* are films in which the camera moves over static illustrations. A few videos are movies based on children's books, performed by actors. Predictably, these selections vary widely in quality.

Some audiovisual media re-creations are artistically well done and deserve to be considered as another means for students to experience literature. It is generally preferable to have students read the book first and form their own images of the story. Then, after viewing the tape, students can make comparisons between the book and the tape.

Audiotapes and videotapes are usually available in school libraries, through school districts' media repositories, or from nearby public libraries. Book clubs sometimes offer audiotapes to teachers with the purchase of a certain number of books by the class.

Responding to Literature

When students experience a story by listening to it, or by reading it, or by viewing it, they may naturally wish to respond or express their reactions to the experience in some way. In sharing their responses with others, students profit by recapturing the experience through translating it to a new form or medium; they develop a better understanding of what they experienced by organizing and deepening their feelings and thoughts on the experience; they discover that other readers' experiences with the same book may not have been the same as theirs; and they bring closure to the experience.

Although it is important to give students opportunities to respond to books, not every book needs or merits a lengthy response. The peals of laughter and the moans of sorrow during the actual reading of the story are sometimes response enough. But with other books, students need opportunities to explore further their thoughts and feelings. Teachers can elicit student responses to literature through oral expression, written expression, and the graphic arts.

Oral Response

Students love to talk, and what better to talk about than a sincerely felt, shared book experience? Rosenblatt (1978) reminds us that no two people have the same prior experiences and that it is the transaction that occurs between the text, the reader, and the present context that provokes a particular response. Teachers may generate opportunities for students to share their individual insights to literary experiences in many different ways.

Discussions   Perhaps the most often used means of eliciting students' responses is through discussions. *Whole-class discussion* usually accompanies the reading aloud of a book to the class. In these discussions, comprehension is assumed and the discussion centers on the different ways students feel and think about the book, its characters, its events, and its outcome. Thus, to stimulate a good class discussion, a teacher will encourage students to share their individual responses to open-ended questions; the teacher will not seek supposedly right answers in order to check comprehension or recall. In a class discussion, the teacher has the pivotal role as discussion leader. The discussion tends to be a teacher-to-students, students-to-teacher format. And with a large class, only some of the students will have an opportunity to express their viewpoints.

Another format for students to discuss their responses to literature is the *literature response group.* In literature response groups, students share their responses with peers about a book they have read as a group or a book read aloud by the teacher to the whole class. One of the goals of literature response groups is to have all children learn to work with one another and to value the opinions and views of others.

Groups can be established by the desire to read the same book, by friendship, by heterogeneous assignment by the teacher, or by random assignment. Small groups are usually set up with two to six students for optimal functioning. Students who have less skill working in groups often function better in dyads or triads. The small group discussion is a student-to-student form of communication that permits students more control over the discussion and more roles to perform as group members. For example, students may assume the role of leader, recorder, arbiter, listener, or devil's advocate. The advantages of small group discussions are that students are in control, have more opportunities to express their opinions, and can become more actively involved. Unless students have been taught to work together, however, groups do not function well. Small group model discussions with the teacher as a participating member and joint planning by teacher and class before groups begin working can enable the group to set rules, goals, and timelines.

Individual conferences between a teacher and a student are another means of discovering students' responses to literature. Although a teacher may choose to set up conferences daily, occasional conferences in which the student comes prepared to talk about a book she has recently finished can be instructive for the teacher and motivating for the student. The conference is focused on what the student thought and felt about the book. Some teachers ask the student to read aloud a favorite part of the story and tell why it was selected. Individual conferences are from five to ten minutes long, and usually end with considering the next book the student will read or the response activity the student has planned.

Eliciting a good discussion with substantial student participation is not an easy art. First of all, it is essential to remember that comprehension of the story is assumed and that the teacher's (or group leader's) purpose is not to test the students on the meaning of the story. Beyond this, certain strategies for promoting discussions need to be considered for use in leading class discussions, in guiding literature response groups, and in interacting with students in individual conferences. Whether you, as the teacher, will be leading the discussion or guiding your students in the art of discussion leader, the questions to be posed are very important.

Questioning   Common sense tells us that a question that can be answered by yes, no, or a single word or phrase will not lead to an interactive discussion. The question, "Did you like the story?" may result in a simple "yes." "Which part of the story did you like best and what did you like about it?" is likely to elicit a more detailed response.

Divergent questions have no one right answer but a number of possible answers. They naturally provoke more discussion than convergent questions for which only one answer is correct. Examples of each of these question types follow. They are tailored to the book *Sylvester and the Magic Pebble* (1969) by William Steig.

- "Was Sylvester turned into a rock or a lion?" ("A rock.") This question is convergent; it can be answered by a single word.
- "What did you think would happen to Sylvester after he became a rock?" ("I thought he would get rolled down the hill and the pebble would tumble on top of him and he would turn back into a donkey." "I thought he would have to be a rock forever." "I thought his dad would find the magic pebble and turn him back into a donkey.") This question is divergent; it stimulates many different answers, each of which is possible or correct. The response to this question results in more than a single word or phrase.
- "Who is the main character of the story?" ("Sylvester.") This convergent question tests the students' literal comprehension of the story and can be answered by only one word. Such a question does not provoke discussion.
- "Do you like Sylvester?" This question, though divergent, can be answered in a word. A better way to phrase this question is, "Why do you like or dislike Sylvester?" or "How do you feel about Sylvester?" The question remains divergent but now may also result in discussion.

The best ideas for questions to stimulate book discussions flow directly from your response to the particular book and why you want the students to experience the book. Usually you will have students read works of fiction for the aesthetic experience they will have with it—enjoyment, appreciation, emotional involvement, deeper understanding of life, and so on. In this case, your questions need to permit students to talk about their experiences. Divergent questions are best suited to this goal. Your questions will tell your students what you believe is important in reading. If your questions are convergent ones about the plot, characters, and setting, then you are telling your students that reading fiction is a type of egg hunt for the particular eggs laid by this author and previously located by you. On the other hand, if you ask divergent questions that permit them to explore their individual experiences with a work of fiction, students will soon discover that you really want to understand their feelings and thoughts about books.

The purpose of reading informational books, though perhaps partially aesthetic, is usually efferent; that is, the reader's attention is centered on what should be retained as a residue after the actual reading event. Locating specific pieces of information to support an argument, or comparing information from two or more sources are examples of reasons for efferent reading of literature. Convergent questions in this case would reflect that purpose and be acceptable. Questions that stimulate more than a single-word answer are still, of course, preferable. Certainly, nonfiction may be read for more than information acquisition, just as fiction may be read for more than aesthetic purposes. For example, historical fiction novels may be read aloud by teachers with a dual goal: involvement in a powerful vicarious experience and acquisition of some understandings about life during a particular era. But keeping in mind the purposes for reading will guide you in formulating good questions.

Taking notes on the interesting, provocative, funny, heart-wrenching, and problematic characters and scenes of a book is a good starting point for question development. Such questions will be specific to a book and are preferable, but formula questions can be adapted to different books and may help you in designing good questions based on specific books. Some formula questions are listed here:

- What important ideas did you find conveyed in this story?
- What made certain parts of this book so funny? Sad? Exciting? Tell which part you are thinking of and why you think it is funny (sad, exciting).
- How do you think the story should have ended, and why do you think so?
- How would you have acted if you had been (*book character*)?
- What do you think the author's main message (theme) was in this story? Explain why you agree or disagree with the message.
- Which part of the story did you like best or least? Why?
- Which character did you like best or least? Why?
- How is this story similar to other ones we have read?
- How is this story similar to (*a specific story*)? Compare the stories and tell which you liked better and why.
- Which character do you identify with? Tell why and how you identify with him or her.
- What has happened in your life that you are reminded of by this story (character, situation)?
- What would you have done in (*character*)'s predicament?
- What do you think about (*character*)?
- What would (*character*) have done if. . . .

Following Up   Another facet of leading a discussion is the follow-up question. Once a student has given an answer, take that answer and build on it with a question that asks the student to expand or carry the answer to another realm. For example, after the student has said that she expected Sylvester to remain a rock forever, you might ask her to explore how Sylvester would adjust to being a rock and whether and how his parents would adjust. In turn, asking other students to tell how and why they believe otherwise about a part of the story is a way to help students discover that each person's experience with the book may be different.

Waiting   What happens if no one answers the question you asked? This is not likely to happen, because students like to talk; but a good discussion leader knows the value of *waiting*. Wait long enough and someone will finally respond. Too often, discussion leaders jump in and answer their own questions before students have had a chance to gather their thoughts on the point being raised. Some teachers find that asking students to jot notes about the book experience during and after reading gives them time to reflect on their experiences with the book and helps them to formulate their thoughts and feelings for later expression during the discussion.

Creative Drama   Creative drama is informal drama that lends itself readily to the reenactment of story experiences. In discussing the features of creative drama, McCaslin (1990) urges teachers and librarians to keep the following in mind:

- The drama is based on a piece of literature.
- Dialogue is created by the actors; lines are not written or memorized.
- Improvisation is an essential element.
- Movement on "stage" by actors is an integral part of creative drama.
- Scenery and costumes are not used, although an occasional prop may assist the children's imaginations.
- Drama is a process rather than a product. It is not performed for an audience, but for the benefit of the participants. Several different dramas or different dramatic interpretations of the same piece of literature can occur simultaneously in the classroom.

Creative drama is an enjoyable and rewarding oral language activity that can be used with students at all grade levels, from kindergarten to high school. A single scene from a chapter book may be enacted, or a picture book or short story may be dramatized in its entirety. The most suitable stories to start with are relatively simple, involving two to six characters and high action. Many folktales fit this description and lend themselves to being enacted.

These are the steps to follow in guiding creative drama in the classroom:

- Once a story is selected, the students listen to it being read to them or they read it independently.
- Next, they decide if they like the story enough to want to act it out. If so, they listen to it again or read it, paying particular attention to the characters and the story scenes in sequence.
- The students then list the characters and the scenes on the chalkboard or on chart paper.
- They cast the play by assigning parts to actors. If enough students are interested in dramatizing the same story, you may want to assign two or more casts of actors immediately. In this way, each cast of characters can observe the performances of the others and learn from them.
- Next, each cast uses the list of scenes to review the plot, ensuring that all actors recall the events. Discuss the characters at this time, too, having students describe the actions, talk, and appearance for each.
- Give the cast of characters a few minutes to decide how to handle the

performance. Then run through it. The first attempt may be a bit bumpy, but by the second time, it usually goes quite smoothly.
- After completing the drama, the class or the group of students then evaluates its success. McCaslin (1990) suggests these questions:
  1. Did they tell the story?
  2. What did you like about the opening scene?
  3. Did the characters show that they were excited (angry, unhappy, etc.)?
  4. When we play it again, can you think of anything that would improve it?
  5. Was anything important left out? (p. 174)

Due to its improvisational nature and absence of costumes and scenery, creative drama appropriately places importance on the learning and experiencing process, not on performance, and it permits drama to become a frequent means of responding to literature in the classroom. Informal performances for the principal, the class next door, and so on, give students additional opportunities for practice and provide them with an opportunity to feel proud of their efforts.

Readers' Theatre Readers' theatre is the oral presentation of literature by two or more actors, and usually a narrator, reading from a script. Children's literary response is made evident through expressive oral reading and group interpretation. This form of response is especially enjoyable for children who are able to read aloud with some fluency. Features typically associated with readers' theatre include the following:

- The readers and narrator typically remain on the "stage" throughout the production.
- Readers use little movement; instead, they suggest action with simple gestures and facial expressions.
- Chairs or stools are used for readers and narrator to sit on, and performers usually remain seated throughout the performance. Sometimes certain readers sit with their backs to the audience to suggest that they are not in a particular scene.
- No costumes or stage settings are necessary, and at most should be suggestive, rather than complete or literal, so as to permit the imaginations of the audience to have full rein. The use of sound effects may enhance the performance and give the impression of a radio play.

Scripts can be developed for readers' theatre by the teacher or by older students adapting a work of literature enjoyed by the class. Picture books readily lend themselves to adaptation, as do short stories. Some teachers have successfully adapted well-selected scenes from a favorite chapter book. The qualities to seek in a promising story are natural-sounding dialogue, strong characterization, drama or humor, and a satisfactory ending. If the original work has extensive dialogue, the script writing is a very easy activity. The script begins with the title of the book being adapted, the name of the author, a list of characters, and usually an opening statement by the narrator. Following the introduction, the dialogue is written into script form, with the narrator scripted for the remaining nondialogue, narrative parts.

<u>Scorpions</u> (adapted from Chapter 3, pp. 15-16)
by Walter Dean Myers
Harper, 1988

CHARACTERS NEEDED: 7

Narrator
Mama
Jamal
Sassy
Mr. Davidson, principal
Mrs. Rich, teacher
Christine, a student

Mama: Jamal, wait for Sassy so you can walk to school with her.

Jamal: I'm going to be late waiting for her.

Mama: Sassy put some vaseline on your face before you leave.

Narrator: Sassy went into the bathroom. Jamal saw her standing in front of the sink and went to the bathroom door to watch her. She took some Vaseline from the jar, rubbed it between her palms, and then put it on her face. She made a tight face as she smoothed it on her cheeks. and squinted her eyes as she put it on the top of her nose. Then she turned toward Jamal and smiled.

Jamal: You think you cute or something?

Sassy: All I know is what I see in the mirror.

Narrator: Sassy walked past her brother.

Jamal: Mama, she think she cute.

Mama: She is cute.

Jamal: No she ain't.

Sassy: Tito think I'm cute.

Jamal: Tito told me you were ugly.

Sassy: No, he didn't, 'cause he told Mary I was the cutest girl in third grade.

Jamal: They must got some ugly girls in the third grade, then.

Mama: Y'all get on to school. And don't fool around on the way.

Etc....

Scripts can also be purchased, but finding scripts that are both well written and adapted from the literature you are using in your classroom may prove difficult. Using any play script you can find defeats the purpose of providing students with an alternate form of response to their literary experiences. Remember: As with most things, developing the first script is the most difficult. Once you have created the first one, you will find out how easy the process is. Intermediate-grade students take readily to script development once they have a model to imitate. Readers' theatre can become a frequently selected response option of literature response groups.

Choice of literature to use can include virtually any literary genre—picture storybooks, novels, biographies, long poems, letters, diaries, and journals. For example, Paul Fleischman's *Bull Run*, an historical novel set during the Civil War, is written as a series of episodes told by different characters at different stages of the war. At the end of the book, the author provides a list of each character's entries for the use of those who wish to produce reader's theatre performances. Variations on readers' theatre can be accomplished through the addition of background music, choral poems, and brief scenes from different stories tied together by a common theme, among other options to enliven this dramatic enactment of literature.

Preparation for a readers' theatre presentation gives students a good opportunity to strengthen their oral reading abilities and to try out their expressive skills. The group typically reads through the script once or twice, and then works on refining the interpretive aspects of each performer. Decisions need to be made on the arrangement of chairs and speakers for greatest visual effect. Following each presentation, an evaluation is made by the group with the goal of improving future performances.

McCaslin (1990) states that "the simplicity of production and effectiveness of result make it [readers' theatre] singularly desirable in schools with inadequate stage facilities and where rehearsal time is at a premium" (p. 263). For these same reasons, readers' theatre is extremely well-suited to classroom reenactments of literary experiences. In readers' theatre, students have the opportunity to translate their experiences with a literary work to a new medium—the medium of drama—with considerable ease and pleasure.

Story Tellings and Retellings   Children who hear good stories read aloud by teachers, librarians, and parents often recapture those happy experiences by making the stories their own through retellings. In addition, in their natural play activities during preschool years, children enjoy role-playing and making up their own stories to tell to a playmate, real or imagined. The foundation for children's storytelling comes from the children's language environment—the talk they have heard and the stories that have been read to them. As young students learn to tell and retell stories, they reinforce their concept of story and are provided with opportunities for oral language development and expansion. Children who can tell a story with a beginning, middle, and an end have the groundwork laid for later writing activities. You will note that story tellings and retellings by children are different in purpose than storytelling by teachers, as discussed in an earlier section of this chapter. Teachers tell stories as one of many ways of sharing literature with their students.

Teachers can foster the telling and retelling of stories by structuring a classroom environment that is conducive to this activity. Setting off an area of the classroom where children can gather for quiet talk, and equipping it with some props such as story puppets, feltboards with cut-out story figures, toy story characters (stuffed animals, dolls, plastic and metal figures), wordless books, and children's favorite storybooks can entice children into telling and retelling their favorite stories. Some children take the book shared by the teacher during storytime and page through it, retelling the story from the pictures; others take story puppets and re-create the story or make up an entirely new adventure with the same characters.

Tape recorders also inspire younger students to record and listen to their favorite stories, while older students find a tape recorder an incentive for developing radio shows based on favorite books. Their favorite readers' theatre performances are well-suited to radio show productions.

Written Response

Written language activities are an important means for students to respond to their experiences with literature.

Expression of Ideas and Feelings   The simplest and most direct way for teachers to elicit written responses to stories is to ask students to write their ideas and feelings about a book listened to or read. Questions to stimulate written response may be formulated according to the same guidelines suggested for designing discussion questions earlier in this chapter. Divergent, open-ended questions, rather than convergent questions, will elicit students' feelings and ideas about a scene, a character, or the story as a whole, and will help students explore their personal involvement with the story.

Each student's writing ability must be considered in selecting an appropriate writing activity. Emergent writers may find it possible to write the name of their favorite character and draw a picture of that character; more able writers may be able to write a detailed character description. A notable children's author, Marion Dane Bauer, has published a book useful to young writers, *What's Your Story?: A Young Person's Guide to Writing Fiction* (1992).

Literature Journals and Records   Some teachers have found a literature journal—in which students make frequent written responses to books read—a motivating tool for students. Teachers read and comment on the entries periodically, and students gain a sense of pride in their reading accomplishments.

In some cases, reactions to books by one student can be enjoyed by the rest of the class. One teacher clipped blank response sheets with columns for responses (Author, Title, Reaction) inside the front cover of books in the classroom collection. After reading the book, a student enters her name and writes views on the book. Other students enjoy reading the book to see if their reaction will be the same. Some teachers have had students write 4" × 6" notecards about each book as it is read. These cards are kept on file in the library corner so that each new reader can add his or her impressions to the card.

Stories as Writing Models   When children read and listen to stories, they accumulate vocabulary, sentence structures, stylistic devices, and story ideas and structures. Well-written stories and poems serve as models for children in their own writing. When an 8-year-old boy who wrote extremely well-developed, interesting stories was asked how he learned to make up such good stories, he replied, "It's really a secret, but I'll tell you if you won't tell my teacher. I don't really make up the stories. When I was little, my mother read lots of books to me; then in school my teachers read a lot more. So what I do is take a beginning from one of the stories, a middle from another, and the end from another. And then I make up a title." Children who have a rich literary background have a well-stocked storehouse of beginnings, middles, and endings to put to use in their story telling and writing.

Modeling after different literary forms can be used to extend book experiences. Writing a story modeled after another story can be an enjoyable re-creation of the experience. In modeling, the student adapts a story form or idea into a new creation. Examples include the following:

- Students create another episode using the same characters.
- Students write a different ending to the story read.
- Students take the perspective of another character in the story and recast the story with a shift in point of view. Two examples of a change in point of view can be found in Jon Scieszka's, *The True Story of the Three Little Pigs* by A. Wolf (1989), which gives the Big Bad Wolf's version, and Scieszka's *The Frog Prince Continued* (1991), which tells the shocking truth about "happily ever after."
- Students develop readers' theatre scripts, writing a story in a new form.
- Students write a prequel to a story.
- Students take a story set in the past and rewrite it with a modern-day setting. Alternatively, a character from the historical narrative can become a visitor to modern times.

Traditional Book Reports   Requiring students to list author, title, date, genre, setting, main characters, and a summary of the plot seldom causes students to delve more deeply into their experiences with literature. Traditional book reports are usually viewed by students as tedious busywork. Although book reports are assigned by teachers in order to cause students to read, students often report that they never read the books they report on, but rather read the bookflap, a page or two at the beginning and end, and write the report. More promising ways to foster the reading habit are through a good read-aloud program, time set aside for silent reading, booktalks about lots of readily available literature, literature response groups in which students can show their excitement for stories, class discussions, and writing activities in which students' thoughts and feelings about books can be expressed.

Recently, some so-called literature response forms or worksheets have been published for use by teachers who adopt literature-based reading approaches. Be cautious in your use of these worksheets. They need to be examined carefully because some of them are little more than disguised book report forms asking for plot, setting, characters, and theme. Such comprehension assessment may be justified occasionally in the reading class, but if your interest is to elicit students' responses to literature, you should stay away from worksheets.

Graphic Arts Response

Most students enjoy arts and crafts. Graphic design and display techniques can therefore be an enjoyable and effective way to communicate literary experiences with other students and to share book experiences with parents and visitors. *Graphic arts response* is the use of different art and graphic design and display techniques to organize, deepen, and bring closure to students' experiences with literature. These activities can be a way for students to recapture the literary experience while translating it to a new medium.

Pictures and Collages   Students can make pictures and collages to illustrate a favorite story or poem. Having a variety of materials available to choose from in designing their re-creations of literature increases students' enthusiasm and creativity. Paints, colored pencils, chalk, crayons, collage materials (cloth, yarn, lace, tissue paper), colored construction paper, and magazines with pictures and printed words for cutting up and shaping into pictures can be kept readily available for use in the classroom. Teachers foster good design by asking students to think about the purpose and desired effects and by pointing out interesting visual elements in other media, especially in picture books. For example, when students observe the different ways illustrators frame their pictures, outline figures, and use blank space and perspective for highlighting an object, they often can replicate and adapt these techniques for their own classroom design projects.

Teachers have often overused the activity of "draw a picture of the story" by assigning it too frequently, by not planning the activity adequately, and by permitting students little or no choice of media and project. An activity repeated to the point of monotony becomes little more than busywork to students. Remember that it may be unnecessary to have a response activity of any kind after reading a book or that a worthy response to a book would be finding another book by the same author and reading it next.

When more active response seems warranted, however, it is important to plan worthwhile ways for students to express those responses. Providing students with a choice of projects and media and then planning collaboratively with the students on the execution of the project are the roles the teacher needs to assume. Your art specialists and school and public librarians can be of great assistance in helping you plan response activities.

Murals   Murals are made from a long roll of paper mounted horizontally on bulletin boards. The entire length of paper is usually divided into sections and often presents a chronology of the story events. Murals may feature a particular theme, such as animals from stories around the world, different kinds of homes the characters live in, personified dolls and toys from a unit on stories with personification, or various ways young story characters have overcome obstacles as they grow and mature. Groups of children decide on the theme or topic, design the segments, and allocate tasks to group members. Sometimes students work directly on the mounted mural; other times they cut it into sections and work at tables then tape it back together for mounting. This device is well-suited for literature response groups whose members collaborate in selecting, planning, and implementing the mural. The product is often dramatic and showy, offering the group members a feeling of real accomplishment.

Roller Movies   This technique produces a simulated movie or filmstrip of a story. The pictures are designed, frame by frame, on a long roll of paper. Once completed, each end of the paper is taped to a dowel rod or broom handle; then the paper is rolled onto the feeder rod so that the beginning frame is viewed first when the paper is unrolled. The ends of each rod are inserted into holes on the sides of a cardboard box so that the paper can be stretched from one roller to the other across the box opening and then rolled to the receiver rod to move the frames along. The box is turned on its side, television style, to face the audience, and the story unfolds as the frames are rolled onto the receiver rod. A script is written by the group to go along with each frame. The need for group collaboration makes this an ideal project for literature response groups. The finished movie lends itself to story retellings.

Dioramas   A diorama is a three-dimensional display in which objects and figures are placed into a background or setting to create a scene. Dioramas are often made in classrooms by using shoeboxes set on the side, providing a framework on which to construct a setting, such as a floor, ceiling, and three walls of a room. Many materials may be used to make the figures, their background, furniture, and clothes, including modeling clay, collage materials, matchboxes, dried leaves, pine straw, and tiny dolls. Dioramas are especially well-suited to individuals and pairs of students who may work alone or cooperatively in selecting and recreating in miniature an important scene from a story.

Books and Big Books   Children can make their own stories and poems into books for a more finished presentation of their writing efforts. There are many different ways to make books in the classroom, ranging from the simple process of stapling together students' separate pictures on a topic with an illustrated cover to the more complex task of developing books with hard covers made of cardboard with pages covered in clear or patterned adhesive paper or fabric, and then sewn together and bound for a "real book" look.

Big Books are often modeled after a favorite picture book enjoyed by the class, with the pictures drawn by students and the text printed by the teacher on 24" × 30" heavy paper or poster board, which is then laminated, bound on metal rings, and hung on an easel. Many schools have laminators for use in these projects. Lamination is also done at many commercial copy and print shops at a moderate cost.

Making books is an activity most suited for individuals or pairs of students. However, a collaborative book organized around a theme or pattern can be made by a larger group in which each member contributes a story or poem. In this type of book, a table of contents with the names of each contributor offers recognition of all students while also calling students' attention to this useful part of a book. When students are first learning the steps of making books, considerable guidance from an adult is required. Parent volunteers and teacher aides can be shown how to provide this assistance. The step-by-step processes of making different types of books can be found in these sources:

- Aliki's *How a Book Is Made* (1984), a 32-page picture book for children, describes the stages of commercial book publishing, including the writing of the manuscript, the drawing of pictures, and the technical processes leading to printed and bound copies.
- Gerry Bohning, Ann Phillips, and Sandra Bryant's *Literature on the Move: Making and Using Pop-Up and Lift-Flap Books* (1993), a 115-page book for teachers and students, with instructions for planning, writing, drawing, and assembling pop-up books.
- Howard Greenfeld's *Books: From Writer to Reader* (1984), a 197-page book more for adult readers, also describes the stages of commercial publishing in a straightforward manner.
- Susan Purdy's *Books for You to Make* (1973), a 96-page book that will prove useful to children and adults, gives well-illustrated, detailed instructions on how to write, design, illustrate, and bind books. Many different bindings, from simple to complex, are described and illustrated.
- Harvey Weiss's *How to Make Your Own Books* (1974) is a fine source for different types of bindings and cover ideas. In addition, many types of books (flip books, scrolls, Japanese-style books, etc.) and how to make them by hand are described and illustrated in this 72-page book.

Completed books need to be displayed for admiration and made available for reading by others. A special place in the reading corner can be reserved to exhibit student-made books.

Newspapers and Newsletters   A collaborative endeavor in which students write about the books they have been reading and tell about their book-related projects can result in class newspapers and newsletters. Each issue of the paper can focus on a different topic, such as favorite authors, illustrators, story characters, and poetic forms. In some intermediate grade classrooms, a different literature response group accepts editing responsibilities for the newsletter each month, selecting the focus, soliciting manuscripts, designing pages, and making editorial decisions. The newsletters are sent home to parents with suggestions of good books to read and new authors to check out. Since computers are generally available in schools, individuals with word processing skills can usually be found, often among the students, to produce interesting newspapers and newsletters.

Time Lines, Maps, Diagrams, and Charts   A type of visual figure that details a period of time covered in a story is a time line. The figure is made by drawing a line on a long strip of mural paper, then placing the dates below the line at scaled intervals. The story events are logged in above the line. This graphic aid organizes the events of the story and can permit the students to compare events from a novel of historical fiction or from a biography with actual dates from history.

Time lines can be excellent visual aids when used in conjunction with reading aloud a progressive plot chapter book. The time line is set up with the dates, then the story events are recorded after each day's reading. The time line can also serve as a reminder of what has happened thus far as a review before beginning the next chapter.

Time lines can also be useful when students are reading a variety of material on a single period of history: biographies, historical fiction novels, and photoessays on World War II, for instance. Historical events from different sources can be compared for authenticity by using parallel time lines or by adding more tiers to the same time line. Individual students may develop time lines to follow the events of an entire series of books, such as science fiction novels and quest adventure stories.

Maps are especially suitable for charting the settings in chapter books of many genres. They can be designed by individuals or groups of students and make interesting and helpful visual aids for telling others about books. Some chapter books in which maps are included as part of the book can be used by students as models to imitate for drawing storymaps on other books. (For example, see the endpapers of *The Nargun and the Stars* [1974] by Patricia Wrightson, *The Book of Three* [1964] by Lloyd Alexander, and *Rabbit Hill* [1944] by Robert Lawson.) Maps are also suitable for laying out the events in picture books and books with a circular journey motif in which the protagonist leaves home, encounters adversity, overcomes it, and returns home.

A *diagram* presents textual material in visual form and can be used to illustrate arrangements and relations within a story. (For example, in *Linnea in Monet's Garden* [Björk, 1987] a family tree of Monet's family is displayed.) Many information books use diagrams, and students can develop ideas for presenting information through diagrams by perusing these books. Another Linnea story, *Linnea's Windowsill Garden*, has a diagram of plants and their seeds. Diagrams can also be developed to show relationships found in book series and long works, such as the Arthurian legends. Diagrams can be used by teachers and students to display the progression of a story, which is especially useful to help students understand unusual plot twists.

Charts give information in table form to show relationships, summarize information, and present facts in a capsule form. (For example, on page 8 of *Linnea's Almanac* [Björk, 1989] a chart showing species of birds and their feeding habits assists readers in the art of feeding winter birds.) When students use nonfiction books for studying content areas, they can be encouraged to consider visual means for presenting and summarizing the information gained.

Displays and Bulletin Boards   Displays are three-dimensional re-creations of a setting, a town, or a battle scene, for instance, placed on a large flat surface, such as a table or piece of plywood. The use of clay and cardboard for figures, papier mache for hills, colored construction paper for lakes and land surfaces, and so on permits students to design impressive displays from story settings. More artistically talented students can be given opportunities to excel in these design activities.

Designing and making bulletin boards provide groups of students with opportunities to demonstrate their book experiences in innovative ways. Planning bulletin boards and displays requires students to select an interesting and worthy focus or message in order to call attention to the display and to get the message across effectively by using only a few words.

Giving students choices of books to read and choices in the ways they respond to them is an essential component of a good curriculum in literature. This chapter presented a smorgasbord of ideas for having students experience literature and respond to those literary experiences.

References

Alexander, L. (1964). *The book of three.* New York: Holt.

Aliki (Brandenberg). (1986). *How a book is made.* New York: Harper & Row.

Bauer, M. D. (1992). *What's your Story?: A young person's guide to writing fiction.* Boston: Houghton.

Björk, C. (1989). *Linnea's almanac.* Illus. by L. Anderson. Translated by J. Sandin. Stockholm: Rabén & Sjögren.

———. (1987). *Linnea in Monet's garden.* Illus. by L. Anderson. Translated by J. Sandin. Stockholm: Rabén & Sjögren.

———. (1988). *Linnea's windowsill garden.* Illus. by L. Anderson. Translated by J. Sandin. Stockholm: Rabén & Sjögren.

Bodart, J. (1980). *Booktalk!* New York: H. W. Wilson.

Bohning, G., A. Phillips, S. Bryant. (1993). *Literature on the move: Making and using pop-up and lift-flap books.* Illus, by S. Bryant. Englewood, CO: Libraries Unlimited.

Browning, E. B. (1902). Reading. In K. D. Wiggins and N. A. Smith, *Golden numbers.* New York: Doubleday.

Cole, B. (1987). *The goats.* New York: Farrar.

Estes, E. (1944). *The hundred dresses.* Illus. by L. Slobodkin. New York: Harcourt.

Fox, P. (1973). *The slave dancer.* New York: Bradbury.

Greenfeld, H. (1989). *Books: From writer to reader.* New York: Crown.

Holdaway, D. (1982). Shared book experience: Teaching reading using favorite books. *Theory into practice, 21,* 293–300.

Hoskisson, K., Sherman, T. M., & Smith, L. L. (1974). Assisted reading and parent involvement. *The reading teacher, 27,* 710–714.

Lawson, R. (1944). *Rabbit hill.* New York: Viking.

Lynch-Brown, C., & Tomlinson, C. M. (1988). *Reading aloud novel-length chapter books: A qualitative study.* Paper presented at the International Reading Association Annual Conference, Toronto.

McCaslin, N. (1990). *Creative drama in the classroom* (5th ed.). New York: Longman.

Myers, W. D. (1988). *Scorpions.* New York: Harper.

Purdy, S. (1973). *Books for you to make.* Philadelphia: Lippincott.

Raskin, E. (1978). *The westing game.* New York: Dutton.

Rosenblatt, L. M. (1978). *The reader, the text, the poem: The transactional theory of the literary work.* Carbondale, IL: Southern Illinois University Press.

Scieszka, J. (1991). *The frog prince continued.* Illus. by S. Johnson. New York: Viking.

———. (1989). *The true story of the three little pigs by A. Wolf.* Illus. by L. Smith. New York: Viking.

Steig, W. (1969). *Sylvester and the magic pebble.* New York: Windmill.

Weiss, H. (1974). *How to make your own books.* New York: Crowell.

Wrightson, P. (1974). *The nargun and the stars.* New York: Atheneum.

Tailpiece

Tongues we use for talking.
Hands we grasp and link.
Feet are meant for walking.
Heads are where we think.
Toes are what we wiggle.
Knees are what we bend.
Then there's what we sit on.
And that's about the end.

—Max Fatchen

In Harrison, M., and C. Stuart-Clark (Eds.). (1988). *The Oxford Treasury of Children's Poems.* Oxford: Oxford University Press.

Children's Book Awards

National, General Awards

The United States

The Caldecott Medal

This award, sponsored by the Association of Library Service to Children Division of the American Library Association, is given to the illustrator of the most distinguished picture book for children published in the United States during the preceding year. Only U.S. residents or citizens are eligible for this award.

1938 ***Animals of the Bible, A Picture Book.*** Text selected from the King James Bible by Helen Dean Fish. Illustrated by Dorothy P. Lathrop. Lippincott (Bible, ages 3–8).

Honor Books:

Seven Simeons: A Russian Tale by Boris Artzybasheff. Viking (Traditional, ages 6–8).

Four and Twenty Blackbirds compiled by Helen Dean Fish. Illustrated by Robert Lawson/Stokes. Lippincott (Traditional, ages 3–6).

1939 ***Mei Li*** by Thomas Handforth. Doubleday (Realism, ages 6–7).

Honor Books:

The Forest Pool by Laura Adams Armer. McKay/Longmans (Realism, ages 6–7).

Wee Gillis by Munro Leaf. Illustrated by Robert Lawson. Viking (Realism, ages 5–7).

Snow White and the Seven Dwarfs. Translated and illustrated by Wanda Gág. Coward-McCann (Traditional, ages 3–6).

Barkis by Clare Turlay Newberry. Harper (Realism, ages 3–7).

Andy and the Lion by James Daugherty. Viking (Fantasy, ages 3–7).

1940 ***Abraham Lincoln*** by Ingri d'Aulaire and Edgar Parin d'Aulaire. Doubleday (Biography, ages 6–8).

Honor Books:

Cock-a-Doodle-Doo by Berta and Elmer Hader. Macmillan (Animal realism, ages 3–7).

Madeline by Ludwig Bemelmans. Viking (Realism, ages 5–7).

The Ageless Story by Lauren Ford. Dodd (Bible, ages 5–8).

1941 ***They Were Strong and Good*** by Robert Lawson. Viking (Biography, ages 6–7).

Honor Book:

April's Kittens by Clare Turlay Newberry. Harper (Realism, ages 3–6).

1942 ***Make Way for Ducklings*** by Robert McCloskey. Viking (Animal fantasy, ages 3–6).

Honor Books:

An American ABC by Maud and Miska Petersham. Macmillan (Alphabet, ages 3–6).

In My Mother's House by Ann Nolan Clark. Illustrated by Velino Herrera. Viking (Informational, ages 6–8).

Paddle-to-the-Sea by Holling Clancy Holling. Houghton (Informational, ages 6–8).

Nothing at All by Wanda Gág. Coward-McCann (Animal fantasy, ages 3–6).

1943 ***The Little House*** by Virginia Lee Burton. Houghton (Fantasy, ages 3–6).

Honor Books:

Dash and Dart by Mary and Conrad Buff. Viking (Realism, ages 3–6).

Marshmallow by Clare Turlay Newberry. Harper (Realism, ages 3–6).

1944 ***Many Moons*** by James Thurber. Illustrated by Louis Slobodkin. Harcourt (Modern folktale, ages 5–7).

Honor Books:

Small Rain: Verses from the Bible. Text arranged from the Bible by Jessie Orton Jones. Illustrated by Elizabeth Orton Jones. Viking (Bible, ages 3–7).

Pierre Pigeon by Lee Kingman. Illustrated by Arnold Edwin Bare. Houghton (Realism, ages 6–7).

The Mighty Hunter by Berta and Elmer Hader. Macmillan (Fantasy, ages 3–6).

A Child's Good Night Book by Margaret Wise Brown. Illustrated by Jean Charlot. Scott (Realism, ages 3–6).

Good Luck Horse by Chih-Yi Chan. Illustrated by Plato Chan. Whittlesey (Traditional, ages 6–7).

1945 ***Prayer for a Child*** by Rachel Field. Illustrated by Elizabeth Orton Jones. Macmillan (Realism, ages 3–6).

Honor Books:

Mother Goose: Seventy-Seven Verses with Pictures. Illustrated by Tasha Tudor. Walck (Traditional, ages 3–6).

In the Forest by Marie Hall Ets. Viking (Fantasy, ages 3–6).

Yonie Wondernose by Marguerite de Angeli. Doubleday (Realism, ages 6–7).

The Christmas Anna Angel by Ruth Sawyer. Illustrated by Kate Seredy. Viking (Modern folktale, ages 6–7).

1946 ***The Rooster Crows*** selected and illustrated by Maud and Miska Petersham. Macmillan (Mother Goose/Nursery rhymes, ages 3–6).

Honor Books:

Little Lost Lamb by Golden MacDonald. Illustrated by Leonard Weisgard. Doubleday (Realism, ages 3–6).

Sing Mother Goose by Opal Wheeler. Illustrated by Marjorie Torrey. Dutton (Nursery songs, ages 3–6).

My Mother Is the Most Beautiful Woman in the World retold by Becky Reyher. Illustrated by Ruth Gannett. Lothrop (Traditional, ages 5–7).

You Can Write Chinese by Kurt Wiese. Viking (Informational, ages 6–8).

1947 ***The Little Island*** by Golden MacDonald. Illustrated by Leonard Weisgard. Doubleday (Fantasy, ages 3–6).

Honor Books:

Rain Drop Splash by Alvin Tresselt. Illustrated by Leonard Weisgard. Lothrop (Informational, ages 5–7).

Boats on the River by Marjorie Flack. Illustrated by Jay Hyde Barnum. Viking (Informational, ages 6–7).

Timothy Turtle by Al Graham. Illustrated by Tony Palazzo. Viking (Animal fantasy, ages 3–6).

Pedro, the Angel of Olvera Street by Leo Politi. Scribner's (Realism, ages 3–6).

Sing in Praise: A Collection of the Best Loved Hymns by Opal Wheeler. Illustrated by Marjorie Torrey. Dutton (Informational, ages 3–8).

1948 ***White Snow, Bright Snow*** by Alvin Tresselt. Illustrated by Roger Duvoisin. Lothrop (Realism, ages 3–6).

Honor Books:

Stone Soup: An Old Tale by Marcia Brown. Scribner's (Traditional, ages 6–8).

McElligot's Pool by Dr. Seuss (pseud. for Theodor Geisel). Random (Fantasy, ages 3–6).

Bambino the Clown by George Schreiber. Viking (Realism, ages 5–7).

Roger and the Fox by Lavinia Davis. Illustrated by Hildegard Woodward. Doubleday (Realism, ages 5–7).

Song of Robin Hood edited by Anne Malcolmson. Illustrated by Virginia Lee Burton. Houghton (Traditional, ages 9–YA).

1949 *The Big Snow* by Berta and Elmer Hader. Macmillan (Animal realism, ages 3–6).

Honor Books:

Blueberries for Sal by Robert McCloskey. Viking (Realism, ages 3–6).

All Around Town by Phyllis McGinley. Illustrated by Helen Stone. Lippincott (Alphabet, ages 3–6).

Juanita by Leo Politi. Scribner's (Realism, ages 3–6).

Fish in the Air by Kurt Wiese. Viking (Fantasy, ages 5–7).

1950 *Song of the Swallows* by Leo Politi. Scribner's (Realism, ages 3–6).

Honor Books:

America's Ethan Allen by Stewart Holbrook. Illustrated by Lynd Ward. Houghton (Biography, ages 6–8).

The Wild Birthday Cake by Lavinia R. Davis. Illustrated by Hildegard Woodward. Doubleday (Realism, ages 5–6).

The Happy Day by Ruth Krauss. Illustrated by Marc Simont. Harper (Animal fantasy, ages 3–6).

Henry-Fisherman by Marcia Brown. Scribner's (Realism, ages 5–7).

Bartholomew and the Oobleck by Dr. Seuss (pseud. for Theodor Geisel). Random (Modern folktale, ages 5–7).

1951 *The Egg Tree* by Katherine Milhous. Scribner's (Realism, ages 3–6).

Honor Books:

Dick Whittington and His Cat. Translated and illustrated by Marcia Brown. Scribner's (Traditional, ages 6–8).

The Two Reds by Will (pseud. for William Lipkind). Illustrated by Nicolas (pseud. for Nicolas Mordvinoff). Harcourt (Fantasy, ages 3–6).

If I Ran the Zoo by Dr. Seuss (pseud. for Theodor Geisel). Random (Fantasy, ages 3–6).

T-Bone, the Baby-Sitter by Clare Turlay Newberry. Harper (Realism, ages 3–6).

The Most Wonderful Doll in the World by Phyllis McGinley. Illustrated by Helen Stone. Lippincott (Realism, ages 6–7).

1952 *Finders Keepers* by Will (pseud. for William Lipkind). Illustrated by Nicolas (pseud. for Nicolas Mordvinoff). Harcourt (Modern folktale, ages 3–6).

Honor Books:

Mr. T. W. Anthony Woo by Marie Hall Ets. Viking (Modern folktale, ages 3–6).

Skipper John's Cook by Marcia Brown. Scribner's (Realism, ages 5–7).

All Falling Down by Gene Zion. Illustrated by Margaret Bloy Graham. Harper (Informational, ages 3–6).

Bear Party by William Pène du Bois. Viking (Animal fantasy, ages 3–7).

Feather Mountain by Elizabeth Olds. Houghton (Modern folktale, ages 5–7).

1953 *The Biggest Bear* by Lynd Ward. Houghton (Realism, ages 3–7).

Honor Books:

Puss in Boots. Translated and illustrated by Marcia Brown. Scribner's (Traditional, ages 5–7).

One Morning in Maine by Robert McCloskey. Viking (Realism, ages 5–7).

Ape in a Cape: An Alphabet of Odd Animals by Fritz Eichenberg. Harcourt (Alphabet, ages 3–6).

The Storm Book by Charlotte Zolotow. Illustrated by Margaret Bloy Graham. Harper (Informational, ages 3–6).

Five Little Monkeys by Juliet Kepes. Houghton (Animal fantasy, ages 3–6).

1954 *Madeline's Rescue* by Ludwig Bemelmans. Viking (Realism, ages 3–6).

Honor Books:

Journey Cake, Ho! by Ruth Sawyer. Illustrated by Robert McCloskey. Viking (Traditional, ages 5–7).

When Will the World Be Mine? by Miriam Schlein. Illustrated by Jean Charlot. Scott (Animal fantasy, ages 3–6).

The Steadfast Tin Soldier by Hans Christian Andersen. Translated by M. R. James. Illustrated by Marcia Brown. Scribner's (Modern folktale, ages 5–7).

A Very Special House by Ruth Krauss. Illustrated by Maurice Sendak. Harper (Fantasy, ages 3–6).

Green Eyes by Abe Birnbaum. Capitol (Animal fantasy, ages 3–6).

1955   *Cinderella, or the Little Glass Slipper* by Charles Perrault. Translated and illustrated by Marcia Brown. Scribner's (Traditional, ages 3–7).

Honor Books:

Book of Nursery and Mother Goose Rhymes compiled and illustrated by Marguerite de Angeli. Doubleday (Nursery rhymes, ages 3–6).

Wheel on the Chimney by Margaret Wise Brown. Illustrated by Tibor Gergely. Lippincott (Realism, ages 6–7).

The Thanksgiving Story by Alice Dalgliesh. Illustrated by Helen Sewell. Scribner's (Historical fiction [USA, 1700s], ages 5–7).

1956   *Frog Went A-Courtin'* retold by John Langstaff. Illustrated by Feodor Rojankovsky. Harcourt (Traditional, ages 3–7).

Honor Books:

Play with Me by Marie Hall Ets. Viking (Realism, ages 3–6).

Crow Boy by Taro Yashima. Viking (Realism, ages 5–7).

1957   *A Tree Is Nice* by Janice May Udry. Illustrated by Marc Simont. Harper (Informational, ages 3–7).

Honor Books:

Mr. Penny's Race Horse by Marie Hall Ets. Viking (Animal fantasy, ages 5–7).

1 Is One by Tasha Tudor. Walck. (Counting, ages 3–6).

Anatole by Eve Titus. Illustrated by Paul Galdone. McGraw (Animal fantasy, ages 5–7).

Gillespie and the Guards by Benjamin Elkin. Illustrated by James Daugherty. Viking (Realism, ages 5–7).

Lion by William Pène du Bois. Viking (Animal fantasy, ages 5–7).

1958   *Time of Wonder* by Robert McCloskey. Viking (Realism, ages 6–8).

Honor Books:

Fly High, Fly Low by Don Freeman. Viking (Animal fantasy, ages 3–6).

Anatole and the Cat by Eve Titus. Illustrated by Paul Galdone. McGraw (Animal fantasy, ages 3–6).

1959   *Chanticleer and the Fox* by Chaucer. Adapted and illustrated by Barbara Cooney. Crowell (Traditional, ages 5–7).

Honor Books:

The House That Jack Built ("La Maison Que Jacques a Bâtie"): A Picture Book in Two Languages by Antonio Frasconi. Harcourt (Informational, ages 5–8).

What Do You Say, Dear? A Book of Manners for All Occasions by Sesyle Joslin. Illustrated by Maurice Sendak. Scott (Fantasy, ages 3–6).

Umbrella by Taro Yashima. Viking (Realism, ages 5–7).

1960   *Nine Days to Christmas* by Marie Hall Ets and Aurora Labastida. Illustrated by Marie Hall Ets. Viking (Realism, ages 3–7).

Honor Books:

Houses from the Sea by Alice E. Goudey. Illustrated by Adrienne Adams. Scribner's (Informational, ages 5–7).

The Moon Jumpers by Janice May Udry. Illustrated by Maurice Sendak. Harper (Realism, ages 3–6).

1961   *Baboushka and the Three Kings* by Ruth Robbins. Illustrated by Nicolas Sidjakov. Parnassus (Traditional, ages 5–7).

Honor Book:

Inch by Inch by Leo Lionni. Obolensky (Animal

fantasy, ages 3–6).

1962 *Once a Mouse* retold by Marcia Brown. Scribner's (Traditional, ages 5–7).

Honor Books:

The Fox Went Out on a Chilly Night: An Old Song by Peter Spier. Doubleday (Traditional, ages 3–6).

Little Bear's Visit by Else Minarik. Illustrated by Maurice Sendak. Harper (Animal fantasy, ages 3–7).

The Day We Saw the Sun Come Up by Alice Goudey. Illustrated by Adrienne Adams. Scribner's (Informational, ages 5–7).

1963 *The Snowy Day* by Ezra Jack Keats. Viking (Realism, ages 3–6).

Honor Books:

The Sun Is a Golden Earring by Natalia Belting. Illustrated by Bernarda Bryson. Holt (Modern folktale, ages 7–10).

Mr. Rabbit and the Lovely Present by Charlotte Zolotow. Illustrated by Maurice Sendak. Harper (Animal fantasy, ages 3–6).

1964 *Where the Wild Things Are* by Maurice Sendak. Harper (Fantasy, ages 3–7).

Honor Books:

Swimmy by Leo Lionni. Pantheon (Animal fantasy, ages 5–7).

All in the Morning Early by Sorche Nic Leodhas (pseud. for Leclaire Alger). Illustrated by Evaline Ness. Holt (Traditional, ages 3–6).

Mother Goose and Nursery Rhymes by Philip Reed. Atheneum (Traditional, ages 3–6).

1965 *May I Bring a Friend?* by Beatrice Schenk de Regniers. Illustrated by Beni Montresor. Atheneum (Fantasy, ages 5–7).

Honor Books:

Rain Makes Applesauce by Julian Scheer. Illustrated by Marvin Bileck. Holiday (Fantasy, ages 5–7).

The Wave by Margaret Hodges. Illustrated by Blair Lent. Houghton (Traditional, ages 6–9).

A Pocketful of Cricket by Rebecca Caudill. Illustrated by Evaline Ness. Holt (Realism, ages 5–7).

1966 *Always Room for One More* by Sorche Nic Leodhas (pseud. for Leclaire Alger). Illustrated by Nonny Hogrogian. Holt (Traditional, ages 3–6).

Honor Books:

Hide and Seek Fog by Alvin Tresselt. Illustrated by Roger Duvoisin. Lothrop (Realism, ages 5–7).

Just Me by Marie Hall Ets. Viking (Realism, ages 3–5).

Tom Tit Tot adapted by Joseph Jacobs. Illustrated by Evaline Ness. Scribner's (Traditional, ages 5–7).

1967 *Sam, Bangs and Moonshine* by Evaline Ness. Holt (Realism, ages 6–8).

Honor Book:

One Wide River to Cross adapted by Barbara Emberley. Illustrated by Ed Emberley. Prentice Hall (Bible, ages 3–6).

1968 *Drummer Hoff* adapted by Barbara Emberley. Illustrated by Ed Emberley. Prentice Hall (Traditional, ages 3–6).

Honor Books:

Frederick by Leo Lionni. Pantheon (Animal fantasy, ages 5–7).

Seashore Story by Taro Yashima. Viking (Realism, ages 6–8).

The Emperor and the Kite by Jane Yolen. Illustrated by Ed Young. World (Modern folktale, ages 5–7).

1969 *The Fool of the World and the Flying Ship: A Russian Tale* by Authur Ransome. Illustrated by Uri Shulevitz. Farrar (Traditional, ages 6–8).

Honor Book:

Why the Sun and the Moon Live in the Sky: An African Folktale by Elphinstone Dayrell. Illustrated by Blair Lent. Houghton (Traditional, ages 6–8).

1970 *Sylvester and the Magic Pebble* by William Steig. Windmill (Animal fantasy, ages 5–7).

Honor Books:

Goggles! by Ezra Jack Keats. Macmillan (Realism, ages 3–6).

Alexander and the Wind-Up Mouse by Leo Lionni. Pantheon (Animal fantasy, ages 3–6).

Pop Corn and Ma Goodness by Edna Mitchell Preston. Illustrated by Robert Andrew Parker. Viking (Modern folktale, ages 5–7).

Thy Friend, Obadiah by Brinton Turkle. Viking (Historical fiction [New England, 1700s], ages 3–7).

The Judge: An Untrue Tale by Harve Zemach. Illustrated by Margot Zemach. Farrar (Modern folktale, ages 5–7).

1971 *A Story, A Story: An African Tale* by Gail E. Haley. Atheneum (Traditional, ages 5–7).

Honor Books:

The Angry Moon retold by William Sleator. Illustrated by Blair Lent. Atlantic/Little, Brown (Traditional, ages 6–8).

Frog and Toad Are Friends by Arnold Lobel. Harper (Animal fantasy, ages 3–7).

In the Night Kitchen by Maurice Sendak. Harper (Fantasy, ages 5–7).

1972 *One Fine Day* by Nonny Hogrogian. Macmillan (Traditional, ages 5–7).

Honor Books:

If All the Seas Were One Sea by Janina Domanska. Macmillan (Traditional, ages 3–6).

Moja Means One: Swahili Counting Book by Muriel Feelings. Illustrated by Tom Feelings. Dial (Counting, ages 5–8).

Hildilid's Night by Cheli Duran Ryan. Illustrated by Arnold Lobel. Macmillan (Modern folktale, ages 3–6).

1973 *The Funny Little Woman* retold by Arlene Mosel. Illustrated by Blair Lent. Dutton (Traditional, ages 5–7).

Honor Books:

Hosie's Alphabet by Hosea Baskin, Tobias Baskin, and Lisa Baskin. Illustrated by Leonard Baskin. Viking (Alphabet, ages 6–9).

When Clay Sings by Byrd Baylor. Illustrated by Tom Bahti. Scribner's (Informational, ages 6–8).

Snow-White and the Seven Dwarfs by the Brothers Grimm. Translated by Randall Jarrell. Illustrated by Nancy Ekholm Burkert. Farrar (Traditional, ages 3–7).

Anansi the Spider: A Tale from the Ashanti adapted and illustrated by Gerald McDermott. Holt (Traditional, ages 6–8).

1974 *Duffy and the Devil* retold by Harve Zemach. Illustrated by Margot Zemach. Farrar (Traditional, ages 6–8).

Honor Books:

Three Jovial Huntsmen adapted and illustrated by Susan Jeffers. Bradbury (Traditional, ages 3–6).

Cathedral: The Story of Its Construction by David Macaulay. Houghton (Informational, ages 8–YA).

1975 *Arrow to the Sun* adapted and illustrated by Gerald McDermott. Viking (Traditional, ages 7–9).

Honor Book:

Jambo Means Hello: Swahili Alphabet Book by Muriel Feelings. Illustrated by Tom Feelings. Dial (Alphabet, ages 6–8).

1976 *Why Mosquitoes Buzz in People's Ears* retold by Verna Aardema. Illustrated by Leo and Diane Dillon. Dial (Traditional, ages 6–8).

Honor Books:

The Desert is Theirs by Byrd Baylor. Illustrated by Peter Parnall. Scribner's (Informational, ages 6–8).

Strega Nona retold and illustrated by Tomie de Paola. Prentice Hall (Traditional, ages 5–8).

1977 *Ashanti to Zulu: African Traditions* by Margaret Musgrove. Illustrated by Leo and Diane Dillon. Dial (Informational, ages 7–11).

Honor Books:

The Amazing Bone by William Steig. Farrar (Fantasy, ages 6–8).

The Contest by Nonny Hogrogian. Greenwillow (Traditional, ages 6–8).

Fish for Supper by M. B. Goffstein. Dial (Realism, ages 3–6).

The Golem: A Jewish Legend retold and illustrated by Beverly Brodsky McDermott. Lippincott (Traditional, ages 6–9).

Hawk, I'm Your Brother by Byrd Baylor. Illustrated by Peter Parnall. Scribner's (Realism, ages 7–9).

1978 *Noah's Ark* by Peter Spier. Doubleday (Bible/Wordless, ages 3–7).

Honor Books:

Castle by David Macaulay. Houghton (Informational, ages 8–YA).

It Could Always Be Worse retold by Margot Zemach. Farrar (Traditional, ages 5–7).

1979 *The Girl Who Loved Wild Horses* by Paul Goble. Bradbury (Traditional, ages 6–8).

Honor Books:

Freight Train by Donald Crews. Greenwillow (Concept, ages 3–6).

The Way to Start a Day by Byrd Baylor. Illustrated by Peter Parnall. Scribner's (Informational, ages 6–9).

1980 *Ox-Cart Man* by Donald Hall. Illustrated by Barbara Cooney. Viking (Historical fiction [New England, 1800s], ages 5–8).

Honor Books:

Ben's Trumpet by Rachel Isadora. Greenwillow (Realism, ages 5–7).

The Treasure by Uri Shulevitz. Farrar (Traditional, ages 6–8).

The Garden of Abdul Gasazi by Chris Van Allsburg. Houghton (Fantasy, ages 6–8).

1981 *Fables* by Arnold Lobel. Harper (Animal fantasy, ages 3–6).

Honor Books:

The Bremen-Town Musicians retold and illustrated by Ilse Plume. Doubleday (Traditional, ages 5–7).

The Grey Lady and the Strawberry Snatcher by Molly Bang. Four Winds (Fantasy/wordless, ages 6–8).

Mice Twice by Joseph Low. Atheneum (Animal fantasy, ages 3–6).

Truck by Donald Crews. Greenwillow (Concept, ages 3–6).

1982 *Jumanji* by Chris Van Allsburg. Houghton (Fantasy, ages 6–8).

Honor Books:

A Visit to William Blake's Inn: Poems for Innocent and Experienced Travelers by Nancy Willard. Illustrated by Alice and Martin Provensen. Harcourt (Biography/Poetry, ages 7–10).

Where the Buffaloes Begin by Olaf Baker. Illustrated by Stephen Gammell. Warne (Traditional, ages 7–10).

On Market Street by Arnold Lobel. Illustrated by Anita Lobel. Greenwillow (Alphabet, ages 4–6).

Outside Over There by Maurice Sendak. Harper (Fantasy, ages 7–10).

1983 *Shadow* by Blaise Cendrars. Translated and illustrated by Marcia Brown. Scribner's (Traditional, ages 8–11).

Honor Books:

When I Was Young in the Mountains by Cynthia Rylant. Illustrated by Diane Goode. Dutton (Realism, ages 7–9).

A Chair for My Mother by Vera B. Williams. Greenwillow (Realism, ages 6–8).

1984 *The Glorious Flight: Across the Channel with Louis Blériot* by Alice and Martin Provensen. Viking (Historical fiction [France, 1909], ages 7–10).

Honor Books:

Ten, Nine, Eight by Molly Bang. Greenwillow (Counting, ages 3–6).

Little Red Riding Hood by the Brothers Grimm. Retold and illustrated by Trina Schart Hyman. Holiday (Traditional, ages 5–8).

1985 *Saint George and the Dragon* adapted by Margaret Hodges. Illustrated by Trina Schart Hyman. Little, Brown (Traditional, ages 9–12).

Honor Books:

Hansel and Gretel adapted by Rika Lesser. Illustrated by Paul O. Zelinsky. Dodd (Traditional, ages 6–8).

The Story of Jumping Mouse retold and illustrated by John Steptoe. Lothrop (Traditional, ages 7–10).

Have You Seen My Duckling? by Nancy Tafuri. Greenwillow (Animal fantasy, ages 4–6).

1986 *The Polar Express* by Chris Van Allsburg. Houghton (Fantasy, ages 5–9).

Honor Books:

The Relatives Came by Cynthia Rylant. Illustrated by Stephen Gammell. Bradbury (Realism, ages 6–9).

King Bidgood's in the Bathtub by Audrey Wood. Illustrated by Don Wood. Harcourt (Fantasy, ages 5–8).

1987 *Hey, Al* by Arthur Yorinks. Illustrated by Richard Egielski. Farrar (Fantasy, ages 7–10).

Honor Books:

The Village of Round and Square Houses by Ann Grifalconi. Little, Brown (Traditional, ages 7–9).

Alphabatics by Suse MacDonald. Bradbury (Alphabet, ages 4–6).

Rumpelstiltskin by the Brothers Grimm. Retold and illustrated by Paul O. Zelinsky. Dutton (Traditional, ages 6–9).

1988 *Owl Moon* by Jane Yolen. Illustrated by John Schoenherr. Philomel (Realism, ages 5–8).

Honor Book:

Mufaro's Beautiful Daughters retold by John Steptoe. Lothrop (Traditional, ages 6–9).

1989 *Song and Dance Man* by Karen Ackerman. Illustrated by Stephen Gammell. Knopf (Realism, ages 7–10).

Honor Books:

Free Fall by David Wiesner. Lothrop (Fantasy/Wordless, ages 7–10).

Goldilocks and the Three Bears retold and illustrated by James Marshall. Dial (Modern Folktale, ages 5–8).

Mirandy and Brother Wind by Patricia McKissack. Illustrated by Jerry Pinkney. Knopf (Traditional, ages 7–9).

The Boy of the Three-Year Nap by Diane Snyder. Illustrated by Allen Say. Houghton (Traditional, ages 7–10).

1990 *Lon Po Po: A Red-Riding Hood Story from China* translated and illustrated by Ed Young. Philomel (Traditional, ages 5–8).

Honor Books:

Hershel and the Hanukkah Goblins by Eric Kimmel. Illustrated by Trina Schart Hyman. Holiday (Modern folktale, ages 7–10).

The Talking Eggs adapted by Robert D. San Souci. Illustrated by Jerry Pinkney. Dial (Traditional, ages 6–9).

Bill Peet: An Autobiography by Bill Peet. Houghton (Biography, ages 7–10).

Color Zoo by Lois Ehlert. Lippincott (Concept, ages 3–6).

1991 *Black and White* by David Macaulay. Houghton (Mystery, ages 8–12).

Honor Books:

Puss 'n Boots by Charles Perrault. Illustrated by Fred Marcellino. Farrar (Traditional, ages 5–7).

"More, More, More." Said the Baby: 3 Love Stories by Vera Williams. Greenwillow (Realism, ages 3–5).

1992 *Tuesday* by David Wiesner. Clarion (Fantasy/Wordless, ages 7–10).

Honor Book:

Tar Beach by Faith Ringgold. Crown (Multicultural [African-American], ages 6–9).

1993 *Mirette on the High Wire* by Emily Arnold McCully. Putnam (Realism, ages 7–9).

Honor Books:

Seven Blind Mice by Ed Young. Philomel (Modern folktale, ages 6–10).

The Stinky Cheese Man and Other Fairly Stupid Tales by Jon Scieszka and Lane Smith. Illustrated by Lane Smith. Viking (Modern folktale, ages 7–11).

Working Cotton by Sherley Anne Williams. Illustrated by Carole Byard. Harcourt (Realism [African-American], ages 7–9).

1994 *Grandfather's Journey* by Allen Say. Houghton (Biography, ages 7–9).

Honor Books:

Peppe the Lamplighter by Elisa Bartone. Illustrated by Ted Lewin. Lothrop (Realism, ages 7–9).

In the Small, Small Pond by Denise Fleming. Holt

(Pattern, ages 5–7).

Owen by Kevin Henkes. Greenwillow (Animal fantasy, ages 5–7).

Raven: A Trickster Tale from the Pacific Northwest by Gerald McDermott. Harcourt (Traditional [Native-American], ages 7–9).

Yo! Yes? by Chris Raschka. Orchard (Realism/ Multicultural, ages 5–7).

1995 *Smoky Night* by Eve Bunting. Illustrated by David Diaz. Harcourt (Realism/Multicultural, ages 6–8).

Honor Books:

Swamp Angel by Anne Isaacs. Illustrated by Paul O. Zelinsky. Dutton (Modern folktale, ages 6–9).

John Henry by Julius Lester. Illustrated by Jerry Pinkney. Dial (Traditional, ages 6–9).

Time Flies by Eric Rohmann. Crown (Wordless, ages 6–9).

The Newbery Medal

This award, sponsored by the Association for Library Service to Children Division of the American Library Association, is given to the author of the most distinguished contribution to children's literature published during the preceding year. Only U.S. citizens or residents are eligible for this award.

1922 *The Story of Mankind* by Hendrik Willem Van Loon. Liveright (Informational, ages 12–YA).

Honor Books:

The Great Quest by Charles Boardman Hawes. Little, Brown (Historical fiction [New England, 1826], ages 11–YA).

Cedric the Forester by Bernard G. Marshall. Appleton (Historical fiction [England, 1200s], ages 11–YA).

The Old Tobacco Shop by William Bowen. Macmillan (Fantasy, ages 9–12).

The Golden Fleece and the Heroes Who Lived before Achilles by Padraic Colum. Macmillan (Traditional fantasy, ages 9–13).

Windy Hill by Cornelia Meigs. Macmillan (Realism, ages 9–12).

1923 *The Voyages of Doctor Dolittle* by Hugh Lofting. Lippincott (Fantasy, ages 8–12).

(No record of the runners-up.)

1924 *The Dark Frigate* by Charles Boardman Hawes. Little, Brown (Historical fiction [England, 1600s], ages 10–YA).

(No record of the runners-up.)

1925 *Tales from Silver Lands* by Charles J. Finger. Illustrated by Paul Honoré. Doubleday (Traditional fantasy, ages 9–YA).

Honor Books:

Nicholas by Anne Carroll Moore. Putnam (Fantasy [Little people], ages 8–11).

Dream Coach by Anne and Dillwyn Parrish. Macmillan (Fantasy, ages 7–11).

1926 *Shen of the Sea* by Arthur Bowie Chrisman. Illustrated by Else Hasselriis. Dutton (Fantasy [Literary tales], ages 9–12).

Honor Book:

The Voyagers by Padraic Colum. Macmillan (Traditional fantasy/Informational, ages 10–12).

1927 *Smoky, the Cowhorse* by Will James. Scribner's (Animal realism, ages 9–12).

(No record of the runners-up.)

1928 *Gay-Neck, The Story of a Pigeon* by Dhan Gopal Mukerji. Illustrated by Boris Artzybasheff. Dutton (Animal realism, ages 9–YA).

Honor Books:

The Wonder Smith and His Son by Ella Young. McKay/Longmans (Traditional fantasy [Ireland], ages 10–YA).

Downright Dencey by Caroline Dale Snedeker. Doubleday (Historical fiction [New England, 1812], ages 9–13).

1929 *The Trumpeter of Krakow* by Eric P. Kelly. Illustrated by Angela Pruszynska. Macmillan (Historical Fiction [Poland, 1400s], ages 11–YA).

Honor Books:

The Pigtail of Ah Lee Ben Loo by John Bennett. McKay/Longmans (Fantasy/Poetry, ages 8–13).

Millions of Cats by Wanda Gág. Coward-McCann (Picture book; Fantasy, ages 5–7).

The Boy Who Was by Grace T. Hallock. Dutton

(Historical fiction [Italy through 3000 years], ages 10–YA).

Clearing Weather by Cornelia Meigs. Little, Brown (Historical fiction [USA, 1787], ages 11–YA).

The Runaway Papoose by Grace P. Moon. Doubleday (Realism/Multicultural, ages 8–11).

Tod of the Fens by Eleanor Whitney. Macmillan (Historical fiction [England 1400s], ages 11–YA).

1930 *Hitty: Her First Hundred Years* by Rachel Field. Illustrated by Dorothy P. Lathrop. Macmillan (Historical fantasy, ages 9–13).

Honor Books:

The Tangle-Coated Horse and Other Tales: Episodes from the Fionn Saga by Ella Young. Illustrated by Vera Brock. Longmans (Traditional, ages 10–13).

Vaino: A Boy of New Finland by Julia Davis Adams. Illustrated by Lempi Ostman. Dutton (Historical fiction [Finland, 1920s], ages 11–YA).

Pran of Albania by Elizabeth C. Miller. Doubleday (Realism, ages 11–YA).

The Jumping-Off Place by Marian Hurd McNeely. McKay/Longmans (Realism, ages 10–YA).

A Daughter of the Seine by Jeanette Eaton. Harper (Biography, ages 12–YA).

Little Blacknose by Hildegarde Hoyt Swift. Illustrated by Lynd Ward. Harcourt (Fantasy, ages 8–11).

1931 *The Cat Who Went to Heaven* by Elizabeth Coatsworth. Illustrated by Lynd Ward. Macmillan (Fantasy, ages 10–13).

Honor Books:

Floating Island by Anne Parrish. Harper (Fantasy, ages 8–11).

The Dark Star of Itza by Alida Malkus. Harcourt (Historical fiction [Mayan Empire], ages 11–YA).

Queer Person by Ralph Hubbard. Doubleday (Historical fiction/Multicultural [Native-American], ages 9–13).

Mountains Are Free by Julia Davis Adams. Dutton (Historical fiction [Switzerland], ages 11–YA).

Spice and the Devil's Cave by Agnes D. Hewes.

Knopf (Historical fiction [Portugal, 1400s], ages 11–YA).

Meggy McIntosh by Elizabeth Janet Gray. Doubleday (Historical fiction [Scotland, USA, 1775], ages 10–YA).

Garram the Hunter: A Boy of the Hill Tribes by Herbert Best. Illustrated by Allena Best (Erick Berry). Doubleday (Realism [Africa], ages 9–13).

Ood-Le-Uk, the Wanderer by Alice Lide and Margaret Johansen. Illustrated by Raymond Lufkin. Little, Brown (Realism [Alaska], ages 11–14.)

1932 *Waterless Mountain* by Laura Adams Armer. Illustrated by Sidney Armer and Laura Adams Armer. McKay/Longmans (Realism/Multicultural [Native-American], ages 9–13).

Honor Books:

The Fairy Circus by Dorothy Lathrop. Macmillan (Fantasy, ages 6–9).

Calico Bush by Rachel Field. Macmillan (Historical fiction, [USA, 1743], ages 9–13).

Boy of the South Seas by Eunice Tietjens. Coward-McCann (Realism, ages 9–12).

Out of the Flame by Eloise Lownsbery. McKay/Longmans (Historical fiction [France, 1500s], ages 10–YA).

Jane's Island by Marjorie Hill Alee. Houghton (Realism, ages 9–13).

The Truce of the Wolf and Other Tales of Old Italy by Mary Gould Davis. Harcourt (Traditional fantasy, ages 8–13).

1933 *Young Fu of the Upper Yangtze* by Elizabeth Foreman Lewis. Illustrated by Kurt Wiese. Holt (Realism, ages 10–YA).

Honor Books:

Swift Rivers by Cornelia Meigs. Little, Brown (Historical fiction [USA, 1835], ages 10–13).

The Railroad to Freedom by Hildegarde Swift. Harcourt (Biography, ages 10–YA).

Children of the Soil by Nora Burglon. Doubleday (Realism, ages 9–12).

1934 *Invincible Louisa: The Story of the Author of "Little Women"* by Cornelia Meigs. Little, Brown (Biography, ages 10–12).

Honor Books:

The Forgotten Daughter by Caroline Dale Snedeker. Doubleday (Historical fiction [Italy, second century B.C.], ages 11–YA).

Swords of Steel by Elsie Singmaster. Houghton (Historical fiction [USA, 1859], ages 11–YA).

ABC Bunny by Wanda Gág. Coward-McCann (Picture book. Fantasy/Alphabet, ages 3–7).

Winged Girl of Knossos by Erik Berry. Appleton (Historical fiction [Ancient Greece], ages 10–YA).

New Land by Sarah L. Schmidt. McBride (Realism, ages 10–YA).

The Apprentice of Florence by Anne Kyle. Houghton (Historical fiction [Italy, 1400s], ages 11–YA).

The Big Tree of Bunlahy: Stories of My Own Countryside by Padraic Colum. Illustrated by Jack Yeats. Macmillan (Fantasy, ages 8–YA).

Glory of the Seas by Agnes D. Hewes. Illustrated by N. C. Wyeth. Knopf (Historical fiction [USA, 1850s], ages 11–YA).

1935 *Dobry* by Monica Shannon. Illustrated by Atanas Katchamakoff. Viking (Realism, ages 9–11).

Honor Books:

The Pageant of Chinese History by Elizabeth Seeger. McKay/Longmans (Informational, ages 11–YA).

Davy Crockett by Constance Rourke. Harcourt (Biography, ages 12–YA).

A Day on Skates: The Story of a Dutch Picnic by Hilda Van Stockum. Harper (Realism, ages 6–8).

1936 *Caddie Woodlawn* by Carol Ryrie Brink. Illustrated by Kate Seredy. Macmillan (Historical fiction [USA, 1860s], ages 9–12).

Honor Books:

Honk: The Moose by Phil Strong. Illustrated by Kurt Wiese. Dodd (Realism, ages 7–11).

The Good Master by Kate Seredy. Viking (Realism, ages 9–11).

Young Walter Scott by Elizabeth Janet Gray. Viking (Biography, ages 11–YA).

All Sail Set by Armstrong Sperry. Winston (Historical fiction [USA, 1851], ages 10–13).

1937 *Roller Skates* by Ruth Sawyer. Illustrated by Valenti Angelo. Viking (Realism, ages 8–10).

Honor Books:

Phoebe Fairchild: Her Book by Lois Lenski. Lippincott (Historical fiction [New England, 1830s], ages 9–12).

Whistler's Van by Idwal Jones. Viking (Realism, ages 9–13).

The Golden Basket by Ludwig Bemelmans. Viking (Realism, ages 6–9).

Winterbound by Margery Bianco. Viking (Realism, ages 11–YA).

Audubon by Constance Rourke. Harcourt (Biography, ages 11–YA).

The Codfish Musket by Agnes D. Hewes. Doubleday (Historical fiction [USA, 1780s], ages 11–YA).

1938 *The White Stag* by Kate Seredy. Viking (Traditional, ages 10–YA).

Honor Books:

Bright Island by Mabel L. Robinson. Random (Realism, ages 11–YA).

Pecos Bill by James Cloyd Bowman. Little, Brown (Traditional, ages 9–YA).

On the Banks of Plum Creek by Laura Ingalls Wilder. Harper (Historical fiction [USA, 1870s], ages 8–11.)

1939 *Thimble Summer* by Elizabeth Enright. Holt (Realism, ages 8–11).

Honor Books:

Leader by Destiny: George Washington, Man and Patriot by Jeanette Eaton. Harcourt (Biography, ages 11–YA).

Penn by Elizabeth Janet Gray. Viking (Biography, ages 11–YA).

Nino by Valenti Angelo. Viking (Realism, ages 9–11).

"Hello, the Boat!" by Phyllis Crawford. Holt (Historical fiction [USA, 1817], ages 9–13).

Mr. Popper's Penguins by Richard and Florence Atwater. Little, Brown (Animal fantasy, ages 7–11).

1940 *Daniel Boone* by James H. Daugherty. Viking (Biography, ages 10–YA).

Honor Books:

The Singing Tree by Kate Seredy. Viking (Historical fiction [Eastern Europe, 1910s], ages 9–12).

Runner of the Mountain Tops by Mabel L. Robinson. Random (Biography, ages 11–YA).

By the Shores of Silver Lake by Laura Ingalls Wilder. Harper (Historical fiction [USA, 1880s], ages 8–10).

Boy with a Pack by Stephen W. Meader. Harcourt (Historical fiction [USA, 1837], ages 9–13).

1941 *Call It Courage* by Armstrong Sperry. Macmillan (Realism, ages 9–12).

Honor Books:

Blue Willow by Doris Gates. Viking (Historical fiction [USA, 1930s], ages 8–11).

Young Mac of Fort Vancouver by Mary Jane Carr. Crowell (Historical fiction [Canada, early 1800s], ages 10–YA).

The Long Winter by Laura Ingalls Wilder. Harper (Historical fiction [USA, 1880s], ages 9–13).

Nansen by Anna Gertrude Hall. Viking (Biography, ages 11–YA).

1942 *The Matchlock Gun* by Walter D. Edmonds. Illustrated by Paul Lantz. Dodd (Historical fiction [Colonial America, 1757], ages 8–11).

Honor Books:

Little Town on the Prairie by Laura Ingalls Wilder. Harper (Historical fiction [USA, 1881], ages 8–10).

George Washington's World by Genevieve Foster. Scribner's (Informational/Biography, ages 10–YA).

Indian Captive: The Story of Mary Jemison by Lois Lenski. Lippincott (Historical fiction [USA, 1750s], ages 9–11).

Down Ryton Water by Eva Roe Gaggin. Illustrated by Elmer Hader. Viking (Historical fiction [England, Netherlands, 1600s], ages 12–YA).

1943 *Adam of the Road* by Elizabeth Janet Gray. Illustrated by Robert Lawson. Viking (Historical fiction [England, 1290s], ages 9–12).

Honor Books:

The Middle Moffat by Eleanor Estes. Harcourt (Realism, ages 8–10).

"Have You Seen Tom Thumb?" by Mabel Leigh Hunt. Lippincott (Biography, ages 10–YA).

1944 *Johnny Tremain* by Esther Forbes. Illustrated by Lynd Ward. Houghton (Historical fiction [Boston, 1770s], ages 12–YA).

Honor Books:

These Happy Golden Years by Laura Ingalls Wilder. Harper (Historical fiction [USA, 1880s], ages 8–10).

Fog Magic by Julia L. Sauer. Viking (Modern fantasy, ages 9–12).

Rufus M. by Eleanor Estes. Harcourt (Realism, ages 8–10).

Mountain Born by Elizabeth Yates. Coward-McCann (Animal realism, ages 9–11).

1945 *Rabbit Hill* by Robert Lawson. Viking (Animal fantasy, ages 7–9).

Honor Books:

The Hundred Dresses by Eleanor Estes. Harcourt (Realism, ages 7–9).

The Silver Pencil by Alice Dalgliesh. Scribner's (Realism, ages 10–YA).

Abraham Lincoln's World by Genevieve Foster. Scribner's (Informational/Biography, ages 10–YA).

Lone Journey: The Life of Roger Williams by Jeanette Eaton. Illustrated by Woodi Ishmael. Harcourt (Biography, ages 13–YA).

1946 *Strawberry Girl* by Lois Lenski. Lippincott (Historical fiction [Florida, early 1900s], ages 8–10).

Honor Books:

Justin Morgan Had a Horse by Marguerite Henry. Follett (Animal Realism, ages 8–10).

The Moved-Outers by Florence Crannell Means. Houghton (Multicultural, ages 10–12).

Bhimsa, the Dancing Bear by Christine Weston. Scribner's (Realism, ages 8–10).

New Found World by Katherine B. Shippen. Viking (Informational, ages 10–YA).

1947 *Miss Hickory* by Carolyn Sherwin Bailey. Illustrated by Ruth Gannett. Viking (Fantasy/Toys and dolls, ages 7–9).

Honor Books:

The Wonderful Year by Nancy Barnes. Messner (Realism, ages 9–12).

The Big Tree by Mary and Conrad Buff. Viking (Informational, ages 9–13).

The Heavenly Tenants by William Maxwell. Harper (Fantasy, ages 10–YA).

The Avion My Uncle Flew by Cyrus Fisher. Appleton (Realism, ages 10–13).

The Hidden Treasure of Glaston by Eleanore M. Jewett. Viking (Historical fiction [England, 1172], ages 10–13).

1948 *The Twenty-One Balloons* by William Pène du Bois. Lothrop (Fantasy, ages 9–11).

Honor Books:

Pancakes-Paris by Claire Huchet Bishop. Viking (Realism, ages 8–11).

Li Lun, Lad of Courage by Carolyn Treffinger. Abingdon (Realism, ages 9–12).

The Quaint and Curious Quest of Johnny Longfoot, The Shoe-King's Son by Catherine Besterman. Bobbs-Merrill (Traditional, ages 8–10).

The Cow-Tail Switch, And Other West African Stories by Harold Courlander and George Herzog. Holt (Traditional, ages 8–13).

Misty of Chincoteague by Marguerite Henry. Illustrated by Wesley Dennis. Rand (Animal realism [horse], ages 9–12).

1949 *King of the Wind* by Marguerite Henry. Illustrated by Wesley Dennis. Rand (Historical fiction [Morocco, Europe, 1700s], ages 9–12).

Honor Books:

Seabird by Holling Clancy Holling. Houghton (Informational, ages 9–12).

Daughter of the Mountains by Louise Rankin. Viking (Realism, ages 9–11).

My Father's Dragon by Ruth S. Gannett. Random (Fantasy, ages 6–9).

Story of the Negro by Arna Bontemps. Knopf (Informational, ages 10–YA).

1950 *The Door in the Wall* by Marguerite de Angeli. Doubleday (Historical fiction [England, 1300s], ages 9–11).

Honor Books:

Tree of Freedom by Rebecca Caudill. Viking (Historical fiction [USA, 1780s], ages 10–12).

The Blue Cat of Castle Town by Catherine Coblentz. McKay/Longmans (Traditional, ages 9–YA).

Kildee House by Rutherford Montgomery. Doubleday (Realism, ages 8–12).

George Washington by Genevieve Foster. Scribner's (Biography, ages 8–11).

Song of the Pines by Walter and Marion Havighurst. Holt (Historical fiction [USA, 1850s], ages YA).

1951 *Amos Fortune, Free Man* by Elizabeth Yates. Illustrated by Nora Unwin. Dutton (Biography, ages 9–11).

Honor Books:

Better Known as Johnny Appleseed by Mabel Leigh Hunt. Lippincott (Biography, ages 11–YA).

Gandhi, Fighter Without a Sword by Jeanette Eaton. Morrow (Biography, ages 11–YA).

Abraham Lincoln, Friend of the People by Clara I. Judson. Follett (Biography, ages 9–13).

The Story of Appleby Capple by Anne Parrish. Harper (Fantasy, ages 6–8).

1952 *Ginger Pye* by Eleanor Estes. Harcourt (Realism, ages 8–10).

Honor Books:

Americans Before Columbus by Elizabeth Chesley Baity. Viking (Informational, ages 10–YA).

Minn of the Mississippi by Holling Clancy Holling. Houghton (Informational, ages 7–9).

The Defender by Nicholas Kalashnikoff. Scribner's (Realism, ages 9–13).

The Light at Tern Rock by Julia L. Sauer. Viking (Realism, ages 7–9).

The Apple and the Arrow by Mary and Conrad Buff. Houghton (Biography, ages 8–10).

1953 *Secret of the Andes* by Ann Nolan Clark. Illustrated by Jean Charlot. Viking (Realism/Multicultural [Native-American], ages 11–13).

Honor Books:

Charlotte's Web by E. B. White. Harper (Animal fantasy, ages 7–9).

Moccasin Trail by Eloise J. McGraw. Coward-McCann (Historical fiction [USA, 1830s], ages 11–YA).

Red Sails to Capri by Ann Weil. Viking (Historical fiction [Italy, 1826], ages 9–11).

The Bears on Hemlock Mountain by Alice Dalgliesh. Scribner's (Historical fiction [USA, 1800s], ages 6–9).

Birthdays of Freedom, Vol. 1 by Genevieve Foster. Scribner's (Informational/Biography, ages 10–13).

1954 And Now Miguel by Joseph Krumgold. Illustrated by Jean Charlot. Crowell (Historical fiction [New Mexico, 1940s], ages 9–12).

Honor Books:

All Alone by Claire Huchet Bishop. Viking (Realism, ages 8–11).

Shadrach by Meindert DeJong. Harper (Animal realism, ages 8–10).

Hurry Home, Candy by Meindert DeJong. Harper (Animal realism, ages 8–10).

Theodore Roosevelt, Fighting Patriot by Clara I. Judson. Follett (Biography, ages 9–11).

Magic Maize by Mary and Conrad Buff. Houghton (Realism, ages 8–11).

1955 The Wheel on the School by Meindert DeJong. Illustrated by Maurice Sendak. Harper (Realism, ages 8–11).

Honor Books:

The Courage of Sarah Noble by Alice Dalgliesh. Scribner's (Historical fiction [USA, 1707], ages 8–10).

Banner in the Sky by James Ramsey Ullman. Lippincott (Historical fiction [Europe, 1860s], ages 10–YA).

1956 Carry On, Mr. Bowditch by Jean Lee Latham. Houghton (Biography, ages 10–13).

Honor Books:

The Golden Name Day by Jennie D. Lindquist.

Harper (Realism, ages 8–11).

The Secret River by Marjorie Kinnan Rawlings. Scribner's (Fantasy, ages 6–9).

Men, Microscopes and Living Things by Katherine B. Shippen. Viking (Informational, ages 10–YA).

1957 Miracles on Maple Hill by Virginia Sorensen. Illustrated by Beth and Joe Krush. Harcourt (Realism, ages 8–10).

Honor Books:

Old Yeller by Fred Gipson. Harper (Animal realism, ages 9–12).

The House of Sixty Fathers by Meindert DeJong. Harper (Historical fiction [China, 1940s], ages 9–13).

Mr. Justice Holmes by Clara I. Judson. Follett (Biography, ages 9–13).

The Corn Grows Ripe by Dorothy Rhoads. Viking (Realism, ages 9–11).

The Black Fox of Lorne by Marguerite de Angeli. Doubleday (Historical fiction [Scotland, tenth century], ages 9–12).

1958 Rifles for Watie by Harold Keith. Illustrated by Peter Burchard. Crowell (Historical fiction, [USA, 1860s], ages 10–YA).

Honor Books:

The Horsecatcher by Mari Sandoz. Westminster (Realism, ages 11–YA).

Gone-Away Lake by Elizabeth Enright. Harcourt (Realism, ages 8–11).

The Great Wheel by Robert Lawson. Viking (Historical fiction [USA, 1890s], ages 9–12).

Tom Paine, Freedom's Apostle by Leo Gurko. Crowell (Biography, ages 11–YA).

1959 The Witch of Blackbird Pond by Elizabeth George Speare. Houghton (Historical fiction [USA, 1680s], ages 12–YA).

Honor Books:

The Family Under the Bridge by Natalie S. Carlson. Harper (Realism, 8–10).

Along Came a Dog by Meindert DeJong. Harper (Animal realism, ages 9–YA).

Chucaro: Wild Pony of the Pampa by Francis Kalnay. Harcourt (Animal realism, ages 9–13).

The Perilous Road by William O. Steele. Harcourt (Historical fiction [USA, 1860s], ages 9–13).

1960 *Onion John* by Joseph Krumgold. Illustrated by Symeon Shimin. Crowell (Realism, ages 9–12).

Honor Books:

My Side of the Mountain by Jean George. Dutton (Realism, ages 10–12).

America Is Born by Gerald Johnson. Morrow (Informational, ages 9–13).

The Gammage Cup by Carol Kendall. Harcourt (Fantasy [little people], ages 9–12).

1961 *Island of the Blue Dolphins* by Scott O'Dell. Houghton (Historical fiction [USA, 1800s]/Multicultural [Native-American], ages 9–13).

Honor Books:

America Moves Forward by Gerald Johnson. Morrow (Informational, ages 9–13).

Old Ramon by Jack Schaefer. Houghton (Realism, ages 10–YA).

The Cricket in Times Square by George Selden. Farrar (Animal fantasy, ages 7–9).

1962 *The Bronze Bow* by Elizabeth George Speare. Houghton (Historical fiction [Jerusalem, 1st century A.D.], ages 12–YA).

Honor Books:

Frontier Living by Edwin Tunis. World (Informational, ages 10–YA).

The Golden Goblet by Eloise J. McGraw. Coward (Historical fiction [Ancient Egypt], ages 10–YA).

Belling the Tiger by Mary Stolz. Harper (Fantasy, ages 7–9).

1963 *A Wrinkle in Time* by Madeleine L'Engle. Farrar (Fantasy [science fiction], ages 9–12).

Honor Books:

Thistle and Thyme by Sorche Nic Leodhas (pseud. for Leclaire Alger). Holt (Traditional fantasy, ages 7–11).

Men of Athens by Olivia Coolidge. Houghton (Biography, ages 11–YA).

1964 *It's Like This, Cat* by Emily Cheney Neville. Harper (Realism, ages 10–YA).

Honor Books:

Rascal by Sterling North. Dutton (Animal realism, ages 9–11).

The Loner by Esther Wier. McKay/Longmans (Realism, ages 9–13).

1965 *Shadow of a Bull* by Maia Wojciechowska. Atheneum (Realism, ages 10–12).

Honor Book:

Across Five Aprils by Irene Hunt. Follett (Historical fiction [USA, 1860s] (ages 10–13).

1966 *I, Juan de Pareja* by Elizabeth Borten de Treviño. Farrar (Biography, ages 10–12).

Honor Books:

The Black Cauldron by Lloyd Alexander. Holt (Fantasy [quest], ages 10–12).

The Animal Family by Randall Jarrell. Pantheon (Fantasy, ages 10–13).

The Noonday Friends by Mary Stolz. Harper (Realism, ages 9–11).

1967 *Up a Road Slowly* by Irene Hunt. Follett (Realism, ages 10–YA).

Honor Books:

The King's Fifth by Scott O'Dell. Houghton (Historical fiction [Spain, 1500s], ages 10–12).

Zlateh the Goat and Other Stories by Isaac Bashevis Singer. Harper (Fantasy, ages 8–11).

The Jazz Man by Mary H. Weik. Atheneum (Realism, ages 9–12).

1968 *From the Mixed-up Files of Mrs. Basil E. Frankweiler* by E. L. Konigsburg. Atheneum (Realism, ages 10–12).

Honor Books:

Jennifer, Hecate, Macbeth, William McKinley, and Me, Elizabeth by E. L. Konigsburg. Atheneum (Realism, ages 9–11).

The Black Pearl by Scott O'Dell. Houghton (Realism, ages 9–11).

The Fearsome Inn by Isaac Bashevis Singer. Scribner's (Fantasy, ages 10–YA).

The Egypt Game by Zilpha Keatley Snyder. Atheneum (Realism, ages 9–11).

1969 *The High King* by Lloyd Alexander. Holt (Fantasy [quest], ages 10–12).

Honor Books:

To Be a Slave by Julius Lester. Dial (Informational, ages 11–YA).

When Shlemiel Went to Warsaw and Other Stories by Isaac Bashevis Singer. Farrar (Fantasy, ages 9–YA).

1970   *Sounder* by William H. Armstrong. Harper (Historical fiction [Southern USA, early twentieth century], ages 10–13).

Honor Books:

Our Eddie by Sulamith Ish-Kishor. Pantheon (Realism, ages 11–YA).

The Many Ways of Seeing: An Introduction to the Pleasure of Art by Janet Gaylord Moore. World (Informational, ages 10–YA).

Journey Outside by Mary Q. Steele. Viking (Fantasy, ages 10–13).

1971   *Summer of the Swans* by Betsy Byars. Viking (Realism, ages 10–13).

Honor Books:

Kneeknock Rise by Natalie Babbitt. Farrar (Fantasy, ages 9–13).

Enchantress from the Stars by Sylvia Louise Engdahl. Atheneum (Fantasy [science fiction], ages 11–YA).

Sing Down the Moon by Scott O'Dell. Houghton (Historical fiction [USA, 1860s], ages 12–YA).

1972   *Mrs. Frisby and the Rats of NIMH* by Robert C. O'Brien. Atheneum (Animal fantasy, ages 10–12).

Honor Books:

Incident at Hawk's Hill by Allan W. Eckert. Little, Brown (Historical fiction [Canada, 1870]/Animal realism, ages 10–12).

The Planet of Junior Brown by Virginia Hamilton. Macmillan (Realism, ages 11–YA).

The Tombs of Atuan by Ursula K. LeGuin. Atheneum (Fantasy [quest], ages 10–YA).

Annie and the Old One by Miska Miles. Little, Brown. (Picture book; Realism/Multicultural [Native-American], ages 8–10).

The Headless Cupid by Zilpha Keatley Snyder. Atheneum (Realism [mystery], ages 10–12).

1973   *Julie of the Wolves* by Jean Craighead George. Harper (Realism/Multicultural [Native-American], ages 10–13).

Honor Books:

Frog and Toad Together by Arnold Lobel. Harper (Picture book; Animal fantasy, ages 3–7).

The Upstairs Room by Johanna Reiss. Crowell (Historical fiction [Holland, 1940s], ages 9–13).

The Witches of Worm by Zilpha Keatley Snyder. Atheneum (Realism, ages 10–12).

1974   *The Slave Dancer* by Paula Fox. Bradbury (Historical fiction [USA, Africa, 1840s], ages 10–13).

Honor Book:

The Dark Is Rising by Susan Cooper. Atheneum/McElderry (Fantasy [quest], ages 11–YA).

1975   *M. C. Higgins, the Great* by Virginia Hamilton. Macmillan (Realism/Multicultural [African-American], ages 10–13).

Honor Books:

Figgs & Phantoms by Ellen Raskin. Dutton (Realism, ages 10–13).

My Brother Sam Is Dead by James Lincoln Collier and Christopher Collier. Four Winds (Historical fiction [Colonial America, 1700s], ages 10–YA).

The Perilous Gard by Elizabeth Marie Pope. Houghton (Historical fiction [England, 1558], ages 12–YA).

Philip Hall Likes Me. I Reckon Maybe by Bette Greene. Dial (Realism/Multicultural [African-American], ages 9–11).

1976   *The Grey King* by Susan Cooper. Atheneum/McElderry (Fantasy [quest], ages 11–YA).

Honor Books:

The Hundred Penny Box by Sharon Bell Mathis. Viking (Realism/Multicultural [African-American], ages 8–11).

Dragonwings by Laurence Yep. Harper (Historical fiction [San Francisco, 1903–1909]/Multicultural [Chinese-American], ages 10–13).

1977   *Roll of Thunder, Hear My Cry* by Mildred D. Taylor. Dial (Historical fiction [Mississippi, 1934]/Multicultural [African-American], ages 9–13).

Honor Books:

Abel's Island by William Steig. Farrar (Animal fantasy, ages 8–10).

A String in the Harp by Nancy Bond. Atheneum/McElderry (Fantasy, ages 11–13).

1978 ***The Bridge to Terabithia*** by Katherine Paterson. Crowell (Realism, ages 9–11).

Honor Books:

Anpao: An American Indian Odyssey by Jamake Highwater. Lippincott (Traditional fantasy/Multicultural [Native-American], ages 10–12).

Ramona and Her Father by Beverly Cleary. Morrow (Realism, ages 7–9).

1979 ***The Westing Game*** by Ellen Raskin. Dutton (Realism [mystery], ages 10–12).

Honor Book:

The Great Gilly Hopkins by Katherine Paterson. Crowell (Realism, ages 9–12).

1980 ***A Gathering of Days: A New England Girl's Journal, 1830–32*** by Joan Blos. Scribner's (Historical fiction [New England, 1830s], ages 11–YA).

Honor Book:

The Road from Home: The Story of an Armenian Girl by David Kherdian. Greenwillow (Historical fiction [Turkey, Greece, 1907–24], ages 11–YA).

1981 ***Jacob Have I Loved*** by Katherine Paterson. Crowell (Historical fiction [USA, 1940s], ages 12–YA).

Honor Books:

The Fledgling by Jane Langton. Harper (Fantasy, ages 9–11).

A Ring of Endless Light by Madeleine L'Engle. Farrar (Fantasy [science fiction], ages 10–12).

1982 ***A Visit to William Blake's Inn: Poems for Innocent and Experienced Travelers*** by Nancy Willard. Illustrated by Alice and Martin Provensen. Harcourt (Picture book/ Poetry, ages 9–11).

Honor Books:

Ramona Quimby, Age 8 by Beverly Cleary. Morrow (Realism, ages 7–9).

Upon the Head of the Goat: A Childhood in Hungary, 1939–1944 by Aranka Siegal. Farrar (Historical fiction, ages 10–13).

1983 ***Dicey's Song*** by Cynthia Voigt. Atheneum (Realism, ages 9–12).

Honor Books:

The Blue Sword by Robin McKinley. Greenwillow (Fantasy [quest], ages 12–YA).

Dr. DeSoto by William Steig. Farrar (Picture book/Animal fantasy, ages 5–8).

Graven Images by Paul Fleischman. Harper (Fantasy, ages 10–12).

Homesick: My Own Story by Jean Fritz. Putnam (Biography, ages 9–11).

Sweet Whispers, Brother Rush by Virginia Hamilton. Philomel (Fantasy/Multicultural [African-American], ages 12–YA).

1984 ***Dear Mr. Henshaw*** by Beverly Cleary. Morrow (Realism, ages 8–10).

Honor Books:

The Sign of the Beaver by Elizabeth George Speare. Houghton (Historical fiction [Colonial America], ages 9–11).

A Solitary Blue by Cynthia Voigt. Atheneum (Realism, ages 11–13).

Sugaring Time by Kathryn Lasky. Photographs by Christopher Knight. Macmillan (Informational, ages 9–13).

The Wish Giver by Bill Brittain. Harper (Fantasy, ages 9–12).

1985 ***The Hero and the Crown*** by Robin McKinley. Greenwillow (Fantasy [quest], ages 12–YA).

Honor Books:

Like Jake and Me by Mavis Jukes. Illustrated by Lloyd Bloom. Knopf (Picture book; Realism, ages 7–9).

The Moves Make the Man by Bruce Brooks. Harper (Realism/Multicultural [African-American], ages 11–YA).

One-Eyed Cat by Paula Fox. Bradbury (Realism, ages 9–12).

1986 ***Sarah, Plain and Tall*** by Patricia MacLachlan. Harper (Historical fiction [USA western frontier, 1800s], ages 8–10).

Honor Books:

Commodore Perry in the Land of the Shogun by Rhoda Blumberg. Lothrop (Informational, ages 9–13).

Dogsong by Gary Paulsen. Bradbury (Realism/Multicultural [Native American], ages 10–13).

1987   *The Whipping Boy* by Sid Fleischman. Greenwillow (Historical fiction [Medieval England], ages 9–11).

Honor Books:

On My Honor by Marion Dane Bauer. Clarion (Realism, ages 8–11).

Volcano: The Eruption and Healing of Mount St. Helens by Patricia Lauber. Bradbury (Informational, ages 8–13).

A Fine White Dust by Cynthia Rylant. Bradbury (Realism, ages 10–12).

1988   *Lincoln: A Photobiography* by Russell Freedman. Clarion (Biography, ages 8–12).

Honor Books:

After the Rain by Norma Fox Mazer. Morrow (Realism, ages 12–YA).

Hatchet by Gary Paulsen. Bradbury (Realism, ages 9–13).

1989   *Joyful Noise: Poems for Two Voices* by Paul Fleischman. Harper (Poetry, ages 9–YA).

Honor Books:

In the Beginning: Creation Stories from Around the World by Virginia Hamilton. Harcourt (Traditional fantasy, ages 9–YA).

Scorpions by Walter Dean Myers. Harper (Realism/Multicultural [African-American, Hispanic-American], ages 10–13).

1990   *Number the Stars* by Lois Lowry. Houghton (Historical fiction [Denmark, 1940s], ages 8–10).

Honor Books:

Afternoon of the Elves by Janet Taylor Lisle. Orchard (Realism, ages 10–13).

Shabanu, Daughter of the Wind by Suzanne Fisher Staples. Knopf (Realism, ages 12–YA).

The Winter Room by Gary Paulsen. Orchard (Realism, ages 10–13).

1991   *Maniac Magee* by Jerry Spinelli. Little, Brown (Realism, ages 9–13).

Honor Book:

The True Confessions of Charlotte Doyle by Avi. Orchard (Historical fiction [England, USA, 1830], ages 10–13).

1992   *Shiloh* by Phyllis Reynolds Naylor. Atheneum (Animal realism, ages 8–10).

Honor Books:

Nothing but the Truth by Avi. Orchard (Realism, ages 10–14).

The Wright Brothers: How They Invented the Airplane by Russell Freedman. Holiday (Informational/Biography, ages 9–12).

1993   *Missing May* by Cynthia Rylant. Orchard (Realism, ages 10–13).

Honor Books:

The Dark-Thirty: Southern Tales of the Supernatural by Patricia McKissack. Knopf (Modern fantasy/Ghost stories [African-American], ages 8–12).

Somewhere in Darkness by Walter Dean Myers. Scholastic (Realism [African-American], ages 11–14).

What Hearts by Bruce Brooks. HarperCollins (Realism, ages 11–14).

1994   *The Giver* by Lois Lowry. Houghton (Modern Fantasy, ages 10–12).

Honor Books:

Crazy Lady by Jane Leslie Conly. HarperCollins (Realism, ages 10–12).

Dragon's Gate by Laurence Yep. HarperCollins (Historical fiction [China, USA West, 1860s], ages 12–14).

Eleanor Roosevelt: A Life of Discovery by Russell Freedman. Clarion (Biography, ages 10–14).

1995   *Walk Two Moons* by Sharon Creech. HarperCollins (Realism [Native American], ages 11–14).

Honor Books:

Catherine, Called Birdy by Karen Cushman. Clarion (Historical fiction, [England, 1200s] ages 10–14).

The Ear, the Eye and the Arm by Nancy Farmer. Orchard (Modern fantasy, ages 10–13).

Boston Globe—Horn Book Awards

These awards, sponsored by *The Boston Globe* and *The Horn Book Magazine,* are given to an author for outstanding fiction or poetry for children, to an illustrator for outstanding illustration in a children's book, and, since 1976, to an author for outstanding nonfiction for children.

1967 Text: *The Little Fishes* by Erik Christian Haugaard. Houghton.

Illustration: *London Bridge Is Falling Down* by Peter Spier. Doubleday.

1968 Text: *The Spring Rider* by John Lawson. Crowell.

Illustration: *Tikki Tikki Tembo* by Arlene Mosel. Illustrated by Blair Lent. Holt.

1969 Text: *A Wizard of Earthsea* by Ursula K. Le Guin. Houghton.

Illustration: *The Adventures of Paddy* Pork by John S. Goodall. Harcourt.

1970 Text: *The Intruder* by John Rowe Townsend. Lippincott.

Illustration: *Hi, Cat!* by Ezra Jack Keats. Macmillan.

1971 Text: *A Room Made of Windows* by Eleanor Cameron. Atlantic/Little.

Illustration: *If I Built a Village* by Kazue Mizumura. Crowell.

1972 Text: *Tristan and Iseult* by Rosemary Sutcliff. Dutton.

Illustration: *Mr. Gumpy's Outing* by John Burningham. Holt.

1973 Text: *The Dark Is Rising* by Susan Cooper. Atheneum/McElderry.

Illustration: *King Stork* by Trina Schart Hyman. Little, Brown.

1974 Text: *M.C. Higgins, the Great* by Virginia Hamilton. Macmillan.

Illustration: *Jambo Means Hello* by Muriel Feelings. Illustrated by Tom Feelings. Dial.

1975 Text: *Transport 7–41-R* by T. Degens. Viking.

Illustration: *Anno's Alphabet* by Mitsumasa Anno. Crowell.

1976 Fiction: *Unleaving* by Jill Paton Walsh, Farrar.

Nonfiction: *Voyaging to Cathay: Americans in the China Trade* by Alfred Tamarin and Shirley Glubok. Viking.

Illustration: *Thirteen* by Remy Charlip and Jerry Joyner. Parents.

1977 Fiction: *Child of the Owl* by Laurence Yep. Harper.

Nonfiction: *Chance, Luck and Density* by Peter Dickinson. Atlantic/Little, Brown.

Illustration: *Granfa' Grig Had a Pig and Other Rhymes* by Wallace Tripp. Little, Brown.

1978 Fiction: *The Westing Game* by Ellen Raskin. Dutton.

Nonfiction: *Mischling, Second Degree: My Childhood in Nazi Germany* by Ilse Koehn. Greenwillow.

Illustration: *Anno's Journey* by Mitsumasa Anno. Philomel.

1979 Fiction: *Humbug Mountain* by Sid Fleischman. Atlantic/Little, Brown.

Nonfiction: *The Road from Home: The Story of an Armenian Girl* by David Kherdian. Greenwillow.

Illustration: *The Snowman* by Raymond Briggs. Random.

1980 Fiction: *Conrad's War* by Andrew Davies. Crown.

Nonfiction: *Building: The Fight Against Gravity* by Mario Salvadori. Atheneum/ McElderry.

Illustration: *The Garden of Abdul Gasazi* by Chris Van Allsburg. Houghton.

1981 Fiction: *The Leaving* by Lynn Hall. Scribner's.

Nonfiction: *The Weaver's Gift* by Kathryn Lasky. Warne.

Illustration: *Outside Over There* by Maurice Sendak. Harper.

1982   Fiction: *Playing Beatie Bow* by Ruth Park. Atheneum.

Nonfiction: *Upon the Head of the Goat: A Childhood in Hungary, 1939–1944* by Aranka Siegal. Farrar.

Illustration: *A Visit to William Blake's Inn: Poems for Innocent and Experienced Travelers* by Nancy Willard. Illustrated by Alice and Martin Provensen. Harcourt.

1983   Fiction: *Sweet Whispers, Brother Rush* by Virginia Hamilton. Philomel.

Nonfiction: *Behind Barbed Wire: The Imprisonment of Japanese Americans During World War II.* by Daniel S. Davis. Dutton.

Illustration: *A Chair for My Mother* by Vera B. Williams. Greenwillow.

1984   Fiction: *A Little Fear* by Patricia Wrightson. McElderry/Atheneum.

Nonfiction: *The Double Life of Pocahontas* by Jean Fritz. Putnam.

Illustration: *Jonah and the Great Fish* retold and illustrated by Warwick Hutton. McElderry/Atheneum.

1985   Fiction: *The Moves Make the Man* by Bruce Brooks. Harper.

Nonfiction: *Commodore Perry in the Land of the Shogun* by Rhoda Blumberg. Lothrop.

Illustration: *Mama Don't Allow* by Thatcher Hurd. Harper.

1986   Fiction: *In Summer Light* by Zibby Oneal. Viking Kestrel.

Nonfiction: *Auks, Rocks, and the Odd Dinosaur* by Peggy Thomson. Crowell.

Illustration: *The Paper Crane* by Molly Bang. Greenwillow.

1987   Fiction: *Rabble Starkey* by Lois Lowry. Houghton.

Nonfiction: *Pilgrims of Plimouth* by Marcia Sewall. Atheneum.

Illustration: *Mufaro's Beautiful Daughters* by John Steptoe. Lothrop.

1988   Fiction: *The Friendship* by Mildred Taylor. Dial.

Nonfiction: *Anthony Burns: The Defeat and Triumph of a Fugitive Slave* by Virginia Hamilton. Knopf.

Illustration: *The Boy of the Three-Year Nap* by Diane Snyder. Illustrated by Allen Say. Houghton.

1989   Fiction: *The Village by the Sea* by Paula Fox. Orchard.

Nonfiction: *The Way Things Work* by David Macaulay. Houghton.

Illustration: *Shy Charles* by Rosemary Wells. Dial.

1990   Fiction: *Maniac Magee* by Jerry Spinelli. Little, Brown.

Nonfiction: *The Great Little Madison* by Jean Fritz. Putnam.

Illustration: *Lon Po Po: A Red-Riding Hood Story from China* retold and illustrated by Ed Young. Philomel.

1991   Fiction: *The True Confessions of Charlotte Doyle* by Avi. Orchard.

Nonfiction: *Appalachia: The Voices of Sleeping Birds* by Cynthia Rylant. Illustrated by Barry Moser. Harcourt.

Illustration: *The Tale of the Mandarin Ducks* retold by Katherine Paterson. Illustrated by Leo and Diane Dillon. Lodestar.

1992   Fiction: *Missing May* by Cynthia Rylant, Orchard.

Nonfiction: *Talking with Artists* by Pat Cummings, Bradbury.

Illustration: *Seven Blind Mice* by Ed Young, Philomel.

1993   Fiction: *Ajeemah and His Son* by James Berry, Harper.

Nonfiction: *Sojourner Truth: Ain't I a Woman?* by Patricia and Fredrick McKissack, Scholastic.

Illustration: *The Fortune-Tellers* by Lloyd Alexander. Illustrated by Trina Schart Hyman, Dutton.

1994 Fiction: *Scooter* by Vera B. Williams, Greenwillow.

Nonfiction: *Eleanor Roosevelt: A Life of Discovery* by Russell Freedman, Clarion.

Illustration: *Grandfather's Journey* by Allen Say, Houghton.

Great Britain

Kate Greenaway Medal

This award, sponsored by the British Library Association, is given to the illustrator of the most distinguished work in illustration in a children's book first published in the United Kingdom during the preceding year.

1957 *Tim All Alone* by Edward Ardizzone. Oxford.

1958 *Mrs. Easter and the Storks* by V. H. Drummond. Faber.

1959 No award

1960 *Kashtanka and a Bundle of Ballads* by William Stobbs. Oxford.

1961 *Old Winkle and the Seagulls* by Elizabeth Rose. Illustrated by Gerald Rose. Faber.

1962 *Mrs. Cockle's Cat* by Philippa Pearce. Illustrated by Anthony Maitland. Kestrel.

1963 *Brian Wildsmith's ABC* by Brian Wildsmith. Oxford.

1964 *Borka* by John Burningham. Jonathan Cape.

1965 *Shakespeare's Theatre* by C. W. Hodges. Oxford.

1966 *Three Poor Tailors* by Victor Ambrus. Hamilton.

1967 *Mother Goose Treasury* by Raymond Briggs. Hamilton.

1968 *Charlie, Charlotte & the Golden Canary* by Charles Keeping. Oxford.

1969 *Dictionary of Chivalry* by Grant Uden. Illustrated by Pauline Baynes. Kestrel.

1970 *The Quangle-Wangle's Hat* by Edward Lear. Illustrated by Helen Oxenbury. Heinemann.

Dragon of an Ordinary Family by Margaret Mahy. Illustrated by Helen Oxenbury. Heinemann.

1971 *Mr. Gumpy's Outing* by John Burningham. Jonathan Cape.

1972 *The Kingdom under the Sea* by Jan Piénkowski. Jonathan Cape.

1973 *The Woodcutter's Duck* by Krystyna Turska. Hamilton.

1974 *Father Christmas* by Raymond Briggs. Hamilton.

1975 *The Wind Blew* by Pat Hutchins. Bodley Head.

1976 *Horses in Battle* by Victor Ambrus. Oxford.

Mishka by Victor Ambrus. Oxford.

1977 *The Post Office Cat* by Gail E. Haley. Bodley Head.

1978 *Dogger* by Shirley Hughes. Bodley Head.

1979 *Each Peach Pear Plum* by Janet and Allan Ahlberg. Kestrel.

1980 *The Haunted House* by Jan Piénkowski. Heinemann.

1981 *Mr. Magnolia* by Quentin Blake. Jonathan Cape.

1982 *The Highwayman* by Alfred Noyes. Illustrated by Charles Keeping. Oxford.

1983 *Long Neck and Thunder Foot*. Kestrel; and *Sleeping Beauty and Other Favorite Fairy Tales*. Gollancz. Both illustrated by Michael Foreman.

1984 *Gorilla* by Anthony Browne. Julia MacRae Books.

1985 *Hiawatha's Childhood* by Errol LeCain. Faber.

1986 *Sir Gawain and the Loathly Lady* by Selina Hastings. Illustrated by Juan Wijngaard. Walker.

1987 *Snow White in New York* by Fiona French. Oxford.

1988 *Crafty Chameleon* by Mwenye Hadithi. Illustrated by Adrienne Kennaway. Hodder & Stoughton.

1989 *Can't You Sleep, Little Bear?* by Martin Waddell. Illustrated by Barbara Firth. Walker.

1990 *War Boy: A Country Childhood* by Michael Foreman. Arcade.

1991   *The Whale's Song* by Dyan Sheldon. Illustrated by Gary Blythe. Dial.

1992   *The Jolly Christmas Postman* by Janet and Allan Ahlberg. Heinemann.

1993   *Zoo* by Anthony Browne. Julia MacRae.

1994   *Black Ships Before Troy* retold by Rosemary Sutcliff. Illustrated by Alan Lee. Frances Lincoln.

Carnegie Medal

This award, sponsored by the British Library Association, is given to the author of the most outstanding children's book first published in English in the United Kingdom during the preceding year.

1937   *Pigeon Post* by Arthur Ransome. Cape.

1938   *The Family from One End Street* by Eve Garnett. Muller.

1939   *The Circus Is Coming* by Noel Streatfield. Dent.

1940   *Radium Woman* by Eleanor Doorly. Heinemann.

1941   *Visitors from London* by Kitty Barne. Dent.

1942   *We Couldn't Leave Dinah* by Mary Treadgold. Penguin.

1943   *The Little Grey Men* by B. B. Eyre & Spottiswoode.

1944   No award

1945   *The Wind on the Moon* by Eric Linklater. Macmillan.

1946   No award

1947   *The Little White Horse* by Elizabeth Goudge. Brockhampton Press.

1948   *Collected Stories for Children* by Walter de la Mare. Faber.

1949   *Sea Change* by Richard Armstrong. Dent.

1950   *The Story of Your Home* by Agnes Allen. Transatlantic.

1951   *The Lark on the Wing* by Elfrida Vipont Foulds. Oxford.

1952   *The Wool-Pack* by Cynthia Harnett. Methuen.

1953   *The Borrowers* by Mary Norton. Dent.

1954   *A Valley Grows Up* by Edward Osmond. Oxford.

1955   *Knight Crusader* by Ronald Welch. Oxford.

1956   *The Little Bookroom* by Eleanor Farjeon. Oxford.

1957   *The Last Battle* by C. S. Lewis. Bodley Head.

1958   *A Grass Rope* by William Mayne. Oxford.

1959   *Tom's Midnight Garden* by Philippa Pearce. Oxford.

1960   *The Lantern Bearers* by Rosemary Sutcliff. Oxford.

1961   *The Making of Man* by I. W. Cornwall. Phoenix.

1962   *A Stranger at Green Knowe* by Lucy Boston. Faber.

1963   *The Twelve and the Genii* by Pauline Clarke. Faber.

1964   *Time of Trial* by Hester Burton. Oxford.

1965   *Nordy Banks* by Sheena Porter. Oxford.

1966   *The Grange at High Force* by Philip Turner. Oxford.

1967   No award

1968   *The Owl Service* by Alan Garner. Collins.

1969   *The Moon in the Cloud* by Rosemary Harris. Faber.

1970   *The Edge of the Cloud* by K. M. Peyton. Oxford.

1971   *The God Beneath the Sea* by Leon Garfield and Edward Blishen. Kestrel.

1972   *Josh* by Ivan Southall. Angus and Robertson.

1973   *Watership Down* by Richard Adams. Rex Collings.

1974   *The Ghost of Thomas Kempe* by Penelope Lively. Heinemann.

1975   *The Stronghold* by Mollie Hunter. Hamilton.

1976   *The Machine-Gunners* by Robert Westall. Macmillan.

1977   *Thunder and Lightnings* by Jan Mark. Kestrel.

1978   *The Turbulent Term of Tyke Tiler* by Gene Kemp. Faber.

1979 *The Exeter Blitz* by David Rees. Hamish Hamilton.

1980 *Tulku* by Peter Dickinson. Dutton.

1981 *City of Gold* by Peter Dickinson. Gollancz.

1982 *The Scarecrows* by Robert Westall. Chatto and Windus.

1983 *The Haunting* by Margaret Mahy. Dent.

1984 *Handles* by Jan Mark. Kestrel.

1985 *The Changeover* by Margaret Mahy. Dent.

1986 *Storm* by Kevin Crossley-Holland. Heinemann.

1987 *Granny Was a Buffer Girl* by Berlie Doherty. Methuen.

1988 *The Ghost Drum* by Susan Price. Faber.

1989 *Pack of Lies* by Geraldine McCaughrean. Oxford.

1990 *My War with Goggle-Eyes* by Anne Fine. Joy Street.

1991 *Wolf* by Gillian Cross. Oxford.

1992 *Dear Nobody* by Berlie Doherty. Hamish Hamilton.

1993 *Flour Babies* by Anne Fine. Hamish Hamilton.

1994 *Stone Cold* by Robert Swindells. Hamish Hamilton.

Canada

Amelia Frances Howard-Gibbon Medal

This award, sponsored by the Canadian Library Association, is given to an illustrator for the most distinguished illustrations in a children's book published in Canada during the preceding year. Only Canadian citizens are eligible for this award.

1971 *The Wind Has Wings* edited by Mary Alice Downie and Barbara Robertson. Illustrated by Elizabeth Cleaver. Oxford.

1972 *A Child in Prison Camp* by Shizuye Takashima. Tundra.

1973 *Au Dé là du Soleil/Beyond the Sun* by Jacques de Roussan. Tundra.

1974 *A Prairie Boy's Winter* by William Kurelek. Tundra.

1975 *The Sleighs of My Childhood/Les Traîneaux de Mon Enfance* by Carlo Italiano. Tundra.

1976 *A Prairie Boy's Summer* by William Kurelek. Tundra.

1977 *Down by Jim Long's Stage: Rhymes for Children and Young Fish* by Al Pittman. Illustrated by Pam Hall. Breakwater.

1978 *The Loon's Necklace* by William Toye. Illustrated by Elizabeth Cleaver. Oxford.

1979 *A Salmon for Simon* by Betty Waterton. Illustrated by Ann Blades. Douglas & McIntyre.

1980 *The Twelve Dancing Princesses* retold by Janet Lunn. Illustrated by László Gál. Methuen.

1981 *The Trouble with Princesses* by Christie Harris. Illustrated by Douglas Tait. McClelland & Stewart.

1982 *Ytek and the Arctic Orchid: An Inuit Legend* by Garnet Hewitt. Illustrated by Heather Woodall. Douglas & McIntyre.

1983 *Chester's Barn* by Lindee Climo. Tundra.

1984 *Zoom at Sea* by Tim Wynne-Jones. Illustrated by Ken Nutt. Douglas & McIntyre.

1985 *Chin Chiang and the Dragon's Dance* by Ian Wallace. Groundwood.

1986 *Zoom Away* by Tim Wynne-Jones. Illustrated by Ken Nutt. Douglas & McIntyre.

1987 *Moonbeam on a Cat's Ear* by Marie-Louise Gay. Stoddard.

1988 *Rainy Day Magic* by Marie-Louise Gay. Hodder & Stoughton.

1989 *Amos's Sweater* by Janet Lunn. Illustrated by Kim LaFave. Douglas & McIntyre.

1990 *Til All the Stars Have Fallen: Canadian Poems for Children* selected by David Booth. Illustrated by Kady MacDonald Denton. Kids Can Press.

1991 *The Orphan Boy* by Tololwa M. Mollel. Illustrated by Paul Morin. Oxford.

1992 *Waiting for the Whales* by Ron Lightburn. Illustrated by Sheryl McFarlane. Orca Books.

1993 *The Dragon's Pearl* by Julie Lawson. Illustrated by Paul Morin. Oxford.

1994 *Last Leaf First Snowflake to Fall* by Leo Yerxa. Groundwood.

Canadian Children's Book of the Year Award

This award, sponsored by the Canadian Library Association, is given to the author of a children's book of outstanding literary merit. Since 1954, an equivalent award has been presented to the author of a children's book published in French. Only Canadian citizens are eligible for these awards.

1947 *Starbuck Valley Winter* by Roderick Haig-Brown. Collins.

1948 *Kristli's Trees* by Mabel Dunham. Hale.

1949 No award

1950 *Franklin of the Arctic* by Richard S. Lambert. McClelland & Stewart.

1951 No award

1952 *The Sun Horse* by Catherine Anthony Clark. Macmillan of Canada.

1953 No award

1954 No English award

   Le Vénérable Francois de Montmorency-Laval by Émile S. J. Gervais. Comité des Fondateurs de l'Église Canadienne.

1955 No award

1956 *Train for Tiger Lily* by Louise Riley, Macmillan of Canada.

   No French award

1957 *Glooskap's Country* by Cyrus Macmillan. Oxford.

   No French award

1958 *Lost in the Barrens* by Farley Mowat. Little.

   Le Chevalier du Roi by Beatrice Clément. Atelier.

1959 *The Dangerous Cove* by John F. Hayes. Copp Clark.

   Un Drôle de Petit Cheval by Hélène Flamme. Leméac.

1960 *The Golden Phoenix* by Marius Barbeau and Michael Hornyansky. Walck/ Oxford.

   L'Été Enchanté by Paule Daveluy. Atelier.

1961 *The St. Lawrence* by William Toye. Oxford.

   Plantes Vagabondes by Marcelle Gauvreau. Centre de Psychologie et de Pédagogie.

1962 No English award

   Les Îles du Roi Maha Maha II by Claude Aubry. Pélican.

1963 *The Incredible Journey* by Sheila Burnford. Little, Brown.

   Drôle D'Automne by Paul Daveluy. Pélican.

1964 *The Whale People* by Roderick Haig-Brown. Collins.

   Férie by Cécile Chabot. Beauchemin.

1965 *Tales of Nanabozho* by Dorothy Reid. Oxford.

   Le Loup de Nöel by Claude Aubry. Centre de Psychologie et de Pédagogie.

1966 *Tiktá Liktak* by James Houston. Kestrel/ Longmans.

   Le Chêne des Tempêtes by Andrée Mallet-Hobden. Fides.

   The Double Knights by James McNeal. Walck.

   Le Wapiti by Monique Corriveau. Jeunesse.

1967 *Raven's Cry* by Christie Harris. McClelland & Stewart.

   No French award

1968 *The White Archer* by James Houston. Academic/Kestrel.

   Légendes Indiennes du Canada by Claude Mélancon. Editions du Jour.

1969 *And Tomorrow the Stars* by Kay Hill. Dodd.

   No French award

1970 *Sally Go Round the Sun* by Edith Fowke. McClelland & Stewart.

   La Merveilleuse Histoire de la Naissance by Lionel Gendron. Les Editions de l'Homme.

1971 *Cartier Discovers the St. Lawrence* by William Toye. Oxford.

   La Surprise de Dame Chenille by Henriette Major. Centre de Psychologie et de Pédagogie.

1972 *Mary of Mile 18* by Ann Blades. Tundra.

No French award

1973 *The Marrow of the World* by Ruth Nichols. Macmillan.

> *Le Petit Sapin Qui a Poussé sur Une Étoile* by Simone Bussières. Laurentiennes.

1974 *The Miraculous Hind* by Elizabeth Cleaver. Holt.

No French award

1975 *Alligator Pie* by Dennis Lee. Macmillan.

No French award

1976 *Jacob Two-Two Meets the Hooded Fang* by Mordecai Richler. McClelland & Stewart.

No French award

1977 *Mouse Woman and the Vanished Princesses* by Christie Harris. McClelland & Stewart.

No French award

1978 *Garbage Delight* by Dennis Lee. Macmillan.

No French award

1979 *Hold Fast* by Kevin Major. Clarke, Irwin.

No French award

1980 *River Runners: A Tale of Hardship and Bravery* by James Houston. McClelland & Stewart.

No French award

1981 *The Violin Maker's Gift* by Donn Kushner. Macmillan.

No French award

1982 *The Root Cellar* by Janet Lunn. Dennys.

No French award

1983 *Up to Low* by Brian Doyle. Douglas & McIntyre.

No French award

1984 *Sweetgrass* by Jan Hudson. Tree Frog Press.

No French award

1985 *Mama's Going to Buy You a Mockingbird* by Jean Little. Penguin.

No French award

1986 *Julie* by Cora Taylor. Western.

No French award

1987 *Shadow in Hawthorn Bay* by Janet Lunn. Dennys.

No French award

1988 *A Handful of Time* by Kit Pearson. Penguin.

No French award

1989 *Easy Avenue* by Brian Doyle. Groundwood.

No French award

1990 *The Sky Is Falling* by Kit Pearson. Penguin.

No French award

1991 *Redwork* by Michael Bedard. Dennys.

No French award

1992 *Eating Between the Lines* by Kevin Major. Doubleday.

No French award

1993 *Ticket to Curlew* by Celia Barker Lottridge. Groundwood.

No French award

1994 *Some of the Kinder Planets* by Tim Wynne-Jones. Groundwood.

No French award

Australia

Australian Children's Books of the Year Awards

The Australian Children's Book Council sponsors three awards for excellence in children's books: The Picture Book of the Year Award; The Children's Book of the Year for Younger Readers (for books that bridge the gap between picture books and longer novels); and The Children's Book of the Year for Older Readers.

Australian Picture Book of the Year Award

1956 *Wish and the Magic Nut* by Peggy Barnard. Illustrated by Shelia Hawkins. Sands.

1957 No award

1958 *Piccaninny Walkabout* by Axel Poignant. Angus & Robertson.

1959–1964 No awards

1965 *Hugo's Zoo* by Elizabeth MacIntyre. Angus & Robertson.

1966–1968 No awards

1969 *Sly Old Wardrobe* by Ivan Southall. Illustrated by Ted Greenwood. Cheshire.

1970 No award

1971 *Waltzing Matilda* by A. B. Paterson. Illustrated by Desmond Digby.

1972–1973 No awards

1974 *The Bunyip of Berkeley's Creek* by Jenny Wagner. Illustrated by Ron Brooks. Kestrel.

1975 *The Man from Ironbark* by A. B. Paterson. Illustrated by Quentin Hole. Collins.

1976 *The Rainbow Serpent* by Dick Roughsey. Collins.

1977 *ABC of Monsters* by Deborah Niland. Hodder & Stoughton.

1978 *John Brown, Rose and the Midnight Cat* by Jenny Wagner. Illustrated by Ron Brooks. Kestrel.

1979 *The Quinkins* written and illustrated by Percy Trezise and Dick Roughsey. Collins.

1980 *One Dragon's Dream* by Peter Pavey. Nelson.

1981 No award

1982 *Sunshine* by Jan Ormerod. Kestrel.

1983 *Who Sank the Boat?* by Pamela Allen. Nelson.

1984 *Bertie and the Bear* by Pamela Allen, Nelson.

1985 No award

   Highly commended: *The Inch Boy* by Junko Morimoto. Collins.

1986 *Felix and Alexander* written and illustrated by Terry Denton. Oxford.

1987 *Kojuro and the Bears* adapted by Helen Smith. Illustrated by Junko Morimoto. Collins.

1988 *Crusher Is Coming!* by Bob Graham. Lothian.

1989 *Drac and the Gremlins* by Allan Baillie. Illustrated by Jane Tanner. Viking/Kestrel.

   The Eleventh Hour by Graeme Base. Viking/Kestrel.

1990 *The Very Best of Friends* by Margaret Wild. Illustrated by Julie Vivas. Margaret Hamilton.

1991 *Greetings from Sandy Beach* by Bob Graham. Lothian.

1992 *Window* by Jeannie Baker. Julia MacRae.

1993 *Rose Meets Mr Wintergarden* by Bob Graham. Viking/Penguin.

1994 *First Light* by Gary Crew. Illustrated by Peter Gouldthorpe. Lothian.

Australian Children's Book of the Year for Younger Readers Award

1982 *Rummage* by Cristobel Mattingley. Illustrated by Patricia Mullins. Angus & Robertson.

1983 *Thing* by Robin Klein. Illustrated by Allison Lester. Oxford.

1984 *Bernice Knows Best* by Max Dann. Illustrated by Ann James. Oxford.

1985 *Something Special* by Emily Rodda. Illustrated by Noela Young. Angus & Robertson.

1986 *Arkwright* by Mary Steele. Hyland House.

1987 *Pigs Might Fly* by Emily Rodda. Illustrated by Noela Young. Angus & Robertson.

1988 *My Place* by Nadia Wheatley and Donna Rawlins. Collins Dove.

1989 *The Best-Kept Secret* by Emily Rodda. Angus & Robertson.

1990 *Pigs and Honey* by Jeanie Adams. Omnibus.

1991 *Finders Keepers* by Emily Rodda. Omnibus.

1992 *The Magnificent Nose and Other Marvels* by Anna Fienberg. Illustrated by Kim Gamble. Allen and Unwin.

1993 *The Bamboo Flute* by Garry Disher. Collins/Angus & Robertson.

1994 *Rowan of Rin* by Emily Rodda. Omnibus.

Australian Children's Book of the Year for Older Readers Award

1946 *Karrawingi, the Emu* by Leslie Rees. Sands.

1947 No award

1948 *Shackleton's Argonauts* by Frank Hurley. Angus & Robertson.

1949 *Whalers of the Midnight Sun* by Alan

Villiers. Angus & Robertson.

1950 No award

1951 *Verity of Sydney Town* by Ruth Williams. Angus & Robertson.

1952 *The Australia Book* by Eve Pownall. Sands.

1953 *Aircraft of Today and Tomorrow* by J. H. and W. D. Martin. Angus & Robertson.

> *Good Luck to the Rider* by Joan Phipson. Angus & Robertson.

1954 *Australian Legendary* by K. L. Parker. Angus & Robertson.

1955 *The First Walkabout* by H. A. Lindsay and N. B. Tindale. Kestrel.

1956 *The Crooked Snake* by Patricia Wrightson. Angus & Robertson.

1957 *The Boomerang Book of Legendary Tales* by Enid Moodie-Heddle. Kestrel.

1958 *Tiger in the Bush* by Nan Chauncy. Oxford.

1959 *Devil's Hill* by Nan Chauncy. Oxford.

> *Sea Menace* by John Gunn. Constable.

1960 *All the Proud Tribesmen* by Kylie Tennant. Macmillan.

1961 *Tangara* by Nan Chauncy. Oxford.

1962 *The Racketty Street Gang* by H. L. Evers. Hodder & Stoughton.

> *Rafferty Rides a Winner* by Joan Woodbery. Parrish.

1963 *The Family Conspiracy* by Joan Phipson. Angus & Robertson.

1964 *The Green Laurel* by Eleanor Spence. Oxford.

1965 *Pastures of the Blue Crane* by Hesba F. Brinsmead. Oxford.

1966 *Ash Road* by Ivan Southall. Angus & Robertson.

1967 *The Min Min* by Mavis Thorpe Clark. Landsdowne.

1968 *To the Wild Sky* by Ivan Southall. Angus & Robertson.

1969 *When Jays Fly to Barbmo* by Margaret Balderson. Oxford.

1970 *Uhu* by Annette Macarther-Onslow. Ure Smith.

1971 *Bread and Honey* by Ivan Southall. Angus & Robertson.

1972 *Longtime Passing* by Hesba F. Brinsmead. Angus & Robertson.

1973 *Family at the Lookout* by Noreen Shelly. Oxford.

1974 *The Nargun and the Stars* by Patricia Wrightson. Hutchinson.

1975 No award

1976 *Fly West* by Ivan Southall. Angus & Robertson.

1977 *The October Child* by Eleanor Spence. Oxford.

1978 *The Ice Is Coming* by Patricia Wrightson. Hutchinson.

1979 *The Plum-Rain Scroll* by Ruth Manley. Hodder & Stoughton.

1980 *Displaced Person* by Lee Harding. Hyland House.

1981 *Playing Beatie Bow* by Ruth Park. Nelson.

1982 *The Valley Between* by Colin Thiele. Rigby.

1983 *Master of the Grove* by Victor Kelleher. Penguin.

1984 *A Little Fear* by Patricia Wrightson. Hutchinson.

1985 *The True Story of Lilli Stubeck* by James Aldridge. Hyland House.

1986 *The Green Wind* by Thurley Fowler. Rigby.

1987 *All We Know* by Simon French. Angus & Robertson.

1988 *So Much to Tell You* by John Marsden. Walter McVitty Books.

1989 *Beyond the Labyrinth* by Gillian Rubinstein. Hyland House.

1990 *Came Back to Show You I Could Fly* by Robin Klein. Viking/Kestrel.

1991 *Strange Objects* by Gary Crew. Heinemann Australia.

1992 *The House Guest* by Eleanor Nilsson. Viking.

1993 *Looking for Alibrandi* by Melina Marchetta. Penguin.

1994   *The Gathering* by Isobelle Carmody. Penguin.

Angel's Gate by Gary Crew. Heinemann.

New Zealand

Russell Clark Award for Illustrations

This award is given to an illustrator for the most distinguished illustrations for a children's book published in New Zealand the previous year. Only citizens or residents of New Zealand are eligible for this award.

1978   *The House of the People* by Ron L. Bacon. Illustrated by Robert F. Jahnke. Collins.

1979   *Kim* by Bruce Treloar. Collins.

1980–1981   No awards

1982   *Mrs. McGinty and the Bizarre Plant* by Gavin Bishop. Oxford.

1983   No award

1984   *The Tree Witches* by Gwenda Turner. Penguin.

1985   *The Duck in the Gun* by Joy Cowley. Illustrated by Robyn Belton. Shortland.

1986   *A Lion in the Night* by Pamela Allen. Hamilton.

1987   *Taniwha* by Patricia Grace. Illustrated by Robyn Kahukiwa. Viking/Kestrel.

1988   *The Magpies* by Denis Glover. Illustrated by Dick Frizzell.

1989   *Joseph's Boat* by Caroline Macdonald. Illustrated by Chris Gaskin. Hodder & Stoughton.

1990   *A Walk to the Beach* by Chris Gaskin.

1991   *Arthur and the Dragon* by David Elliot. Steck-Vaughn.

1992   *One Lonely Kakapo* by Sandra Morris. Hodder & Stoughton.

1993   *Lily and the Present* by Christine Ross. Methuen.

1994   *Hinepau* by Gavin Bishop. Ashton Scholastic

Esther Glen Award

This award is given to an author for the most distinguished contribution to New Zealand children's literature during the previous year. Only New Zealand citizens or residents are eligible.

1945   *The Book of Wiremu* by Stella Morice. Angus & Robertson.

1946   No award

1947   *Myths and Legends of Maoriland* by A. W. Reed. Reed.

1948–1949   No awards

1950   *The Adventures of Nimble, Rumble and Tumble* by Joan Smith. Paul's Book Arcade.

1951–1958   No awards

1959   *Falter Tom and the Water Boy* by Maurice Duggan. Paul's Book Arcade.

1960–1963   No awards

1964   *The Story of a Little Boy* by Leslie C. Powell. Paul's Book Arcade.

1965–1969   No awards

1970   *A Lion in the Meadow* by Margaret Mahy. Dent.

1971–1972   No awards

1973   *The First Margaret Mahy Story Book* by Margaret Mahy. Dent.

1974   No award

1975   *My Cat Likes to Hide in Boxes* by Eve Sutton and Lynley Dodd. Hamish Hamilton.

1976–1977   No awards

1978   *The Lighthouse Keeper's Lunch* by Ronda Armitage. Deutsch.

1979   *Take the Long Path* by Joan de Hamel. Lutterworth.

1980   No award

1981   *The Year of the Yelvertons* by Katherine O'Brien. Oxford.

1982   *The Haunting* by Margaret Mahy. Dent.

1983   *Jacky Nobody* by Anne de Roo. Methuen.

1984   *Elephant Rock* by Caroline Macdonald. Hodder.

1985   *The Changeover* by Margaret Mahy. Dent.

1986   *Motherstone* by Maurice Gee. Oxford.

1987   No award

1988   *Alex* by Tessa Duder. Oxford.

1989   *The Mangrove Summer* by Jack Lazenby. Oxford.

1990   *Alex in Winter* by Tessa Duder. Oxford.

1991   *Agnes the Sheep* by William Taylor. Scholastic.

1992   *Alessandra: Alex in Rome* by Tessa Duder. Oxford.

1993   *Underrunners* by Margaret Mahy. Hamish Hamilton.

1994   *A Dolphin in the Bay* by Diana Noonan. Omnibus/Ashton Scholastic.

Awards for a Body of Work

Hans Christian Andersen Award

This international award, sponsored by the International Board on Books for Young People, is given every two years to a living author and, since 1966, to a living illustrator whose complete works have made important international contributions to children's literature.

1956   Eleanor Farjeon (Great Britain)

1958   Astrid Lindgren (Sweden)

1960   Erich Kästner (Germany)

1962   Meindert DeJong (USA)

1964   René Guillot (France)

1966   Author: Tove Jansson (Finland)

Illustrator: Alois Carigiet (Switzerland)

1968   Authors: James Krüss (Germany) and José Maria Sanchez-Silva (Spain)

Illustrator: Jirí Trnka (Czechoslovakia)

1970   Author: Gianni Rodari (Italy)

Illustrator: Maurice Sendak (USA)

1972   Author: Scott O'Dell (USA)

Illustrator: Ib Spang Olsen (Denmark)

1974   Author: Maria Gripe (Sweden)

Illustrator: Farshid Mesghali (Iran)

1976   Author: Cecil Bödker (Denmark)

Illustrator: Tatjana Mawrina (USSR)

1978   Author: Paula Fox (USA)

Illustrator: Otto S. Svend (Denmark)

1980   Author: Bohumil Riha (Czechoslovakia)

Illustrator: Suekichi Akaba (Japan)

1982   Author: Lygia Bojunga Nunes (Brazil)

Illustrator: Zbigniew Rychlicki (Poland)

1984   Author: Christine Nöstlinger (Austria)

Illustrator: Mitsumasa Anno (Japan)

1986   Author: Patricia Wrightson (Australia)

Illustrator: Robert Ingpen (Australia)

1988   Author: Annie M. G. Schmidt (Netherlands)

Illustrator: Dušan Kalláy (Czechoslovakia)

1990   Author: Tormod Haugen (Norway)

Illustrator: Lisbeth Zwerger (Austria)

1992   Author: Virginia Hamilton (USA)

Illustrator: Kveta Pacovská (Czechoslovakia)

1994   Author: Michio Mado (Japan)

Illustrator: Jörg Müller (Switzerland)

Laura Ingalls Wilder Award

This award, sponsored by the Association for Library Service to Children of the American Library Association, is given to a U.S. author or illustrator whose body of work has made a lasting contribution to children's literature. Awarded every five years until 1980, the award is now given every three years.

1954   Laura Ingalls Wilder

1960   Clara Ingram Judson

1965   Ruth Sawyer

1970   E. B. White

1975   Beverly Cleary

1980   Theodor S. Geisel (Dr. Seuss)

1983   Maurice Sendak

1986   Jean Fritz

1989   Elizabeth George Speare

1992   Marcia Brown

1995   Virginia Hamilton

NCTE Excellence in Poetry for Children Award

For the list of award winners, see Chapter 3, page 47.

Awards for Specific Genres or Groups

Mildred L. Batchelder Award

This award, sponsored by the ALA's Association for Library Service to Children, is given to the American publisher of a children's book considered to be the most outstanding of those books originally published in a country other than the United States in a language other than English, and subsequently translated and published in the United States during the previous year.

1968   *The Little Man* by Erich Kästner. Translated from German by James Kirkup. Illustrated by Rick Schreiter. Knopf.

1969   *Don't Take Teddy* by Babbis Friis-Baastad. Translated from Norwegian by Lise Sömme McKinnon. Scribner's.

1970   *Wildcat Under Glass* by Alki Zei. Translated from Greek by Edward Fenton. Holt.

1971   *In the Land of Ur: The Discovery of Ancient Mesopotamia* by Hans Baumann. Translated from German by Stella Humphries. Illustrated by Hans Peter Renner. Pantheon.

1972   *Friedrich* by Hans Peter Richter. Translated from German by Edite Kroll. Holt.

1973   *Pulga* by Siny Rose Van Iterson. Translated from Dutch by Alexander and Alison Gode. Morrow.

1974   *Petros' War* by Alki Zei. Translated from Greek by Edward Fenton, Dutton.

1975   *An Old Tale Carved Out of Stone* by Aleksandr M. Linevski. Translated from Russian by Maria Polushkin. Crown.

1976   *The Cat and Mouse Who Shared a House* written and illustrated by Ruth Hürlimann. Translated from German by Anthea Bell. Walck.

1977   *The Leopard* by Cecil Bödker. Translated from Danish by Gunnar Poulsen. Atheneum.

1978   No award

1979   *Konrad* by Christine Nöstlinger. Translated from German (Austrian) by Anthea Bell. Illustrated by Carol Nicklaus. Watts.

Rabbit Island by Jörg Steiner. Translated from German (Swiss) by Ann Conrad Lammers. Illustrated by Jörg Müller. Harcourt.

1980   *The Sound of Dragon's Feet* by Alki Zei. Translated from Greek by Edward Fenton. Dutton.

1981   *The Winter When Time Was Frozen* by Els Pelgrom. Translated from Dutch by Raphael and Maryka Rudnik. Morrow.

1982   *The Battle Horse* by Harry Kullman. Translated from Swedish by George Blecher and Lone Thygesen-Blecher. Bradbury.

1983   *Hiroshima No Pika* written and illustrated by Toshi Maruki. Translated from Japanese through Kurita-Bando Literary Agency. Lothrop.

1984   *Ronia, the Robber's Daughter* by Astrid Lindgren. Translated from Swedish by Patricia Crampton. Viking.

1985   *The Island on Bird Street* by Uri Orlev. Translated from Hebrew by Hillel Halkin. Houghton.

1986   *Rose Blanche* by Christophe Gallaz and Roberto Innocenti. Translated from French by Martha Coventry and Richard Graglia. Illustrated by Roberto Innocenti. Creative Education.

1987   *No Hero for the Kaiser* by Rudolf Frank. Translated from German by Patricia Crampton. Illustrated by Klaus Steffans. Lothrop.

1988   *If You Didn't Have Me* by Ulf Nilsson. Translated from Swedish by Lone Thygesen-Blecher and George Blecher. Illustrated by Eva Eriksson. McElderry.

1989   *Crutches* by Peter Härtling. Translated from German by Elizabeth D. Crawford. Lothrop.

1990   *Buster's World* by Bjarne Reuter. Translated from Danish by Anthea Bell. Dutton.

1991   *A Hand Full of Stars* by Rafik Schami. Translated from German by Rika Lesser. Dutton.

Honor Book:

Two Short and One Long by Nina Ring Aamundsen. Translated from Norwegian by the author. Houghton.

1992   *The Man from the Other Side* by Uri Orlev. Translated from Hebrew by Hillel Halkin. Houghton.

1993 No Award

1994 *The Apprentice* by Pilar Molina Llorente. Illustrated by Juan Ramón Alonso. Translated from Spanish by Robin Longshaw. Farrar.

Honor Books:

Anne Frank, Beyond the Diary: A Photographic Remembrance by Ruud van der Rol and Rian Verhoeven. Translated from Dutch by Tony Langham and Plym Peters. Viking.

The Princess in the Kitchen Garden by Annemie and Margriet Heymans. Translated from Dutch by Johanna H. Prins and Johanna W. Prins. Farrar.

1995 *The Boys from St. Petri* by Bjarne Reuter. Translated from Danish by Anthea Bell. Dutton.

Coretta Scott King Awards

These awards, founded to commemorate Dr. Martin Luther King, Jr., and his wife, Coretta Scott King, for their work in promoting peace and world brotherhood, are given to an African-American author and, since 1974, an African-American illustrator whose children's books, published during the preceding year, made outstanding inspirational and educational contributions to literature for children and young people. The awards are sponsored by the Social Responsibilities Round Table of the American Library Association.

1970 *Martin Luther King, Jr.: Man of Peace* by Lillie Patterson. Garrard.

1971 *Black Troubador: Langston Hughes* by Charlemae Rollins. Rand.

1972 *17 Black Artists* by Elton C. Fax. Dodd.

1973 *I Never Had It Made* by Jackie Robinson as told to Alfred Duckett. Putnam.

1974 Author: *Ray Charles* by Sharon Bell Mathis. Crowell.

Illustrator: The same title, illustrated by George Ford.

1975 Author: *The Legend of Africana* by Dorothy Robinson. Johnson.

Illustrator: The same title, illustrated by Herbert Temple.

1976 Author: *Duey's Tale* by Pearl Bailey. Harcourt.

Illustrator: No award

1977 Author: *The Story of Stevie Wonder* by James Haskins. Lothrop.

Illustrator: No award

1978 Author: *Africa Dream* by Eloise Greenfield. Day/Crowell.

Illustrator: The same title, illustrated by Carole Bayard.

1979 Author: *Escape to Freedom* by Ossie Davis. Viking.

Illustrator: *Something on My Mind* by Nikki Grimes. Illustrated by Tom Feelings. Dial.

1980 Author: *The Young Landlords* by Walter Dean Myers. Viking.

Illustrator: *Cornrows* by Camille Yarbrough. Illustrated by Carole Bayard. Coward.

1981 Author: *This Life* by Sidney Poitier. Knopf.

Illustrator: *Beat the Story-Drum, Pum-Pum* by Ashley Bryan. Atheneum.

1982 Author: *Let the Circle Be Unbroken* by Mildred D. Taylor. Dial.

Illustrator: *Mother Crocodile: An Uncle Amadou Tale from Senegal* adapted by Rosa Guy. Illustrated by John Steptoe. Delacorte.

1983 Author: *Sweet Whispers, Brother Rush* by Virginia Hamilton. Philomel.

Illustrator: *Black Child* by Peter Mugabane. Knopf.

1984 Author: *Everett Anderson's Good-Bye* by Lucille Clifton. Holt.

Illustrator: *My Mama Needs Me* by Mildred Pitts Walter. Illustrated by Pat Cummings. Lothrop.

1985 Author: *Motown and Didi* by Walter Dean Myers. Viking.

Illustrator: No award

1986 Author: *The People Could Fly: American Black Folktales* by Virginia Hamilton. Knopf.

Illustrator: *Patchwork Quilt* by Valerie

Flournoy. Illustrated by Jerry Pinkney.

1987   Author: *Justin and the Best Biscuits in the World* by Mildred Pitts Walter. Lothrop.

Illustrator: *Half Moon and One Whole Star* by Crescent Dragonwagon. Illustrated by Jerry Pinkney. Macmillan.

1988   Author: *The Friendship* by Mildred D. Taylor. Illustrated by Max Ginsburg. Dial.

Illustrator: *Mufaro's Beautiful Daughters: An African Tale* retold and illustrated by John Steptoe. Lothrop.

1989   Author: *Fallen Angels* by Walter Dean Myers. Scholastic.

Illustrator: *Mirandy and Brother Wind* by Patricia McKissack. Illustrated by Jerry Pinkney. Knopf.

1990   Author: *A Long Hard Journey* by Patricia C. and Fredrick L. McKissack. Walker.

Illustrator: *Nathaniel Talking* by Eloise Greenfield. Illustrated by Jan Spivey Gilchrist. Black Butterfly Press.

1991   Author: *Road to Memphis* by Mildred D. Taylor. Dial.

Illustrator: *Aïda* retold by Leontyne Price. Illustrated by Leo and Diane Dillon. Harcourt.

1992   Author: *Now Is Your Time! The African-American Struggle for Freedom* by Walter Dean Myers. HarperCollins.

Illustrator: *Tar Beach* by Faith Ringgold. Crown.

1993   Author: *The Dark-Thirty: Southern Tales of the Supernatural* by Patricia McKissack. Knopf.

Illustrator: *Origins of Life on Earth: An African Creation Myth* by David A. Anderson. Illustrated by Kathleen Atkins Smith. Sight Productions.

1994   Author: *Toning the Sweep* by Angela Johnson. Orchard.

Illustrator: *Soul Looks Back in Wonder* compiled and illustrated by Tom Feelings. Dial.

1995   Author: *Christmas in the Big House, Christ-*

mas in the Quarters by Patricia C. McKissack and Fredrick L. McKissack. Illustrated by John Thompson. Scholastic.

Illustrator: *The Creation* by James Weldon Johnson. Illustrated by James E. Ransome. Holiday.

Edgar Allan Poe Award (Mystery)—Best Juvenile Novel Category

This award, sponsored by the Mystery Writers of America, is given to the author of the best mystery of the year written for young readers.

1961   *The Mystery of the Haunted Pool* by Phyllis A. Whitney. Westminster.

1962   *The Phantom of Walkaway Hill* by Edward Fenton. Doubleday.

1963   *Cutlass Island* by Scott Corbett. Atlantic/Little.

1964   *The Mystery of the Hidden Hand* by Phyllis A. Whitney. Westminster.

1965   *The Mystery at Crane's Landing* by Marcella Thum. Dodd.

1966   *The Mystery of 22 East* by Leon Ware. Westminster.

1967   *Sinbad and Me* by Kin Platt. Chilton.

1968   *Signpost of Terror* by Gretchen Sprague. Dodd.

1969   *The House of Dies Drear* by Virginia Hamilton. Macmillan.

1970   *Danger at Black Dyke* by Winifred Finlay. Phillips.

1971   *The Intruder* by John Rowe Townsend. Lippincott.

1972   *Night Fall* by Joan Aiken. Holt.

1973   *Deathwatch* by Robb White. Doubleday.

1974   *The Long Black Coat* by Jay Bennett. Delacorte.

1975   *The Dangling Witness* by Jay Bennett. Delacorte.

1976   *Z for Zachariah* by Robert C. O'Brien. Atheneum.

1977   *Are You in the House Alone?* by Richard Peck. Viking.

1978 *A Really Weird Summer* by Eloise Jarvis McGraw. Atheneum.

1979 *Alone in Wolf Hollow* by Dana Brookins. Clarion.

1980 *The Kidnapping of Christina Lattimore* by Joan Lowery Nixon. Harcourt.

1981 *The Seance* by Joan Lowery Nixon. Harcourt.

1982 *Taking Terri Mueller* by Norma Fox Mazer. Avon.

1983 *The Murder of Hound Dog Bates* by Robbie Branscum. Viking.

1984 *The Callender Papers* by Cynthia Voigt. Atheneum.

1985 *Night Cry* by Phyllis Reynolds Naylor. Atheneum.

1986 *The Sandman's Eyes* by Patricia Windsor. Delacorte.

1987 *Other Side of Dark* by Joan Lowery Nixon. Delacorte.

1988 *Lucy Forever and Miss Rosetree, Shrinks* by Susan Shreve. Holt.

1989 *Megan's Island* by Willo Davis Roberts. Atheneum.

1990 No award

1991 *Stonewords* by Pam Conrad. Harper.

1992 *Wanted ... Mud Blossom* by Betsy Byars. Delacorte.

1993 *Coffin in a Case* by Eve Bunting. Harper-Collins.

1994 *The Twin in the Tavern* by Barbara Brooks Wallace. Atheneum.

1995 *The Absolutely True Story ... How I Visited Yellowstone Park with the Terrible Rubes* by Willo Davis Roberts. Atheneum.

Scott O'Dell Award for Historical Fiction

This award, donated by the author Scott O'Dell and administered by Zena Sutherland of the University of Chicago, is given to the author of a distinguished work of historical fiction for children or young adults set in the New World and published in English by a U.S. publisher.

1984 *The Sign of the Beaver* by Elizabeth George Speare. Houghton.

1985 *The Fighting Ground* by Avi (Wortis). Harper.

1986 *Sarah, Plain and Tall* by Patricia MacLachlan. Harper.

1987 *Streams to the River, River to the Sea: A Novel of Sacagawea* by Scott O'Dell. Houghton.

1988 *Charlie Skedaddle* by Patricia Beatty. Morrow.

1989 *The Honorable Prison* by Lyll Becerra de Jenkins. Lodestar.

1990 *Shades of Gray* by Carolyn Reeder. Macmillan.

1991 *A Time of Troubles* by Pieter van Raven. Scribner's.

1992 *Stepping on the Cracks* by Mary Downing Hahn. Clarion.

1993 *Morning Girl* by Michael Dorris. Hyperion.

1994 *Bull Run* by Paul Fleischman. Harper-Collins.

1995 *Under the Blood-Red Sun* by Graham Salisbury. Delacorte

Orbis Pictus Award

This award, sponsored by NCTE's Committee on Using Nonfiction in the Elementary Language Arts Classroom, is given to an author in recognition of excellence in writing of nonfiction for children published in the United States in the preceding year.

1990 *The Great Little Madison* by Jean Fritz. Putnam.

Honor Books:

The Great American Gold Rush by Rhoda Blumberg. Bradbury.

The News About Dinosaurs by Patricia Lauber. Bradbury.

1991 *Franklin Delano Roosevelt* by Russell Freedman. Clarion.

Honor Books:

Arctic Memories by Normee Ekoomiak. Holt.

Seeing Earth from Space by Patricia Lauber. Orchard.

1992 *Flight: The Journey of Charles Lindbergh* by Robert Burleigh. Illustrated by Mike Wimmer. Philomel.

Honor Books:

Now Is Your Time: The African-American Struggle for Freedom by Walter Dean Myers. HarperCollins.

Prairie Vision: The Life and Times of Solomon Butcher by Pam Conrad. HarperCollins.

1993   ***Children of the Dustbowl: The True Story of the School at Weedpatch Camp*** by Jerry Stanley. Random.

Honor Books:

Talking with Artists by Pat Cummings. Bradbury.

Come Back, Salmon by Molly Cone. Sierra.

1994   ***Across America on an Emigrant Train*** by Jim Murphy. Clarion.

Honor Books:

To the Top of the World: Adventures with Arctic Wolves by Jim Brandenburg. Walker.

Making Sense: Animal Perception and Communication by Bruce Brooks. Farrar.

1995   ***Safari Beneath the Sea*** by Diane Swanson. Photographs by the Royal British Columbia Museum. Sierra Club.

Honor Books:

Wildlife Rescue: The Work of Dr. Kathleen Ramsay by Jennifer Dewey. Boyds Mills.

Kids at Work by Russell Freedman. Photographs by Lewis Hine. Clarion.

Phoenix Award

This award, sponsored by the Children's Literature Association, is given to the author of a book first published 20 years earlier. The book must have been originally published in English and cannot have been the recipient of a major children's book award.

1985   ***Mark of the Horse Lord*** by Rosemary Sutcliff. Walck.

1986   ***Queenie Peavy*** by Robert Burch. Viking.

1987   ***Smith*** by Leon Garfield. Constable.

1988   ***The Rider and His Horse*** by Eric Christian Haugaard. Houghton.

1989   ***The Night Watchman*** by Helen Cresswell. Macmillan.

1990   ***Enchantress from the Stars*** by Sylvia Louise Engdahl. Macmillan.

1991   ***A Long Way from Verona*** by Jane Gardam. Macmillan.

1992   ***A Sound of Chariots*** by Mollie Hunter. Harper.

1993   ***Carrie's War*** by Nina Bawden. Puffin.

1994   ***Of Nightingales That Weep*** by Katherine Paterson. Harper.

Other Notable Book Exhibitions and Awards

Biennale of Illustrations Bratislava

This biannual international exposition of books was begun in 1967 and is held in Bratislava, Czechoslovakia. A Grand Prix and five honor book awards are given to children's books for excellence in illustration.

American Institute of Graphic Arts Book Show

This annual book show features approximately 100 books, both children's and adult, selected for excellence in design and manufacture. Lists of books selected each year can be found in AIGA Graphic Design USA (Watson-Guptil).

New York Times Best Illustrated Children's Books of the Year

Sponsored by *The New York Times*, this list of 10 books appears annually in the *Times*. A three-member panel of experts chooses the books.

International Reading Association Children's Book Award

Sponsored by the Institute for Reading Research and administered by the International Reading Association, this international award is given annually to an author for a first or second book that shows unusual promise in the children's book field.

International Board on Books for Young People Honor List

Sponsored by the International Board on Books for Young People (IBBY), this biennial list is composed of three books (one for text, one for illustration, and one for translation) from each IBBY National Section to represent the best in children's literature published in that country in the past two years.

The books selected are recommended as suitable for publication worldwide.

State Children's Choice Award Programs

ARIZONA: "Arizona Young Readers Award," founded 1977. (Grades K–4)

ARKANSAS: "Charlie May Simon Children's Book Award," founded 1970. (Grades 4–6)

CALIFORNIA: "California Young Reader Medals," founded 1975. (Four divisions: primary, intermediate, junior high, senior high)

COLORADO: "Colorado Children's Book Award," founded 1976. (Elementary grades); "Blue Spruce Award," founded 1985. (YA)

FLORIDA: "Florida Reading Association Children's Book Award," founded 1987. (Grades K–2); "Sunshine State Young Reader's Award," founded 1984. (Grades 3–8)

GEORGIA: "Georgia Children's Book Award," founded 1969. (Grades 4–8); "Georgia Children's Picture Storybook Award," founded 1976. (Grades K–3)

HAWAII: "Nene Award," founded 1964. (Grades 4–6)

ILLINOIS: "Rebecca Caudill Young Readers' Book Award," founded 1988. (Grades 4–8)

INDIANA: "Young Hoosier Award," founded 1975. (Two divisions: Grades 4–6, Grades 6–8)

IOWA: "Iowa Children's Choice Award" founded 1980. (Grades 3–6); "Iowa Teen Award," founded 1985. (Grades 6–9)

KANSAS: "William Allen White Children's Book Award," founded 1953. (Grades 4–8)

KENTUCKY: "Kentucky Bluegrass Award," founded 1983. (Division one, Grades K–3; Division two, Grades 4–8)

MARYLAND: "Maryland Children's Book Award," founded 1988. (Grades 3–6)

MASSACHUSETTS: "Massachusetts Children's Book Award," founded 1976. (Grades 4–6)

MICHIGAN: "Michigan Young Readers' Awards," founded 1980.

MINNESOTA: "Maud Hart Lovelace Book Award," founded 1979. (Grades 3–8)

MISSOURI: "Mark Twain Award," founded 1971. (Grades K–8)

NEBRASKA: "Golden Sower Award for Fiction," founded 1981. (Grades 4–6); "Golden Sower Award for Picture Book," founded 1983. (Grades K–3)

NEW HAMPSHIRE: "Great Stone Face Award," founded 1980. (Grades 4–6)

NEW JERSEY: "Garden State Children's Book Awards," founded 1977. (Three divisions: Easy to Read, Younger Fiction, Younger Nonfiction)

NEW MEXICO: "Land of Enchantment Book Award," founded 1981. (Grades 4–8)

NEVADA: "Nevada Young Readers' Award," founded 1988. (Three divisions: Grades K–3, 4–6,YA)

NORTH DAKOTA: "Flicker Tale Children's Book Award,"founded 1978. (Two categories: picture book and intermediate book)

OHIO: "Buckeye Children's Book Awards," founded 1982. (Three divisions: Grades K–2, 3–5, 6–8)

OKLAHOMA: "Sequoyah Children's Book Award," founded 1959. (Grades 3–6); "Sequoyah Young Adult Book Award," founded 1988. (Grades 7–9)

PACIFIC NORTHWEST: (Alaska; Alberta, Canada; British Columbia, Canada; Idaho; Montana; Oregon; Washington) "Pacific Northwest Young Reader's Choice Award," founded 1940. (Grades 4–8)

PENNSYLVANIA: "Keystone to Reading Book Award," founded 1984.

SOUTH CAROLINA: "South Carolina Children's Book Award," founded 1976. (Grades 4–8); "South Carolina Young Adult Book Award," founded 1980. (Grades 9–12)

SOUTH DAKOTA: "Prairie Pasque Children's Book Award," founded 1987. (Grades 4–6)

TENNESSEE: "Volunteer State Book Award," founded 1979. (Four divisions: Grades K–3, 4–6, 7–9, 10–12)

TEXAS: "The Texas Bluebonnet Award," founded 1979. (Grades 3–6)

UTAH: "Utah Children's Book Award," founded 1980. (Grades 3–6)

VERMONT: "Dorothy Canfield Fisher Children's Book Award," founded 1957. (Grades 4–8)

VIRGINIA: "Young Reader Award of the State of Virginia," founded 1981. (Four divisions: Grades Ps–3, 4–6, 7–9, 10–12)

WASHINGTON: "Washington Children's Choice Picture Book Award," founded 1982. (Grades K–3)

WEST VIRGINIA: "West Virginia Children's Book Award" founded 1984. (Grades 3–6)

WISCONSIN: "Golden Archer Award," founded 1974. (Grades 4–8); "Little Archer Award," founded 1976. (Grades K–3)

WYOMING: "Indian Paintbrush Book Award," founded 1986. (Grades 4–6); "Soaring Eagle Young Adult Book Award," founded 1988. (Two divisions: Grades 7–9, Grades 10–12)

Appendix B

Professional Resources

Compiled and Annotated by
Marie Louise Sorensen

Professional Readings

Books

Bader, B.(1976). *American Picture Books from Noah's Ark to the Beast Within.* New York: Macmillan.

This critical, comprehensive history of art in children's picture book publishing in the United States is particularly valuable because we often take for granted the seemingly unlimited capabilities of art reproduction available to us today. Bader describes the achievements of artists by putting them in the perspective of advances in reproduction techniques as they became available to the publishing industry.

Barton, B., & Booth D. (1990). *Stories in the Classroom: Storytelling, Reading Aloud, and Roleplaying with Children.* Portsmouth, NH: Heinemann.

The authors suggest a variety of follow-up activities to help teachers create and enrich their classrooms with what the authors refer to as the "storying" experience. Included are ideas for finding appropriate stories.

Bauer, C. F. (1993). *New Handbook for Storytellers: With Stories, Poems, Magic and More.* Illustrated by L. Bredeson. Chicago: American Library Association.

Bauer uses storytelling to introduce her listeners to children's literature. She includes sections on

getting started, sources for stories, multimedia approaches, and planning programs. This updated version of Bauer's 1977 classic handbook includes many new books in its expanded bibliographies.

Bauer, M. D. (1992). *What's Your Story? A Young Person's Guide to Writing Fiction.* New York: Clarion.

Bauer provides clear information on the elements of fiction, with chapters on the development of character, theme, plot, story tension, point of view, and dialogue, as well as practical advice on revision.

Benedict, S., & Carlisle, L. (Eds.). (1992). *Beyond Words: Picture Books for Older Readers and Writers.* Portsmouth, NH: Heinemann.

Suggesting that readers are never too old to enjoy a good picture book, this collection contains essays in which many individual contributors describe the various ways in which they have used picture books in middle grades, junior high, and high school. Contributors range from high school students to college professors.

Bodart, J. R. (Ed.). (1985–1993). *Booktalk!* (Vols. 2–5). New York: H. W. Wilson.

———. (Ed.). (1995). *Booktalking the Award Winner: 1992–1993.* New York: H.W. Wilson

These resources explain the what, how, and why of booktalking, followed by prepared booktalks for all ages and audiences.

Bohning, G., Phillips, A., & Bryant, S. H. (1993). *Literature on the Move: Making and Using Pop-Up and Lift-Flap Books*. Englewood, CO: Libraries Unlimited.

Clear directions, which can be followed by children, are provided for making eight basic types of engineered (movable) pages with variations for each. The authors include thematic ideas to help teachers generate interest in reading and writing through the production of books.

Bromley, K. D. (1991). *Webbing with Literature: Creating Story Maps with Children's Books*. Boston: Allyn and Bacon.

Bromley defines semantic webbing and explains the use of webs to enhance children's comprehension of literature in grades K–8. She includes chapters on the selection of quality literature and various ways of helping children respond to literature. The author also provides examples of webs for 50 award-winning books with additional brief annotations for another 145 books.

Carlsen, G. R., & Sherrill, A. (1988). *Voices of Readers: How We Come to Love Books*. Urbana, IL: National Council of Teachers of English.

The authors have excerpted from and categorized autobiographical statements about development as readers written by Carlsen's students over a period of thirty years. The presentation and the analysis of these quotations in the readers' own words provide a compelling list of conditions that promote the making of readers.

Chatton, B. (1993). *Using Poetry across the Curriculum: A Whole Language Approach*. Phoenix, AZ: Oryx Press.

Chatton suggests many ways in which children can be captivated by poetry. To encourage the integration of poetry into all subject areas, the book is divided into broad curricular areas, with many subtopics. Each category includes lists of appropriate poetry along with the bibliographic information needed to locate the suggested poems. Indexes enable users to find the work of individual poets, favorite poems, and particular topics.

Cullinan, B. E. (Ed.). (1987). *Children's Literature in the Reading Program*. Newark, DE: International Reading Association.

———. (Ed.). (1992). *Invitation to Read: More Children's Literature in the Reading Program*. Newark, DE: International Reading Association.

Advocating the incorporation of children's literature into the reading program on all grade levels, these books include chapters of many well-known contributors who discuss a variety of aspects of literature-based reading, including implementation.

Esbensen, B. J. (1975). *A Celebration of Bees: Helping Children Write Poetry*. Minneapolis: Winston Press.

Emphasizing that children's first experiences in writing poetry should be in group sessions, this teacher shares practical ideas that will help move children toward individual poetry writing.

Fiore, C. D. (1994). *Programming for Introducing Adults to Children's Literature* (new ed.). Chicago: American Library Association.

This pamphlet suggests several valid ways in which public librarians might introduce adults to children's literature both for their own enjoyment and as material to use with their children. Especially useful are the "Guidelines for Book Discussions" attributed to Ginny Moore Kruse and Kathleen T. Horning of the Cooperative Children's Book Center in Madison, Wisconsin.

Glazer, J. I. (1991). *Literature for Young Children* (3rd ed.). New York: Merrill/Macmillan.

Well-written children's literature has much to offer children as they develop and grow. Those who work with preschool and primary-grade children will benefit from the research cited by Glazer and from her recommendations for integrating literature into programs for young children.

Hall, S. (1990, 1994). *Using Picture Storybooks to Teach Literary Devices: Recommended Books for Children and Young Adults* (Vol. 1 & 2). Phoenix, AZ: Oryx Press.

The author explains how picture books can be used to teach complex literary devices and then organizes annotations of recommended books by those devices. Curriculum tie-ins are often suggested. Artistic styles and techniques are defined, identified for each book, and then listed by style or technique.

Hancock, J., & Hill, S. (Eds.). (1987). *Literature-Based Reading Programs at Work*. Portsmouth, NH: Heinemann.

This book from Australia suggests solutions to the possible problems encountered when teachers implement a literature-based reading program. The authors also discuss how teachers' beliefs affect how they help children learn.

Hansen, J. (1987). *When Writers Read.* Portsmouth, NH: Heinemann.

Hansen describes the change—in both adults and children—that resulted when teachers and researchers working together in an elementary school discovered that the same principles used in the process approach to the teaching of writing could be applied to the teaching of reading. The author compares her current thinking with the way she used to do things as a classroom teacher in the late 1960s and 1970s, emphasizing how children can be encouraged to develop strategies to help them learn to read.

Harris, V. J. (Ed.). (1993). *Teaching Multicultural Literature in Grades K–8.* Norwood, MA: Christopher-Gordon Publishers.

Knowledgeable authors representing a wide range of expertise have written essays for this book on important issues concerning the field of multicultural children's literature. Selection criteria are discussed, and many recommended books and authors are highlighted.

Heard, G. (1989). *For the Good of the Earth and Sun: Teaching Poetry.* Portsmouth, NH: Heinemann.

Heard, a poet, describes her experiences with helping children and teachers learn about the process of writing poetry.

Hickman, J., & Cullinan, B. E. (Eds.). (1989). *Children's Literature in the Classroom: Weaving Charlotte's Web.* Needham Heights, MA: Christopher-Gordon Publishers.

Hickman, J., Cullinan, B. E., & Hepler, S. (Eds.). (1994). *Children's Literature in the Classroom: Extending Charlotte's Web.* Norwood, MA: Christopher-Gordon Publishers.

These books are a tribute to Charlotte Huck written by her former students, with chapters on picture books, fantasy, historical fiction, and poetry, as well as sections on many aspects of implementing a literature-based reading program.

Hopkins, L. B. (1987). *Pass the Poetry, Please!* (revised, enlarged, and updated). New York: Harper & Row.

Hopkins introduces his favorite works by twenty contemporary poets and enthusiastically makes

suggestions for helping children appreciate poetry at home, in the classroom, and in the library. Bibliographies are included.

Janeczko, P. B. (1994). *Poetry from A to Z: A Guide for Young Writers.* New York: Bradbury Press.

Janeczko selects poems and has the poets talk about their writing, but he also has many suggestions of his own for middle-graders who would like to try writing poetry and for the teachers who would encourage them.

Jobe, R., & Hart, P. (1991). *Canadian Connections: Experiencing Literature with Children.* Markham, Ontario: Pembroke Publishers Limited.

Jobe and Hart list what they consider to be key books by Canadian authors, and then they provide examples of plans for exploring some of these books with students aged 9 through 12 years. Lists of additional recommended books by Canadian authors are included.

Johnson, T. D., & Louis, D. R. (1987). *Literacy Through Literature.* Portsmouth, NH: Heinemann.

These Canadian-based authors share many ideas for introducing children to literature and then relate such activities to underlying assumptions and beliefs about how children learn to read.

Johnson, T. D., & Louis, D. R. (1990). *Bringing It All Together: A Program for Literacy.* Portsmouth, NH: Heinemann.

In their second book of suggestions for those planning a literature program for the classroom, the authors discuss the theory behind their ideas, explaining that when readers begin to understand the philosophy on which literature programs are based, they will be able to develop and implement their own ideas.

Kimmel, M. M., & Segal, E. (1988). *For Reading Out Loud! A Guide to Sharing Books with Children* (revised and expanded). New York: Delacorte.

Compiled by librarians who know and love books, this handbook includes comments on 125 books recommended for preschoolers and 175 for school-age listeners. The annotations, listed alphabetically by title, include estimates on how much time to allow for reading selections aloud.

Koch, K. (1970). *Wishes, Lies, and Dreams: Teaching Children to Write Poetry.* New York: Harper.

Koch describes how he worked with inner-city children who had never done much writing of any kind and encouraged them to express themselves by writing down their feelings.

———. (1973). *Rose, Where Did You Get That Red? Teaching Great Poetry to Children.* New York: Random House.

Koch explains his approach to exposing children to adult poetry by providing samples of the lessons he used followed by examples of the poetry his students wrote in response. He includes an anthology of additional poetry.

Kulleseid, E. R. & Strickland, D. S. (1989). *Literature, Literacy, and Learning: Classroom Teachers, Library Media Specialists, and the Literature-Based Curriculum.* Chicago: ALA.

After concisely explaining the theory and research behind literature-based reading programs, the authors describe the partnership of the school library media specialist and the classroom teacher. The Appendix includes a viewer's guide to a video produced by Encyclopedia Britannica Educational Corporation (1990, No. 4594) for use in conjunction with this booklet.

Lamme, L. L., Krogh, S. L., & Yachmetz, K. A. (1992). *Literature-Based Moral Education: Children's Books & Activities for Teaching Values, Responsibility, & Good Judgment in the Elementary School.* Phoenix, AZ: Oryx Press.

After reviewing the knowledge base on children's developmental understanding of moral issues, the authors provide annotations of books they recommend for teaching children about such things as responsibility, respect for others, sharing, truthfulness, and solving conflicts peacefully.

Lehr, S. S. (1991). *The Child's Developing Sense of Theme: Responses to Literature.* New York: Teachers College Press.

Based on her studies of the responses to literature by children ranging from pre-school age to fourth graders, Lehr discusses what she has learned about how children make meaning in the books they read. Classroom profiles give examples of the kinds of discussions that can be held with children about books.

Livingston, M. C. (1991). *Poem Making: Ways to Begin Writing Poetry.* New York: HarperCollins Publishers.

This poet's ideas about the process of writing poetry will cause children and teachers alike to look at poetry differently after reading this book. Poems by a great number of well-known poets are used as examples. The poetry is indexed by first line, title, author, and type.

Lukens, R. J., & Cline, R. K. J. (1995). *A Critical Handbook of Literature for Young Adults.* New York: HarperCollins College Publishers.

Lukens and Cline have collaborated to help prepare teachers and librarians who work with junior high school students to be able to discuss critical elements of literature with their young adult readers. Recommended books are cited at the end of each chapter.

McClure, A. A. (1990). *Sunrises and Songs: Reading and Writing Poetry in an Elementary Classroom.* Portsmouth, NH: Heinemann.

This book describes how two teachers guided their fifth- and sixth-grade students into writing and reading poetry over a period of a year.

McConaghy, J. (1990). *Children Learning Through Literature: A Teacher Researcher Study.* Portsmouth, NH: Heinemann.

This Canadian teacher describes her development in ability to help her first graders learn to read and write through the use of literature. McConaghy emphasizes children's responses to books as meaning-making experiences, and she also describes her own growth as a teacher.

McCracken, R. A., & McCracken, M. J. (1986). *Stories, Songs, and Poetry to Teach Reading and Writing: Literacy Through Language.* Chicago: American Library Association.

This book is designed to help teachers, librarians, and parents of young children understand that reading and writing are natural processes. The suggestions provided emphasize the concept that children can learn to read in much the same way that they learn to talk.

Moss, J. F. (1994). *Using Literature in the Middle Grades: A Thematic Approach.* Norwood, MA: Christopher-Gordon Publishers, Inc.

Moss believes that teachers who read and regard literature as important will be able to bring literature into the lives of their students. She then explains how she integrates content matter and language arts by setting up literature units around a topic, genre, literary theme, or narrative element. Examples of the particular themes of focus units for which Moss shares resource ideas in the work include war and peace, problems of immigrants, and survival stories.

Neuman, J. (Ed.). *Whole Language: Theory in Use.* Portsmouth, NH: Heinemann.

Includes essays on a variety of topics in which experienced teachers explain how their classroom practices have been affected by their understanding of whole language theory.

Pellowski, A. (1984). *The Story Vine: A Source Book of Unusual and Easy-to-Tell Stories from Around the World.* Illustrated by Lynn Sweat. New York: Macmillan.

Pellowski cites sources and uses drawings to illustrate how she tells some of her favorite stories with the aid of authentic props, such as string figures and pictures.

———. (1990). *The World of Storytelling: A Practical Guide to the Origins, Development, and Applications of Storytelling* (expanded and revised edition). New York: H. W. Wilson.

Pellowski provides comprehensive information about the oral tradition and the history of storytelling. She stresses the responsibility of the storyteller to know and present background information about the various cultures from which stories are selected for telling. Bibliographies list books, articles, and manuals on storytelling, as well as a list of storytelling festivals held around the world.

Rhodes, L. K., & Dudley-Marling, C. (1988). *Readers and Writers with a Difference: A Holistic Approach to Teaching Learning Disabled and Remedial Students.* Portsmouth, NH: Heinemann.

Rhodes and Dudley-Marling share strategies that have worked in their classrooms and offer recommendations for choosing reading materials. They explain how to use predictable books and include an expanded bibliography of Rhodes' 1981 list of such books.

Robb, L. (1994.) *Whole Language, Whole Learners: Creating a Literature-Centered Classroom.* New York: Morrow.

A master teacher, Robb offers sound advice about whole language and literature-based teaching for

primary, intermediate, and middle-school grades. She provides a wealth of examples from her own classroom and numerous vignettes about literature written by outstanding authors and illustrators of children's books.

Routman, R. (1988). *Transitions: From Literature to Literacy.* Portsmouth, NH: Heinemann.

Explaining how she came to change the way she helps children learn to read, the author describes reading and writing as processes, and includes a section on evaluation. The last hundred pages are devoted to resources for the teacher, including an excellent bibliography of professional books and journal articles.

———. (1991, 1994). *Invitations: Changing as Teachers and Learners K–12.* Portsmouth, NH: Heinemann.

In her second book, Routman provides additional assistance to teachers committed to improving the way they teach. Having observed the teachers in her school district struggle with change, Routman believes that the issues all teachers confront are similar, regardless of what grade or age they teach. The comprehensive, annotated bibliography of blue resource pages at the back has been updated for the 1994 edition.

———, with Hepler, S., Milz, V., & Noble, D. (1994). *The Blue Pages: Resources for Teachers from Invitations.* Portsmouth, NH: Heinemann.

For those people already owning copies of Routman's Transitions *(1988) or* Invitations *(the 1991 edition), it is now possible to purchase the updated and expanded blue resource pages separately. This is a valuable tool for teachers who incorporate literature into their classrooms.*

Rudman, M. K. (1995). *Children's Literature: An Issues Approach* (3rd ed.). White Plains, NY: Longman.

Rudman discusses criteria for evaluating children's books dealing with issues affecting our society today, such as siblings, adoption, divorce, sexuality, aging, death, heritage, and war and peace. Each chapter includes adult resources on the topic being considered as well as annotations describing recommended books for children.

———. (1993). *Children's Literature: Resource for the*

Classroom (2nd ed.). Norwood, MA: Christopher-Gordon Publishers.

The chapters in this book were written by authorities involved in various aspects of children's literature. Evaluation, selection, censorship, and literature in the reading program are addressed. This edition also includes a new chapter on global education and a bibliography of multicultural literature that advocates searching for universals as well as appreciating differences.

Saltman, Judith. (1987). *Modern Canadian Children's Books: Perspectives on Canadian Culture*. Toronto: Oxford University Press.

This brief survey traces the historical developments in Canadian children's literature during the major growth years from 1975 to 1985, highlighting contemporary trends and discussing significant titles in each of the major genres. Bibliographic information accompanies each chapter. Indexes by title, author, and illustrator are included.

Sims, R. (1982). *Shadow and Substance: Afro-American Experience in Contemporary Children's Fiction*. Urbana, IL: NCTE.

Sims analyzed 150 books of realistic fiction about the African-American experience that were written for children and published in the United States between 1965 and 1979. Her well-written narrative puts into historical context societal changes as they were reflected in those books.

Trelease, J. (1989). *The New Read-Aloud Handbook* (2nd rev. ed.). New York: Viking Penguin.

This bestseller of practical suggestions has helped Trelease become a spokesperson for reading aloud. He annotates three hundred of his favorite read-alouds, giving the listening level of each. Many of the annotations include suggestions of other books by the same author.

Trousdale, A. M., Woestehoff, A. S., & Schwartz, M. (Eds.). (1994). *Give a Listen: Stories of Storytelling in School*. Urbana, IL: National Council of Teachers of English.

In this edited collection of stories, elementary-through university-level teachers write of their classroom experiences using storytelling both as a way to teach and to learn.

Tunnell, M. O., & Ammon, R. (Eds.). (1993). *The Story of Ourselves: Teaching History through Children's Literature*. Portsmouth, NH: Heinemann.

The contributors to this collection of essays write in support of teachers who would like to incorporate children's literature into their history or social studies programs. The perspectives of some well-known writers of historical fiction are included, and practical classroom suggestions are offered by teachers. An annotated bibliography of American historical literature for young readers is included.

Veatch, J. (1968). *How to Teach Reading with Children's Books* (2nd ed.). New York: Richard C. Owen.

This pamphlet provides a straightforward, simple explanation of how to set up a classroom instructional reading program with trade books. Veatch explains her "rule of thumb" that will help children determine whether a book they have chosen will be too difficult for them to read.

Wood, K. D., with Moss, A. (Eds.). (1992). *Exploring Literature in the Classroom: Contents and Methods*. Norwood, MA: Christopher-Gordon Publishers.

Examining what to teach as well as how to teach, experts in their fields provide perspectives on a variety of literacy issues, including the place of today's basal readers in literature-based reading programs and the current status of multiethnic literature.

Books about the History of Children's Literature

Bingham, J., & Scholt, G. (1980). *Fifteen Centuries of Children's Literature: An Annotated Chronology of British and American Works in Historical Context*. Westport, CT: Greenwood.

Gillespie, M. C. (1970). *History and Trends: Literature for Children*. Dubuque, IA: Brown.

Marshall, M. R. (1982). *An Introduction to the World of Children's Books: Books about the History of Children's Literature*. Aldershot, England: Gower.

Meigs, C., Eaton, A. T., Nesbitt, E., & Vigeurs, R. H. (1969). *A Critical History of Children's Books in English* (rev. ed.). New York: Macmillan.

Smith, E. S. (1980). In M. Hodges & S. Steinfirst (Eds.), *The History of Children's Literature* (rev. ed.). Chicago: ALA.

Journal Articles

Altwerger, B., Edelsky, C., & Flores, B. M. (1987). "Whole Language: What's New?" *The Reading Teacher, 41,* 144–154.

The authors explain that whole language is not a practice but a set of beliefs based on certain ideas that they list here. The authors clearly describe what whole language is and is not and provide definitions for terms frequently used.

Bigelow, W. (1992). "Once upon a Genocide: Christopher Columbus in Children's Literature". *Language Arts, 69,* 112–120.

The author critiques eight children's biographies of Columbus, compares them with the historical record, and then analyzes the influence these accounts may have on young readers. Especially concerned that portrayals of Columbus's relationship to Native Americans may be perceived as justifying racism, Bigelow suggests more appropriate ways to teach Columbus.

Byrnes, D. A. (1988). "Children and Prejudice." *Social Education, 52,* 267–271.

Although most multicultural educational programs at the elementary school level aim to promote understanding of other cultures, Byrnes feels that teachers should also teach children about prejudice and discrimination. She recommends specific activities and strategies for teachers to use to reduce children's prejudices.

Cohen, D. H. (1968). "The Effect of Literature on Vocabulary and Reading Achievement." *Elementary English, 45,* 209–213, 217.

This landmark study is often cited because it demonstrates that spending classroom time reading aloud to second-graders from low socio-economic backgrounds results in significant increases in vocabulary, word knowledge, and reading comprehension.

DeFord, D. E. (1981)."Literacy: Reading, Writing, and Other Essentials." *Language Arts, 58,* 652–658.

DeFord studied three first-grade classrooms where different approaches to reading and writing were emphasized. Analysis of samples of these children's writing indicated that the writing of the children in the whole language classroom reflected familiarity with a greater variety of literary forms, such as stories, poetry, and newspaper reports. DeFord recommends that reading and writing be taught as interactive processes.

Durkin, D. (1961). "Children Who Read Before Grade One. *The Reading Teacher, 14,* 163–166.

When Durkin looked for factors that might explain why the forty-nine children identified for this study had learned to read before they started first grade, she found that they all had been read to regularly at home, some since the age of two. This was one of the first studies to recognize this important correlation.

Eldredge, J. L., & Butterfield, D. (1986)."Alternatives to Traditional Reading Instruction." *The Reading Teacher, 40,* 32–37.

Teachers who want to use children's literature to help children learn to read will find support in this research, which found more significant gains in achievement and attitudes toward reading in second-grade classrooms where literature was part of the reading instruction program than in those classrooms relying on basal instruction.

Flood, J., & Lapp, D. (1994)."Teacher Book Clubs: Establishing Literature Discussion Groups for Teachers." *The Reading Teacher, 47,* 574–576.

The authors suggest that when teachers participate in book club discussions on a regular basis and become aware of their own literacy processing, they also develop a greater understanding of teaching and learning.

Goodman, K. S. (1986). "Basal Readers: A Call for Action." *Language Arts, 63,* 358–363.

Although basal readers dominate reading instruction in the United States, Goodman points to an ever-widening gap between the methods employed in basal readers and the latest theory and research in reading instruction. Perhaps partly because of recommendations such as Goodman's, today's basal reading programs have improved and now include more children's literature.

Goodman, K. S. (1988)."Look What They've Done to Judy Blume!: The 'Basalization' of Children's Literature." *The New Advocate, 1,* 29–41.

Goodman suggests that if we accept the idea that children learn to read by reading, we should offer them authentic children's literature rather than adaptations that have been rewritten under the mistaken notion that they can be made easier to read by controlling vocabulary.

Holdaway, D. (1982). "Shared Book Experience: Teaching Reading Using Favorite Books." *Theory into Practice, 21,* 293–300.

Holdaway explains the rationale and research behind what he called the "shared book experience," a form of natural literacy learning that has become widely used in classroom literature programs planned for young children, both in New Zealand and the United States.

Horning, K. (1993). "The Contributions of Alternative Press Publishers to Multicultural Literature for Children." *Library Trends, 41,* 524–540.

Horning profiles several alternative, or independently owned, small publishers and describes the nature of the literature each publishes for children. Special attention is given to presses owned and operated by Native Americans and African Americans. The theme of the Winter 1993 issue of Library Trends *in which this article appears is "Multicultural Children's Literature in the United States."*

Huck, C. S. (1982). "I Give You the End of a Golden String." *Theory into Practice, 21,* 315–321.

Huck cites research that firmly supports her plea for making children's literature the central part of programs for helping children learn to read. She also thoroughly describes the aesthetic aspects of developing in children a love for literature that will help them become lifelong readers.

Jalongo, M. R., & Creany, A. D. (1991)."Censorship in Children's Literature: What Every Educator Should Know." *Childhood Education, 67(3),* 143–148.

The authors of this article explain the complex distinctions between censorship, selection, and self-censorship. After pointing out the main reasons children's books are censored, they provide suggestions about how educators can be prepared to handle censorship controversies should they occur.

Kutiper, K., & Wilson, P. (1993)."Updating Poetry Preferences: A Look at the Poetry Children Really Like." *The Reading Teacher, 47,* 28–35.

The authors believe that teachers who are aware of children's poetry preferences will be able to plan classroom experiences that will broaden their students' appreciation for a diverse array of poetry.

Lamme, L. L., & Ledbetter, L. (1990). "Libraries: The Heart of Whole Language." *Language Arts, 67,* 735–741.

Focusing on the changed role of the school librarian in whole language schools, the authors describe some of the many ways in which teachers and librarians can collaborate to maximize the use of a school's library media resources for the benefit of everyone in the school.

Larrick, N. (1965)."The All-White World of Children's Books." *Saturday Review of Literature, 11,* 63–65, 84–85.

This landmark article describes a study Larrick made of children's books published between 1962 and 1964 in which she found very little mention of people of color in the texts or illustrations. Articles reporting on the status of multicultural literature often cite this article, which described some of the negative stereotypes that were prevalent in the early 1960s. Many years later, publishers and editors told Larrick of the impact this article had, for her study resulted in an increased sensitivity to books by and about minorities.

Rasinski, T. V., & Padak, N. D. (1990). "Multicultural Learning Through Children's Literature." *Language Arts, 67,* 576–580.

Teachers who use children's literature as part of a multicultural curriculum are challenged to broaden their expectations of the role of that literature in their programs. These authors suggest ways we can encourage our students to engage in constructive action regarding multiethnic issues, including civil rights.

Rhodes, L. K. (1981). "I Can Read! Predictable Books as Resources for Reading and Writing Instruction." *The Reading Teacher, 34,* 511–518.

Rhodes explains the characteristics of predictable books and demonstrates how such books can be used as resources for reading and writing instruction with young children. The article includes a bibliography of predictable books, which Rhodes updated in 1988. (See Rhodes and Dudley-Marling, Readers and Writers with a Difference, *in the first section of this appendix.)*

Rudman, M. K., & Rosenberg, S. P. (1991). "Confronting History: Holocaust Books for Children." *The New Advocate, 4,* 163–177.

Suggestions for evaluating books about the Holocaust are given, followed by descriptions of several recommended fiction and nonfiction books on the topic. A bibliography of additional titles is also included.

Swibold, G. V. (1984)."Textbooks Need Trade Books: One Librarian's Case Study." *Top of the News, 41*, 93–98.

Swibold, a school library media specialist, describes how she found trade books to use in conjunction with her school's fifth- and sixth-grade social studies texts. She points out that children's learning can be greatly enhanced when trade books are used in addition to social studies textbooks.

Trousdale, A. (1989)."Who's Afraid of the Big, Bad Wolf?" *Children's Literature in Education, 20(2)*, 69–79.

The author reports on how some young children responded to fearful elements in fairy tales. Trousdale explains why she feels that it may be a mistake to remove violence from fairy tales.

Tunnell, M. O., & Jacobs, J. S. (1989). "Using 'Real' Books: Research Findings on Literature Based Reading Instruction." *The Reading Teacher, 42*, 470–477.

Tunnell and Jacobs looked at a number of studies that directly compared literature-based reading programs with basal instruction. They also looked at research reports on the reading growth of children in whole language classrooms where real literature was prevalent. Tunnell and Jacobs concluded that children's literature is a viable alternative approach to the teaching of reading.

Journals and Periodicals

Book Links: Connecting Books, Libraries, and Classrooms. A bimonthly magazine published by Booklist Publications, an imprint of the American Library Association, 50 E. Huron St., Chicago, IL 60611.

Started in 1991, Book Links *publishes articles with suggestions for exploring a particular theme through literature. Descriptions of books, strategies for stimulating classroom discussion about them, and activities for student involvement are among the offerings.*

Bookbird: World of Children's Books. Published quarterly by IBBY, the International Board on Books for Young People, Nonnenweg 12 Postfach, CH-4003 Basel, Switzerland. For subscriptions write to Bookbird, P. O. Box 3156, West Lafayette, IN 47906, USA.

This English-language journal includes articles, authors' and illustrators' portraits, reports and announcements, and reviews of children's books and professional literature of international interest. Authors are from the sixty member nations of IBBY.

Children's Literature in Education: An International Quarterly. Published by Human Sciences Press, Inc. 233 Spring Street, New York, NY 10013-1578.

The types of articles published in this journal include interviews with authors and illustrators, and articles by or about them; accounts of classroom practice involving literature or the reading process, critical evaluation of literature; and analysis or commentary on social issues as reflected in books.

Journal of Children's Literature. Journal of the Children's Literature Assembly of the National Council of Teachers of English, published and sent to CLA members twice a year. NCTE members may join the Children's Literature Assembly by obtaining the name and address of the current Membership Chair of CLA. Write to NCTE, 111 Kenyon Road, Urbana, IL 61801.

The Journal of Children's Literature *solicits and publishes manuscripts regarding any aspect of children's literature, as well as reviews of children's books and professional resources. News and items of interest to members are also featured.*

The Dragon Lode. The Journal of the Children's Literature and Reading Special Interest Group of the International Reading Association is published three times a year for members. IRA members may join this interest group by obtaining the name and address of its current Membership Chair from IRA, 800 Barksdale Road, P.O. Box 8139, Newark, DE 19714-8139.

The Dragon Lode publishes articles about children's literature and the teaching of it, classroom ideas, and book reviews of books published internationally as well as in the United States.

JOYS, Journal of Youth Services in Libraries. Quarterly journal of the Association for Library Service to Children and the Young Adult Library Services Association, divisions of the American Library Association, 50 Huron St., Chicago, IL 60611.

JOYS' goal is to provide news and information about both of the above named professional library associations and to inform librarians who work with children and/or young adults about current practices in both specialties. Teachers as well as librarians will find the thorough reviews of professional resources helpful.

Language Arts. Published monthly, September through April, by the National Council of Teachers of English, for its members. For membership information, write NCTE, 1111 Kenyon Road, Urbana, IL 61801-1096.

Language Arts publishes themed issues on topics relating to the content and teaching of English and the language arts, with the contributed articles often being written by classroom teachers. Regular features include author profiles, annotations of children's books, reviews of professional resources, and commentaries on trends in the field.

The New Advocate for Those Involved with Young People and Their Literature. Published quarterly since 1988 by Christopher-Gordon Publishers, 480 Washington Street, Norwood, MA 02062.

The New Advocate contains articles on using children's literature in the classroom and often includes author or illustrator profiles. Reviews of children's books and literature resources for teachers appear in each issue.

The Reading Teacher. A journal of the International Reading Association, published monthly eight times during the school year. For information on joining the IRA and subscribing to its journals, write to IRA, 800 Barksdale Road, P.O. Box 8139, Newark, DE 19714-8139.

The Reading Teacher contains articles that reflect current theory, research, and practice regarding the teaching of reading. Regular columns deal with instructional issues, practical ideas for classroom use, and evaluation of children's trade books and professional resources.

The United States Board on Books for Young People, Inc. (USBBY) Newsletter. Published twice a year by the U.S. section of the International Board on Books for Young People (IBBY). To join USBBY and receive the newsletter, write for the address of the current USBBY Secretariat, c/o International Reading Association, P.O. Box 8139, Newark, DE 19714-8139.

This newsletter includes news and articles concerning national and international activities related to children's literature. It also includes reviews of international children's books.

The Web: Wonderfully Exciting Books. Published three times a year by Ohio State University, Room 220, Ramseyer Hall, 29 West Woodruff, Columbus, OH 43210

Each issue includes a "web of possibilities," along with reviews of books on a related theme stressing ideas for using books in the classroom. Write to the above address for a list of the topics of back issues that are available for purchase.

Information on Authors and Illustrators

"American Writers for Children, 1990–1960." (1983). J. Cech (ed.). *Dictionary of Literary Biography, 22.* Detroit: Gale Research.

"American Writers for Children Before 1900." (1985). G. E. Estes (Ed.). *Dictionary of Literary Biography, 42.* Detroit: Gale Research.

"American Writers for Children Since 1960: Fiction." (1986). G. Estes (ed.). *Dictionary of Literary Biography, 52.* Detroit: Gale Research.

These volumes profile writers and illustrators whose work is primarily for children; they are written for the adult student of children's literature. The most recent volume of the Dictionary of Literary Biography *indexes the entire series.*

Children's Literature Review: Excerpts from Reviews, Criticism, and Commentary on Books for Children and Young People, 1–35 (1976–1995). Detroit: Gale Research.

This reference provides information about authors and illustrators, often in their own words, as well as excerpts from reviews of their work. Each volume contains a cumulative index to authors and titles, with the most recent volumes including a cumulative index of nationalities. Students writing reports on authors and their work are shown the correct way to credit the original sources for information obtained from this series.

Cummings, P. (Compiler-Ed.). (1992). *Talking with Artists.* New York: Bradbury.

Biographical essays written by fourteen well-known children's book illustrators are followed by the answers they provided to questions about their work and their lives. Samples of their early artistic work as well as some of their published illustrations, with information included about the medium used, will make this innovative book useful for teachers as well as students.

Janeczko, P. B. (Selector). (1990). *The Place My Words Are Looking For: What Poets Say about and through Their Work.* New York: Bradbury Press.

This anthology includes comments about the work of more than forty poets in their own words, as well as examples of their poetry.

Junior Book of Authors (1951), *More Junior Authors* (1963), and the *Third, Fourth, Fifth,* and *Sixth Book of Junior Authors and Illustrators.* (1972–1989). S. H. Holtze. (Ed.). New York: H. W. Wilson.

This reference includes biographical sketches of authors and illustrators written for young people; each book's index is cumulative. Most entries include a photograph, selected list of works, and sources for additional information.

Marantz, S., & Marantz, K. (1992). *Artists of the Page: Interviews with Children's Book Illustrators.* Jefferson, NC: McFarland & Company, Inc., Publishers.

This book provides an in-depth look at how thirty-one British and American artists do their work. Some of the people profiled for this book were interviewed when they came to Ohio for children's literature conferences, but when possible, Sylvia and Kenneth Marantz met with the artists in their studios. The answers to the questions the authors asked provide insights into how these illustrators work.

Martin, D. (1990). *The Telling Line: Essays on Fifteen Contemporary Book Illustrators.* New York: Delacorte.

Martin gets at the history of British children's picture book illustration by discussing publishing trends, printing techniques, and changing art styles in the field in the course of his interviews with fifteen major graphic artists, including Raymond Briggs, Helen Oxenbury, and Brian Wildsmith.

Rollock, B. (1988). *Black Authors and Illustrators of Children's Books. A Biographical Dictionary.* New York: Garland Publishing.

This short work includes brief biographical information about 115 black authors and illustrators who were included because they are making literary history in the world of children's books.

Something about the Author Autobiography Series, 1–20 (1986–1995). Detroit: Gale Research.

Autobiographical information has been provided by authors and illustrators for this series. A cumulative index in each volume includes entries appearing in all of Gale Research's books on authors and illustrators.

Something about the Author: Facts and Pictures about Authors and Illustrators of Books for Young People, 1–81 (1971–1995). Detroit: Gale Research.

This series includes comprehensive information about authors and illustrators, written for young people. A cumulative index is included in the odd-number volumes after Volume 57. Volumes 50 (1988) and 54 (1989) also include a cumulative character index, featuring many well-known library characters.

Bibliographies: Annual Lists

"CCBC Choices."

This is an annual spring annotated booklist, published by and for the members of the Friends of the CCBC, Inc. (Cooperative Children's Book Center). Introductory information explains the book-selection criteria and also provides statistics on how many books for children were published that year, how many were written or illustrated by minorities, and how many were published by small presses. For information about CCBC publications and/or membership in the Friends, send a self-addressed stamped envelope to Friends of the CCBC, P.O. Box 5288, Madison, WI 53705-0288.

"Children's Choices."

This yearly list of newly published books, chosen by young readers themselves, appears each October in The Reading Teacher *as a project of the International Reading Association/Children's Book Council Joint Committee. Single copies are available for a self-addressed, 9" × 12" envelope, stamped with first-class postage for four ounces, from Children's*

Choices, International Reading Association, P.O. Box 8139, Newark, DE 19713-8139.

"Notable Children's Books."

This annual American Library Association list is compiled during the ALA midwinter meeting by a committee of the Association for Library Service to Children (ALSC), which is organized each year for that purpose. The list, which is not annotated, appears in the March issue of School Library Journal *and also in the March 15th issue of* Booklist *as part of the news from the ALA midwinter meeting. Copies of this and other awards lists are available from the ALA. Write for price list and/or catalog to ALA Graphics, American Library Association, 50 E. Huron St., Chicago, IL 60611.*

"Notable Children's Books in the Language Arts (K–8)."

The books on this annual list, which appears in each October issue of Language Arts, *have been designated as outstanding tradebooks for enhancing language awareness among students in grades K–8 by a committee of the Children's Literature Assembly of the National Council of Teachers of English.*

"Notable Children's Trade Books in the Field of Social Studies." (This list appears in the April/May issue of *Social Education.*)

"Outstanding Science Trade Books for Children." (This list appears in the March issue of *Science and Children.*)

Both of these annual lists are available from the Children's Book Council. Send for their current materials brochure, available for a first-class stamped, self-addressed, business-size envelope. CBC Order Center, 350 Scotsland Road, Orange, NJ 07050.

"Teachers' Choices."

This yearly list includes books recommended by teachers. It appears each November in The Reading Teacher, *along with an explanation of how they were chosen. It is another project of the International Reading Association. Single copies are available for two-ounce postage on a 9" × 12" self-addressed envelope. The address is the same as for "Children's Choices."*

"Young Adults' Choices."

The books on this annual list were selected by readers in middle, junior high, and senior high schools.

It appears in the October issue of The Reading Journal, *the journal for secondary teachers published by the International Reading Association. Single copies available as per "Children's Choices."*

Bibliographies

Barstow, B., & Riggle, J. (1995). *Beyond Picture Books: A Guide to First Readers* (2nd ed.). New York: R. R. Bowker.

This work annotates 2,000 recommended books, published between 1951 and 1995, intended for beginning readers of first- or second-grade children. They are indexed by subject, title, illustrator, readability, and series. Also included is a list of two hundred titles that the authors consider outstanding.

Children's Book Review Index. (1975–1994) Detroit: Gale Research.

This annual work indexes the reviews appearing in two hundred periodicals. Although it contains no actual reviews, this work compiles those citations appearing in Book Review Index, *which locates reviews of books written for children and young adults. A five-volume master cumulation of book reviews that appeared from 1965 to 1984 is available. The entries are arranged by title under author, with separate indexes of titles and illustrators.*

Children's Books: Awards & Prizes. (1992). Children's Book Council (Compiler-Ed.). New York: The Children's Book Council, Inc.

Nearly two hundred major domestic and international children's book awards and prizes are identified in this frequently revised book. A complete list of winners from each award's inception through the spring of 1992 is included, as well as a description of each award along with the sponsor's address.

Children's Books in Print. (Published annually). New York: R. R. Bowker.

This is an index of juvenile titles that are listed in publishers' catalogs as "in print," but it does not always include books from smaller publishing companies. Access is by title, author, or illustrator. Prices and ISBN (International Standard Book Number) numbers are given for library binding, trade, and/or paperback editions, thus indicating which are available. This work includes a separate listing of addresses of publishers.

The Children's Catalog. (16th ed.). (1991). J. Yaakov (Ed.). New York: H. W. Wilson.

Part 1 lists books and magazines recommended for preschool children through sixth-graders, as well as useful professional resources, in a classified catalog format arranged by Dewey Decimal System, fiction, story collections, and easy books. The descriptive entries often include quotations from book reviews. Part 2 helps the user locate entries through one alphabetical, comprehensive key that includes author, title, subject, and analytical listings. A new edition is published every five years, with supplements being sent to subscribers annually. Wilson offers other similar print media catalogs, one for junior high and another for high school readers.

Dreyer, S. S. (1977, 1981, 1985, 1989). *The Bookfinder: A Guide to Children's Literature about the Needs and Problems of Youth Aged 2–15.* Circle Pines, MN: American Guidance Service.

Arranged so that users can locate books on a particular subject relating to children's needs and problems, Dreyer provides critical annotations for each of the suggested books. The third edition features a cumulative subject index of the first three volumes, covering books published through 1982. The fourth edition covers 731 additional books published from 1983 to 1986.

———. (1992). *The Best of Bookfinder: A Guide to Children's Literature about Interests and Concerns of Youth Aged 2–18.* Circle Pines, MN: American Guidance Service.

This version included 676 annotations from the earlier volumes of Bookfinder. *Ninety percent of these books are fiction, and most were still in print in 1992.*

The Elementary School Library Collection: A Guide to Books and Other Media. (19th ed.). (1994). L. Lee (Ed.). Williamsport, PA: Brodart.

In addition to books and periodicals, this work also recommends all kinds of nonprint media and resources for teachers and parents. A classified arrangement features entries in catalog-card format that provide critically descriptive annotations as well as such information as priority for acquisition and estimates of reading level and interest level. The work is indexed by subject, title, author, and illustrator. A revised edition is issued biennially.

Cagnon, A., & Cagnon, A. (Eds.). (1988). *Canadian Books for Young People: Livres Canadiens pour la Jeunesse* (4th ed.). Toronto: University of Toronto Press.

This concise book includes brief annotations, with suggested reading levels, of the best Canadian books printed in English and French. The work includes reference works and magazines, and is indexed by title and author.

Horning, K. T. (Ed.). (1991). *Alternative Press Publishers of Children's Books: A Directory* (4th ed.). Madison, WI: Friends of the CCBC, Inc.

This directory lists names and addresses of small presses in the United States and Canada that publish one or more books for children and indicates the type of books published by each.

Lima, C. W., & Lima, J. A. (1993). *A to Zoo: Subject Access to Children's Picture Books (4th ed.).* New York: R. R. Bowker.

This index indicates the subject matter of 14,000 picture books for children with access through author, illustrator, and title, as well as 800 subjects. An introductory chapter provides information on the genesis of the English language picture book.

NCTE bibliography series (National Council of Teachers of English):

Adventuring with Books: A Booklist for Pre-K–Grade 6 (10th ed.). (1993). J. M. Jensen & N. L. Roser (Eds.). Urbana, IL: NCTE.

Books for You: A Booklist for Senior High Students (11th ed.). (1992). S. Wurth (Ed.). Urbana, IL: NCTE.

High Interest—Easy Reading: A Booklist for Junior and Senior High Students (6th ed.). (1990). W. G. McBridge (Ed.). Urbana, IL: NCTE.

Kaleidoscope: A Multicultural Booklist for Grades K–8. (1994). R. Sims-Bishop (Ed.). Urbana, IL: NCTE.

Your Reading: A Booklist for Junior High and Middle School Students (9th ed.). (1993). C. A. Webb (Ed.). Urbana, IL: NCTE.

All of these books include annotated listings of fiction and nonfiction books recommended for children and young people in the grades specified in each title. The books in each index are grouped by appropriate topic. The latest addition to this series is Kaleidoscope, *which focuses on books celebrating cultural diversity and includes an introductory section on selecting multicultural books. All of these works are indexed by subject, author, and title;* Adventuring with Books *and* Kaleidoscope *are also indexed by illustrator.*

Pilla, M. L. (1990). *The Best: High/Low Books for Reluctant Readers.* Englewood, CO: Libraries Unlimited.

This index contains brief annotations of 374 quality books that are of interest to reluctant readers. The work is indexed by title, subject, grade level, and reading level.

Stoll, D. R. (Ed.). (1994). *Magazines for Kids and Teens: A Resource for Parents, Teachers, Librarians, and Kids!* Newark, DE: International Reading Association.

Co-published by the Educational Press Association of America, this updating of Magazines for Children *describes 249 magazines geared toward children from ages 2 to 17. Information concerning circulation, cost, and frequency of publication is included, as well as indexes of age levels, subjects, and whether the magazine publishes readers' writing.*

Subject Guide to Children's Books in Print (Published annually). New York: R. R. Bowker.

This comprehensive reference provides a subject approach to children's books in print. Headings are based on the Sears list of subject headings with additional entries from the Library of Congress. A directory of publishers and distributors is included.

Sutherland, Z., Hearne, B., & Sutton, R. (1991). *The Best in Children's Books: The University of Chicago Guide to Children's Literature 1985–1990.* See also earlier volumes edited by Zena Sutherland (1973, 1980, 1986) covering, respectively, books published between 1966 to 1972, 1973 to 1978, 1979 to 1984. Chicago: University of Chicago Press.

Compiled from reviews of books originally designated as "recommended" in the Bulletin of the Center for Children's Books, *each volume annotates the best books published Xduring the inclusive years. Annotations are arranged alphabetically by author's name with indication of probable grade level use. The books are indexed by title, developmental values, curricular use, and subject matter, as well as reading level.*

Bibliographies: Special Topics

Adamson, L. G. (1987). *A Reference Guide to Historical Fiction for Children and Young Adults.* New York: Greenwood Press.

————. (1994). *Recreating the Past: A Guide to American and World Historical Fiction for Children and Young Adults.* New York: Greenwood Press.

Especially useful for teachers interested in augmenting the study of particular periods of history with literature, Adamson provides readers with plot summaries of well-written historical fiction. The two books are organized differently, but both provide information about reading and interest levels as well as setting dates and locales. The newer work is more comprehensive in its coverage and appendices, but for those who own it, the older work will still be helpful.

The Black Experience in Children's Books. (1994). S. Pine (Ed.). New York: The New York Public Library.

This periodically revised pamphlet briefly annotates folklore, fiction, and nonfiction, written for children from preschool to age 12, that portrays African-American life. The titles are arranged by genre, and the Coretta Scott King Award winners are listed.

Friedberg, J. B., Mullins, J. B., & Sukiennik, A. W. (1992). *Portraying Persons with Disabilities: An Annotated Bibliography of Nonfiction for Children and Teenagers.* New Providence, NJ: R. R. Bowker.

Aiming to familiarize readers with nonfiction titles that foster positive attitudes toward human differences, this work organizes annotations by broad categories of disabilities. The indexes—by author, title, and subject—also list works that were in the same authors' 1985 edition, titled Accept Me As I Am. *Other useful features are a bibliography of reference books on disabilities and a chronology of events that have influenced the disabled.*

Hartman, D. K., & Sapp, G. (1994). *Historical Figures in Fiction.* Phoenix: Oryx Press.

This reference is designed to help locate fictional biographies of famous and not-so-famous individuals from history. Reading levels, awards the book may have won, and a list of review sources are included for each title.

Jenkins, E. C., & Austin, M. C. (1987). *Literature for Children about Asians and Asian Americans: Analysis and Annotated Bibliography, with Additional Readings for Adults.* New York; Greenwood Press.

The annotations are arranged by country and then by genre; introductory historical information is provided about each country. The copy is computer generated.

Kobrin, B. (1988). *Eyeopeners! How to Choose and Use Children's Books about Real People, Places, and Things.* New York: Penguin Books.

Kobrin shares her enthusiasm for five hundred interesting informational books that she has annotated and organized for access through what she calls her "Quick-Link Index." For information about a subscription to Korbrin's newsletter, which provides information on current nonfiction books, write to The Kobrin Letter, 732 Greer Road, Palo Alto, CA 94303.

Kruse, G. M., & Horning, K. T. (1991). *Multicultural Literature for Children and Young Adults: A Selected Listing of Books 1980–1990 by and about People of Color* (3rd ed.). Madison, WI: Wisconsin Department of Public Instruction.

This reference annotates recently published multicultural books recommended for their high quality by the Children's Cooperative Book Center. The work includes information about the selection process, a list by racial/ national background of some authors and illustrators whose works are included, a list of titles divided into the ethnic/cultural groups depicted in those books, and a brief bibliography of recommended adult resources.

The Newbery and Caldecott Awards: A Guide to the Medal and Honor Books. (1994). Chicago: American Library Association.

This annual guide includes annotations on each of the award winners and honor books, as well as information concerning the criteria on which the awards are based. One of its most useful features is an article in which Christine Behrmann discusses the difficulty of determining the media used in the early Caldecott award-winning books and then goes as far as she can toward making those determinations.

Robertson, D. (1992). *Portraying Persons with Disabilities: An Annotated Bibliography of Fiction for Children and Teenagers.* New Providence, NJ: R. R. Bowker.

Plot descriptions and analyses of works of fiction published from 1982 through 1991 are annotated in this work. Because Bowker considers this reference work a continuation of Notes from a Different Drummer *and* More Notes from a Different Drummer *(by Barbara Baskin and Karen Harris, 1977 & 1984), the books annotated in those books have been indexed in this volume. Taken together, these three works provide information about the patterns and trends of dealing with the disabled in our society.*

Rochman, H. (1993). *Against Borders: Promoting Books for a Multicultural World.* Chicago: American Library Association.

Explaining that multiculturalism refers not only to people of color, Rochman recommends books which she hopes will help junior and senior high school students break down borders and cross cultures. The essays in part one are interspersed with the kinds of booktalks for which Rochman is known. The annotations in part two are meant to serve as a resource for studies of related issues such as apartheid, the Holocaust, and various ethnic groups in the United States.

Rudman, M. K., Gagne, K. D., and Bernstein, J. E. (1993). *Books to Help Children Cope with Separation and Loss: An Annotated Bibliography* (4th ed.). New York: R. R. Bowker.

This reference work summarizes, evaluates, and indicates reading and interest level for 750 fiction and nonfiction books dealing with temporary and tragic losses. Over half of the titles are new to the 4th edition. The 3rd edition (by Joanne Bernstein and Masha K. Rudman, 1989) is still useful for books published between 1983 and 1988.

Schon, I. (1978–1993). *Books in Spanish for Children and Young Adults: An Annotated Guide* (Series I–IV). Metuchen, NJ: Scarecrow Press.

Each volume covers a three-year period. These are selection guides for books in Spanish written by Hispanic authors for children, preschool through high school. The list is comprehensive and includes some negative reviews because not all of the included books are recommended. The entries are arranged by country and topic; most originate in Latin America or Spain.

Slapin, B., & Seale, D. (1991). *Through Indian Eyes: The Native Experience in Books for Children* (Vol. 3). Philadelphia: New Society Publishers.

This is a reprint of Volume 2 with some additions. The entries provide detailed, critical content analysis, from an American Indian perspective, of children's books dealing with Native-American themes. Also included are essays by Native-American writers and educators, and bibliographies of recommended books.

Verrall, C., & McDowell, P. (1990). *Resource Reading List 1990: Annotated Bibliography of Resources by and about Native People.* Toronto, Ontario: Canadian Alliance in Solidarity with the Native Peoples.

This annotated bibliography of nonprint media and books for children and teenagers indicates the degree to which Native Peoples were involved in the creation of each listed item.

Review Journals

Appraisal: Science Books for Young People. Published quarterly by the Children's Science Book Review Committee, a nonprofit organization sponsored by the Science Education Department of Boston University School of Education and the new England Roundtable of Children's Librarians. Diane Holzheimer, Editor, 605 Commonwealth Avenue, Boston, MA 02215.

This journal presents lengthy, thorough, critical reviews, one written by a children's librarian and one by a subject specialist for each science book considered. The reviews are arranged alphabetically by author's name; ratings are given. A separate section contains reviews of books issued as part of a series.

Booklist. Published twice monthly September through June and monthly in July and August by American Library Association, 50 E. Huron St., Chicago, IL 60611.

Booklist reviews current print and nonprint materials for children and adults that are worthy of consideration for purchase by small and medium-sized public libraries and school media centers. Inclusion in Booklist is a recommendation for library purchase. Reviews of children's books are presented by age and grade levels. Subject lists of good books in particular fields are often presented. Audiovisual media and reference books are reviewed in separate sections.

The Bulletin of the Center for Children's Books. Published monthly except August by the University of Illinois Press, 1325 S. Oak, Champaign, IL 61820.

This publication reviews current children's books, with adverse as well as favorable reviews, assigning a recommendation code to each. An age or grade level is given to each book, and annotations include information on curricular use, developmental values, and literary merit. Reviews are arranged alphabetically by the author's last name. An annual index by title, author, and illustrator is included in the July/August issue.

Children's Book News. Quarterly newsletter published by the Canadian Children's Book Center, 35 Spadina Road, Toronto, Ontario M5R 2S9.

This newsletter features articles and reviews; it lists all children's books published in Canada. Subscribers also receive Our Choice: Your Annual Guide to Canada's Best Children's Books, *which contains brief reviews of the three hundred best Canadian children's books of the year.*

The Horn Book Guide to Children's and Young Adult Books. Published twice a year in March and September by the Horn Book, Inc., 11 Beacon Street, Suite 1000, Boston, MA 02108.

First published in 1990, The Horn Book Guide *contains brief reviews of all hardcover children's trade books published in the United States during the previous six months. Fiction is organized by age, and nonfiction by Dewey Decimal System. Within each category, the reviews are arranged by ratings and then by the author's name. If a book was reviewed in* The Horn Book Magazine, *information is provided so that the complete review may be consulted. Author, illustrator, and subject indexes are also included.*

The Horn Book Magazine. Published six times a year by the Horn Book, Inc., 11 Beacon Street, Suite 1000, Boston, MA 02108.

The Horn Book Magazine *includes detailed reviews of children's books deemed the best in children's literature by the editorial staff. It provides information about reissues, paperbacks, and books in Spanish. It also contains articles about literature and interviews with authors. The Newbery and Caldecott acceptance speeches are features in the*

July/August issue. An annual index appears in the November/December issue.

School Library Journal: The Magazine of Children's, Young Adult, and School Librarians. A Cahners/ R. R. Bowker Publication, published monthly. For subscription information, write to School Library Journal, P.O. Box 1978, Marion, OH 43305-1978.

This journal prints reviews, written by practicing librarians, of most children's books published. It includes both negative and positive reviews. It also includes news from the field and articles of interest to school librarians. An index appears each December; that issue also features a "Best Books" section.

Professional Organizations

American Library Association. 50 E. Huron Street, Chicago, IL 60611. Special Divisions: Association for Library Service to Children, Young Adult Library Services Association

Children's Book Council. 568 Broadway, Room 706, New York, NY 10012

Children's Literature Association. 210 Education Department, Purdue University, West Lafayette, IN 47907

Cooperative Children's Book Center. Friends of the CCBC, P.O. Box 5288, Madison, WI 53705-0288

International Reading Association. 800 Barksdale Road, P.O. Box 8139, Newark, DE 19714-8139. Special Interest Group: Children's Literature and Reading

National Council of Teachers of English. 1111 W. Kenyon Road, Urbana, IL 61801-1096. Special Interest Group: Children's Literature Assembly

United States Board on Books for Young People. USBBY Secretariat, International Reading Association, P.O. Box 8139, Newark, DE 19714-8139.

Index to Children's Books and Authors

Strugnell, Ann, 115, 143, 152
Stuart-Clark, Christopher, 63, 294
Stuart Little (White), 134
Stupids Have a Ball, The (Allard), 88
Suetake, Kunihiro, 64
Sugaring Time (Lasky), 34, 191, 199
Sukey and the Mermaid (San Souci), 94
Suleiman the Elephant (Rettich), 238
Sullivan, Charles, 228
Summer Day, A (Florian), 87
Summer of My German Soldier (Greene), 167, 175, 253, 256
Summer of the Monkeys (Rawls), 143, 151, 159
Summer of the Swans, The (Byars), 143, 151, 156
Summer to Die, A (Lowry), 153
Sunday's Child (Mebs), 237
Sundvall, Viveca, 238
Sun Horse, Moon Horse (Sutcliff), 172
Sunrises and Songs: Reading and Writing Poetry in an Elementary Classroom (McClure et al.), 59
Sun's Day, The (Gerstein), 87
Sun, The (Simon), 196
Sun, the Wind, and the Rain, The (Peters), 195
Supermarket, The (Rockwell & Rockwell), 198
Super Super Superwords (McMillan), 87
Surprise Picnic, The (Goodall), 84
Surprises (Holman), 64
Surtsey: The Newest Place on Earth (Lasky), 195
Sutcliff, Rosemary, 104, 107, 112, 137, 165, 171–73, 224, 234, 252
Sutherland, Zena, 16, 84
Suzuki, Mamoru, 238
Svedberg, Ulf, 238
Swamp Angel (Isaacs), 91, 133
Swan (Lewis), 194
Swann, Brian, 66
Swans (Scott), 195
Sweet Dreams, 150
Sweetest Fig, The (Van Allsburg), 72, 95
Sweetgrass (Hudson), 164, 174, 230
Sweet, Melissa, 91
Sweet, Ozzie, 195
Sweet Valley Twins, 150
Sweet Whispers, Brother Rush (Hamilton), 132, 136
Swenson, May, 65
Swift, Jonathan, 124, 126, 217
Swiftly Tilting Planet, A (L'Engle), 138
Swimmy (Lionni), 12, 23, 72, 82, 92
Swindells, Robert, 234
Swirsky, Michael, 235
Swiss Family Robinson (Wyss), 144–45
Switching Well (Griffin), 136
Swope, Sam, 95
Sword and the Circle, The (Sutcliff), 112
Sword in the Tree, The (Bulla), 165
Sydney, Herself (Rodowsky), 154
Sylvester and the Magic Pebble (Steig), 12, 17, 24, 94, 281, 293

Table Where Rich People Sit, The (Baylor), 89
Tackle Without a Team (Christopher), 158

Tafuri, Nancy, 66, 83, 86–88
Tail Feathers from Mother Goose: The Opie Rhyme Book (Opie & Opie), 84
Tail Toes Eyes Ears Nose (Burton), 83
Taina, Hannu, 99, 238
Take a Look: An Introduction to the Experience of Art (Davidson), 199
Take a Walk in Their Shoes (Turner), 193, 226
Takeshita, Fumiko, 238
Take Wing (Little), 157
Talbert, Marc, 153, 170, 177
Tale of Peter Rabbit, The (Potter), 74, 78, 82, 93, 124, 128, 217
Tale of the Mandarin Ducks, The (Paterson), 99, 117
Tale of the Unicorn, The (Preussler), 237
Tales for a Winter's Eve (Watson), 95
Tales from Gold Mountain: Stories of the Chinese in the New World (Yee), 175, 222, 227, 234
Tales from Grimm (Gág), 115
Tales from the Enchanted World (Williams-Ellis), 118
Tales Mummies Tell (Lauber), 191
Tales of a Fourth Grade Nothing (Blume), 151, 154
Tales of a Gambling Grandma (Khalsa), 228, 232
Tales of Moominvalley, The (Jansson), 125
Tales of Mother Goose (Perrault), 76, 105, 217
Tales of Pan (Gerstein), 114
Tales of the Greek Heroes (Green), 111
Tales of Uncle Remus, The: The Adventures of Brer Rabbit (Harris; Lester), 104, 116, 209, 225
Talisman of Death (Jackson & Livingstone), 131146
Talking Earth, The (George), 230
Talking Eggs, The: A Folktale from the American South (San Souci), 104, 117, 222
Talking Peace: A Vision for the Next Generation (Carter), 196
Talking with Artists (Cummings), 184, 199
Tall Book of Mother Goose, The (Rojankovsky), 84
Tall Tale America: A Legendary History of Our Humorous Heroes (Blair), 112
Tam Lin (Cooper), 113
Tam Lin (Yolen), 118
Tangled Fortunes (Mahy), 153, 233
Taran Wanderer (Alexander), 137
Tar Beach (Ringgold), 94, 221, 226
Taronga (Kelleher), 232
Tashjian, Virginia, 118
Taste of Blackberries, A (Smith), 154
Taste of Salt: A Story of Modern Haiti (Temple), 158
Taste of Smoke, A (Bauer), 135
Tate, Joan, 235
Tattercoats (Steel), 118
Taxis and Toadstools (Field), 49
Taylor, Ann, 49
Taylor, C. J., 104, 118, 231
Taylor, Jane, 49, 67

Taylor, Mildred D., 164–67, 171, 176, 204, 207, 210, 221–22, 226
Taylor, Sydney, 144–46, 153
Taylor, Theodore, 157, 159, 176
Teague, Mark, 134
Teammates (Golenbock), 188, 193
Teeth of the Gale, The (Aiken), 173
Tehanu: The Last Book of Earthsea (Le Guin), 137
Tejima, Keizaburo, 95, 118, 238
Teller of Tales (Brooke), 133
Telling of the Tales, A: Five Stories (Brooke), 133
Tell Me a Story, Mama (Johnson), 91
Tell Me Everything (Coman), 155
Tempering, The (Skurzynski), 174
Temple, Frances, 158, 164, 172
Temple, Lannis, 196
Ten Harmsel, Henrietta, 66
Ten, Nine, Eight (Bang), 80, 86
Ten Sly Piranhas: A Counting Story in Reverse (Wise), 86
Ten Small Tales (Lottridge), 233
Ten Tall Tales (Bird), 112
Teskey, Donald, 164, 173
Testa, Fulvio, 86, 88, 95, 119
Thai, Ted, 226
Thanksgiving Poems (Livingston), 65
Thank You, Jackie Robinson (Cohen), 158
That Dreadful Day (Stevenson), 95
That Julia Redfern (Cameron), 151–52
That Scatterbrain Booky (Hunter), 175
That's Good, That's Bad (Cuyler), 97
That Was Then, This Is Now (Hinton), 155
Thayer, Ernest Lawrence, 49, 67
14th Emergency, The (Byars), 155
18th Emergency, The (Byars), 148
Then Again, Maybe I Won't (Blume), 148, 155
There's a Monster Under My Bed (Howe), 91
There's a Nightmare in My Closet (Mayer), 93
Theseus and the Minotaur (Fisher), 110, 112, 252
Theseus and the Minotaur (Hutton), 112
Thesman, Jean, 154, 157
Thidwick the Big-hearted Moose (Seuss), 94
Thiele, Colin, 151, 157, 224, 234
Things I Want, The: Poems for Two Children (Shaw), 61
Things That Go (Rockwell), 199
Thinking Big: The Story of a Young Dwarf (Kuklin), 197
Third Eye (Duncan), 136
Third Gift, The (Carew), 113
This Is Betsy (Wolde), 88
This Is the Way We Go to School: A Book about Children around the World (Baer), 196
This Little Nose (Ormerod), 82
This Little Pig-a-Wig and Other Rhymes about Pigs (Blegvad), 63
This Same Sky: A Collection of Poems from Around the World (Nye), 66
This Star Shall Abide (Engdahl), 138
This Time of Darkness (Hoover), 131, 138
This Time, Tempe Wick? (Gauch), 164, 172

Subject Index

ABC books. *See* Alphabet books
Abstract art, 35
Acceptance by peers, 147–148
Adjustment stories, 144
Adolescent issues stories, 148, 155
Adventure stories. *See* Survival and
    adventure stories
Aesthetic reading, 9
African-American literature, 208–10,
    224–26
    authors, notable, 221–22
    illustrators, notable, 221–22
    poets, 50
African Imprints Library Services, 215
Alliteration, definition of, 45
Alphabet books, 16, 76–77, 85–86
Alternative family, 147
Amelia Frances Howard-Gibbon Award,
    14*t*, 71
American Library Association, 13
Animal fantasies, 127–28, 133–34. *See also*
    Beast tales
Animal stories, 146, 150, 158–59
Animated videos, 279
Antagonist, 30
Anthology(ies), 42, 62–63
Applied sciences, 189, 199
Appraisal: Children's Science Books, 183
Art appreciation
    literature as teaching material for, 8–9
    and picture books, 69–70
Arte Publico, 205
Artistic media, 35–36
Artistic styles, 34–35
Asian-American literature, 210–11,
    226–27
    authors, notable, 222
    illustrators, notable, 222
Assisted reading, 276–77
Association of Jewish Libraries Awards,
    211
Assonance, definition of, 45
Atheneum/Margaret K. McElderry
    Books, 215
Audiotapes, 279
Authentic biography, 186
Author(s), notable
    of historical fiction, 170–71
    of international literature, 222–24
    of modern fantasy, 132–33
    of multicultural literature, 221–22
    of nonfiction, 190–91
    of picture books, 80–82
    of realistic fiction, 151
    organizing curriculum by, 240–41
    school visits by, 260
Autobiography, definition of, 179

Baby books, 75, 82–83
Backdrop setting, 30

Ballad, 52–54
Basal reading program, 245–47
Beast tales, 108. *See also* Animal fantasies
Bias. *See also* Stereotyping
    in historical fiction, 165
    in history, 162–163
Bibliographies, 15
Bibliotherapy, 278–79
Biennale of Illustrations Bratislava (BIB),
    218
Big Books, 276
    made by students, 290–91
Biography(ies), 178–99. *See also* Nonfiction
    authentic, 186
    biographical fiction, 187
    collected, 188
    complete, 188
    fictionalized, 187
    partial, 188
    picture books, 180
    series, 188
    types of, 186–88
Biological sciences, 188–89, 193–95
Black Butterfly, 205
Board books, 16, 75
Book(s), 25–40
    acquisition for classroom, 251
    choosing. See Selection
    format of, 36–38
    made by students, 290–91
    mode of delivery of, 11
    organizing curriculum by, 241–42
    visual elements of, 32–34
Book awards, 14*t*
    as guides for choosing books, 13–15,
        144, 163, 183, 205, 215
Book binding, 38
Bookbird: World of Children's Books,
    214–15, 218
Book clubs, 258
Bookfairs, 258–59
Book Links, 15
Booklist, 14, 215
Book reports, 288–89
Bookstores, school, 258–59
Book talks, 273–74
    example, 274
Bulletin boards, 293
Bulletin of the Center for Children's Books,
    14

Caldecott Medal, 14*t*, 71, 207
Canadian Library Awards, 14*t*
Canon, literary, 254
Carnegie Medal, 14*t*
Cartoons, 35
Castle tales, 108
Censorship, 11–13, 130
    books subjected to attempts of, 12
    publications about, 13

Chapbooks, 105
Chapter book(s), 17
    nonfiction, 180
    reading aloud 270–72
Character(s), 28–30
    antagonist, 30
    balance of male and female, 38
    flat, 29
    minor or secondary, 29
    protagonist, 29
    round, 29
Character development, 29
Character foil, 29–30
Characterization, 29
Charts, 271, 292
Child(ren)
    knowledge of, in choosing books, 10
Childhood, theories of, 73
Children's Book Council, lists of books, 15
Children's Book Press, 205
Children's Catalog, 21
Children's literature. *See also* Literature
    content of, 2–3
    definition of, 2–3
    for the developing child, 15–19
    genres of. See Genre(s)
    quality of, 3
    research in, 21–22
    values to children, 4–5
Choosing books for children, 10–11. *See*
    also Selection
    resources for, 13–15
Choral poetry, 57–58
    arrangements of, 57
    memorization of, 57
    performance of, 58
    selection of, 57
Chronological plot, 27
Cinquains, definition of, 52
Civil Rights Movement, 207
Classroom
    assessment of, 262–64
    design, for literature curriculum,
        247–50
    interactive, 247, 249f
    literature-based reading, elements of,
        244–45
    storytelling area, 287
    traditional, 247, 248f
Classroom interest inventory, 20–21
Classroom library, development of,
    250–51
Cloth books, 75
Collages, 289
Color, 33
Composition, 34
Concept books, 16, 77, 87–88
Conceptual difficulty, definition of, 11
Concrete poetry, 54–55
Conferences, teacher–student, 280

This page constitues a continuation of the copyright page.

Acknowledgements

Front End Page: "Books Fall Open." From *One at a Time* by David McCord. Copyright 1965, 1966 by David McCord. By permission of Little, Brown and Company.

Pages 1–2: "Give Me Books, Give Me Wings." Reprinted with permission of Margaret K. McElderry Books for Young Readers, an imprint of Simon & Schuster Children's Publishing Division. From *I Never Told and Other Poems* by Myra Cohn Livingston. Copyright © 1992 by Myra Cohn Livingston.

Page 44: "Song of the Train." From *One at a Time* by David McCord. Copyright 1952 by David McCord. By permission of Little, Brown and Company.

Page 45: "Slowly." From The Wondering Moon. Published by William Heinemann Ltd. Copyright © The Estate of James Reeves, 1950.

Pages 50–1: "Giraffes." From *Triptich* by Sy Kahn. By permission of the author, 1212 Holcomb St., Ravenshille House, Port Townsend, WA, 98368.

Pages 51–2: "The Broken Legg'd Man." From *The Things I Want: Poems for Two Children*. Copyright 1967 by the John M. Shaw Collection, Florida State University Library. Reprinted with permission.

Page 54: "Small Bird, Forgive Me." From *More Cricket Songs*, Japanese Haiku translated by Harry Behn. Copyright © 1971 by Harry Behn. Reprinted by permission of Marian Reiner.

Page 54: "Last Day of School." From *Cold Stars and Fireflies: Poems of the Four Seasons* by Barbara Juster Esbensen. Copyright © 1984 by Barabara Juster Esbensen.

Page 68: "My Book!" by David L. Harrison from *Somebody Catch My Homework*. Published by Wordsong, Boyds Mills Press, Inc. Reprinted by permission.

Page 100: "Listen!" by Walter de la Mare. From *Poems for Children*. Copyright 1930 by Society of Authors. Reprinted by permission of the Literary Trustees of Walter de la Mare and the Society of Authors as their representative.

Page 120: "Silverly." From *Jelly Belly*. Copyright © by Dennis Lee. Reprinted by permission of the publisher.

Page 139: "Listening to Grownups Quarreling." From the *Marriage Wig and Other Poems*. Copyright © 1968 by Ruth Whitman. Reprinted by permission of Harcourt Brace & Company.

Page 160: "Ancestors" by Greg Cohoe. From *Whispering Wind* by Terry Allen. Copyright © 1972 by the Institute of American Indian Arts. Used by permission of Doubleday, a division of Bantam Doubleday Dell Publishing Group, Inc.

Page 178: "Questions at Night." From *Rainbow in the Sky* by Louis Untermeyer. Copyright 1975 by Harcourt Brace & Company and renewed 1963 by Louis Untermeyer. Reprinted by permission of the publisher.

Page 200–1: "Human Family." From *I Shall Not Be Moved* by Maya Angelou. Copyright © by Maya Angelou. Reprinted by permission of Random House, Inc.

Page 294: "Tailpiece." From *Wry Rhymes for Troublesome Times*. Published by Kestrel Books. Copyright © Max Fatchen, 1983.

Back End Page: "After the End." From *Always Wondering* by Aileen Fisher. Copyright © 1991 by Aileen Fisher.